gauguin
AND THE ORIGINS OF **SYMBOLISM**

gauguin
AND THE ORIGINS OF **SYMBOLISM**

Editor
Guillermo Solana

Richard Shiff
Guy Cogeval
María Dolores Jiménez-Blanco

Philip Wilson Publishers
in association with
Museo Thyssen-Bornemisza
and Fundación Caja Madrid

Published in conjunction with the exhibition
Gauguin and the origins of Symbolism,
28 September 2004–9 January 2005
Museo Thyssen-Bornemisza, Madrid
Fundación Caja Madrid, Madrid
Curator: Guillermo Solana

Texts
Guillermo Solana
Richard Shiff
Guy Cogeval
María Dolores Jiménez-Blanco

Edition
Museo Thyssen-Bornemisza
Fundación Caja Madrid
Philip Wilson Publishers

Editorial Co-ordination
Museo Thyssen-Bornemisza

Translations
Ana María Beaven
Laura Suffield

Production
Philip Wilson Publishers

Design
Anikst Design
James Warner

Cover design
Pep Carrió / Sonia Sánchez

Typesetting
Lucam

Colour Separation
Articolor Italia (Verona, Italy)

Printing and binding
Editoriale Lloyd (Trieste, Italy)

ISBN (English paperback edition) 84-96233-13-8
ISBN (English hardback edition) 0 85667 595 5

Printed in Italy

Lenders to the Exhibition

ARGENTINA
BUENOS AIRES — Museo Nacional de Bellas Artes

CANADA
MONTREAL — The Montreal Museum of Fine Arts
OTTAWA — National Gallery of Canada

DENMARK
COPENHAGEN — Ny Carlsberg Glyptothek
Ordrupgaard
FREDERIKSSUND — J. F. Willumsens Museum

EGYPTE
CAIRO — Mahmoud Khalil Museum

FRANCE
ALBI — Musée Toulouse-Lautrec
BREST — Musée des beaux-arts de Brest
STRASSBOURGH — Musée d'Art Moderne et Contemporain
LYON — Musée des Beaux-Arts
PARIS — Bibliothèque nationale de France
Galerie Bères
Institut national d'histoire de l'art, Bibliothèque, collections Jacques Doucet
Musée des Arts décoratifs
Musée d'Orsay
Musée du Louvre
Musée Maillol
Petit Palais, Musée des Beaux-Arts de la Ville de Paris
Musée Picasso
QUIMPER — Musée des Beaux-Arts de Quimper
RENNES — Musée des beaux-arts de Rennes
SAINT-GERMAIN-EN-LAYE — Musée Départemental Maurice Denis "Le Prieuré"

GERMANY
COLOGNE — Wallraf-Richartz Museum-Fondation Corboud
HAMBURG — Hamburger Kunsthalle
KARLSRUHE — Staatliche Kunsthalle
MUNICH — Bayerische Staatgemäldesammlungen, Neue Pinakotek
STUTTGART — Staatsgalerie
WUPPERTAL — Von der Heydt Museum

GREAT BRITAIN
CAMBRIDGE — Fitzwilliam Museum
EDINBURGH — National Gallery of Scotland
SOUTHAMPTON — Southampton City Art Gallery

ITALY
MILAN — Galleria d'Arte Moderna, Collezione Grassi

IRELAND
DUBLÍN — National Gallery of Ireland

LIECHTENSTEIN
SCHAAN — Hilti Art Foundation

RUSSIA
MOSCOW — State Pushkin Museum of Fine Arts

SPAIN
BARCELONA — Museu Nacional d'Art de Catalunya
Museu Picasso
BILBAO — Museo de Bellas Artes de Bilbao
MADRID — Colección Carmen Thyssen-Bornemisza
Museo Nacional Centro de Arte Reina Sofía
VALENCIA — IVAM, Instituto Valenciano de Arte Moderno, Generalitat Valenciana

SWEDEN
GOTEBORG — Göteborgs Konstmuseum

SWITZERLAND
GENEVA — Association des Amis du Petit Palais
MARTIGNY — Fondation Pierre Gianadda
ZURICH — Kunsthaus Zürich

THE NETHERLANDS
AMSTERDAM — Van Gogh Museum (Vincent van Gogh Foundation)
BRUSSELS — Musées royaux des Beaux-Arts de Belgique
GOOREIND — Triton Foundation
ROTTERDAM — Museum Boijmans Van Beuningen

UNITED STATES
CLEVELAND — The Cleveland Museum of Art
FORT WORTH — Kimbell Art Museum
HARTFORD — Wadsworth Atheneum Museum of Art
INDIANAPOLIS — Indianapolis Museum of Art
KANSAS CITY — The Nelson-Atkins Museum of Art, Kansas City, Missouri
NEWARK — The Newark Museum
NEW YORK — The Metropolitan Museum of Art
Solomon R. Guggenheim Museum
PORT WASHINGTON — Nassau County Division of Museum Services at the Sand Point Preserve
SAN FRANCISCO — Fine Arts Museums of San Francisco
SAINT LOUIS — The Saint Louis Art Museum
WASHINGTON — National Gallery of Art
WEST PALM BEACH — Norton Gallery of Art

PRIVATE COLLECTIONS
María Amalia Lacroze de Fortabat
E. W. K. Collection
Jan and Marie-Anne Krugier-Poniatowski Collection
Reytenbagh Collection
William Kelly Simpson Collection, New York
Eugene V. Thaw, New York

The Museo Thyssen-Bornemisza and the Fundación Caja Madrid would like to thank the Spanish Embassy in Egypt, Cairo; The Fine Arts Society Plc., London; Agencia Española de Cooperación Internacional, Ministerio de Asuntos Exteriores, Madrid; Galleria Pieter Coray, Montagnola; Christies' New York; Sotheby's New York; Archives Vuillard, Paris; Galerie Bellier, Paris and Galerie Malingue, Paris, for their collaboration in this project. As well as thanking all those private collectors that wish to remain unknown and whose generosity has made this exhibition possible.

Acknowledgements:

Ilrina Antonova
Ermanno A. Arslan
Kosme de Barañano
Christoph Becker
Luc Bellier
Alberto G. Bellucci
Brent R. Benjamin
Fernanda Bennett
Jacques de la Béraudière
Anisabelle Berès
Hugo Bongers
Juan Manuel Bonet
Christian Briend
Rainer Budde
Bernhard Bürgi
Helena Bussers
Françoise Cachin
Eduard Carbonell i Esteller
André Cariou
Philippe Cazeau
Consuelo Ciscar
Michael Clarke
Timothy Clifford
Guy Cogeval
Pieter Coray
William Cordia
Tim Craven
Gilles Chazal
Anne-Marie Chevrier
Mathias Chivot
Cyanne Chutkow
Françoise Daniel
Agnès Delannoy
Lisa Dennison
Cara D. Denison
C. P. E. Dercon
Danièle Devynck
François Ditesheim
Benjamin Doller
Sabine Fehlemann
Evelyn Ferlay
Maria Teresa Fiorio
Birgitta Flensburg
Maria Fratelli
Björn Fredlund
Flemming Friborg
Anne-Birgitte Fonsmark
Robert Futernick
Belén Galán
Claude Ghez
Léonard Gianadda
Emmanuel Guigon
José Antonio Hernández Solórzano
Anthony G. Hirschel
Danielle Hodel
William Holmes
Christian von Holst
Siegmar Holsten
Jean-Nöel Jeannerey
Pablo Jiménez Burillo
Samuel Josefowitz
Joachim Kaak
Koiki Kabayama
Ronda Kasl
Raymond Keaveney
E. W. Kornfeld
Thomas Krens
Leila Krogh
Jan y Marie-Anne Krugier Poniatowski
María Amalia Lacroze de Fortabat
Christopher Larsen
Steingrim Laursen
Ellen W. Lee
Katherine Lee Reid
John Leighton
Serge Lemoine
Faith Lewis
Pedro López Aguirrebengoa
Olivier Lorquin
Daniel Malingue
Francine Mariani-Ducray
Ana Martínez de Aguilar
Andrew McIntosh Patrick
Tom Meganck
Philippe de Montebello
Dalia Mustafa
Ahmed Nawar
María Teresa Ocaña
Christina Orr-Cahall
Harry S. Parker
Sue Ellen Paxson
Vincent Pomarède
Tatiana Potapova
Timothy F. Potts
Martine Poulain
Earl A. Powell III
Gérard Regnier
Francis Ribemont
Duncan Robinson
William Robinson
María José Salazar
Béatrice Salmon
Carmen Sánchez
Alain Schnapp
Uwe M. Schneede
Klaus Schrenk
Michael Semff
Jesús Silva
William Kelly Simpson
Susan Alyson Stein
Mary Anne Stevens
Mary Sue Sweeney Price
Alain Tarica
Antoine Terrasse
Eugene Victor Thaw
Pierre Théberge
Carmen Thyssen-Bornemisza
Gary Tinterow
Javier Viar
Françoise Viatte
Dina Vierny
Roger Ward
Uwe Wieczorek
Marc F. Wilson

Index

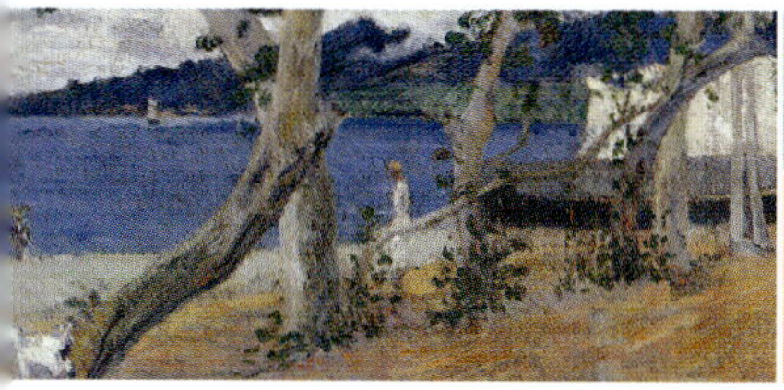
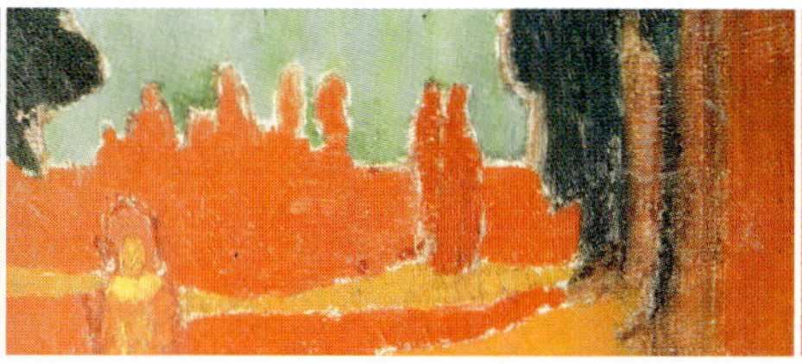
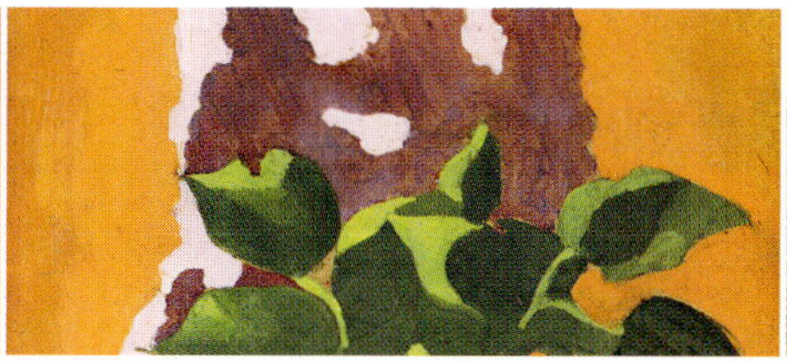
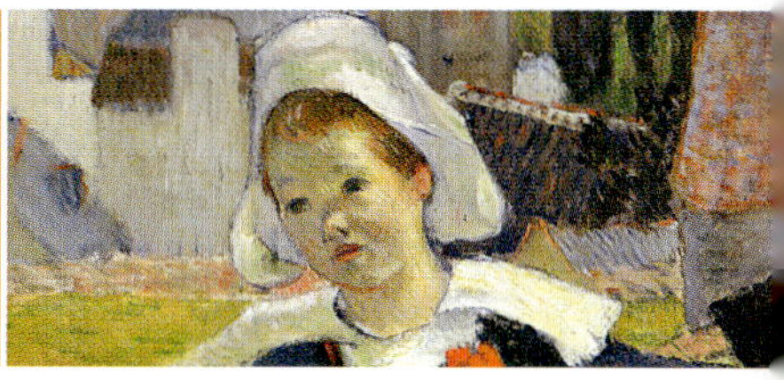

Forewords

Essays

Catalogue

The exhibition *Gauguin and the Origins of Symbolism*, with Prof. Guillermo Solana as curator and organised by the Museo Thyssen-Bornemisza and the Fundación Caja Madrid, is a new initiative within the collaboration agreement signed by these two institutions, aimed at reviewing and popularising certain aspects of modern art.

Whereas *Form* analysed the influence of classicism on modern art and *Musical Analogies* highlighted the role of music in the development of abstract language in painting, *Gauguin and the Origins of Symbolism* is centred around the crucial moment when Paul Gauguin and some of his contemporaries began to move away from Impressionism, developing a new pictorial language under the influence of Symbolism. By freeing themselves from nature as a model and conceiving the work of art as a product of their creative imagination, these artists opened the way for the avant-gardes of the early 20th century.

The exhibition, divided in nine sections, is organised around a series of successive *encounters* between Gauguin and his masters and pupils. The almost two hundred works are distributed in two different spaces; the first six sections, showing the evolution of Gauguin and his contemporaries between 1884 and 1891, are exhibited at the Museo Thyssen-Bornemisza, and the three last sections, dedicated to Gauguin's influence on the artists of Pont-Aven and the Nabis circle, are shown at the *Casa de las Alhajas*, headquarters of the Fundación Caja Madrid, where a room is devoted to Gauguin's influence in Spain.

Bringing together these masterworks has only been possible thanks to the collaboration of many museums and collections, which have generously lent their paintings for this exhibition, and to the efforts and keen interest of many people. As President of the Board of Trustees of the Museo Thyssen-Bornemisza, I wish to express my gratitude to all of them. I would also like to thank the Fundación Caja Madrid for its important financial contribution which has been essential to the success of this ambitious project.

Carmen Calvo Poyato
Minister of Culture

The Fundación Colección Thyssen-Bornemisza and the Fundación Caja Madrid have been maintaining a close cultural collaboration which has set itself as its main task since 2003 the organisation of joint exhibitions in the headquarters of both institutions.

The exhibition *Gauguin and the Origins of Symbolism* that we now present constitutes a new stage of these joint exhibitions which began with *Musical Analogies. Kandinsky and his Contemporaries* (2003) and continued with *Willi Baumeister* (2003-2004).

Gauguin and the Origins of Symbolism is an exhibition with an international character, showing the changes brought about by the Parisian avant-garde, which was mostly impressionist, as a reaction to the appearance of the symbolist movement during the 1880s. Centred on Gauguin, the exhibition analyses his relationship with some of his predecessors, such as Pissarro, Degas, Renoir or Van Gogh, as well as the mark he left on various groups that followed him; it closes with a reference to the Spanish connections between Gauguin and several artists up to Picasso.

As usual within our joint programme, the exhibition is accompanied by a series of lectures and a symposium in which several Spanish and foreign specialists will analyse the figure of Gauguin with the greatest scientific rigour.

This exhibition is the result of a thorough intellectual plan for which we are indebted to Guillermo Solana, Curator of the exhibition, and to Richard Shiff, Guy Cogeval and María Dolores Jiménez Blanco, members of the editorial team for the catalogue, as well as to the generosity and collaboration of all the museums and private collections which have kindly lent us their valuable works. The English edition of the catalogue will guarantee its international diffusion.

The opening of the exhibition *Gauguin and the Origins of Symbolism* constitutes a great organisational challenge and a major cultural investment for the two institutions behind it, the Fundación Colección Thyssen-Bornemisza and the Fundación Caja Madrid. With this project, they have achieved their most ambitious goals.

Miguel Blesa de la Parra
President of the Board of Trustees of the Fundación Caja Madrid

An anti-modern future

In 1883 Gauguin was working with Pissarro as an artist totally identified with the ideas of Impressionism. In 1888, however, he painted *The Vision after the Sermon*, a work that the critic Albert Aurier acclaimed as the model of a new type of painting. In contrast to Impressionism's 'painting of sensations', Aurier described this as 'painting of ideas'. While it is not clear that Gauguin was completely aware of this himself, the change that took place in this brief five-year period was one of the most significant within the history of art. It was not limited to Gauguin's personal development, nor to the field of painting, but rather formed part of a broader movement: it was influential for literary creation, and affected the beliefs, ideas and attitudes of an entire generation. Going further, if required to pin down the origins of the avant-garde as it was understood and experienced by the young artists of the early 20th century, we would have to point to that critical thresh old of the mid-1880s.

In terms of the history of painting as a series of movements, the process to which I refer above could be described as the transition from Impressionism to Symbolism. However, art history has always had a somewhat vague idea of Symbolism, a movement whose role in the development of the avant-garde has been problematic for numerous art historians. Whatever the case, the present exhibition focuses on a series of specific transformations in the practice of painting, a line of development in which Gauguin played a key role.

Originating from within Impressionism, these transformations affected both the devices and strategies of painting itself, as well as its relations with its social and cultural context. In both areas, the result was a radical critique of the two basic principles of Impressionism: the belief that painting had to be reinvented in the name of something approximating a 'natural gaze', and the belief that it had to integrate itself into modern life. Through the successive sections of the exhibition, Guillermo Solana demonstrates Gauguin's developing critique of these two principles. Partly as a consequence of his encounters with Pissarro, Cézanne, Degas and Bonnard, Gauguin developed a new pictorial language which relied on the subjective randomness of colour and line in contrast to the supposed objectivity of the Impressionist gaze. At the same time – and here his relations with Van Gogh were crucial – he broke away from modern life to propose a new return to origins. Conceived of in terms of a flight, this return initially relied on the motifs of a pastoral tradition deriving from Antiquity and still present in modern European culture. In a later phase, the amenable tone of this pastoral evocation gave way to an emphasis on the diabolical and a fierce conflict between the artist and modern life with its rationalism. The paradoxical fact that this anti-modern conflict was waged in the name of the future was the key to its fascination for the young artists of the 20th century.

Tomàs Llorens
Chief Curator Museo Thyssen-Bornemisza

The Faun Awakes

Gauguin and the revival of the pastoral

GUILLERMO SOLANA

In memory of my father

Paul Gauguin is seated in front of his easel, brush in hand and looking into a mirror which we cannot see. He seems trapped in the narrow space of the attic room, between the sturdy beam, the chair and the easel. The light divides his face into two and gives it a double expression: half sombre and half expectant. Like the face, the painting itself is ambiguous; although modelled with chiaroscuro in grey-brown tones, here and there we see touches of pure, bright red pigment, while on the wall behind, the brushstrokes are aligned in parallel in the manner of Cézanne.

Gauguin's *Self-Portrait* [cat. 1] was painted in May 1885 in Copenhagen, a city in which the artist felt ill at ease and whose inhabitants he described in the following terms: 'The most terrible cannibal is nothing compared to a Danish property owner'.[1] He had decided to devote himself completely to painting a year and a half earlier. 'My wife, the family, in fact everyone throws this cursed painting back in my face, saying that it's shameful not to earn a decent living. But a man's faculties are not enough for two activities and I can only do one: paint'.[2] Gauguin and his children lived off the French lessons that his wife Mette gave at home. The painter was confined to this small upstairs room, as the drawing room was used by Mette and her pupils, some of whom were from the upper ranks of the Danish aristocracy. Gauguin only had himself as model and he spent the day alone, painting his own portrait.[3] Before long he would leave Copenhagen for Paris, in a separation from his family that would eventually become permanent.

When we encounter the artist again, in a second *Self-Portrait* [cat. 48], he is barely recognisable. His gaze and pose are more confident, even a touch arrogant. His hair and beard have grown, giving him the air of a Bohemian dandy. He no longer wears the traditional suit seen in Copenhagen, but rather an embroidered jacket and a shirt with a yellow yoke. This is in fact typical Breton dress, the region where Gauguin had worked for lengthy periods and where his painting underwent a radical change of direction. His intention here seems to be to pay homage to the Breton peasants, still bound to their language, their Catholic faith and their ancient traditions and superstitions. In a letter to his friend Schuffenecker, Gauguin declares his passion for this region: 'You are a devotee of Paris. I am rather for the country. I love Brittany: there I find the wild, the primitive. When my clogs ring out on the granite floor I hear the mute, dull and powerful sound that I am seeking in painting…'[4] As if to emphasise this quest for the rustic, Gauguin has used a jute canvas with a thick weave.

It is impossible to state precisely when this self-portrait was created. It may have been in Brittany in the spring of 1888, or more likely in Arles in December during the last few days

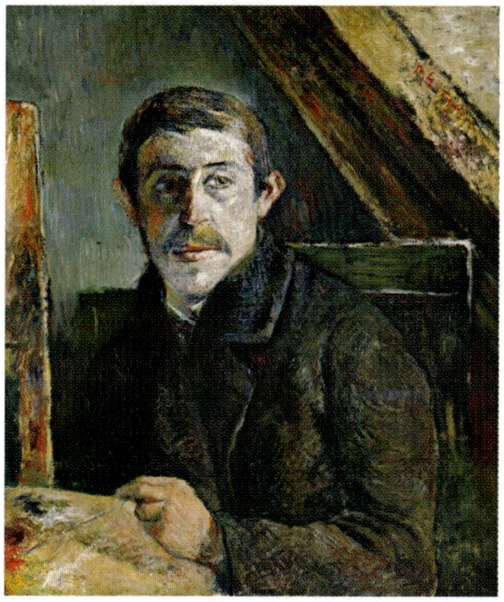

Paul Gauguin
Self-Portrait in front of the Easel, 1885
[cat. 1]

1. 'Le plus terrible cannibale n'est rien comparé à un propriétaire danois.' Letter to Pissarro, end of May 1885, in *Correspondance de Paul Gauguin*. Victor Merlhès (ed.). Fondation Singer-Polignac, Paris, 1984, vol. I, p. 108.
2. 'Ma femme la famille tout le monde enfin me met sur le dos cette maudite peinture prétendant que c'est une honte de ne pas gagner sa vie. Mais les facultés d'un homme ne peuvent suffire à 2 choses et moi je nepuis faire q'une chose peindre.' Letter to Pissarro, end of May 1885, ibid, vol. I, p. 108.
3. Gauguin, Paul: *Paul Gauguin mon père*. Paris, Les éditions de France, 1938, p. 82.
4. 'Vous êtes parisianiste. Et à moi la campagne. J'aime la Bretagne, j'y trouve le sauvage, le primitif. Quand mes sabots résonnent sur ce sol de granit, j'entends le ton sourd, mat et puissant que je cherche en peinture…' Letter to Schuffenecker, end of February or beginning of March 1888, in *Correspondance de Paul Gauguin*, *op. cit.*, vol. I, p. 172.

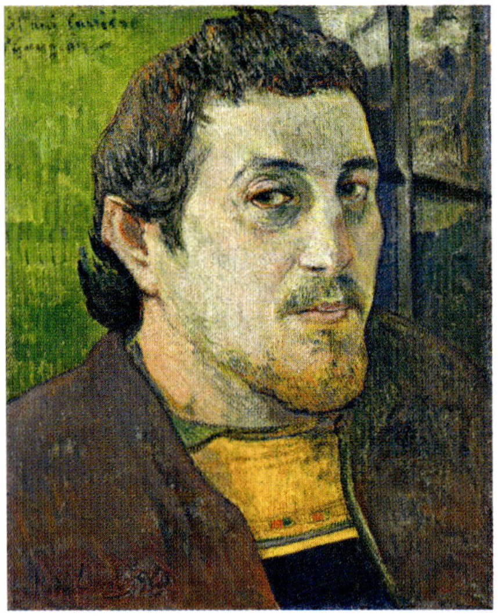

Paul Gauguin
Self-Portrait, 1888
[cat. 48]

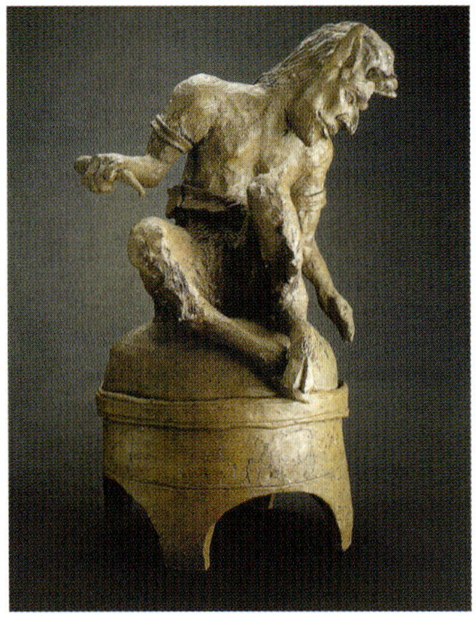

Paul Gauguin
The Faun, 1886
Unglazed stoneware with touches of gold gilding. 47 cm
Chicago, The Art Institute of Chicago (Estate of Suzette Morton Davidson; Major Acquisitions Centennial Endowment, 1997.88)

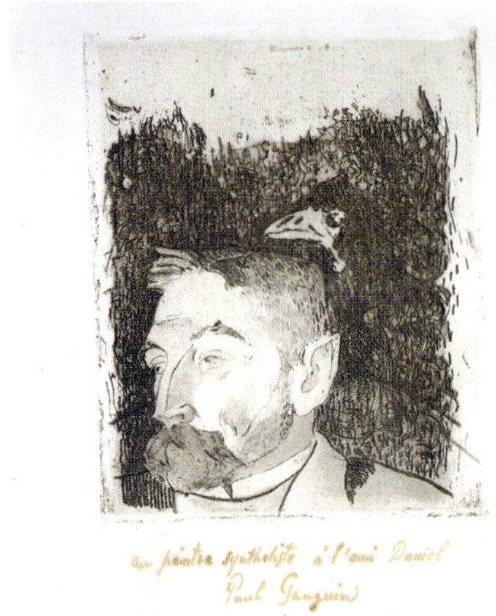

Paul Gauguin
'Au Poéte Synthetiste...', Portrait of Stéphane Mallarmé, 1891
Pen and ink on paper. 18.2 x 14.3 cm
Paris, Institut national d'histoire de l'art, Bibliothèque, collections Jacques Doucet

that Gauguin spent with Van Gogh in the Yellow House.[5] 'On several occasions', Gauguin wrote, 'Vincent called me the man who comes from afar and will go far'.[6] In line with this idea of a wandering destiny, the image is of everywhere and nowhere. The landscape seen through the window is of neither Brittany or Provence; the misty sky, the purple mountain and the tall trees are more suggestive of the landscapes of Martinique which the artist had painted in 1887.[7] This painting seems to be an evocation or a tropical reverie that looks forward to the Tahiti landscapes.

The face has a green tinge, as if all of the natural world outside were reflected in it. It is modelled in green tones against the green background of the wall. We could almost say that Gauguin has seen himself in the mirror as the green man, that fantastical figure with a face made of leaves who appears in the corners of medieval churches carved in stone or in stained glass windows. A pointed ear can be seen protruding from his hair, seemingly announcing the sitter's hybrid nature, between man and beast. Gauguin's first piece of ceramic, made in 1886, was of a faun with large ears. It is unlikely that the artist had read Nathaniel Hawthorne's novel *The Marble Faun*, whose hero was a man who resembled Praxiteles's faun. But he certainly did know Mallarmé's *L'Après-midi d'un faune*, which its own author would dedicate years later to Gauguin with the words: 'To the wild man and

5. In the catalogue raisonné of Gauguin's paintings, the painting entitled *Autoportrait à Lezaven* is dated to the spring of 1888 in Lezaven, Brittainy (Wildenstein, Daniel: *Gauguin. Premier itinéraire d'un sauvage. Catalogue de l'oeuvre peint (1873-1888)*. Text and research Sylvie Crussard. Documentation and chronology Martine Heudron. Skira / Seuil / Wildenstein Institute, 2001). According to Douglas W. Druick and Peter Kort Zegers, it was painted in December 1888 in Arles (in Druick, Douglas W. and Kort, Peter: *Van Gogh and Gauguin. The Studio of the South*. Chicago, The Art Institute of Chicago - Van Gogh Museum, Amsterdam. Thames & Hudson, 2001, pp. 247 and 390–91).
6. 'Vincent m'appelle quelquefois l'homme qui vient de loin et qui ira loin.' Letter to Schuffenecker, around 20 December 1888, in *Correspondance de Paul Gauguin*, *op. cit.*, vol. I, p. 306.
7. Druick, D. and Zegers, P. K.: *Van Gogh and Gauguin. The Studio of the South*, *op. cit.*, p. 247.

bibliophile. His friend Stéphane Mallarmé'.[8] Gauguin would draw Mallarmé with these same pointed ears.

There are various possible ways to describe the transformation that has taken place between the first self-portrait and the second: as the metamorphosis of a budding painter into a fully formed artist; of a bourgeois into a colourful bohemian; of a civilised European into a would-be native of a lost region. However, we might also say simply that Paul Gauguin, the former stockbroker, has become a faun.

Voyage to Arcadia

From his exile in Tahiti, in the last days of 1892, Gauguin described to his friend Daniel de Monfried a painting that he had just completed and of which he was particularly pleased. 'Exceptionally, I have given it a French title: *Pastorales tahitiennes*, as I did not find a corresponding title in Canac'.[9] Why did he need to use a European word – pastoral – for an Oceanic painting? This was not the first time that Gauguin had employed the term. Years before, in 1889, he had entitled a print from the *Suite Volpini* with the name of *Pastorales Martinique*, evoking his trip to the Antilles.

These titles suggest a paradox. Gauguin has come down to us as the personification of the *Überläufer*, the cultural refugee, fleeing from European civilisation to find shelter in a different and alien culture. However, when this fugitive comes to give a name to the experience of passage towards the other, he makes use of a concept – the pastoral – derived from Greco-Latin antiquity and one which embodies better than any other the classical values of the western tradition. The origins of the pastoral date back to the third century BC, when Theocritus wrote his *Idylls* for the sophisticated readers of Alexandria, some of them dealing with the subject of Sicilian shepherds. Two centuries later, Virgil created the definitive treatment of the genre in his *Bucolics*, in which he and his friends appeared transformed into shepherds. Virgil's example offered the Renaissance a fruitful model, taken up by Petrarch, Boccaccio, Agnolo Poliziano and above all Jacopo Sannazaro, with his enormously successful *Arcadia*, as well as Garcilaso de la Vega, Torquato Tasso and others. The eclogues of these poets juxtapose the ideal simplicity of rural life with the pointless sophistication of the city and court. The shepherd is the pure, simple man, free of ambition, greed, adulation and envy, and remote from the intrigues and corruption of urban and court society.

A parallel and equally fruitful tradition of the pastoral exists in painting. This was formulated in Renaissance Venice by Giorgione and Titian, and continues in the work of the Carracci and Domenichino, Poussin, Claude, Rubens and Rembrandt, up to Watteau, Boucher and Fragonard.[10] If we look as far as the nineteenth century we see that leading

8. Manceron, Gilles: 'Segalen et Gauguin', in *Gauguin. Actes du colloque Gauguin*. Paris, Musée d'Orsay, 11–13 January 1989. Paris, La Documentation Française, 1991, p. 47.
9. 'Par extraordinaire je lui ai mis un titre français: Pastorales tahitiennes; ne trouvant pas en canaque un titre correspondant.' Letter to Monfreid, end of December 1892, *Lettres de Paul Gauguin à Daniel de Monfreid*. Précédées d'un hommage par Victor Segalen. Georges Crès, Paris, 1919, p. 103.
10. See exh. cat. *Places of Delight. The Pastoral Landscape*. The Phillips Collection in association with the National Gallery of Art, Washington, 1988.

figures such as Constable, Corot and Puvis de Chavannes would appear to confirm the survival of the bucolic genre. However, not even these exceptional artists were able to stem the irresistible process of decline which the pastoral suffered from the Romantic era onwards, at a time of crisis for classical humanism and its values. In mid-century-landscape painting and the representation of rural subjects, the fragile conventions of the pastoral gave way to the innovations of realism, while its bucolic ideals seemed out of date in the light of new scientific and ideological concerns such as ethnographic documentation, patriotic exaltation and a desire for social redemption, among others.

The pastoral of the primitive

Surprisingly, however, the pastoral – seemingly doomed to extinction around 1850 – enjoyed a revival in modern art. In 1946, the critic Clement Greenberg observed: 'What characterises painting in the line Manet to Mondrian – as well as poetry from Verlaine through Mallarmé to Apollinaire and Wallace Stevens – is its pastoral mood'.[11] Greenberg formulated this thesis so that he could then go on to condemn the drift in twentieth-century art, which he saw as having abandoned its pastoral origins, moving into a Baroque mode and into an expression of emotional violence. Greenberg identified this abandonment of the pastoral with the crisis of avant-garde art. The pastoral implies two conditions and two complementary attitudes: on the one hand, a dissatisfaction with the prevailing customs within social structures and venues, and on the other, a faith in the stability of that society. 'One flees to the shepherds from the controversies that agitate the market place. But this flight – which takes place in art – depends inevitably upon a feeling that the society left behind will continue to protect and provide for the fugitive, no matter what differences he may have with it.'[12] For Greenberg, 'pastoral security' symbolised the necessary relation between the autonomy of art and the continuity of bourgeois society, which the wars and revolutions of the nineteenth century had placed in jeopardy.

Without mentioning Greenberg, Lawrence Gowing once again set out and also added further detail to this relationship between the pastoral and the origins of the modern in European art. Gowing maintained that following decades of oblivion, the arcadian ideal was revived by 'the non-conforming talents that sought an enterprising alternative to the relics of Impressionist realism in the 1880s'.[13] The pastoral tradition became a source of inspiration for the masters of Post-impressionism: Gauguin, Seurat, even Matisse, as according to Gowing it was the pastoral idea which prevented Matisse's 'proto-fauvism' of the 1890s from turning into 'a thoroughly muddled proto-expressionism'. With regard to Gauguin, Gowing stated that the artist went to paint in Brittany, summoned by the pastoral tradition and that he renewed that tradition in a new guise, 'the pastoral of the primitive', which would survive into the twentieth century.[14]

11. 'What characterises painting in the line Manet to Mondrian – as well as poetry from Verlaine through Mallarmé to Apollinaire and Wallace Stevens – is its pastoral mood.' Review of Exhibitions of Hyman Bloom, David Smith, and Robert Motherwell', *The Nation*, 26 January 1946. Republic in Greenberg: *The Collected Essays and Criticism*. 1939–1969. Chicago and London, The University of Chicago Press, 1986–1993, vol. 2, p. 51.
12. 'One flees to the shepherds from the controversies that agitate tha market place. But this flight – which takes place in art – depends inevitably upon a feeling that the society left behind will continue to protect and provide for the fugitive, no matter what differences he may have with it.' In Greenberg, C.: *Collected Essays and Criticism*, *op. cit.*, vol. II, p. 52.
13. 'The nonforming talents that sought an enterprising alternative to the relics of Impressionist realism in the 1880s'. Gowing, Lawrence: 'The Modern Vision', cat. cit., *Places of Delight. The Pastoral Landscape*, p. 238.
14. Ibid.

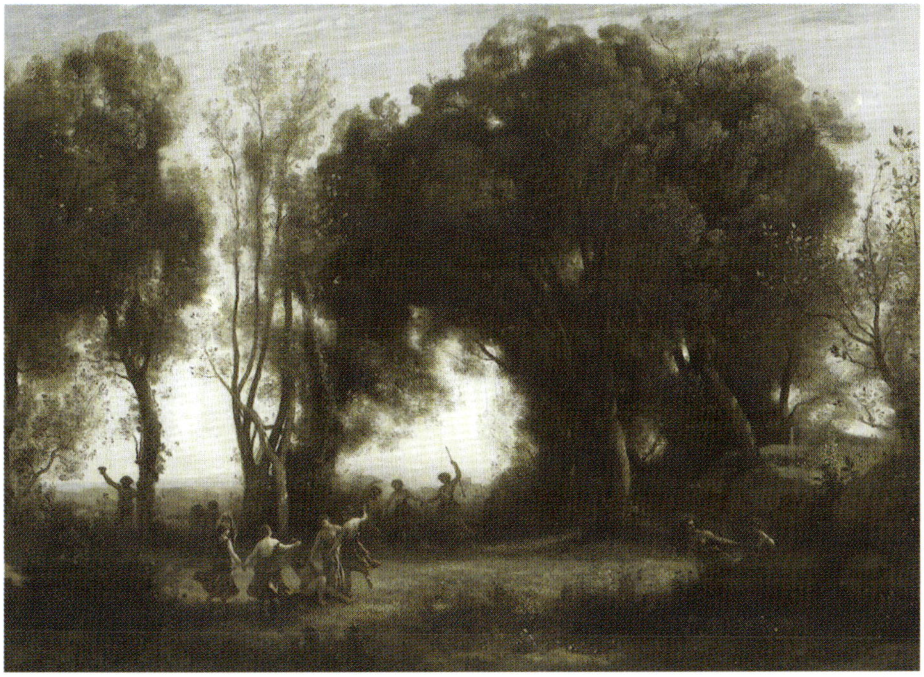

Camille Corot
A Morning. Dance of the Nymphs, 1850
Oil on canvas. 97 x 132 cm
Paris, Musée d'Orsay

Gowing's formula, 'the pastoral of the primitive', allows us to understand Gauguin's pilgrimages to Brittany, to Martinique, even to Tahiti and the cannibal islands – the Marquesas – no longer as the product of a unique individual psychology, but rather as an option always inherent in the western tradition. Gauguin's words when he stated his longing to disappear in the forests of an Oceanic island to live there on ecstasy, calm and art[15] are not the mere random thoughts of an eccentric. Rather, they are the literal (too literal, perhaps) realisation of the cliché of the Valley of Tempe, the *locus amoenus* located in the middle of a wild forest, described so many times from Theocritus's famous *Idyll* on the Dioscuri onwards. Setting Gauguin within the pastoral tradition allows us a new reading of 'primitivism' which goes beyond the Romantic stereotypes that have prevailed in the literature on the artist for the past century.

One of the most surprising indications of the continuity between the classical pastoral tradition and Gauguin's primitivism is to be found in his commentaries on Corot's work. We know that Corot was Gauguin's first reference point when he began painting around 1873. Long after he abandoned a superficial imitation of his style, however, Corot would continue to be a model for Gauguin in the most personal and profound sense. In December 1888, when he had already taken his most important step – the break with Impressionism and with the entire tradition of European art from the Renaissance onwards – Gauguin was moved when he recalled the work of Corot. He regarded Corot

15. 'Puisse venir le jour (et peut-être bientôt) où j'irai m'enfuir dans les bois sur une île de l'Océanie, vivre là d'extase, de calme et d'art.' Letter to Mette, February 1890, *Lettres de Gauguin à sa femme et à ses amis*. Maurice Malingue (ed.). Paris, Bernard Grasset, 1946 (reprinted 1998), p. 184.

not so much as a forerunner of realism and Impressionism, but rather the Hellenising and Virgilian painter. 'In a landscape by Corot', Gauguin wrote, 'there are trees, ivy, clear water in which the nymphs come to bathe at their ease. Corot's nymphs dance like nymphs and not like the mortals of today. Everything grows, calmly and meditatively, and no one has ever drowned in the deep waters. Corot's entire soul has passed through his landscapes; the air breathes goodness, while the slender tree trunks express grace and nobility. He has understood Greece with its delights taken from nature'.[16]

A further evocation of Corot's nymphs reappears later in a passage of *Avant et Après*, Gauguin's autobiography which he wrote at the end of his life and left among his unpublished papers. I refer to the paragraph which starts with a famous confession: 'Sometimes I have gone far back, further than the horses of the Parthenon... to the rocking horse of my childhood, the good wooden horse.' This passage is always, however, quoted without the phrase that follows it: 'I have dawdled among Corot's nymphs dancing in the sacred woods of Ville d'Avray'.[17]

For Gauguin, these nymphs were linked in some obscure way to his attempts to return to the origins of artistic expression. It is thus not surprising that they appear a third time, in another passage in *Avant et Après*, mingled with the verses from *L'Après-midi d'un faune* and with his experiences of Oceania: 'These nymphs, I would like to preserve them – and he preserved them, this adorable Mallarmé: happy, guardians of love, of flesh and of life, near the ivy which twines around Corot's great oaks in Ville d'Avray, with its golden tones, its deep, animal odour; here and elsewhere, timeless tropical flavours, even in eternity'.[18]

A journey

The present exhibition covers Gauguin's activities from the moment when he became a professional artist to his departure for Tahiti in April 1891. By the time of his emigration to the South Seas, the artist's stylistic and ideological evolution was almost completed. It is thus in the preceding period, the key years between 1884 and 1890, that we witness the laborious process by which Gauguin absorbed artistic influences, formulated his style, progressed in his quest for the primitive and fully developed the idea of *Synthetism* as a pictorial concept parallel to the Symbolist aesthetic.

This period can be seen as a coherent phase with a beginning, development and end. The succeeding sections of this exhibition follow Gauguin's journey through his encounters with the contemporary artists who contributed to the formulation of his style and thinking, in particular five leading names: Pissarro, Cézanne, Degas, Émile Bernard and Vincent van Gogh. His work under the guidance of Pissarro in the Pointoise circle would set Gauguin out on the path leading back from the urban world to the rural one. Cézanne's

16. 'Dans un paysage de Corot, il y a des arbres, des lierres, des eaux limpides où les nymphes viennent se baigneur à leur aise. Les nymphes de Corot dansent en nymphes et non pas comme des mortelles d'aujourd'hui, Tout pousse avec sérenité et recueillement et les eaux profondes n'ont jamais noyé personne. Toute l'âme de Corot a passé dans ses paysages; l'air respire la bonté, tandis que ses troncs d'arbres élancés y respirant la grâce et la noblesse. Il a compris la Grèce avec ses joies tirées de la nature.' Letter to Schuffenecker, around 20 December 1888, in *Correspondance de Paul Gauguin*, *op. cit.*, vol. I, p. 306.

17. 'Quelquefois je me suis reculé bien loin, plus loin que les chevaux du Parthénon... jusqu'au dada de mon enfance, le bon cheval de bois. / Je me suis attardé aux nymphes de Corot dansant dans les bois sacrés de Ville-d'Avray.' Gauguin: *Avant et après* [1902–1903]. Preface by Jean-Marie Dallet. Éditions de La Table Ronde, Paris, 1994, p. 33.

18. 'Ces nymphes, je les veux perpétuer... et il les a perpétuées, cet adorable Mallarmé; gaies, vigilantes d'amour, de chair et de vie, près du lierre qui enlace à Ville d'Avray les grands chênes de Corot, aux teintes dorées, d'odeur animale, pénétrantes; saveurs tropicales ici comme ailleurs, de tous les temps, jusque dans l'éternité.' Gauguin, P.: ibid., p. 236.

new understanding of pictorial composition, his structured brushstroke and decorative calligraphy would offer the artist the first model for moving beyond Impressionism. With Degas, Gauguin re-learned how to draw the figure, the distortions that had to be applied to the human form in order to fit it into the pictorial space. Other younger artists, such as Émile Bernard and Vincent van Gogh, would help him to bring about his definitive break with Impressionism and create a new artistic model.

These various artistic encounters resulted in the gradual formation of 'the pastoral of the primitive'. Dr Johnson's ironic and caustic definition of the genre as 'a decadent affectation of crudeness'[19] might be of use when following Gauguin's steps. Rhetorical tradition recommended a simple, pared-down style for bucolic subjects: *pastorali vitae convenit stilus humilis*. In order to represent the Arcadia embodied by the Breton peasant women or natives of Martinique (and later the women of Tahiti), Gauguin needed a simple style, which for a late nineteenth-century artist meant a *simplified* style. Primitivism is the tendency towards a second state of innocence, the route towards a reclaimed rather than natural ingenuity. Rusticity and roughness can only be achieved by shedding a great deal, from the photographic illusionism of some realist artists to the virtuoso brushwork of some of the Impressionists. Gauguin gradually forged his *stilus humilis* not just with the help of his contemporaries, but also by looking to Byzantine painting, Romanesque sculpture, early Renaissance painters, Japanese prints, Breton crucifixion groups, and temple reliefs in Java. To do so he explored the variety of archaising materials and techniques that he needed: painting in wax, preparations without oil and unvarnished surfaces, glazed ceramics and wood carving.[20]

The 'pastoral of the primitive' created by Gauguin between 1884 and 1885 and developed in his Martinique and Breton painting between 1886 and 1888 would undergo a crisis around 1889–90. As a result of his intention to empathise with the primitive world of Brittany, he developed an anti-naturalist and visionary type of painting linked to literary symbolism, but it is precisely this *surnaturalisme* (to use Baudelaire's term) which ended by muddying the purity of the pastoral mode. In Brittany, as in Martinique, Gauguin believed he had discovered a world of perfect innocence, a prelapsarian world, prior the Fall. However, from 1888, with the appearance of Christian subjects and ideas, the notions of evil and guilt perverted this paradisical innocence. Pastoral inspiration would appear again later in Gauguin's Tahitian paintings, but profoundly altered by that major crisis.

1. The circle of Pissarro

In a humorous drawing made years after the event, Georges Manzana, one of Pissarro's sons, evoked a happy picnic with a group of painters on a river bank in the summer of 1881. Seated in the centre is the patriarch of the group, Camille Pissarro. Next to him are

19. 'A decadent affectation of crudeness', in Johnson, Samuel: 'Pastoral Poetry I,' in *Rambler* no. 36, 21 July 1750. Republished in *Eighteenth Century Critical Essays*, Scott Elledge (ed.). Ithica, Cornell University Press, 1961, 11, 579.
20. Jirat-Wasiutyski , Vojtêch and Newton, H. Travers Jr.: *Technique and Meaning in the Paintings of Paul Gauguin*. Cambridge University Press, 2003.

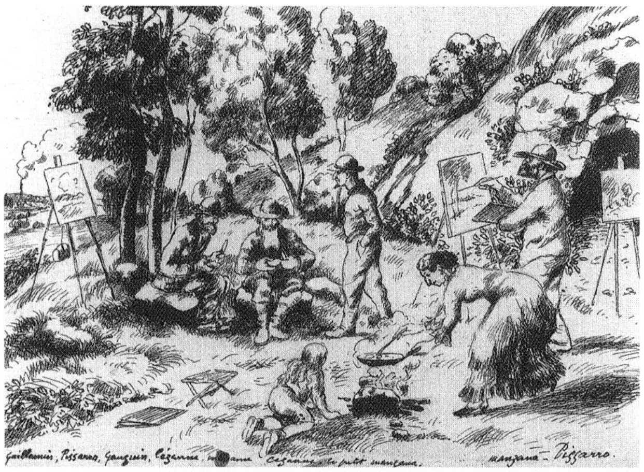

George Manzana-Pissarro
Impressionist Picnic, 1881
(Guillaumin, Pissarro, Gauguin, Cézanne, Mme. Cézanne, *le petit* Manzana)
Pen and ink
Private Collection

Armand Guillaumin and Paul Gauguin. A little further on, painted in front of an easel is Cézanne with his wife cooking on an improvised stove. While the scene did not in fact take place quite in this way, we know that its protagonists worked together that summer on the banks of the Oise. It reflects the high point of that small artists' colony which formed around the Pissarro home in Pontoise.

Pissarro was the only master, in the sense of teacher, of the Impressionist group, for the reason that he was always ready to *learn from* artists younger than himself. This was the case with Cézanne, who worked intermittently with him for a decade, and with Seurat and his friends Signac and Luce, whom he joined in the Neo-Impressionist group. Pissarro helped Van Gogh to adapt himself to Impressionism and in his last years was even able to offer some useful advice to the young Henri Matisse. Many years after his personal rupture with the great patriarch, Gauguin acknowledged his debt to him: 'If one examines Pissarro's work as a whole, despite its fluctuations [...] one finds not just an excessive artistic will which never contradicts itself, but also an essentially intuitive art of fine lineage. [...] He has looked at everyone, you say! And why not? Everyone has also looked at him but renounced him. He was one of my masters and I do not renounce him'.[21]

While Gauguin came to painting as a pure autodidact, Pissarro helped him to become a real painter. He was the ideal guide to initiate Gauguin into the pastoral tradition which the younger artist had already discerned in the work of Corot. In contrast to Degas or Renoir, who were essentially urban artists, or even Monet and Sisley, whose landscapes were seen through the gaze of the city-dweller, Pissarro was the Impressionist artist most interested in rural life. While Monet frequented the Normandy beaches crowded with summer visitors or the bends of the Seine peopled by Parisians on Sunday outings, Pissarro preferred country vegetable plots and village paths. His gaze was, however, totally

21. 'Or, si l'on examine l'art de Pissarro dans son ensemble malgré ses fluctuations [...] on y trouve non seulement une excessive volonté artistique qui ne se dément jamais, mais encore un art essentiellement intuitif de belle race. [...] Il a regardé tout le monde, dites-vous! Pourquoi pas? Tout le monde l'a regardé aussi mais le renie. Ce fut un de mes maîtres et je ne le renie pas.' In Gauguin, P.: *Racontars de rapin* [1902]. Monaco, Editions Sauret, 1993, pp. 30–31.

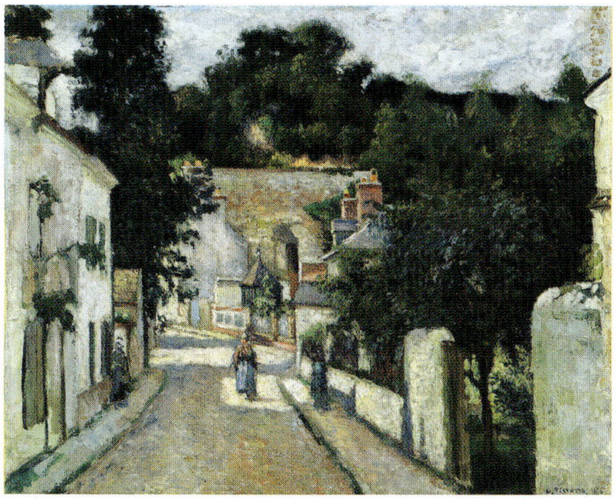

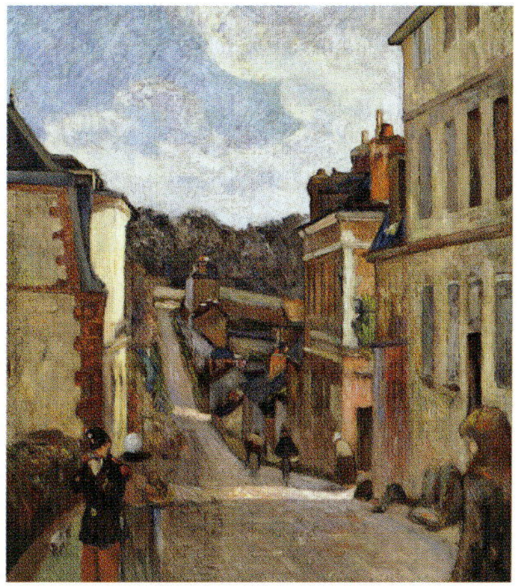

Camille Pisssarro
Rue de l'Hermitage, in Pontoise, 1875
[cat. 3]

Paul Gauguin
Rue Jouvenet in Rouen, 1884
[cat. 4]

distinct from the rhetoric of that poet of peasant life par excellence, Millet. 'Far from expressing the soul and life of the peasants as Millet did [...]', wrote Maurice Denis, '[Pissarro] observed them with the curiosity of a Gauguin avid for the exotic'.[22] Following Denis, we can play with this idea of the exchange of roles between master and pupil, interpreting Pissarro from the standpoint of Gauguin. Like Gauguin later on, Pissarro would come to feel the desire to turn rustic and somewhat primitive: 'I am of a rustic temperament, melancholic, coarse and wild in appearance, only pleasing from a distance'.[23] Like Gauguin, Pissarro had grown up far from Europe, in the tropics, and was of mixed-race background. Anticipating Gauguin, Pissarro also sought his models outside the tradition of western art, in the art of other cultures, as he shows in his advice to his son: 'Look at the Persians, the Chinese, the Japanese, formulate your taste from the really strong men, always go to the source: in painting the primitives, in sculpture the Egyptians, in miniature the Persians'.[24]

Gauguin worked with Pissarro in Pontoise in 1881, in 1882 and for the last time in the summer of 1883. At the end of that year he decided to *devote* himself to painting, and in January 1884 he went to live with his family in Rouen, where he hoped to meet wealthy collectors. This was the start of his first truly productive period. He still felt insecure about his technique and execution and accepted the advice and corrections that Pissarro offered him, as we know from letters of this period.[25] A marked parallel can be detected between Gauguin's work in Rouen and Pissarro's in Pontoise. Pissarro's work in Pontoise is located on the dividing line between the rural and the urban, a division which would become more defined years later. The same was also the case with Gauguin's work in Rouen. The two artists focused on transitions, on the passages between inhabited areas and nature and between architecture and vegetation, such as rivers and bridges, market gardens and above all paths, possibly the key motif of their landscapes. Their paintings

22. 'Bien loin d'exprimer l'âme et la vie des paysans comme fit Millet [...], il les observa avec la curiosité d'un Gauguin avide d'exotisme.' In 'Camille Pissarro' [1903], in Denis, M.: *Le Ciel et l'Arcadie*. Jean-Paul Bouillon (ed.) Paris, Hermann, 1993, p. 83.
23. 'Je suis de tempérament rustique, mélancolique, d'aspect grossier et sauvage, et ce n'est qu'à la longue que je puis plaire'. Letter of 20 November 1883, *Correspondance de Camille Pissarro*. Janine Bailly-Herberg (ed.). Paris, Presses Universitaires de France, 1980, vol. 1, p. 190.
24. 'Regarde les Persans, les Chinois, les Japonais, forme-toi le goût aux hommes vraiment forts, c'est toujours à la source qu'il faut aller: en peinture les Primitifs, en sculpture les Égyptiens, en miniature les Persans.' Letter from Pissarro to Lucien, 25 June 1883, ibid., vol. I, p. 164.
25. Letter to Pissarro, in Rouen, around mid-May 1884, *Correspondance de Paul Gauguin*, *op. cit.*, vol. I, p. 63.

always feature small figures coming and going on the path or road, in constant movement from the city to the countryside or vice versa.

Both Pissarro's *Rue de l'Hermitage, in Pontoise* (1875) [cat. 3] and Gauguin's *Rue Jouvenet in Rouen* (1884) [cat. 4] depict settings familiar to each artist, as they represent the area around their respective houses. In both cases, the light from the streets crossing at right angles establishes a measured *andante* rhythm receding into the distance. There, in the background the urban area meets a horizon of vegetation: nature envelops the architecture. In fact, however, the opposite case is the more common one, in which the houses are shifted towards the background. Pissarro painted *The Cabbage Field, Pontoise* (1873) [cat. 5] in a part of Pontoise known as 'Le Chou' (The Cabbage). In this autumn landscape only the small, scarcely visible figures of three peasants people what appears to be a scene of total bucolic solitude. However, through the curtain of trees we can make out houses on the hill. This ambiguity seems even more thought-out in *A Street in Rouen* (1884) [cat. 6], a work by Gauguin that may have been exhibited (although it is difficult to be sure) in the eighth Impressionist exhibition of 1886, and which produces the impression of a purely rural landscape. In fact, however, it depicts an empty plot of urban land: the trees on the right are those of a cemetery near the artist's house.[26] Both Pissarro and Gauguin offer us the chance to follow these changing perspectives in parallel, this game of hide-and-seek which consists of looking at the country from the city and (not) looking at the city from the country.

Cézanne's formula

Among Gauguin's relationships with the regulars of Pissarro's circle, the one with Cézanne is the most difficult to pin down (there is no surviving correspondence between them, nor any indication that they may have become friends), but it was also the most important. The Cézanne whom Gauguin met in 1881 in Pontoise was ten years older than Gauguin and much more developed with regard to the formulation of his own style. Gauguin envied his 'secret formula' as he jokingly put it to Pissarro in June 1881: 'Has M. Césanne [sic] found the precise formula for a work accepted by everyone? If he finds the recipe for compressing the exaggerated expression of all his sensations into a single and unique procedure, I beg of you to make him talk about it in his sleep, by giving him one of those mysterious homeopathic drugs and come to Paris as soon as possible to tell me about it'.[27] Gauguin's students recalled how he would sometimes set to work saying 'Let's do a Cézanne'.[28] It is hardly surprising that all this encouraged Cézanne's paranoid tendencies, the sensation of being persecuted and exploited. Towards the end of his life he would repeat often the phrase: 'I just had one little feeling, and M. Gauguin stole it from me'.[29]

What Gauguin envied above all in Cézanne was his discovery of a method for moving beyond Impressionism, which by that point had begun to degenerate into a mannered

26. Wildenstein, D.: *Gauguin. Premier itinéraire d'un sauvage. Catalogue de l'oeuvre peint (1873–1888), op. cit.*, vol. I, p. 142

27. 'Mr Césanne a-t-il trouvé la formule exacte d'une oeuvre admise par tout le monde? S'il trouvait la recette pour comprimer l'expression outrée de toutes ses sensations dans un seul et unique procédé je vous en prie tâchez de le faire causer pendant son sommeil en lui administrant une de ces drogue mystérieuses et homéopathique et venez au plus tôt à Paris nous en faire part.' Letter to Pissarro, June 1881, in *Correspondance de Paul Gauguin*, *op. cit.*, vol. I, p. 21.

28. 'Allons faire un Cézanne'; declaration by Paul Sérusier quoted in Chassé, Charles : *Gauguin et son temps*, Paris, 1955, p. 50.

29. 'Je n'avais qu'une petite sensation, Monsieur Gauguin me l'a volée!' in Gustave Geffroy: *Claude Monet. Sa vie, son oeuvre* [1924]. Macula, Paris, 1980, p. 328. Maurice Denis recoge otra versión más elaborada que le contó Octave Mirbeau: 'Ah! ce Gauguin! J'avais une petite sensation et il me l'a prise. Il l'a menée en Bretagne, à la Martinique, à Tahiti, oui, dans tous les paquebots!' in Denis, M: *Journal*, Paris, La Colombe, 1957–1959; vol. II, p. 46.

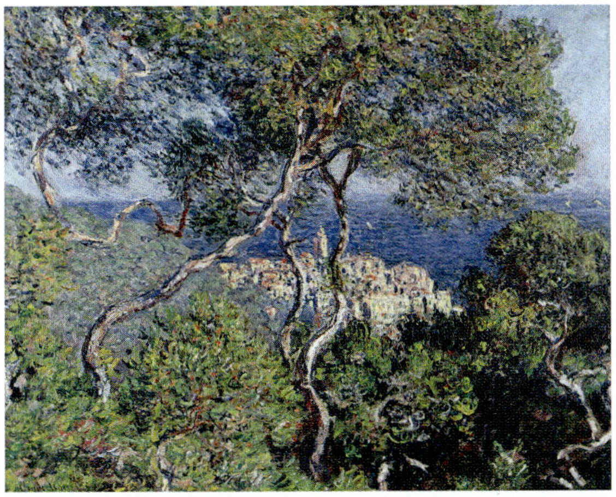

Claude Monet
Bordighera, 1884
Oil on canvas. 65 x 81 cm
Chicago, Art Institute of Chicago

style. One day in July 1884, Gauguin visited the exhibition in the Durand-Ruel gallery of around twenty works by Monet, most painted in Bordighera between January and April of that year. Although he acknowledged Monet's 'great qualities', and admired his 'remarkable' execution, Monet's delight in this brilliance of handling seemed to Gauguin a dangerous path to pursue. To counterbalance this impression, when he left the Durand-Ruel gallery, Gauguin went into Père Tanguy's shop and was fascinated to find there four paintings by Cézanne painted in Pontoise: 'marvels of an essentially pure art and one which one never tires of looking at'.[30]

In discussing Cézanne's influence on Gauguin, elements such as the ordering of the brushstroke into parallel vertical or diagonal lines and the geometrical simplification of the outlines of the objects are frequently mentioned. However, what Gauguin learned from Cézanne cannot simply be reduced to this. The major theme of a Cézanne-like still life by Gauguin such as *The White Bowl* (1886) [cat. 11] is a Baroque interplay of the ambiguities between appearance and reality. The printed wallpaper so often found in the background of works by Cézane, for example his *Fruit Bowl, Plate and Apples* (1879–1880) [cat. 13], is used by Gauguin to create a sort of dance between the flowers in the vase, their image in the mirror and the flowers on the wallpaper. The real flowers are located on the borderline between two illusions: the reflection on one side and the wallpaper on the other. It is as if Gauguin were thinking about the nature and limits of pictorial illusionism.

The wallpaper is also a protagonist in some of the portraits of this period. *The Landlord's Daughter* (1886) [cat. 9], if its traditional title is not misleading, must be a portrait of the daughter of the street advertising firm director in which Gauguin found himself obliged to work in the winter of 1885–1886 in order to relieve his somewhat desperate financial situation. A sort of 'cosmetic' counterpoint which animates the face of the sitter is

30. 'Voilà des merveilles d'un art essentiellement pur et qu'on ne se lasse pas de regarder.' Letter to Pissarro, around 10 July 1884, in *Correspondance de Paul Gauguin*, *op. cit.*, vol. I, p. 65.

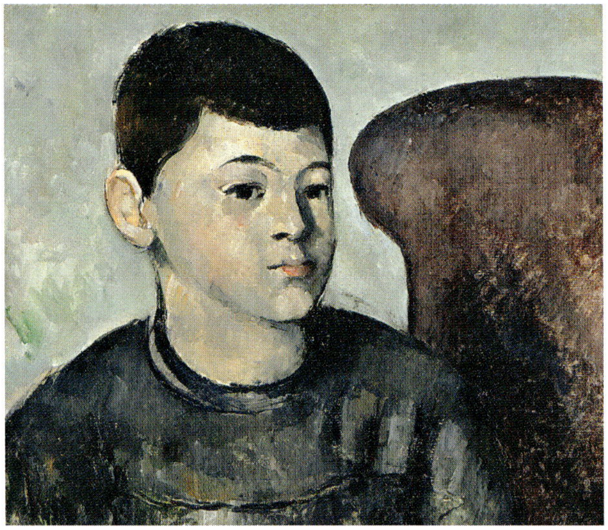

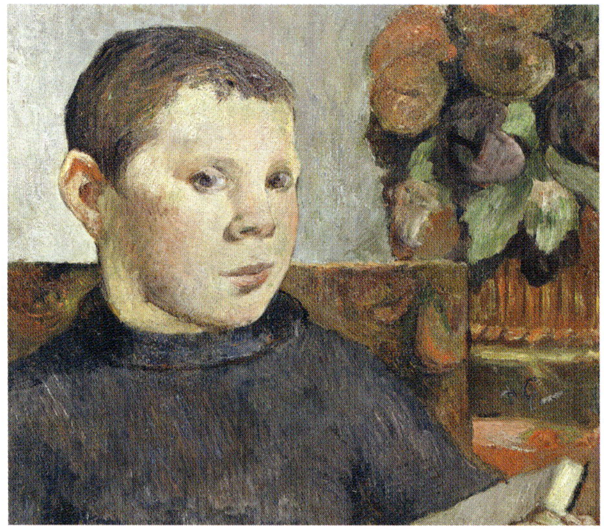

Paul Cézanne
The Artist's Son in a Red Armchair, 1881–1882
Oil on canvas. 34 x 37.5 cm
Paris, Musée de l'Orangerie

Paul Gauguin
Clovis, c. 1886
(detail)
[cat. 10]

established between the cold, greenish flowers, the wallpaper and the strong red of the shawl, the latter in turn emphasising the red of her lips. The sketchy flowers, like the curls that fall over her forehead, give a coquettish air to this young woman who, despite her lack of beauty, looks out and smiles at the spectator with a seeming desire to seduce. Between this rhetoric of seduction and the sobriety of the portraits of Madame Cézanne, with her expressionless eyes and her mute, mask-like face, there is a huge gulf.

However, other portraits reveal a much greater affinity with Cézanne. The Portrait of *Clovis* (cat. 10) must also have been painted in the winter of 1885–1886, which Gauguin spent in Paris with his six-year-old son Clovis, whom he had brought with him from Denmark. The artist's letters to his wife offer us a moving testimony of the miserable existence of father and son during those months, living in an unfurnished house, at times with nothing more than a little bread and sausage for dinner. The letters also describe Clovis's sadness, how he frequently asked when his mother was arriving and how he became accustomed to play alone in a corner so as not to disturb his father. They tell of how the child fell ill and of Gauguin's desperate search for work. All these moving details are notably absent in the painting. Gauguin clearly abandons here the type of psychological portrait that had prevailed in the nineteenth century and rethinks the genre from the starting point of purely visual values. His Clovis seems close to Cézanne's portrait of his son Paul (*The Artist's Son in a Red Armchair*, 1881–1882). Like Cézanne, Gauguin simplifies the line and gives the sitter a monumental, hieratic quality. The figures are made more legible at the expense of superficial likeness, with the nose and the distance between the eyes made larger, and the hands and head made more vigorous, the latter as round as if carved in stone. While Cézanne's portrait of his son establishes a contrast between the contiguous curves of the head and chair, Gauguin finds his counterpart for Clovis's head in the basket of flowers which is not a real basket of flowers but rather a decorative finial at the top of the stairs: a bouquet as stone-like as the head of the child itself.[31]

2. Landscape and Arabesque

> 'In the centre of the Paradise, Ygdrasil, the logarithmic tree, sunk its roots of life into the soil, and the thick shadow of its leaves moved over the grass around it where the lone Night spread out. Leaning against its trunk in the shadow was the book of the Mystery, which set out the truth that had to be known. And in the course of the day, the wind, breathing on the leaves of the tree, spelled out the required hieroglyphics.'
>
> André Gide, *Le traité du Narcisse*.[32]

The first time that Gauguin's name appeared alongside those of the Impressionists was in the fourth exhibition held by that group in 1879. The single work he exhibited on that occasion was not in fact a painting but a marble bust of his eldest son, Emil, which was not included in the catalogue as the artist had only been invited to take part very shortly before the opening. However, 'M. Gauguin' does appear in the same catalogue as the owner of three exhibited paintings by Pissarro. One of them was *Woodland Scene (Spring)* (1878) [cat. 16], entitled then *Landscape in February. Women Returning from the Fountain* whose bare, slender trees against the luminous sky gave the composition a delicate, measured rhythm.[33] This device, which Pissarro used on other occasions, had a primarily formal function. In the same way that Manet used the rail in *The Balcony*, or the large metal railings of the Gare Saint-Lazare in *The Railway*, Pissarro used this screen of trees to *support* the scene on the picture surface. The spectator's gaze, rather than losing itself and disappearing into the distance, is obliged to pause in a nearer plane. At the same time, the interlaced, aligned trees imbue the landscape with a certain lyrical tone. The poet and critic Albert Aurier (who would be the great champion of Gauguin's art) noted that in Pissarro's landscapes, 'the monotonously curving lines of the grove of willows, the curtain of poplars, help to create the impression of a tender rural peacefulness'[34] (another confirmation of the pastoral mode, we might suggest).

The device of the tree trunks and branches as a support for the composition would later be developed by Cézanne. Gauguin owned a work by the artist with 'the trees aligned like soldiers and the shadows projected in succession like a flight of steps'.[35] Cézanne explored all the possibilities that trees offered: the aligned, parallel trunks and the sinuous branches, trees as classical columns or forming pointed arches or cross-vaulting, Gothic filigree against blue sky. However, along with these variations on the structure of the picture surface, the tree could also be an isolated entity, a hero in plant-form dominating the landscape, like the solitary tree next to the pond of the Jas de Bouffan, or the great pine

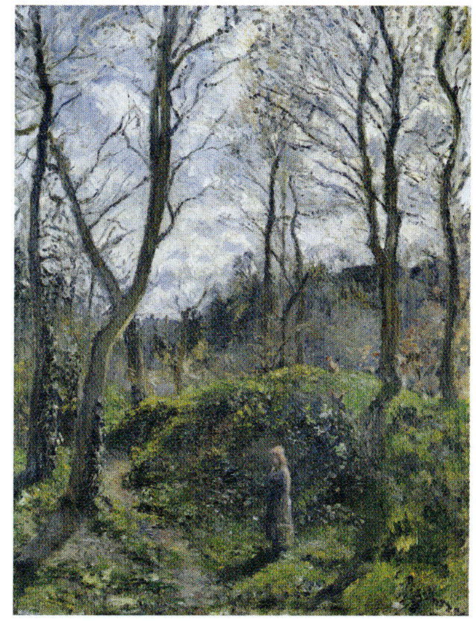

Camille Pissarro
Woodland Scene (Spring), 1878
[cat. 16]

31. Wildenstein, D.: *Gauguin. Premier itinéraire d'un sauvage*, *op. cit.*, vol. 1, p. 250.
32. 'Au centre de l'Eden, Ygdrasil, l'arbre logarithmique, plongeait dans le sol ses racines de vie, et promenait sur la pelouse autour, l'ombre épaisse de son feuillage où s'éployait la seule Nuit. Dans l'ombre, contre son tronc, s'appuyait le livre du Mystère — où se lisait la vérité qu'il faut connaître. Et le vent, soufflant dans les feuilles de l'arbre, en épelait, le long du jour, les hiéroglyphes nécessaires.' In Gide, André: *Le traité du Narcisse*. 1891.
33. Bodelsen, Merette: 'Gauguin collector', in *The Burlington Magazine*, September 1970, pp. 590–616.
34. 'Les lignes monotonement courbes du buisson des saules, du rideau des peupliers, concourent à une impression de paix rural, attendrissante.' 'Camille Pissarro', in Aurier, Albert: *Textes critiques 1889–1892. De l'impressionnisme au symbolisme*. École nationale supérieure des Beaux-Arts, Paris, 1995, p. 56.
35. 'Les arbres rangés comme des soldats et les ombres portées en gradin comme un escalier.' Letter to Pissarro, between 25 and 29 July 1883, in *Correspondance de Paul Gauguin*, *op. cit.*, vol. I, p. 51.

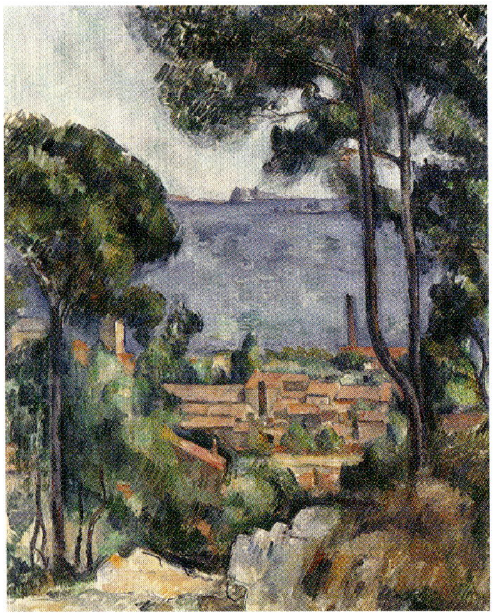 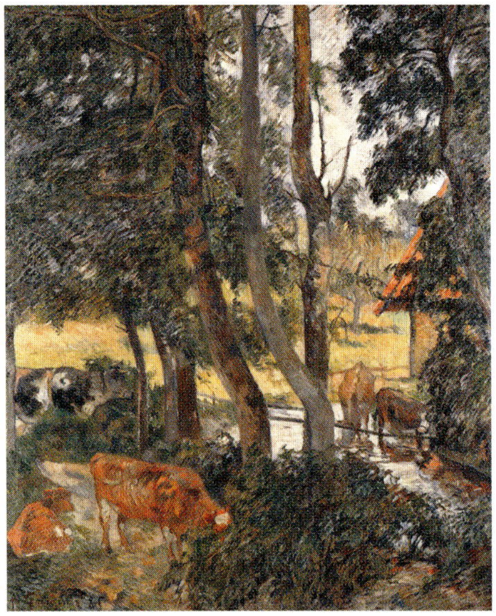 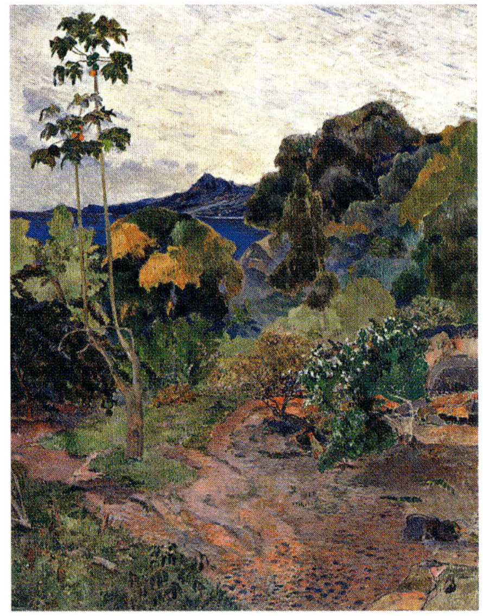

Paul Cézanne
View of L'Estaque, 1883–1885
[cat. 21]

Paul Gauguin
Cows at the Watering-place, 1885
[cat. 22]

Paul Gauguin
Tropical Vegetation, Martinique, 1887
Oil on canvas. 116 x 89 cm
Edinburgh, National Gallery of Scotland

which rises up on the flat Provençal plain and rivals the Mont Saint-Victoire behind it in symbolic power. Gauguin's painting also features these two possibilities: the tree as a structure within the landscape, and the tree as a sign that it has freed itself from the landscape and stands above it. In *An Orchard Under the Church of Bihorel* (1884) [cat. 18] the central tree, with its radial structure, is the framework that supports the dense mass of vegetation. In *The Fire at the River Bank* (1886) [cat. 19] an almost identical organisation of the branches is to be seen, but this time raised up on the horizon, delineating its arabesque like a signature against the sky.

This exaltation of the tree as an isolated sign appears in a work by Cézanne that seems to have been particularly influential for Gauguin: his *View of L'Estaque* (1883–1885) [cat. 21]. The lines of the very long, slim trunks spring from their bases together, then separate into a graceful curve and continue in parallel lines towards the sky. The vertical format, unusual in a landscape, further reinforces the ascending sensation of this hairpin form that is both two trees and one at the same time (and which also appears in some of Cézanne's drawings, such as *Trees and Roofs* (1882–1883) [cat. 20]. Gauguin undoubtedly had this *View of L'Estaque* in mind when he painted *Cows at the Watering-place* (1885) [cat. 22], set in the meadows near Dieppe. The Cézanne-like brushwork which Gauguin used for the dense foliage of the forest, is always mentioned in relation to this painting, but it is not, however, the most interesting aspect of Cézanne's influence. The 'hairpin' of trees taken from the *View of L'Estaque* and reinforced with the parallel lines of other trunks, becomes a powerful central band that traverses and dominates the composition from top to bottom.

The interest in these trees in L'Estaque is related to a particular interpretation of Cézanne's use of drawing. Around 1884–1885, Gauguin was fascinated by graphology, analysing Pissarro's character on the basis of his handwriting and asking others for samples of their hand. 'You see', he wrote, 'how thought has a direct influence on writing. Do you have a letter by Césanne [sic]?.'[36] In January 1885, in a letter to Schuffenecker which is one of the first statements of his personal aesthetic, Gauguin offers a discourse on the various types of lines (noble lines and deceitful lines, the straight line as a symbol of the infinite and the curved line as a symbol of the limited), and argues that an artist's drawing can be read according to the rules of graphology: 'Take Césanne [sic] the misunderstood; he cultivates the essentially mystical nature of the Orient [...] in the guise of the mystery and weighty tranquility of the man who lies down to dream'.[37] The reference here to the 'mystical nature of the Orient' would be repeated by Gauguin on another occasion when he referred to the sinuous ornamental lines of old Persian art in the Dieulafoy Collection in the Louvre. Speaking of them, he observed that 'one needs immense genius to imagine flowers that are muscles of animals or muscles that are flowers. All the dreaming, mystical Orient is to be found there'.[38] We can associate the Oriental mysticism which Gauguin believed he could see in the work of Cézanne with that 'song of the arabesque', that Matisse referred to in praise of the artist.[39]

The Tree of Paradise

Like an obsessive motif, Cézanne's 'hairpin' tree form reappears once more in Gauguin's painting, in one of the masterpieces of his stay in Martinique in 1887: *Tropical Vegetation*. In Gauguin's Martinique canvases, the atmospheric landscape of Impressionism gives way to a vision which is marked by an emphasis on the decorative surface. In this view of the bay of Saint-Pierre, with the sea and Mount Pelée in the background, the artist has hidden the city of Saint-Pierre between the luxuriant vegetation in order to create a landscape untouched by human presence. The rich palette of greens and blues with touches of crimson and orange and the parallel brushstrokes in the manner of Cézanne give the painting the feel of an Oriental carpet, as has often been observed. And within the dense network that covers the picture surface we see two extended branches of a papaya tree, like a liberated sign. The way of drawing its parallel lines, which join together to form a sort of bow, anticipates Victor Horta's iron columns, Henry van de Velde's candelabra, or other examples of Art Nouveau metalwork. While Octave Mirabeau saw in Gauguin's Martinique landscapes 'an almost religious mystery, a sacred abundance of Eden,'[40] this papaya tree is the tree of paradise which summarises the entire mythical and legendary character of the tropical island.

The trees with their calligraphic presence are to be found in almost all the Martinique works. Possibly the finest example is *The Inlet of Saint-Pierre seen from the Anse Turin*

36. 'Vous voyez que la pensée influe directement sur l'écriture. Avez-vous une lettre de Césanne.' Letter to Pissarro, end of November to beginning of December 1884, in *Correspondance de Paul Gauguin*, *op. cit.*, vol. I, p. 77.

37. 'Voyez Césanne [sic] l'incompris; la nature essentiellement mystique de l'Orient, [...] il affectionne sous la forme le mystère et la tranquillité lourde de l'homme couché pour rêver.' Letter to Schuffenecker, 14 January 1885, ibid., *Correspondance de Paul Gauguin*, vol. I, p. 88.

38. 'Il a fallu un immense génie pour imaginer des fleurs qui soient des muscles d'animaux ou des muscles qui soient des fleurs. Tout l'Orient mystique rêveur se retrouve là-dedans.' Gauguin, P.: 'Notes sur l'art à l'Exposition universelle', in *Le Moderniste illustré*, 4 July 1889, p. 86.

39. 'Le chant de l'arabesque' is a phrase quoted in Diehl, Gaston : *Henri Matisse*. Paris, Pierre Tisnée, 1954, quoted in Matisse, H.: *Écrits et propos sur l'art*. Dominique Fourcadem (ed.). Paris, Hermann, 1992, p. 134.

40. 'Il y a dans ces sous-bois aux végétations, aux flores monstrueuses, aux formidables coulées de soleil, un mystère presque religieux, une abondance sacrée d'Éden.' 'Paul Gauguin' [1891], in Mirbeau, Octave : *Des artistes*. Hubert Juin. (preface). Paris, Union Générale d'Éditions, 1986, p. 126.

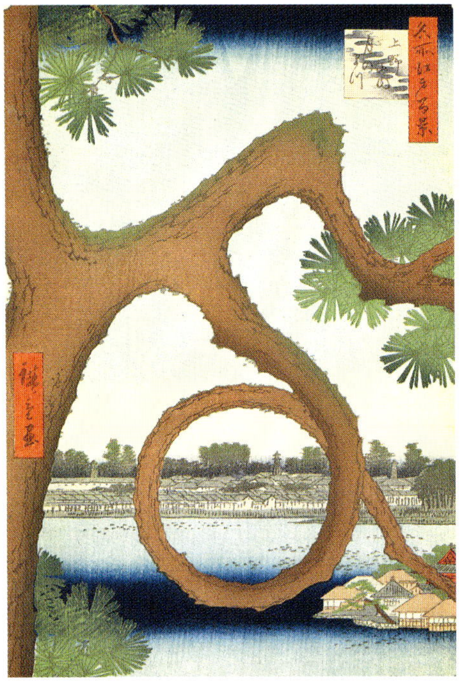

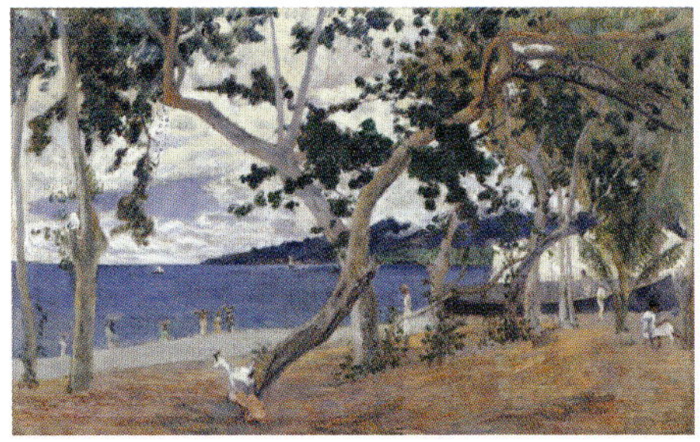

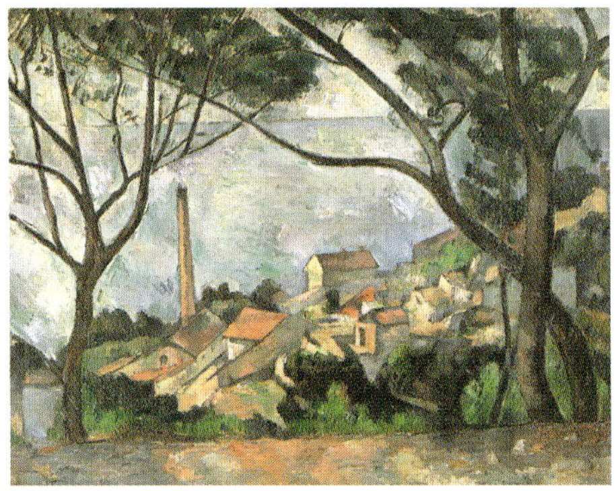

Utagawa Hiroshige
Moon Pine, Ueno, 1857
No. 89 from 'One Hundred Famous Views of Edo'
Woodblock print. 36 x 23,5 cm.
Brooklyn, The Brooklyn Museum of Art (Gift of Anna Ferris 30,1478.89)

Paul Gauguin
The Inlet of Saint-Pierre seen from the Anse Turin, 1887
[cat. 23]

Paul Cézanne
The Sea at L'Estaque, 1879
Oil on canvas. 92 x 73 cm
Paris, Musée Picasso

(1887) [cat. 23]. As in *Tropical Vegetation*, in this work the city of Saint-Pierre remains hidden, here behind the outcrop of white rock extending into the sea. The human and animal figures to be found in other Martinique compositions have been relegated to the distance in order to focus on the trunks and branches of the vines which interlace in the foreground. This emphasis on the arabesque of the trees has been associated with the prints of Hokusai and Hiroshige. However, at this point Gauguin does not seem to have been interested in Japanese art (which he only turned to in 1888), and it is more convincing to relate it once again to Cézanne, for example the serpentine interlaced branches of the trees in *The Sea at L'Estaque* (1878–1879). As with Cézanne's sinuous branches, Gauguin's trees frame the background landscape with the volcano below the cloudy sky and the bustle of people on the beach. However, the interlaced vine branches in the foreground also have a symbolic value: the large x-shape which they create literally blots out the realistic aspect of the landscape and transforms nature into a fantastical stage set. The vines are a door, a sort of gateway which blocks or allows access into a distant and mythical domain. Their sinuous feminine curves summarise the sensual, eroticised landscape of the tropical paradise.

The tree as a sign will reappear on numerous occasions in Gauguin's work, up to his late Oceanic paintings. We encounter it once more in the diagonal trunk that crosses *The Vision after the Sermon* (1888) [cat. 41], dividing the canvas and separating the real from the imaginary. It is present again in *Shepherds in a Meadow* (1888) [cat. 26], in which the

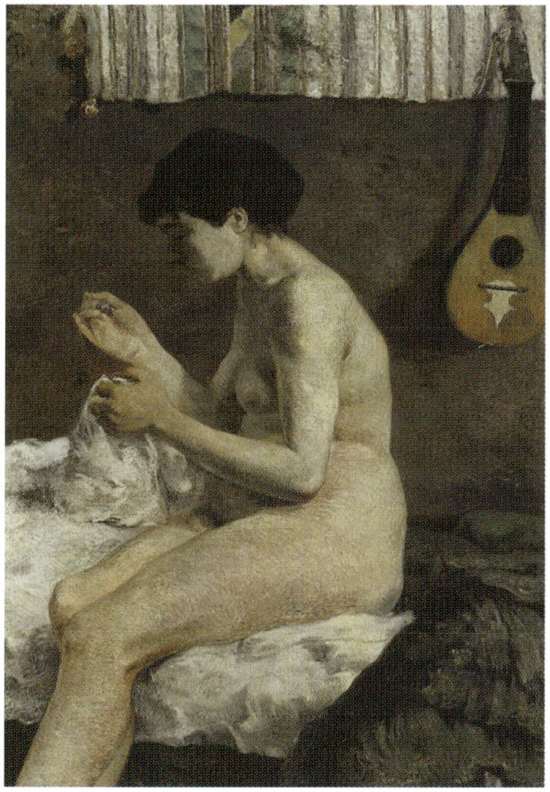

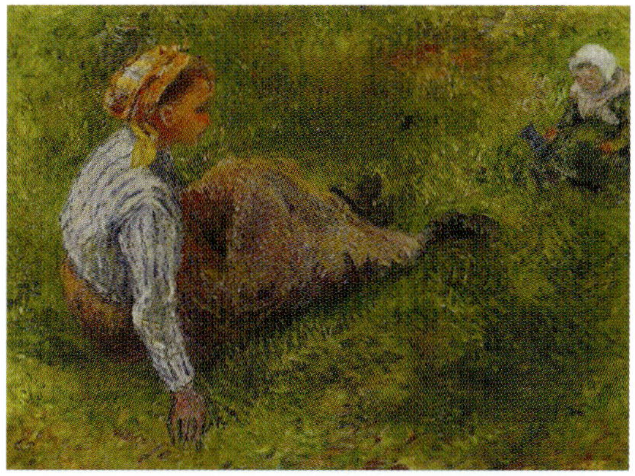

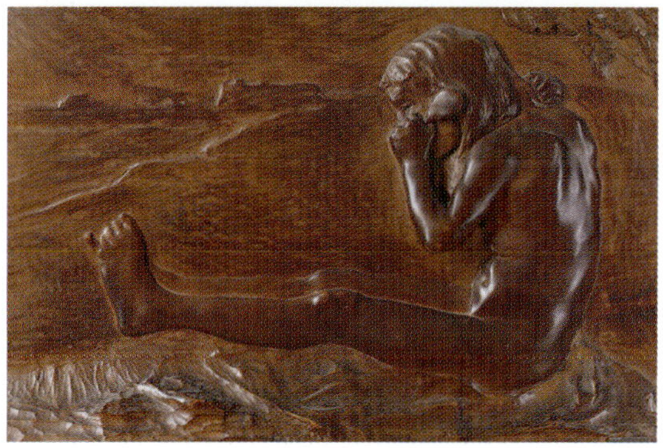

Paul Gauguin
Study of a Nude. Suzanne Sewing, 1880
Oil on canvas. 111,4 x 79.5 cm
Copenhagen, Ny Carlsberg Glyptotek

Camille Pissarro
Sitting Peasant with Infant, 1881
Oil on canvas
Private Collection

Paul Gauguin
La Toilette, 1882
[cat 28]

intimacy between the human figures is reflected in the entire natural setting, both in the bull and cow resting on the grass and in the two tall trees, one of which leans towards the other. Lastly, in *Christ in the Garden of Olives* (1889) [cat. 68] the motif appears once more as a sad, charred remnant of the tree of Paradise.

3. The nude and the dance

A largely overlooked early work by Gauguin is, in fact, crucial for deciphering the development of the 'pastoral of the primitive' in his work. This is a carved wood relief entitled *La Toilette* [cat. 28], dated 1882 and dedicated 'à mon ami Pissarro'. Although Pissarro's letter acknowledging this gift has not survived, we do have Gauguin's reply to it: 'I am totally abashed and blushing to read your compliments regarding the wood carving which I sent you; I am happy that you liked it'.[41] Pissarro undoubtedly grasped the homage that was intended by the gift: the girl in *La Toilette* evokes the figures of seated peasants on the grass which are so common in his work of that period (see for example, *Seated Peasant with Child* of 1881). While taking his former teacher as his starting point, here Gauguin goes much further in his simplification of the anatomy, anticipating his later evolution towards primitivism and synthetism.

41. 'Je suis tout confus et rouge en lisant vos compliments à propos du bois que je vous ai envoyé; je suis heureux qu'il vous plaise'. Letter to Pissarro, 9 November 1882, in *Correspondance de Paul Gauguin*, *op. cit.*, vol. I, p. 35.

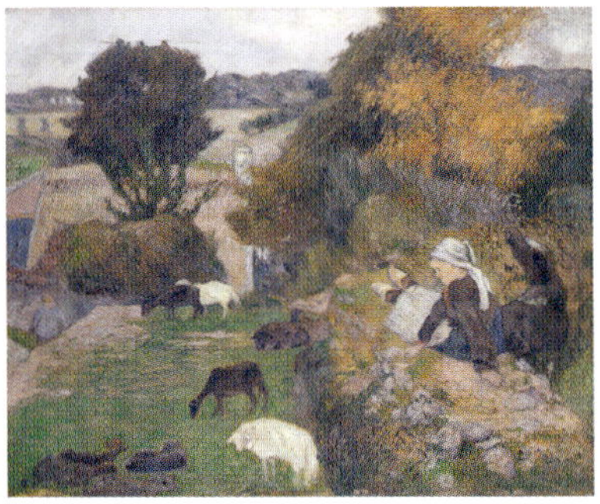

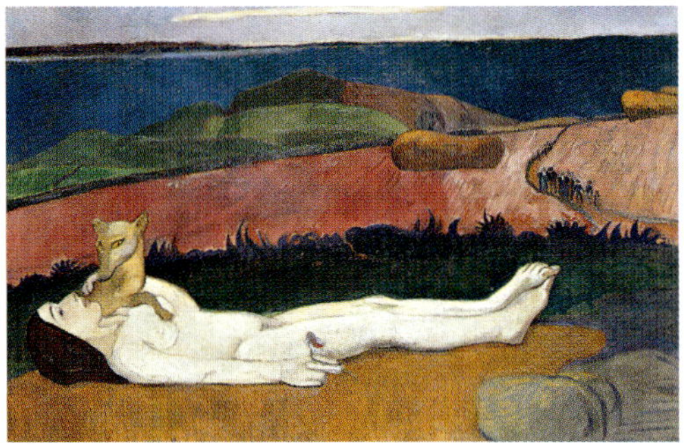

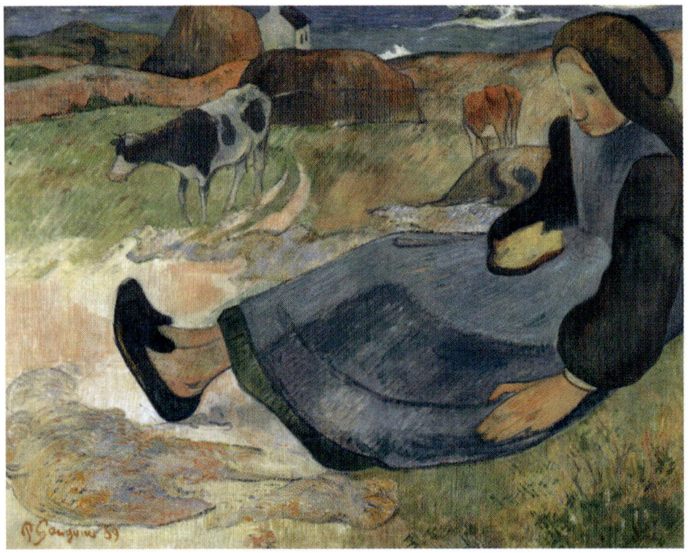

Paul Gauguin
Breton Sheperdess, 1886
Oil on canvas. 60 x 73 cm
Newcastle upon Tyne, The Laing Art Gallery, Tyne & Wear Museums

Paul Gauguin
The Loss of Virginity, 1890–1891
Oil on canvas. 90 x 130 cm
Norfolk, Chrysler Museum, Gift of Walter P. Chrysler, Jr.
71.510

Paul Gauguin
Seated Breton Girl, 1889
Oil on canvas. 71.5 x 90.5 cm
Copenhagen, Ny Carlsberg Glyptotek

The nude is a rare subject in Gauguin's early work. One exception is the famous *Suzanne Sewing* (1881) which drew Huysman's praise.[42] *La Toilette* is the exact opposite of that painting: rather than an adult woman, we have an adolescent; rather than working, the sitter focuses on her body; rather than an interior, the setting is a sketchy landscape. While *Suzanne Sewing* is a late sample of naturalist painting, *La Toilette* contains the seed of the future development of the 'pastoral of the primitive'. The naked girl in a landscape, identified with the earth, is a symbolic subject that Gauguin would explore a decade later in *Loss of Virginity* (1890). The angular, androgynous body and the stiff pose appear again, for example, in one of the *Young Breton Bathers* of 1888 [cat. 36]. Also important is the monstrous, grotesque foot that terminates the body and recalls numerous examples of archaic sculpture, from figures on Romanesque capitals to Hindu temple reliefs. The exaggeratedly large hands and feet reappear in *Breton Bathers* and *The Wrestlers* (1880), as well as *Loss of Virginity* (1890–1891) as a sign of regression, the indication of a rough, primitive nature.

42. 'L'Exposition des Independants en 1881', in Huysmans, Joris-Karl: *L'art moderne. Certains*. Hubert Juin (preface). Paris, Union Générale d'Éditions, 1975, pp. 239–43.

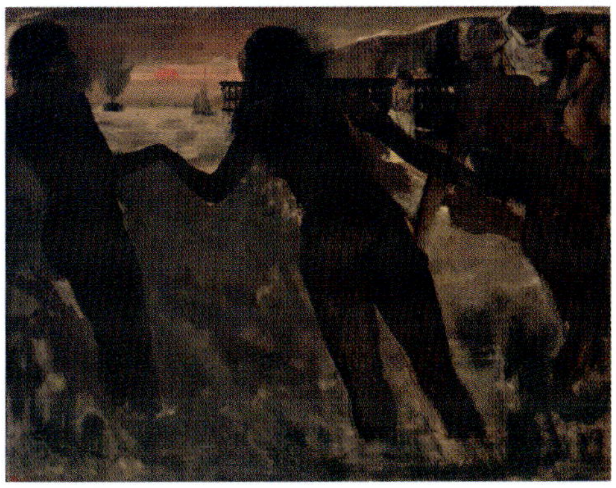

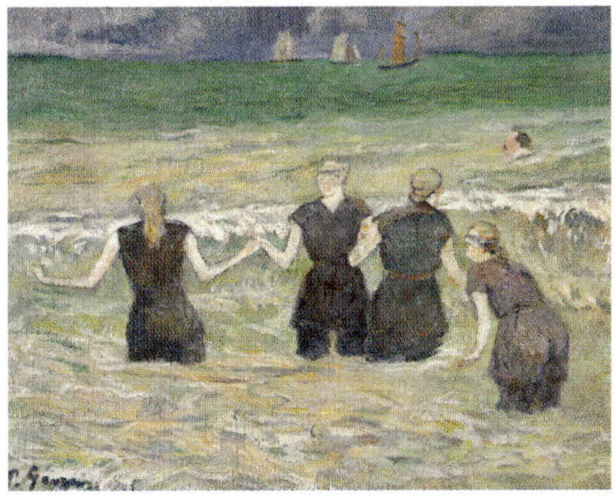

Edgar Degas
Peasant Girls bathing in the Sea at Sunset, 1875–1876
[cat 29]

Paul Gauguin
Bathers at Dieppe, 1885
Oil on canvas. 38 x 46 cm
Tokyo, The National Museum of Western Art

Learning from Degas

The brilliant precedent of *La Toilette* was not, however, followed up. Four years would pass before Gauguin would once more turn to the nude and to the human figure in general. I do not refer by this to the small figures that are always to be found as accessories in his landscapes, but rather to large-scale figural compositions. Towards the mid-1880s, other artists associated with Impressionism, such as Pissarro, Renoir and the young Seurat, were all tempted to undertake ambitious figure subjects. Gauguin did not look to any of these artists, however, but focused instead on Degas. Pissarro and Degas represented two rival leaderships within the Impressionist group, and while Gauguin had aligned himself with one of them, he had kept his distance from the other, frequently accusing him of intrigues and of sabotaging the Impressionist group's exhibitions.[43] Following his break with Pissarro in 1886, however, the result of the older artist's association with the Neo-Impressionist group, the way was opened for a closer association with Degas, and in the autumn of 1886 Pissarro commented sarcastically on this new relationship.[44]

One of Gauguin's first references to Degas in his correspondence relates to his talents in drawing: 'Manet assumed the uniform of leader; now that he has died, Degas will take over from him, and this is an impressionist who draws!'.[45] Inevitably, drawing was what interested Gauguin in Degas. For him, Degas' draughtsmanship had a negative aspect: its naturalist aspect, which Gauguin graphically called the 'bad odour of the model'.[46] At the same time, however, Degas was the master who did not fear to disobey nature and subject human anatomy to whatever distortions were required. Émile Bernard noted that in 1886, Gauguin 'spoke above all about Degas, for whose aesthetic distortion he had the greatest respect'.[47] Over time Gauguin would assemble his own pantheon of great masters of drawing, whom he appreciated in terms of their distortion of the figure: Botticelli, Cranach, Delacroix and Ingres. Degas was the last in this tradition.

43. See for example the letter to Pissarro of late May 1885, *Correspondance de Paul Gauguin*, *op. cit.*, vol. I, p. 107.
44. 'Gauguin est redevenu très intime de Degas et va le voir souvent, curieux, n'est-ce pas, cette bascule des intérêts!' Letter from Pissarro to his son Lucien, 23 November 1886, *Correspondance de Paul Gauguin*, vol. I, p. 141.
45. 'Manet avait endossé l'uniforme de chef maintenant qu'il est mort Degas va lui succéder et c'est un impressioniste qui *dessine*!' Letter to Pissarro, around 7 May 1883, in *Correspondance de Paul Gauguin*, *op. cit.*, vol. I, p. 43.
46. 'Il [Degas] ne trouve pas en effet dans mes toiles ce qu'il voit lui (la mauvaise odeur du modèle).' Letter to Émile Bernard, November 1889, in *Lettres de Gauguin à sa femme et à ses amis*, *op. cit.*, p. 174.
47. Bernard, E: 'Concernant Paul Gauguin', *Nouvelle revue d'Égypte*, January 1904, p. 8. Cited in Wildenstein: *Gauguin. Premier itinéraire d'un sauvage*, *op. cit.*, vol. II, p. 303.

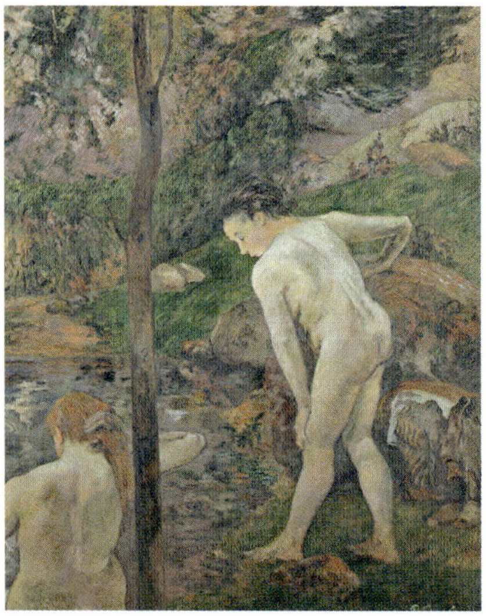

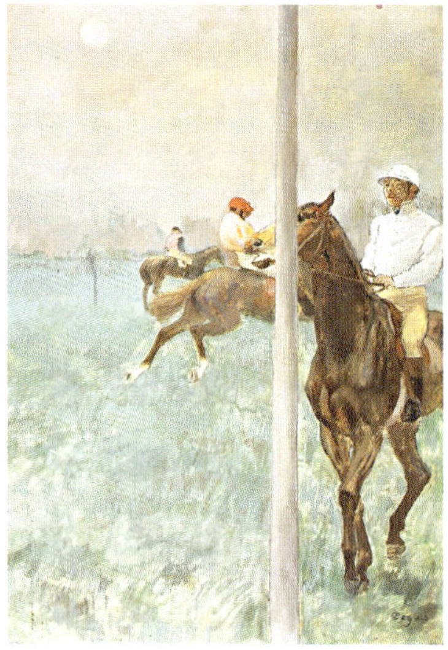

Paul Gauguin
Two Bathers 1887
[cat. 35]

Edgar Degas
Jockeys before the Race, c. 1869–1870
Oil, gouache and pastel on canvas. 107 x 73 cm
Birmingham, University of Birmingham,
The Barber Institute of Fine Arts

Gauguin's large figural compositions up to 1888 are devoted to two subjects typical of Degas: bathing and the dance. In a work that can be seen as a forerunner, *Bathers at Dieppe* (1885), the two subjects are combined. A work by Degas is usually cited as a precedent for this painting, *Peasant Girls Bathing in the Sea at Sunset* (1875–1876) [cat. 29]. This is a pastoral dance with the air of a primitive ritual, more redolent of Gauguin than many works by the artist himself, more *sauvage* than the paintings of the official savage. Normally, however, the subjects of bathing and the dance have a different character in Degas's work: his bathers and dancers move across the parquet of Parisian interiors. Gauguin would translate them into a new, bucolic context.

The women seen washing themselves, drying or arranging their hair in Degas' pastels, shrouded in the shadowy light of their apartments, are now transformed into outdoor bathers. The figures in *Two Bathers* (1887) [cat. 35] recall precedents in the work of Degas (such as the pastel of *Woman Washing Herself with a Sponge*, of 1887 [cat. 34], but transposed to a wooded landscape on the outskirts of Pont-Aven. The critic Fénéon described these two figures and the marked contrast between them: 'One of them, cut in two at waist level by the water, has splendidly drawn shoulders, an opulent bourgeois form: on the grass, a timid little maid with short, rigid hair and a stupid mouth, looks at her, trembling and hesitant to take the last step, her left hand on her knee – she swings her hips. A slender trunk, like a smooth straight shaft, already seen in Cézanne, separates and divides the canvas into two compartments'.[48] This trunk which divides the image into two (and which had also appeared in the work of Degas, for example *Jockeys before the Race*, Barber Institute, Birmingham), emphasises the contrast between the two women, the androgynous one and the sensual red-head. The undergrowth conceals a third figure: that of a deer,

48. 'L'une, que sectionne à la ceinture l'eau, développe un large dessin d'épaules, une architecture d'opulente bourgeoise; sur le pré, une pantoise petite servante, aux courts cheveux raides, à l'ahuri museau, la regarde grelotter, et, hésitante à faire le dernier pas, la main gauche au genou, — hanche. Un grêle, rectiligne et lisse fût, déjà vu dans Cézanne, les sépare et divise la toile en deux caissons.'Aux magasins des marchands de tableaux' [1888], in Fénéon: *Oeuvres plus que complètes*. Halperin, Joan U. (ed.). Gineva-Paris Chroniques d'art. Librairie Droz, 1970, p. 95.

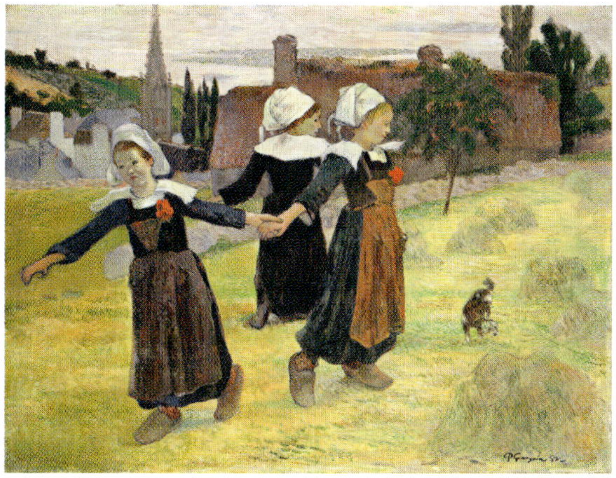

31. Paul Gauguin
Breton Girls Dancing, 1888
[cat 31]

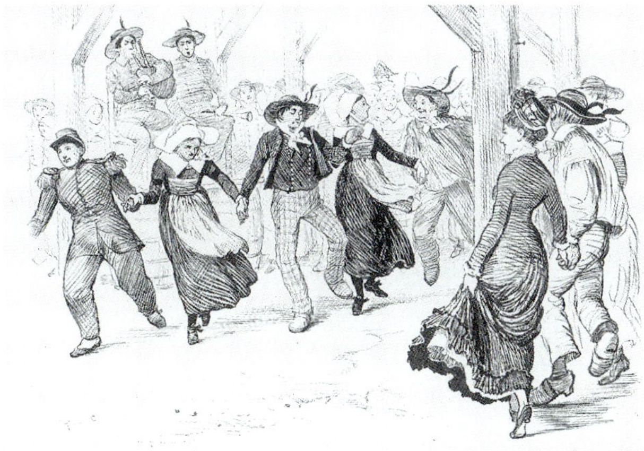

Randolph Caldecott
'Gavotte'
Illustration of the work by Blackburn: *Breton Folk An Artistic Tour in Brittany* (1880)
London, Victoria and Albert Museum

which could be a satyrical symbol of Eros. The scene is perhaps a distant evocation of the traditional iconography of Adam and Eve in Paradise, located on either side of the Tree of Knowledge. It is as if these two bathers were an eccentric parody of the First Couple.

With regard to the other subject, the dance, Gauguin also translates what he borrows from Degas into a new setting. *Breton Girls Dancing* (1888) [cat. 31], which Gauguin described in a letter to Theo van Gogh as 'a Breton gavotte danced by three young girls in the middle of the hay',[49] seems to derive from an illustration by Caldecott for Blackburn's book *Breton Folk: An Artistic Tour in Brittany*.[50] Disregarding the picturesque detail of Caldecott's print, with its theatrical details of set and clothing, Gauguin focuses on the essential: the minimal group of the three girls, like three young Graces, stripped of any festive context that would explain their gaiety.

This removal of context around the figures makes them almost as unreal as Corot's dancing nymphs, so beloved of Gauguin. The isolation between the girls, who are shown looking outwards, emphasises the static and monumental character of each figure. This is particularly the case with the one seen frontally, who recalls one of Degas' ballerinas in second position (*Dancer*, c. 1878 [cat. 30]). This figure also offers us a particularly illuminating example of Degas' influence. Some time after completing the painting, Theo van Gogh found a buyer for it, and asked Gauguin if he would alter a detail that did not please this collector, specifically the girl's right arm, which ended near the edge of the painting with an outsized hand. This monstruous hand which Gauguin ultimately

49. 'Je suis en train de faire une gavotte bretonne dansée par 3 petites filles au milieu des foins [...]. Ce tableau me paraît original et j'en suis assez content au point de vue du dessin.' Letter to Théo van Gogh, around 15–18 June 1888, in *Correspondance de Paul Gauguin*, *op. cit.*, vol. I, p. 151.
50. It has been noted that Gauguin appreciated the graphic works of Caldecott. See Wildenstein, D.: *Gauguin. Premier itinéraire d'un sauvage*, *op. cit.*, vol. 1, p. 267.

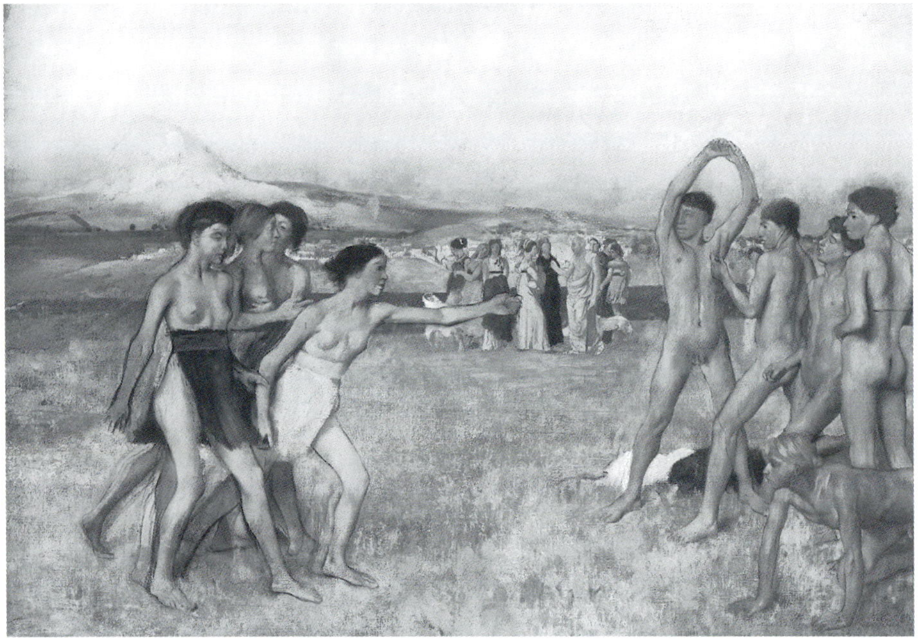

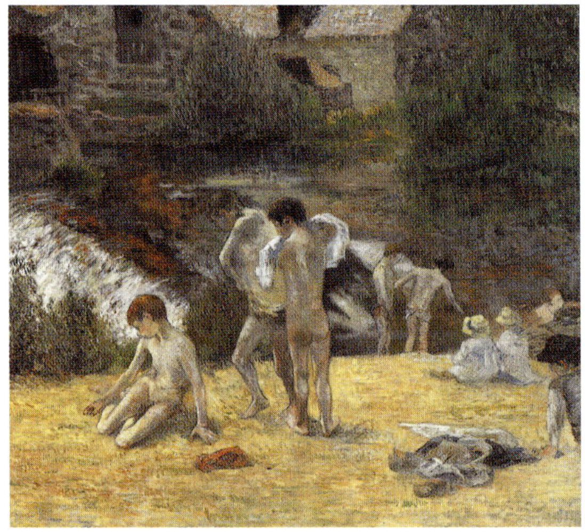

Edgar Degas
Young Spartans Exercising, 1860
Oil on canvas. 109 x 155 cm
London, The National Gallery

Paul Gauguin
The 'Moulin du Bois d'Amour' Bathing Place, 1886
Oil on canvas. 60 x 73 cm
Hiroshima, Hiroshima Museum of Art

'corrected' recalls once again *La Toilette*, and the large feet and hands of primitive figures. Gauguin explained that he had made the girl's hand disproportionate 'in order to balance the dance which has an s-shape'.[51] We can find no better example of one of those *artistic distortions* of which Degas was the master, and which subordinated the delineation of each figure to the rhythm and arabesque of the overall composition.

Puer eternus

The pastoral was traditionally linked to the idea of youth and adolescence, ages expressive of innocence and purity prior to the Fall. The shepherd is the eternal youth – the *puer eternus*. *Breton Girls Dancing* [cat. 31], like the paintings that follow it, focuses on the outdoor activities of adolescents. *Young Breton Bathers* [cat. 36], painted in late June or early July 1888, is located in a bathing spot at the Moulin-Neuf, one of the flour mills on the banks of the Aven, where Gauguin had already painted in the summer of 1886, producing his '*Moulin du Bois d'Amour' Bathing Place* in a style that can still be called Impressionist. If we compare that painting with *The Two Bathers*, mentioned earlier, we see certain similarities between the compositions, such as the opposition between the two figures and the dividing tree, here shifted further back. However, the psychological or social nuances have gone, as well as any narrative pretext. The two boys are isolated from each other, each self-absorbed. The figures derive from a large charcoal drawing and have almost the feel of academic nude studies. An unorthodox and archaicising type of academic study, we might add, which, with its thin, angular bodies recalls the *Young Spartans Exercising* (1860).

51. 'Je vais m'occuper du tableau à retoucher; évidemment la main qui arrive dans le cadre prend beaucoup d'importance et je la croyais nécessaire ainsi pour équilibrer la danse qui a la forme d'un S. Mais comme ce sont des toquades de peintre et non d'amateur je tâcherai d'y remédier ou plutôt atténuer.' Letter to Théo van Gogh, 14 November 1888, in *Correspondance de Paul Gauguin*, *op. cit.*, vol. I, p. 282.

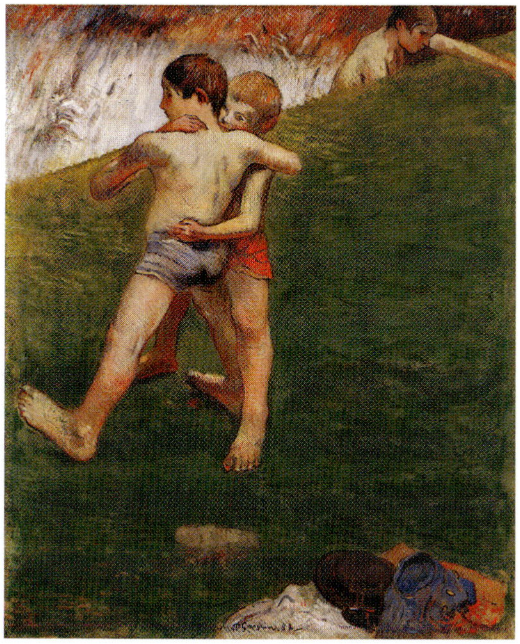

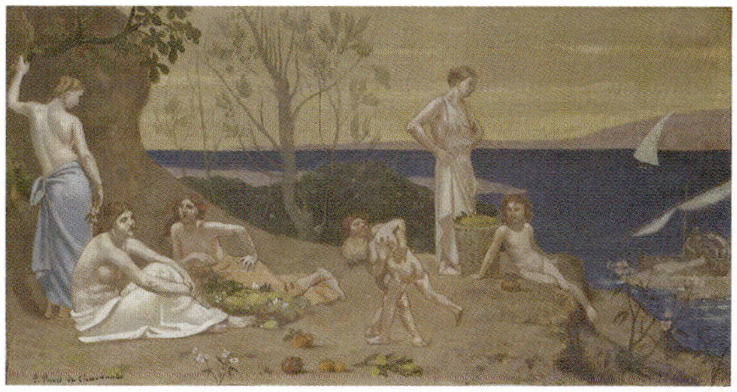

Paul Gauguin
Young Wrestlers, 1888
Oil on canvas. 93 x 73 cm
Private Collection

Pierre Puvis de Chavannes
Pleasant Land, 1882
Oil on canvas. 25.8 x 47.3 cm
New Haven, Conn., Yale University Art Gallery
(The Mary Gertrude Abbey Fund)

Gauguin returns to the figures and setting in this work in another painting of the same format with which it seems to form a pendant: *Young Wrestlers*, depicting the traditional Breton wrestling known as *gouren*. When he completed this painting in early July, the artist explained to Schuffenecker: 'I have just made some nudes that you will like. Not at all like Degas - / The last one is a scene of two young boys near the river – completely Japanese for a savage [deleted: Frenchman] from Peru'.[52] Gauguin thus confirms at a later date his gravitation towards Degas evident in the earlier nudes. Also, the off-centre composition and fragmentation of the image contradict Gauguin's statement that he had liberated himself completely from Degas, as he claims here. With regard to the reference to the 'Japanese', this is also highly significant; up to now Gauguin's allusions to Japanese art were limited to the occasional print included in his still lifes. But this plunging view with its notably high horizon, and use of a low vanishing point is a synthesis of Japanese compositional devices.

If the paintings of Breton girls and boys of 1888 exude eroticism, it is one not contaminated by adult passions: the artist himself stands aside from the scene, not mingling with it, as a purely Platonic spectator. However, in 1889, when Gauguin returned to the subject of bathers in his *Nude Breton Boy* [cat. 59], everything had changed. The boy's body lacks the naturalness of the bathers of the previous year, and the frontal pose implies that he is inevitably conscious of being painted. The viewpoint, as well as stripping away any last vestige of spatial depth, suggests the artist's omnipotence over his model. The face and hands appear reddened by the sun, while the rest of the body is white, implying an

52. 'Aussi je viens de faire quelques nus dont vous seres content. Et ce n'est pas du tout du Degas – Le dernier est une lutte de 2 gamins près de la rivière – tout à fait japonais par un Français sauvage du Perou'. Letter to Schuffenecker, 8 July 1888, ibid, vol. I, pp. 197–98.

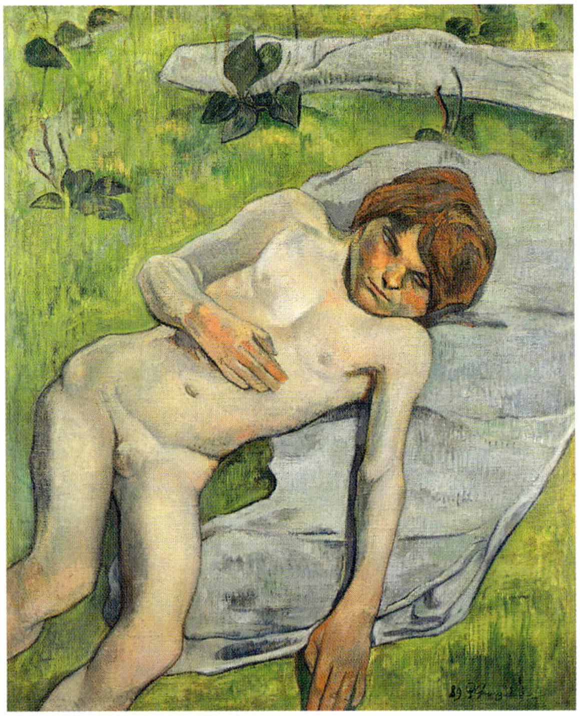

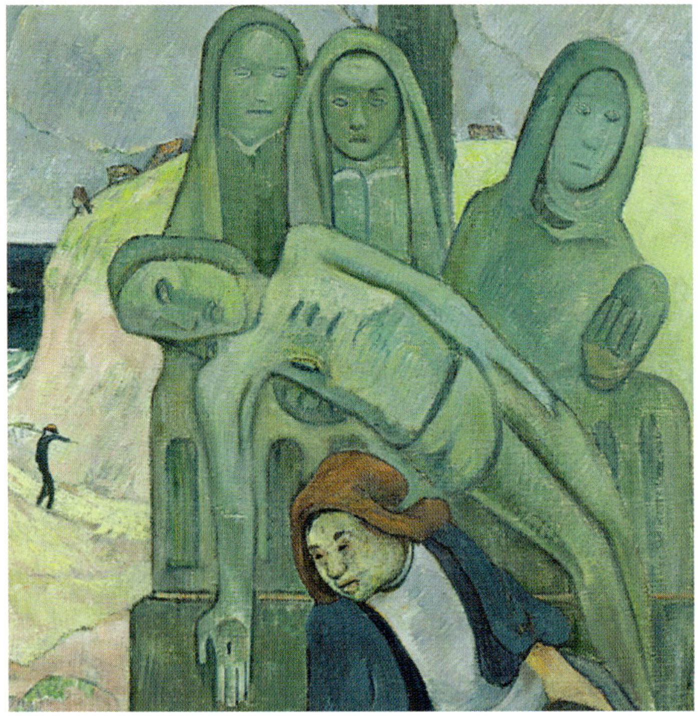

Paul Gauguin
Nude Breton Boy
[cat. 59]

Paul Gauguin
The Green Christ, 1889
(detail)
Oil on canvas. 92 x 73 cm
Brussels, Musées royaux des Beaux-Arts de Belgique

'undressed' rather than nude model, although the red colour of the face might also suggest a blush of shame and anger. The oblique set of the eyes, the fox-like gaze suggestive of a malignant animal that Gauguin uses with other models (such as his portraits of the painter Meyer de Haan), suggest that the boy turns against the painter-voyeur who has imposed his authority over him. Something disturbing has infiltrated the pastoral environment, a certain perversion. The body seems crushed against the ground like an insect, with the limbs almost dislocated, suggesting some of Klimt and Schiele's drawings with their similar charge of disturbing sexuality. What is odd is that this pose repeats the position of Christ in the *Pietà* of the Nizon Calvary group, which Gauguin would also use that same year in his *Green Christ*.[53] By simply changing the context, the artist had discovered the possibility of modifying the meaning of the images, converting the sacred into the profane or transforming a funerary monument into a dubious erotic image.

4. The Vision

> 'The country people, of course, cherish the unlovely idols of an earlier time, such as those which Pausanias found still devoutly preserved in Arcadia. Athenaeus tells the story of one who, coming to a temple of Latona, had expected to find some worthy presentiment of the mother of Apollo, and laughed on seeing only a shapeless wooden figure.'
>
> Walter Pater, 'Winckelmann', *The Renaissance*.[54]

53. Delouche, Denise: 'Gauguin au regard des autres peintres, ses prédécesseurs en Bretagne', in Delouche (ed.): *Pont-Aven et ses peintres*, Presses Universitaires de Rennes 2, l'Institut Culturel de Bretagne, Rennes, 1986, p. 62.
54. The country people, of course, cherish the unlovely idols of an earlier time, such as those which Pausanias found still devoutly preserved in Arcadia. Athenaeus tells the story of one who, coming to a temple of Latona, had expected to find some worthy presentment of the mother of Apollo, and laughed on seeing only a shapeless wooden figure.' Pater, Walter: 'Winckelmann', in *The Renaissance*.

The first indications of Gauguin's shift away from Impressionism appear at a very early date, in a letter to Pissarro of 1881. They take the form of an attack against Monet and Sisley: '*A note* of plein air can be an agreeable thing here and there, but it doesn't constitute an entire painting, and the proof is that you take the trouble to make one'.[55] The Impressionist aesthetic had blurred the difference between *étude* and *tableau*; Gauguin, in contrast, considered that the painting had to be constructed, and for this reason he encouraged Pissarro to 'work more in the studio', creating 'things matured beforehand from the viewpoint of composition and setting'.[56]

In line with this idea, Gauguin developed a working method which consisted of producing 'documents' (sketches or studies) which he compiled for use in later paintings. In 1884, for example, he wrote to Pissarro: 'I started a large number of things which I wish to show you, I hope you will find them interesting, I am not looking for results, they are documents which I am keeping for later'.[57] Gauguin would remain faithful to this method for the rest of his career. His documents are of human figures and animals which he later incorporated into landscape settings. He used this archive of motifs with enormous freedom, increasing or diminishing the size of the figures, inverting them or combining them with others. As with Rodin, Gauguin created his compositions on the basis of fragments, which he reused and re-combined in different works, often far apart chronologically.

As was the case with Rodin, this method inevitably affected the connection or lack of connection between the various elements that made up the composition, questioning that congruity between figures and landscape which was the norm for realist and Impressionist painters. The result at times approximates a collage. This effect is particularly visible in *Breton Women by a Bend in the Road* [cat. 40], painted in Pont-Aven in the late winter or early spring of 1888. The monumental figure in the foreground is taken from a large pastel which apparently dates from 1886. The marked outline and disproportion between the foreground group and the elements of the landscape provokes a violent rupture between the figures and the background. We might say that these Breton women are not located within the landscape, but rather stand in front of a backdrop or theatrical curtain. It would be possible to change the landscape background for a different one without changing anything essential in the composition. *Breton Women at the Bend in the Road* thus anticipates the non-naturalist organisational principle of the painting that Gauguin would use in his most crucial work, *The Vision after the Sermon* [cat. 41].

Cloisonnisme

However, the style of *Breton Women at the Bend in the Road* is still an Impressionist one. To make the jump to the *Vision after the Sermon* Gauguin required the stimulus of an

55. '*Une note* de plein air peut être une jolie chose par-ci par-là mais celà ne constitue complètement un *tableau* et la preuve c'est que vous vous donnez la peine d'en faire.' Letter to Pissarro, August or September 1881, in *Correspondance de Paul Gauguin, op. cit.*, vol. I, p. 22.

56. 'Quant à ce qui est de vous, je crois qu'il est temps (si toutefois c'est votre tempérament) de faire *plus à l'atelier* mais alors des choses mûries à l'avance au point de vue de l'arrangement et de la *scène*.' Letter to Pissarro, May–June 1882, ibid., vol. I, p. 29.

57. 'Tâchez de venir dimanche prochain j'ai bien des choses *commencées* à vous faire voir j'espère que celà vous intéressera ce ne sont pas des résultats que je cherche ce sont des documents que je range pour plus tard.' Letter to Pissarro, May–June 1882, ibid, vol. I, p. 29.

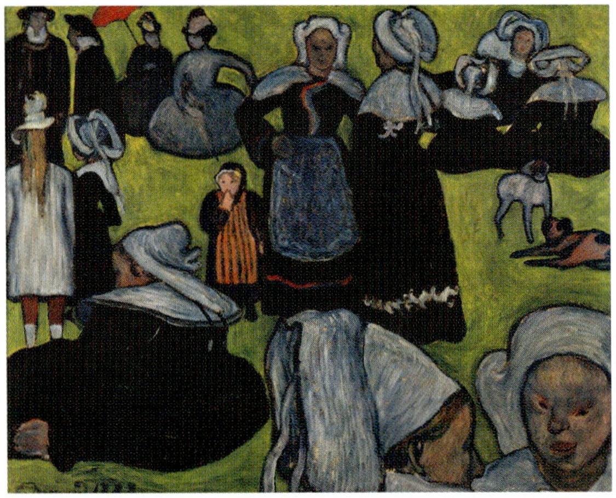

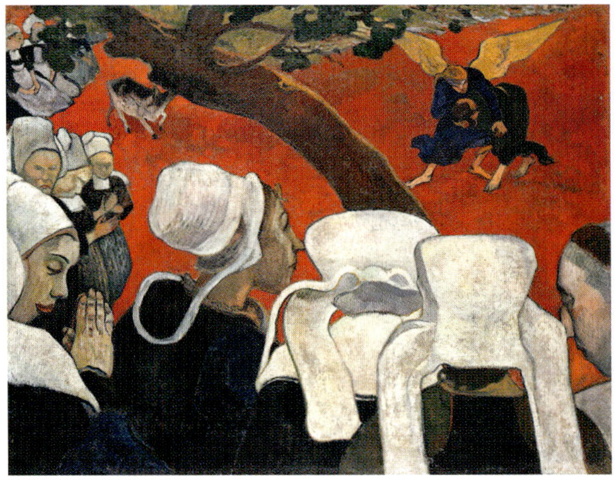

Émile Bernard
Breton Women in the Meadow, 1888
[cat. 38]

Paul Gauguin
Vision after the Sermon, 1888
[cat. 41]

external factor, a sort of catalyst. A few days before 15 August 1888, Pont-Aven saw the arrival of Émile Bernard, a young artist whom Gauguin had met and appreciated for his daring.[58]

The year before in Paris, Bernard had worked with another painter, Louis Anquetin, in a collaboration that had given rise to a new pictorial style representing a clear break with Impressionism. In March 1888, the critic Édouard Dujardin baptised this style with the name of 'cloisonnisme'. The name derived from the technique of cloisonné enamelling, in which the surface to be worked is divided into compartments by strips of metal so that the colours of the enamel remain separate during firing. Pictorial cloisonnisme was characterised by the concept of isolating areas of flat colour between pronounced outlines: Dujardin pointed to the *images d'Épinal* and to Japanese art as the models, in which lines were drawn first then the colours filled in. He could also have mentioned stained-glass windows as another source of inspiration. Overall, Dujardin emphasised the 'hieratic quality' of the line and colour in this new style and its decorative effect. The cloisonniste painter had freed himself from the slavery of appearance and illusionism in order to try and 'set down, with the fewest possible lines and characteristic colours, the intimate reality, the essence of the object'.[59]

All these features are to be found in a painting which Émile Bernard painted in Pont-Aven in the summer of 1888: *Breton Women in the Meadow* [cat. 38]. Gauguin came to own the painting as the result of an exchange of works and took it with him to Arles, where Van Gogh made a copy of it [cat. 39]. Before this, however, Gauguin had created another work which Bernard considered to be directly inspired by his. In the words of the artist himself: 'The Pont-Aven Pardon had just taken place, and I had painted, taking the local costume as my subject, a sunny meadow with a preconceived idea in yellow, decorated with Breton headdresses and groups in blue-black. This painting was taken by Gauguin as the basis for

58. 'Le petit Bernard est ici et a rapporté [...] des choses intéressantes. En voilà un qui ne redoute rien.' Letter to Schuffenecker, 14 August 1888, *Correspondance de Paul Gauguin*, vol. I, p. 210.
59. Dujardin: 'Aux XX et aux Indépendants. Le Cloisonnisme', in *La Revue Indépendante*, March 1888, p. 489.

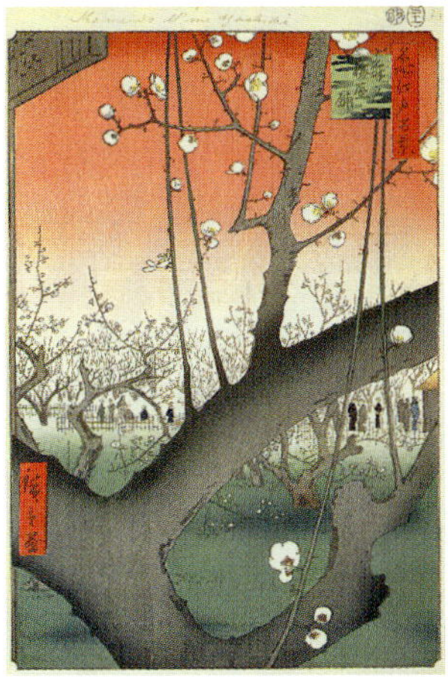

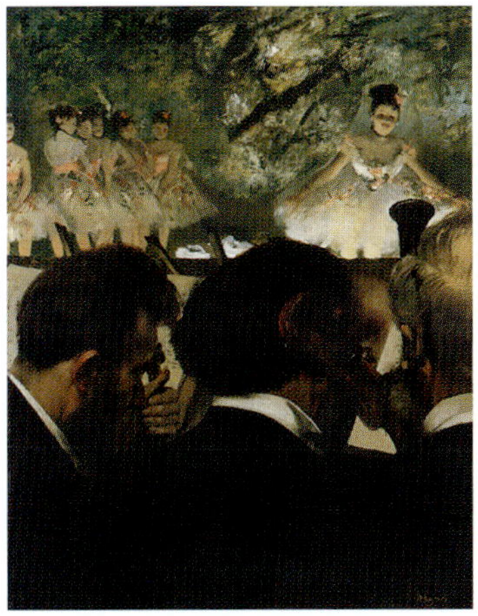

Utagawa Hiroshige
Plum Estate, Kameido, 1857
No. 30 from 'One Hundred Famous Views of Edo'
Woodblock print. 36 x 23.5 cm
Brooklyn, The Brooklyn Museum of Art
(Gift of Anna Ferris 30,1478.30)

Edgar Degas
Musicians of the Orchestra, 1872
Oil on canvas. 69 x 49 cm
Frankfurt, Städdesches Kunstinstitut und Städtische Galerie

his *Vision after the Sermon*, in which the headdresses are also the main motif [...] This painting of flat colours created a contrast to the point of negation with Paul Gauguin's previous works, and he came close to the point of resembling my *Breton Women in the Meadow*'.[60]

The Vision after the Sermon depicts a group of Breton women who have listened to the priest's sermon and subsequently witness an apparition in the meadow of the biblical combat between Jacob and the Angel; some of them watch absorbed while others pray with closed eyes. Gauguin explained the work in a letter to Schuffenecker: 'This year I have sacrificed everything, execution, colour, for style, wishing to impose on myself something different to that which I already know how to do'.[61] We might ask to what extent this style was determined by Bernard's influence. In the *Vision* we encounter undeniable affinities with *Breton Women in the Meadow*: the flat, uniform background, the colours enclosed within simplified outlines painted in black and Prussian blue, as well as the caricatural faces of the Breton women and the large stylised headdresses. Merette Bodelsen has noted that from 1886 Gauguin was experimenting with techniques of decorative painting on ceramic and that these experiments could have led him to cloisonnisme independently of Bernard.[62]

Whatever the case, there are certain key differences between Gauguin's painting and Bernard's which are worth pointing out. This is apparent above all in the colour, which is much bolder in *The Vision after the Sermon*, more unreal than Bernard's greenish yellow. Here we find a pure vermilion that Gauguin had already used in his still life *Fête Gloanec* (1888). A more fundamental difference is the composition: Bernard's painting is characterised by the absence of any spatial organisation, while in the *Vision after the Sermon* we can recognise a coherently applied principle. The figures of the Breton women are arranged in a line, leading the gaze to the left from the foreground into the distance.

60. 'Le Pardon de Pont-Aven venait d'avoir lieu, et j'avais peint, me servant comme thème du costume local, une prairie ensoleillé de parti pris jaune historiée de coiffes bretonnes et de groupes noir-bleu. De ce tableau Gauguin partir et fit la Vision du sermon tableau dans lequel les coiffes formaient également le motif principal. [...] Ce tableau à teintes plates tranchait comme une négation sur les oeuvres précédentes de Paul Gauguin, il se rapprochait jusqu'à la ressemblance de mes "Bretonnes dans la Prairie"'. Bernard, É. 'Note sur l'école dite de Pont-Aven', in *Mercure de France*, December 1903, pp. 679–80.
61. 'J'ai fait pour une église un tableau naturellement il a été refusé aussi je le renvoie à Van Gogh. Inutile de vous le décrire vous le verrez. J'ai cette année tout sacrifié l'exécution la couleur pour le style voulant m'imposer autre chose que ce que je sais faire.' Letter to Schuffenecker, 8 October 1888, in *Correspondance de Paul Gauguin*, *op. cit.*, vol. I, pp. 248–49.
62. Bodelsen, Merete: 'The Missing Link in Gauguin's Cloisonism', in *Gazette des Beaux-Arts*, 53, May–June 1959, pp. 329–44.

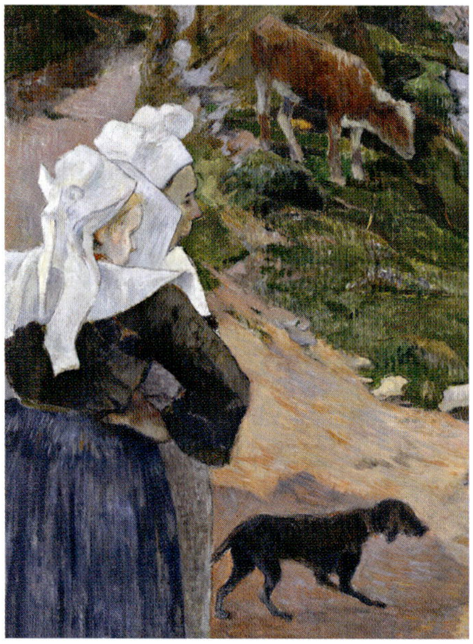 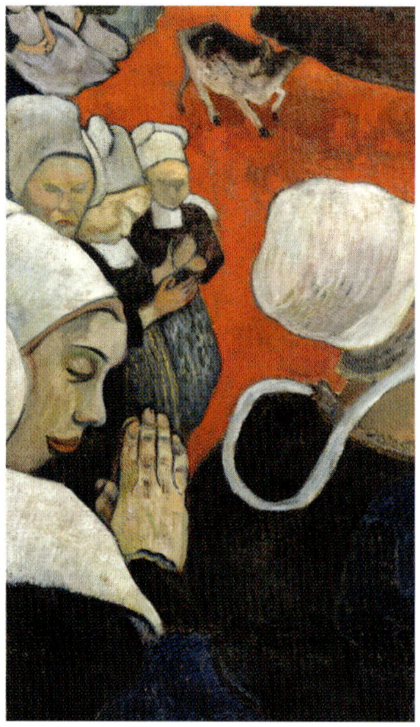

Paul Gauguin
Breton Women by a Bend in the Road, 1888
(detail)
[cat. 40]

Paul Gauguin
The Vision after the Sermon, 1888
(detail)
[cat. 41]

The tree that crosses the painting in a diagonal line separates the women from the group of wrestlers (inspired by Japanese prints), dividing the scene into two worlds: the real and the imaginary. This opposition between earthly reality and the vision is emphasised by the difference of scale and of treatment between the foreground and the background. The Breton women painted in the foreground are modelled bodies with some volume, but the group of wrestlers is a small, flat image.

A precedent for this contrast between the foreground and the distance has been detected in the work of Degas, for example, in his *Musicians of the Orchestra* (1870–1871, Frankfurt, Städtische Galerie im Städelschen Kunstinstitut).[63] Amishai-Maisels has suggested that Gauguin may have been inspired by the heads of praying women in stained-glass windows in a church,[64] while Michael Hogg has suggested that the visionary scene of combat is an image on a wall, possibly projected by a magic lantern, like those used in the catechism.[65] Despite the naivety of these hypotheses (in that they presume the need for a real situation as a model for the painting), the conjectures of these two scholars denote a key point. The unique composition of the *Vision after the Sermon* does not in fact derive from Bernard's *Breton Women* in *the Meadow*, but rather from a painting by Gauguin that we have already looked at, painted long before Bernard arrived at Pont-Aven: *Breton Women by a Bend in the Road* [cat. 40]. This group of peasant women on the road, with their traditional costume and headdresses in the foreground, anticipates almost literally the left half of the *Vision after the Sermon*. Furthermore, the relationship between the women in the foreground and the calf slightly further in, with its disproportion of scale, is

63. Mark, Roskill : *Van Gogh, Gauguin and the Impressionist Circle*. Greenwich (Conn.), New York Graphic Society, 1970, p. 170.
64. Amishai-Maisels, Ziva : *Gauguin's Religious Themes*. New York & London, Garland Publishing Inc., 1985, pp. 28–30.
65. Michel, Hoog: *Gauguin: vie et oeuvre*. Office du Livre, Fribourg, 1987, p. 77.

maintained in the *Vision*. One might say that *Breton Women by a Bend in the Road* was the dress-rehearsal for this strange relationship between figures and background, this effect of cinematographic transparency, this strange spatial division which produces the unreal feel of the *Vision after the Sermon*.

A religious painting

We still need to look at the most crucial difference between the *Vision after the Sermon* and *Breton Women in the Meadow*. While Bernard would try to brush over it years later, adding the sub-title of *The Pardon in Pont-Aven* to his painting in order to introduce a religious reference, his painting was in fact a simple genre scene, of the pastoral type. The *Vision after the Sermon*, in contrast, was conceived of as a religious painting. Gauguin confirmed this in a letter to Van Gogh: 'I have just done a religious painting very badly but which was interesting to do and which I like. I want to give it to the church at Pont-Aven. Naturally they don't want it [...] I think I have reached in the figures a great rustic and superstitious simplicity. [...] For me, in this painting, the landscape and the fight only exist in the imagination of the praying people after the sermon, hence the unnatural and disproportionate contrast between the real people and the fight in its landscape'.[66]

At this point we encounter a strange *chiasmus*, an exchange of roles between the two artists. Bernard was a devout Catholic, inclined to mysticism. We know little of Gauguin's beliefs, but up to the summer of 1888 he had not shown any signs of religious interests. However, it is Gauguin and not Bernard who chooses a biblical motif and a supernatural apparition as his subject. Had Gauguin undergone some sort of conversion of the type so common at the end of the century, such as those of Barbey d'Aurevilly, Verlaine, Léon Bloy, Huysmans and Paul Bourget? Or is this in fact a swindle on the artist's part? Pissarro was inclined to the latter view: 'Gauguin is not a soothsayer', he wrote in a letter to his son, 'he is a trickster who has detected a retrograde movement on the part of the bourgeoisie, the result of the great ideas of solidarity that spring up in the people, an unconscious but fruitful idea and the only legitimate one! The Symbolists are just the same! What do you think? ... They have to be fought like the plague!.[67]

If, as Pissarro thought, this was all a deliberate deceit, it has to be said that Gauguin took a lot of trouble over it. Not only did he go to the church at Pont-Aven to offer his painting, but, following its rejection, he then tried to donate it to the church at Nizon (where he went in the company of Bernard and other painter friends, such as Laval and Sérusier). Again he was unsuccessful. At that point he wrote to Theo van Gogh: 'The church painting will be sent to you and you can exhibit it. Sadly, it is made for a church and what works there does not have the same effect as in this setting of stained glass, stones etc... as in a salon'.[68] It has recently been pointed out that the technique used by Gauguin in the *Vision*,

66. 'Je viens de faire un tableau religieux très mal fait mais qui m'a intéressé à faire et qui me plaît. Je voulais le donner à l'église de Pont-Aven. Naturellement on n'en veut pas. [...] Je crois avoir atteint dans les figures una grande simplicité rustique et superstitieuse. [...] Pour moi dans ce tableau le paysage et la lutte n'existent que dans l'imagination des gens en prière par suite du sermon c'est pourquoi il y a contraste entre les gens nature et la lutte dans son paysage non nature et disproportionnée.' Letter to Vincent, around 25–27 September 1888, in *Correspondance de Paul Gauguin*, *op. cit.*, vol. I, pp. 230–32.

67. 'Gauguin n'est pas un voyant, c'est un malin qui a senti un retour rétrograde de la bourgeoisie en arrière par suite des grandes idées de solidarité qui germent dans le peuple, idée inconsciente mais féconde et la seule légitime! Les symbolistes sont dans le même cas! Qu'en penses-tu?... Aussi il faut les combattre comme le peste!' Letter to Lucien, 20 April 1891, in *Correspondance de Camille Pissarro*, *op. cit.*, vol. III: Éditions du Valhermeil, Paris, 1988, p. 66. A week later he would repeat the same arguments: Letter to Lucien, 13 May 1891, ibid, vol. III, p. 82.

68. 'Le tableau d'église vous sera remis et vous pourrez le montrer. Malheureusement il est fait pour une église et ce qui va là n'a pas le même effet dans cet entourage de vitraux pierres etc.. que dans celui d'un salon' Letter to Théo van Gogh, 7/8 October 1888, in *Correspondance de Paul Gauguin*, *op. cit.*, vol. I, pp. 247–48.

with wax as a binding agent for the thickest paint layers, suggesting religious and ancient paintings, was intended to give the work the character of an icon or cult image.[69]

It is as exaggerated to assume a religious conversion as it is to think that Gauguin was attempting to perpetrate a fraud here. The spiritual background to the *Vision* is real and, like its style and technique, ultimately derives from the artist's primitivist leanings. The key is to be found in Gauguin's words to Van Gogh quoted above: 'I think that in the figures I have achieved a great rustic and superstitious simplicity'.[70] The *Vision* was intended to be an expression of the *genius loci*, the ancestral spirit of Brittany, of that religious atavism which all contemporary writers referred to as one of the key characteristics of Breton peasants.[71]

This apparent effort to become a sort of interpreter or medium of Breton *Volksgeist* does not imply, however, that Gauguin in any way sacrificed his pride as an artist. His efforts to give the painting to local churches rather suggests an emphasis on the omnipotent power of the artist, as if he felt himself capable of creating the gods of the community. Four years after the artist's death, the writer Victor Segalen wrote a story about Gauguin's life among the Maoris. His argument focused on the contrast between the destructive influence of civilisation and the redemptive influence of an artist over a dying race. In Segalen's story, Gauguin created some gods for the Maoris, which were so real and believable that the natives acknowledged them as their own.[72] It is not impossible that Gauguin's had something like Segalen's idea in mind when he painted the *Vision after the Sermon*.

Creative power

The issue, then, is whether we can link the religious inspiration of the *Vision* to an exaltation of the creative power of the artist. In mid-August 1888, at the same time that Bernard arrived in Pont-Aven, Gauguin wrote a letter to his friend Schuffenecker that contained a sort of programmatic declaration: 'A word of advice, don't copy too much from life – Art is an abstraction; take it from nature, dreaming before it and think more about the creation than the result, it is the only way to ascend towards God, acting like our divine master, creating'.[73] The analogy between the power of the artist and divine creation is presented in this passage as an antidote against aesthetic naturalism. Following this line of argument, the choice of a religious theme, and in particular of a supernatural apparition, as the subject of the *Vision*, acquires a new polemical meaning, opposing naturalism and Impressionism. Baudelaire had already maintained that the decline of religious art in bourgeois society was not due to a loss of faith on the part of the artists, but to the waning of their imagination, and he had recommended a *surnaturalisme* against all forms of realism.[74]

Moreover, the subject matter of Gauguin's painting, the combat between Jacob and the Angel, could be interpreted as referring to artistic creation. It appears that Gauguin

69. Jirat-Watsiutynski, Vojtech and Newton, Travers: 'Tradition et innovation dans la technique picturale de Paul Gauguin', in *Gauguin. Actes du colloque Gauguin*, *op. cit.*, pp. 71–72.
70. 'Je crois avoir atteint dans les figures una grande simplicité rustique et superstitieuse.' Letter to Vincent, around 25–27 September 1888, in *Correspondance de Paul Gauguin*, *op. cit.*, vol. I, pp. 230–32.
71. In an exhaustive study on Brittany published in 1885, Henri Baudrillart referred to the 'goût porté jusqu'à la passion pour le surnaturel qu'on a toujours remarqué dans la Bretagne rural' (Baudrillart, H.: *Les populations agricoles de la France. Tome 1, Normandie et Bretagne, passé et présent*. Librairie Guillaumin, Paris, 1885, p. 377) while elsewhere he explained that 'l'imagination porté au merveilleux, au surnaturel, par suite aux légendes, en est un des caractères les plus prononcés [of the Breton spirit]', p. 417.
72. Segalen, Victor: *Gauguin dans son dernier décor et autres textes de Tahiti*. Fontfroide, Bibliothèque artistique et littéraire, 1986, pp. 53–54.
73. 'Un conseil, ne copiez pas trop d'après nature. L'art est une abstraction; tirez-la de la nature en rêvant devant et pensez plus à la création qu'au résultat c'est le seul moyen de monter vers Dieu en faisant comme notre divin maître créer.' Letter to Schuffenecker, 14 August 1888, in *Correspondance de Paul Gauguin*, *op. cit.*, vol. I, p. 210.
74. Baudelaire, Ch.: *Critique d'art suivi de Critique musicale*. Claude Pichois. (ed.), Paris, Gallimard, 1992, pp. 288–89.

discovered the symbolic possibilities of this subject in the work of Victor Hugo. In Hugo's novel *Les Miserables*, which Gauguin was reading in early July 1888, the episode of Jacob's combat appears as a metaphor for man's internal struggle with his own conscience.[75] Even more relevant, however, is the reference to Jacob and the angel in another book by Hugo, *Les Contemplations*. In a poem entitled 'Insomnia' (in the third part of the book under the revealing heading 'Combats and Dreams') the poet describes how an unknown spirit, a 'mysterious master' awakens him in the middle of the night to oblige him to write, setting up a relationship between 'the idea' and 'the flesh', between the body and the soul: 'and the angel clasped Jacob, and the soul supports the body'.[76] Victor Merlhès, who has compiled an index of allegorical interpretations of the fight between Jacob and the Angel, has referred to the Romantic interpretation in which the story symbolises the struggle of the creative genius.[77]

The Vision after the Sermon finally became the prototype of a new concept of painting which Gauguin (without formally defining it) baptised 'synthetism' and which aimed to be a global alternative to Impressionism in painting. In 1891, the young poet and critic Gabriel-Albert Aurier published an essay in the *Mercure de France* entitled 'Symbolism in Painting: Paul Gauguin', which starts in fact with a lengthy and lyrical description of *The Vision after the Sermon*. The first part of Aurier's text is a critique of the Impressionist aesthetics, which he sees as nothing more than another variant of realism, albeit a more subjective one: 'Pissarro, Claude Monet, undoubtedly translate forms and colours in a way different to Courbet, but essentially, like Courbet, even more than Courbet, they only translate form and colour. The bedrock and underlying goal of their art is the material thing, the real thing'. Aurier goes on to set out a new programme: 'In the eyes of the artist, in fact [...] objects cannot have value as objects. They can only appear to him as signs. They are the letters of a vast alphabet which only the man of genius can spell out. To write his thoughts, his poem, with these signs, remembering that the sign, as vital as it is, is nothing in itself, and that the idea is everything, this, then, is the artist's task'.[78] Aurier contrasts the perceptualist concept of painting with a semiotic one: he opposes the idea of painting as a register of visual sensations with the notion of painting as hieroglyphic, as the symbolic handwriting of ideas. His argument is basically determined by his intent to annex Gauguin's pictorial ideas to a literary movement, Symbolism, which was starting to show signs of staleness by 1891. The title of the article itself is revealing in this sense, as Aurier avoids the term 'Synthetism' and reduces Gauguin's contribution to that of the translation of poetic *Symbolism* into painting.

It is difficult to know how far Gauguin identified himself with the theoretical content of Aurier's text; but he was certainly interested in its practical effect. Prior to his departure for Tahiti, the artist was courted, honoured and fêted in the various Symbolist circles,

75. The image appears in the fifth section of the book, Book VI, Chap IV.
76. Hugo, V.: *Les contemplations*. Léon-Paul Fargue (preface). Pierre Albouy (ed.), Paris, Gallimard, 2002, pp. 162ff.
77. In *Correspondance de Paul Gauguin*, *op. cit.*, vol. I, p. 501 note 277.
78. 'Aux yeux de l'artiste, en effet [...] les objets ne peuvent avoir de valeur en tant qu'objets. Ils ne peuvent lui apparaîtres que comme des *signes*. Ce sont les lettres d'un immense alphabet que l'homme de génie seul sait épeler. Écrire sa pensée, son poème, avec ces signes, en se rappelant que le signe, pour indispensable qu'il soit, n'est rien en lui-même et que l'idée seule est tout, telle apparaît donc la tâche de l'artiste'. 'Le symbolisme en peinture, Paul Gauguin' [1891], in Aurier, Albert: *Textes critiques 1889–1892. De l'impressionnisme au symbolisme*. École nationale supérieure des Beaux-Arts, Paris, 1995, p. 33.

including Mallarmé's. The critic Fénéon wrote later that as a result Gauguin became 'prisoner of the literati'.[79] For his part, Pissarro explained to his son that Gauguin had 'manoeuvred by low means to have himself chosen (that is the word) as a man of genius, and very adroitly'.[80]

5. Eve and the Gods

There is one detail from the *Vision after the Sermon* which deserves comment in relation to the painting's symbolic content. Two silhouettes in profile flank the group of women in the foreground like a pair of donors. The one on the right is a priest and that on the left a Breton woman who stands out from the other visionaries. Ziva Amishai-Maisels has convincingly argued that the figure of the priest is a self-portrait of Gauguin, while the woman on the right depicts Madeleine Bernard,[81] sister of Émile, who had arrived with her mother in Pont-Aven around 14 August 1888. At that point Madeleine was 17, and had blue eyes, blond hair and an intelligent and expressive gaze. The 'very beautiful and very mystic' Madeleine, as her brother described her, fell in love with Brittany. She loved to wear the traditional costume of Pont-Aven and to pray in the local church. 'Naturally', Bernard continued, 'Gauguin, consoled by my sister, who had the character of a true saint and artist, fell in love with her and considered running away with her, but my father intervened in time'.[82] After M. Bernard put an end to the relationship, Gauguin wrote Madeleine a couple of letters in which his passion is sublimated into an offer of a purely spiritual friendship. For all these reasons, it would not be at all surprising if the figure of Madeleine was included in the *Vision* along with that of the artist, framing the symbolic combat in a sort of mystical marriage.

The presence of these two figures in the *Vision* opens up a new perspective on Gauguin's later work. The inclusion of the artist himself in the picture anticipates a whole series of paintings in which Gauguin would combine his self-portrait with religious iconography: images in which he presents himself in the guise of the Redeemer, or the Tempter, the Messiah or the Anti-Christ, developing a personal mythology to suit his requirements. In addition, the figure of Madeleine, beyond the biographical anecdote, indicates the new role cast for women in the 'symbolic way' that Gauguin had embarked upon. While his painting was already dominated by female figures, from the *Vision* onwards, woman would be the *intercessor* for establishing a relationship with the sacred, be it in a divine or a devilish form.

Perversity and irony

During the key weeks of the summer of 1888, Gauguin and Bernard both made portraits of Madeleine. Bernard painted her lying on the ground, in a dreamy, contemplative pose [cat. 55], and again in a more conventional half-length portrait [cat. 54]. Both paintings include part of the Bois d'Amour converted into a sacred grove, a subject dear to the

79. 'La proie des littérateurs', 'M. Gauguin' [1891], in Fénéon, F.: *Oeuvres plus que complètes*, *op. cit.*, vol. I, p. 192.
80. 'Si tu savais avec quelle platitude Gauguin a agi pour arriver à se faire élire (c'est le mot) homme de génie, et cela fort adroitement.' In *Correspondance de Camille Pissarro*, *op. cit.*, vol. III, p. 81.
81. Amishai-Maisels, Z.: *Gauguin's Religious Themes*, *op. cit.*, p. 31.
82. 'Naturellement, Gauguin, consolé par ma soeur, qui avait un vrai caractère de sainte et d'artiste, tomba amoureux d'elle et songea à l'enlever; mais mon père s'interposa à temps' Cited in Wildenstein, D.: *Gaugiun. Premier itinéraire d'un sauvage*, *op. cit.*, vol. II, p. 444.

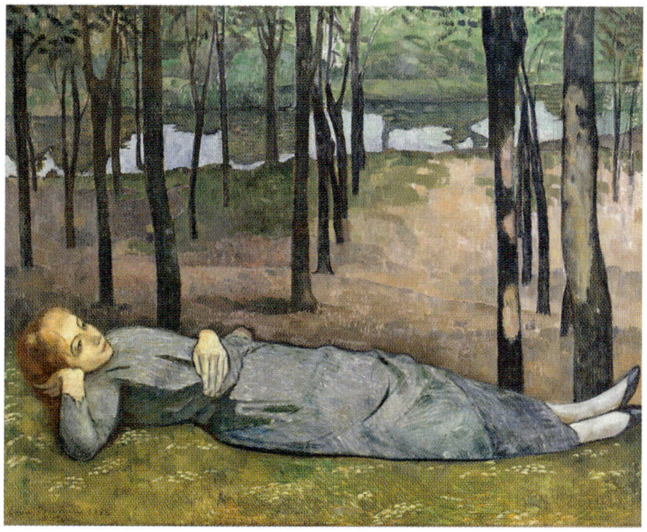

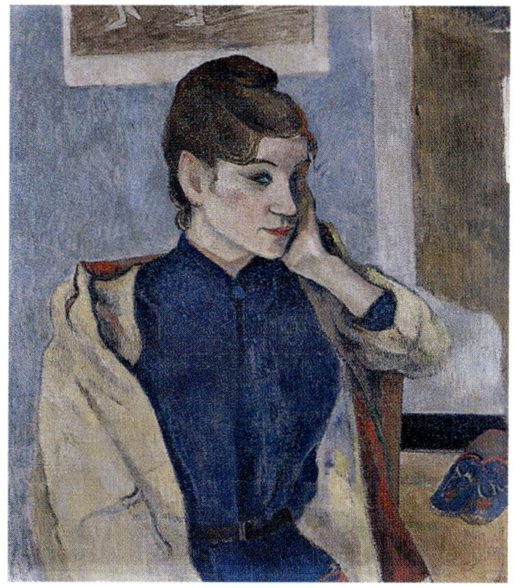

Émile Bernard
Madeleine in the Bois d'Amour, 1888
[cat. 55]

Paul Gauguin
Madeleine Bernard, 1888
Oil on canvas. 72 x 58 cm
Musée de Grenoble

Symbolists and in perfect harmony with the sitter's own mystical inclinations. However, Gauguin's portrait of Madeleine expresses very different thoughts. Her almond-shaped eyes, her slanted gaze, the insinuating smile and above all that pointed ear of a female faun (of the type we mentioned above in Gauguin's self-portrait) do not convey Bernard's idea of her as an innocent spiritual creature, but rather show her as a wily seductress and a somewhat perverted young woman.

This perversity which Gauguin saw in Madeleine can undoubtedly be linked to the Symbolist fascination for the *femme fatale* found in both literature and art. Beyond any specific moral content, however, this perversity is the expression of a shift in the direction of Gauguin's imagery, which, in line with his new 'symbolic way', would systematically explore the concept of irony, using *antiphrasis*, the inversion of the literal or normal meaning of images. The same irony that Gauguin used in his confrontation with Bernard would reappear in his pictorial dialogue with Van Gogh during the months they spent together in Arles, once again in relation to the female portrait. Marie Ginoux, wife of the owner of the Café de la Gare (where Van Gogh had rented a room between May and September), agreed to be painted by the two artists, and one day in early November she presented herself at the Yellow House dressed in her traditional costume of Arles. During the hour in which she posed for them, Van Gogh painted a rapid and hasty oil sketch. Soon after, he executed a second and more highly elaborated version of the subject, which is the painting that interests us here. The silhouette of *L'Arlesienne. Madame Ginoux* [cat. 51], with its concave outlines, reveals the influence of both Japanese prints and the typical costume of the Breton women as seen in *The Vision after the Sermon*. On the table are some books (novels) which were normal accessories in Van Gogh's paintings, symbolising the spiritual

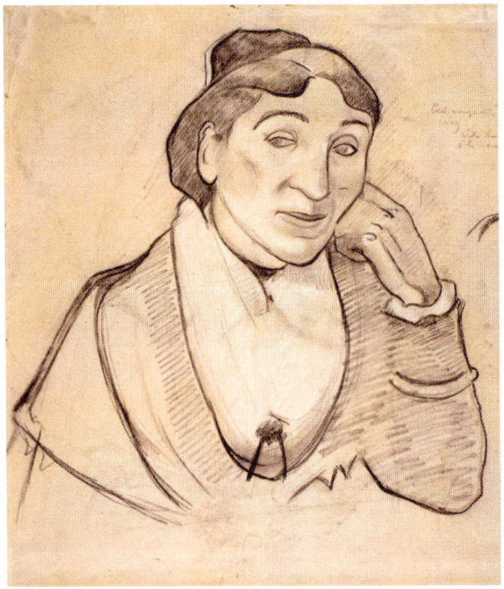

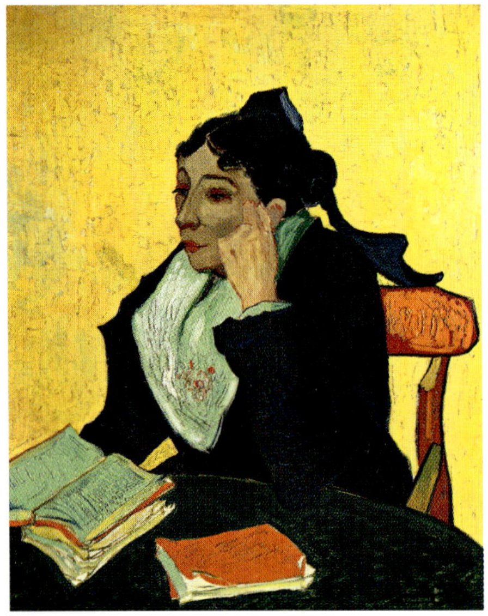

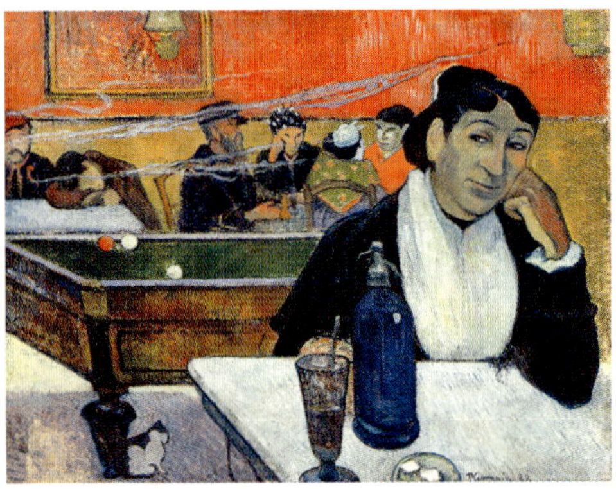

Paul Gauguin
L'Arlésienne. Madame Ginoux, 1888
[cat. 50]

Vincent Van Gogh
L'Arlésienne. Madame Ginoux. 1888
[cat. 51]

Paul Gauguin
At the Café, 1888
Oil on jute. 72 x 92 cm
Moscow, State Pushkin Museum of Fine Arts

preoccupations of the modern age. Van Gogh's Madame Ginoux, with her hand on her cheek and her distant gaze, represents the melancholy and tormented soul of a modern woman.

In contrast to the *seriousness* of this portrait, the drawing which Gauguin made at the same time gives the sitter a certain insinuating charm [cat. 50]. This drawing is not intended as an independent work: rather it is one of those documents which the artist used in his compositions. Gauguin inserted it into a painting which represented the same night-time café that Van Gogh had already painted but 'with figures seen in the brothels'.[83] In this painting Madame's Ginoux's expression has been subtly modified and now has an enigmatic and spiteful smile. Dominating the scene as the owner of the café, she is surrounded by the tendrils of smoke that suggest the murky and sordid atmosphere of the bar. Behind her, at the other tables are some of the local people of Arles whom Van Gogh had portrayed, such

83. Van Gogh, letter to Bernard B 19a. In *Correspondance complète de Vincent van Gogh, enrichie de tous les dessins originaux*. M. Beerblock and L. Roelandt (translation). Georges Charensol (introduction and annotations). Paris, Gallimard-Grasset, 1960.

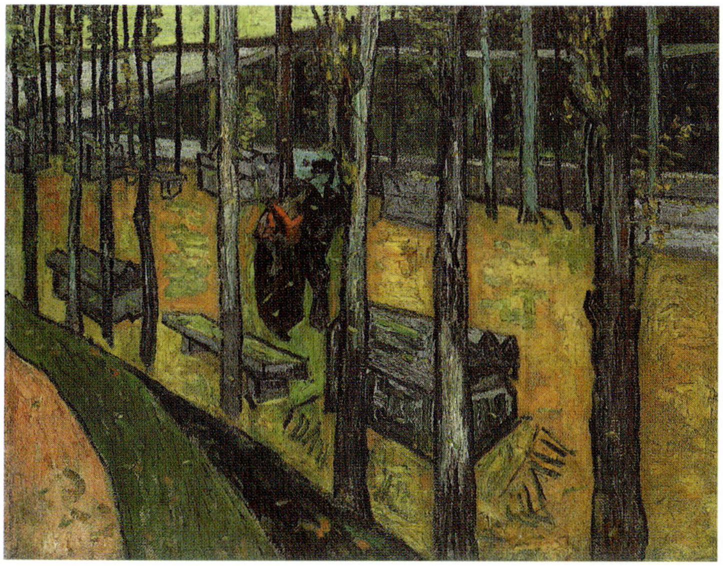

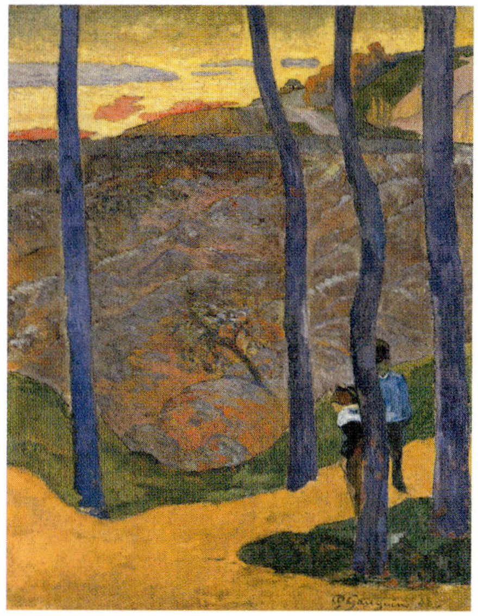

Vincent van Gogh
Falling Leaves (Les Alyscamps), 1888
Oil on jute. 72 x 91 cm
Private Collection

Paul Gauguin
The Blue Trees, 1888
[cat. 43]

as lieutenant Milliet or the famous M. Roulin, seated in the company of three prostitutes. Once again, moral perversity is no more than the effect of irony, capable of subverting the meaning of any image through a change in a figure or its context, however minimal.

During the Arles period, Gauguin's irony was directed above all against Van Gogh's innocent optimism and enthusiasm, but also, in an oblique way, against the bucolic universe that Gauguin himself had constructed in Brittany. In contrast to its bright luminosity he projected a dense web of shadows: suggestions of mysteries, suspicions, threats. In the painting *The Blue Trees* [cat. 43], the combination of blue trunks and yellow sky recalls Van Gogh's *Falling Leaves, Alyscamps* (1888), which decorated Gauguin's bedroom in the Yellow House. However, while Van Gogh used his trees to frame a pair of lovers, Gauguin uses them as the setting for an uncertain, troubling relationship.[84] The mysterious couple whom he depicts as semi-hidden among the trees comprises a working man in a cap and blue blouse, represented with his hands in his pockets and his legs separated, and a small local woman who walks along slightly bent, as if trying to slip away unnoticed. The troubling sensation that the scene arouses is confirmed by the title which Gauguin gave the painting when it was exhibited in Brussels in February 1889: *Vous y passerez, la belle* ('Your turn will come, pretty one').

The ironic revision of pastoral clichés could acquire notably different tones. *Washerwomen in Arles* [cat. 42] was Gauguin's second canvas on a subject which Van Gogh had already treated. Starting from an innocent, harmless pretext, he took pleasure in creating an almost indecipherable composition, filled with visual and narrative enigmas. Hovering

84. Druick, D. and Zegers, P.K.: *Van Gogh and Gauguin. The Studio of the South*, cat. cit., p. 224.

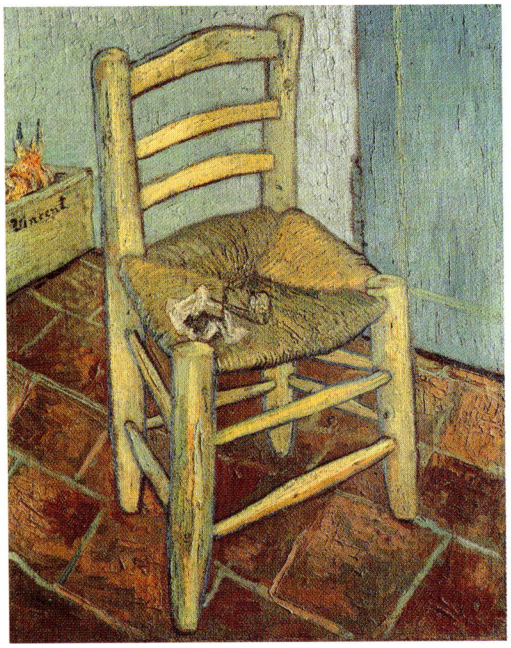

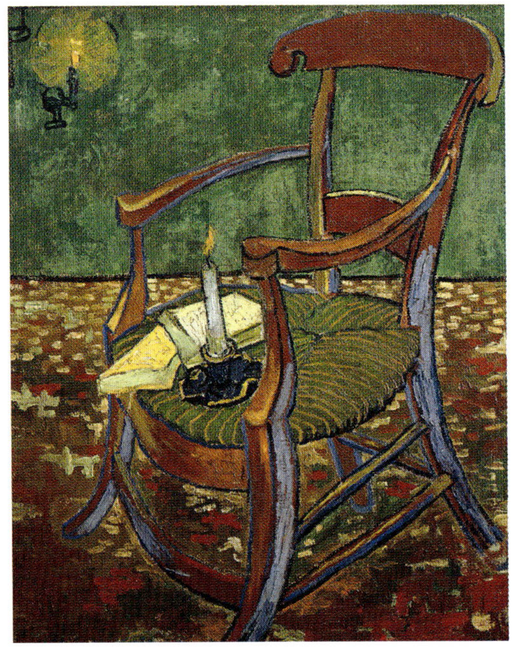

Vincent van Gogh
Van Gogh's Chair, 1888
Oil on jute. 93 x 73,5 cm
London, The National Gallery

Vincent van Gogh
Gauguin's Chair, 1888
[cat. 49]

over the woman washing is the disturbing figure of a bent old woman who casts a large and seemingly living shadow. In the foreground is a goat who seems like a pet. The old woman is the origin of an entire series of hooded silhouettes which culminate in the *tupapaus*, the terrifying apparitions in Gauguin's Tahiti paintings. What magic spell is this figure preparing? The painter Daniel de Monfreid, one of Gauguin's last close friends, simply stated: 'There is no subject in this painting, but the colours sound out a powerful fanfare, and the figures, with their simplified drawing, have so little of the human that they must be from another mysterious and terrible world'.[85]

Van Gogh himself also saw Gauguin's artistic personality as shrouded in an air of mystery. In late November 1888, Van Gogh executed two still lifes which functioned as two symbolic portraits of himself and his companion, using a familiar symbol which he was particularly attracted to – that of the empty chair. Van Gogh's chair, with its straight legs and back and the lone accessory of the pipe and tobacco, is intended to express a rough, simple, manly character. In contrast, *Gauguin's Chair* [cat. 49] (which Van Gogh had bought specially for him) is represented with curving, enveloping lines. The curves were intended to harmonise with Gauguin's room, which Van Gogh had wanted to decorated like 'a boudoir of a really artistic woman'.[86] Two novels lie on the chair, symbols of the poetic gifts that Van Gogh considered Gauguin to be such a master of. In contrast to the daytime clarity that bathes Van Gogh's chair, in the depiction of Gauguin's armchair the lighted candle and the lamp on the wall create a night-time atmosphere. The range of greens and reds is comparable

85. 'Il n'y a pas de sujet dans cette toile, mais les couleurs sonnent une fanfare puissante, et les figures, dans leur dessin simplifié, restent si peu humaines qu'elles semblent venues d'un autre monde mystérieux et terrible.' Monfreid, G.-Daniel de : 'Paul Gauguin', in *La Revue provinciale*, November 1903, p. 386.
86. Letter to Théo 534, in *Correspondance complète de Vincent van Gogh*, *op. cit.*, vol. III, p. 192.

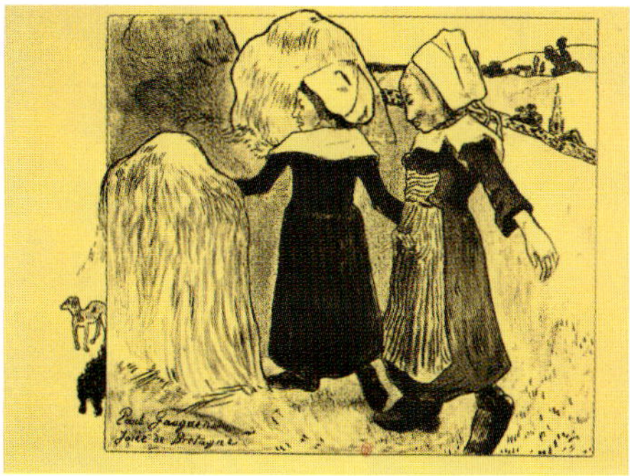

Paul Gauguin
The Joys of Brittany, 1889
Suite Volpini
[cat. 72]

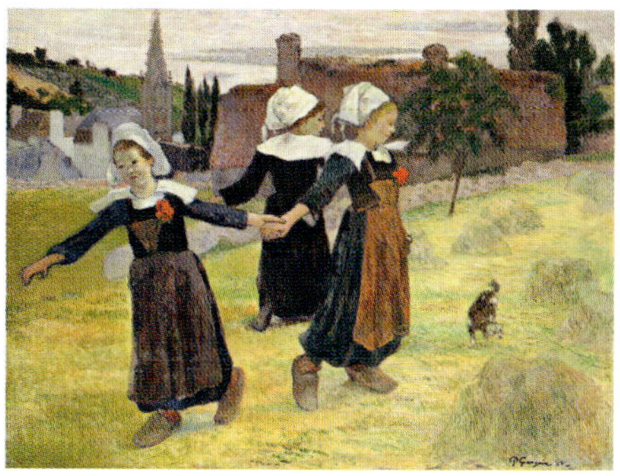

Paul Gauguin
Breton Girls Dancing, 1888
[cat. 31]

to the atmosphere of another painting by Van Gogh, his *Night Café*, which aimed to evoke night-time figures and emotions.

Interlude: the *Suite Volpini*

On his return to Paris at Christmas 1888, following his adventure in Arles, Gauguin created a series of prints using the zincograph technique which Émile Bernard had tried out some months previously. The resulting album would be shown in the exhibition which Gauguin and his friends organised in the spring in the Café des Arts (owned by a certain Volpini), located inside the 1889 *Exposition Universelle* complex, and with the title of 'Exhibition of the Impressionist and Synthetist Group'. The *Suite Volpini*, which consists of scenes of Brittany, Martinique and Arles, has always troubled scholars in its apparent lack of thematic unity. For Caroline Boyle-Turner, the suite is a sample of various themes taken from earlier works, a sort of 'showcase' which Gauguin designed in order to sell his recent paintings.[87] With regard to a linking thread in the set, Boyle-Turner only ventures a vague one: 'the idea of people as a reflection of their environment'.[88] Richard Brettell has emphasised certain aspects of the *Suite Volpini* which differentiate it from a merely reproductive and commercial project. For Brettell, the prints are not based literally on earlier paintings (except in a couple of cases), but are rather very free reinterpretations. When suggesting an overall interpretation for the suite, Brettell is not as adventurous, limiting himself to an

87. Boyle-Turner, Caroline: *Gauguin and the School of Pont-Aven. Prints and Paintings*. Douglas Druick (introduction). London, Royal Academy of Arts – Weidenfeld and Nicolson, 1986, p. 38.
88. 'He was intrigued by the idea of people as a reflection of their environment. This formed a theme in many of his paintings, and is the thread that unifies his Volpini album. Ibid., p. 42.

interesting list: 'images of transgression, growth, nudity, adolescence, old age, prayer, desperate cleanliness and spoiled paradise. At each level, the world represented is compromised by doubt, and Gauguin's cover reveals that doubt in a self-conscious way'.[89] More recently, Douglas Druick and Peter Kort Zegers summarised the content of the series as touching on the issues of 'sexuality, good and evil, innocence and guilt'.[90]

Venturing to go beyond these ideas and to suggest a unified interpretation of the Volpini album, we might say that the suite is in fact a *compendium of the pastoral world and its fall*. Leaving aside for the moment the cover, the other ten images in the set are clearly divided into two equal and symmetrical groups of five images each. The first of these, consisting of three prints of Brittany (*The Joys of Brittany*, *Breton Bathers*, *Breton Women by a Gate*) and two of Martinique (*Martinique Pastoral* and *The Grasshoppers and the Ants*), is apparently devoted to an exaltation of the bucolic life. The other group consists of five mysterious, sombre or tragic images which act as the dark side of the pastoral: the two prints devoted to *Dramas of the Sea* in Brittany, and the three on subjects from Arles: *Old Women from Arles*, *Washerwomen* and *Human Misery*.

The *Suite Volpini* thus depicts the dialectic of the pastoral and the anti-pastoral, of idyll and tragedy. However, the marvellous complexity of the series is not exhausted in this initial suggestion, and once again we need to consider Gauguin's use of ironic devices. In the group of 'positive' prints, the artist introduces some subtle alterations with regard to the original paintings, confusing their meanings. For example, in *The Joys of Brittany* [cat. 72] the two dancing girls, derived from the *Dance of the Breton Girls*, have changed appearance radically. Now they seem to wear masks that transform them into monstrous, primitive creatures, almost forerunners of the *Demoiselles d'Avignon*. In *Breton Bathers* [cat. 73], the figure of the woman entering the water, taken from the painting of *The two Bathers*, is now outlined against the background of an ominous black cloud, like a great cloud of smoke. In *The Grasshoppers and the Ants - Memories of Martinique* [cat. 80], the moralising fable that contrasts idleness and work corrupts the purity of the surroundings.

Finally, the print on the cover (a design for a plate individualised by hand-colouring with watercolour and gouache) is a sort of emblem summarising the paradoxes within the album. The apparently simple image in fact condenses a complex process of iconographic elaboration with three different phases. The first stage, underlying the image, is a representation of a young country girl with a goose, a characteristic motif in the Brittany paintings. In a second stage, this pastoral motif becomes the mythological scene of Leda and the swan (with two small swans alluding to the Dioscuri). But the association does not end here: the elegant curve of the swan's neck suggests a small snake winding around the edge of the roundel. This is the biblical Serpent, whose appearance (completed by an

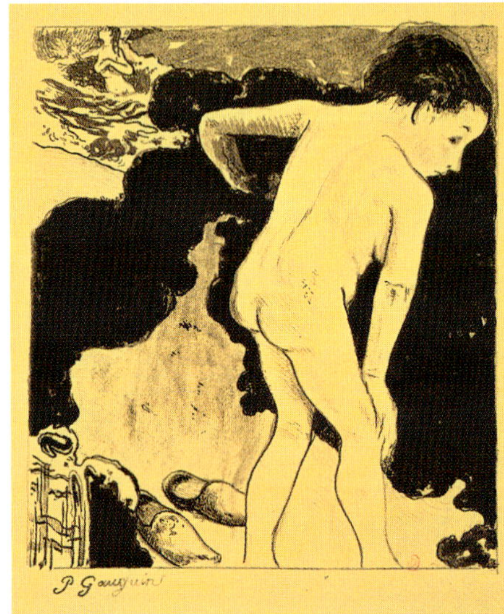

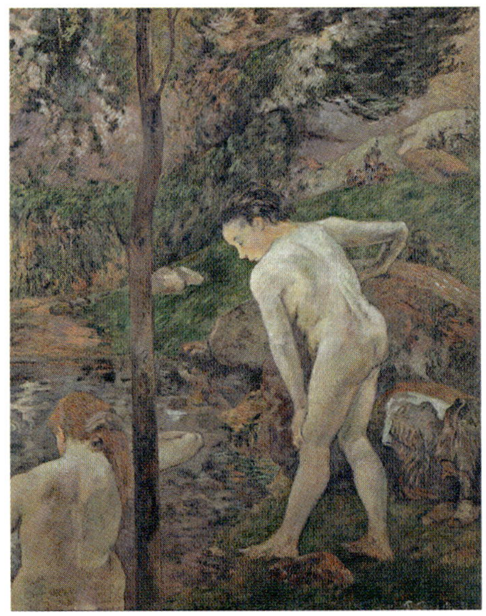

Paul Gauguin
Breton Bathers, 1889
Suite Volpini
[cat. 73]

Paul Gauguin
Two Bathers, 1887
[cat. 35]

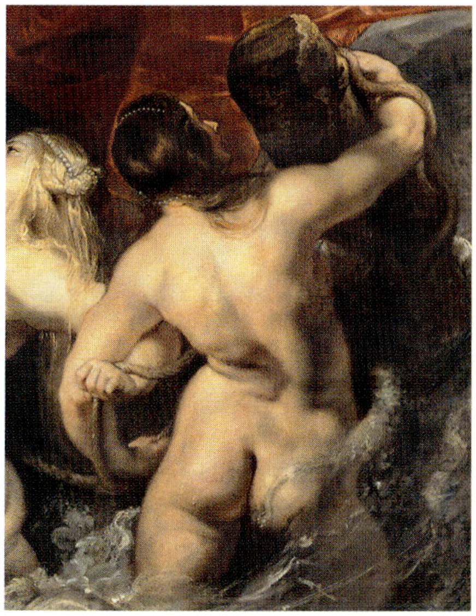

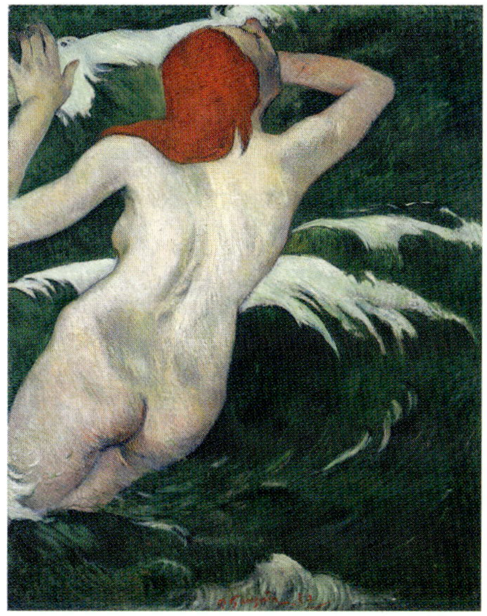

Peter Paul Rubens
The Landing of Marie de Medici at Marseilles, 1622–1625 (detail)
Oil on canvas. 394 x 295 cm
Paris, Musée du Louvre

Paul Gauguin
In the Waves (Ondine), 1889
[cat. 57]

apple) turns Leda into Eve, and the erotic pagan image into a Christian one of the Fall. The ironic and perverse sense of the transformation is underlined by the motto (written in reverse) of the Order of the Garter: 'Homis [sic] soit qui mal y pense', meaning 'Evil be to him who evil thinks'.

Eve

It is in fact this image of Eve at the moment of Temptation that would be the pivot for a large number of Gauguin's works in 1889, acting as a veritable symbol of the crisis of the pastoral. One of the most interesting works exhibited at the Café Volpini was a small pastel of Eve beneath the Tree of Knowledge and the serpent, with an inscription in Creole, the language of the natives of Martinique: *Pas écouter li li menteur* (Do not listen to the liar). The figure of that Breton Eve was taken from a 'poor wretched woman' (in Gauguin's words) who appears with her head leaning on her hands in the middle of the harvest in his painting *Human Misery*, painted in Arles.[91] If this figure represents a seduced and abandoned peasant, as it would seem to, in his Breton Eve Gauguin decided to raise the anecdotal, genre element to the timeless dignity of myth. The hands on the face in *Human Misery* have combined with the foetal position of a Peruvian mummy which the artist had seen in Paris in the Ethnographical Museum in the Trocadero. Thus modified, like a symbol of the link between temptation, sin and death, the image reappears in the painting *Life and Death* (1889) [cat. 63].

Various elements link *Life and Death* to another painting of this period, initially titled *In the Waves* but later exhibited as *In the Waves (Ondine I)* [cat. 57]. The particular importance

89. Brettel, Richard; Cachin, Françoise; Stuckey, Charles F. and Frèches-Thory, Claire: *The Art of Paul Gauguin*. Washington, National Gallery of Art – Chicago, The Art Institute of Chicago, p. 132.
90. Druick, D. and Zegers, P.K.: *Van Gogh and Gauguin. The Studio of the South*, cat. cit., p. 277.
91. 'Ce n'est pas une nature privée d'intelligence, de grâce et de tous les dons de la nature. C'est une femme.' Letter to Schuffenecker, 20 December 1888, in *Correspondance de Paul Gauguin*, vol. I, p. 306.

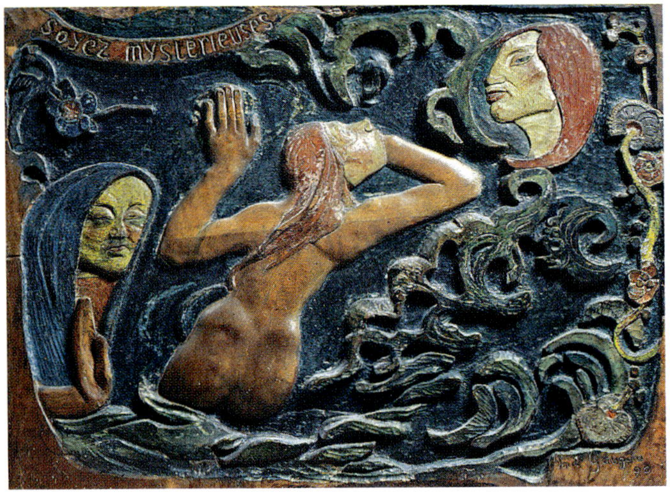

Paul Gauguin
Be Mysterious, 1890
Painted linden panel. 73 x 95 cm
Paris, Musée d'Orsay

of this work for Gauguin can been appreciated in the way he selected it as the background for a self-portrait painted that same year [cat. 56]. *In the Waves* has been related to nudes by Degas and Delacroix, but if one had to find a single precedent, it would be the figure of one of the nereids that welcome the ship in *The Landing of Marie de Medici in Marseilles* by Rubens. Obviously, the powerful volumes of the figure's back in Rubens' work have been flattened, creating a silhouette laminated against the decorative design of the waves. The waving, fluid movement of the nereid has become a broken line, and the overflowing voluptuousness a more uncertain, mysterious kind of eroticism. The secret of this eroticism lies in the unrealistic pose: it has been said that the figure in *In the Waves* is eating her own arm. This pose reappears, albeit more frontally, in the relief *Be Mysterious* (1890), which conveys a stronger impression of a limb penetrating the open mouth, suggesting a barely concealed act of fellatio.

We can now return to the painting *Nude Breton Boy*, which we contrasted earlier with the bathers of 1888. Although it has never previously been suggested, it seems highly likely that *In the Waves* and *Breton Boy* constitute a pair, forming a sort of diptych. Painted around the same time, on canvases of the same format, the two paintings have the same flat green backgrounds (the sea and the grass respectively), decorated with white (the crests of the waves and the sheet). Against this background the nude figure is stretched out diagonally, with its limbs arranged in unnatural positions. *In the Waves* and *Breton Boy* could be read as two complementary visions, the two faces of a single fantasy of sexual submission.

Lesser gods

The 1889 *Exposition Universelle* was held on the Champs de Mars, at the foot of Eiffel's *Three hundred metre Tower*. It celebrated colonial conquests in pavilions devoted to the

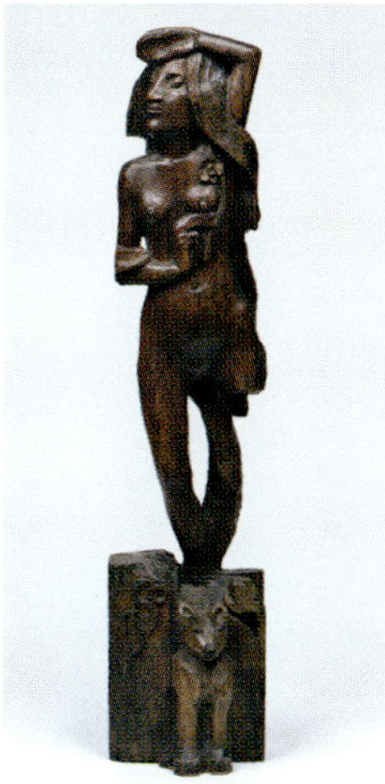

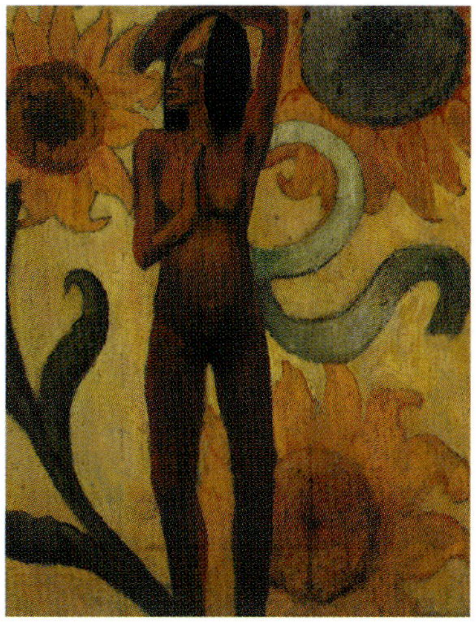

Paul Gauguin
Lust, 1890
[cat. 65]

Paul Gauguin
Nude with Sunflowers (*The Carribean Woman)*
1889
Oil on wood. 62.2 x 52 cm
Private Collection

remotest regions of Asia and the Pacific, allowing Gauguin to make the fascinating discovery of Indian, Cambodian and Javanese art.[92] In the following months, the impact of that encounter would make its mark on a series of works which combined eroticism and religious symbolism. The first of these works is a watercolour, a mysterious image presided over by the word 'Ictus' and the pictogram of a fish [cat. 66]. Both signs, the image and the word (the Greek acrostic that refers to Christ) were suggested to Gauguin by a letter from Van Gogh.[93] The androgynous female nude that appears between the two signs combines elements of various cult religions. Seated in a semi-lotus position, one of her arms stretches out in a Buddhist gesture, while the other evokes the crucifixion. The work testifies to the attraction Gauguin felt for religious syncretism and esoteric theories (such as theosophy) which the painter would develop systematically in Polynesia, both in his art and his writings. In the text *The Catholic Church and Modern Times* (1897–1898: subsequently reworked with the title *The Modern Spirit and Catholicism*) Gauguin emphasised the coincidences between Christian doctrine and Egyptian, Persian, Hindu, Chinese and, naturally, Tahitian beliefs.[94]

Religious and artistic syncretism are both to be found in two statuettes. These are fetish-like figures of erotic divinities with connotations of perversity. *Lust* (1890) [cat. 65] is the second version of a statuette which broke, and which can be related to the painting *Nude with Sunflowers* (1889) that formed part of the decoration painted by Gauguin for the dining-room of Marie Henry's inn at Le Pouldu. The pose of the slim figure is inspired by the *mudrâs* or symbolic poses of the Javanese dancers that had so fascinated Gauguin (and Rodin) at the 1889 Universal Exhibition, and by figures from the reliefs at Angkor Vat reproduced in plaster in the Cambodian pavilion. In contrast to the sinuous sensuality of *Lust*, the so-called *Black Venus* [cat. 64] represents an opposing female ideal, massive and

92. 'Dans le village de Java il y a des danses Hindous. Tout l'art de l'Inde se trouve là et les photographies que j'ai du Cambodge se retrouvent là textuellement.' Letter to Émile Bernard, March 1889, in *Lettres de Gauguin à sa femme…, op. cit.*, p. 157.
93. Letter from Vincent to Gauguin, 23 or 24 January 1889, in *Paul Gauguin: 45 Lettres à Vincent, Théo et Jo van Gogh*. Douglas Cooper (introduction and annotations). 'S-Gravenhague, Staatsuitgeverij, Lausana, Bibliothèque des arts, 1983, pp. 270–71.
94. In *Avant et après* he will insist in the coincidences between the Vedas, Buddah and the Bible: *Avant et après, op. cit.*, pp. 171–75.

opulent. Their sources are, however, almost the same: the hieratic pose, the hairstyle, the long earrings, the bracelets and the bands around the body were inspired by a photograph of an ancient Javanese sculpture of Vishnu. Gauguin, however, introduces an unexpected feature. A lotus flower climbs around the goddess's leg, comparable to the phallic cobra that symbolises fecundity. The stem springs from a decapitated head which the goddess, like a sinister Salome, holds in her lap: a head that clearly bears the features of Gauguin.

Self-Portrait as Christ

The self-portrait included in the *Black Venus* sets the image of the artist within a primitive, religious context, a strategy already announced in the *Vision after the Sermon*. However, the full identification of the artist with the god, the theomorphic self-portrait (a genre whose precedents ran from Dürer to Courbet) would only appear in Gauguin's painting with his *Christ in the Garden of Olives* [cat. 68], of June 1889. The choice of that particular gospel episode may have been inspired by various sources – firstly, by Breton crucifixion groups, which always included a representation of *The Agony in the Garden*. In addition, the subject was favoured by Romantic poets (such as Lamartine and Musset, Vigny and Gerard de Nerval) and painters (including Goya, Delacroix and Corot). For the most radical of these artists, the anguish of Christ undoubtedly revealed not just the human condition but also the absence or inexistence of God. The figure of the desperate, defeated Christ was a powerful metaphor for the tragic condition of the poet or the modern artist. In October 1889 (i.e. after Gauguin had painted the *Christ in the Garden of Olives*), Aurier expanded on this subject in his poem 'La montagne de doute', in which the poet appears as a Christ-Prometheus figure condemned to be crucified for having given the holy wine to the people.[95] Gauguin's painting is inspired by this attitude, and evokes a number of passages from his letters in which the painter exalts Christ as the supreme artist ('What an artist, this Christ who has sculpted in all humanity!')[96] and compares the suffering of the modern painter to that of Christ's Passion ('What a long calvary is the life of the artist!').[97] Not even in a context such as this, however, does Gauguin refrain from introducing an element of irony. His Jesus's most notable feature is the red hair, a stigma traditionally associated with Judas: thus in a single figure he paradoxically represents both betrayer and betrayed.[98]

The use of red hair was also an allusion to Gauguin's friend Van Gogh, a justifiable one in that Gauguin knew that his friend had preceded him in an attempt to depict the subject of the Agony in the Garden. Between June and July 1888 and again at the end of the year, Van Gogh had executed two studies on this theme which featured Christ and an angel. He destroyed them immediately afterwards, however, alleging that he did not wish to paint figures of any importance without a model.[99] When Van Gogh came across Gauguin and Bernard's efforts at biblical subjects (Bernard having painted his own *Christ on the Mount*

95. On Aurier's poem, see Loevgren, *Genesis of Modernism, Seurat, Gauguin, Van Gogh and French Symbolism in the 1880s*. Bloomington – London, Indiana University Press, 1971, p. 138.
96. 'Quel artiste, ce Jésus qui a taillé en pleine humanité.' Letter to Schuffenecker, end of August 1888, in *Correspondance de Paul Gauguin*, *op. cit.*, vol. I, p. 216.
97. 'C'est un long calvaire à parcourir que la vie d'artiste!' Letter to Vincent van Gogh, around 7–9 September 1888, ibid., vol. I, p. 220.
98. During their period together in Arles, Gauguin and Van Gogh visited together the Montpellier Museum, where they looked at a painting by Antoine Verdier which represented the red-headed Bruyas as Christ with a crown of thorns. Druick, D. and Zegers, P. K: *Van Gogh and Gauguin. The Studio of the South*, cat. cit., p. 255.
99. See the letters to Théo nos. 505 and 540 in *Correspondance complète de Vincent van Gogh*, *op. cit.*

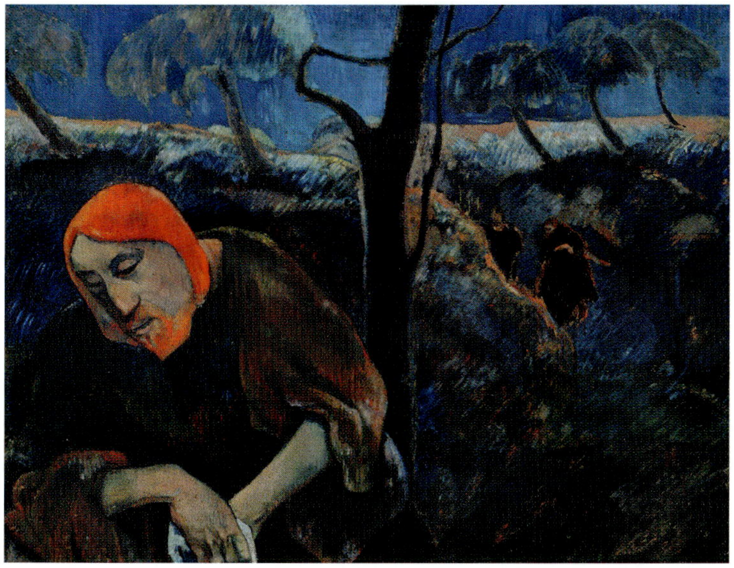

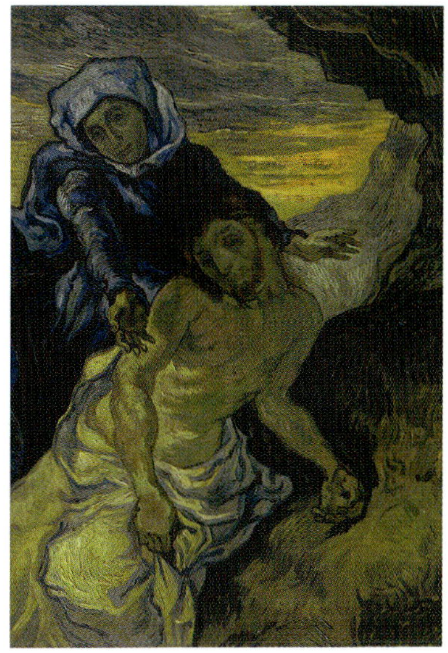

Paul Gauguin
Christ in the Garden of Olives, 1889
[cat. 68]

Vincent van Gogh
Pietà (after Eugène Delacroix), 1889
Oil on canvas. 73 x 60.5 cm
Amsterdam, Van Gogh Museum
(Vincent van Gogh Foundation)

of Olives later in 1889), he took issue with them. For Van Gogh, Bernard and Gauguin's religious paintings were no more than an artificial return to medieval tapestries and primitive paintings, comparable to the Pre-Raphaelites' anaemic figures. Van Gogh contrasted the only healthy religious painting that he knew, that of Rembrandt and Delacroix, with these decadent inventions. As if to confirm this thesis, in September 1889, Van Gogh painted his own theomorphic self-portrait in the form of a modified version of Delacroix's *Pietà*.

But the true alternative that Van Gogh offered to Gauguin's and Bernard's icons was completely different. In a letter to Bernard written from the asylum at Saint-Rémy where he was interned, Van Gogh described to him a landscape that he had painted of the garden there. This was an allegorical landscape with a great destroyed tree, and Van Gogh explained that 'to give an impression of anguish, one can aim to do so without aiming directly at the historical garden of Gesthemane'.[100] Over the course of the summer and autumn of 1889, Van Gogh systematically painted olive trees in the surrounding area. In November he wrote to his brother: 'This month I have worked in the olive groves, as they (Gauguin and Bernard) made me furious with their Christs in the garden, where there is nothing observed. In my case of course it is not a question of doing anything from the Bible, and I have written to Bernard and also to Gauguin that I believe our duty is thinking and not dreaming, and for that reason I was so astonished by their work, and that they had let themselves go in that direction'.[101] Van Gogh's obstinate resistance to biblical subjects has been attributed to his agitated state resulting from his mental illness, during which he suffered periods of crisis with religious visions and anxieties. However, the artist's attitude coincides perfectly with that of another painter working in Provence, the

100. 'Pour donner une impression d'angoisse, on peut chercher à le faire sans viser droit au jardin de Gethsemani historique.' Letter to Émile Bernard B 21, early December 1889, ibid. vol. III, p. 414.
101. 'C'est que j'ai travaillé ce mois-ci dans les vergers d'oliviers, car ils m'avaient fait enrager avec leurs Christs au jardin, où rien n'est observé. Bien entendu chez moi il n'est pas question de faire quelque chose de la Bible — et j'ai écrit à Bernard et aussi à Gauguin, que je croyais que la pensée et non le rêve étaity notre devoir, que donc j'étais étonné devant leur travail de ce qu'ils se laissent aller à cela.' Letter to Théo no. 615, 21 November 1889, ibid, vol. III, p. 407.

elderly Paul Cézanne. Years later Cézanne confided to his friend Joachim Gasquet: 'You will remember what Jacobo de Voragine had to say, that on the night on which the Saviour was born all the vines flowered in Palestine [...] We, the painters, should paint these vines flowering rather than the clouds of trumpeting angels announcing the Messiah'.[102]

It is almost impossible not to see Van Gogh's reaction to Gauguin's *Christ in the Garden of Olives* as a sort of poetic justice: as Gauguin had subjected various icons of his friend Vincent to a sort of ironic deconstruction, so Van Gogh's response was to some extent a dose of his own medicine. We might see an irresistible and involuntary irony in these olive trees that claim to be Agonies in the Garden without Christ or angels, religious paintings but ones stripped of biblical allusions.

6. In the wake of Gauguin: from Pont-Aven to the Nabis

'After Manet, he [Gauguin] is the French painter who has been most influential. What Manet was to the generation of 1870, Gauguin was to that of 1890'.[103] These words of Maurice Denis are witness to the strangest paradox that we can associate with Gauguin: that a painter so radically individualist became something like the founder of a school. It is difficult to decide how much was involuntary and how much deliberate in this paradox. On the one hand, Gauguin exuded a personal charisma which attracted young artists. But on the other, it appears that he soon grasped the benefits which that charisma could bring him within the context of his difficult professional circumstances. Gauguin appreciated that the degree of recognition of his own work depended to some extent on the disciples which he managed to recruit. During his first stay in Brittany in 1886, Gauguin already boasted of being the most hated and the most admired among the Pont-Aven artists' colony, of the arguments which he provoked, and how the other painters debated the words of advice he offered.[104] Pissarro sarcastically commented that Gauguin preached in Brittany, with a following of young men who listened to him like a master: Gauguin had achieved enormous influence with his commendable labour 'in the art of creating sects'.[105]

Starting with his very first followers whom he found in Pont Aven in 1886 – Charles Laval and a certain Puigadeau, nicknamed 'Picolo' – Gauguin's band would grow on his successive return trips to Brittany. First there was Émile Bernard, who never wished to be a disciple of Gauguin, but an equal, and later numerous others, some of them locals such as Armand Séguin and Maxime Maufra, and others from farther away, such as the Dutch artists Jacob Meyer de Haan and Jan Verkade, the Englishman Robert Bevan and the Irishman Roderic O'Conor, among others. Although the term Pont-Aven School has survived, it was in fact a varied and incoherent group which never really became a school, as its members dispersed every time Gauguin disappeared from the scene (as he did in

102. 'Vous devez vous rappeler ce que raconte Jacques de Voragine, que la nuit de la naissance du Sauveur les vignes fleurirent dans toute la Palestine. [...] Nous peintres, nous devons plutôt peindre la floraison de ces vignes que les tourbillons d'anges qui trompettent le Messie.' Gasquet, Joachim: *Cézanne* [1921]. Paris, Encre marine, 2002, p. 310.
103. 'Depuis Manet, il [Gauguin] est le peintre français qui eut la plus grande influence. Ce que fut Manet, pour la génération de 1870, Gauguin le fut pour celle de 1890.' La peinture' [1905], in Denis, M.: *Le Ciel et l'Arcadie*, *op. cit.*, p. 85.
104. See the letters to Mette of end of July 1886, in *Correspondance de Paul Gauguin*, vol. I, pp. 133, 137.
105. Letter to Lucien, 22 January 1887, in *Correspondance de Camille Pissarro*, *op. cit.*, vol. II, p. 119.

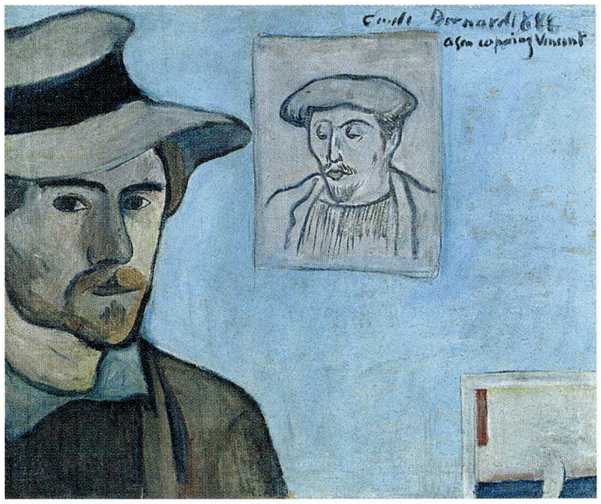

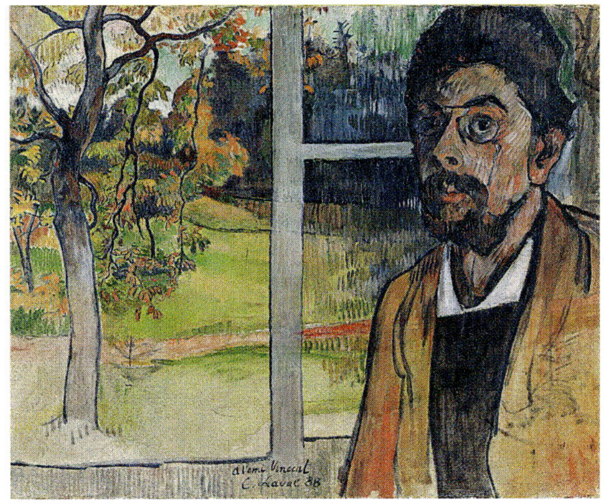

Émile Bernard
Self-Portrait with Portrait of Gauguin, 1888
Oil on canvas. 46.5 x 55.5 cm
Amsterdam, Van Gogh Museum
(Vincent van Gogh Foundation)

Charles Laval
Self-Portrait, 1888
Oil on canvas. 50 x 60 cm.
Amsterdam, Van Gogh Museum
(Vincent van Gogh Foundation)

1891 and again in 1895). Some of his followers in Brittany abandoned their emulation of the master to return to their earlier pictorial styles, while others joined a new and more stable group established in Paris around the figure of Paul Sérusier.

Experiments and decoration

In the summer of 1888 – according to an anecdote that has been repeated to the point of cliché – the young Sérusier, an intellectually avid student painter, visited the village of Pont-Aven. There he met Gauguin and became interested in his new ideas on painting. In the nearby Bois d'Amour, on a small panel, Sérusier painted a landscape following Gauguin's instructions. Gauguin apparently asked Séruiser: 'How do you see that tree? [...] Is it green? Well put green, the most beautiful green on your palette; and that shadow, more like blue? Don't hesitate to paint it as blue as possible'.[106]

When Sérusier returned to Paris, he showed the panel to his fellow students at the Académie Julian (Maurice Denis, Pierre Bonnard, Paul Ranson, and Henri-Gabriel Ibels), who received it as a revelation. With his reputation as an erudite polyglot (he was said to command Latin, Arabic and Hebrew), philosopher and theologian, Sérusier became the guru to a group of young artists. They took the name of Nabis, deriving from the Hebrew word meaning 'prophets'. This initial group of painters associated with the Académie Julian subsequently expanded to include Édouard Vuillard and Ker-Xavier Roussel (former companions of Denis in the Lycée Condorcet), while later arrivals included the Swiss artist Félix Vallotton, and the Hungarian Rippl-Ronaï, and the sculptors Lacombe and Maillol. Half in jest and half seriously, the prophets adopted the paraphernalia of a secret society or mystic brotherhood: they wore oriental costumes, wrote letters in a pompous, archaic style, and invented new names for themselves: Sérusier was the *nabi à la barde rutilante*, Denis the *nabi aux belles icones*, Bonnard the *nabi japponard*, and Vuillard the *nabi zouave*.

106. 'La influence de Paul Gauguin' [1903], in Denis, M.: *Le Ciel et l'Arcadie*, *op. cit.*, p. 8.

Among the young initiates, the small landscape which they called the *Talisman* [cat. 84] provoked a veritable outburst of experiments, from Denis' *Patches of Sun on the Terrace* (1890) [cat. 85] with its almost unrecognisable setting, to Vuillard's *Octagonal Self-Portrait* (1890) [cat. 82] and *Lilacs* (1890) [cat. 87], and Roussel's *The Fisherman* (1890–91) [cat. 86]. These small-format paintings, flat and almost abstract in style, were experiments in pure colour as a means of translating sensations onto the picture plane. These experiments, whose radical nature would not be surpassed until the arrival of Fauvism or that of abstract painting, literally illustrated the famous inaugural definition offered by the theoretician of the group, Maurice Denis, in 1890: 'Remember that a painting – before it is a horse or a battle, a naked woman or a story of any type – is essentially a flat surface covered with colours arranged in a certain order'.[107]

Later, throughout the 1890s, these experiments would be replaced by large format compositions of declared decorative intent. The Nabis were fascinated by early Renaissance Italian frescoes, Japanese screens, and by Puvis de Chavannes' large allegorical compositions, and had read Aurier's article in which he praised Gauguin's abilities as a decorative painter. Sérusier fostered the primacy of large-scale mural painting, and produced his *Apple Harvest* [cat. 106]. Denis, Bonnard, Vuillard and Roussel embarked on large commissions for the homes of their wealthy patrons and protectors. However, the tendency towards decoration was also evident in their easel works, in Denis' famous *Madame Ranson with Cat* (1892) [cat. 110] or *The Muses* [cat. 111], in which the sacred grove has been domesticated and become an elegant private park. Some of the Nabis, such as Lacombe and Maillol, were literally inspired by works by Gauguin, submitting them to a new process of decorative simplification.

The contrast between the early colour experiments on a small scale and the large decorative compositions, so characteristic of the overall evolution of the Nabis group, is perfectly reflected in the two artistic principles set out by the group's theoretician, Maurice Denis: *subjective deformation* and *objective deformation*. The principle of subjective deformation or theory of the equivalents affirms that 'the emotions or states of mind provoked by whatever spectacle' arouse 'in the artist's imagination signs or visual equivalents capable of reproducing those emotions or states of mind without the need to reproduce the initial spectacle'.[108] In the name of expression that principle authorised all intensification or exaggeration (of colour, physiognomies, etc.) to the point of caricature. However, as a necessary 'corrective' to these expressionist excesses, and as a compensation for them, Denis added another principle, that of objective deformation, which imposed on the artist the need for a 'decorative, aesthetic and rational composition', and obliged him to 'transpose everything into Beauty.[109]

107. 'Se rappeler qu'un tableau —avant d'être un cheval de bataille, une femme nue, ou une quelconque anecdote— est essentiellement une surface plane recouverte de couleurs en un certain ordre assemblées'. 'Définition du néo-traditionnisme' [1890], ibid., p. 5.
108. 'Les émotions ou états d'âme provoqués par un spectacle quelconque, comportaient dans l'imagination de l'artiste des signes ou équivalents plastiques capables de reproducire ces émotions ou états d'âme sans qu'ils soit besoin de fournir la copie du spectacle initial; qu'à chaque état de notre sensibilité devait correspondre une harmonie objective capable de le traduire.' De Gauguin et de Van Gogh au classicisme' [1909], ibid, p. 162.
109. 'La *déformation objective* obligeait à son tour l'artiste à tout transposer en Beauté'. 'De Gauguin et de Van Gogh au classicisme' [1909], ibid., p. 163.

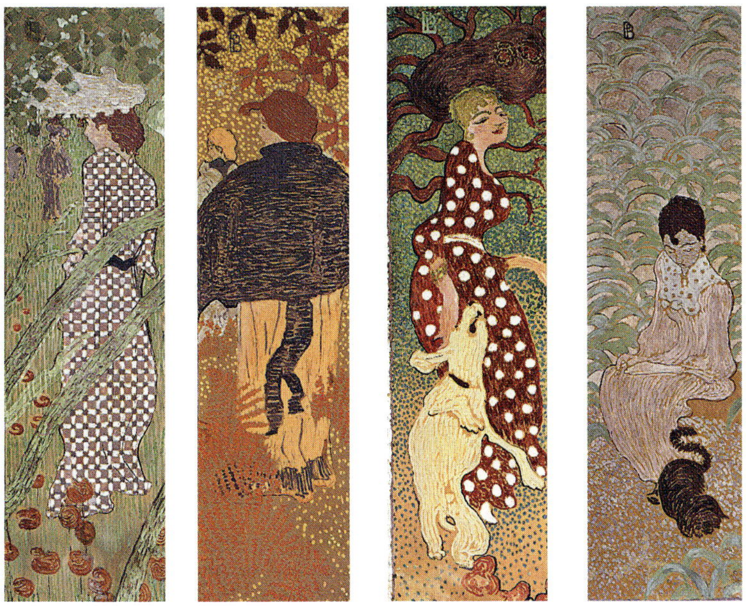

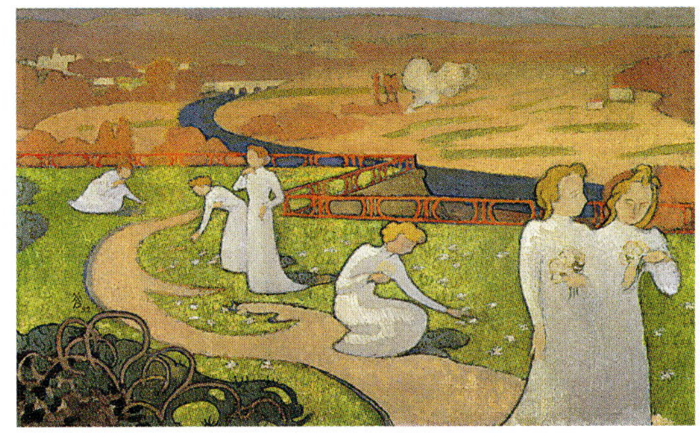

Pierre Bonnard
Women in the Garden, 1891
4 decorative panels,
Oil on paper on canvas. 160 x 48 cm each
Paris, Musée d'Orsay

Maurice Denis
April, 1892
Decorative panel from the series *Sujet poétique*
Oil on canvas. 38 x 61 cm
Otterlo, Kröller-Müller Museum Collection

Two trends

The core group of the Nabis was profoundly imbued with spiritual interests: Sérusier managed to combine theosophy and Christianity, Maurice Denis was a fervent Catholic, while Ranson was passionately interested in esoteric doctrines, all three turning to religious and archaic symbolic subjects remote from the modern world. Other Nabis, however, were less interested in such matters: Bonnard and Vuillard painted street scenes, parks and domestic interiors. These painters were not interested in abstract speculations, but in their own perceptions. Their sense of modern life set them apart from any nostalgic, archaising recreation. They looked to Japanese art, to Degas and Lautrec, admiring their capacity for observation, their manner of representing certain movements and gestures synthetically, and their feeling for modern life.

In March 1899, as the Nabis decade was reaching an end, Maurice Denis characterised the two tendencies into which the group had divided itself in words that also testify to the rupture brought about in French culture as a result of the 'Dreyfus Affair'. The first of these two trends, represented by Sérusier, Ranson and Denis himself, could be distinguished by its inclination towards pure colours, a symbolic emphasis, the importance given to the human figure and, in general, by a simplicity of 'Latin taste'. The other trend, represented by Vuillard and Bonnard, inclined towards darker tones, towards images observed from life, was less interested in the figures and in drawing, and tended towards complication, in a reflection of 'Semite taste'.[110]

110. Denis: *Journal*, vol. I, p. 150.

However, the gap between the two halves of the Nabi group, between Catholic and Jewish members, religious and secular, archaic and modern, speculative and observing types, had not been as visible or as evident at the start of the decade as these later reflections suggest. While Denis in his painting cultivated muses and fairies, Annunciations and the holy women at the sepulchre, he remained apart in his theories from any complicity with idealising Symbolism as represented, for example, by Albert Aurier. In his 'Notes on Religious Painting' (1896), Denis maintained that synthetism or pictorial Symbolism was not born from any idealising theory, but was rather the 'immediate result of positivist philosophies', and that it was 'the most strictly scientific artistic tendency': 'Those who began it were the landscape painters, the still life painters, and absolutely not the 'painters of the soul'.'[111] In addition, we should add that Denis's famous definition of a painting, quoted above, came close (as its author later acknowledged) to the one proposed by Taine, the patron saint of aesthetic positivism in his *Philosophy of Art*: 'A painting is a coloured surface in which the different tones and different degrees of light are distributed with a certain criteria'.[112]

Bonnard, Vuillard and mystery

In addition, Bonnard and Vuillard, despite their apparent segregation, fully shared the spirit of the Nabis. Maurice Denis maintained that Bonnard unconsciously and effortlessly applied the complimentary principles of 'subjective deformation' and 'objective deformation'.[113] Expressive difference and decorativeness converge in the early work of Bonnard and Vuillard and both painters transformed people and everyday things into sinuous, graceful, dancing silhouettes imbued with both dazzling ornamental qualities and with a kind of phantasmal spirit. This is the case, for example, with a composition such as *Two Dogs playing* [cat. 116] by Bonnard. The painter's interest in the children and small animals goes hand in hand with a tendency to give the inanimate elements the appearance of living beings. An example of this is *Woman Putting on her Stockings* (1893) [cat. 119], by the same artist, in which the stocking breaks free from the woman and becomes a living creature, a sort of snake. Bonnard and Vuillard's silhouettes, submerged in shadow or bathed in lamplight, have something of ghosts, or *revenants*. In Vuillard's *Woman in an Interior* (1893) [cat. 120] the head retains some volume but it is attached to a body which is pure, insubstantial shadow.

All of Vuillard's work is a *voyage autour de ma chambre*. However, this focus on the intimate is not an exaltation of comfort, of the predicted order, of domestic routine. For the artist, the bourgeois interior is the least familiar and strangest domain, a jungle that needs to be explored. 'I had the feeling' André Gide wrote in *Les Cahiers d'André Walter*, 'of seeing only the half of things. I believed that the others had been initiated into rituals that they hid from me because I was too young. When I entered, conversations would cease in my presence: at times I came across signs that I was the only one who did not understand,

111. 'Certes non, ce n'était pas une théorie idéaliste. Résultat immédiat des philosophies positives, alors en vogue, et des méthodes d'induction que nous eûmes en si grand respect, ce fut bien la tentative d'art la plus strictement scientifique. Ceux qui l'ont inauguré étaient des paysagistes, des nature-mortistes, pas du tout des "peintres de l'âme."' 'Notes sur la peinture religieuse' (1896), in Denis: *Le Ciel et l'Arcadie*, p. 36.

112. 'Un tableau est une surface colorée, dans laquelle les divers tons et les divers degrés de lumière sont répartis avec un certain choix; voilà son être intime', quoted in Denis, M.: *Le Ciel et l'Arcadie*, *op. cit.*, p. 216.

113. '[...] les deux déformations objective et subjective, il les pratique sans penser. [...] oui, les deux déformations, celle qui de chacune de ses toiles fait un tapis de couleur rare, et celle qui leur donne le charme de poèmes délicats, elles sont l'armature invisible d'une oeuvre qui, par ailleurs, est le triomphe net de tes dons prodigieux et de ta souriante fantaisie.' In Denis, M.: 'L'époque du symbolisme' [1934], in *Le ciel et l'Arcadie*, *op. cit.*, p. 216.

and sometimes when I went to bed, I suspected that mysterious things happened while I was sleeping'.[114] Vuillard's interiors also suggest these sensations: low-voiced conversations, stifled complaints, murmurings, a feeling of the unsaid and the secret all around.

This manner of representing everyday people and objects is fully in line with the central thesis of literary Symbolism which took allusion or suggestion as the key to poetic diction. 'To name an object', wrote Mallarmé in his famous reply to Jules Huret's survey, 'is to take away three-quarters of the pleasure of the poem, which consists of the pleasure of gradually becoming aware: to *suggest*, that is the dream. The symbol constitutes the perfect use of that mystery: to gradually evoke an object in order to reveal a state of mind, or, in contrast, to select an object and extract a state of mind from it through a series of decipherings'.[115] Many years before, almost at the outset of his career, Gauguin had written a simpler phrase: 'Poetry begins where mystery is born'.[116]

In 1892, when Gauguin had already left Europe for the islands of the Pacific, Paul Ranson referred to him as 'The Nabi on a mission in Tahiti'.[117] In the meantime, the exiled artist wrote in a suspicious, untrusting tone about his followers. Recalling how earlier critics had taken him as a disciple of Anquetin and Bernard, he predicted: 'Tomorrow I will turn into a follower of Bernard and Sérusier'.[118] Gauguin suspected that Sérusier wished to replace him as master and he renounced 'the whole Sérusier, Denis and company lot'.[119] Nonetheless, leaving aside paranoid suspicions, Gauguin had a basic confidence in his artistic heirs. In his discussion of the 'music of the painting' that appears in his last text, *Racontars de rapin*, Gauguin firmly states: 'Bonnard, Vuillard, Sérusier, to mention some young artists, are musicians and you can be sure that coloured painting is entering a musical phase'.[120] Despite all his suspicions, at the end of his life, Gauguin valued his legacy as a teacher higher than his own work. In his last letters from the Marquesas Islands his confessed to his friend Monfreid: 'You know what I have long wished to establish: the *right* to risk everything. My abilities [...] have not brought about great results, but the machine is set in motion. The public owes me nothing as my pictorial work is only relatively good, but the painters who are now benefiting from that freedom owe me something'.[121]

114. 'J'avais le sentiment de ne voir qu'une moitié des choses. Je croyais les autres initiés à des rites qu'on me cachait parce que j'étais trop jeune. Quand j'entrais, les conversations se taisaient devant moi, parfois je surprenais des signes que j'étais seul à ne pas comprendre, et, le soir surtout, quand je m'en allais dormir, je soupçonnais que des choses très mystérieuses se passaient pendant mon sommeil.' Gide, A.: *Les cahiers d'André Walter. Avec des fragments inédits du Journal*. Claude Martin (ed.). Paris, Gallimard, 1986, p. 214.

115. 'Nommer un objet, c'est supprimer les trois-quarts de la jouissance du poème qui est fait du bonheur de deviner peu à peu; le *suggérer*, voilà le rêve. C'est le parfait usage de ce mystère qui constitue le symbole: évoquer petit à petit un objet pour montrer un état d'âme, ou, inversement, choisir un objet et en dégager un état d'âme, par une série de déchiffrements.' 'Réponse à l'enquête de Jules Huret sur l'évolution littéraire' (1891), Mallarmé, Stéphane: *Igitur. Divagations. Un coup de dés*. Preface by Yves Bonnefoy. Paris, Gallimard, 1976, p. 392.

116. 'La poésie commence où naît le mystère'. Draft of a letter of late 1884, sold at Christie's, Geneva, 14 May 2001; quoted in Wildenstein, D.: *Gauguin. Premier itinéraire d'un sauvage. Catalogue de l'oeuvre peint (1873–1888)*, *op. cit.*, vol. I, p. XXXIII.

117. 'Le Nabi en mission à Tahiti', letter from Ranson to Verkade, October–November 1892, quoted in Mauner, George L.: *The Nabis: Their History and their Art, 1886–1896*. New York and London, Garland Publishing, 1978, p. 282.

118. 'Demain je deviendrai élève de Bernard et de Sérusier.' Letter to Monfreid, March 1897, *Lettres de Paul Gauguin à Daniel de Monfreid*, *op. cit.*, p. 168.

119. Letter to Monfreid, January 1900, ibid., pp. 268–69. 'Toute la bande Sérusier, Denis et Cie'. Letter to Monfreid July 1898, ibid., p. 219.

120. 'Ne vous y trompez pas, Bonnard, Vuillard, Sérusier, pour citer quelques jeunes, sont des musiciens, et soyez persuadés que la peinture colorée entre dans une phase musicale.' Gauguin, P.: *Racontars de rapin* [1902]. Monaco, Editions Sauret, 1993, p. 45.

121. 'Vous connaissez depuis longtemps ce que j'ai voulu établir: le *droit* de tout oser: mes capacités [...] n'ont pas donné un grand résultat, mais cependant la machine est lancée. Le public ne me doit rien puisque mon oeuvre picturale n'est que relativement bonne, mais les peintres qui, aujourd'hui, profitent de cette liberté, me doivent quelque chose.' Letter to Monfreid, October 1902, in *Lettres de Paul Gauguin à Daniel de Monfreid*, *op. cit.*, p. 348.

The primitive of everyone else's way

RICHARD SHIFF

'I remain the primitive of the way I discovered. ... I am the primitive of my own way. ... Someone else will do what I could not do. Perhaps I am only the primitive of a new art.'

Paul Cézanne, c. 1904, quoted by witnesses.[1]

'Primitive art originates in the mind and puts nature to its use.'

Paul Gauguin, c. 1890, quoted by Charles Morice.[2]

'Today's direction in art, indicated first by Pissarro, was then rectified by Cézanne, as Gauguin showed us. [Gauguin] was my liberator as well as that of many others.'

Paul Sérusier, 1905.[3]

If we accept Cézanne's word 'primitif', he discovered the way to a new art but failed to command it. He remained the 'primitive', the one who inaugurates a method without perfecting it or realising its implications. 'Will I reach the goal I've sought so much and so long pursued', he asked in September 1906, only a month before he died. 'I'm working from nature as always, and I think I'm making some slow progress.'[4] Cézanne continued to distrust his results, leaving many canvases in an unfinished state. In this respect his progress was as 'slow' as he claimed. Perhaps his sense of 'working from nature' prevented him from proceeding along the path he had already cleared. Doubting his innovations but never questioning his definition of painting – 'the concrete study of nature' – Cézanne may have misconceived the significance of the art that his years of practice gradually brought into being.[5] From Gauguin's position, Cézanne's painting represented human feeling, not nature.

In 1905, Paul Sérusier suggested as much when he responded to a survey not only on Cézanne but also on Gauguin, who had died in 1903. His statement offered a condensed history of Symbolism in modern art. First, Pissarro's painting had demonstrated the expressive power of an accentuated brushstroke. Next, Cézanne had released the stroke from its task of description, enhancing that power. Yet because Cézanne did this unknowingly, it was left to Gauguin to announce the discovery: the modern painter's mark was liberated from any naturalistic function, like the primitive artist's mark, which was 'primitive' by the very fact that it never developed analogous concerns.[6] No longer in the service of nature – to the contrary, served by nature – modern painting had now established a direct link to the imagination and its associated emotions. In words of his own, Sérusier repeated the lesson of Gauguin's Cézanne: 'He is a pure painter ... Of an ordinary painter's apple, you say "I could take a bite out of it." Of Cézanne's apple, you say "How beautiful!"'[7] With the viewer responding emotionally to a specific configuration of line and color, the sensation of beauty – or simply sensation itself –became the primary meaning of Cézanne's form. His 'apple' was not an apple to eat, but an imaginative fantasy to

1. 'Je reste le primitif de la voie que j'ai découverte': Paul Cézanne, quoted in Émile Bernard, 'Souvenirs sur Paul Cézanne et lettres inédites', in *Mercure de France* 69, n.1, 16 October 1907), p. 614. Cézanne, who often spoke with deep irony, was aware that Bernard regarded himself as a respectful follower. If Cézanne actually said that he remained the 'primitive' of his own style, this would have been flattering to Bernard (whose artistic ambitions were evident), for he would inherit the master's technique and assume responsibility for perfecting it. 'Je suis le primitif de ma propre voie [...] Un autre fera ce que je n'ai pu faire. Je ne suis, peut-être, que le primitif d'un art nouveau': Paul Cézanne, quoted in Joachim Gasquet, in *Cézanne*, Paris: Bernheim-Jeune, 1926 [1921]), pp. 70, 208 (emphasis added). Gasquet referred to the first of these two statements as 'reported' (presumably by Bernard); he incorporated the second 'Un autre fera ...') into the end of an imaginary dialogue with Cézanne. With regard to the first variant, Gasquet commented that it reflected humility, even self-deprecation, because Cézanne actually disdained primitive style, that is, the style of the European 'Primitives', such as Giotto. To the contrary, Bernard had once chosen to relate Cézanne's stylistic manner, at times 'rude', at other times 'charmingly puerile', to these same European 'primitive masters'. (Bernard, Émile: 'Paul Cézanne', in *Les hommes d'aujourd'hui* 8, no. 387. February–March 1891): n.p. Unless otherwise noted, all translations are by the author. I thank James Lawrence, Katie Robinson Edwards, Alexander Dumbadze and especially Elizabeth C. Childs for aid in research.
2. 'L'art primitif procède de l'esprit et emploie la nature': Paul Gauguin, quoted in Charles Morice, in *Paul Gauguin*, Paris, H. Floury, 1919, p. 22. Variants of this thought appear in statements by Gauguin's followers among the Symbolists and Nabis. For example, Maurice Denis wrote: 'For the artist, nature becomes a state of his own subjectivity'. (Denis, Maurice: 'De Gauguin et de Van Gogh au Classicisme', 1909, in *Théories 1890–1910: Du Symbolisme et de Gauguin vers un nouvel ordre classique*, Paris, Rouart et Watelin, 1920, p. 275). With regard to the timing of Gauguin's statement, Morice implies that it was made in late 1889, when he first encountered the painter; but Isabelle Cahn and others date their initial meeting to late 1890. This seems correct given Gauguin's movements between Brittany and Paris during the two years. On Gauguin's complicated relationship with Morice, see Cahn, Isabelle: 'Noa Noa: The Voyage to Tahiti', Mark Polizzotti, trans., in Shackelford, George T. M. and Frèches-Thory, Claire, eds.: *Gauguin Tahiti*, Boston, MFA Publications, 2004, pp. 94–98; Wadley, Nicholas, *Noa Noa: Gauguin's Tahiti*, Oxford, Phaidon, 1985, pp. 100–107.

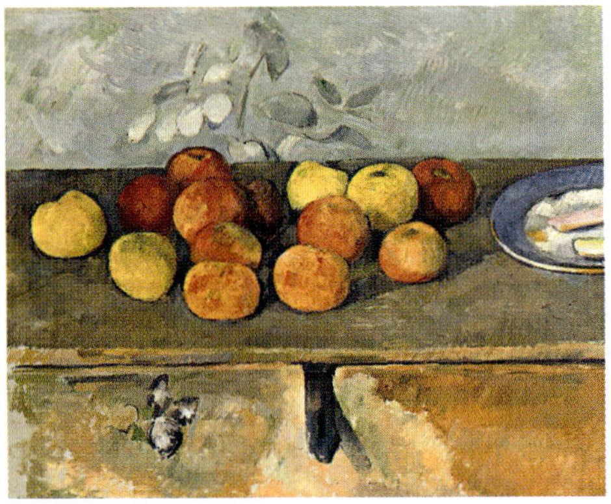

Paul Cézanne
Still Life with Compotier,
1879–1880
Oil on canvas. 44 x 55 cm
Paris, Musée national de l'Orangerie
(Jean Walter and Paul Guilaume Collection)

dream. In the Symbolist painting that Gauguin and Sérusier conceived, dreaming replaced eating and every other banal aspect of existence. Such a condition changes the quality of living.

Hard to live

Gauguin's interest in Cézanne developed when he painted beside both Pissarro and Cézanne at Auvers in 1881, observing first-hand Cézanne's application of discrete, parallel strokes. (This interest was never reciprocated; Cézanne disapproved of the linear 'abstraction' and unmodulated colour apparent in the style Gauguin derived from him.)[8] Whatever Cézanne happened to do and say in 1881 led Gauguin to understand the separate, juxtaposed marks as the painter's successive 'sensations.'[9] Gauguin either adopted, appropriated, or stole Cézanne's technique – the choice of verb would depend on the attitude or allegiance of whoever was telling this story – and along with Cézanne's mark came his sensation.[10] 'Forthright, uniform, supple, and grand', was Maurice Denis's description of Gauguin's own brushstroke; and he added immediately that its character had been 'acquired evidently from Cézanne.'[11] 'Gauguin, absolutely the first in this respect, had a limitless admiration for Cézanne.'[12]

Gauguin perceived that the patterning of Cézanne's side-by-side marks, their orientation in relation to the picture surface, did not necessarily follow the volumetric contouring of the cultivated fields, the trees, or the still-life objects being represented. An apple was round; its constituent marks might be vaguely rectilinear. Beyond the fact that Cézanne's technique defied the conventions of naturalistic imitation, it bore a remarkable implication: 'sensation' was no longer something to be recorded (as a view or "study" of nature) but something independently created (as the painter's internalised vision or dreamlike, imaginative projection [rêve]). This was noted by Émile Bernard, who in 1891 became the first to devote an interpretive essay to Cézanne; like Sérusier, Bernard had been a member

3. 'Ce mouvement [actuel], dirigé d'abord par Pissarro, fut rectifié ensuite par Cézanne, que Gauguin nous révéla. [Gauguin] fut mon libérateur et celui de beaucoup d'autres': Paul Sérusier, statement of 1905, in Dagen, Philippe (ed.): *La peinture en 1905: l'Enquête sur les tendances actuelles des arts plastiques' de Charles Morice*, Paris, in Lettres Modernes, 1986, p. 74 (sentence order reversed). Compare Paul Sérusier, letter to Maurice Denis, 27 November 1907, in Sérusier, Paul: *A B C de la Peinture, suivi d'une correspondance inédite*, (ed.), H. Boutaric, Paris: Floury, 1950, p. 132: 'It was not until after he was familiar with Pissarro that Cézanne became aware of his mission. Parallel to the evolution of Gauguin, sharing the same beginning (Pissarro), Cézanne evolved further. This is not an end [*réalisation*]; instead he shows the way [*c'est un jalon*] for those to come.'

4. Letter from Paul Cézanne to Émile Bernard, 21 September 1906, quoted in Rewald, John (ed.): *Paul Cézanne, correspondance*, Paris, Grasset, 1978, pp. 326–27. Cézanne's irony (compare note 1, above) may lie behind his reference to 'slow progress'; perhaps the modesty he professed was false. Nevertheless, in this instance his sincerity is likely, given his rapidly failing health and awareness that many aspects of his cumulative artistic project remained unresolved.

5. 'L'étude concrète de la nature', letter from Cézanne to Émile Bernard, 12 May 1904, in Rewald: *op. cit.*, p. 302.

6. Compare Denis: 'De la gaucherie des Primitifs' (1904), in *Théories 1890–1910…*, *op. cit.*, pp. 174, 176: 'Every Primitive [those who initiate an art, such as Giotto] views nature like the savage [those living in a wild or uncivilized state] … he makes the image of things conform to the idea he has of them.'

7. For Sérusier's statement, see Denis, 'Cézanne' (1907), in *Théories 1890–1910…*, *op. cit.*, p. 252. Denis himself commented that 'facing [a] Cézanne, we think only of the painting; neither the object represented nor the artist's subjectivity hold our attention', p. 247.

8. On Cézanne's dissatisfaction with Gauguin's art and with the use of linear contour, see his letters to Bernard, 15 April 1904, 23 October 1905, Rewald: *op. cit.*, pp. 300, 315. On Gauguin's unmodulated colour, see Cézanne's words as reported in Bernard: *op. cit.*, p. 400.

9. See letter from Paul Gauguin to Camille Pissarro, July 1881, in Merlhès, Victor (ed.): in *Correspondance de Paul Gauguin (1873–1888)*, Paris, Fondation Singer-Polignac, 1984, p. 21.

10. See, for example, Mirbeau, Octave: 'Préface du catalogue du Salon d'automne 1909', 'Cézanne' (1914), *Combats esthétiques*, (ed.), Pierre Michel and Jean-François Nivet, 2 vols., Paris, Séguier, 1993, 2, pp. 485, 528; Bernard: *op. cit.*, p. 400.

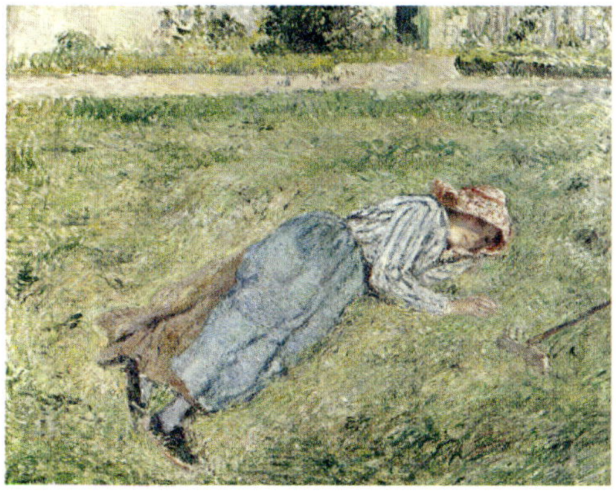

Camille Pissarro
The Rest, Young Peasant Girl Lying in the Grass, 1882
Oil on canvas. 63 x 78 cm
Bremen, Kunsthalle

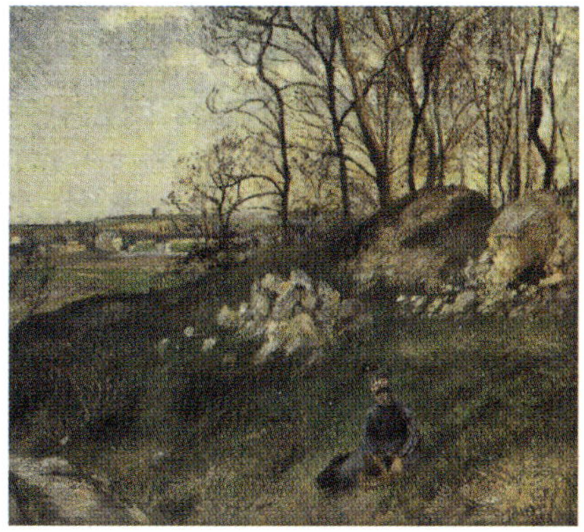

Camille Pissarro
The Quarry of Le Chou, Pontoise, 1882
Private Collection

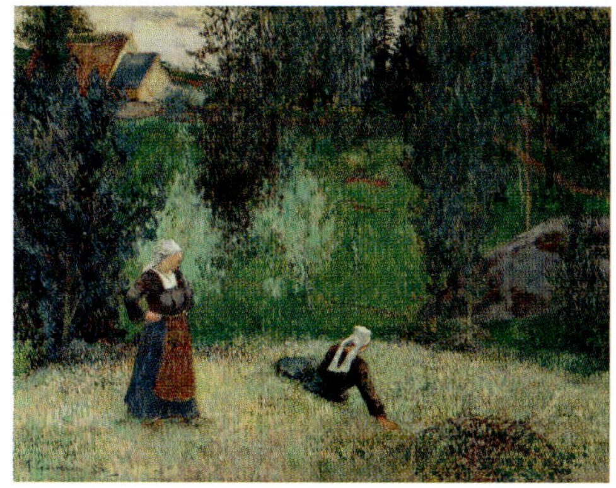

Paul Gauguin
Early flowers, 1888
Oil on canvas. 70 x 92 cm
Zurich, Kunsthaus Zürich

of the 'School of Pont-Aven' during the late 1880s (see *Madeleine in the Bois d'Amour*, 1888 [cat. 55]). He developed his interest in Cézanne prior to meeting Gauguin, but Gauguin caused that interest to deepen. Unlike Gauguin's focus on the system of marking, Bernard's view of Cézanne's style featured its abstracted form, a kind of geometric reduction: his apples were 'round as if drawn with a compass;' his pears were 'triangular'. But the significance remained the same – creative expression beyond or apart from nature. In Bernard's words, Cézanne 'opened to art this amazing door: painting for itself.'[13]

The blunt juxtaposition of variously coloured strokes (the feature Gauguin stressed) was much more insistent in Cézanne's painting than in Pissarro's. This increased the chromatic energy of each individual hue; accordingly, Cézanne's imaginative vision became that much more moving, its emotional force intensified. The effect that Cézanne produced in *Three Bathers* (c. 1876–1877) [cat. 46] or *View of L'Estaque* (c. 1883–1885) [cat. 21], Gauguin self-consciously adapted to his own expressive purposes in *An Orchard Under the Church of Bihorel* (1884) [cat. 18], *River Under the Trees* (1887) [cat. 24], *Breton Women by a Bend in the Road* (1888) [cat. 40], and *Still Life with Peaches* (c. 1889).

In 1885 Gauguin reflected on his new practice, indicating that the technique of juxtaposed strokes was at its core: 'People complain about our unblended colours, set one against the other. ... [Yet] a green beside a red does not yield a reddish brown, as in physical mixture, but rather two vibrant notes.'[14]

At issue in Gauguin's response to Cézanne were two distinct but related applications of the concept of the primitive (or primitiveness). First, the term would be applied to art that

11. Denis: 'L'influence de Paul Gauguin' (1903), *Théories 1890–1910..., op. cit.*, p. 170.
12. Denis: 'Cézanne', *Théories 1890–1910..., op. cit.*, p. 253.
13. Bernard, Émile: 'Paul Cézanne' (1891), n.p. Compare Bernard, Émile: 'Paul Cézanne', in *L'Occident* 6, July 1904, p. 21: 'The more [Cézanne] works, the more his work removes itself from the external view [and] the more he abstracts the picture.'
14. Gauguin, Paul: 'Notes synthétiques', 1885, in *Oviri: Ecrits d'un sauvage*, ed. Daniel Guérin, Paris, Gallimard, 1974, p. 24.

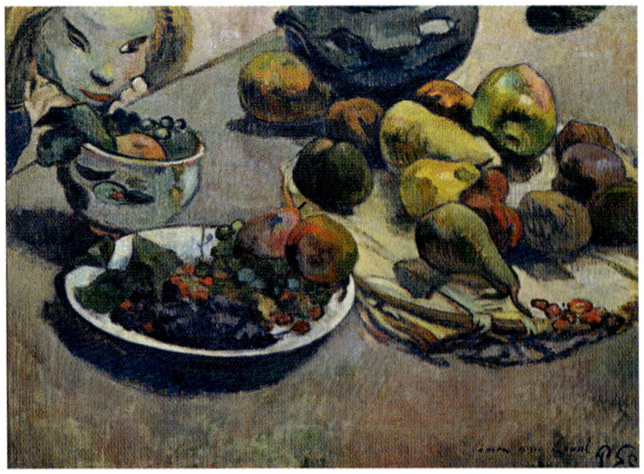

Paul Gauguin
Still Life with Fruits, 1888
Oil on canvas. 43 x 58 cm
Moscow, The State Pushkin Museum of Fine Arts

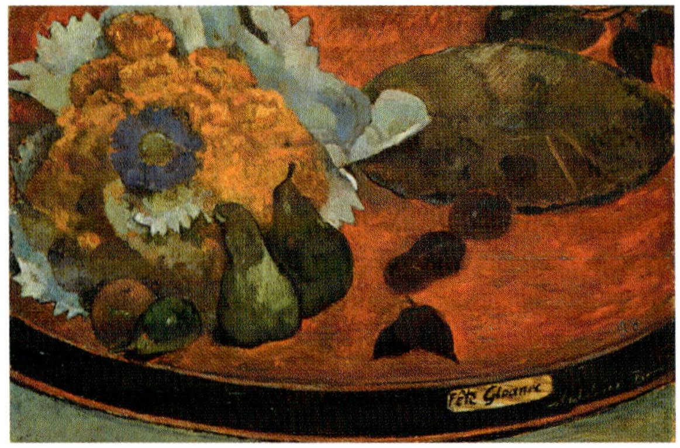

Paul Gauguin
Still Life 'Fête Gloanec', 1888
Oil on panel. 38 x 53 cm
Orleans, Musée des Beaux-Arts

possessed qualities associated with 'primitive' expressiveness (often linked in turn to the native societies that Europeans were colonising). Second, it would designate the 'primitive' status of the initiator of any radically original form of art (from anonymous Egyptian sculptors, to Gothic stonemasons, to Giotto, to Cézanne himself).[15] In Gauguin's view, Cézanne was at least doubly primitive. He was the 'primitive' of something more than a new technique or type of form; he had invented a new kind of artistic expressiveness. Or perhaps he had redeemed an old, exhausted naturalistic art, returning it to a fecund state of savagery, recovering its wildness. A stubborn Cézanne never seemed to grasp what he had done. Only Gauguin understood the potential significance of the achievement. Unlike Cézanne, he had no doubt about the expressive validity of the method they were sharing.

By the late 1880s, Gauguin had purchased several Cézannes for his personal collection and was proclaiming Cézanne's genius to anyone who would listen.[16] His impromptu lessons emphasised that the technical details of painting, when sufficiently liberated from illustrational requirements, would convey emotional and psychological force independent of formulaic narrative and thematic content (which he called 'literature', or superficial anecdote).[17] According to Gauguin, the motivation for primitive art was spiritual, speculative, and above all emotional. Primitive art had its origin in the mind and its expression proceeded directly through colour and form as much as through the freely imagined subjects that transformed an artist's mundane experience of nature. All this was to be clearly distinguished from the empirical and utilitarian concerns that guided the realism of conventional painting and sculpture.

15. *Primitif* also had a third sense; it could designate a technical practice that was naïve or imperfected (or one that resembled naïve practice in others). With this connotation, Cézanne, possibly ironically, told visitors to his studio in 1905, 'Je suis un primitif'; see Rivière, R. P. and Schnerb, J. F.: 'L'atelier de Cézanne', in *La grande revue* 46, 25 December 1907, p. 813.
16. See Bodelsen, Merete: 'Gauguin, the Collector', in *Burlington Magazine* 112, September 1970, pp. 605–6; Merlhès: *op. cit.*, pp. 386–87; Denis, Maurice: 'L'aventure posthume de Cézanne', in *Prométhée* 6, July 1939, p. 195.
17. See letter from Gauguin to Emile Schuffenecker, 14 January 1885, in Merlhès: *op. cit.*, pp. 87–89; Gauguin, Paul: 'Armand Seguin', in *Mercure de France* 13, February 1895, p. 223.

Sérusier was among those who received Gauguin's direct instruction, especially in October 1888 when he painted a small landscape in the Bois d'Amour at Pont-Aven in the older artist's presence [cat. 84]. Each of its coloured strokes was distinct, with the hues correspondingly exaggerated and therefore emotionally resonant. Sérusier's painting (which remained unfinished) came to be known as the *Talisman*, because he used it to convey the understanding – beyond any ordinary words and beyond 'literature' – that Gauguin, his 'liberator', had conveyed to him.[18] Sérusier would later say of Cézanne: '[He] cannot be described with words. He is too pure a painter.'[19] Gauguin had probably said something very similar.

Despite the acknowledged chain of leadership (from Pissarro the Impressionist, to Cézanne the anti-Impressionist, to Gauguin the Symbolist, and finally to Sérusier, Bernard, Denis, and their associates), Gauguin never received unqualified approval, perhaps because he was truly 'wild' (*sauvage*). This was a description he often applied to himself: 'Puvis [de Chavannes] is Greek [civilized] whereas I am a savage, a wolf in the woods without a collar.' Puvis explains his idea,' Gauguin insisted; and it was an idea that corresponded to a preexisting symbol (in effect, Puvis was an allegorist).

But Gauguin painted his idea, discovering its symbolic form as he proceeded.[20] His identification with the wildness of the proverbial wolf suggested a lack of social constraint or socialisation. More significantly, wildness connotes imaginative freedom: 'let your thoughts run wild', we sometimes say; and uncharted, untamed land is called wilderness or simply 'the wild'. A man in the wild, *un sauvage*, is not out of control, although he may be uncontrollable. In this sense, Gauguin's originality was 'wild' – unbounded and impossible to comprehend. He tested himself in all materials and moved confusingly in many expressive directions (see *Window Box with Breton Scenes* (1886) [cat. 182]; *Black Venus* (1889) [cat. 64]).

Odilon Redon described him as 'full of gifts, capriciously expressed in diverse mediums ... Do not look for perfection in Gauguin [because] the powerful stream of his production prevents him from achieving it.'[21] Cézanne denied himself success because of nagging doubts about how his painting related to nature. Ironically, having set external nature aside in order to free his imaginative forces, Gauguin may have failed because of his own hyperactivity. Meeting continual resistance to his multifaceted creative provocations, he led a hard life. For him, living was difficult – just living.

Gauguin's difficulties are apparent even to those who would never subscribe to a romantic, mythologised account of modern art, which consigns creative artists to suffer the abuse, disdain and neglect of a philistine public. Charles Morice – Gauguin's literary

18. See Boyle-Turner, Caroline: 'Sérusier's *Talisman*', in *Gazette des beaux-arts* 105, May–June 1985, pp. 191–96.
19. Letter from Sérusier to Maurice Denis, 27 November 1907, in Sérusier: *op. cit.*, p. 131.
20. Letter from Gauguin to Charles Morice, July 1901, in Malingue, Maurice (ed.): *Lettres de Gauguin à sa femme et à ses amis*, Paris, Bernard Grasset, 1946, pp. 300–301 (emphasis added). Compare Gauguin, letter to André Fontainas, March 1899, in Malingue: *op. cit.*, 289; Fontainas, André: 'Art moderne', *Mercure de France* 29, January 1899, pp. 235–38, 240–41 (on Gauguin and Puvis). Gauguin was adept at defending himself and attacking others through his writing, not only in the form of letters but also in essays; see Childs, Elizabeth C.: 'Gauguin as Author: Writing the Studio of the Tropics', *Van Gogh Museum Journal*, 2003, pp. 70–87.
21. Odilon Redon, statement in Charles Morice, (ed.), 'Quelques opinions sur Paul Gauguin', in *Mercure de France* 48, November 1903, pp. 428–29.

collaborator, eventual biographer, and something of a mythologizer – dated the artist's 'solitude and misery' to the day he decided to end his career in finance and devote his life to painting.[22] Although unusually resourceful in managing his new art career, Gauguin was nearly always in debt and often felt betrayed by the dealers, collectors and critics he believed were controlling his market. His habitually aggressive behaviour negated the benefits of his charisma and charm. Appraising his qualities in 1903, Denis listed his 'nexhaustible imagination'" but also his 'spitefulness' and 'capacity for alcohol.',[23] Gauguin, in other words, tended to get into fights. He cultivated lasting friendships with fellow artists and writers, but generated just as many cases of enmity.

Luck often turned against Gauguin, even when it seemed to be with him. After a disappointing response to two exhibitions of his work in 1889, he found a source of enthusiastic support in the young critic Albert Aurier, a friend of Sérusier. In the March 1891 issue of *Mercure de France*, Aurier promoted Gauguin as the exemplary Symbolist painter, describing the 'glowing vermilion earth' that animated *The Vision After the Sermon* [cat. 41] and calling its creator 'the initiator of a new art [who] knows how to read the abstract meaning in every object in nature.'[24]

Aurier's second article on Symbolist painters (April 1892) reconfirmed Gauguin's Symbolist identity, characterizing his art as 'Platonism plastically interpreted by a wild man [*un sauvage*] of genius.'[25] Gauguin, so to speak, was a genius in 'the wild.' At that time, he was on his first visit to Tahiti (April 1891 to July 1893), where he was enacting the theoretical links between *primitif*, *sauvage* and *Symboliste*. Calling Gauguin a Platonist made him appear more philosophical and programmatic than he was, but Aurier's position was true to the artist in stressing as the source of his expression imaginative fantasies, dreams and emotionally evocative ideas, as opposed to delimited observations of the external environment.[26] Having received word in distant Tahiti that Aurier was continuing to praise him, Gauguin was inspired to proclaim his Symbolist leadership even more boldly: 'I created this movement in painting and many young [artists] benefit from it ... Nothing in them comes from them; it comes from me.'[27]

In October 1892, however, Aurier died suddenly from typhoid fever; and Gauguin lost his most effective literary ally. Aurier's successor at *Mercure de France* was Camille Mauclair, who would declare that Gauguin's theoretical statements on the topic of pictorial expression were 'as naïve as they are useless'. In this respect, Gauguin's theory was hardly different from his pictures: 'his dogs painted red, his cabbage-green trees, his pink skies.'[28] To Aurier such exaggerated, simplified color conveyed the kind of 'abstract meaning' (*signification abstraite*) he advocated, 'the ever-changing drama of abstractions' – pure ideas, symbols, at once intellectualised and spiritualised.[29] To Mauclair, these claims were nonsense.

22. Morice, Charles: 'Paul Gauguin', in *Mercure de France* 48, October 1903, p. 103.
23. Denis: 'L'influence de Paul Gauguin', in *Théories 1890–1910..., op. cit.*, p. 168.
24. Aurier, G.-Albert: 'Le Symbolisme en peinture: Paul Gauguin', in *Mercure de France* 3, March 1891, pp. 155, 159, 163. See also Émile Bernard's letter to Aurier, 1890, asking for the earliest possible publication of Aurier's planned article on Gauguin; in Malingue: *op. cit.*, pp. 329–30.
25. Aurier, G.-Albert: 'Les peintres symbolistes', 1892, in *Oeuvres posthumes*, ed. Rémy de Gourmont, Paris, *Mercure de France*, 1893, p. 305.
26. The theoretical gap between Aurier and Gauguin might be stated this way: although both acknowledged the individualizing quirks of an artist's personal style, Aurier thought of the artist as perceiving a Platonic, mystical, universalizing Idea and shaping the pictorial image to express it; whereas Gauguin's 'idea' was his own projection, as personalized as the style used to render it. See Aurier: 'Le Symbolisme en peinture: Paul Gauguin,' *op. cit.*, p. 162; and note 2, above, as well as my references to projection in the text to follow.
27. 'Ce mouvement je l'ai créé en peinture et beaucoup de jeunes gens en profitent ... Et rien en eux ne vient d'eux cela vient de moi', letter from Paul Gauguin to Mette Gauguin, May 1892, in Malingue: *op. cit.*, p. 226.
28. Mauclair, Camille: 'Choses d'art', in *Mercure de France* 14, June 1895, pp. 358–59.
29. Aurier: 'Le Symbolisme en peinture: Paul Gauguin', *op. cit.*, p. 164.

Aurier may have impressed Gauguin, but many others were either puzzled by or actively refuted his analysis. Among them was Pissarro, whom Aurier faulted (along with Impressionism in general) for concentrating on the material aspects of reality. Pissarro, in turn, took offense at the critic's use of the concept of *émotivité*, which, for an artist, is both a sensitivity to emotional stimulation and the capacity to project emotion. Aurier identified Gauguin with *émotivité*, while implying that Pissarro lacked it. With regard to subjectivity or emotional content, Pissarro saw little fundamental difference between the old Impressionism and the new Symbolism; both were, or should be, imaginative in their content, individualistic yet fully rational in their technique.[30] Pissarro presented the matter to his son Lucien, who observed that *émotivité* was just another word for what the Impressionists had always called 'sensation' – an impassioned, personalised, emotional act of perception (ironically, this was what Gauguin supposedly 'stole' from Cézanne).[31] Pissarro inferred from Aurier's 'Le Symbolisme en peinture' that with so much emphasis on intellectual musing and fantasy – bordering on religiosity, which Pissarro abhorred – art would lose its physical involvement with material form. It would become all conception and no execution, no work. Pissarro concluded that if Aurier's position were taken to its inherent 'absurdity', artists would "no longer need to draw or paint."[32]

At one point, the writer Octave Mirbeau, friend of Pissarro and occasional supporter of Gauguin, encountered Aurier on the street: 'I explained to him that [you were] a great idealist', Mirbeau reported to Pissarro in December 1891. Mirbeau was implying that, like Pissarro, he failed to see any clear division between Impressionist and Symbolist ends. To this, as to all that Mirbeau asserted, Aurier placidly concurred, as if unable to articulate a contrary opinion: 'Smiling stupidly, he agrees with everything.' With the same sarcastic exasperation, Mirbeau suggested that 'all this Gauguinesque foolishness' (*gauguineries*) instilled in him the desire to contemplate 'a cabbage leaf'.[33] Cabbage was unpretentious, something familiar to ordinary working men, and a subject Pissarro treated with dignity.

Gauguin was no Pissarro. Although sympathetic to the class that socialists knew as 'the people' – agricultural labourers, fishermen, machine workers, washerwomen – Gauguin never identified with them. He was an artist: a poet, yet not a literary man. Pragmatic and often engaged with social causes, he nevertheless entertained a rather romanticised view of the plight of the modern artist within an unaccepting bourgeois society. Resistance from the likes of Pissarro and Mirbeau – both socialist-anarchists who on occasion supported him – only reinforced Gauguin's beleaguered attitude. He was at odds with the world, often rejected by the very people who should have understood him, the sophisticated, free-thinking painters and writers. He knew that his life would be hard, for creativity was not his society's reigning quality. Like Vincent van Gogh, Gauguin saw

30. For extended analysis of the convergence of the theoretical positions of the Impressionist and Symbolist painters during the 1880s and 1890s, see Shiff, Richard: *Cézanne and the End of Impressionism*, Chicago, University of Chicago Press, 1984, pp. 3–52 (English edition); *Cézanne y el fin del impresionismo*, trans. Daniel Aguirre Oteiza and Mariano Pozas, Madrid, A. Machado Libros, 2002, pp. 29–88, 289–99 (Spanish edition); Hobbs, Richard (ed.): 'To Move the Eyes: Impressionism, Symbolism, and Well-Being, c. 1891', in *Impressions of French Modernity*, Manchester, Manchester University Press, 1998, pp. 190–210; See also Kearns, James: *Symbolist Landscapes*, London, Modern Humanities Research Association, 1989.
31. Letter from Camille Pissarro to Lucien Pissarro, 20 April 1891, in Bailly-Herzberg, Janine (ed.): *Correspondance de Camille Pissarro, III, 1891–1894*, Paris, Editions du Valhermeil, 1988, p. 66; letter from Lucien Pissarro to Camille Pissarro, May 1891, in Thorold, Anne (ed.): *The Letters of Lucien to Camille Pissarro, 1883–1903*, Cambridge, Cambridge University Press, 1993, p. 217. Pissarro annotated his copy of Aurier's March 1891 essay on Gauguin and Symbolism, indicating his reaction; see Thomson, Belinda: 'Camille Pissarro and Symbolism: some thoughts prompted by the recent discovery of an annotated article', *Burlington Magazine* 124, January 1982, pp. 14–23. Aurier had written a complimentary (but pretentious) review of Pissarro in 1890, to which, coincidentally, he appended a note of praise for Gauguin: see Aurier, G. Albert: 'Camille Pissaro [sic]', in *La revue indépendante* 14, March 1890, pp. 503–15. On the matter of Gauguin's 'theft', see note 10, above.
32. Handwritten marginal note on Pissarro's copy of Aurier: 'Le Symbolisme en peinture', *op. cit.*, p. 159.
33. Letters from Octave Mirbeau to Camille Pissarro, 14 and 16 December 1891, in Pierre Michel and Jean-François Nivet (ed.): *Octave Mirbeau, correspondance avec Camille Pissarro*, Tusson, Du Lérot, 1990, pp. 75, 77–78 (original emphasis). Compare Pissarro's reply to Mirbeau, 17 December 1891, in Bailly-Herzberg: *op. cit.*, p. 169.

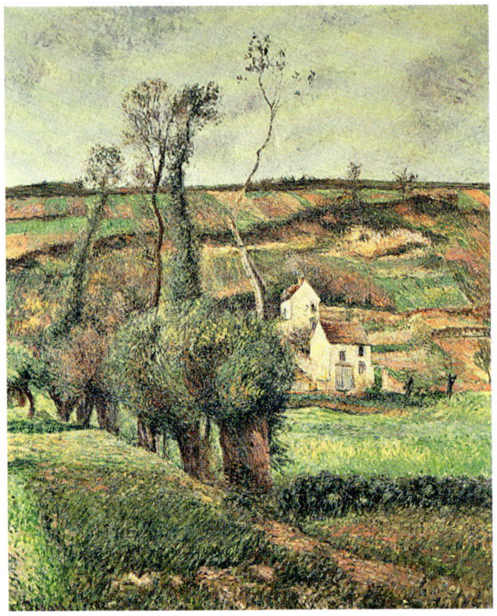

Camille Pissarro
La Cote du Chou, Pontoise, 1882
Oil on canvas. 80 x 65 cm
Private Collection

himself as an outsider, even an outcast, isolated – but isolated by willful choice and temperament, *un isolé* (as Aurier referred to both van Gogh and Gauguin).[34]

Circumstances nevertheless may have turned out even worse than Gauguin expected. During his final years in relative neglect in Oceania – 'overcome by misery and beset by premature aging' (his own description) – he had little hope of gaining general recognition or comprehension. 'With a few words I can explain my painting to you', he told Morice in 1901, acknowledging the writer's refined intelligence, 'but, with regard to the public, why should my brush, otherwise free of all restraint, be obligated to open everyone's eyes?'. Gauguin's art required its viewers to be willing to experience 'emotion first; understanding afterward.'[35] It was indeed hard to go on living, at least for those like him, wild primitives among the pacified urbanites and colonials who believed that they understood everything already, and therefore resisted all new feeling. In 1891 Aurier referred to such a world as 'our imbecilic society of bankers and engineers.'[36] When he made this complaint, it was already a cliché; and in 1901, when Gauguin wrote to Morice from Tahiti, it was still more so.

Gustave Kahn, a literary acquaintance of Gauguin (but not one of his advocates), used 'Difficulty of Living' as the title of an essay for the second issue of *Le Symboliste*, the journal he directed. What caused the presumed 'difficulty'? 'Living is living only when creating or preparing for creation', Kahn proclaimed. 'Everything else is merely to exist like a stone or to vegetate like a plant.' The organisation of modern society, the writer suggested, offered

34. Under the category of 'Les Isolés', Aurier conceived of a series of essays on contemporary painters; see Aurier, G. Albert: 'Les Isolés: Vincent van Gogh', in *Mercure de France* 1, January 1890, pp. 24–29. On the need of artists to isolate themselves, see Aurier: 'Essai sur une nouvelle méthode de critique', 1892, in *Oeuvres posthumes*, *op. cit.*, pp. 186–88. On Gauguin's need specifically, see C. Childs, Elizabeth: 'Seeking the Studio of the South: Van Gogh, Gauguin, and Avant-Garde Identity', in Homburg, Cornelia (ed.): *Vincent van Gogh and the Painters of the Petit Boulevard*, Saint Louis, Saint Louis Art Museum, 2001, p. 146: 'Gauguin, like Van Gogh, was more successful as a loner than a collaborator'.
35. Letter from Paul Gauguin to Charles Morice, July 1901, in Malingue: *op. cit.*, pp. 300–302.
36. Aurier: 'Le Symbolisme en peinture: Paul Gauguin', *op. cit.*, p. 165.

a plan for surviving rather than for living; it produced the passivity and monotony of a stupefied, stone-like existence. Neither the science of the Academy, nor the economics of the State, nor the religion of the Church, but only art would remedy the urban ills brought by bourgeois society. 'The aristocracies are gone', Kahn noted, 'and their descendants have only their arms, the hunt, horsemanship, mere pastimes.' An ascendant bourgeoisie 'imposes its sense of tactful conduct and good taste. Its triumph is stagnation.' With 'financial matters' as the single topic taken seriously, bourgeois conversation became 'a steady flow of anodyne pleasantries'. As for the working class, it was suffering from 'a diet of intoxicants [and] the depression resulting from the monotony and degradation of mechanised labor.'[37] Kahn published this barrage in October 1886, the month in which Gauguin completed his first campaign of painting in Brittany. There he had been seeking his 'primitive' way, stimulated by lingering thoughts of Cézanne and the customs and artifacts of the rude Breton culture, so different from what he experienced in Paris.

To abstract, to isolate

Statements by French artists and critics active during the last quarter of the nineteenth century make frequent use of the words *abstraire* (to abstract), *abstrait* (abstract), and *abstraction* (abstraction), as well as, occasionally, *s'abstraire* (to become mentally abstracted, or to withdraw or isolate oneself). These terms convey the sense of a circumscribed reduction – the isolation, but also intensification and concentration, of a form or a feeling. Writing from Brittany in August 1888, Gauguin advised fellow painter Emile Schuffenecker: 'Art is an abstraction; draw it out from nature in dreaming (*rêvant*) before nature, and think more of [this act of] creation than of what will result.'[38] With his reference to 'dreaming', Gauguin alludes to a kind of wakeful, but abstracted, projection of his thoughts upon the surrounding environment. As he told Morice in 1890: 'Primitive art originates in the mind and puts nature to its use.'[39] Projective dreaming allowed Gauguin to 'see' his world poetically, taking from it – drawing from it, extracting – the core of its suggestiveness. A particular colour might evoke the emotionality (Aurier's *émotivité*) associated with a particular object; but such colour would not derive exclusively from the object, for it would exist as well in the eye and mind of the artist. When Gauguin viewed his model in nature, he projected its image, which was his dream.

As a theorist, Morice wrote about the power of this kind of 'suggestiveness'.[40] He was no doubt inspired by his mentor Stéphane Mallarmé who, despite accusations of obscurity, spoke of the reciprocity of the symbol with remarkable clarity. Here are Mallarmé's words from an interview of 1891: 'To *suggest* (the object), there you have the dream (*rêve*). This is the perfect use of the mystery that constitutes the symbol: gradually to evoke an object in order to show a state of mind, or, inversely, to choose an object and, by a series of decipherments, to abstract (release, separate out) from it (en dégager) a state of mind.'[41]

37. Kahn, Gustave: 'Difficulté de vivre', in *Le Symboliste* 1, 15–22 October 1886, p. 1.

38. 'L'art est une abstraction; tirez-la de la nature en rêvant devant et pensez plus à la création qu'au résultat': Letter from Gauguin to Emile Schuffenecker, 14 August 1888, in Merlhès: *op. cit.*, p. 210. Compare Gauguin: 'Armand Seguin', *op. cit.*, p. 223: 'To paint what you dream is an act of sincerity'. On the significance of 'sincerity', see Shiff: *op. cit.*, (English ed.), p. 33; Shiff: *op. cit.*, (Spanish ed.), p. 66.

39. See note 2, above. Gauguin's position is reflected negatively by a timely statement Mirbeau made to Claude Monet: 'We are completely in agreement: in painting, it is through the eyes that thought should be stimulated' (Letter from Octave Mirbeau to Claude Monet, 10 February 1891, in Michel, Pierre and Nivet, Jean-François (ed.): *Octave Mirbeau, correspondance avec Claude Monet*, Tusson: Du Lérot, 1990, p. 118). At this moment, Mirbeau and Monet had been having a friendly dispute over their somewhat different estimations of Gauguin's talents. But they agreed, in contrast with Gauguin, that the source of painting must be vision, not thought (although neither position was uncomplicated).

40. Morice, Charles: *La littérature de tout à l'heure*, Paris, Perrin, 1889, pp. 377–79; statement of 1891, in Huret, Jules: *Enquête sur l'évolution littéraire*, Paris, Charpentier, 1913, p. 85.

41. Stéphane Mallarmé, statement of 1891, in Huret, *op. cit.*, p. 60 (original emphasis). At Morice's instigation, Mallarmé introduced Gauguin to Mirbeau, who then wrote in support of funding the painter's journey to Tahiti in 1891; see Morice: *Paul Gauguin*, *op. cit.*, pp. 81–82.

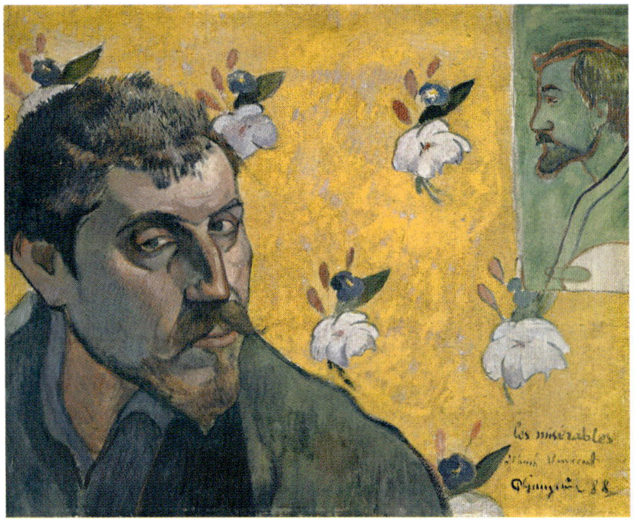

Paul Gauguin
Self-Portrait, Les Misérables, 1888
Oil on canvas. 45 x 55 cm
Amsterdam, Van Gogh Museum
(Vincent van Gogh Foundation)

By this process of projection and extraction, an artistic image became what Gauguin called 'an abstraction'. As a drawing-away or drawing-from, abstraction isolates the points of contact between a subject (the artist) and an object ('nature'). When Aurier referred to 'the symbolism of the abstract elements of design', his word *abstrait* indicated that the expressive factor in visual art could be drawn or separated out, isolated and hence intensified to create a specific emotional and ideational effect.[42] To use a colour without concern for its naturalism (whatever in nature it might resemble) would abstract from the general experience of that colour its specifically expressive, 'symbolic' quality.[43] Gauguin's kind of abstraction – as opposed to the rule-bound, academic abstraction of 'official' art – touched on emotions that lay beyond the intellectual comprehension of ordinary referential language.[44] This is why he told Morice that his viewers needed to experience 'emotion first; [rational] understanding afterward.'[45] In 1888 Gauguin described the self-portrait he was sending to van Gogh in anticipation of their planned painting campaign in Arles: 'Its design is totally special (a complete abstraction).'[46]

Here the descriptive term 'special' indicates that the form is specific to Gauguin's thinking, his dreaming. His design is abstracted from nature, but only as a result of his having projected his abstract thought upon nature. His approach to writing was analogous: 'I wish to write the way I make my paintings, that is, by my fantasy, according to the moon [emotion], and to find the title [understanding] long afterward.'[47]

Commenting on Gauguin's art after his return from Tahiti in 1893, Morice gave a *de facto* description of the process of abstraction, the act of creation of which Gauguin had advised Schuffenecker from Brittany, five years previously: 'With incredible rapidity, a

42. Aurier: 'Les peintres symbolistes', *op. cit.*, p. 302. Compare the words of van Gogh, who in 1888 referred to 'the symbolic meaning that the abstract and mystical design of the Italian Primitives can contain'; letter from Vincent van Gogh to Émile Bernard, beginning of August 1888, in *Correspondance complète de Vincent Van Gogh*, ed. Georges Charensol, 3 vols., Paris, Grasset, 1960, 3, p. 157.
43. Compare Denis's account of 'the definition of Symbolism as we understood it around 1890', which he related to Cézanne's distinction between 'reproducing' an object and 'representing' it. Representation would not depend on any naturalistic resemblance (Denis: 'Cézanne', in *Theories 1880–1910…*, *op. cit.*, p. 253).
44. Denis thought of 'abstract' in the academic sense when he wrote that Cézanne's 'formulations are luminous, concise: never abstract' (Denis: 'Cézanne', in *Theories 1880–1910…*, *op. cit.*, p. 260). For Denis's use of *abstraction* in its various pejorative senses (as mental distraction and intellectual confusion), see Denis: 'La réaction nationaliste' (1905), in *Théories 1890–1910…*, *op. cit.*, pp. 195–96. Compare also Ernest Chesneau, for whom 'abstract' refers to a conventional or standard conception and a philosophical ideal, 'la réalité abstraite de la nature' (Chesneau, Ernest: 'Les peintres impressionnistes', in *Paris-Journal*, 7 March 1882, p. 1).
45. 'Emotion d'abord! compréhension ensuite': letter from Gauguin to Charles Morice, in Malingue: July 1901, p. 301.
46. Letter from Paul Gauguin to Emile Schuffenecker, 8 October 1888, in Merlhès: *op. cit.*, p. 249.
47. Gauguin, Paul: *Avant et après*, Taravao, Editions Avant et Après, 1989, p. 8. Gauguin dated this manuscript 1903.

painter's brain projects its thought upon the view – whether a person's face or a landscape – and to reclaim this thought, to extract it from the spectacle, painters cut away, simplify, synthesise, eliminating everything that would interfere with a plain vision of the object ... Try to recognize in an objective view of nature the landscape where Gauguin saw only his thought!'[48] Morice's commentary corresponds not only with Gauguin's beliefs but with the writer's earlier account of Symbolist literature, for which he used examples from painting: 'If Corot and Cazin "copy" the same landscape, neither will their landscapes resemble each other, nor will one "copied" with the aid of a photographic lens resemble either of the other two – only vaguely. Strictly speaking, no exact description is ever possible. ... Art is essentially subjective. The appearance of things is only a symbol; the artist's mission is to interpret it. Things acquire truth only in him, they have only an internal truth.'[49] We comprehend external reality only as it is abstracted, isolated as an 'internal truth' that the activity of an artist creates. Performing the abstraction ourselves, we become artists.

Early in the evolution of his thinking, but already affected by Gauguin, Sérusier stressed the element of personality (*personnalité*) in his exposition of a Symbolist aesthetic. This factor was usually called 'temperament' by naturalists, but they too sometimes referred to personality.[50] Regardless of which word was used, both naturalists and Symbolists shifted the sense of personality from a limited array of human types to an unlimited set of individuals. Given Morice's account, personality or temperament would explain the difference between landscapes by Corot and Cazin; each necessarily expressed something of his individuality, even when dealing with a general truth.

In October 1889, Sérusier wrote to Denis: 'Personality [in art] is an abstract thing.' With his phrase *une chose abstraite*, he implied that every personality escaped concrete definition. Personality could not be developed in a professional atelier, as if it were an effect to be cultivated by the flourishes of a brush. In fact, the more an artist neglected manual facility, the more evident the element of personality might become, even as maladroitness increased. 'Given a certain amount of lines and colours that form a harmony,' Sérusier reasoned, 'there is an infinity of ways of arranging them.' Personality would determine which configuration out of the many harmonious ones – which specific form abstracted from the general field of aesthetically satisfying forms – would appear as the artist's projection of the scene or theme. Yet the abstracted configuration would be independent of the theme; otherwise, Sérusier warned, art would 'fall into illustration'.[51] Cézanne's apple – 'How beautiful!' – exhibited little facility, no perfection, and was hardly illustrational.[52]

Less than a year after Sérusier formulated his thoughts, Denis published his own Gauguinesque definition of painting, which has often been regarded as a theory – fif-

48. Morice: 'Paul Gauguin', *op. cit.*, p. 294.
49. Morice: *La littérature de tout à l'heure*, *op. cit.*, pp. 165–66 (original emphasis).
50. See Shiff: *op. cit.*, (English ed.), pp. 27–38, 88–89; Shiff: *op. cit.*, (Spanish ed.), pp. 59–72, 130–31.
51. Letter from Paul Sérusier to Maurice Denis, undated (October 1889), in Sérusier: *op. cit.*, pp. 44–45.
52. See note 7, above.

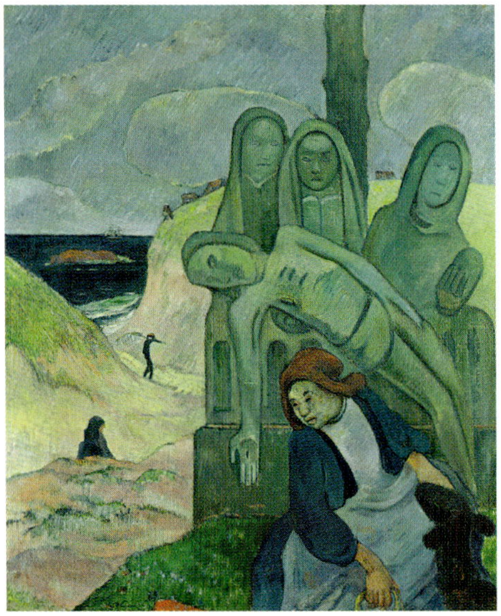

Paul Gauguin
The Green Christ, 1889
Oil on canvas. 92 x 73 cm
Brussels, Musées royaux des Beaux-Arts de Belgique

teen years before the fact – of twentieth-century formalist and abstract art (see Denis, *Patches of Sun on the Terrace* (1890) [cat. 85]). With his simple qualifier 'certain' *(certain)*, Denis incorporated Sérusier's notion of infinitely varied personality: 'Recall that a painting – before being a battle horse, a nude woman, or some anecdote – is essentially a planar surface covered with colors arranged in a certain order.'[53] Denis never specified how the 'certain order' should appear because every artistic personality projects its dream differently. An artist's colours (the abstracted material factor) express the artist's thought and vision (the abstracted psychological factor). The result might prove to be either universalising or isolating. In his essay of 1890, Denis cited Gauguin's Calvaire as a work for which the meaning did not come 'through the motifs represented from nature, but through the representation itself, its forms and colouration.'[54] This is what many critics were calling *Symbolisme*; on this occasion, Denis named it *Néo-traditionnisme*.

At the beginning of the twentieth century, Denis (like Kahn and Gauguin before him) observed that his society was being dehumanised by the leveling effects of modern urban life – mechanisation, standardization and social regulation – all leading to impoverishment of both intellectual and spiritual experience. Because life was hard, sensitive souls turned to art: 'We live in the museums, the theatres, the concert halls, amidst the sensations of art: there we gradually lose the sense of [real] life; our sensibility increasingly requires purely aesthetic feelings.' Denis argued that, for better or worse, the artistic remedy seemed to lie in an 'abstract ideal, the expression of inner

53. Denis: 'Définition du Néo-traditionnisme' (1890), in *Théories 1890–1910…*, *op. cit.*, p. 1. For this wording, see also Denis: 'Préface de la IXe Exposition des peintres impressionnistes et symbolistes' (1895), 'A propos de l'Exposition de Charles Guérin' (1905), in *Théories 1890–1910…*, *op. cit.*, pp. 26, 143. Like Cézanne, Denis came to question and even disapprove of the trend he appeared to inaugurate. When he remarked in 1905 that 'the representational arts are evolving toward abstraction', he was already becoming dubious of the cultural benefit (Maurice Denis, statement of 1905, in Dagen: *op. cit.*, p. 60).
54. Denis: 'Définition du Néo-traditionnisme', *Théories 1890–1910…*, *op. cit.*, p. 10.

[mental] life or a simple decoration for the pleasure of the eyes.'[55] This 'ideal' would assume many material forms, the many different instances of 'a certain order.' Cézanne was exemplary because his marks appeared independent of mimetic function and were also aggressively physical, as Gauguin had emphasised in his appropriation of his elder's primitive way. Cézanne created an emotionally engaged, material abstraction of the painting process. His materialism was aestheticised and humanised, intense in both sensation and spirit; and its energy countered the vegetative character of bourgeois life, its stone-like existence.

Once manifested as a technique and articulated as a critical principle, material abstraction of Cézanne's kind had no clear limit, whether physical or conceptual. With the advent of Henri Matisse's Fauvism and the emerging primitivistic Cubism of Pablo Picasso – styles perceived to derive from both Cézanne and Gauguin – Denis decided that 'abstraction' had shifted from a liberated aesthetic expression to an intellectual aberration. Much of the new art, especially Matisse's, had become so completely a product of mental conception that it seemed to eliminate any accompanying emotion: 'painting apart from any contingency, painting in itself, the pure act of painting, [lacking] our instinct for nature.'[56] 'Abstraction' and 'form' had been pushed so far that neither sensible reason nor human feeling, but only misguided theories, could justify the new practices. Denis excluded Cézanne from these accusations, explaining that he had never 'compromised' his pictorial synthesis 'with any [conceptualised] abstraction'; despite its abstraction of the means, Cézanne's art redeemed itself by remaining rooted in nature.[57] (Recall Pissarro's complaint about Aurier, that he would induce painting to lose all physicality.) Of the two master figures, Cézanne and Gauguin, it was the latter who had carried abstraction to the breaking point: 'He rendered Cézanne's models flat... The reconstruction of art that Cézanne had begun with the materials of impressionism, Gauguin continued with less feeling but more theoretical rigor.'[58] Under Gauguin's leadership, the art properly called 'abstract' had been reduced to a product of theory; it was no longer emotional projection, no longer a liberating dream. Gauguin's old collaborator Morice was sensitive to this realignment of authority, which critics cited while pitting one modernist hero against the other. Morice urged his colleagues to avoid such partisan division: 'Gauguin and Cézanne were two of the greatest artists. The first accomplished something; the second [Cézanne] indicated it.'[59] Against the obstacles that bourgeois society set in the way, Cézanne and Gauguin equally furthered the cause of living.

But they were not always such equals, even for Morice who admired them both. If Denis favoured Cézanne over Gauguin, it could be argued that Morice favored Gauguin over Cézanne. He expressed a certain ambivalence toward Cézanne's cultural and

55. Denis: 'A propos de l'exposition de Charles Guérin', in *Théories 1890–1910..., op. cit.*, pp. 143–44.
56. Denis: 'De Gauguin, de Whistler et de l'excès des théories' (1905), in *Théories 1890–1910..., op. cit.*, p. 208.
57. Denis: 'Cézanne', in *Théories 1890–1910..., op. cit.*, p. 260.
58. Denis: 'De Gauguin et de Van Gogh au classicisme', *Théories 1890–1910..., op. cit.*, pp. 270–71.
59. Charles Morice 'Art moderne: la grande querelle', *Mercure de France* 70, 1 December 1907, p. 547.

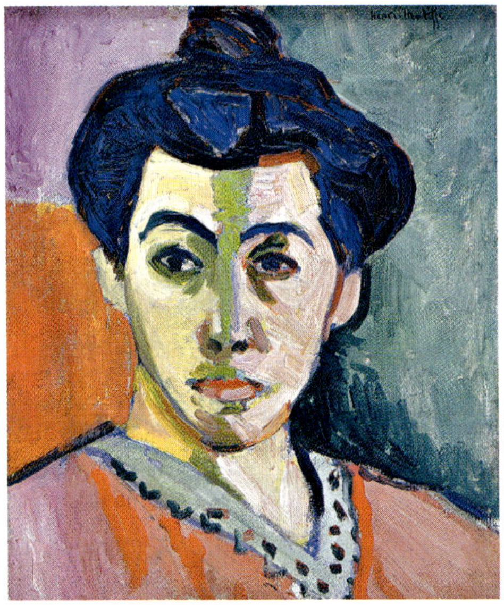

Henri Matisse
Portrait of Madame Matisse: the Green Line, 1905
Oil on canvas. 40.5 x 32.5 cm
Copenhagen, Statens Museum for Kunst
(J. Rump Collection)

psychological difficulties, not unrelated to the type of reservation Denis felt when he regarded Matisse. Several months after Cézanne's death, Morice wrote: 'We hardly dare say that Cézanne lived; he [only] painted. ... His is an art of separation ... painting estranged from the course of life, painting with the [sole] aim of painting ... This separation [amounts to] a tacit protest.'[60] Like Denis, like Kahn, like Gauguin, Morice believed that scientism, materialism and technocratic efficiency were deadening all spiritual life. The situation tempted artists to abandon the decaying remains of humanistic principle and withdraw into pure sensory experience. Cézanne purged his life – a life that amounted to painting, because he had no other life – of all social and 'moral values', for which he substituted 'colour values'.[61]

In lieu of intellectual and ethical abstractions, the painter produced colour abstractions. Cézanne did not lack political, religious or philosophical beliefs, but he appeared resigned to the fact that theoretical and ideological concerns could no longer guide his or any other artistic practice. The technique of painting – isolated from its representational content, abstracted, and linked only to the sensing hand of the artist – became the means of a 'tacit protest'. To the sensitive critic, it signalled the corruption of the intellectual and moral bases of modern society. Acknowledging Cézanne's impenetrable mystery, Morice added parenthetically: 'Was [his protest] fully conscious? I don't know.'[62]

In the case of Gauguin, however, we do know: he understood what he was doing. Morice noted Gauguin's ability to reproduce an alien style with precision, controlling

60. Morice, Charles: 'Paul Cézanne', in *Mercure de France* 65, 15 February 1907, pp. 577, 593 (original emphasis).
61. Morice, Charles: 'Le XXIe Salon des Indépendants', in *Mercure de France* 54, 15 April 1905, p. 552.
62. Morice: 'Paul Cézanne', *op. cit.*, p. 593.

the influence of his own personality; referring to a related capacity to manipulate, Pissarro called Gauguin a 'schemer'.[63] With his refined intelligence and precise but intentionally unrefined language, Gauguin could articulate a 'Symbolist' position as clearly as Morice, Aurier, Sérusier or Denis. He had actively determined to be 'primitive', projecting his thoughts and emotions into painting without concern for conventional decorum. Neither his hard life (self-imposed?) nor his psychological self-isolation prevented him from recognising Cézanne's radical inventiveness. He abstracted from Cézanne's way its most meaningful and productive elements. Gauguin's Cézanne retained the primitive, isolating mystery yet was sufficiently inviting to encourage everyone else to follow. By following Cézanne, they followed Gauguin. In this Morice was correct: Cézanne indicated; Gauguin realised.

63. Morice, Charles: 'Salons et Salonnets', in *Mercure de France* 10, January 1894, p. 68; Pissarro, letter to Lucien Pissarro, 20 April 1891, in Bailly-Herzberg: *op. cit.*, p. 66.

The Path of the Avant-Garde

GUY COGEVAL

According to tradition, the golden legend of the Nabis was born in the fall of 1888. It was then that Paul Sérusier returned from Pont-Aven and presented his friends with his magical *Bois d'amour*, painted on the cover of a cigar box. This small landscape, with its boldly pure colours, placed side by side with little regard for transition, completely shattered traditional modes of representation, including those of Impressionism. Gauguin's famous advice to the young painter hardly needs repeating.[1] But in this little sketch alone, which it is now widely agreed anticipated by some fifteen years the Fauvist landscapes of Derain and Vlaminck – proof that not all platitudes are false – can be measured the scale of the revolution that was occurring between Pont-Aven and Paris. Among young artists of the time, Gauguin's name seems to have symbolised a new era. Generationally speaking, Gauguin could have been the Nabis' father, and his influence over them was rooted in the weight of his superior experience. His verbal persuasiveness also had a powerful effect, as did his sense of comedy and even his braggadocian certitudes.

Bois d'amour was immediately labelled *The Talisman* by the Nabis, a name that emphasised its putative magical powers. Maurice Denis, passionate chronicler of Nabis activities, described the work's impact in these immortal words: 'And so we realised that every work of art was a transposition, a caricature, the impassioned equivalent of a sensation experienced.'[2] For many months, the language of rapture and ecstasy infused the discourse of these young artists, the self-proclaimed 'Nabis' (*nebiim*, a Hebrew word meaning 'prophets' or 'visionaries'). With the exception of the somewhat older Paul Ranson, most of the group had known each other since their days at the Lycée Condorcet, between 1885 and 1888. Most, too, were from middle-class families – Maurice Denis and Édouard Vuillard alone were from rather humbler backgrounds – and, in contradiction of the enduring image of the misunderstood artist, were positively disposed towards the artistic careers of their offspring.

Members of the bourgeoisie who ridiculed their own social class, part of the artistic vanguard who yet displayed a certain cultural conformism (although was it conformist, in 1890, to appreciate Wagner, Puvis de Chavannes, Schuré and Debussy?), these artists constitute from the late 1880s to around the turn of the century the most cohesive group of the post-Impressionist avant-garde. Stylistic similarities united the Neo-Impressionists, successors to Seurat, while a sort of regional fraternity bound the Pont-Aven group. Only the Nabis, however, embarked on a genuinely collective artistic project that encompassed painting and the decorative arts, sculpture and literature, theatrical design and illustration.

1. 'How do you see this tree?', Gauguin had asked, regarding a corner of the Bois d'amour. 'Is it really green? Then put green, the most beautiful green from your palette. And this shadow, rather blue? Don't be afraid to paint it as blue as possible.' Reported by Denis, Maurice: *Théories*, Paris, 1920, p. 167.
2. Denis, ibid.

Like all avant-garde groups composed of very young artists (the Jeunes-France group of the Romantic era and the later English Pre-Raphaelites are both examples), the Nabis had a tendency to operate like a secret society and to indulge in elaborate initiatory rituals, a tendency reinforced by the esoteric inclinations of Ranson and Sérusier, the two spiritual guides of the early years. The studio at 25 Boulevard du Montparnasse, where, summoned by Ranson, they met regularly from 1889, became their 'Temple'. Their letters were often oddly dated – 'Day of Venus, one hour before the setting of Helios, completed on the Lord's day', for instance – and accompanied by the message 'In your palm, my word and my thought'. Its rather juvenile trappings situated Nabi culture somewhere between the *bal des quat'zarts*[3] and the most cerebral form of the Symbolism whose shadow then lay across Europe. The miracle, in fact, is that *despite* the burden of the group's ritualism, its members became, with only a few exceptions, such great artists. One thing is clear: the positivist, scientistic atmosphere that still reigned during their formative years was hardly likely to temper the group's propensity for provocation.

France of the late 1880s was still under the imperturbable sway of Salon art – a skilful blend of Academicism and Realism that bore the weight of official commissions. The gradual critical acceptance of Impressionism was a slow process, and the Nabis – still frequenters of the studios of Bouguereau and Cormon, those paragons of *pompier* art – knew very little about it. Generally speaking, art critics were extremely hostile to new trends. Many years after having acted as the enlightened defender of Manet, Monet and Renoir, Émile Zola responded to the irruption of new painting at the Salon of 1896 with the following words: 'At the Salon, there is no longer anything but t*aches*, a portrait is just a *tache*, figures are just *taches*, trees, houses, continents and seas are nothing but *taches*...And they are really disconcerting works, these multicoloured women, these purple landscapes and orange horses, which are presented to us with the scientific explanation that they are the way they are because of such and such a reflection or such and such a decomposition of the solar spectrum. Oh, the ladies who have one cheek blue in the moonlight and the other vermilion under the shaded light of a lamp! Oh, the landscapes where the trees are blue, the water red and the sky green! It's awful, awful, awful!'[4] Gauguin had already anticipated and responded to such puritanical indignation by affirming that his yellow Christs, pink skies and red dogs were 'necessary' and therefore 'absolutely intentional'. Taking full advantage of the new freedom, Verkade silhouetted green trees against the blossoms of his *Lilacs* [cat. 87]. Provocation – both visceral and cerebral – was rife. Naturally enough, the advocates of a realistic, 'slice of life' artistic approach were unable to connect with a younger generation that revelled in an iconography of dreams, imbued with an overt sensuality and expressed in a synthetic technique that was drifting swiftly towards abstraction.

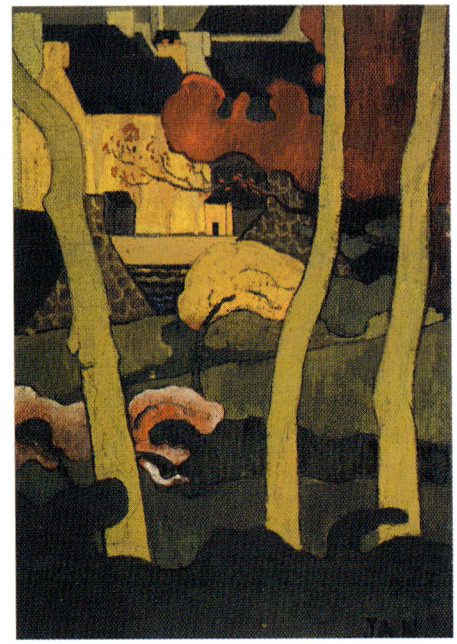

Jan Verkade
Decorative Landscape, 1891–1892
Oil on canvas on panel. 74 x 51 cm
Private Collection

3. A famous and scandalous dance which was part of the *Moulin Rouge* show, in which nakes dancers performed (N. d. T.).
4. Zola, Émile: in *Le Figaro*, 2 May, 1896. Quoted in Zola, Émile: *Le Bon Combat*, Paris, 1974, pp. 261–62.

With his plea for a 'surface covered with colours assembled in a certain order' and his early, resolutely pre-Fauvist works, Maurice Denis emerges as the frontrunner of this *tachiste* avant-garde. *Easter Morning*, *The Orchard*, the pre-Jawlenskian *At the Train Window* – these experimental works, spare and violent, offer clear proof of Denis's leading role. Close behind him was Vuillard, whose youthful journal betrays a similar quest for a scientific method of organising colours and creating tonal transitions: 'A form, a colour only exists in relation to another. Form alone does not exist. We conceive only of relations.'[5]

The pursuit of a synthetic art capable of evolving gradually towards abstraction nonetheless did not preclude an idealistic worldview. An assembler of colours, Maurice Denis was also an 'assembler of dreams' in the style of Gustave Moreau, that reluctant leader of the Symbolists for whom art was an attempt to 'render virtually visible the inner flashes that come from we know not where, that are almost divine in their apparent insignificance'.[6] This duality of (in fact complementary) goals had already found definitive and perfect visual expression in Paul Gauguin's *The Vision after the Sermon* (1888) [cat. 41], presented at the Café Volpini during the Paris Universal Exposition of 1889. An expression of primitive Breton Christianity, a vehicle for simple beliefs transformed into a shared inner vision, this painting had a profound and permanent effect on all the Nabis – witness *The Pardon at Perros* by Denis and *Apple Harvest* by Sérusier [cat. 106]. It derived its impact from a distortion of perspective and a compartmentalised separation of the figures that made it, at the turn of the century, a key point of entry to modern art.

In spite of the differences between the most esoteric of the Nabis (Ranson and Sérusier) and the most secular (Bonnard and Vallotton), the group as a whole seems to have shared an adherence to the basic principles of Symbolism, including the belief that all human beings are surrounded by a kind of magnetic field, an invisible aura that is the intangible expression of their deepest passions and feelings. Most of the Nabis held to the Symbolist idea that 'natural objects are signs of ideas, that the visible is the manifestation of the invisible; that sounds, colours and words have a miraculously expressive value quite apart from representation. Quite apart even from the literal meaning of words.'[7] They displayed in varying degrees the same sense of the forest's mystery, and a similar taste for medieval and ancient legend;
but their main contribution to painting was the notion of the abstract and rhythmic organisation of figures and ground on the pictorial surface. In fact, it was in their Symbolist guise that the group attached the most violent criticism: 'Who is showing us a new conception of life? – After Mr. Gauguin, a precursor (!), people are talking of Mr. Sérusier, Mr. Vuillard, Mr. Émile Bernard, Mr. Verkade, and Symbolism triumphs.

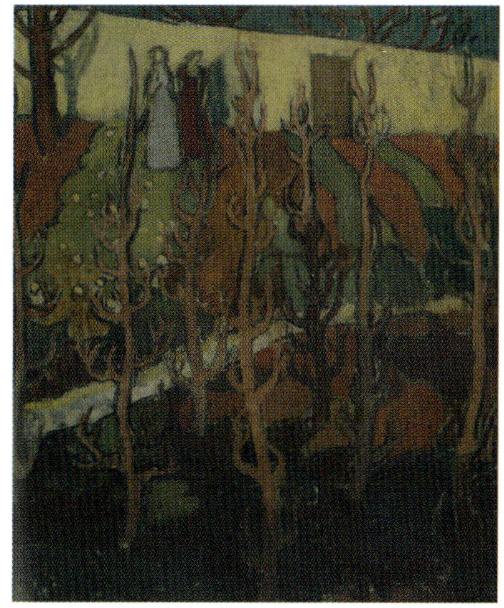

Maurice Denis
The Orchard, c. 1892
Oil on panel. 57 x 47 cm
Neuss, Clemens-Sels Museum

5. Vuillard, Édouard: *Journal*, 20 November, 1888.
6. Moreau, Gustave: *L'Assembleur de rêves*, Fontfroide, 1984, p. 29.
7. Denis, Maurice: 'Étude sur la vie et l'œuvre de Paul Sérusier', in *ABC de la peinture*, Paris, 1942, p. 64.

What a joke! The much-vaunted mysticism is nothing but a sham, the last resort of faithless times.'[8]

Deaf to such derision, the Nabis persisted in conceiving of the painting as an enigma. Their view is manifest in Maurice Denis's *Sunlight on the Terrace* (1890), Ker-Xavier Roussel's *Fisherman* [cat. 86] and Vuillard's *The Lady of Fashion* [cat. 121] and *Au Divan japonais* – all works whose meaning, never entirely defined, emerges painfully from doubt, that 'doubt, accumulation of nights past'[9] which Mallarmé had so recently raised. Other contemporary branches of the avant-garde were deeply impressed by the complex virtuosity of these experiments. As Paul Signac wrote of Vuillard in his dairy, 'His figures are shapeless – he can draw admirably, and if he makes neither mouths, nor hands, nor feet, it is because he doesn't want to.'[10] The gradual decoding of the signs arranged on the surfaces of these small compositions reveal them to be not simply sketches or unfinished exercises, but rather talismans, secret treasures full of meaning that glow with their own light, the light of the 'inner need' that Kandinsky would refer to a couple of decades later. It is certainly an inner life awaiting revelation that is evoked by Nabi portraits; in Bonnard's *Berthe Schoedlin*, for example, a border of flowers transforms the subject's appearance in the window of the painting into a veritable *advent*. A mysterious and explosive inner life is also suggested by Vuillard's *Octagonal Self-portrait* [cat. 82], which not only 'foreshadows Fauvism' but, with its outrageous collaging of pink, yellow and peacock blue, shocks the eye in very much the same way as an *Orange Marilyn* by Warhol.

Symbolist culture was also marked by a powerful return to the values of Christianity, coupled with a highly instinctive use of colour. Adopting a Denisian tone, Vuillard wrote in his journal, 'the purer the elements, the purer the work...; the more mystical painters are, the more brilliant the colours (reds, blues, yellows), the more materialist painters are, the more they use dark colours (earths, ochres, bituminous blacks).'[11] As early as 1850, Dante Gabriel Rossetti's *Ecce ancilla domini* had served as a manifesto for the Pre-Raphaelites' move back towards Fra Angelico, towards, in fact, the simplicity of means employed in the painting of the Quattrocento. The Italian Divisionists, closer to the Nabis, exploited a certain Catholic pathos in their painting, as Segantini's *Il dolore confortato dalla fede* (1895) clearly illustrates. In contrast to his friends Ranson and Roussel, avowed free-thinkers, Maurice Denis was eager to express his catholic convictions. At the age of only fourteen, he wrote in his journal, 'I went to the Salon yesterday and came away with a troubled mind. There will never be a place there for me! Yes, I have to be a Christian painter, I have to celebrate all the miracles of Christianity, I feel that I must.[12] The emotional power of Denis's painting is also rooted in the conciseness of his Symbolist language, a subtle blend of neo-medieval Synthetism and sophisticated Japanism: the unrealistic flowering trees in *Easter Morning* thus play the same role as

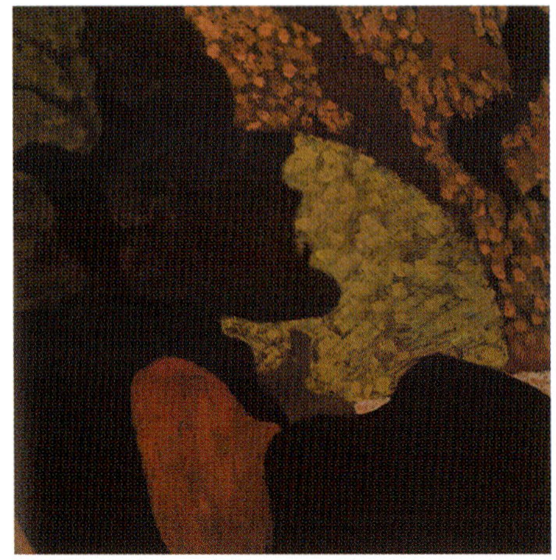

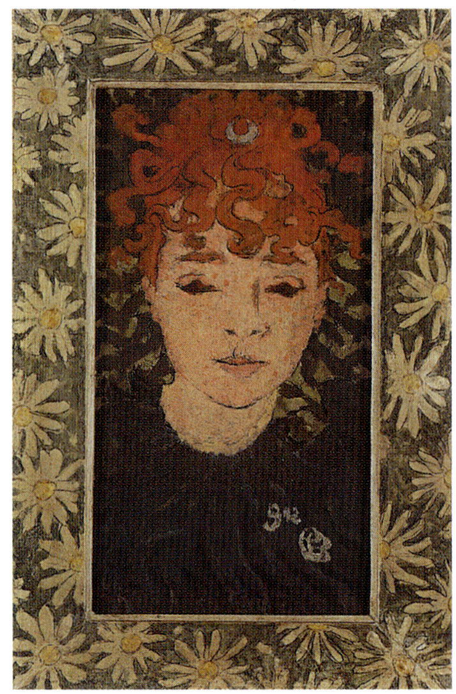

Édouard Vuillard
At the Divan Japonais, 1890–1891
Oil on panel. 21 x 20 cm
Private Collection

Pierre Bonnard
Portrait of a Young Girl (Berthe Schaedlin), 1892
Oil and ink on canvas. 29.5 x 16 cm
D. W. Collection

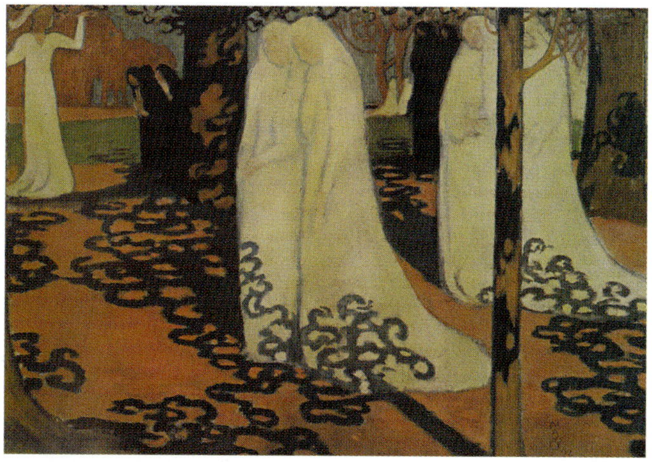

Maurice Denis
The Procession Under the Trees, 1892
Oil on canvas. 56 x 81.2 cm
M. and Mme Arthur G. Altschul Collection

the hypnotic interlacing of *The Procession under the Trees*, where – to quote Thadée Natanson's perfect description – 'on the purity of the dresses and the heat of the sand, the shadow of the foliage embroiders the pretty torment of its blue design'.[13]

Generally speaking, the Nabis belonged to a generation that believed in the eschatological power of images. Even when illustrating Symbolism's darker themes (as embodied in Maeterlinck's *Les Aveugles* and *L'Intruse*, for instance, for which they created the sets at the Théâtre d'Art in 1891), they always retained a sense of optimism. On the other hand, Nabi Symbolism sometimes strayed well into the realm of the absurd, as witness the adventure of Alfred Jarry's *Ubu Roi*, in which they were all involved. But they never lapsed into what German and Austrian artists of the period labelled *Kulturpessimismus*. Their vision of the world always evaded the inevitable catastrophe, and their art, sensitive and intellectual, was invariably imbued with a sort of benevolence towards reality, a total confidence in life. It was no doubt this latter quality that, at the dawn of the twentieth century, lent their creative approach its unifying logic.

8. Merki, Charles: 'Apologie pour la peinture', in *Mercure de France*, no. 42, June 1893, p. 153.
9. Mallarmé, Stéphane: *L'après-midi d'un faune*.
10. Signac, Paul: 'Extraits du Journal Inédit de Paul Signac: II, 1897–1898', 16 February 1898, in *Gazette des Beaux-Arts*, April 1952, p. 302.
11. Vuillard, Édouard: *Diario*, 31 August, 1890.
12. Denis, Maurice: *Journal*, vol. 1, May 22, 1885, Paris, 1957, p. 59.
13. Natanson, Thadée: 'IX° exposition de la Société des Artistes Indépendants', in *La Revue Blanche*, Paris, 1st quarter 1893 (reprint edition, Geneva, 1972–1973, vol. 4, p. 274).

On Gauguin and Synthetism in Spanish art

MARÍA DOLORES JIMÉNEZ-BLANCO

Every time the arrival of international artistic novelties in Spanish art is studied, it is usually said that this happens late and, particularly, in a confused way. Generally, this is also the case of Synthetism. Every attempt at analysing its influence on Spanish art finds an initial obstacle in the difficulty to demarcate and define what is understood by Synthetism applied to the context of Spanish art. If by Synthetism we understand exclusively the pictorial approach which came out of the conversations and exchanges between Gauguin and other younger painters, fundamentally Émile Bernard, during the summer of 1888 in Pont-Aven, its influence in Spain will be strongly reduced, apart from the fact that the map drawn will not correspond to the peculiarity of Spanish art of that time. On the contrary, the only reasonable possibility is to start from the certain fact that the echo of Synthetism in Spain can rarely be separated from a wider view of Post-impressionism. In this sense, what stands out clearly is a more widespread influence of the figure of Gauguin – whose mythical character grew enormously in a few years – linked to that of the Nabi aesthetics, and also sometimes to the impact of Van Gogh.

In addition, the effects of Synthetism – with the previously mentioned adherences – on Spanish art spread to the 1910s and 1920s, when other movements had already shaken the Parisian avant-gardes, and when the so-called 'return to order' also demanded a new debate on the relationship between art and history. Thus, certain aspects of Fauvism and others related to Cubism, the two important avant-gardes previous to World War I, overlapped in certain artists, and even in certain works, with Synthetism as a liberating influence which triggered new artistic possibilities. In other cases, Synthetism was linked to the problem of the articulation between Primitivism and Classicism as forms of modernity. This review of the effects of Synthetism on Spanish art, necessarily limited and schematic, can only reflect this situation.

Overlapping legacies

In 1919, sixteen years after Gauguin's death, a set of nineteen of his oils present in the *Exposición Internacional de Pintura y Escultura* in Bilbao constituted his most substantial contribution to an international exhibition, which confirmed this artist as a fundamental reference for the renovation of Spanish art of that period. It was an eclectic exhibition, in which the most recent avant-gardes were absent, but which could still appear as refreshingly innovative in an artistic scene like the Spanish one, where the late arrival of Post-impressionism in its different forms still overlapped with both Fauvism and Cubism, as well as with the so-called 'return to order'.

That substantial show of Gauguin's works was the official culmination of a process which had started in the 1890s, when a few Spanish artists installed in Paris had begun to discover in the myth of Gauguin a key to modernity, at the same time as it was

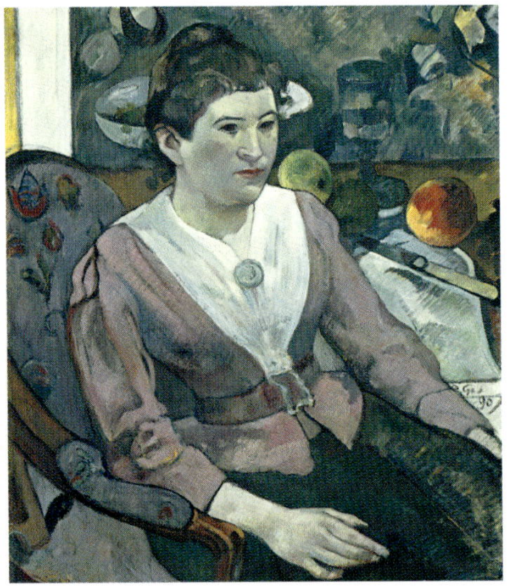

Paul Gauguin
Woman Seated in Front of a Still Life by Cezanne, 1890
Oil on canvas. 65.3 x 54.9 cm
Chicago, The Art Institute of Chicago.
(Joseph Winterbothan Collection, 1925.753)

being discovered in the French capital itself. But in the 1919 Bilbao exhibition works by Émile Bernard, Sérusier, Bonnard, Vuillard and Valloton also stood out, which was highly significant, as it shows that although Gauguin was the undisputed prophet of the new art, for the young painters and critics his legacy was inseparable both from the synthetic aesthetics and from its Nabi progeny. Together, these formed, in their eyes, what was somewhat improperly known as the 'aesthetics of Pont-Aven'.

Actually, Gauguin himself, with his unhidden desire to become the martyr of modern art, had foretold that something like this would happen. In many occasions he had declared in his letters his certainty regarding the future appreciation of his work on the part of generations of painters to come, but also his fear regarding the doubts that would arise in attributing to him the rightful merits. The year before his death he expressed this to his friend Monfreid:

> 'You have known for some time that I have wished to establish the right to venture on anything; my abilities (bearing in mind that my financial difficulties have been excessive for this purpose) have not produced an important result; however, the machine has got started. The public owe me nothing, as my artistic production is only relatively good, but the painters who today enjoy that freedom do owe me something.'
>
> It is true that many imagine that all this happened by itself. At the same time, I do not ask them for anything, and my conscience is enough to reward me.'[1]

1. Letter to Monfreid, Marquesas Islands, October 1902, in Paul Gauguin: *Oviri: Ecrits d'un sauvage*. Translated from the Spanish version, (*Escritos de un salvaje*, Madrid, Itsmo, 2000) (prol. by Miguel Morán, ed. and notes by Miguel Morán Turina; trans. by Marta Sánchez–Eguibar), pp. 220–21.

What is certain is that Synthetism very soon became a key influence for the artists eager for innovations in late nineteenth-century Paris, and his wake can be followed throughout the artistic production of various decades. The famous exhibition held in 1889 at the Café Volpini (Café des Arts), in which the title 'synthetist' appeared for the first time, was seen as a revelation by young painters like Sérusier, who shortly afterwards considered Gauguin as his master, and who soon became the link between the Pont-Aven group and the artists who founded the Nabi movement, bringing about their 'conversion'.[2] In opposition to the primitivist and melancholic spiritualism of the former, the work of the latter had a more literary, programmatic aspect, while at the same time it emphasised the decorative aspect of painting by building the work as a flat coloured image. But, in spite of all the differences, both groups shared a vision of painting that advocated the intensification of the expressive means, replacing the image with the symbol, the representation of nature with the idea. The synthetist painters of Pont-Aven and the Nabi therefore shared an artistic concept that was clearly related to Symbolism, and what is important to emphasise here is that their legacies appear to be inextricably intertwined for the future generations.

In opposition to the pseudoscientific and sensorial analysis of Impressionism, Synthetism proposes an abstract image, different from perceivable reality. It is an image that resulted from a series of choices, from a mental and spiritual synthesis, in which pure colour was exalted and form was simplified, mostly by drawing inspiration from Japanese prints, but also from a certain neo-traditionalism which admired medieval art, as expressed in its paintings and sculptures as well as in its enamels and stained-glass windows with marked outlines in black or blue (*cloisonné*). It is a synthetic vision that 'tries not to dissociate the content, treated in a symbolic manner, from the formal expression'.[3]

As has already been said, in its immediately subsequent reception, the new vision also ended up mixing itself with the expressive exuberance of Vincent Van Gogh, whose personal and artistic connections with the Pont-Aven group had been very close. This artistic concept, impassioned and arbitrary but also concerned with purely formal matters, ended up becoming one of the dominating influences among the most progressive circles – which were still a minority – on the European art scene in the last decade of the nineteenth and the first of the twentieth century.

In 1919, the same year of the Bilbao exhibition, Juan de la Encina, one of the most influential art critics in Spain at the time and partly responsible for the style of that exhibition, published a book entitled *La Trama del Arte Vasco* (The Weaving of Basque Art). His aim was to define a differentiated modern school of Basque art, and at the same time

2. Goldwater, Robert: 'From Synthetism to Symbolism', in *Symbolism*. Icon Editions, 1984, pp. 73 and ff.
3. Cariou, André: '1888: secondo soggiorno di Gauguin. L'invenzione del sintetismo', in *Gauguin e la Bretagna*, Geneva-Milan, Skira, 2003, pp. 69 and ff.

analyse its sources. In that text, Juan de la Encina clearly points out the influence of Gauguin and of his synthetist stylisation not only on the pioneering generations of Basque modernity, but also on the more recent ones, placing in the same Gauguinian genealogy artists like Durrio, Echevarría and Arteta. Juan de la Encina summarises Gauguin's art in the following words:

> 'Above all, the rhythm of simplified forms, the restrained and potent harmonies of colour, obtained through oppositions of flat shades. That, in the outside. As to the intimate meaning of the work, the feeling – the beginning and the end of art in the impressionists – can at the most be the means of transmission of thought.'[4]

It is interesting to note that those same words could be applied to some of the Basque artists commented in the book, from Echevarría to Iturrino; but also that later, when Juan de la Encina talked about Arteta, he could not say whether he found in that artist a direct influence of Gauguin, or of something which could be explained as 'an influence diffused in the modern circles',[5] thus pointing to the problem of the confusion or the overlapping of Gauguin's legacy – not only artistic but also emotional – with that of his synthetist and Nabi followers.

Other important critics of the time, as cosmopolitan, informed and conservative as Juan de la Encina, show in their writings the importance of Synthetism in the art scene of the first decades of the twentieth century. This is the case of Joan Sacs (a pseudonym of the painter Feliu Elías, who signed his caricatures as Apa), for example, in the article entitled 'El valor de l'art modern' (The value of modern art). Although he commented on the dissatisfaction he felt with regard to the trends of modern art that followed Impressionism, what we are interested in is that he referred to Synthetism as the most conspicuous of them, identifying it with the synthetic spirit of the time.[6] In fact, that expressionist aesthetics, which links a spiritualist yearning to the tendency to simplify form and experiment with it, can be understood as the visual distillation of a spirit that characterised the whole period; this is particularly true if we consider that its wish to return to the origins, to extol the primitive, is in tune with other research which was being developed also in the scientific and academic fields: the initial stages of culture, like the tribal systems, prehistory and childhood, roused great interest at the time. In the field of art, this concern was translated into primitivism, into the search for primeval systems of representation, an essential characteristic of which is precisely a synthetic spirit. Synthetism, therefore, was seen as something representative of the period, as part of the *zeitgeist*.

A few months later Joan Sacs also published an article which was entitled 'Gauguin i el primitivisme' (Gauguin and Primitivism). In it he relates the best of Gauguin's

4. Encina, Juan de la: *La Trama del Arte Vasco*, 1919. Facsimile edition, Museo de Bellas Artes de Bilbao, 1998, p. 38
5. Ibid., p. 35
6. Sacs, Joan: 'El valor de l'art modern', in *Revista Nova*, n. 3, Barcelona, 25 April 1914, pp. 3–4.

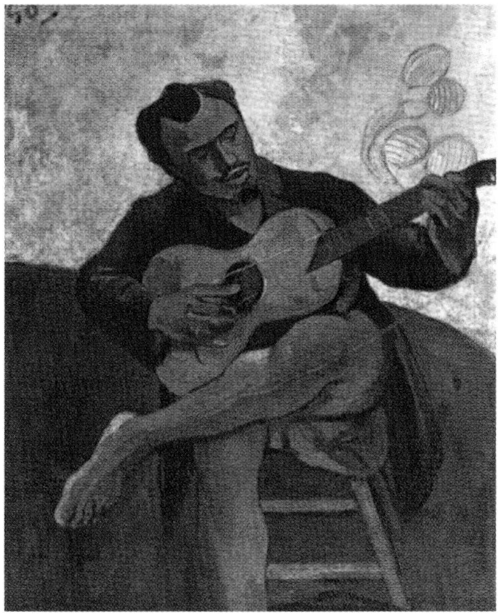

Paul Gauguin
The Guitar Player, c. 1894
Oil on canvas. 90 x 72 cm
London, private collection on loan at The National Gallery

primitivist legacy with the fauvist movement, but not so much for its wild nature, as for the way in which it reflected the same ideal of classicist exaltation not only on the part of Gauguin, but also of Ingres. Joan Sacs' approach reveals the extent to which Gauguin's legacy, Synthetism and the first avant-gardes appear intertwined within that primitivist spirit which attempted to reconcile itself with classicism in the context of the noucentist circles of Barcelona. But we should not forget the wider European context of the return to order, in which only two years before, Maurice Denis, a Nabi painter and theoretician, had emphasised the connection between Classicism and Gauguin's Primitivism and in a book entitled *Théories 1890–1910: Du Symbolisme et de Gauguin vers un nouvel ordre classique,* which gathered his critical writings of several years.[7] Although the title and date, 1912, seem to allude to an evolution in European sensibility, the book in actual fact dealt with the definition of concepts like Symbolism, Primitivism and Classicism, apparently disparate but actually inseparable. Denis suggested that the latter two are but two sides of the same coin, of the same problem, which can be summed up in a harmonious relation with nature, in nostalgia for a Golden Age.[8]

Durrio, the mediator

The process of absorption of the synthetist proposal, of its archaic expressiveness and its radical decorativism as a trigger of the modernising process of Spanish painting at the turn of the century, finds an exceptional mediator in the sculptor, goldsmith and ceramist from Bilbao Paco Durrio (1868–1840). There is clear evidence of the friendship

7. Denis, Maurice: *Théories 1890–1910: Du Symbolisme et de Gauguin vers un nouvel ordre classique*, Paris, Rouart et Watelin, 1920. Spanish version: *Teorías. 1890–1910. Del simbolismo y de Gauguin hacia un nuevo orden clásico* Prol. and trans. by José España. Buenos Aires, El Ateneo, 1944.
8. Bozal, Valeriano: 'Clásicos y salvajes', in *Los primeros diez años. 1900–1910, los orígenes del arte contemporáneo*. Madrid, Visor, 1991, pp. 123 and ff.

and mutual admiration that existed between Durrio and Gauguin, which apparently went back to the autumn of 1886, when they met, probably through Émile Bernard, in the workshop directed by the ceramics artist Ernest Chaplet. This friendship deepened particularly during Gauguin's stay in Paris from 1893 to 1895, during the interval between his two sojourns in Tahiti.[9] In those years, Durrio and Gauguin shared a workshop, as well as an interest in the techniques of sculptural ceramics and in primitivist forms. We know that Gauguin remembered Durrio for the rest of his life, and that he painted his portrait in the work entitled *The Guitar Player*, now at the National Gallery in London. For his part, Durrio became a true 'apostle of Gauguin',[10] not only showing the mark of the melancholic symbolism and of the primitivist iconography of the painter of the southern seas in his own oeuvre as a ceramist, sculptor and goldsmith, but also actively and enthusiastically disseminating his master's work among other artists. Durrio insisted on familiarising painters like Zuloaga and Picasso with Gauguin's legacy and Synthetism at a time when they were still being absorbed by the Parisian circles themselves. Later, when other avant-garde movements had assimilated and radicalised many of Gauguin's original approaches, Durrio helped promote his oeuvre on a larger scale both in Spain and in Paris. In order to do this, he ensured Gauguin would be present in various exhibitions held in the Basque country, like the *Primera Exposición de Arte Moderno* in Bilbao in 1900 and the 1919 *Exposición Internacional de Pintura y Escultura* mentioned above. Similarly in Paris, he lent a large number of works signed by Gauguin for the retrospective exhibition of the artist organised at the *Salon d'Automne* in 1906, which had such a great impact on Picasso. These works were part of a substantial collection that Durrio had received from Gauguin himself before his departure for Tahiti in 1895, and which grew with later contributions sent from Polynesia. He had settled with them in Montparnasse, where various Spanish artists were able to see them. Apart from the famous and often reported episode in which a bohemian and caricaturised Manolo Hugué sold to Vollard the paintings of the French master during Durrio's absence, we know for example that artists such as Zuloaga and Uranga were able to see them personally, as they shared a house with Durrio until 1901. Others, like the painter Iturrino and the sculptor Mogrobejo, went there frequently. Later, when Durrio moved to Montmartre, also Picasso and Vázquez Díaz, among many, frequented his workshop. There, they were introduced to Gauguin's oeuvre and were able to listen to Durrio's praise of it.

Picasso, the heir

After Gauguin's departure for Tahiti in 1895 and, in particular, after his death on the Marquesas Islands in 1903, Durrio looked for his successor among the new artists, and thought he had found him in Picasso. With the intention of bringing about a true reincarnation, Durrio tried to introduce Picasso to the subject of sculptural ceramics in

9. Barañano, Kosme: 'Orfebrería y cerámica', in *Escultores y orfebres. Francisco Durrio, Pablo Gargallo, Julio González, Manolo*. Valencia, Obra Social y Cultural de Bancaixa, 1993, p. 17.
10. Pingeot, Anne: 'La maison de jouir 1901–1902' in *Gauguin Tahiti. L'Atelier des tropiques*, Paris, Réunion des Musées Nationaux, 2003, p. 314.

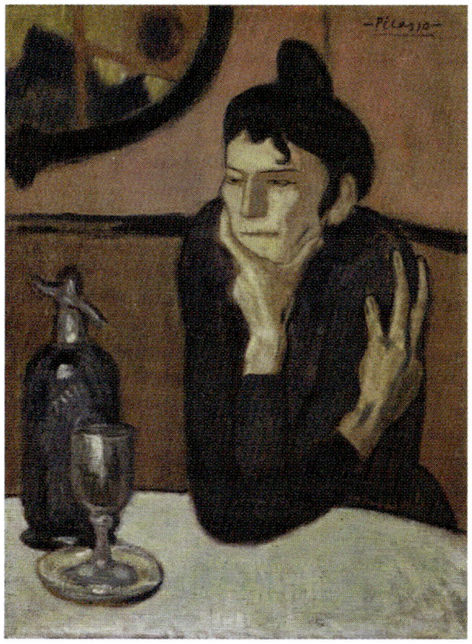

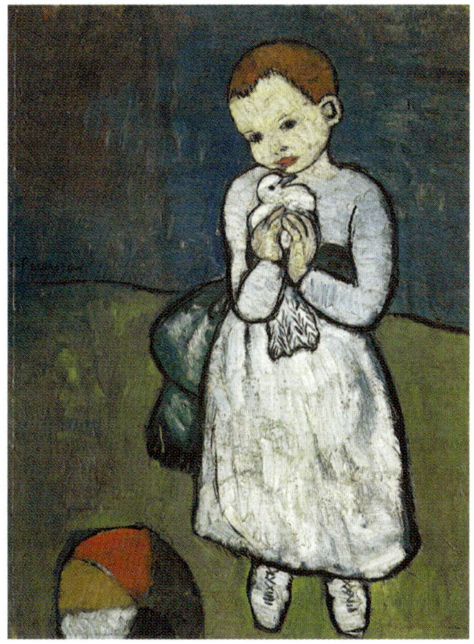

Pablo Picasso
The Absinthe Drinker, 1901
Oil on canvas. 73 x 54 cm
St Petersburg, The Hermitage Museum

Pablo Picasso
Child with a Dove, 1901
Oil on canvas. 73 x 54 cm
London, The National Gallery

which Gauguin achieved the organic integration of colour and shape. Like Gauguin, Picasso had a strong sense of independence and, again like Gauguin, he always took an ambiguous stand with respect to his own place in art history: an initiator, breaker and revolutionary, he never ceased to consider the legacy of a past that included both Iberian and African art, el Greco as well as Ingres, and Degas as well as Gauguin himself, from whom he was taking over now.

The relationship between colour and feeling which Gauguin had expressed in his writings, his synthetic primitivism, his melancholy, were already showing up in paintings like *Sick woman at Saint-Lazare, moonlight*, now at the Detroit Museum of Art, and *The Absinthe Drinker*, from the Hermitage, both painted in Paris in 1901, as well as in the mysterious and attractive *Harlequin* of 1901, at The Metropolitan Museum, New York, whose floral freeze seems to allude directly to Gauguin's Synthetism, and in some still lifes of the same period. However, other paintings of 1901, like *Child with a Dove*, now at the National Gallery in London, or *The Tub*, in the Phillips Collection in Washington, seem to point more directly, in their theme and their decorativism, to the Nabi aesthetics. In any case, beyond the visual echoes of Synthetism, there exists a coincidence, in Picasso's works, between the spirit that inspires them and that of Gauguin. During his stay in le Pouldu, in Brittany, Gauguin – ill and destitute – had expressed his conviction that his art emanated from sadness and pain: an expressionist concept of art that could easily fit Picasso's oeuvre of that initial period. And Picasso's closeness to Gauguin's work and spirit increased in the

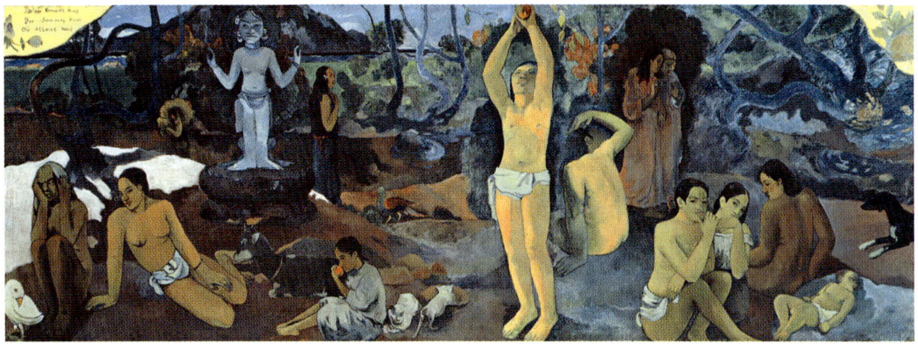

Paul Gauguin
D'où venons-nous? Que sommes-nous? Ou allons-nous?, 1897
Oil on canvas. 139.1 x 374.6 cm
Boston, Museum of Fine Arts
(Tomkins Collection 36.270)

following years. In 1902, on the occasion of his exhibition in the Parisian gallery of Berthe Weill, Picasso obtained a highly favourable review from Charles Morice, which pleased him particularly as it came from a friend of Gauguin's. It seems that it was once again Durrio who induced Morice to visit the exhibition. And the latter not only wrote about Picasso, but he also gave him a copy of *Noa-Noa*, the book by Gauguin that Morice had completed. Richardson has pointed out the great benefit Picasso obtained from this book, full of illustrations that would soon be reflected in the oeuvre of the artist from Malaga. It is clear that Gauguin's primitivist impetus, together with many other sources, were behind the works of Picasso dating from those years. But his identification with Gauguin went deeper, to the extent that he was convinced that Gauguin 'was the explorer whose traces should be followed through the sacred woods'.[11]

Picasso's real fascination with Gauguin came about in particular with his contemplation of the retrospective exhibition held in the *Salon d'Automne* in 1906, to which Durrio had contributed. Picasso had not been able to visit the exhibitions held three years before in Vollard's gallery and in the *Salon d'Automne*, as he was then in Barcelona. There, he had been working on various fundamental sources, among which stood out El Greco, Puvis de Chavanne and, primarily, Gauguin. Thus, between the spring and summer of 1903 he executed in Barcelona a painting with ambitious symbolist claims, pompously entitled *La Vie*, which in its meaning could be considered as a counterpart to Gauguin's *D'ou venons nous? Que sommes-nous? Ou allons-nous?* of 1897. This hypothesis is reinforced by the figures curled up in the background, direct references to those that appear in Gauguin's painting.

Picasso, who had returned to Paris in 1904 knowing that he was leaving Barcelona behind forever, had settled in the studio that Durrio had vacated in the Bateau Lavoir in Place Ravignan. The following year, after a trip around Holland, he had given Durrio his painting *La belle Holandaise*, his masterpiece from that period, so that he could hang it next to his Gauguins, which proves not only that he was proud of it, but also that he

11 .Richardson, John: *Picasso. Una biografía. Vol. I, 1881–1906*. Madrid, Alianza, 1991, pp. 263 and ff. See also the chapter 'La huella de Gauguin', pp. 455 and ff.

found a certain parallel between that work, with its stylised and synthetic construction of the figure with the white cap, and those of Gauguin.

1906 became a crucial year for Picasso: his closeness to the circle of the Stein brothers, and his consequent contact with artists like Matisse and Derain, had a triggering significance. From then on, he ceased to be the leader of a small group of Spanish artists in Montmartre and became a prominent member of the new Parisian avant-garde. Vollard then decided to buy all the works that Picasso had in his studio, which enabled him to sojourn in the village of Gósol, in the Pyrenees, between May and October 1906. There, he painted a work that finally freed itself of the remains of the end-of-the-century artificiousness and the literary style of his pink period. He now approached deliberately harsh forms, which brought together Classicism and Primitivism in a synthesis that owed as much to Gauguin as to Maillol. In fact, the latter had visited with great enthusiasm the synthetist exhibition at the Volpini café in 1889, which revealed to him Gauguin as a true master.[12] Gósol was for Picasso what Brittany had been for Gauguin: an uncontaminated, innocent place, where he could experiment free from inhibitions, far from the pressures of Paris. Eugenio Carmona has recently pointed out the transcendence of Picasso's sojourn in Gósol, which meant 'Picasso's wish to re-found his oeuvre from his first meeting with Primitivism, [which] turned out to be a transforming force for the whole of 20th century art'.[13] It was precisely after that liberating and fruitful experience that Picasso contemplated, ecstatic, Gauguin's works in the *Salon d'Automne*, which caused in him a deep impact and confirmed his aspirations. It was then that he painted works like *Watering-place* and *Boy Leading a Horse*, probably as a response to *Riders on the Beach*, one of Gauguin's last works and a perfect example of the fusion between Primitivism and Classicism on which Picasso wanted to base his new art. Shortly after, *Les Demoiselles d'Avignon* showed that the interests of Picasso were shifting direction, placing Classicism in the background, though he never abandoned it. In any case it is interesting to point out here, next to the sources of inspiration habitually put forward for this work – El Greco, African and Oceanic art, Catalan Romanesque and Iberian art, etc. – one more: the *Bathers* that Émile Bernard painted in Pont-Aven in 1889.

In any case, if *Les Demoiselles d'Avignon* points in the direction of Cubism, it can be said that the lesson of synthetic Primitivism, with its effect of simplifying forms and its concept of a picture as the abstract image of reality, is not absent from it. That affinity comes out, in fact, in the combined influence of both movements in later artists.

Gauguin, Synthetism and Spanish art

We have mentioned the mediation played by Durrio in order to guarantee Gauguin's presence in Basque art exhibitions, as well as his active participation in the

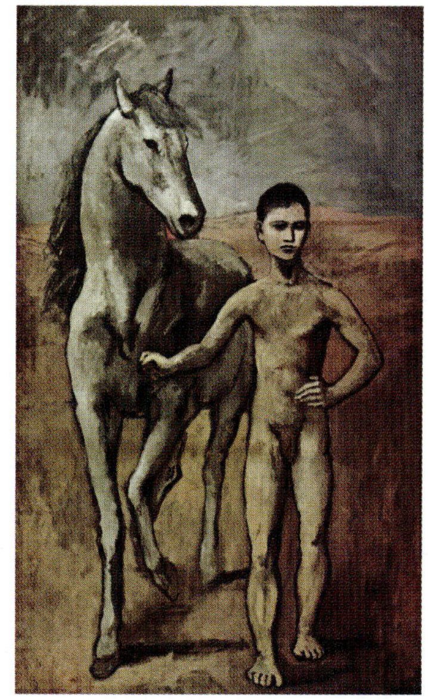

Pablo Picasso
Boy Leading a Horse, 1906
Oil on canvas. 220.3 x 130.6 cm
New York, The Museum of Modern Art
(Donated by William S. Paley)

12. Rewald, John: *El postimpresionismo de Van Gogh a Gauguin*. Madrid, Alianza, 1982, p. 223.
13. Carmona, Eugenio: ' Novecentismo y vanguardia en las artes plásticas españolas 1906–1926', in *La generación del 14. Entre el novecentismo y la vanguardia (1906–1926)*. Madrid, Fundación Cultural Mapfre Vida, 2002, pp. 13 and ff.

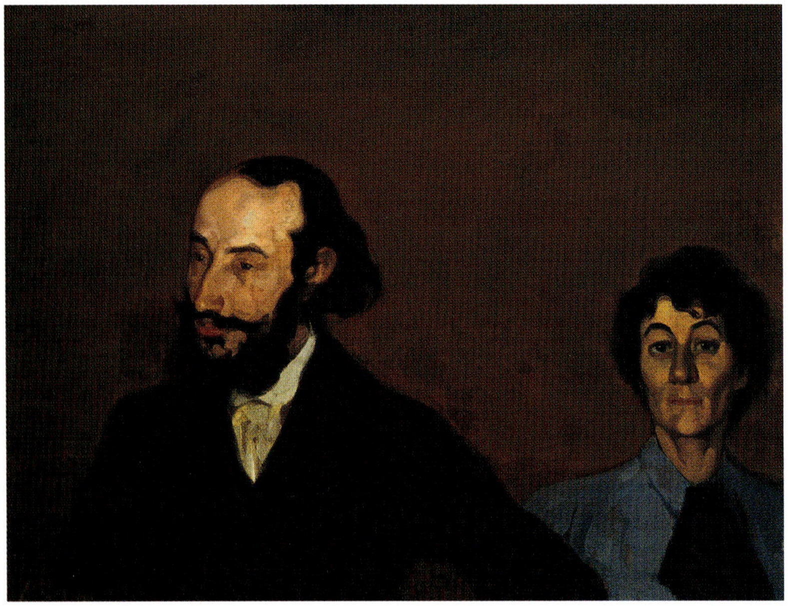

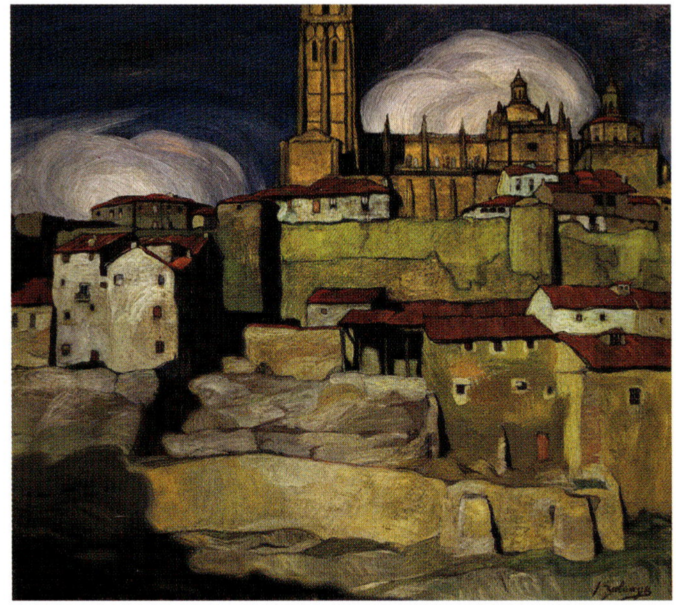

Ignacio Zuloaga
Portrait of Charles Morice and his Wife, 1889
Oil on canvas. 70 x 90 cm
Zumaia, Museo Zuloaga

Ignacio Zuloaga
Segovia Cathedral, 1909
Oil on canvas. 92 x 99 cm
Pedraza, Museo Zuloaga

organisation of other important exhibitions of his works in Paris, in order to ensure the diffusion of Gauguin's oeuvre. This was particularly true among his young compatriots, who also found in turn-of-the-century Paris other opportunities to familiarise themselves with Gauguin's oeuvre – shows which undoubtedly Durrio encouraged them to attend. It is the case of the exhibitions held in 1898, 1903 and 1910 at Ambroise Vollard's gallery, in rue Lafitte, or of the one organised the year of his death, 1903, in a room at the *Salon d'Automne*, marking the beginning of a deferred public recognition which arrived, in particular, after the much larger exhibition of Gauguin's works at the 1906 *Salon d'Automne*.

Among the Basque artists who arrived in Paris around 1890, and who therefore received the impact of Synthetism at the same time as the French painters, we should mention first of all Ignacio Zuloaga (1870–1945), who began, at the end of 1889, a decisive sojourn in the French capital. He missed the exhibition at the Volpini Café, which had taken place during the previous summer. But we know that shortly after his arrival he was in contact with artistic circles close to the painters who took part in that show. He then had a close relationship with Maxime de Thomas, one of the artists associated with the Breton group, marrying his sister Valentine. In 1891 he managed to take part in a collective exhibition organised at the Le Barc gallery in Bouteville together with Gauguin, Van Gogh, Toulouse-Lautrec and Émile Bernard. Apparently, he already knew Gauguin, but he did not meet Émile Bernard – the painter who claimed to be the author of Synthetism – until 1895 in Seville. However, the influence of Synthetism in general, and of Bernard in particular, can be seen in his elegant *Portrait of the Marquis of Villamarciel* (c. 1893); the wood in the background seems to refer directly to Bernard's oil entitled *Madeleine au Bois d'Amour*, of 1888. In 1898, the *Portrait of Charles Morice and his Wife* also shows, both in its iconography and in its stylised compositional simplification, his particular adherence to Synthetism. Charles Morice, who became one of the most important supporters Zuloaga could count on in France, was a poet and an art critic for *Mercure de France*, and he added his comments to the text initially prepared by Gauguin for *Noa-Noa*, thus creating between them the book that was meant to explain and render more attractive for the European public the environment in which Gauguin's Polynesian oeuvre was conceived. A superficial glance at this and other works by Zuloaga would make us think that the tendency to use dark colours, which gradually characterised his work, drew him away from the visual point of view and aesthetics of the bright colours created in Pont-Aven. However, the wish for a formal synthesis, the expressionist character, which is visionary beyond the visual, the deliberate primitivist harshness and the cloisonné (or outlines) typical of the Pont-Aven aesthetics, have a clear echo in works like *Segovia Cathedral* (1909), and in particular in *Palace of La Granja* (1912), to mention but two examples.

Closer to the typical colour of Breton Synthetism is the palette of Francisco Iturrino (1864–1924). Iturrino is usually considered to be the Spanish artist closest to Fauvism, the movement that inherited the chromatic freedom and stylisation of Synthetism and Gauguin's wild primitivism. He was therefore close to Fauvism, in the wake of the artistic vision that had surged in Brittany in 1888. But Iturrino's relationship with Synthetism did not wait for the fauvist explosion at the *Salon d'Automne* of 1905. *Couple on a Horse*, of 1898, now at the Musée d'Ixelles, shows that he needed no mediation. From very early on, Francisco Iturrino was in contact with the Nabi group and with Ambroise Vollard's gallery, which at the time was showing Paul Gauguin's oeuvre in Paris. Iturrino exhibited there in 1901, next to a younger, and at the time less known, artist called Picasso. Not waiting for the exhibition to close, Iturrino travelled to Spain and during the first years of the century looked for his own primitivist paradises in Andalusia and in the Basque country, although he still went back and forth to Paris, where he was already a known artist. Some time later, his paintings with orientalist subjects, resulting primarily from a trip with Matisse around Andalusia and North Africa, show in their distinctively fauvist style his debt to the synthetic spirit of Pont-Aven. Paintings like *The Harem*, 1911–15, in the Museo de Vitoria, which depicted many women in white head-dresses, clearly reminds us of Émile Bernard's *Les Bretonnes dans la Prairie*, which since its creation had become the programmatic work of Synthetism.

The other 'fauve' of Basque art, Juan de Echevarría (1875–1931), reflected more strongly the impact of Synthetism. But Echevarría, sensitive to the meaning of expressive freedom, widened his assimilation of post-impressionist approaches to include also Van Gogh[14]. Echevarría developed a type of painting that Pío Baroja described in terms of a chromatic harmony that recalls a musical composition.[15] Terms which almost paraphrase Gauguin himself when he describes what he himself calls the 'music of the painting':

> 'There is an impression that results from particular dispositions of colour, of light and of shade. It is what is called the music of the painting. [...] Here is the root of the true superiority of painting with regard to other forms of art, since emotion directly addresses the spirit.'[16]

It is true that both in his landscapes and in his still lifes and figures, Echevarría went for that musicality, for the expressive intensity and formal freedom of Synthetism. In a recent piece of writing, Guillermo Solana correctly points out the relationship that existed between specific works by Echevarría and by Gauguin and Van Gogh,[17] so it is not necessary to go into the subject here. What is interesting is that this closeness is maintained across various decades. We only need to mention outstanding works by Echevarría, like *Madame Julie* (1912), *Gypsy Woman from Granada* (1915), and *Gypsies Standing in a Ring* (c. 1925), to realise the clear impact not only of Synthetism, but also of Gauguin's Tahitian oeuvre. In the field of figure painting, perhaps the work which most clearly shows his connection with Gauguin is *Naked Mestizo Woman*, of 1923. In it, Echevarría refers not only to works painted by Gauguin in Polynesia – like *Te arii vahine* (1896), and *Manao Tupapau*, of 1892 – but also, via them, to Manet's *Olympia*, which had inspired them in the first place. Also in Echevarría's landscapes we find examples of an image built from areas of arbitrary colour, in a bright palette, which accentuate the flat character of the painting in a way very similar to that used by the artists of Pont-Aven. This can clearly be seen in *Landscape of Pampliega* (c. 1908), and also in other works executed in the same place in the 1920s. But it is in the still life genre where perhaps the closeness to Gauguin – and to other darker synthetists, like the Dutch painter Meyer de Haan – becomes more evident, both in the choice and disposition of the objects, and in the expressive use of colour. Significantly, one of Echevarría's still lifes closest to the visionary and expressive spirit both of Gauguin and of Van Gogh is *Still Life with Statues by Durrio*, of 1909. It is impossible not to mention Durrio when referring to other examples, such as *Still Life with Quimper Pitcher*, housed in the Berkeley Art Museum, dated in 1889, one of Gauguin's seldom shown still lifes. This painting was part of the collection of the Basque sculptor and ceramist, and shows strong formal and compositional similarity to a few of Echevarría's works, even to some made later in his life, like *Still Life with Japanese Print* (c. 1922). This suggests that the closeness can be extended to all of Echevarría's still lifes, and this may be the closest approximation to the synthetist image in the whole of Spanish art of that time.

14. Van Gogh's closeness to the aesthetics of Pont-Aven is a fact acknowledged by critics and historians, given his continuous contact and exchange of opinions with the most outstanding members of the group, which has clear consequences on his oeuvre. In the catalogue of the exhibition entitled *Gauguin e la Bretagna*, mentioned above, André Cariou wrote: 'Gauguin rimase deluso de Arles e dal Midi, e rimpiangeva la Bretagna. Vincent rimase fortemente impressionato dal sintetismo inventato a Pont-Aven, con la sua eliminazione de le ombre, con i contorni sottolineati, i colore in campiture piatte e l'essecuzione a memoria. (...) A buon diritto si tende spesso ad associare Van Gogh alla scuola di Pont-Aven, sebbene l'artista non abbia mai visto la Bretagna' (p. 75) ['Gauguin was disappointed with Arles and the Midi, and missed Brittany. Vincent was deeply impressed by the Synthetism invented in Pont-Aven, with the elimination of shades, with the strong outlines, the colours applied in flat areas and the execution from memory. [...] Van Gogh is quite rightly often associated with the Pont-Aven school, in spite of the fact that the artist never visited Brittany'].
15. Baroja, Pío: *Desde la última vuelta del camino. Memorias. Galería de tipos de la época*, Madrid, Biblioteca Nueva, 1947, pp. 267 and ff.
16. Gauguin, Paul: 'Cosas diversas' (1896–1898), in *Escritos de un salvaje*, *op. cit.*, p. 158.
17. Solana, Guillermo: 'El desollado', in *Juan de Echevarría (1875–1931)*, Madrid, Fundación Cultural Mapfre Vida and Bilbao, Museo de Bellas Artes, 2004, pp. 39 and ff.

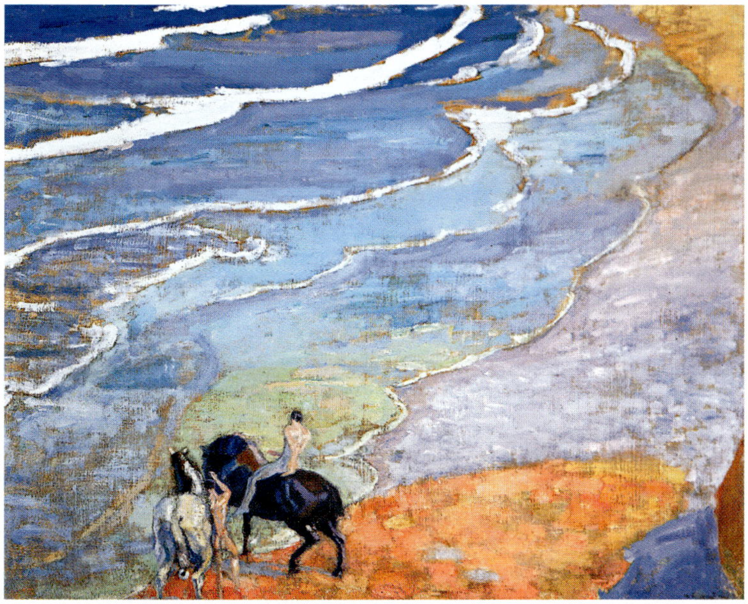

Daniel Vázquez Díaz
The Sea, 1908
Oil on canvas. 103 x 133 cm
Madrid, Museo Nacional Centro de Arte Reina Sofía

Thus, in the case of Iturrino and Echevarría, the influence of Synthetism is mixed with that of Fauvism, which followed Expressionism and implied a radicalisation of some of the ideas of Synthetism. But the assimilation of the synthetist proposal into subsequent avant-garde formulas could also concern other aspects of the distancing from traditional mimesis that this movement implied: those related to the analysis of form, and its geometrisation, used in the construction of an abstract image that does not describe reality but creates its visual parallel. This was done by Daniel Vázquez Díaz (1882–1969), an Andalusian painter in contact with the Basque artists as a result of his summer sojourns in Fuenterrabía and of the good reception he received from Basque art critics. In one of his articles, Vázquez Díaz recalled his visits to Durrio's studio during his stay in Paris, when Durrio spoke to him with passion about Gauguin, even though he no longer possessed his collection of works by this artist.[18] Always attentive to the most recent trends, but deep down still conservative, Vázquez Díaz reflects in paintings like *Joy in the Basque Countryside*, of 1918, a particular fusion between the synthetist legacy and the more recent Cubist movement – which had already become a thing of the past – and which he had adapted to suit his own needs without moving too far away from Cézanne. This particular mild translation of Cubism, which builds rather than decomposes, is exemplified here by a greater geometrisation of the schematising approach already proposed by Émile Bernard and Paul Gauguin in their works of 1888. In any case, Vázquez Díaz's painting shows perfectly his personal combination of the formulas of modernity and traditional art that characterises Vázquez Díaz's entire oeuvre, which is generically modern, but never takes risks.

18. Vázquez Díaz, Daniel: 'El escultor Francisco Durrio'. Originally published in ABC, 23 March 1958, and reproduced in Jiménez-Blanco, María Dolores: *Daniel Vázquez Díaz. Mis contemporáneos*, Madrid, Fundación Cultural Mapfre Vida, pp. 200–02.

Within this tendency to borrow from Synthetism in particular the sense of formal organisation we could place Aurelio Arteta (1879–1940), another initiator of modernity in Spain, whose work preceding World War I tended to include the decorativism and the classicist grandeur typical of the cycles of traditional Italian frescoes in the synthetic style and the chromatism of the post-impressionist art of Pont-Aven. This can be seen in works like *On the Way to the Market*, of 1913, and *To the Market* (c. 1913–1915).

But the influence of Gauguin and of Synthetism on Basque art extends to many other artists. One of them is Ramón de Zubiaurre (1882–1969) who, together with his brother Valentín, epitomized for art historians a type of genre painting that extolled what was then known as the 'Basque race' – an expression coined by Juan de la Encina with more cultural than ethnic connotations. Like all leitmotifs, this one contains some truth, but it is such a simplification that it misses many interesting nuances. Ramón de Zubiaurre's interest in synthetist and Nabi aesthetics is patent, for example, in a screen of c. 1910-1911 recently exhibited in Madrid.[19] Characteristics like cloisonné, formal simplification, the construction of the image starting from planes of colour, and Japanese influence are all evident, as is an Arcadian vision of nature that is unquestionable if difficult to define. I have no evidence that Zubiaurre was familiar with the screens made twenty years before by the Nabi artists, or those painted by Émile Bernard,[20] but in any case we can say that he seems to apply to the Basque landscape and architecture Bernard's approach to the Breton landscape and way of living. Even his manner of depicting the figures in works like *The Basque Sailor Shanti Andía the Temerary* (c. 1924), as isolated and strongly coloured elements, and his tight control over the composition, conferring to it a strong decorative value similar to that of Japanese prints, point to a more generalised influence of Synthetism in Zubiaurre's oeuvre. On their part, Julián de Tellaeche (1884–1958), Gustavo de Maeztu (1887–1947), and Ramiro Arrúe (1892–1971) later incorporated in their visual description of the Basque reality some aspects of Synthetism in a perhaps more anecdotic way, as a technical formula devoid of its initial meaning.

Among the Catalans, the other important colony of Spanish artists in Paris, the presence of Synthetism is more difficult to define, maybe not just because it was mixed with the other forms of Post-impressionism that marked the Parisian avant-gardes, but also because, already in the first years of the twentieth century, it overlapped the stylisation and organising vision typical of Catalan Noucentism, a project of national modernity based on a form of Mediterranean classicism understood as a harmonious relationship with nature.

Durrio frequented the *bande catalane* particularly after 1901, when he moved to the studio at the Bateau Lavoir, which he later passed on to Picasso. Artists like Anglada

19. Carmona, Eugenio and Jiménez-Blanco, María Dolores: *La Generación del 14. Entre el novecentismo y la vanguardia (1906–1926)*, Madrid, Fundación Cultural Mapfre Vida, 2002, pp. 212–13.
20. Like those entitled *The Four Seasons* and *The Miserable Woodcutters*, both of 1891 and in private collections. Like Zubiaurre's work, both are made up of four vertical panels. Those of Bernard and that of Zubiaurre describe a more or less idealised rural environment. The difference is clear, however, in the essential presence of figures in the case of Bernard, and in their absence in that of Zubiaurre.

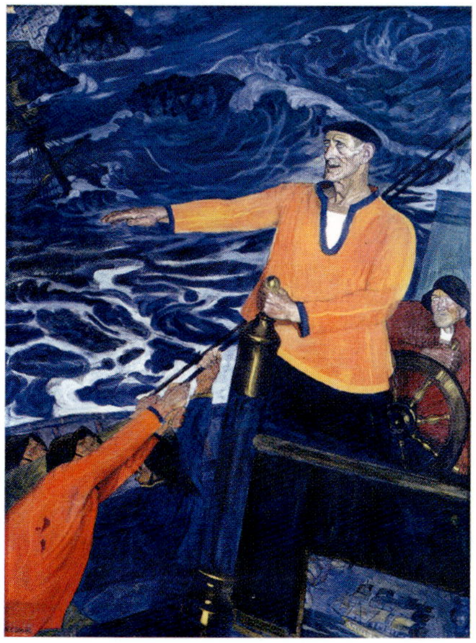

Ramón de Zubiaurre
The Basque Sailor Shanti Andía the Temerary, c. 1924
Oil on canvas. 228 x 118 cm
Madrid, Museo Nacional Centro de Arte Reina Sofía

Camarasa, Rusiñol and Casas were already at the peak of their career. All of them had built their success on a personal synthesis of the different post-impressionist proposals, among which was Synthetism, although it was not predominant. Modern and complacent at the same time, they occasionally created images which owed as much to art-nouveau decorativism as to Nabi aesthetics. In this context we can also understand the work of the younger refined painter and illustrator Pere Torné-Esquius (1879–1936), some of whose images can be seen as a Catalan counterpart to those of Bonnard and Vuillard.

But it was other artists younger than Anglada, Rusiñol and Casas who answered to the name of *bande catalane*. They were artists closer to Durrio and they provided fertile ground for his proselytising labour. Thus, the sculptures of Julio González, Manolo Hugué and Gargallo, in addition to those of the Basque artist Nemesio Mogrobejo (1875-1910), tended more to the primitivist-classicist symbolism of Gauguin's later work than to the pure Synthetism of his Breton period. That Gauguin's influence was passed on through the eyes of Durrio can be seen in reliefs like *Eve*, by the sculptor Mogrobejo. A better known example is the pictorial and sculptural oeuvre of Julio González (1876–1942) – as well as his work on precious metals – previous to his collaboration with Picasso at the end of the 1920s. The same can be said about the Catalan sculptor Manolo Hugué (1872–1945), who did not hesitate to sell Durrio's collection of works by Gauguin to Vollard in Durrio's absence. His views on Classicism included, as did Gauguin's, artistic forms different from those typical of the Greco-Roman period. He created a style which lay between archaic and primitive, echoing that dull noise of clogs on a wooden floor which, for Gauguin, symbolised acoustically the idea of Breton Primitivism.[21]

In 1896 another artist from the same generation as these two arrived in Paris. He was soon to show a sensitivity towards the forms of Post-impressionism and apply to his paintings the possibilities they offered. This artist was Joaquim Sunyer (1874-1956), later destined to become the visual interpreter of Noucentism. Initially, he expressed his fascination with Parisian life in engravings showing the evident mark of Daumier and Steinlen. Towards 1905, however, his interest in textures and his sense of ornamentation, inspired by the Nabi artists Vuillard and Bonnard, became more pronounced in his paintings. This can be seen in *Woman Sewing* (1905), in *The Mirrors,* of 1905–1907, and in *The Make-up*, of 1907. Such closeness did not go unnoticed, since in 1904 he had taken part in a collective exhibition in the Rive Gauche gallery with Vuillard which, incidentally, also included works by Matisse and Marquet. Sunyer had by then settled in Montmartre, very near the Bateau Lavoir, and had a close relationship with some of the artists marked by Synthetism: not only did he know Picasso, but also Maillol, and he was a friend of Vázquez Díaz, Zuloaga, Canals and Rusiñol.

It is usual for Sunyer's biographers to point out the indisputable impact that his visit to Cézanne's retrospective exhibition in the *Salon d'Automne* of 1906 had upon him, but we should also mention the exhibition dedicated to Gauguin in the same *Salon*, which also affected him and many of his Catalan friends. Indeed, close observation reveals that it is a combination of both approaches which seems to animate the works he executed in the following years, when he came in contact with the uncontaminated paradise that he discovered upon his return to Catalonia in 1908. Surrounded by coastal and rural Catalonia, so distant from the sophistication of Paris, Sunyer removed from his art the Nabi multicolouring typical of his previous works, creating an essential image, of formal economy and primitivist appearance. This happens in *Sant Sebastià, Sitges* (1909), and in *Mediterranean Life* (1909), where the exaltation of primeval landscape and traditional lifestyles recalls – both in naïf spirit as in visual formula – the images of Breton Synthetism. It can be said that Sunyer's proposal reaches its height in the works *Pastoral* and *Mediterranean* (1910–1911), extolled by the poet Joan Maragall on the occasion of his exhibition at the Faianç Catalá in 1911. As if he was closing the circle, Sunyer created in those paintings an image that embodies a perfect fusion between the visual synthesis of the Pont-Aven group, with its connotations of medievalist primitivism and of hymn to the origins, and the spiritual and formal charge of classicism. Such classicism emerged then not only as harmony with nature, but also in an acceptance of Mediterranean culture as the heir of its Latin past, in a way not dissimilar to what

21. Gauguin, Paul: letter to Schuffenecker, Pont-Aven, 29 February 1888, in *Escritos de un salvaje, cit.*, p. 52.

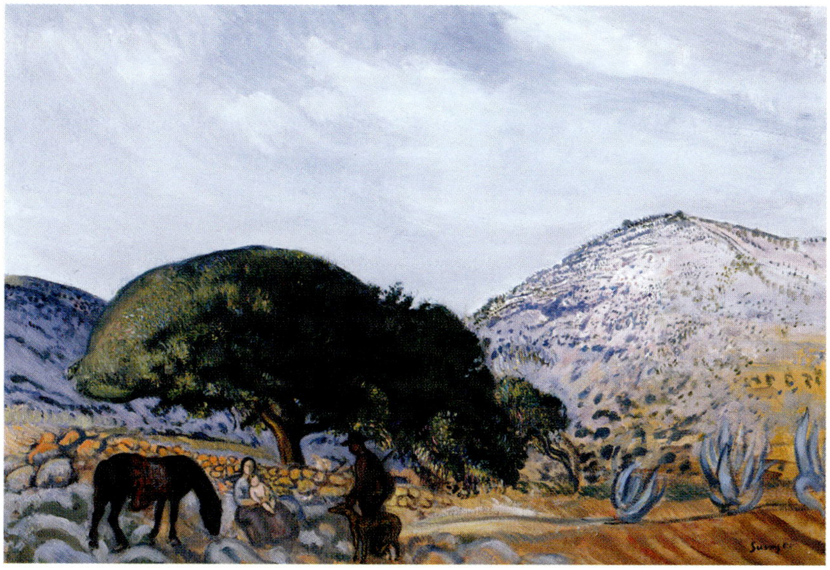

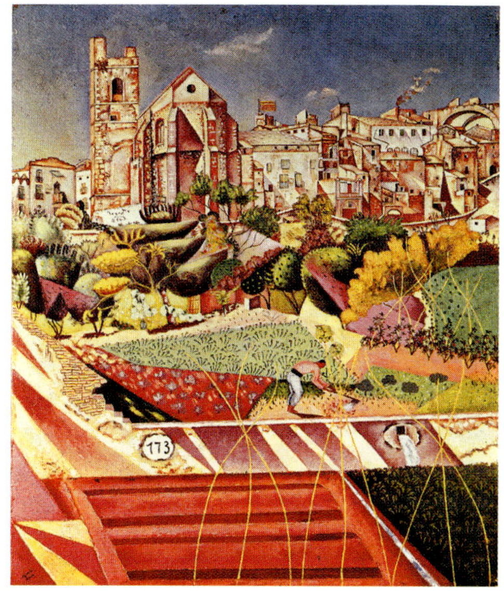

Joaquim Sunyer
Landscape with a Family of Peasants, c. 1908–1911
Oil on canvas. 75 x 106 cm
Carmen Thyssen-Bornemisza Collection

Joan Miró
Montroig, Village and Church, 1919
Oil on canvas. 73 x 60 cm
Private Collection

had already been established by Puvis de Chavannes. Sunyer thus seemed to answer the aspirations of Maurice Denis' book containing his critical writings of a whole decade, which appeared a year later, in 1912.[22]

On 14 August 1888, just when he was debating with Bernard and other painters in Brittany a new artistic concept which the following year would be called Synthetism, Gauguin wrote to his friend the painter Schuffenecker:

> 'My advice. Don't paint too much from nature. Art is an abstraction, draw it out from nature by dreaming in front of it, and think more about the act of creation than about what will result.'[23]

Gauguin, Bernard and a few young painters had found in the Breton landscape the roots of a new aesthetics that joined colour and emotion, establishing a new relationship between art and feeling, which became one of the pillars of modern art. Its mark is visible in movements and artists of the twentieth century, from the classical avant-gardes to abstraction. In the case of Spanish art, in addition to the ones mentioned above, we could add an interminable list of artists including Evaristo Valle, Nicanor Piñole, Castelao, Barradas, Torres García, Marià Andreu, Enric C. Ricart and the young Miró, who looked at Synthetism and made the most of its lessons in their search for a modern artistic form capable of freeing them from the slavery of mimesis without separating them from representation, and of separating them from the visual to gain the freedom of the visionary. At last, Gauguin was right.

22. See note 7.
23. Gauguin, Paul: letter to Schuffenecker, Pont-Aven, 14 August 1888, in *Escritos de un salvaje*, *op. cit.*, p. 55.

Bouvet - Bouvet, F.: *Bonnard L'œuvre gravé.* Paris, 1981

Dauberville - Dauberville, Jean and Henry: *Bonnard. Catalogue Raisonné de l'oeuvre peint* [revisé et augmenté par Michel et Guy-Patrice Dauberville], vol. I 1888-1905. Paris, Bernheim-Jeune, 1992

Faille - Faille, J.-B. de la: *The Works of Vincent van Gogh. His Paintings and Drawings.* Amsterdam, 1970

Field/Strauss/Wagstaff - Field, Richard S.; Strauss, Cynthia L. and Wagstaff Jr., Samuel J.: *The Prints of Armand Seguin 1869-1903.* Davison Art Center, Wesleyan University, Middletown, Ct, s. f. (c. 1964). 1980

Gray - Gray, Christopher: *Sculpture and Ceramics of Paul Gauguin.* Baltimore, 1963 (New York, 1980)

Guérin - Guérin, M.: *L'Œuvre gravé de Gauguin.* Paris, 1927

Pissarro/Venturi - Pissarro, Ludovico Rodo and Venturi, Lionello: *Camille Pisarro. Son Art, son oeuvre.* Paris, Paul Rosenberg, 1939 (2001)

Luthi - Luthi, Jean-Jacques: *Emile Bernard : catalogue raisonné de l'oeuvre peint.* Paris, c. 1982

Rewald - Rewald, John: *The Paintings of Paul Cézanne. A Catalogue Raisonné.* New York, 1996

Salomon/Cogeval - Salomon, Antoine and Cogeval, Guy: *Vuillard. The Inexhaustible Glance. Critical Catalogue of Paintings and Pastels.* Paris/Milan, 2003, Vol. 1, 2, 3

Wildenstein 1964 - Wildenstein, Georges: *Gauguin.* Paris, 1964

Wildenstein 2001 - Wildenstein, Daniel: Gauguin. *Premier itinéraire d'un savage. Catalogue de l'oeuvre peint (1873-1888).* Paris/Milan, 2001

Zervos - Zervos, Christian: *Pablo Picasso*, Vols. I to XXXIII. Paris, 1932

Catalogue

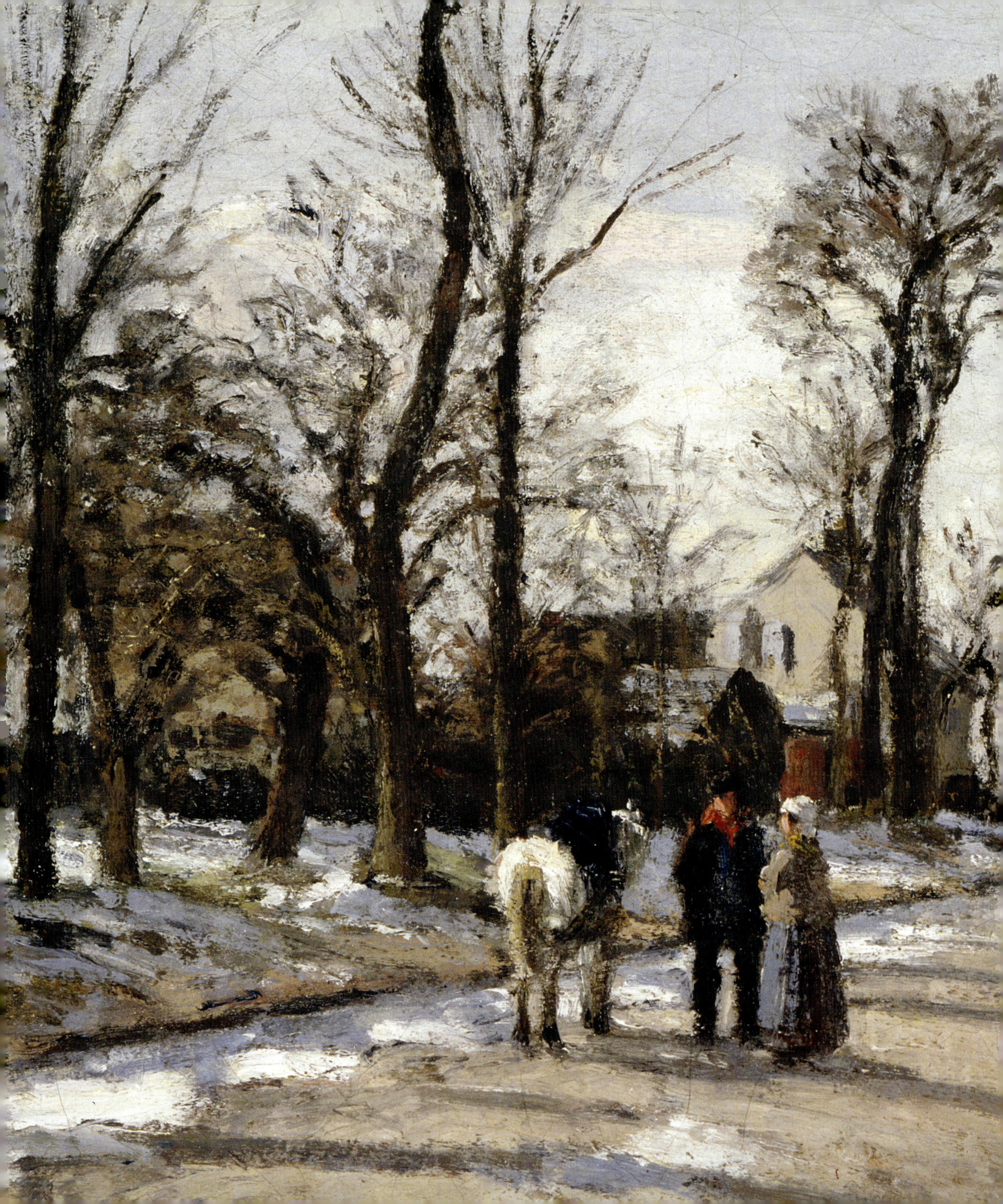

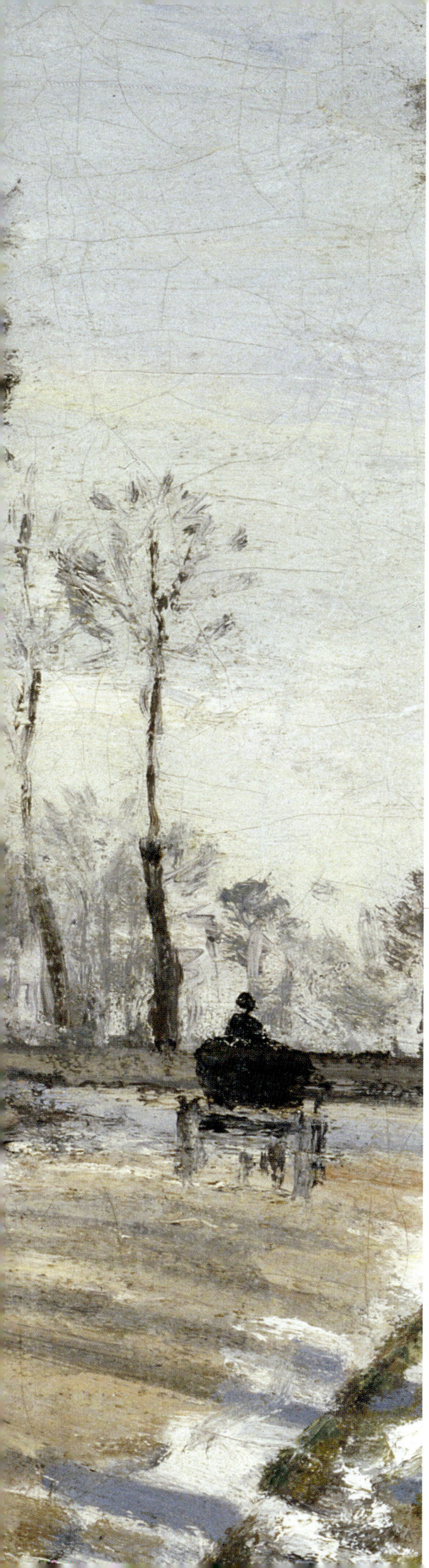

Camille Pissarro
Route, Winter Sun and Snow, c. 1870
(detail)
[cat. 2]

1. The Circle of Pissarro

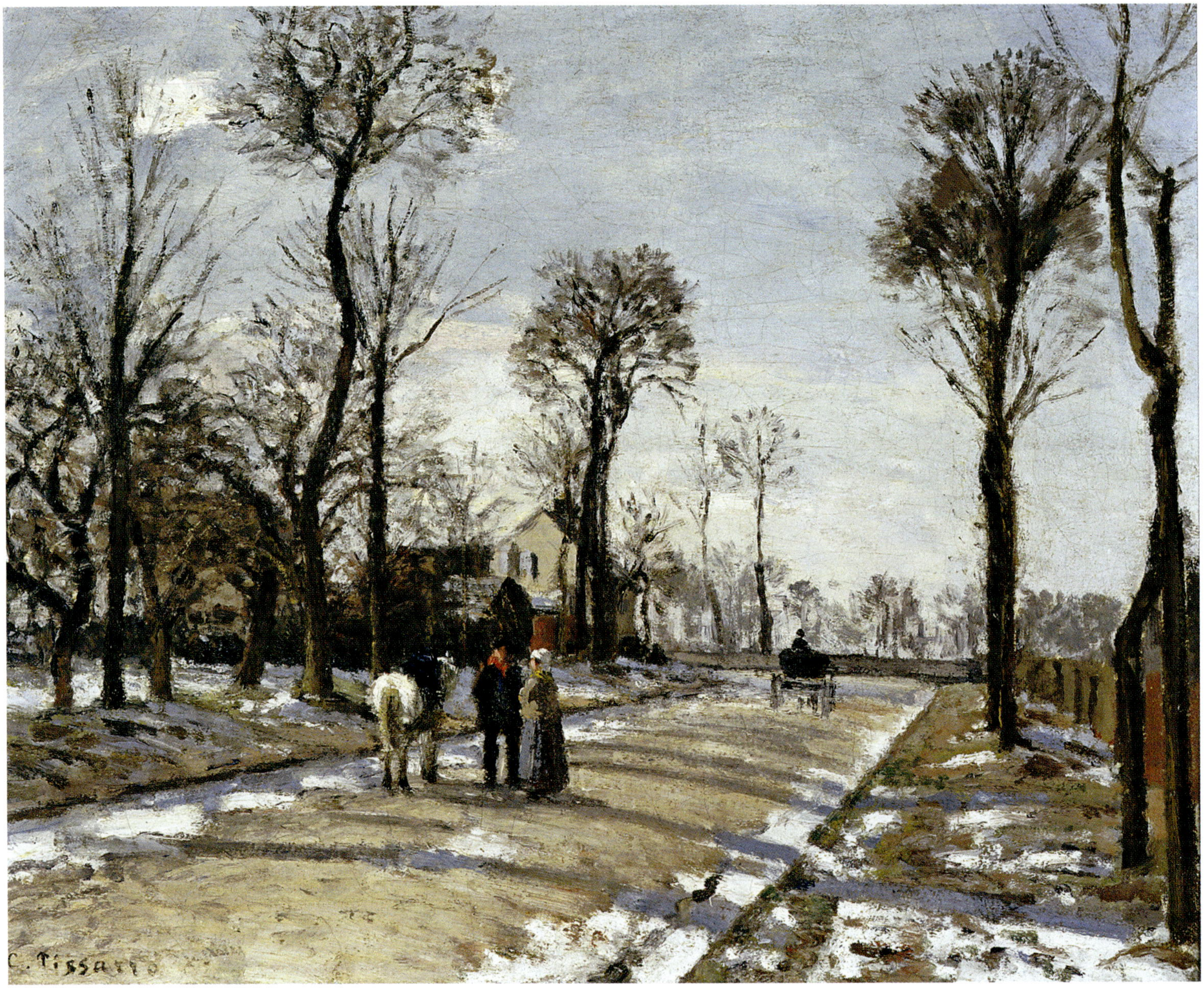

2. Camille Pissarro
Route, Winter Sun and Snow, c. 1870
(Route, soleil d'hiver et neige)
Oil on canvas. 46 x 55.3 cm
[Pissarro/Venturi n. 136]
Carmen Thyssen-Bornemisza Collection
on loan at the Museo Thyssen-Bornemisza, Madrid

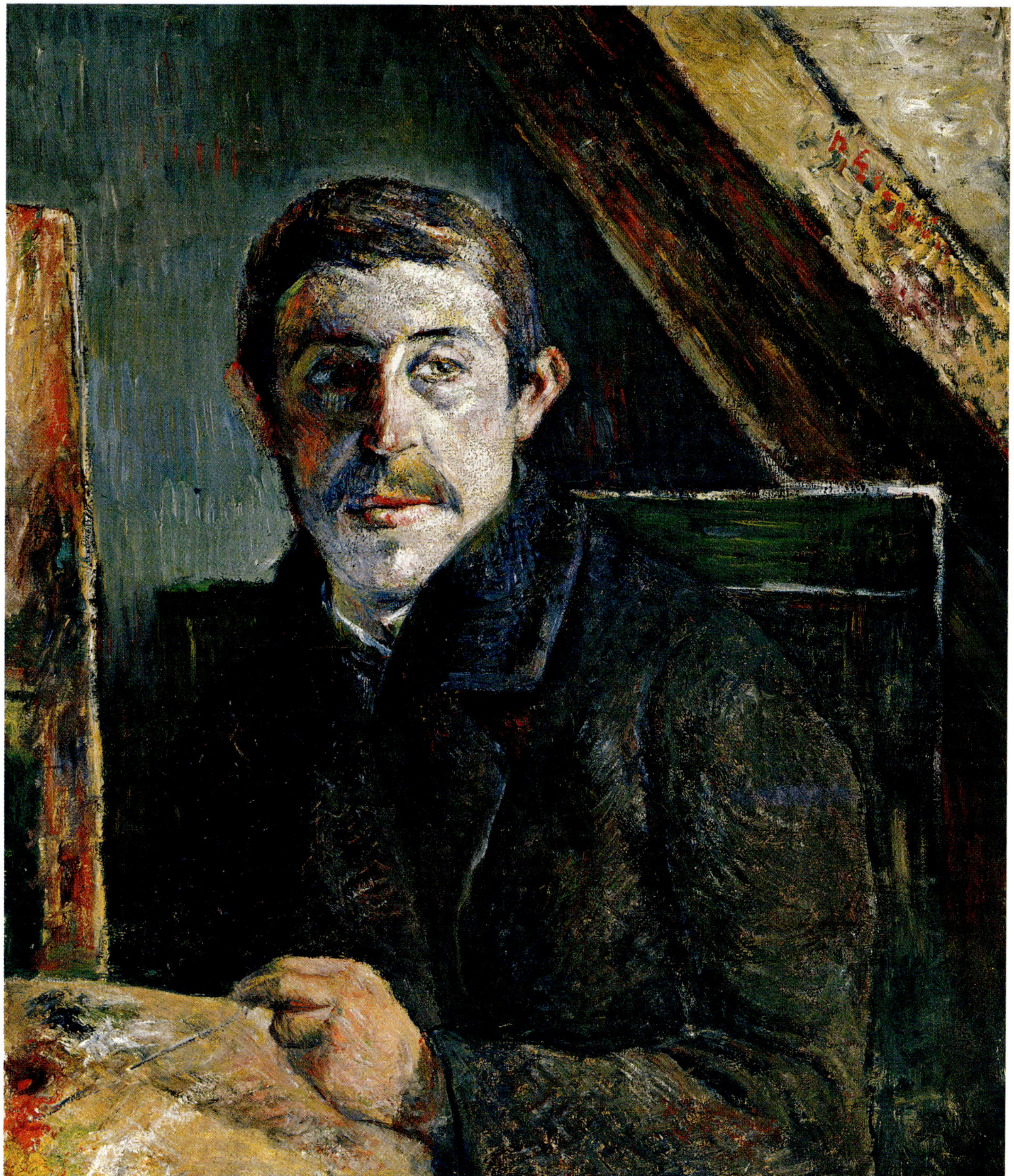

1. Paul Gauguin
Self-Portrait in front of the Easel, 1885
(Autoportrait au chevalet)
Oil on canvas. 65.5 x 54.5 cm
[Wildenstein 2001 n. 165]
Kimbell Art Museum, Fort Worth, Texas

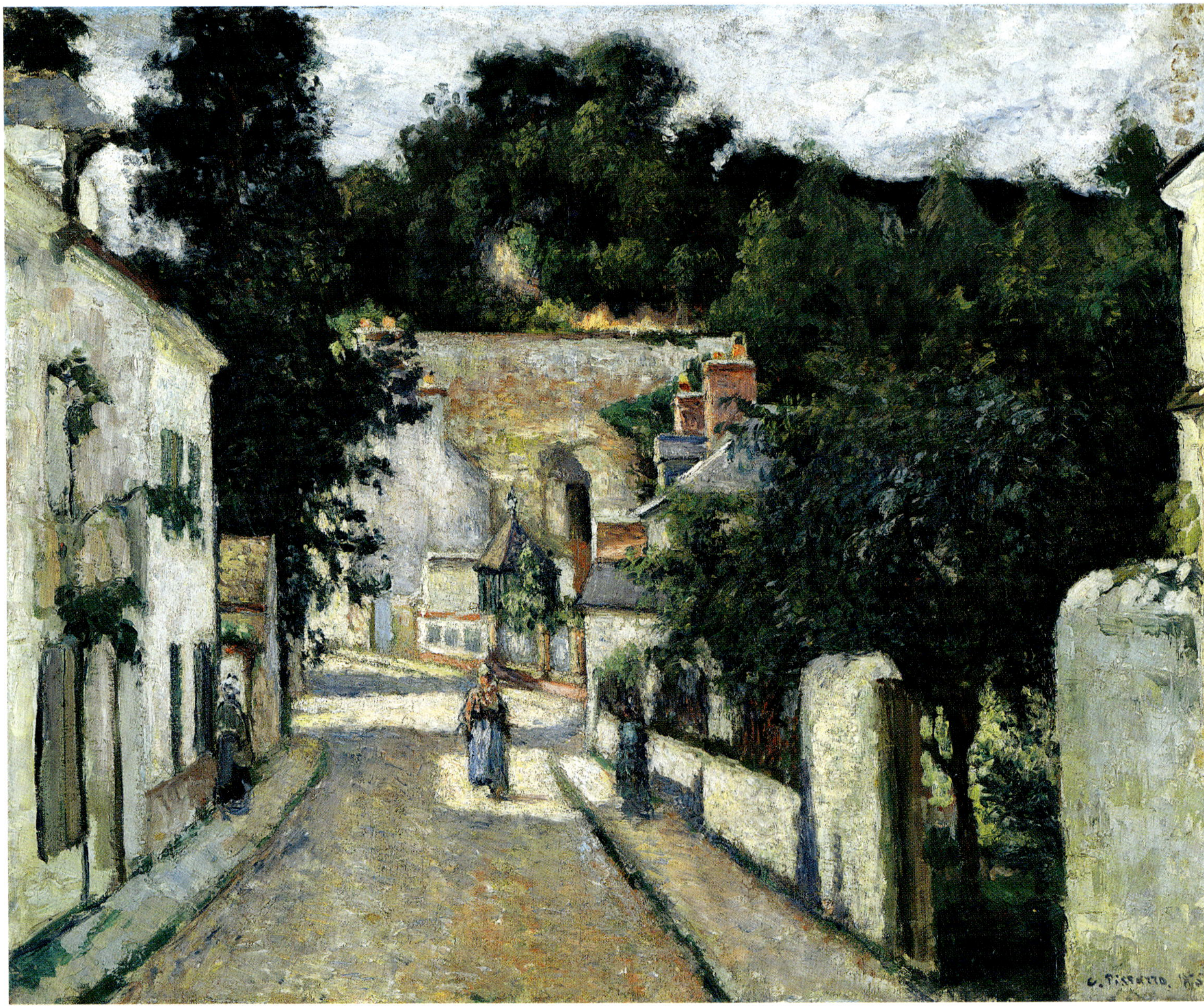

3. Camille Pissarro
Rue de l'Hermitage, in Pontoise, 1875
(Rue de l'Hermitage, à Pontoise)
Oil on canvas. 58.4 x 69.9 cm
[Pissarro/Venturi n. 305]
National Gallery of Canada, Ottawa. Purchased 1946

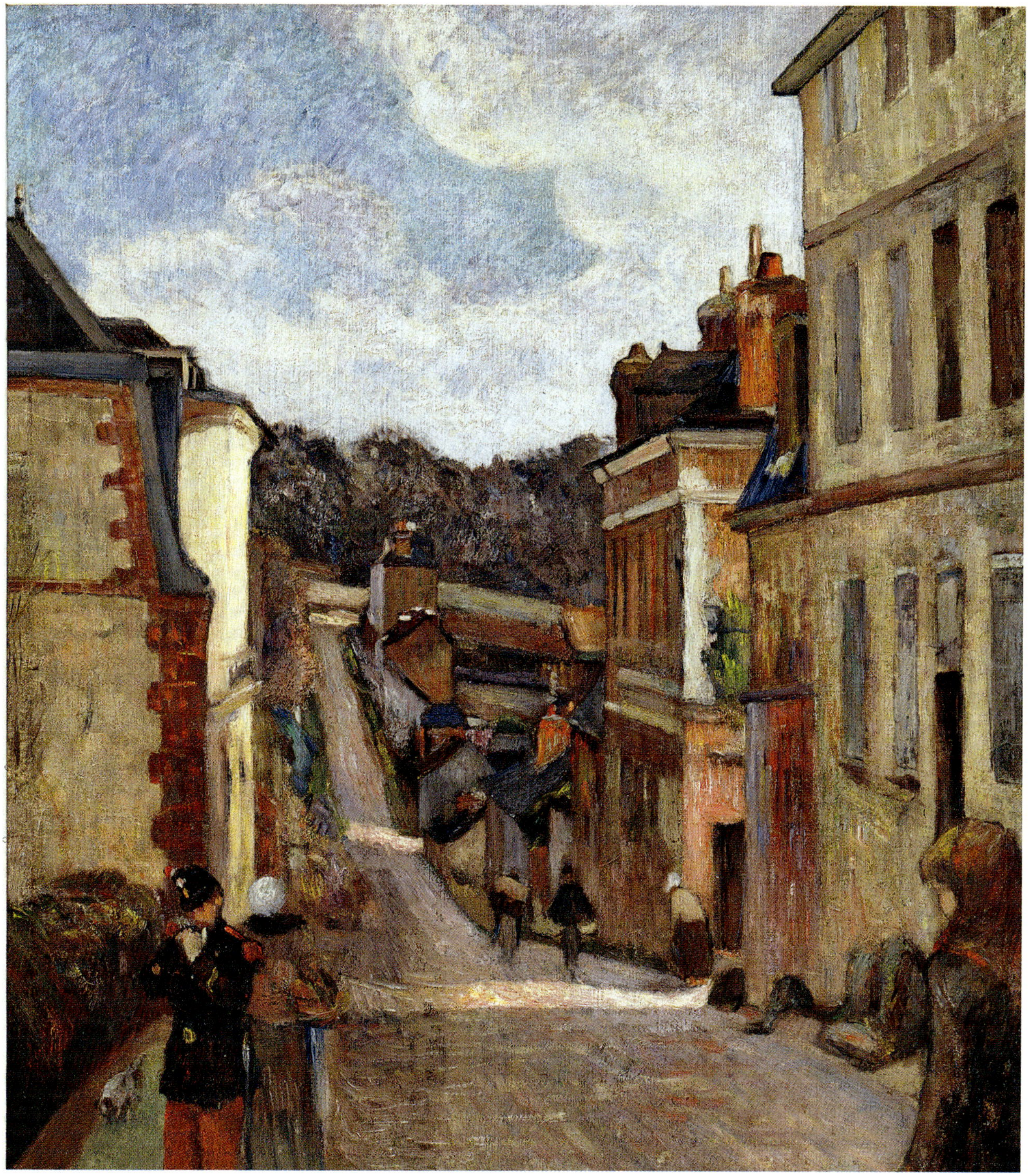

4. Paul Gauguin
Rue Jouvenet in Rouen, 1884
(La rue Jouvenet à Rouen)
Oil on canvas. 55 x 48.5 cm
[Wildenstein 2001 n. 115]
Carmen Thyssen-Bornemisza Collection
on loan at the Museo Thyssen-Bornemisza, Madrid

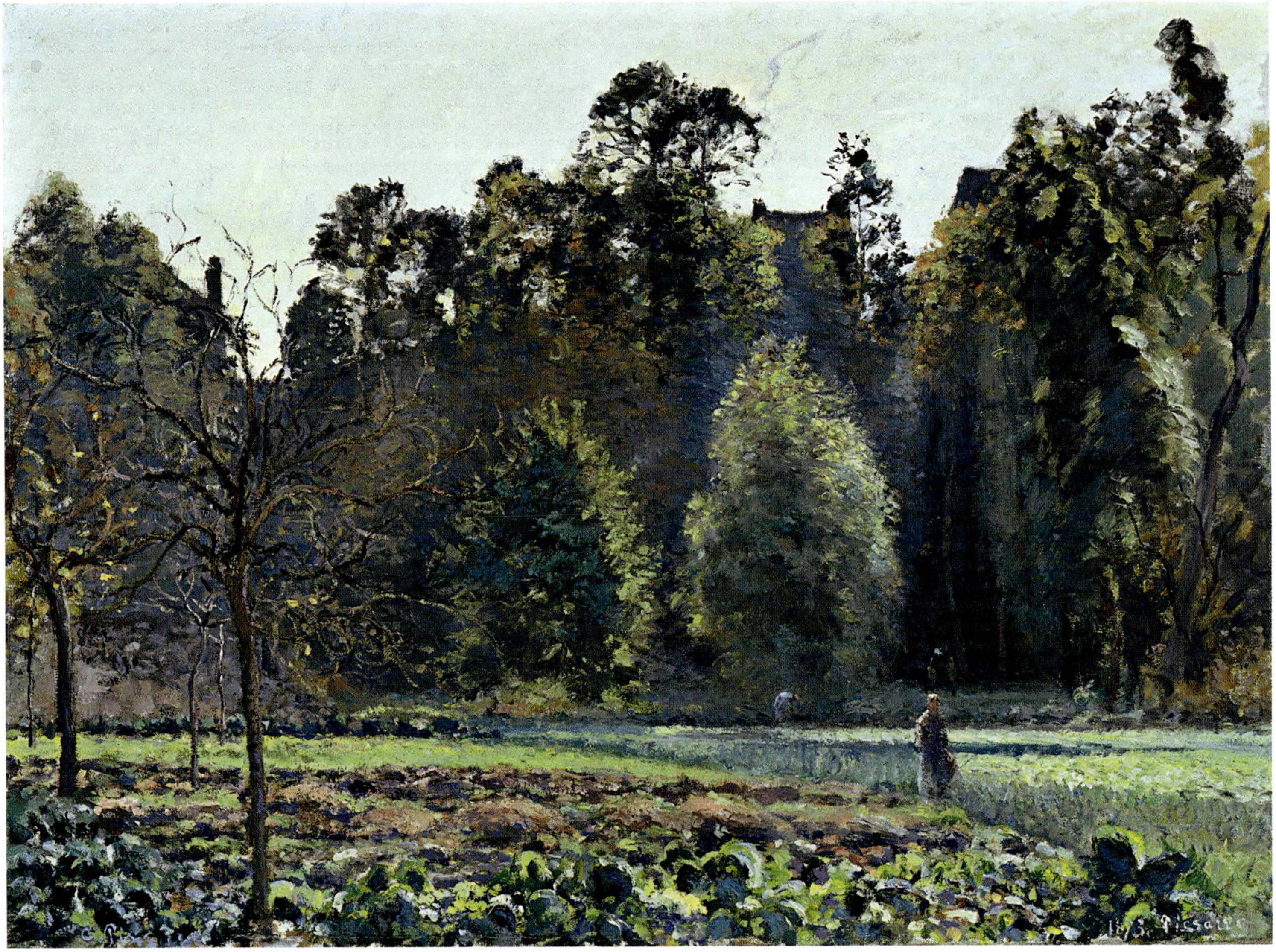

5. Camille Pissarro
The Cabbage Field, Pontoise, 1873
(Le champ de choux, Pontoise)
Oil on canvas. 60 x 80 cm
[Pissarro/Venturi n. 230]
Carmen Thyssen-Bornemisza Collection
on loan at the Museo Thyssen-Bornemisza, Madrid

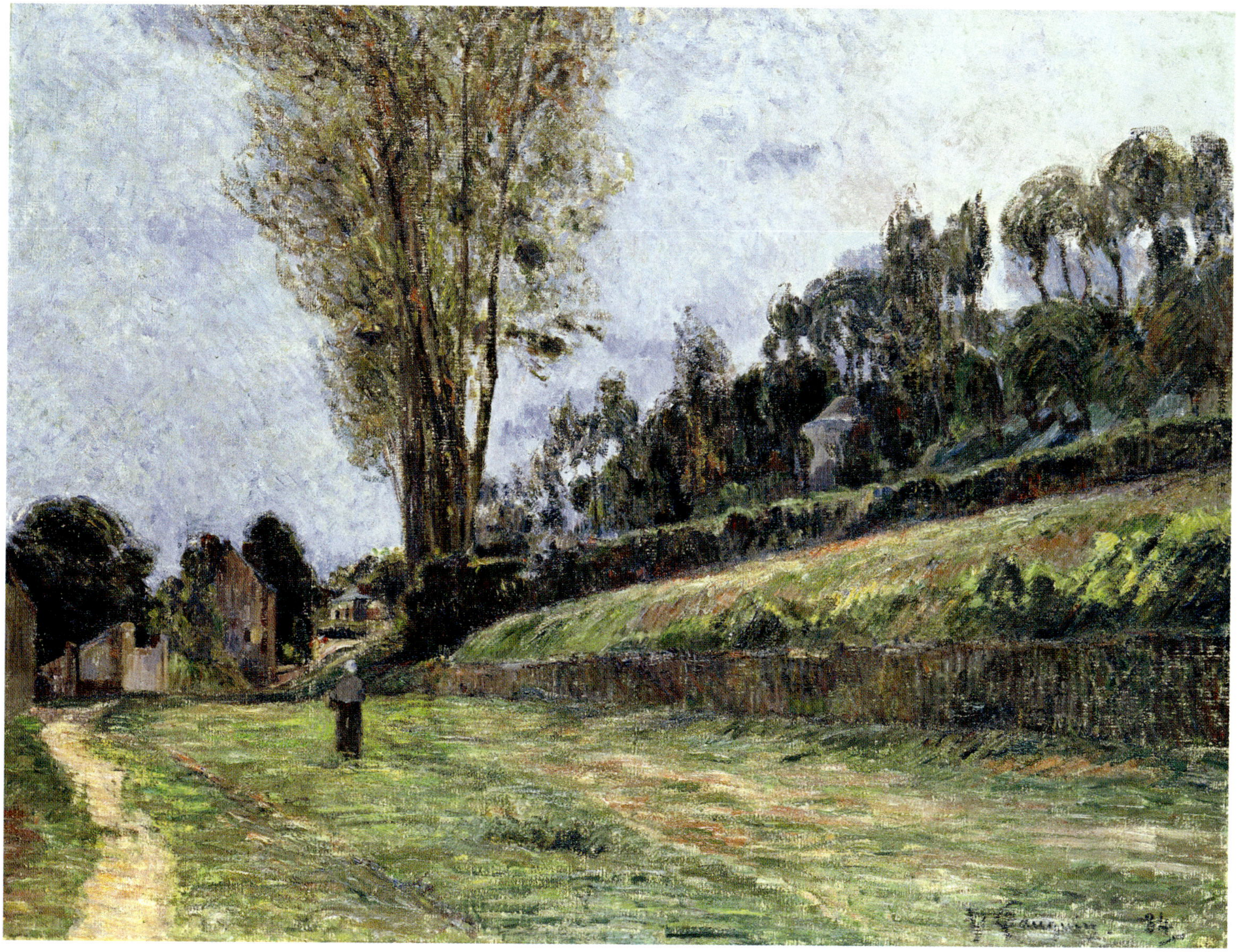

6. Paul Gauguin
A Street in Rouen, 1884
(Une rue à Rouen)
Oil on canvas. 73 x 92 cm
[Wildenstein 2001 n. 122]
Museo Thyssen-Bornemisza, Madrid

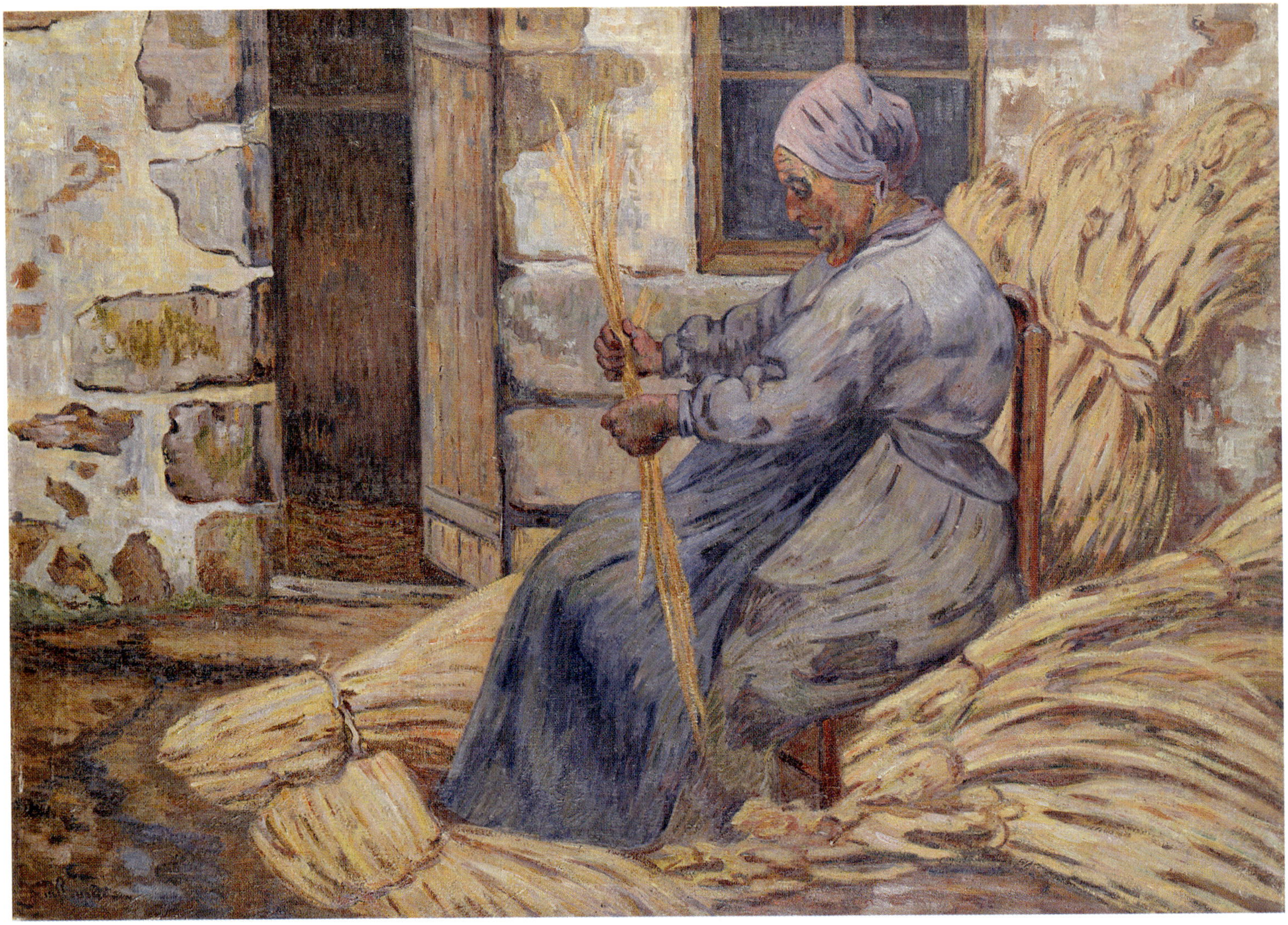

8. Armand Guillaumin
Woman Sheaving in Damiette, 1884
(La vanneuse à Damiette)
Oil on canvas. 81 x 110 cm
Association des Amis du Petit Palais, Geneva

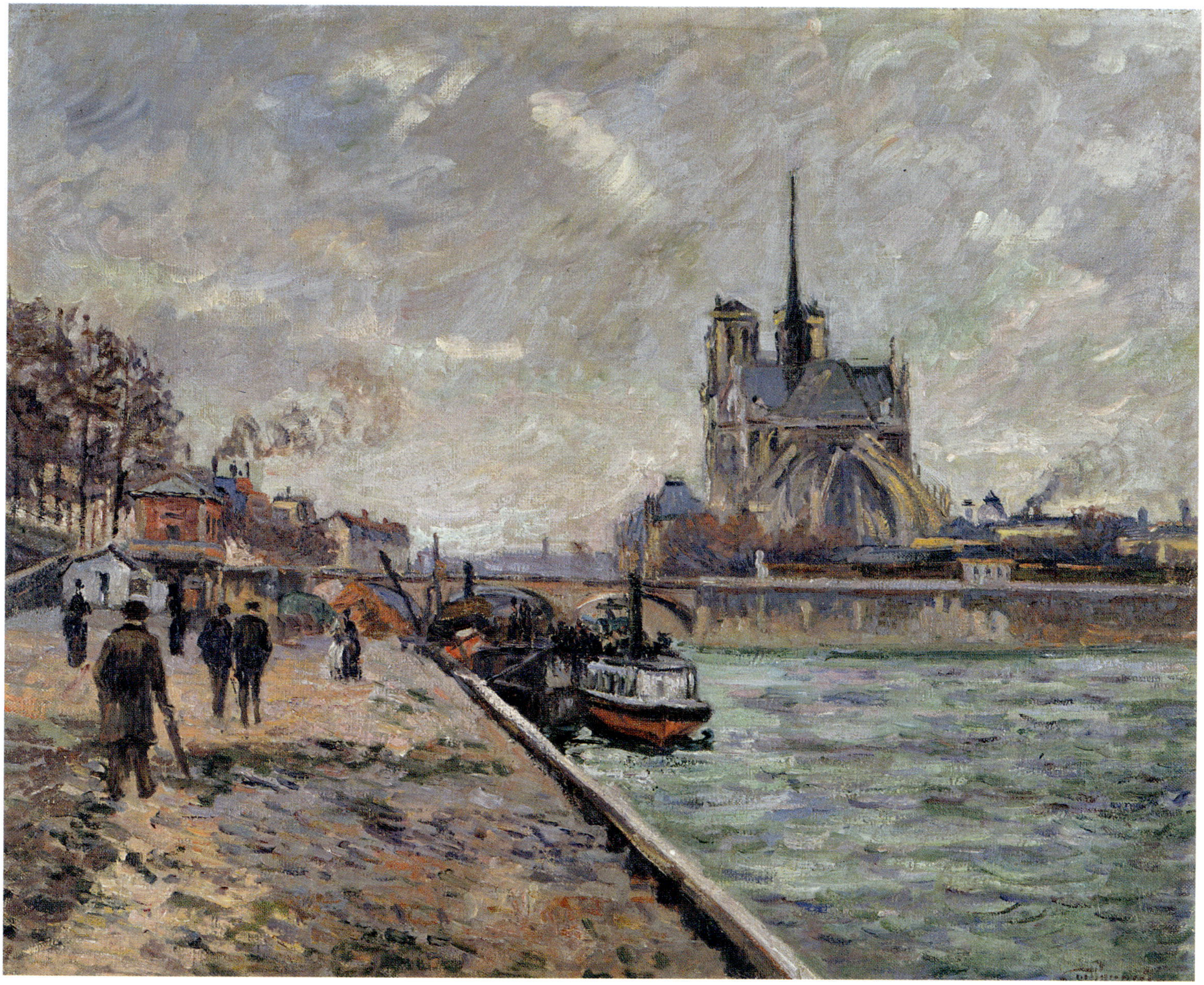

7. Armand Guillaumin
The Bridge of the Archbishop's Palace and the Apse of Notre-Dame, Paris, c. 1880
(Le Pont de l'Archevêché et le chevet de Notre Dame de Paris)
Oil on canvas. 54 x 65 cm
Carmen Thyssen-Bornemisza Collection
on loan at the Museo Thyssen-Bornemisza, Madrid

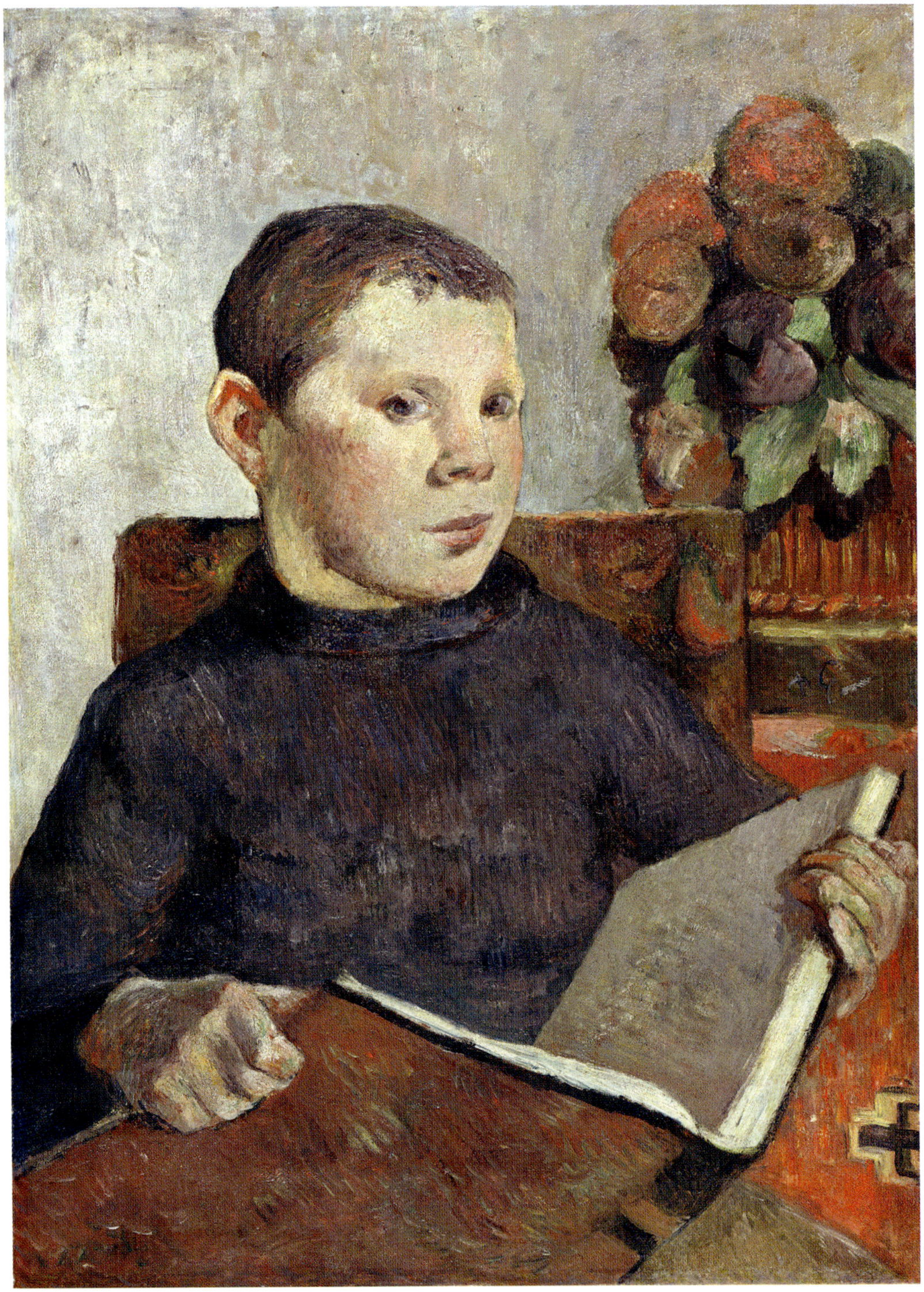

10. Paul Gauguin
Clovis, c.1886
Oil on canvas. 56.5 x 41 cm
[Wildenstein 2001 n. 208]
Collection of The Newark Museum,
Gift of Mrs Lloyd Westcott, 1960

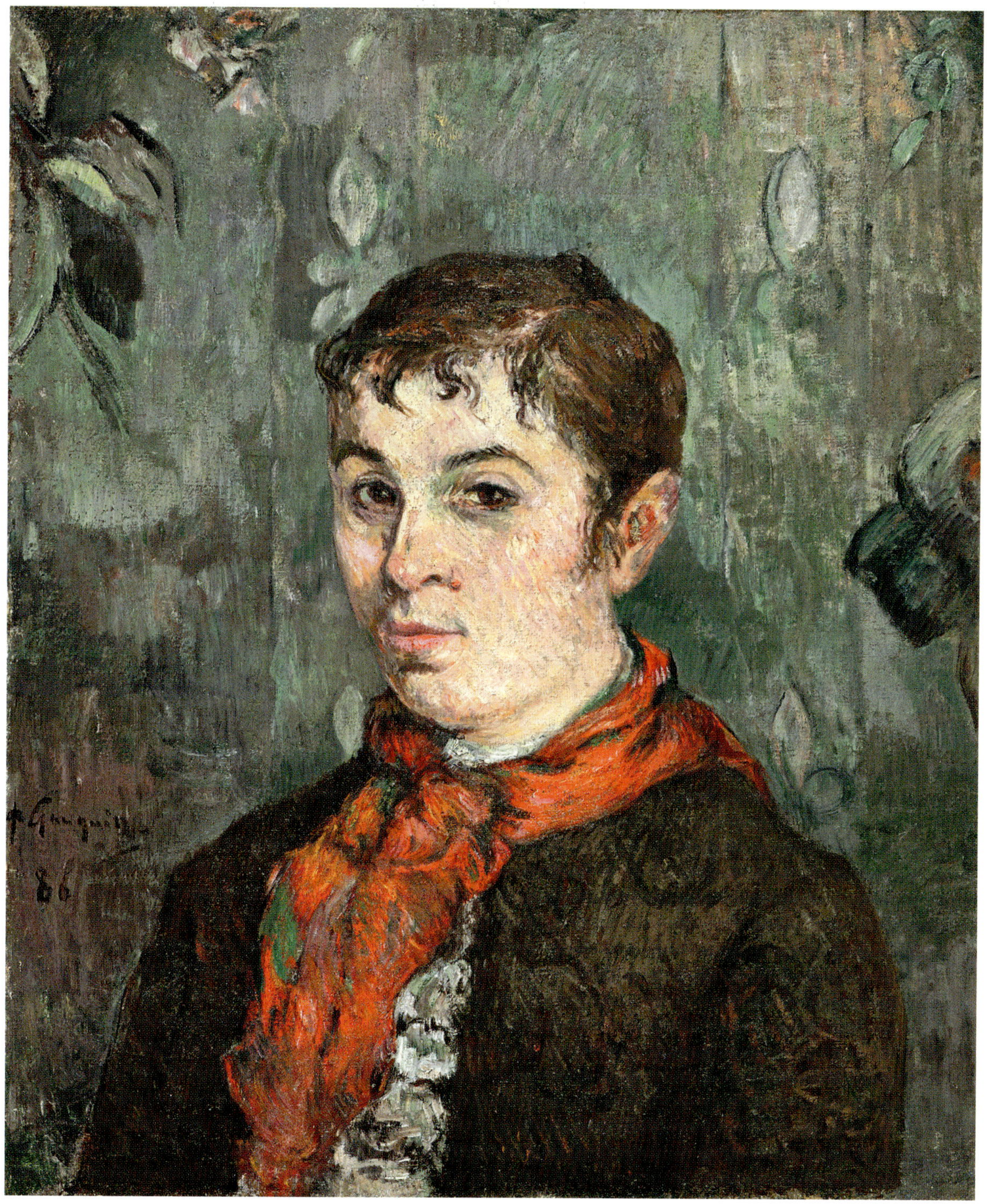

9. Paul Gauguin
The Landlord's Daughter, 1886
(La fille du patron)
Oil on canvas. 55.5 x 46 cm
[Wildenstein 2001 n. 207]
Musée Départemental Maurice Denis 'Le Prieuré',
Saint-Germain-en-Laye

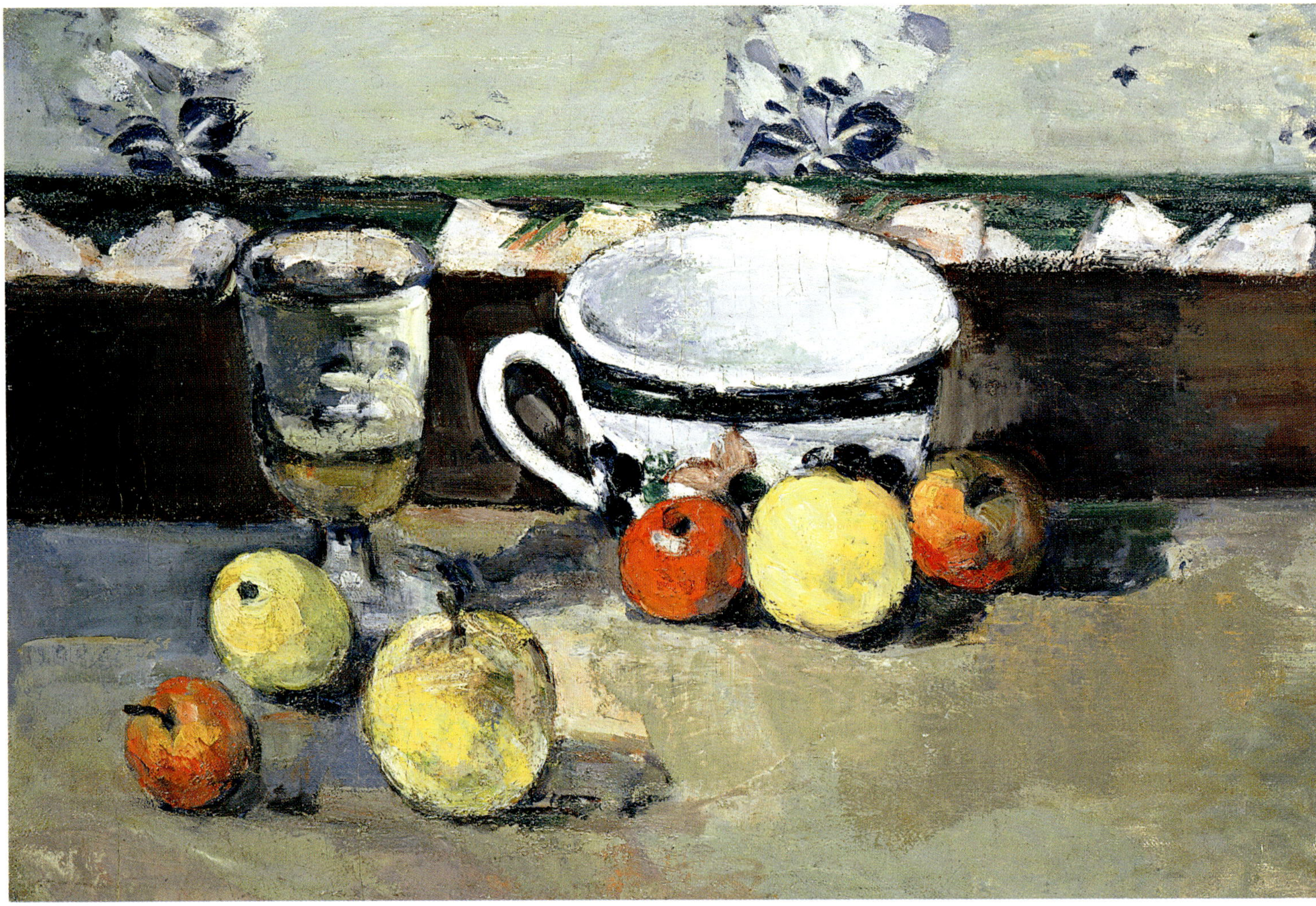

12. Paul Cézanne
Cup, Glass and Fruit II, c. 1877
(Tasse, verre et fruits, II)
Oil on canvas. 34 x 46 cm
[Rewald n. 320]
Jan and Marie-Anne Krugier-Poniatowski Collection

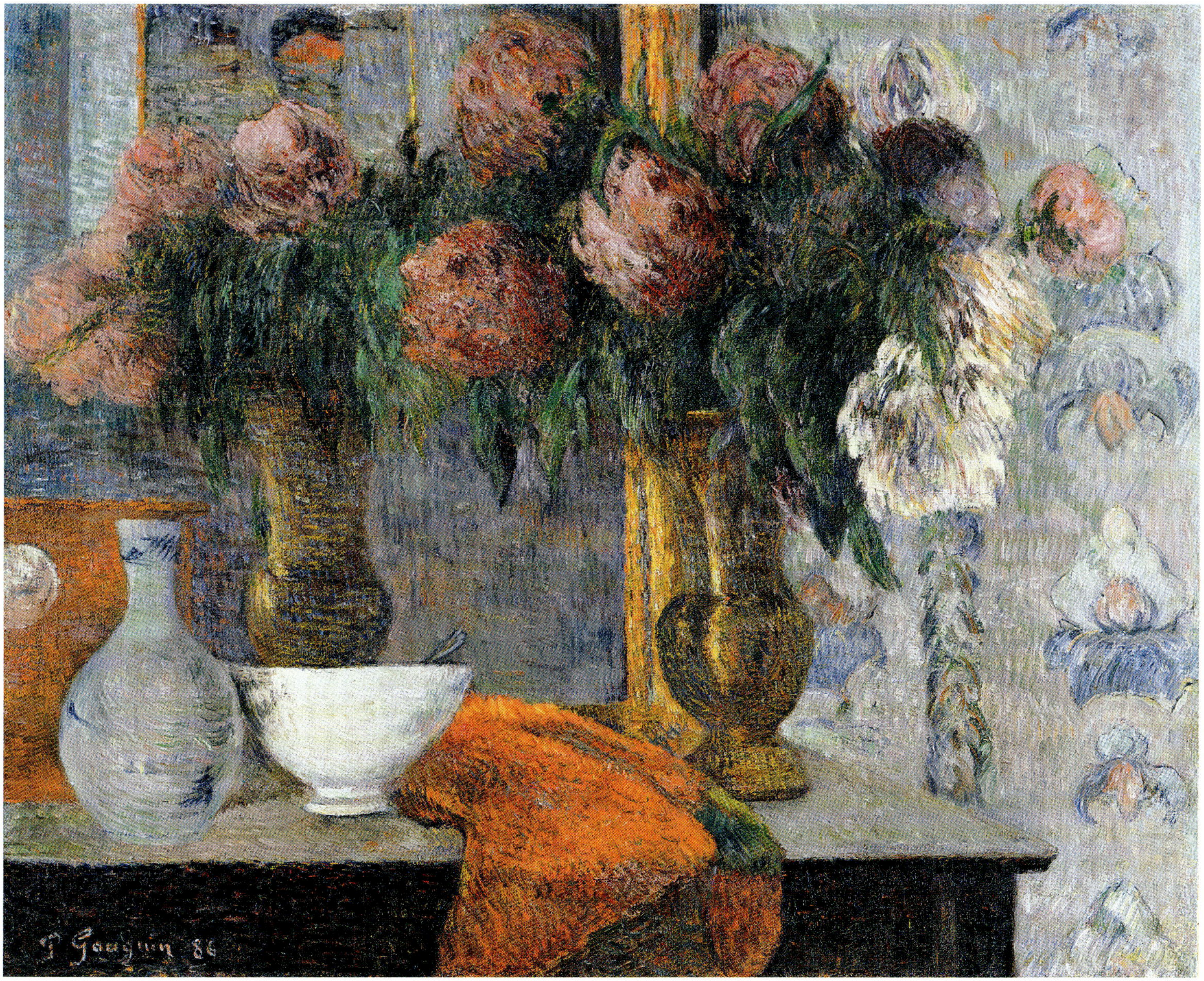

11. Paul Gauguin
The White Bowl, 1886
(Le bol blanc)
Oil on canvas. 59.5 x 72 cm
[Wildenstein 1964 n. 211]
Kunsthaus Zürich

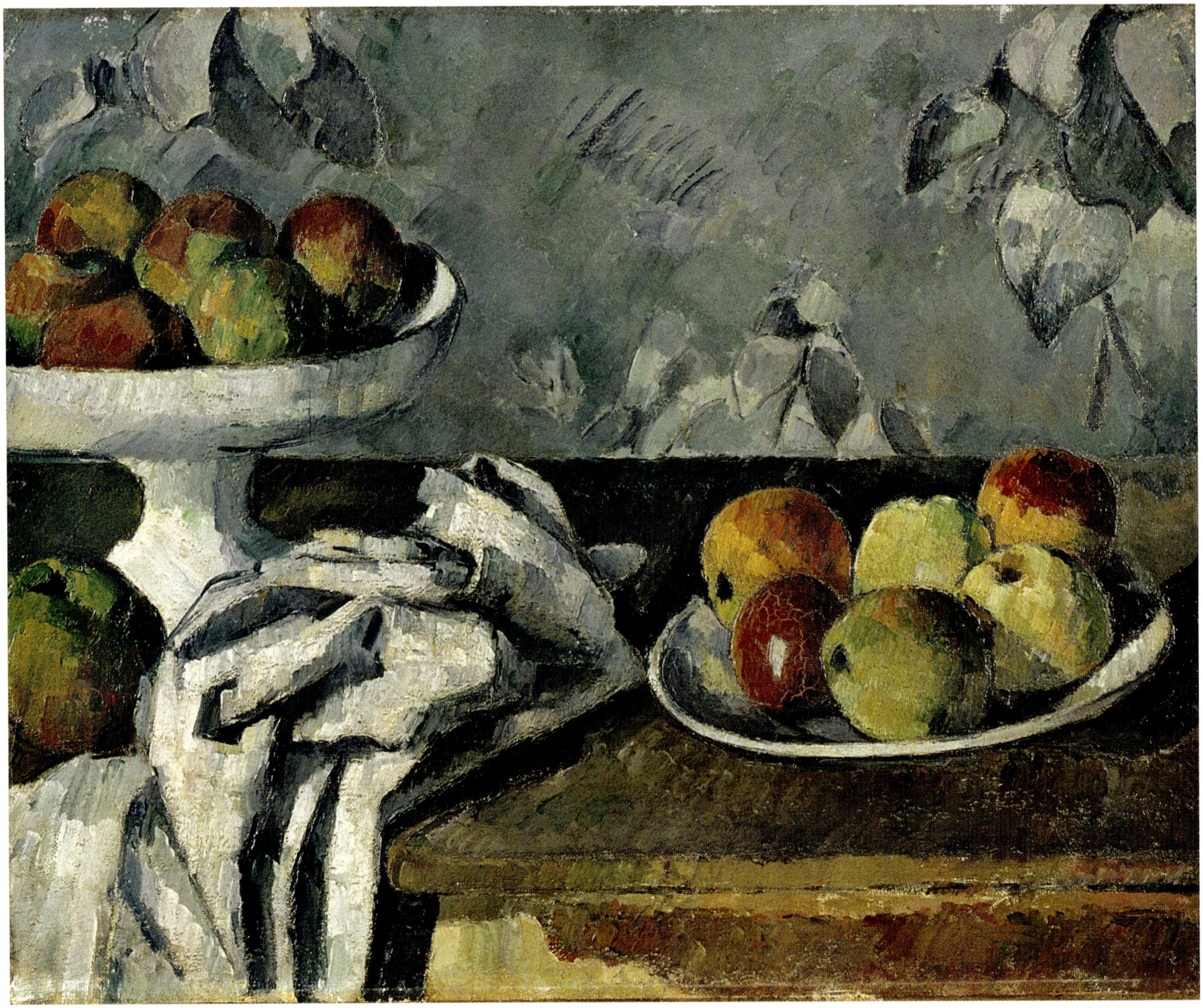

13. Paul Cézanne
Fruit Bowl, Plate and Apples, 1879–1880
(Compotier, assiette et pommes)
Oil on canvas. 43.5 x 54 cm
[Rewald n. 419]
Ny Carlsberg Glyptotek, Copenhagen

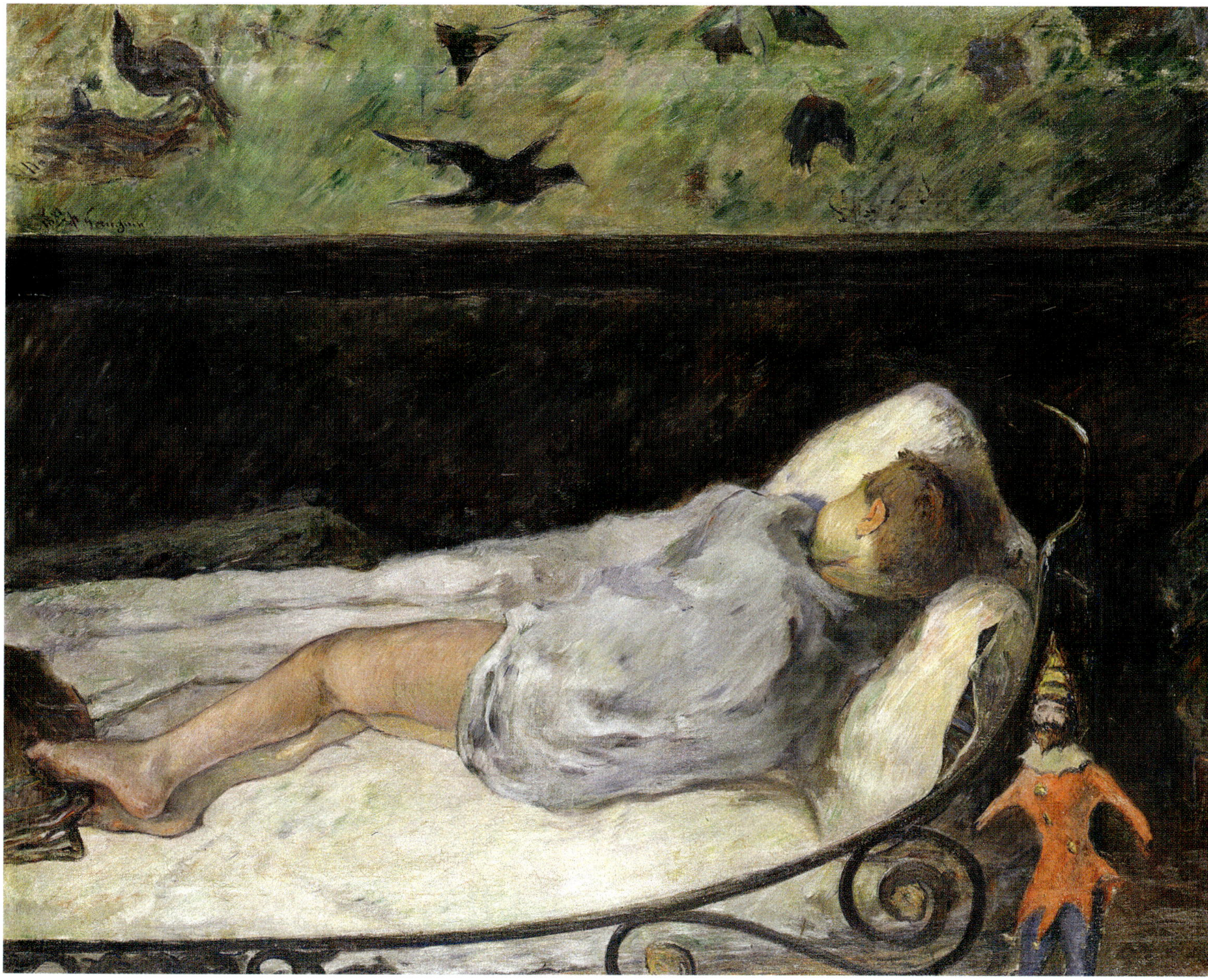

14. Paul Gauguin
The Little One is Dreaming, 1881
(La petite rêve)
Oil on canvas. 59.5 x 74.5 cm
[Wildenstein 2001 n. 75]
Ordrupgaard, Copenhagen

15. Paul Gauguin
Lilacs, 1885
(Bouquet de lilas)
Oil on canvas. 34.9 x 27 cm
[Wildenstein 2001 n. 168]
Carmen Thyssen-Bornemisza Collection
on loan at the Museo Thyssen-Bornemisza, Madrid

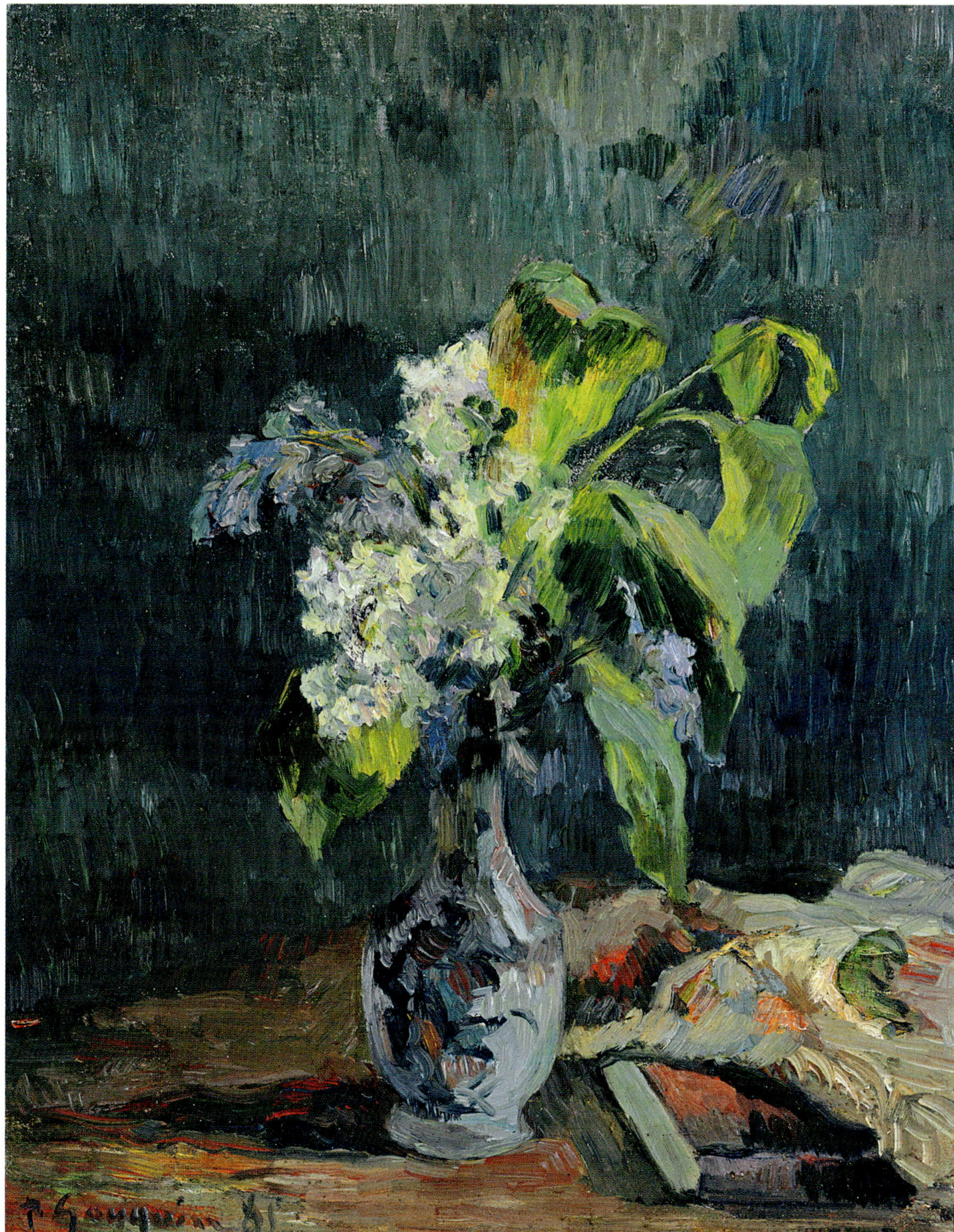
P. Gauguin 85

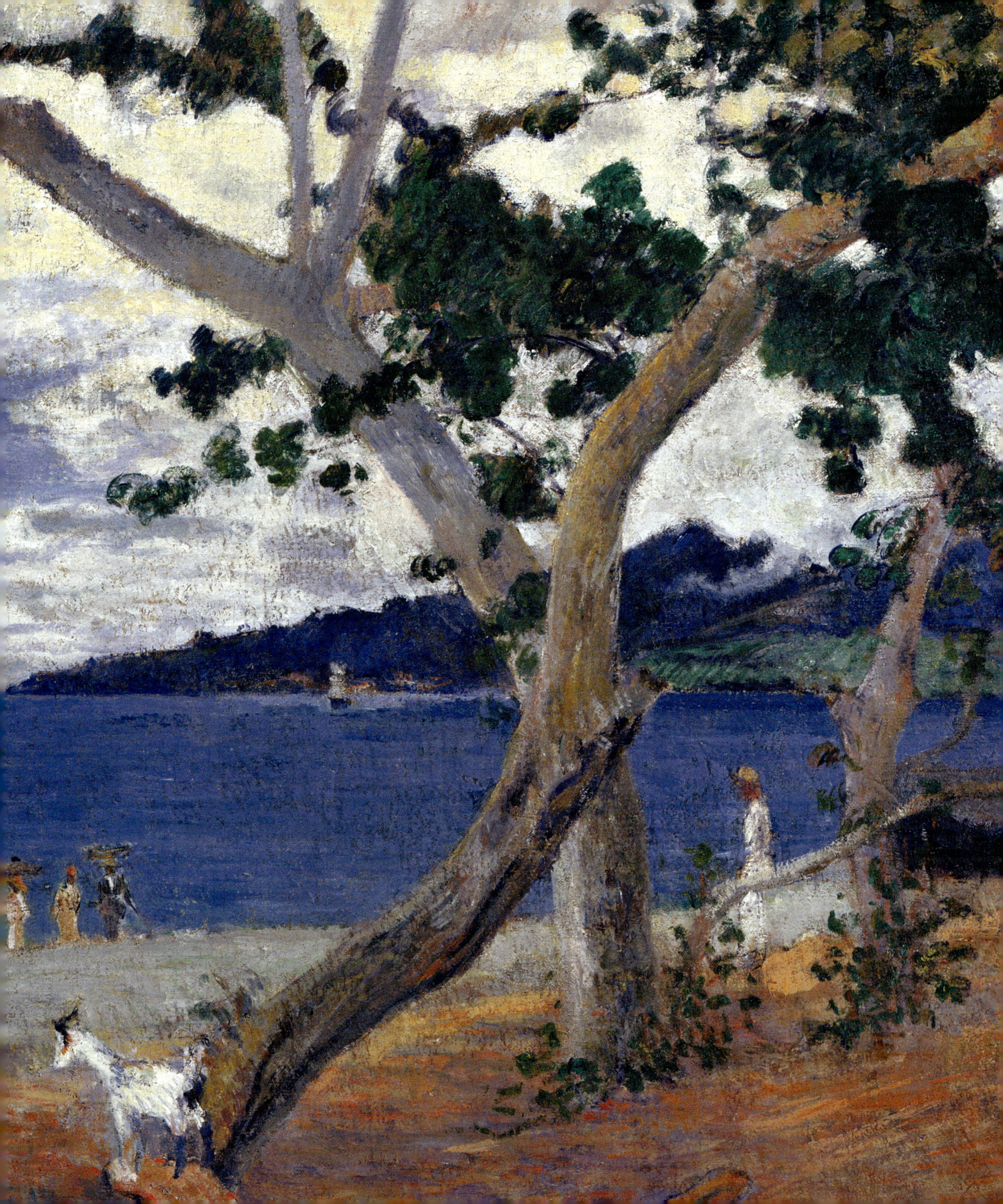

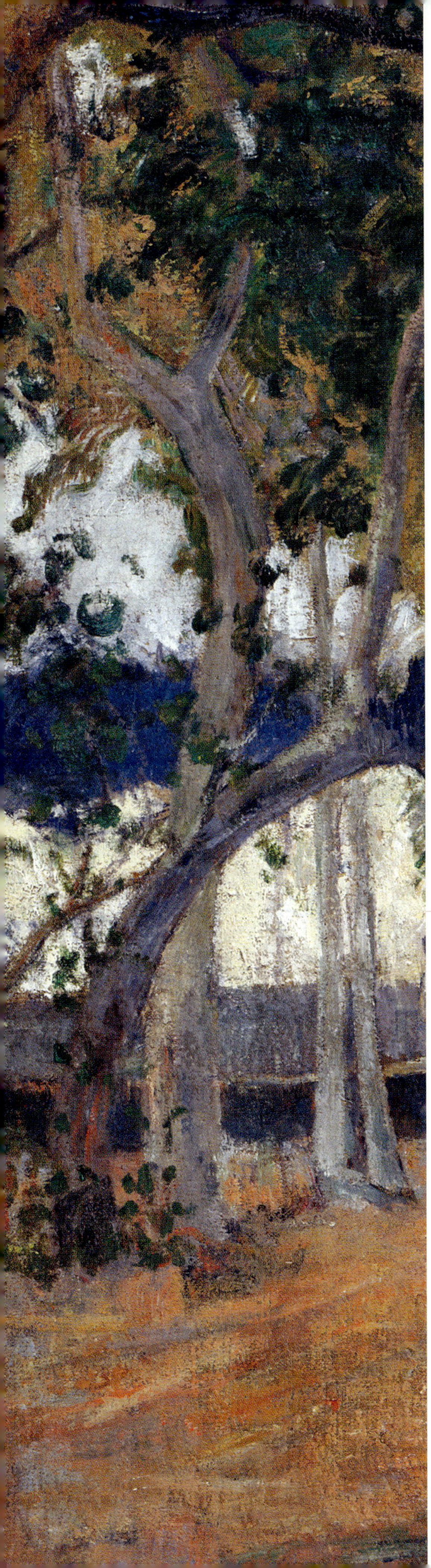

Paul Gauguin
The Inlet of Saint-Pierre seen from the Anse Turin, 1887
(detail)
[cat. 23]

2. Landscape and Arabesque. From Cézanne to Martinique

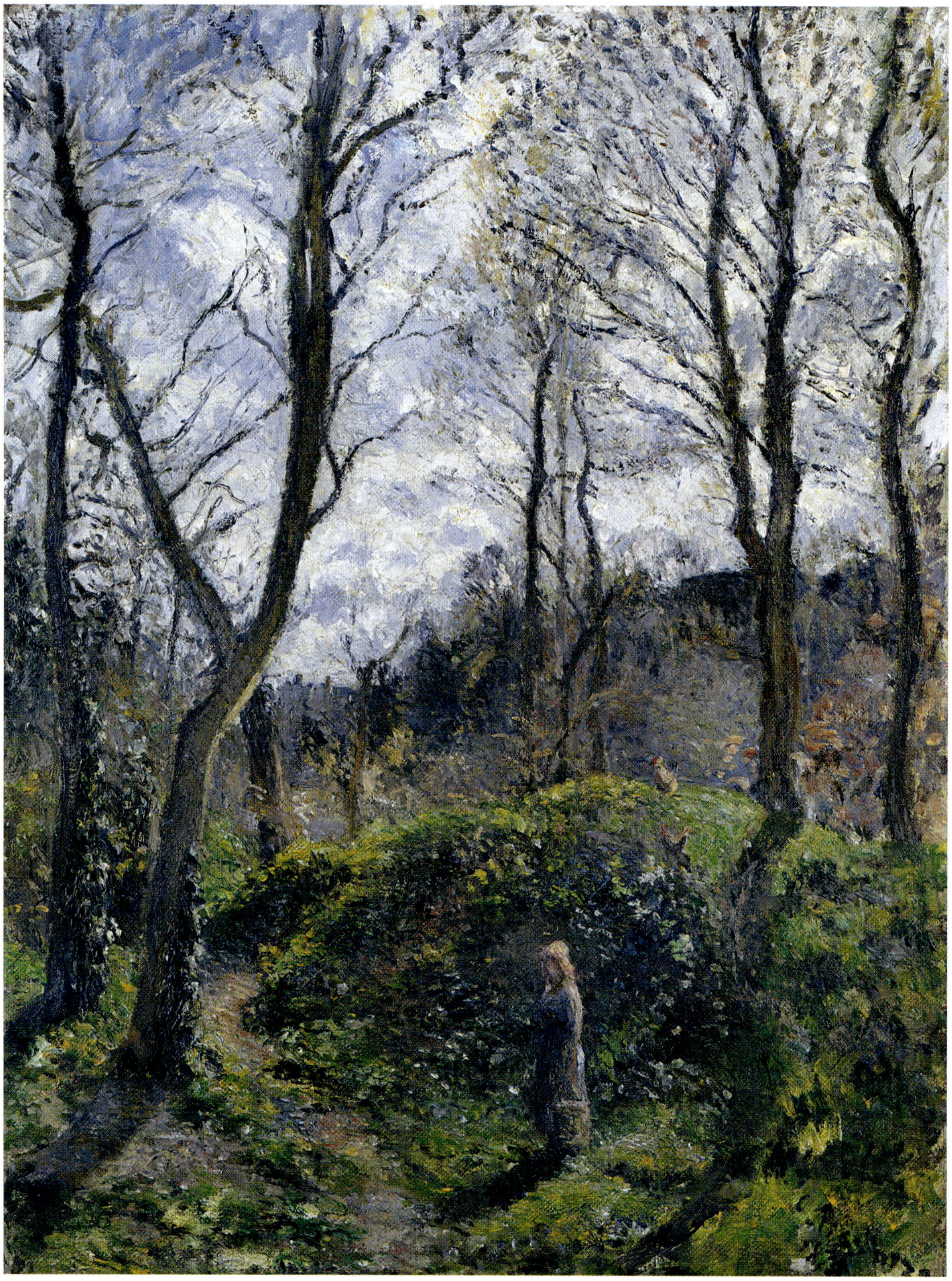

16. Camille Pissarro
Woodland Scene (Spring), 1878
(Paysage avec de grands arbres [Printemps])
Oil on canvas. 73 x 54 cm
[Pissarro/Venturi n. 480]
Ny Carlsberg Glyptotek, Copenhagen

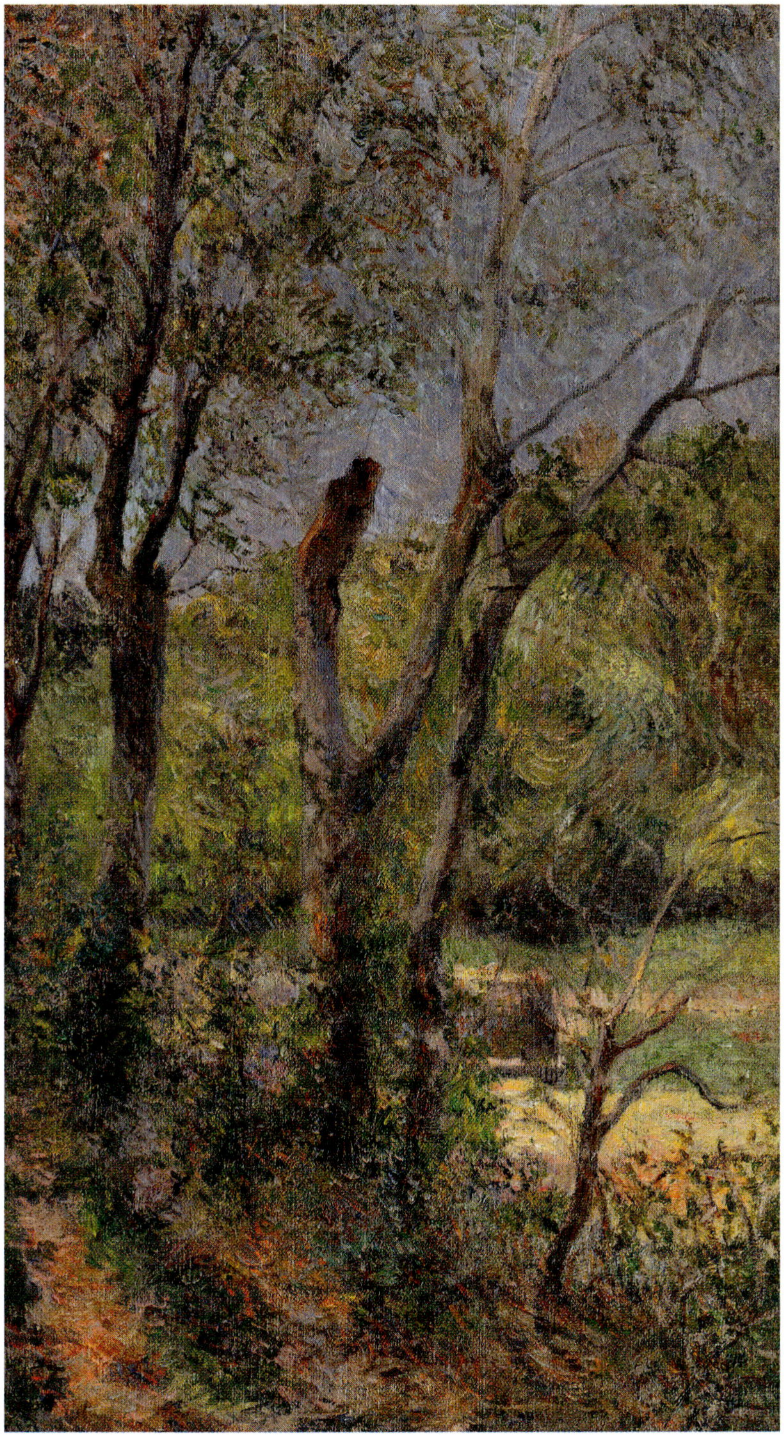

17. Paul Gauguin
The Willows, 1885
(Les saules)
Oil on canvas. 89.5 x 48 cm
[Wildenstein 2001 n. 200]
Private Collection. In deposit at the Musée
Départemental Maurice Denis 'Le Prieuré', St Germain en Laye, c. 1994

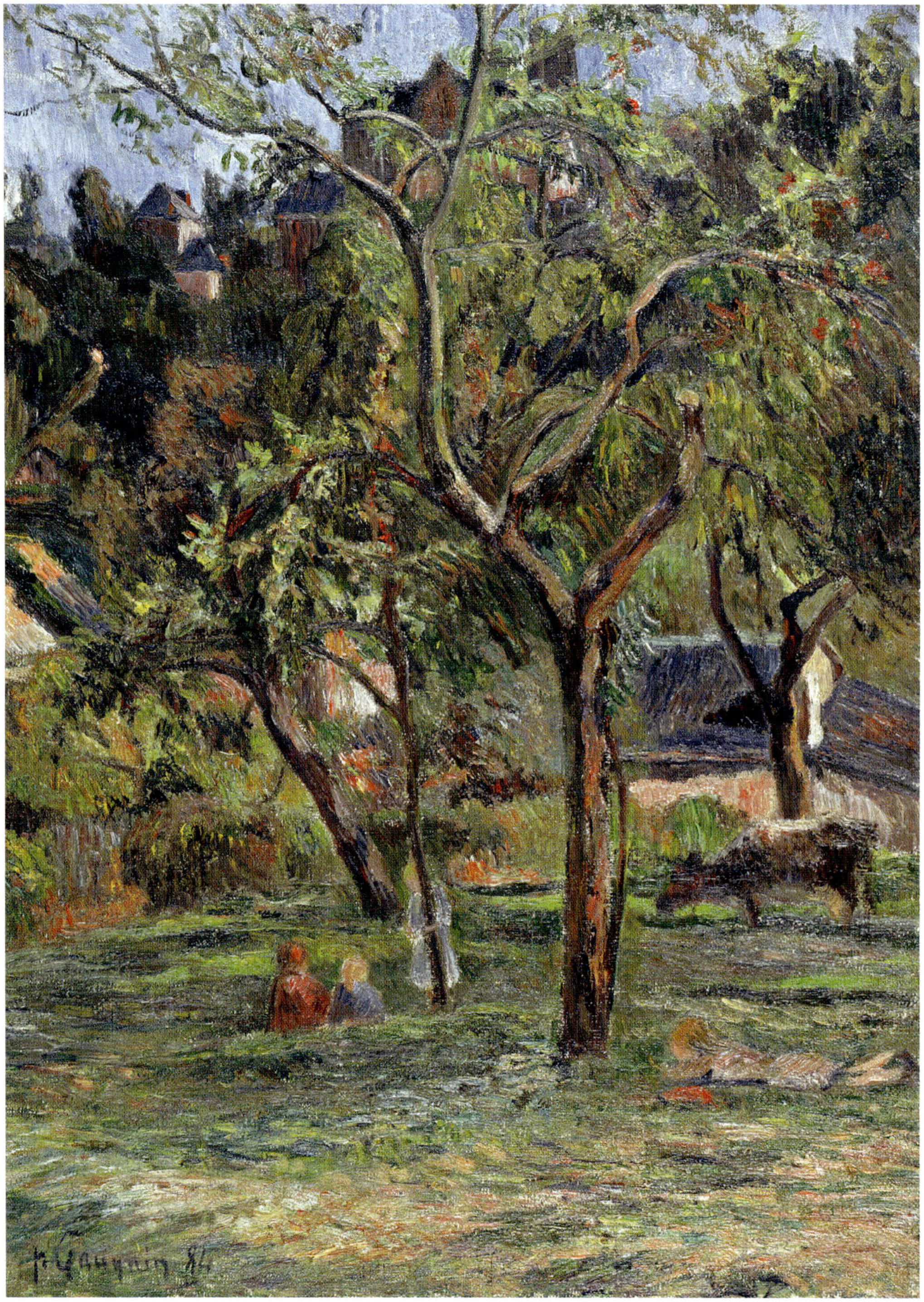

18. Paul Gauguin
An Orchard Under the Church of Bihorel, 1884
(Un verger au-dessous de l´église de Bihorel)
Oil on canvas. 65.5 x 46 cm
[Wildenstein 2001 n. 132]
Carmen Thyssen-Bornemisza Collection
on loan at the Museo Thyssen-Bornemisza, Madrid

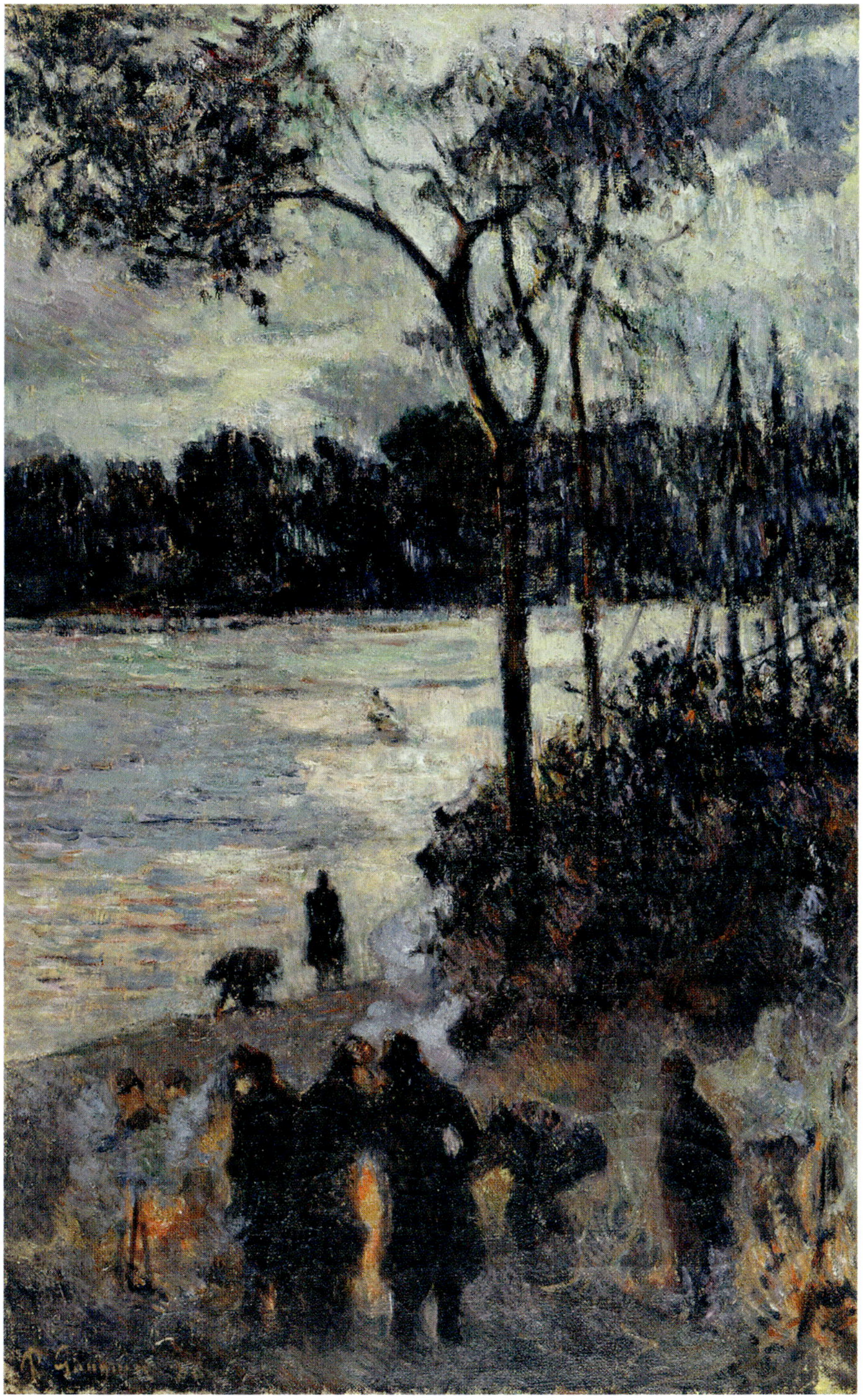

19. Paul Gauguin
The Fire at the River Bank, 1886
(Le feu au bord de l'eau)
Oil on canvas. 60 x 38 cm
[Wildenstein 2001 n. 211]
Carmen Thyssen-Bornemisza Collection
on loan at the Museo Thyssen-Bornemisza, Madrid

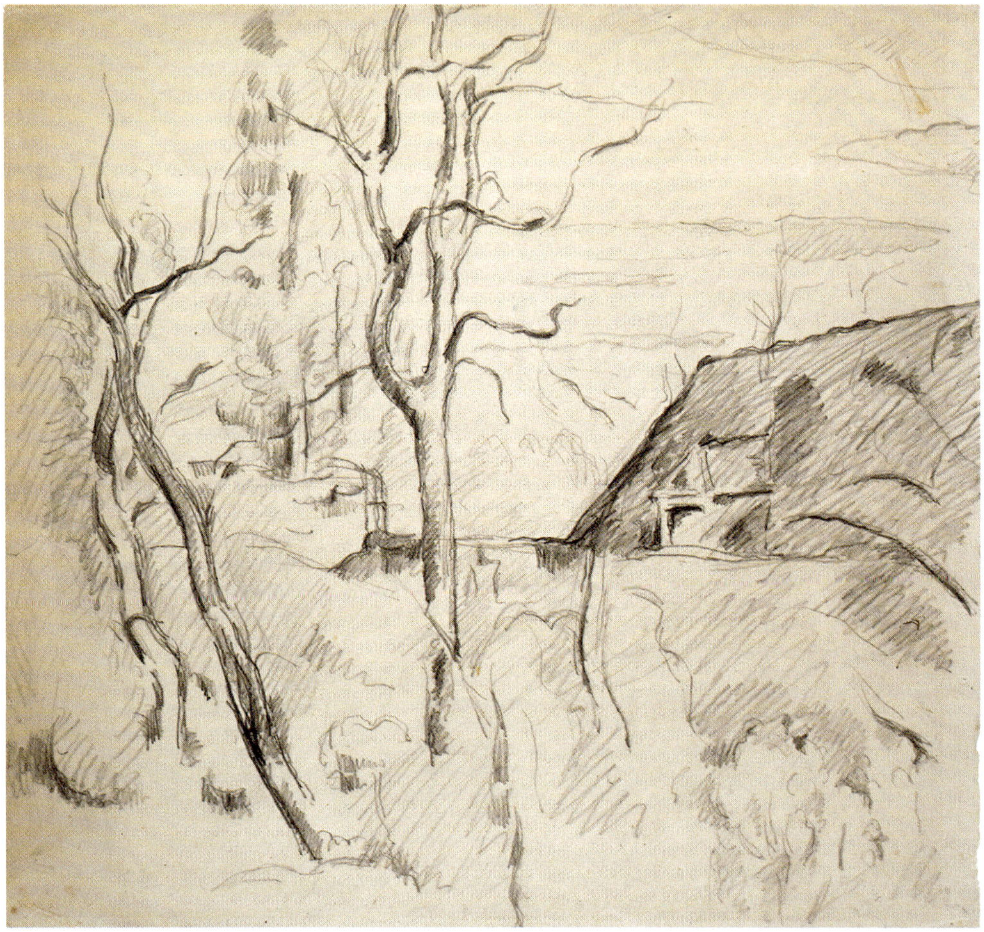

20. Paul Cézanne
Trees and Roofs, 1882–1883
(Arbres et Toits)
Pencil on paper. 32.6 x 34.5 cm
Museum Boijmans Van Beuningen, Rotterdam

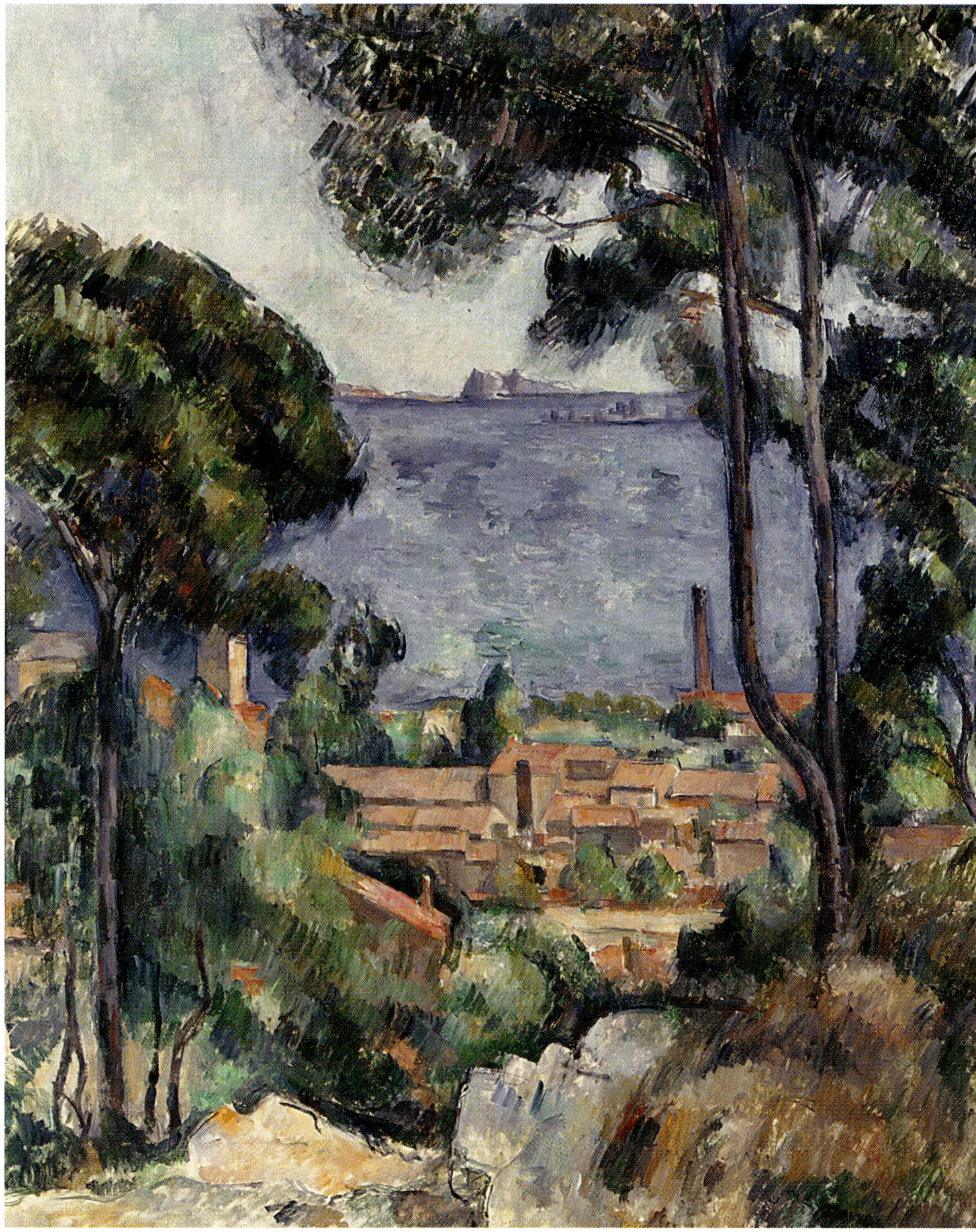

21. Paul Cézanne
View of L'Estaque, 1883–1885
(Vue de L'Estaque)
Oil on canvas. 71 x 57.7 cm [Rewald n. 531]
Private Collection, on loan to the Fitzwilliam Museum, Cambridge

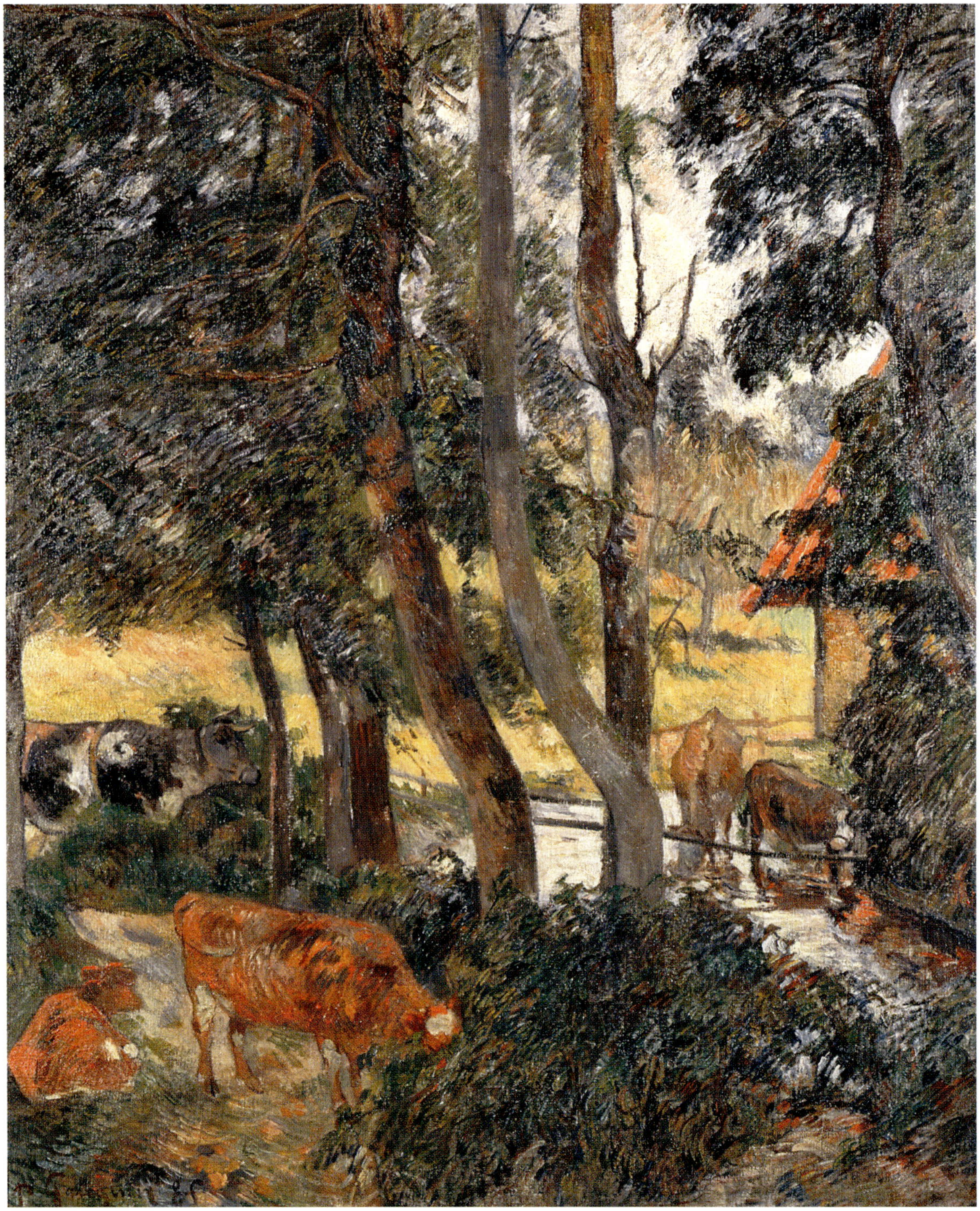

22. Paul Gauguin
Cows at the Watering-place, 1885
(Vaches à l'abreuvoir)
Oil on canvas. 81 x 65 cm
[Wildenstein 2001 n. 192]
Civica Galleria d'Arte Moderna, Raccolta Grassi, Milan

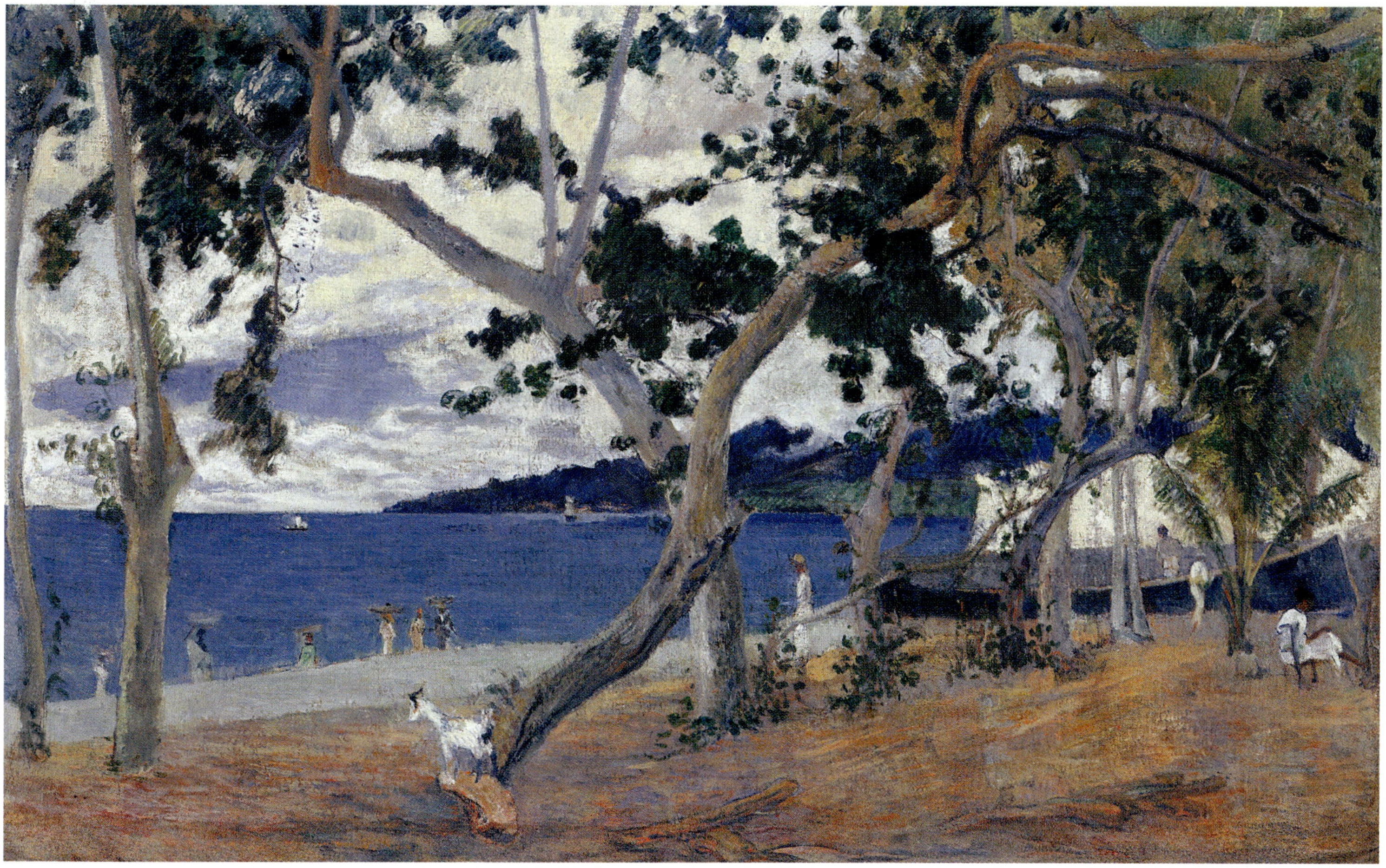

23. Paul Gauguin
The Inlet of Saint-Pierre seen from the Anse Turin, 1887
(La rade de Saint-Pierre vue de l'Anse Turin)
Oil on canvas. 54 x 90 cm
[Wildenstein 2001 n. 242]
Ny Carlsberg Glyptotek, Copenhagen

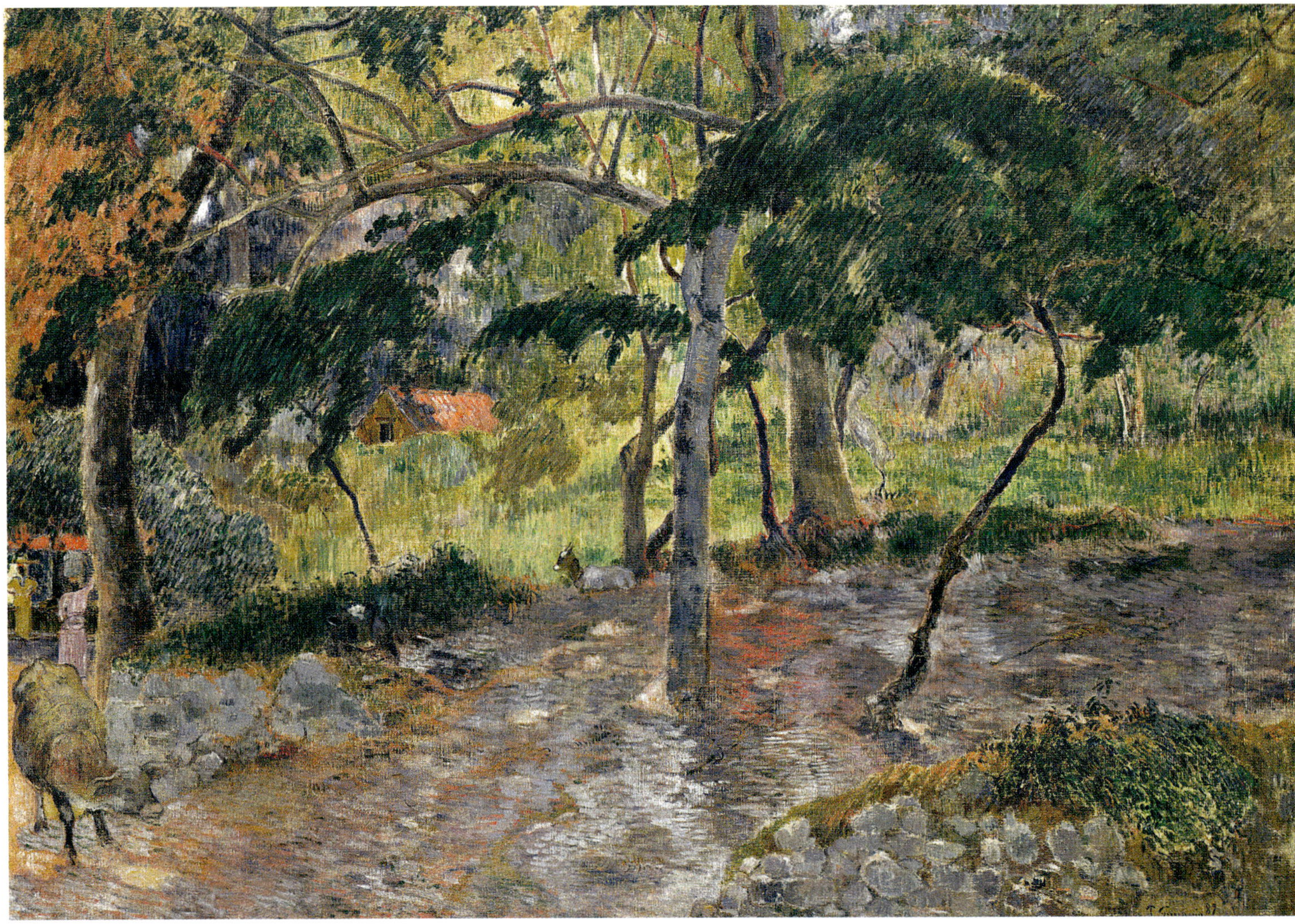

24. Paul Gauguin
River under the Trees, Martinique, 1887
(Cours d'eau sous les arbres, Martinique)
Oil on canvas. 90 x 116 cm
[Wildenstein 2001 n. 246]
Bayerische Staatgemäldesammlungen, Neue Pinakotek, Munich

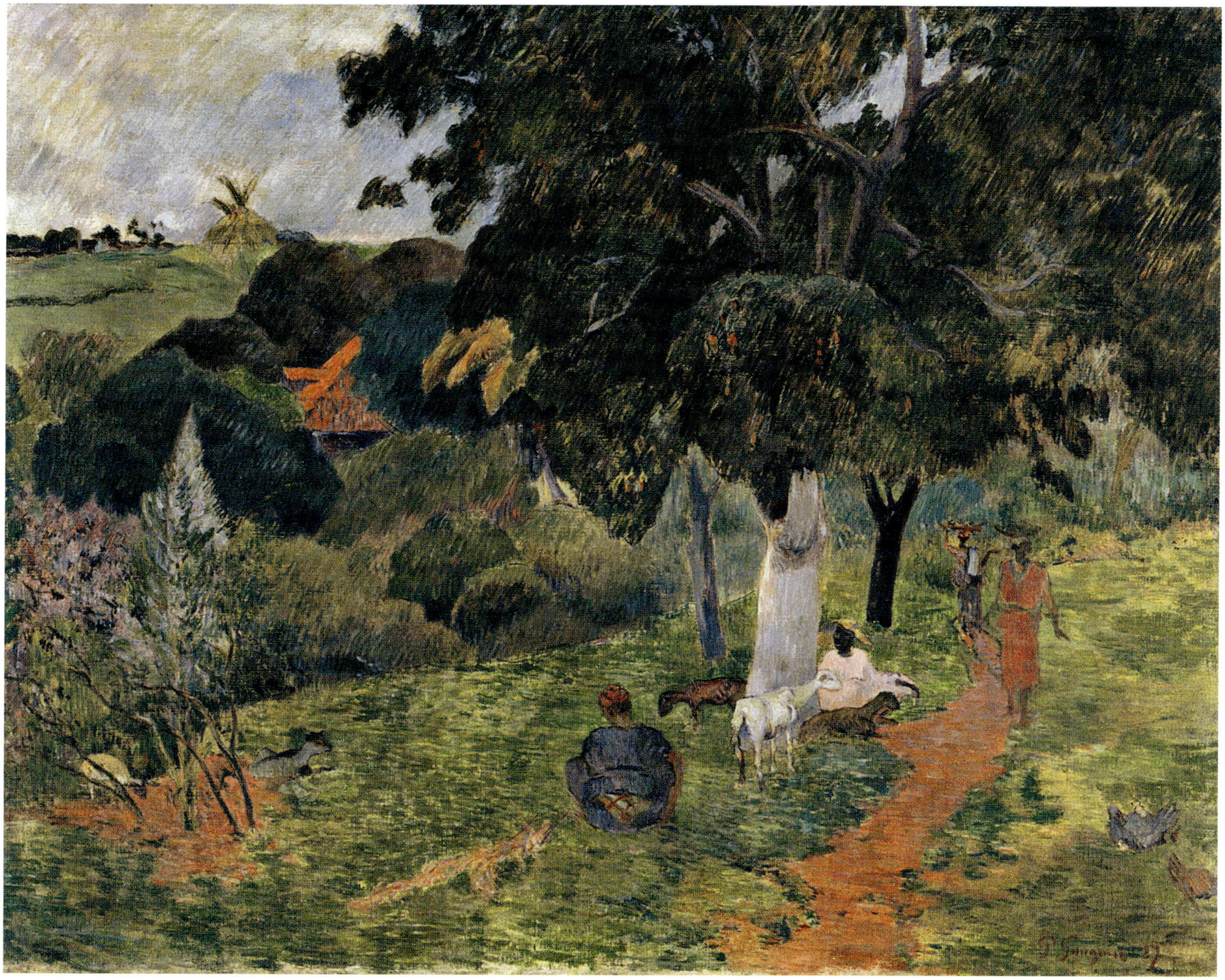

25. Paul Gauguin
Coming and Going, Martinique, 1887
(Allées et Venues. Martinique)
Oil on canvas. 72.5 x 92 cm
[Wildenstein 2001 n. 245]
Carmen Thyssen-Bornemisza Collection
on loan at the Museo Thyssen-Bornemisza, Madrid

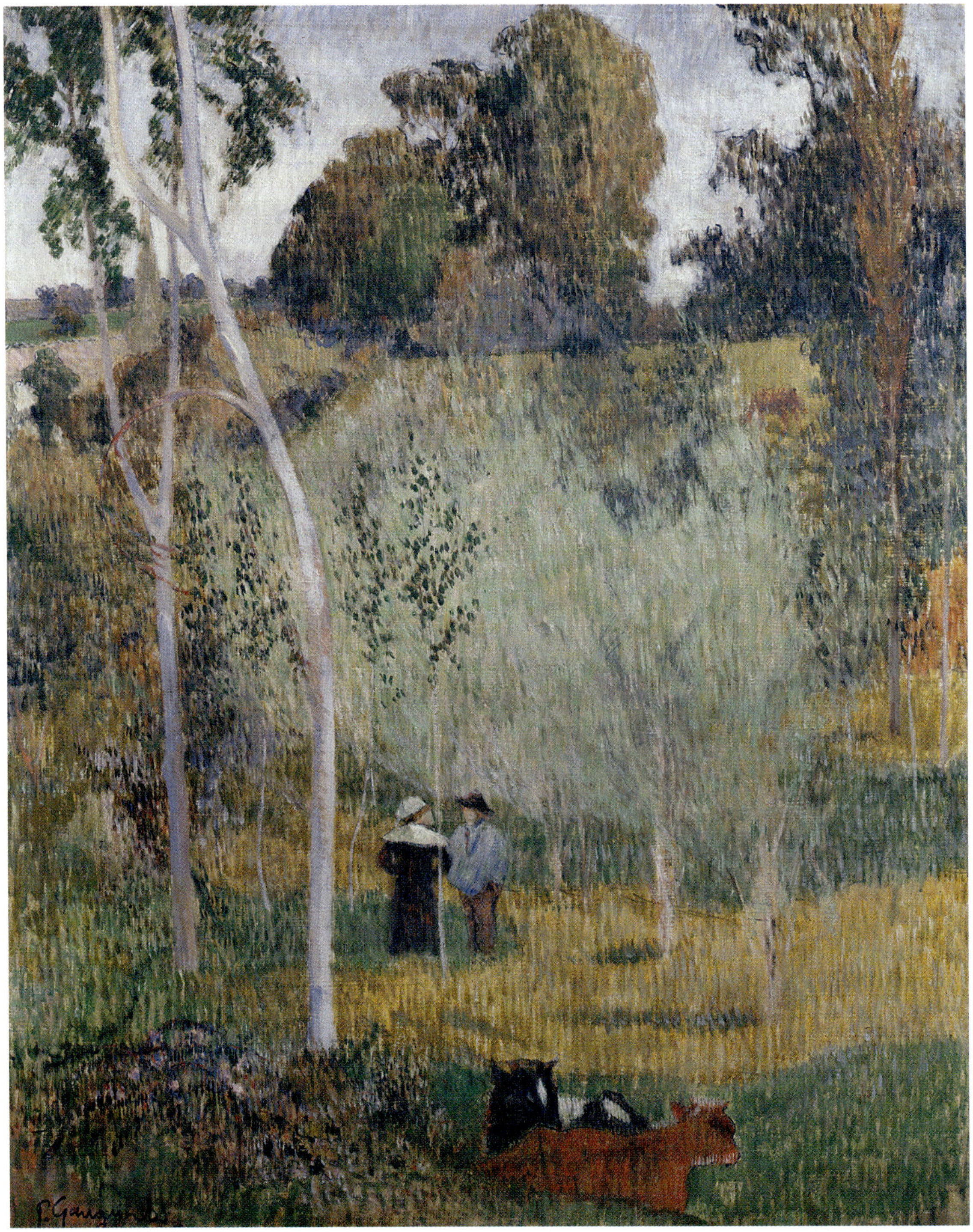

26. Paul Gauguin
Shepherds in a Meadow, 1888
(Berger et bergère dans le pré)
Oil on canvas. 92 x 73 cm
[Wildenstein 2001 n. 280]
Musées royaux des Beaux-Arts de Belgique, Brussels
Inv. 5092

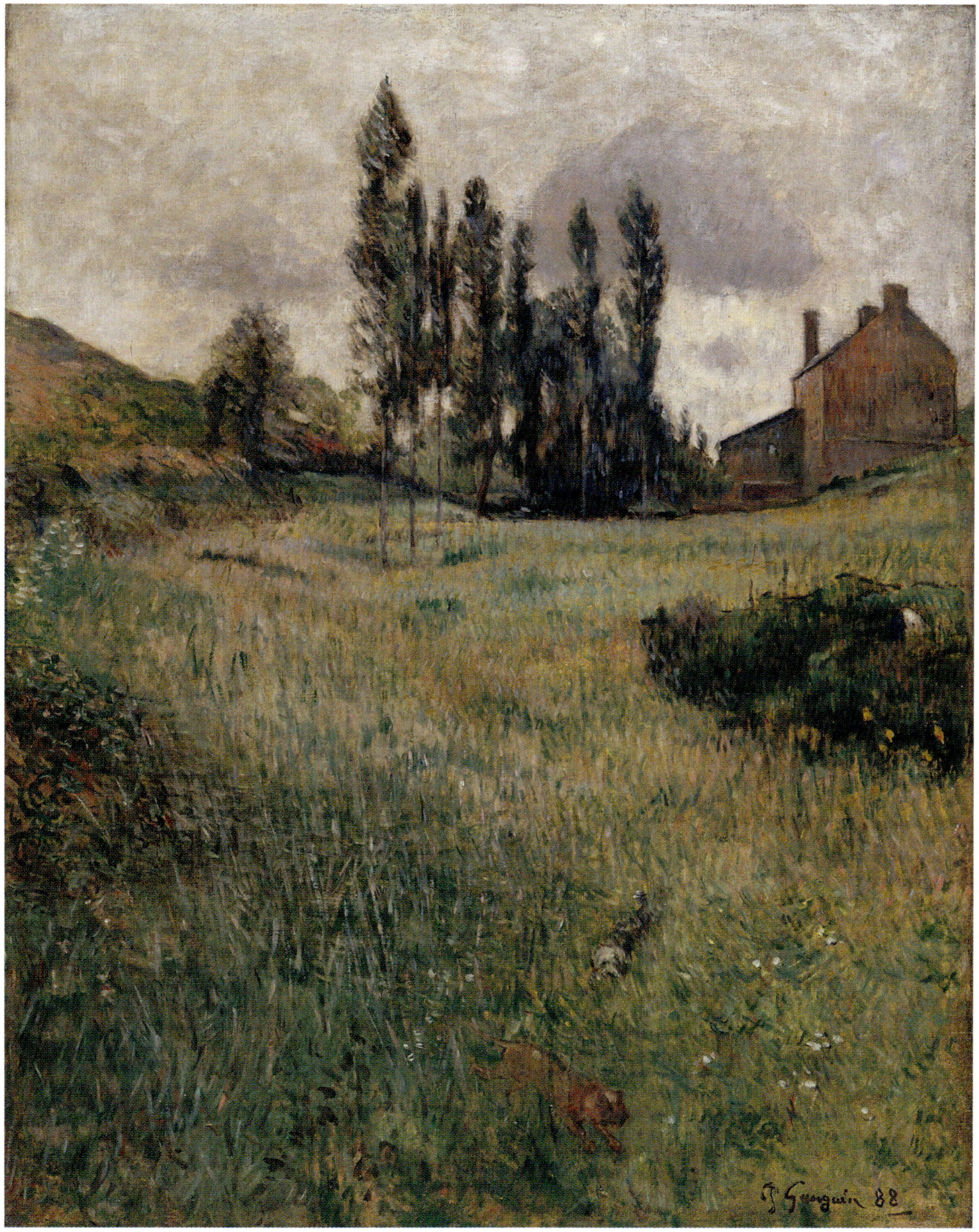

27. Paul Gauguin
Dogs Running in a Meadow, 1888
(Course de chiens dans la prairie)
Oil on canvas. 92 x 72.5 cm
[Wildenstein 2001 n. 282]
Carmen Thyssen-Bornemisza Collection
on loan at the Museo Thyssen-Bornemisza, Madrid

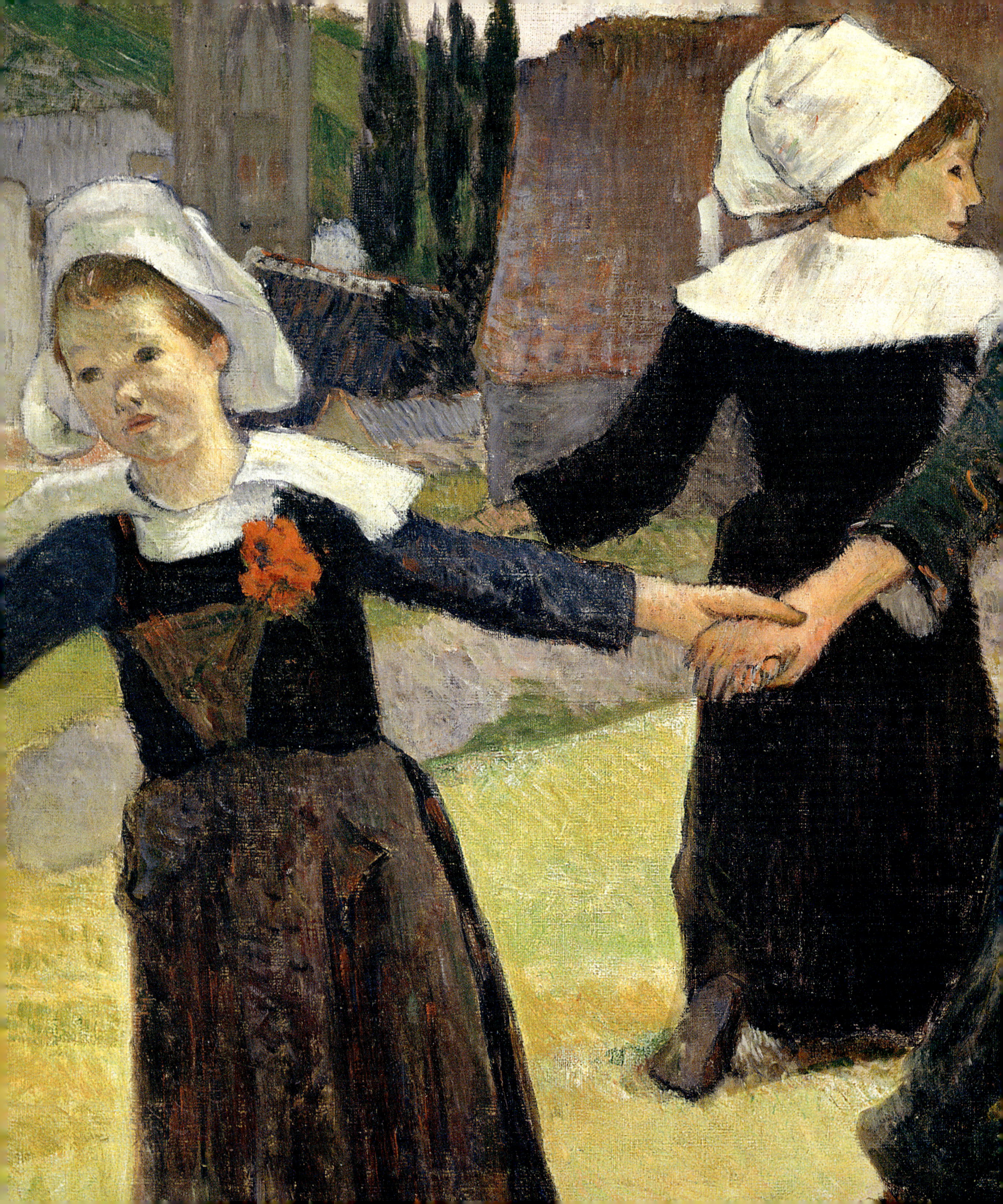

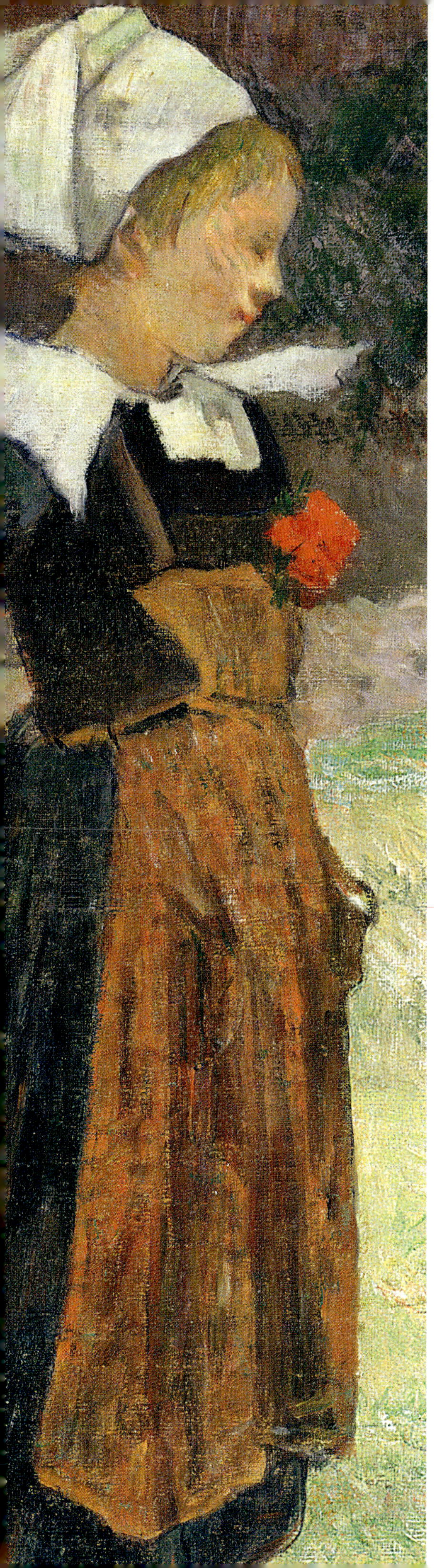

Paul Gauguin
Breton Girls Dancing, 1888
(detail)
[cat. 31]

3. Degas, Nude and Dance

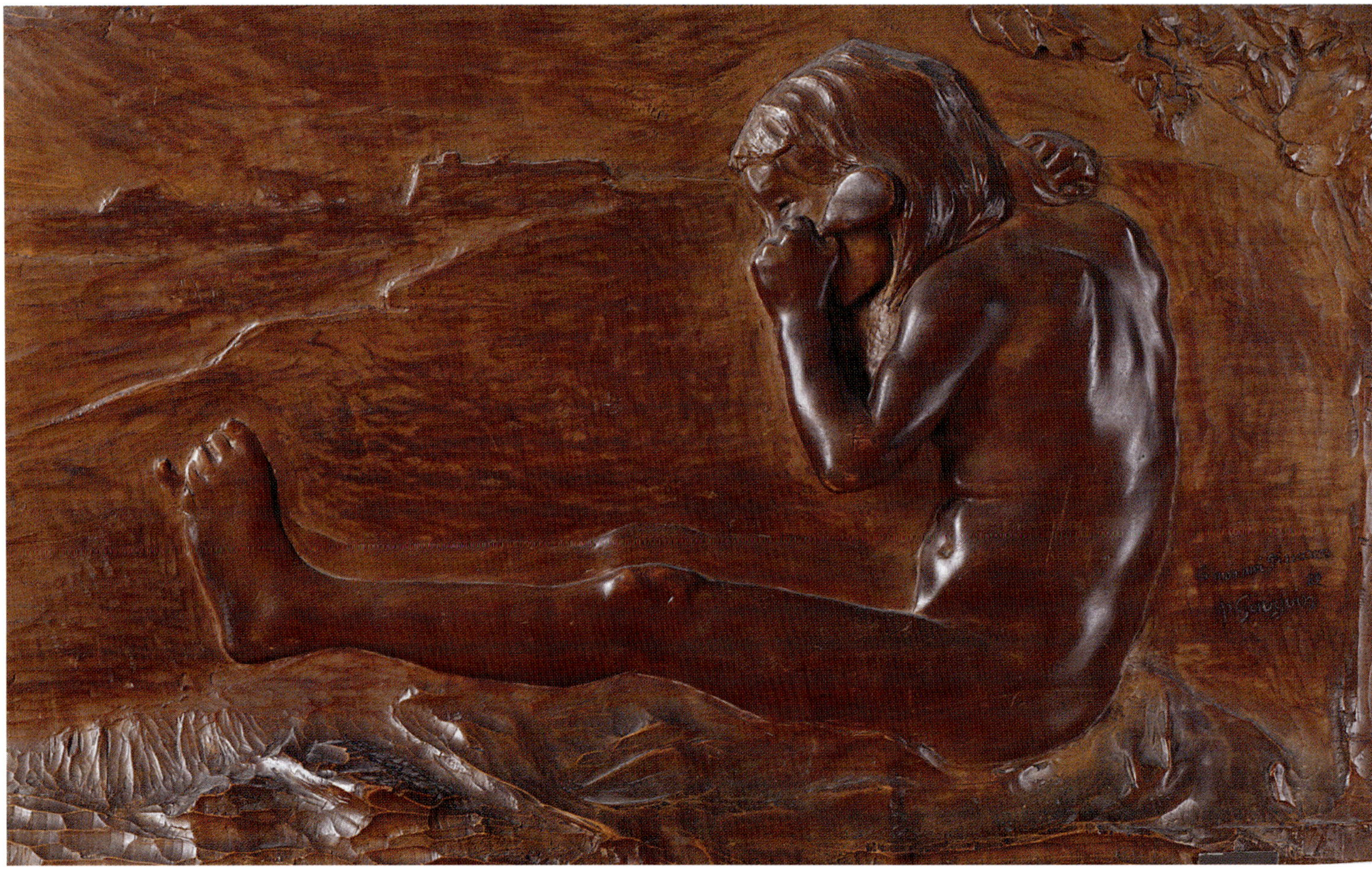

28. Paul Gauguin
La Toilette, 1882
Low relief in pear wood. 34 x 55 x 7 cm
[Gray n. 7]
Musée d'Art Moderne et Contemporain, Strasbourg

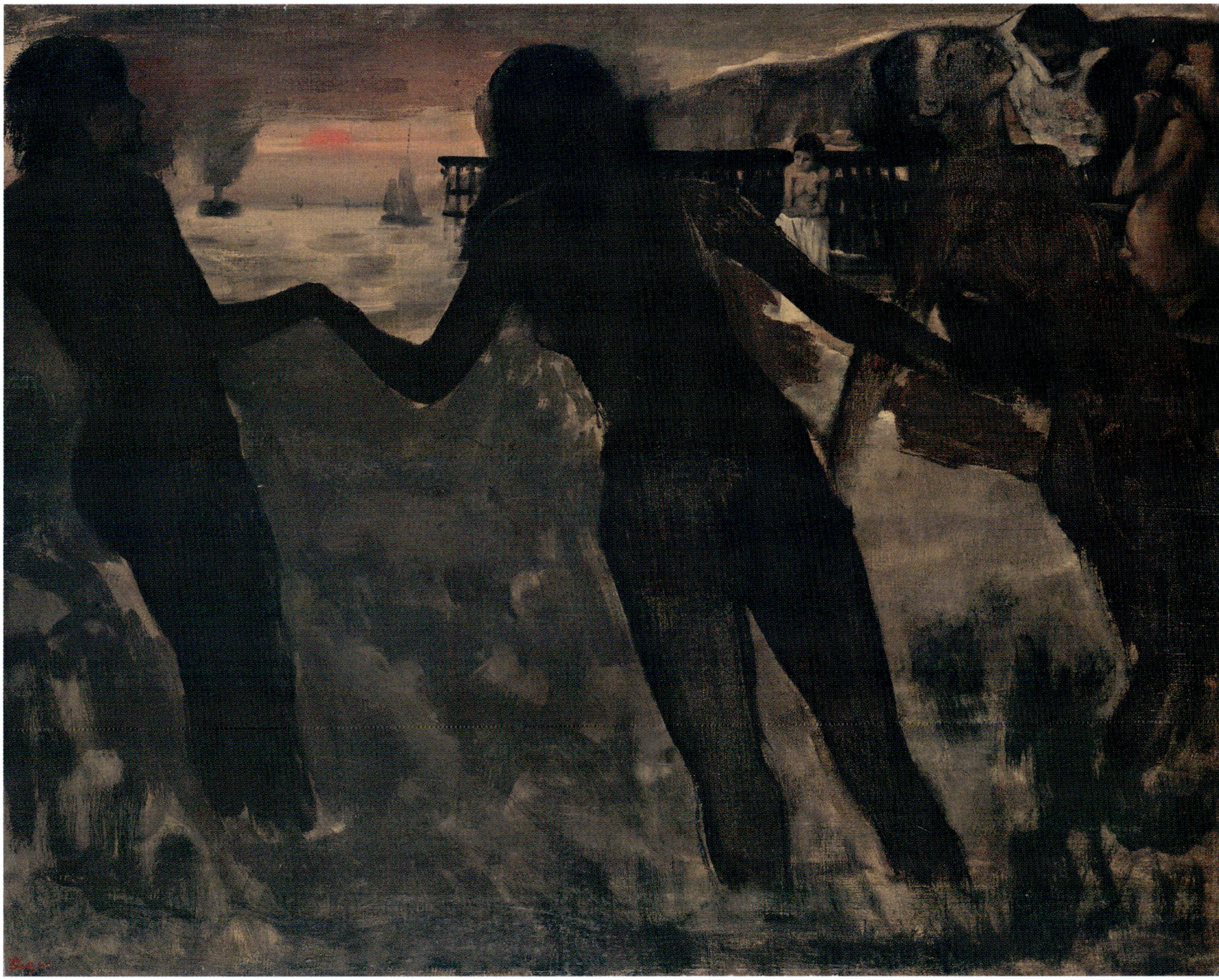

29. Edgar Degas
Peasant Girls Bathing in the Sea at Sunset, 1875–1876
(Petites paysannes se baignant à la mer vers le soir)
Oil on canvas. 61 x 81 cm
[Lemoisne n. 377]
Private Collection

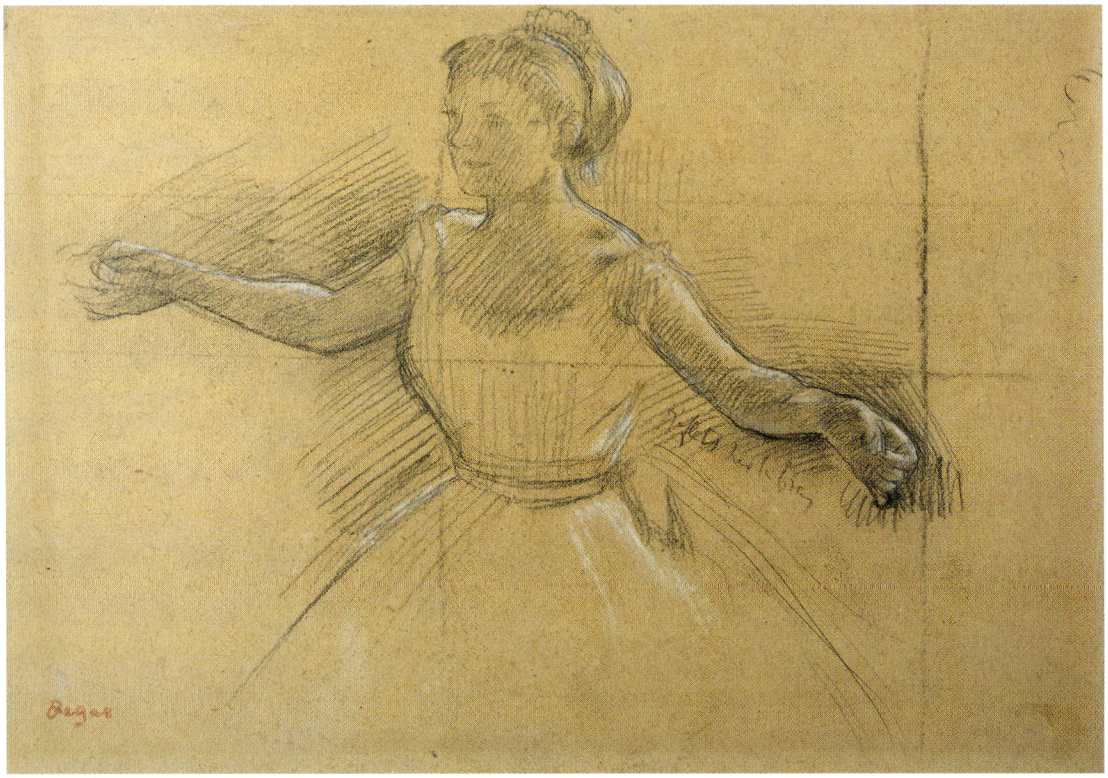

30. Edgar Degas
Dancer, c. 1878
(Danseuse)
Black chalk and white highlights on paper. 23.5 x 32.5 cm
Eugene V. Thaw, New York

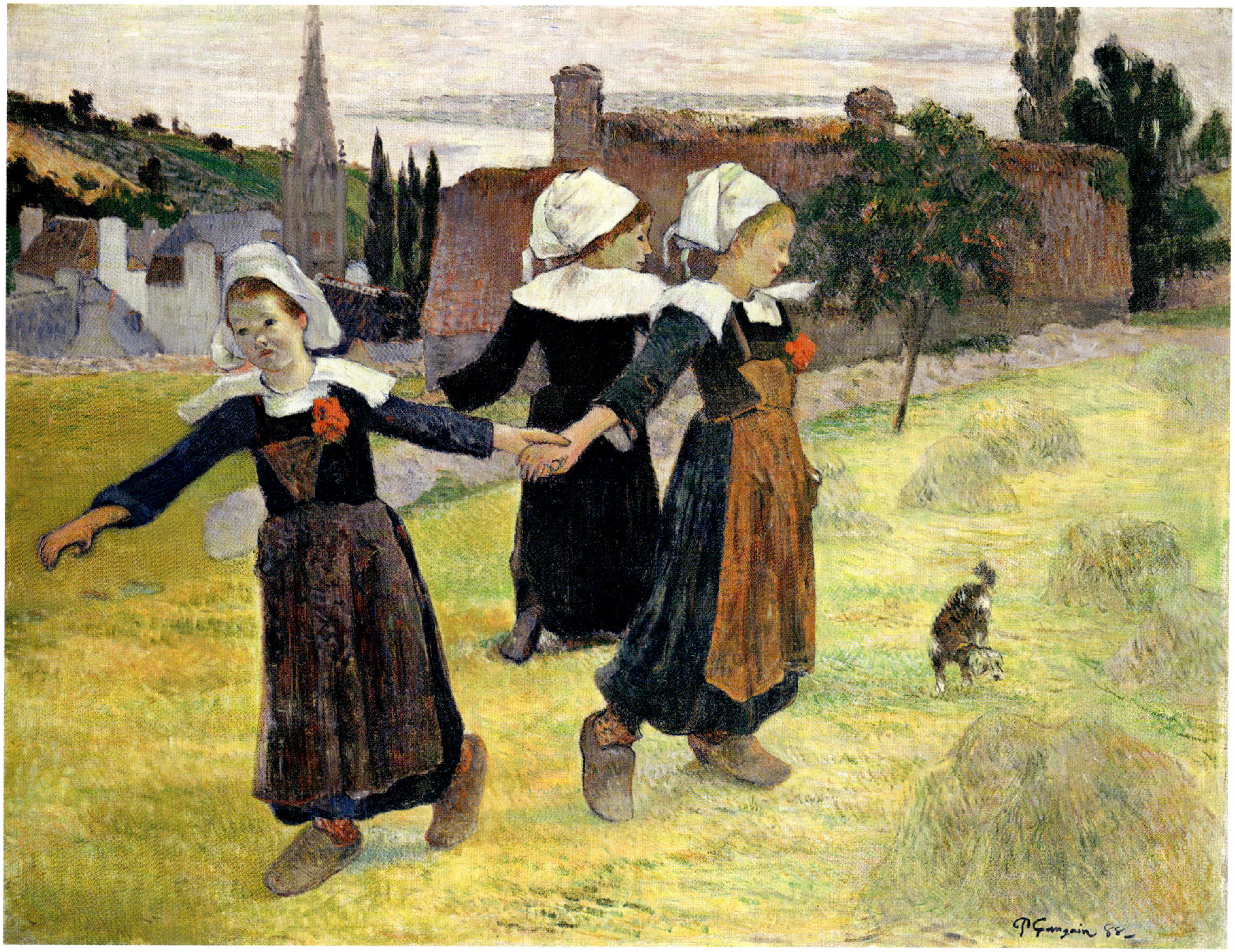

31. Paul Gauguin
Breton Girls Dancing, 1888
(La Ronde des petites Bretonnes)
Oil on canvas. 71.5 x 93 cm
[Wildenstein 2001 n. 296]
National Gallery of Art, Washington
(Collection of Mr and Mrs Paul Mellon, 1983.1.19)

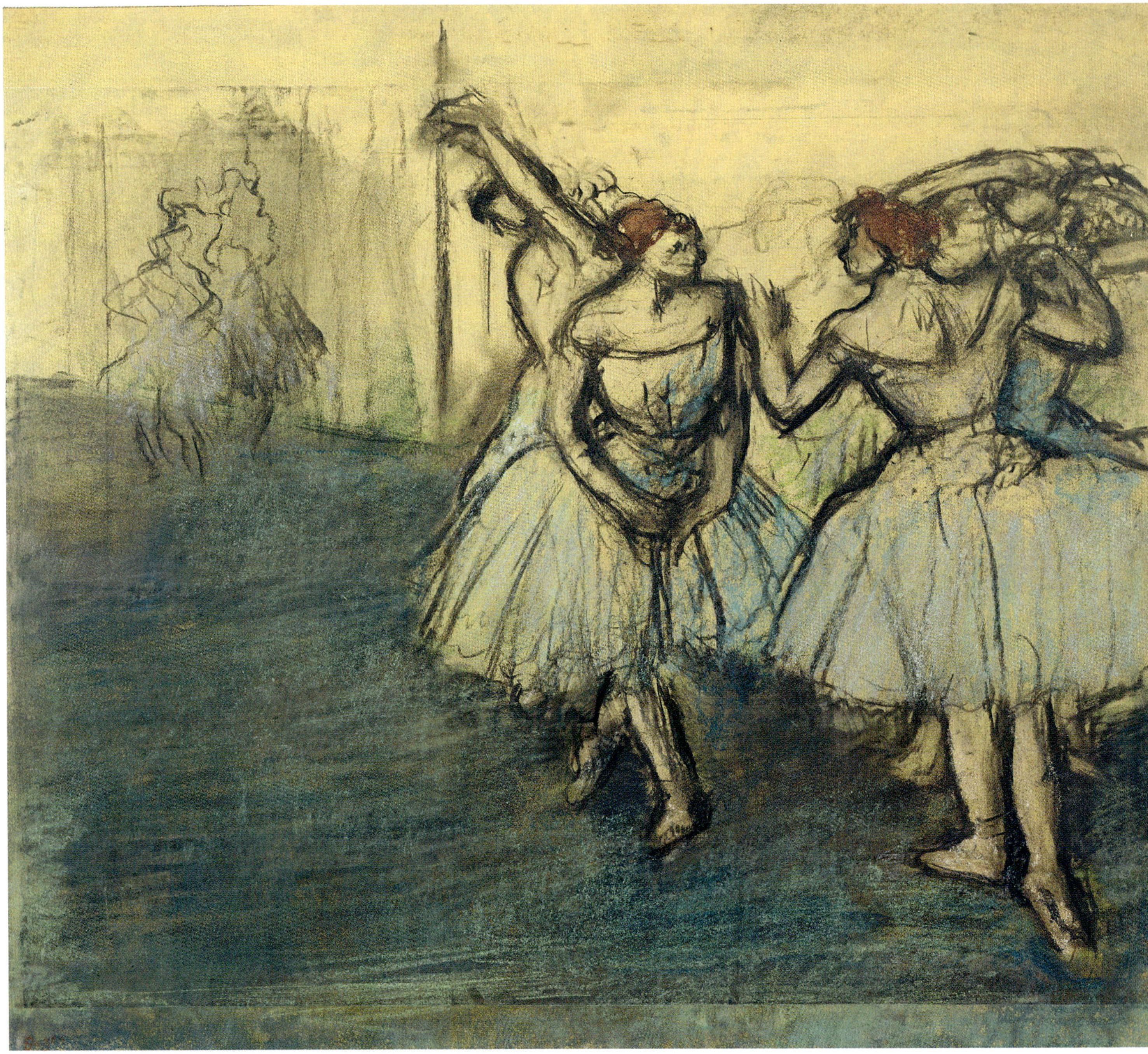

32. Edgar Degas
Dancers on Stage, 1906–1908
(Danseuses en scène)
Charcoal and pastel with tracing paper added
above and below. 65 x 70 cm
[Lemoisne n. 1462]
Von der Heydt Museum, Wuppertal

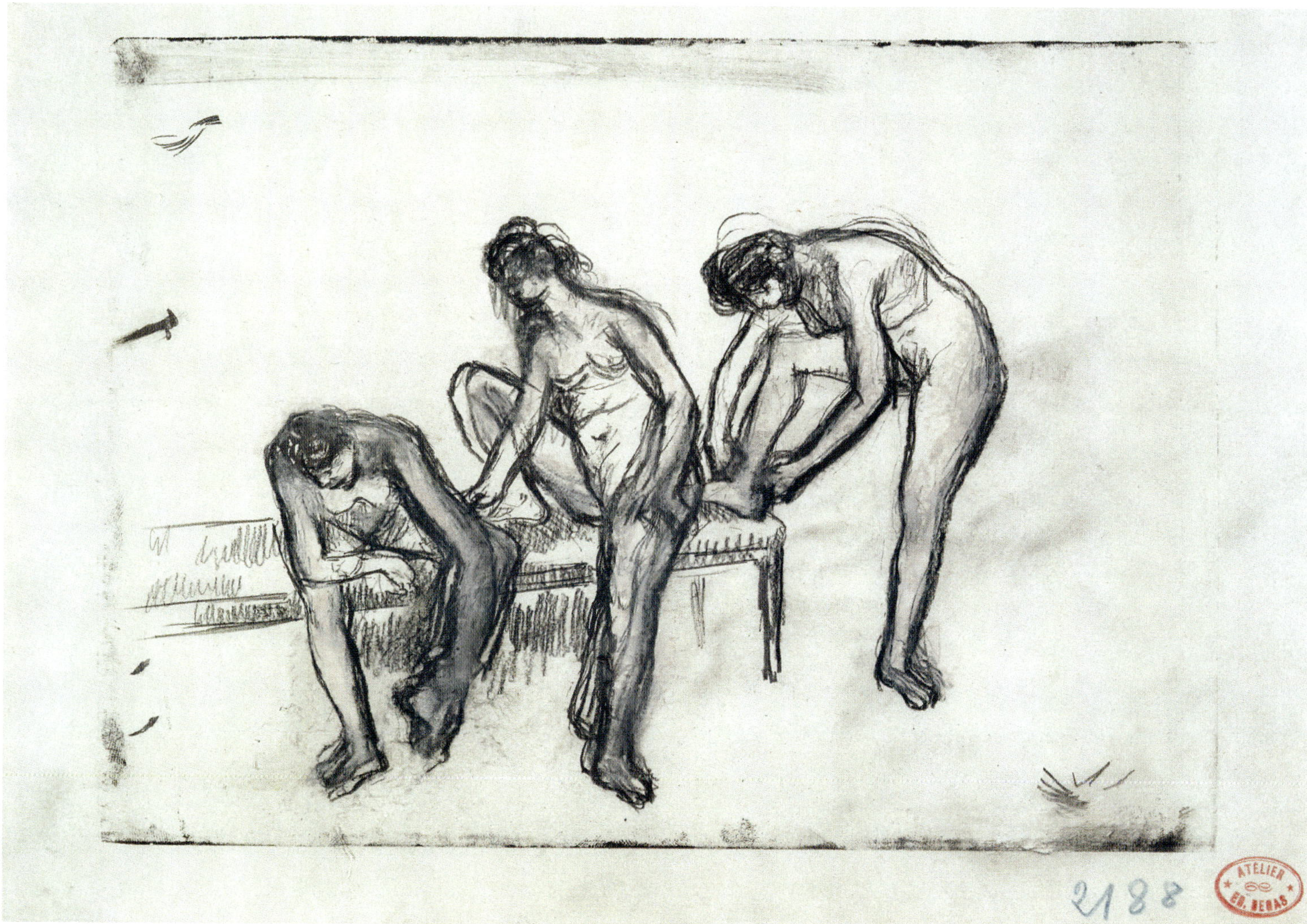

33. Edgar Degas
Three Nude Dancers, Resting, c. 1891–1892
(Trois danseuses nues, au repos)
Black pencil and pastel on lithograph. 19.7 x 27 cm
E. W. K Collection

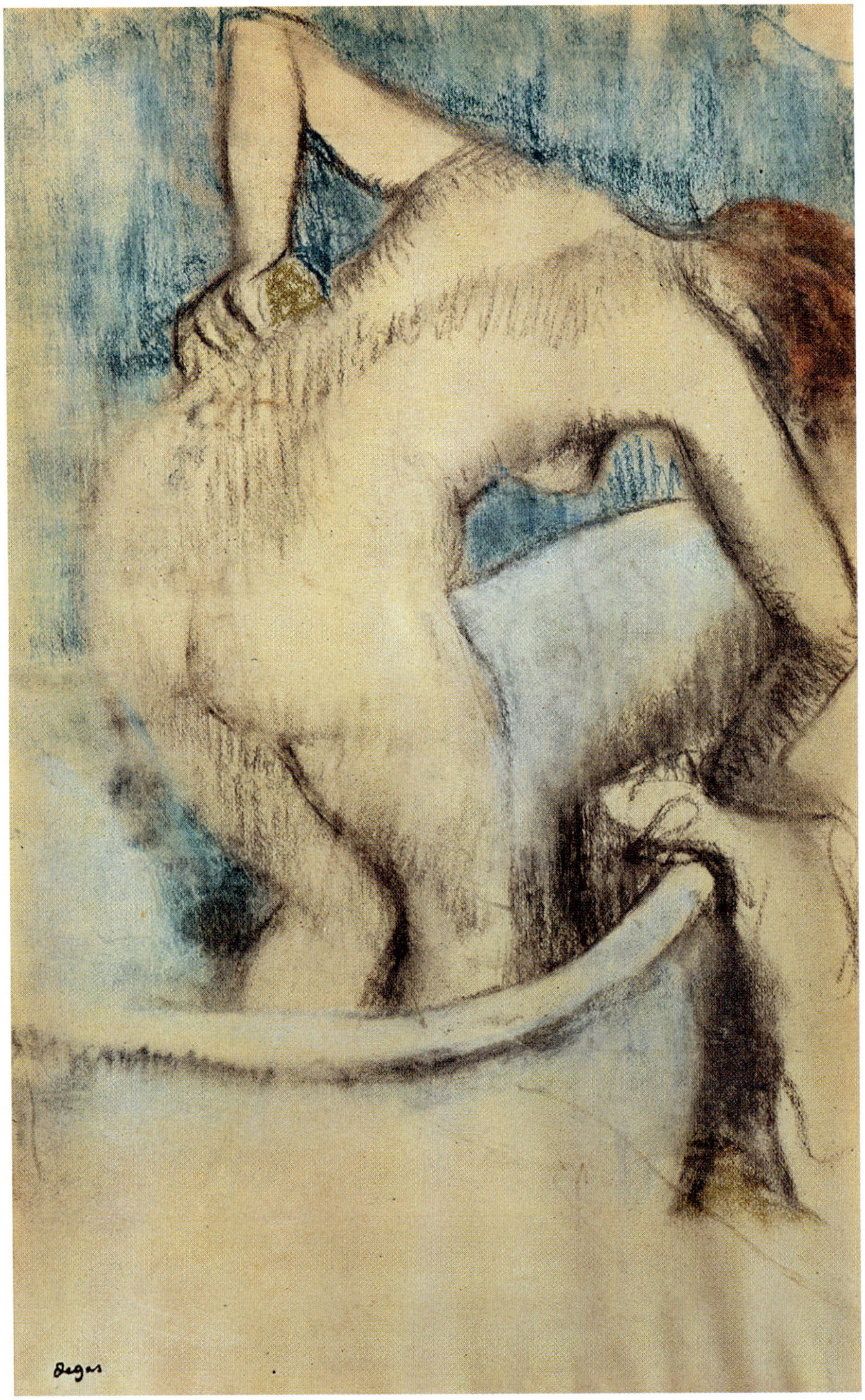

34. Edgar Degas
Woman Washing herself with a Sponge, c. 1887
(Le bain, femme s'épongeant)
Pastel and charcoal on paper. 58 x 35.5 cm
[Lemoisne n. 915]
Private Collection. Courtesy Pieter Coray

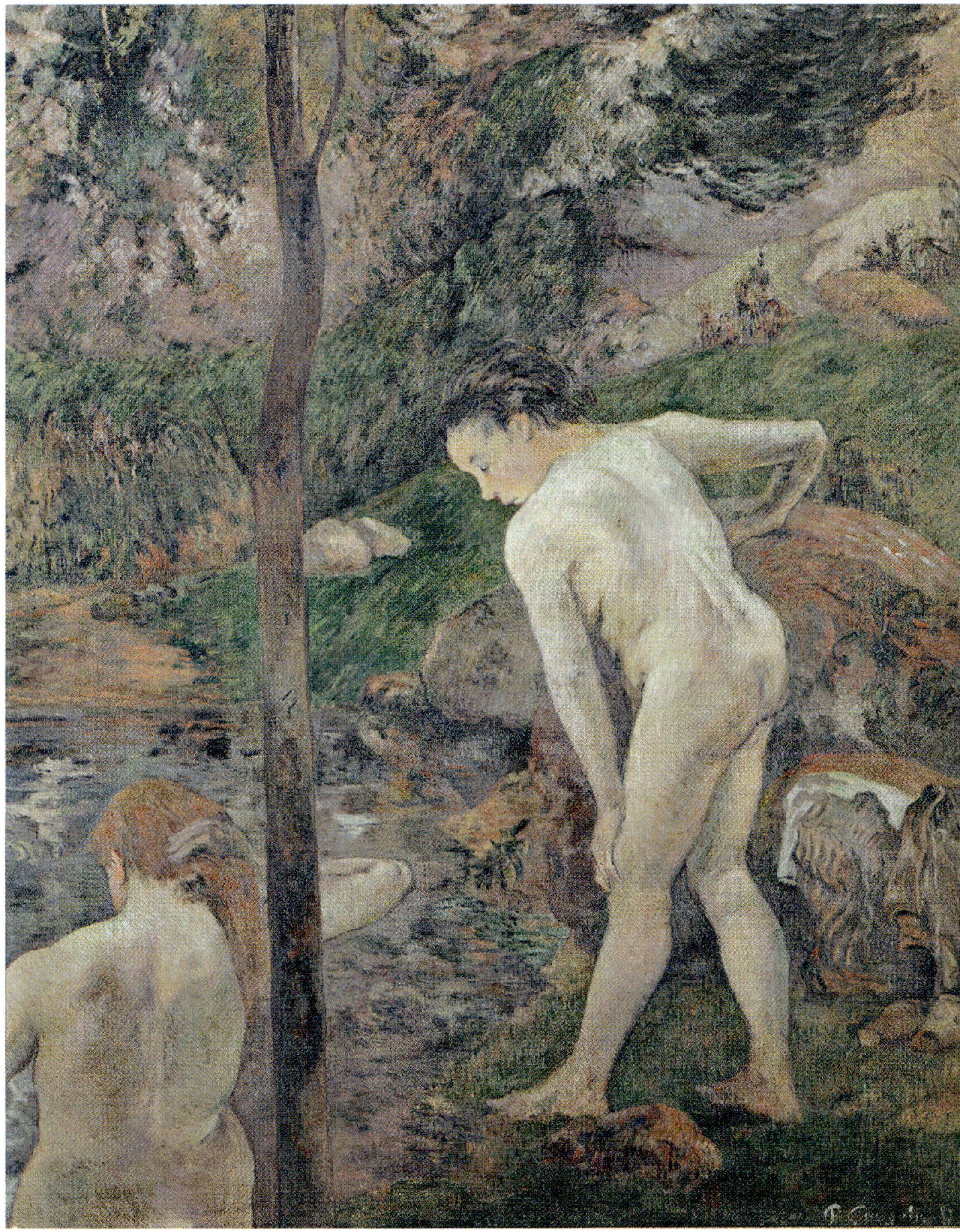

35. Paul Gauguin
Two Bathers, 1887
(Deux baigneuses)
Oil on canvas. 87.5 x 70 cm
[Wildenstein 2001 n. 241]
Museo Nacional de Bellas Artes, Buenos Aires

36. Paul Gauguin
Young Breton Bathers, 1888
(Jeunes baigneurs bretons)
Oil on canvas. 92 x 73 cm
[Wildenstein 2001 n. 298]
Hamburger Kunsthalle, Hamburg

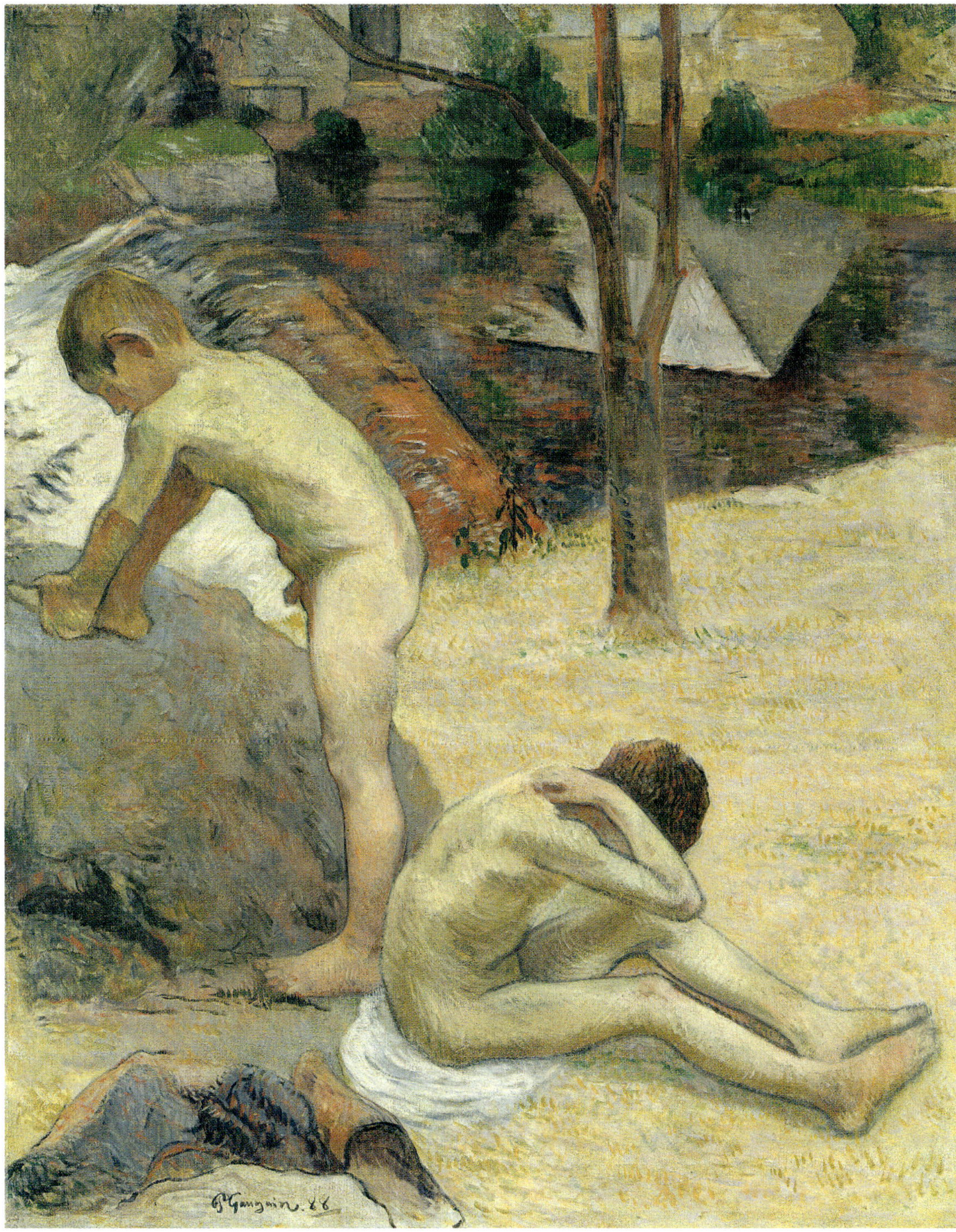

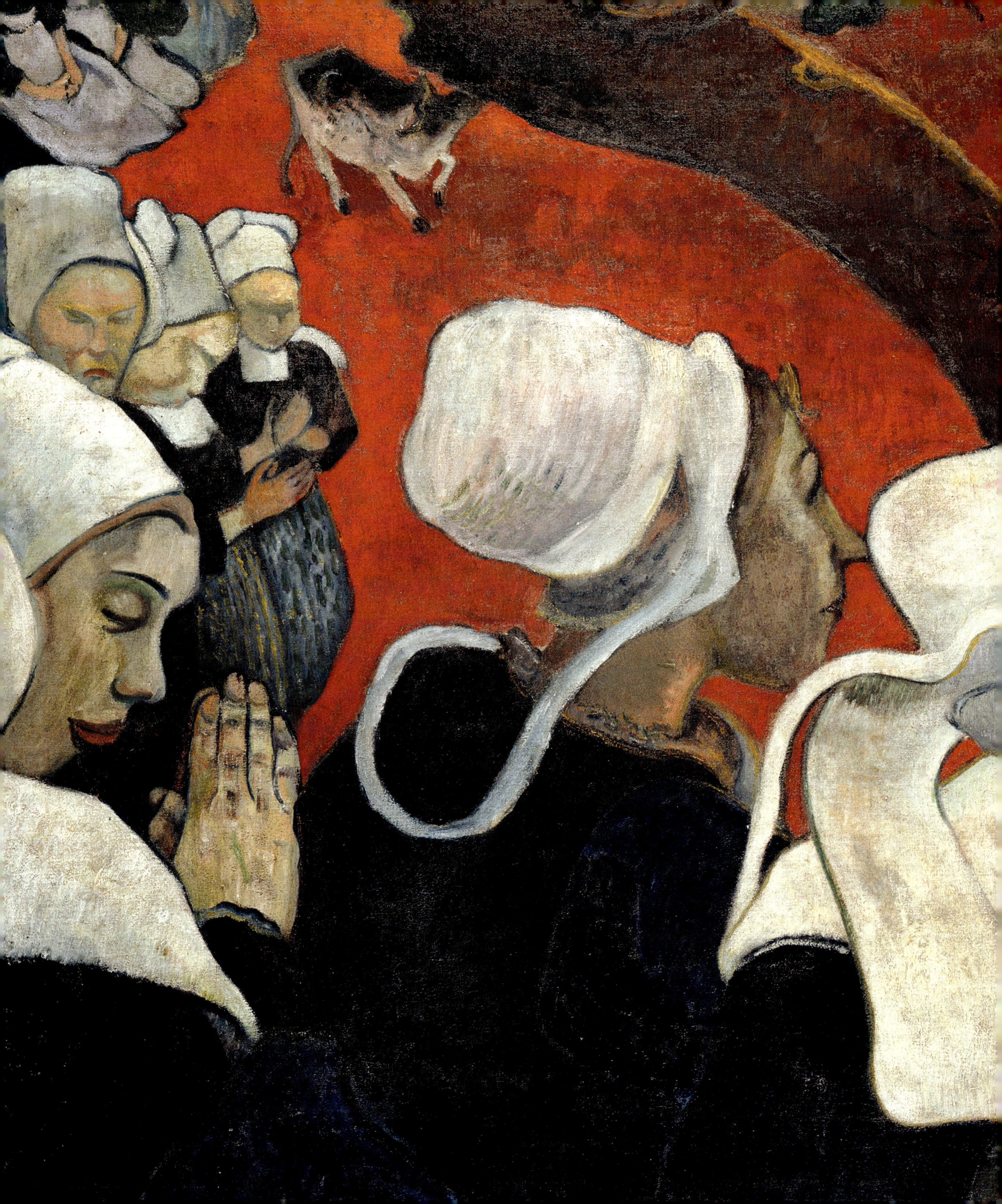

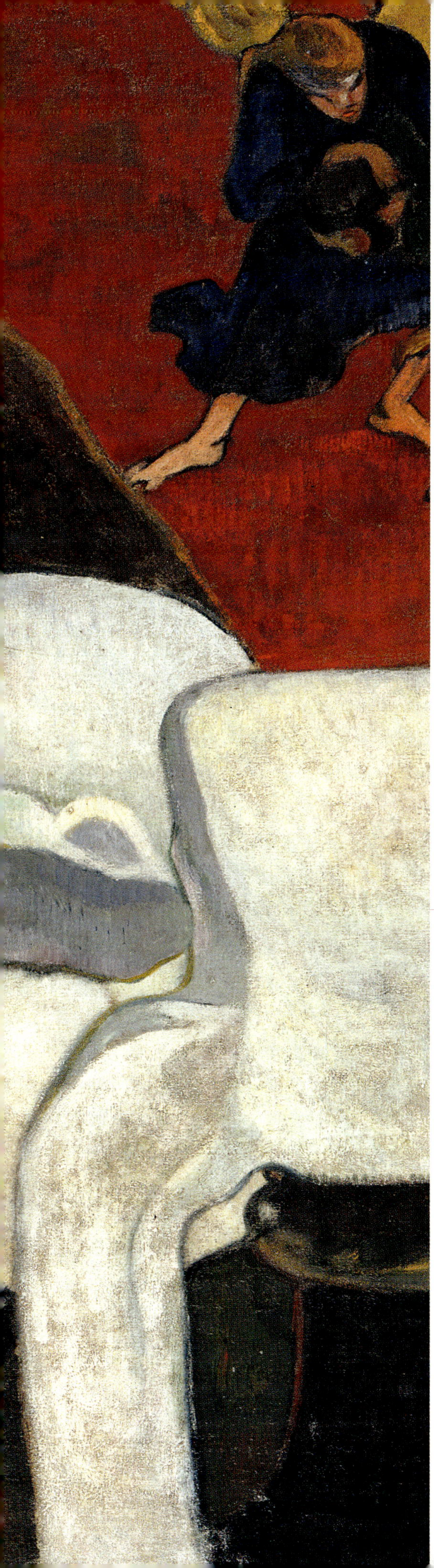

Paul Gauguin
The Vision after the Sermon, 1888
(detail)
[cat. 41]

4. The Vision. From Cloisonnisme to Synthetism

37. Louis Anquetin
Avenue de Clichy, 1887
Oil on canvas. 69 x 53 cm
Wadsworth Atheneum Museum of Art, Hartford, CT.
(The Ella Gallup Sumner and Mary Catlin Sumner Collection Fund)

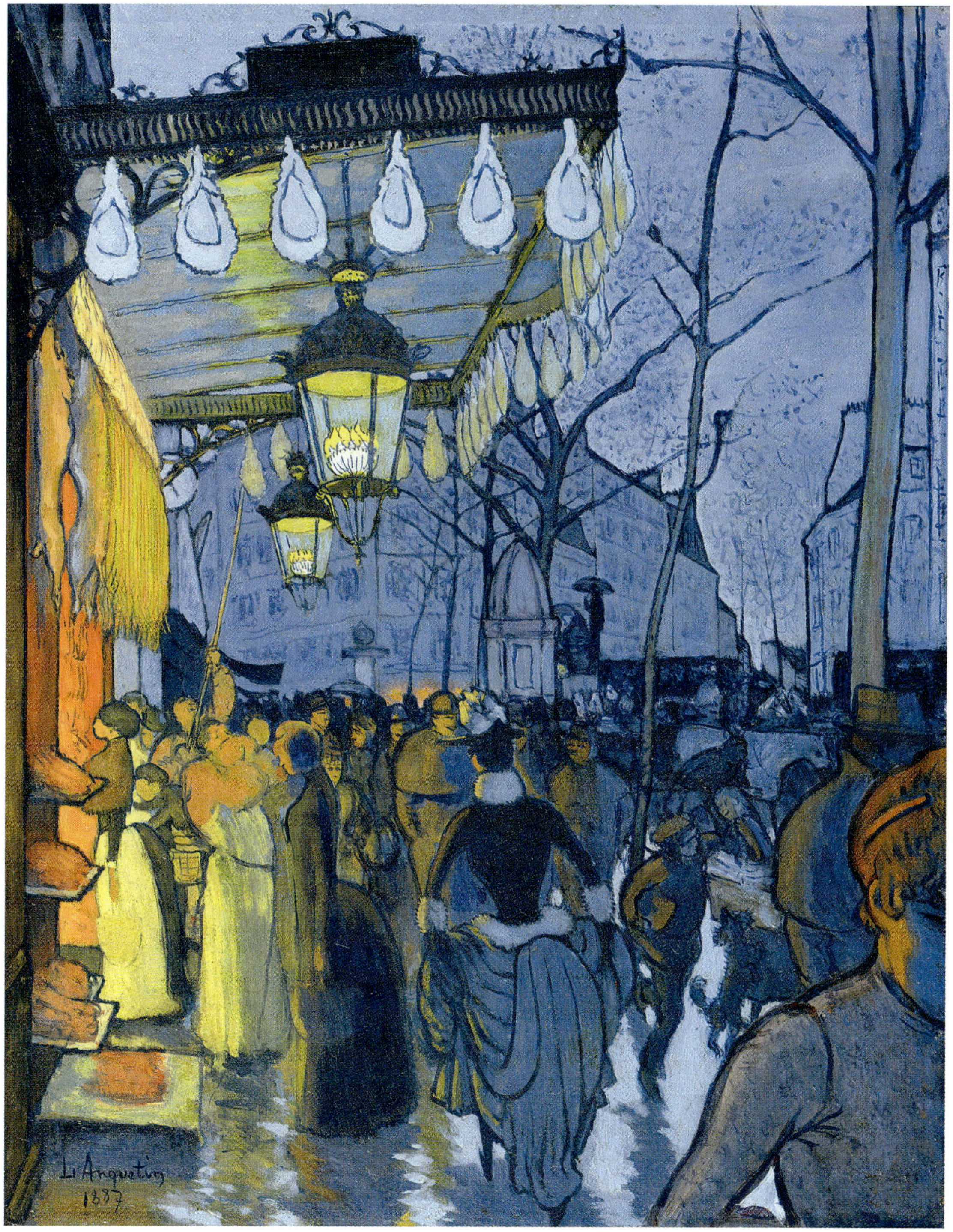
L. Anquetin
1887

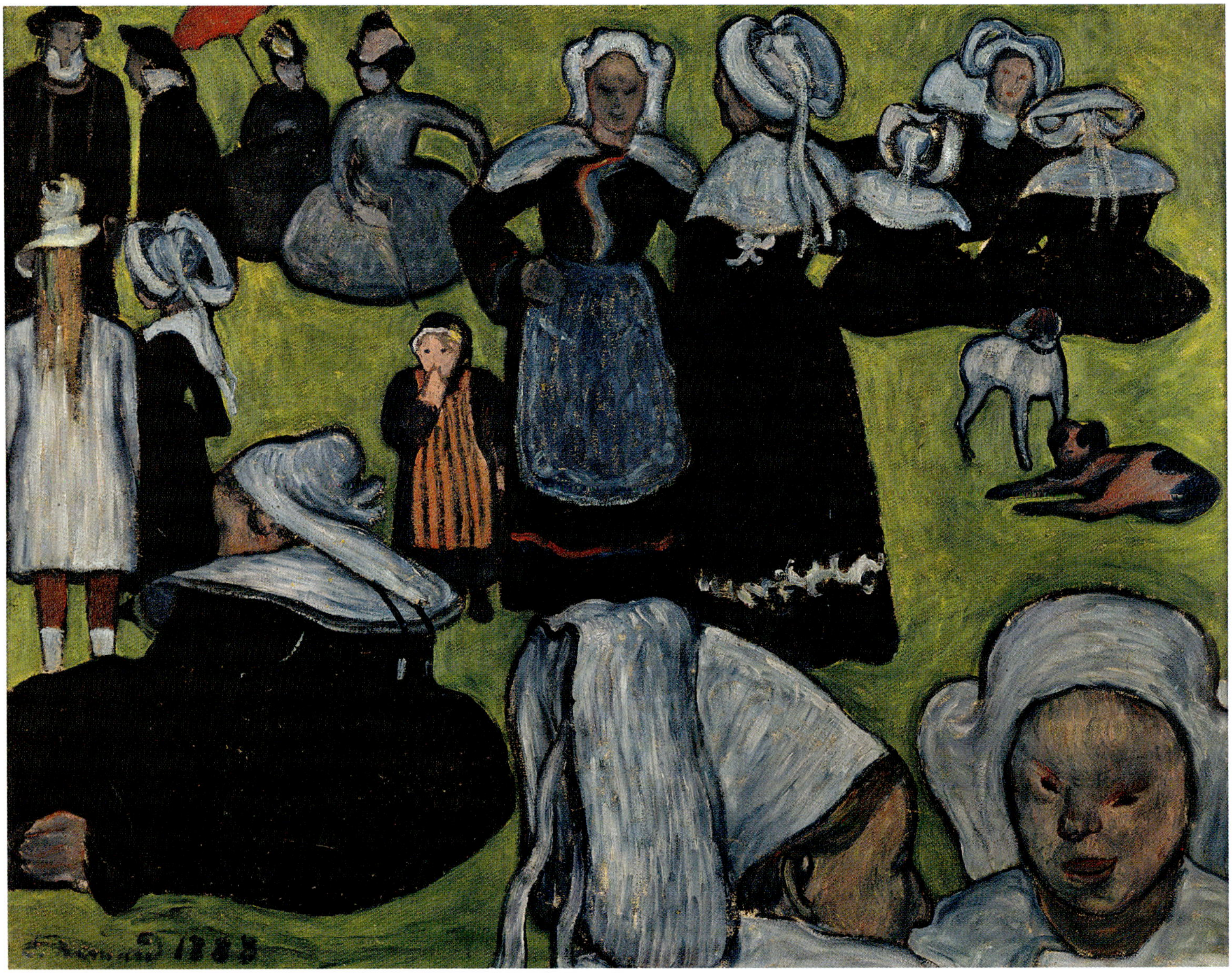

38. Émile Bernard
Breton Women in the Meadow, 1888
(Bretonnes dans la prairie)
Oil on canvas. 74 x 92 cm
[Luthi n. 114]
Private Collection

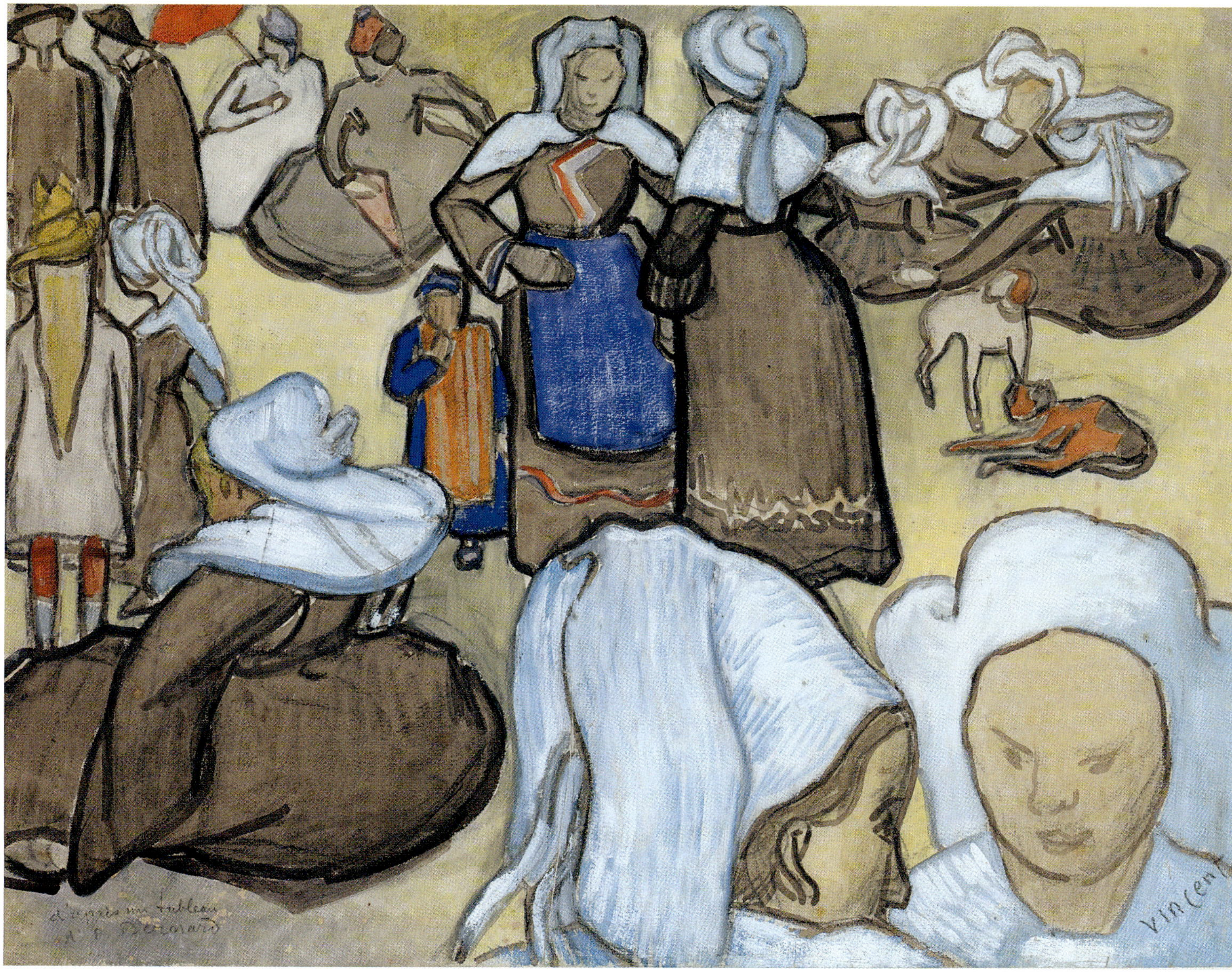

39. Vincent van Gogh
Breton Women in the Meadow (after Bernard), 1888
(Bretonnes dans la prairie, après Bernard)
Oil, pencil and watercolour on canvas. 47.5 x 62 cm
[Faille n. 1422]
Civica Galleria d'Arte Moderna, Raccolta Grassi, Milan

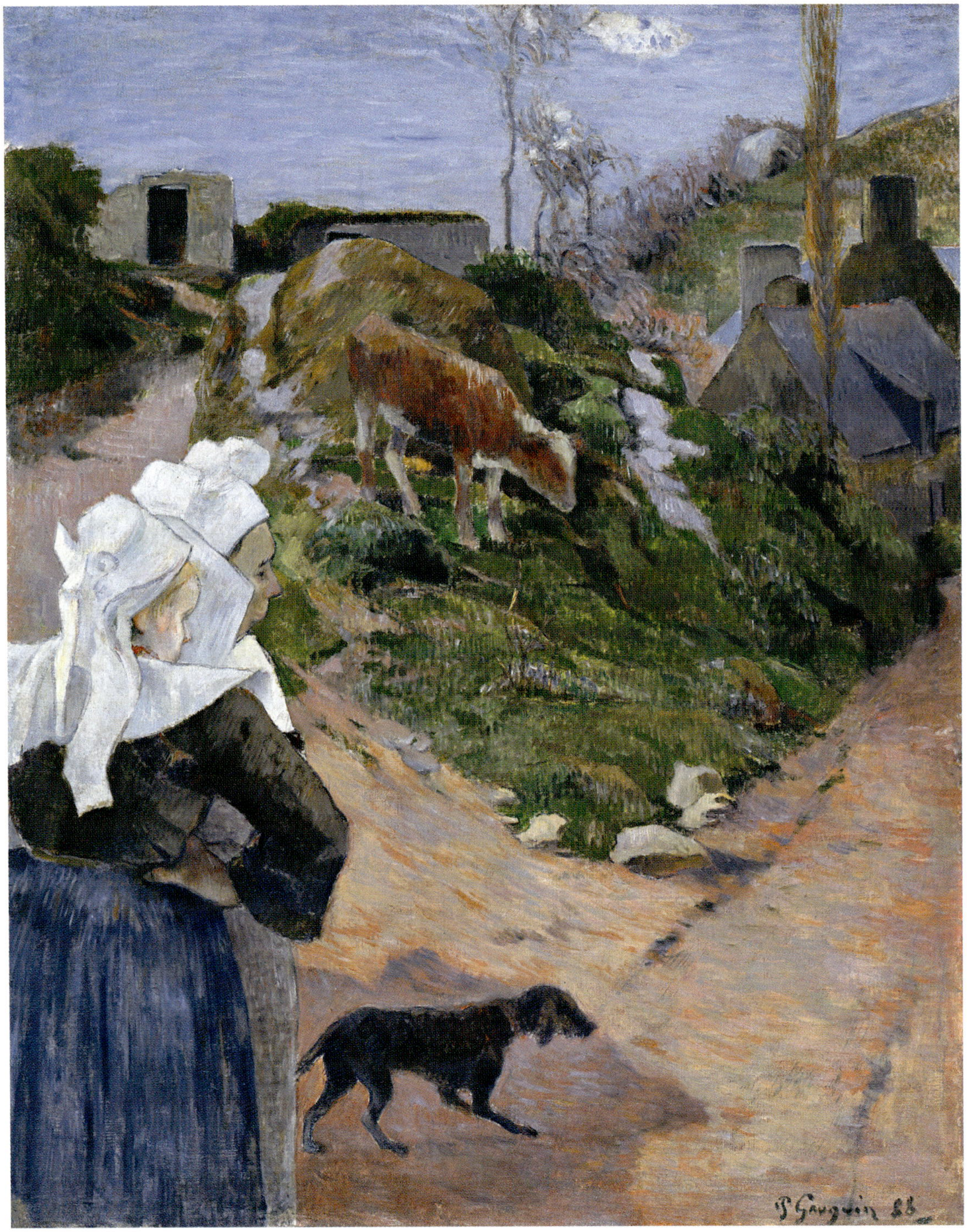

40. Paul Gauguin
Breton Women by a Bend in the Road, 1888
(Bretonnes au tournant d'une route)
Oil on canvas. 91 x 72 cm
[Wildenstein 2001 n. 271]
Ny Carlsberg Glyptotek, Copenhagen

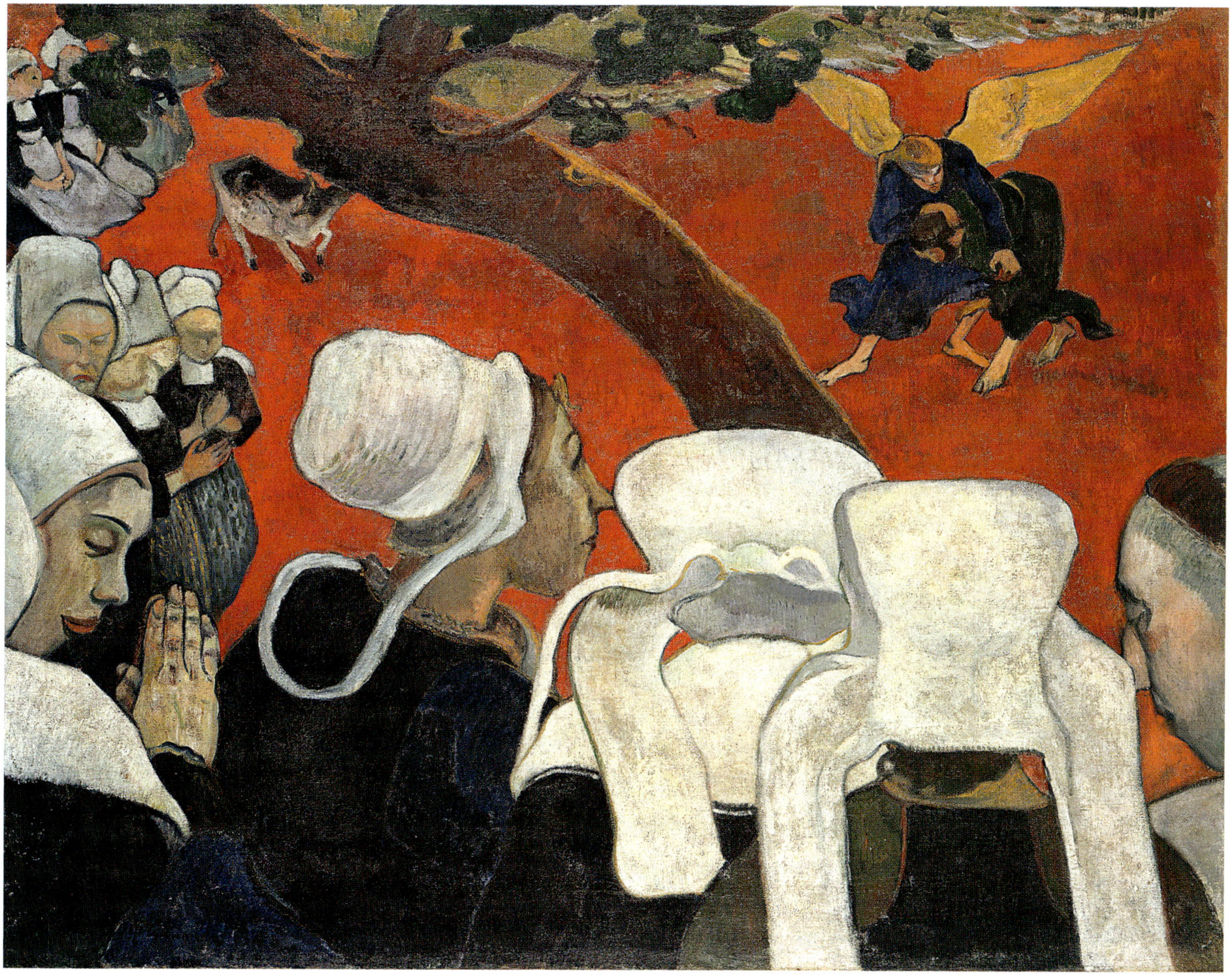

41. Paul Gauguin
The Vision after the Sermon, 1888
(La vision du sermon)
Oil on canvas. 73 x 92 cm
[Wildenstein 2001 n. 308]
National Gallery of Scotland, Edinburgh

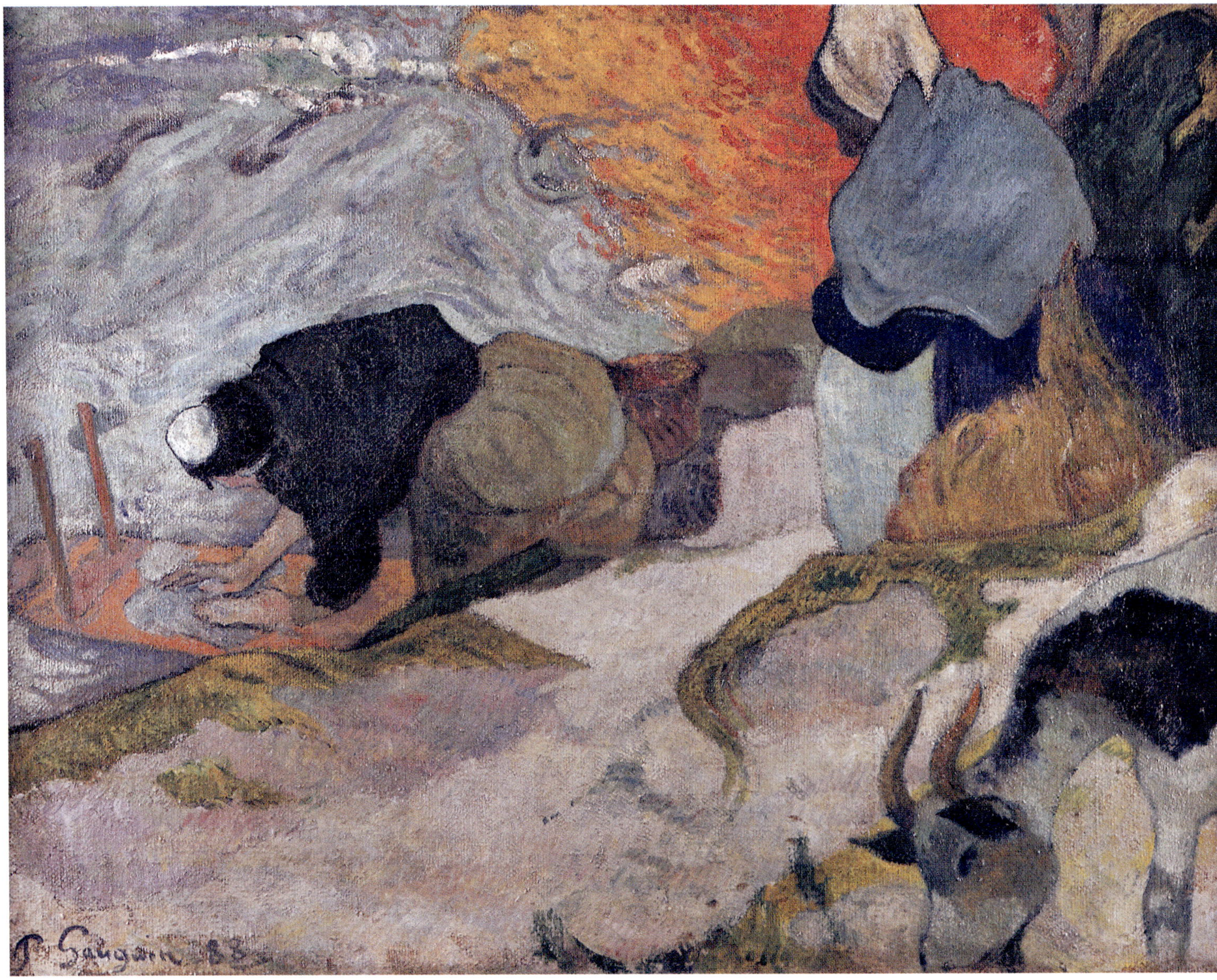

42. Paul Gauguin
Washerwomen in Arles, 1888
(Les lavandières à Arles)
Oil on jute. 73 x 92 cm
[Wildenstein 2001 n. 325]
Museo de Bellas Artes de Bilbao

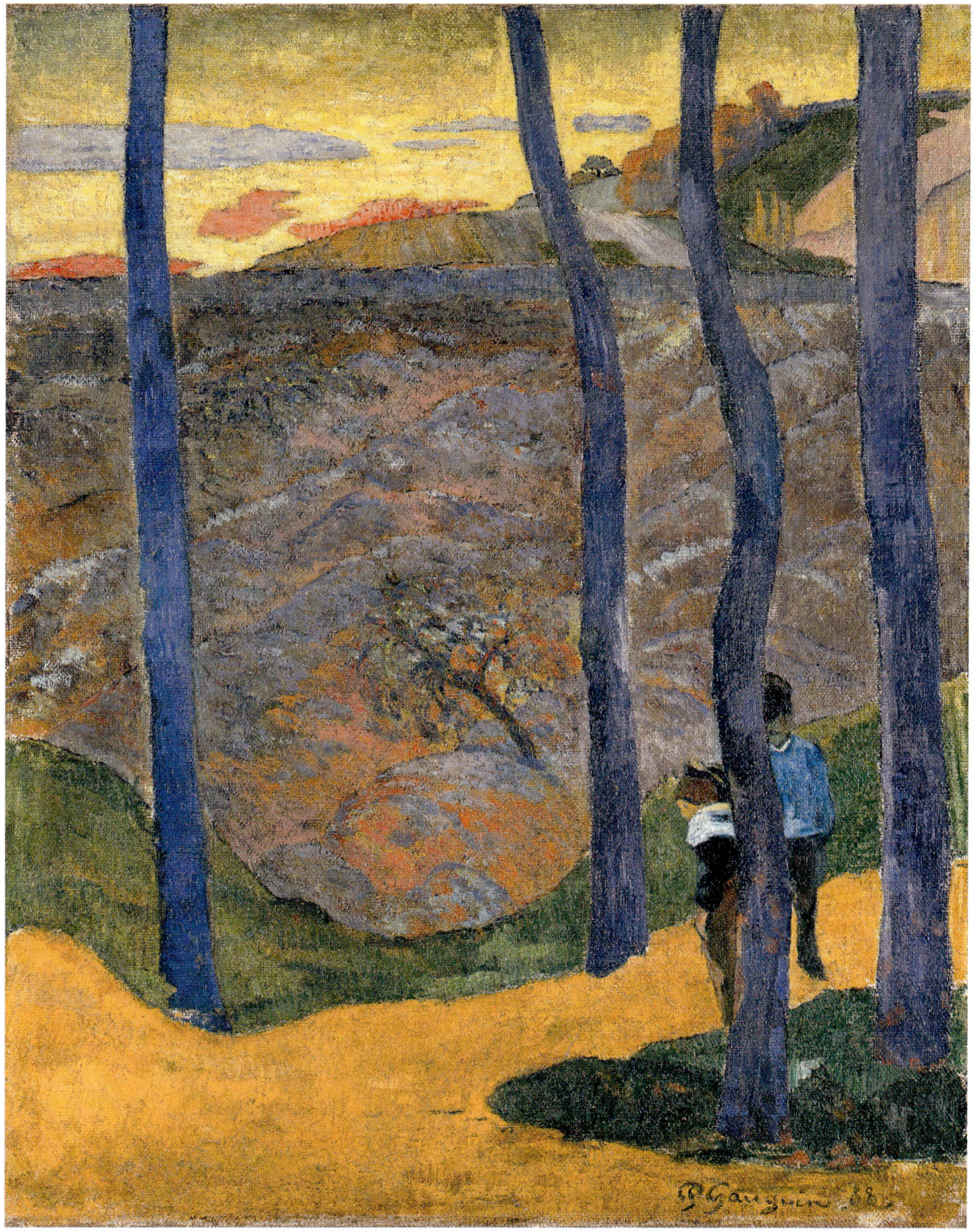

43. Paul Gauguin
The Blue Trees, 1888
(Les Arbres bleus)
Oil on jute. 92 x 73 cm
[Wildenstein 2001 n. 319]
Ordrupgaard, Copenhagen

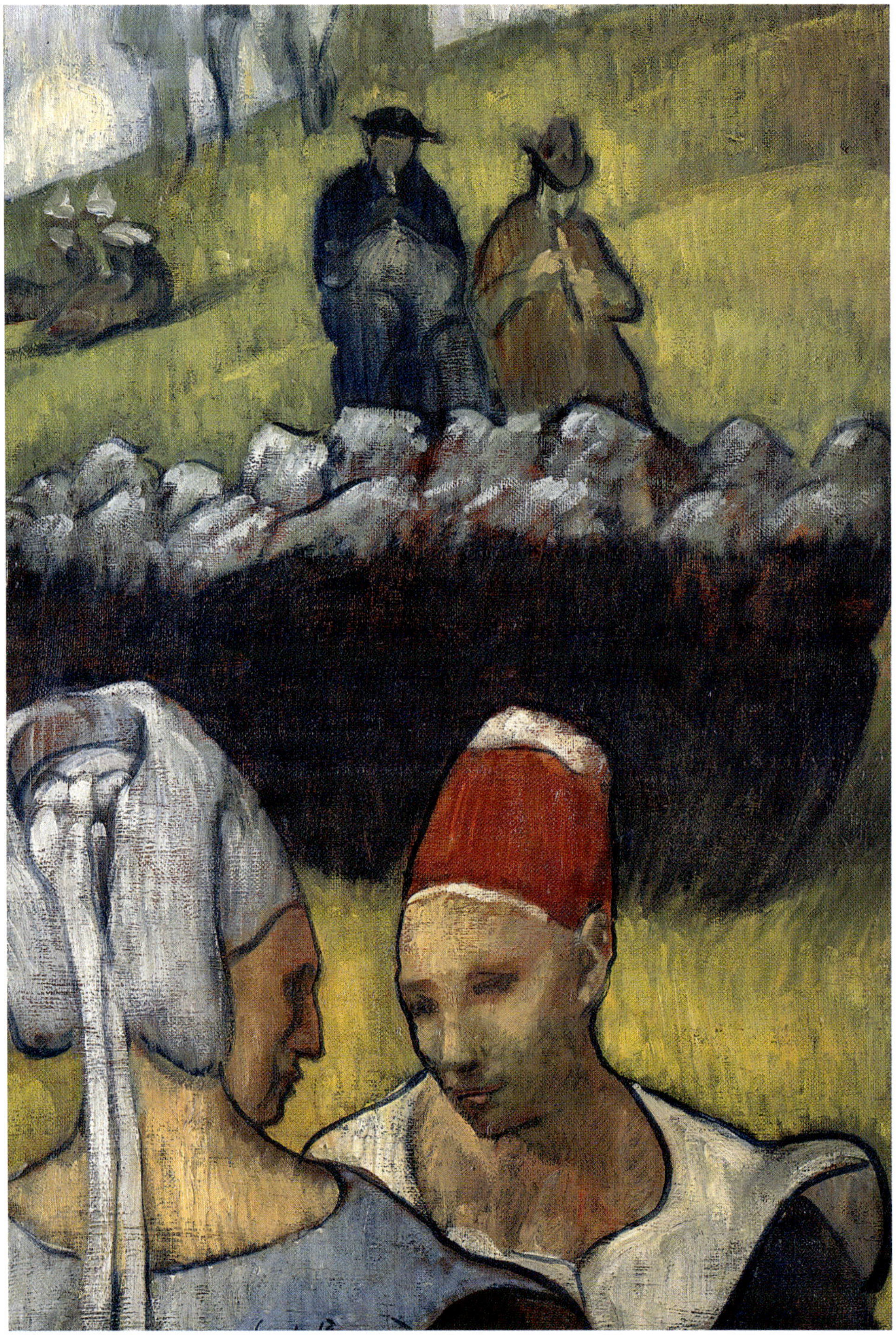

44. Émile Bernard
Study of Breton Women or *Breton Women Dancing*, 1888–1890
(Etude de Bretones ou La Ronde bretonne)
Oil on canvas. 81 x 54 cm
[Luthi n. 334]
Musée des Beaux-Arts de Quimper

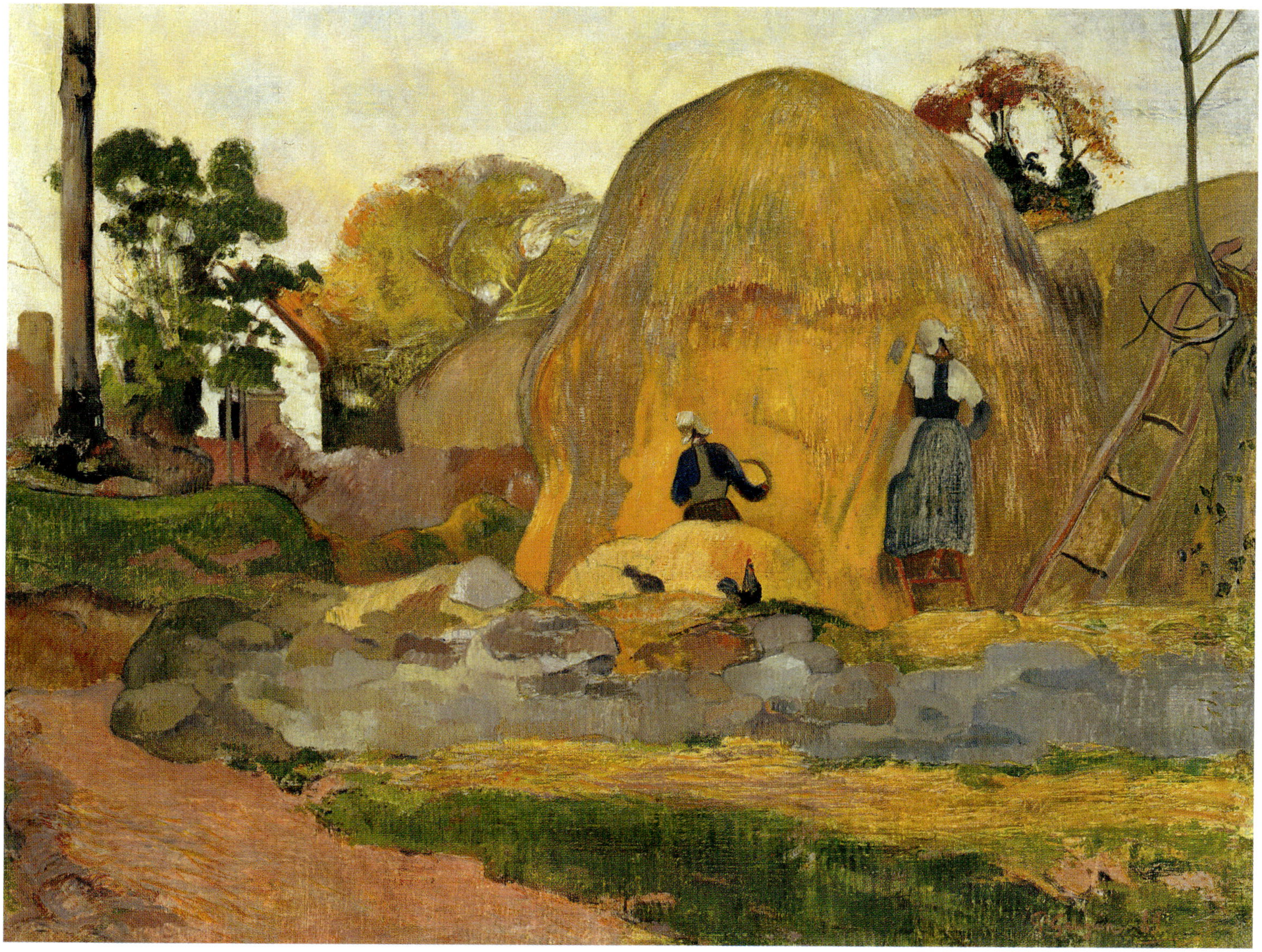

45. Paul Gauguin
The Yellow Haystacks, 1889
(Les meules jaunes)
Oil on canvas. 73 x 92 cm
[Wildenstein 1964 n. 351]
Musée d'Orsay, Paris
Donated with right of usufruct by
Mme Huc de Monfreid, 1951, entry in 1968

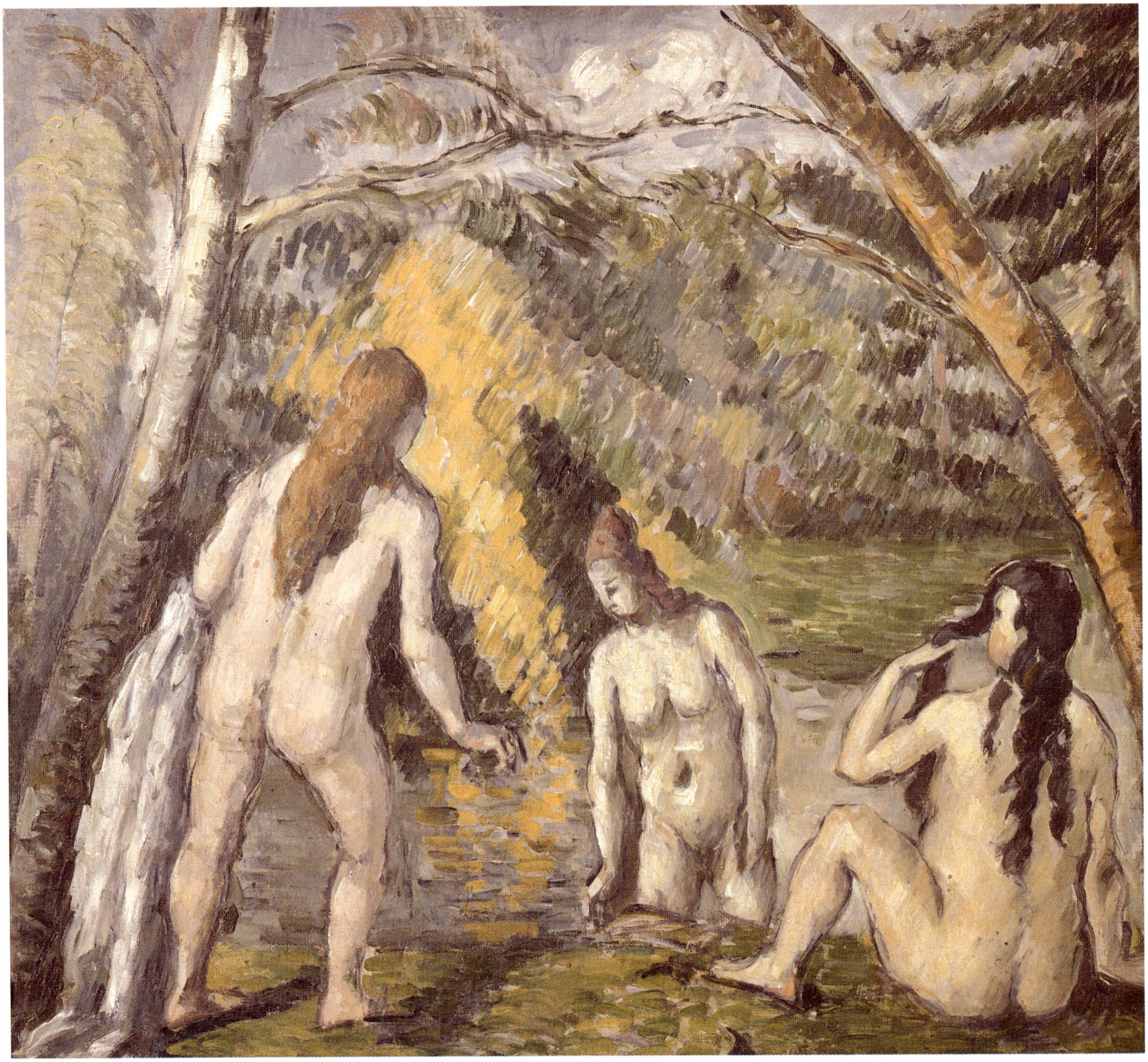

46. Paul Cézanne
Three Bathers, 1876–1877
(Trois baigneuses)
Oil on canvas. 52 x 55 cm
[Rewald n. 360]
Petit Palais, Musée des Beaux-Arts de la Ville de Paris

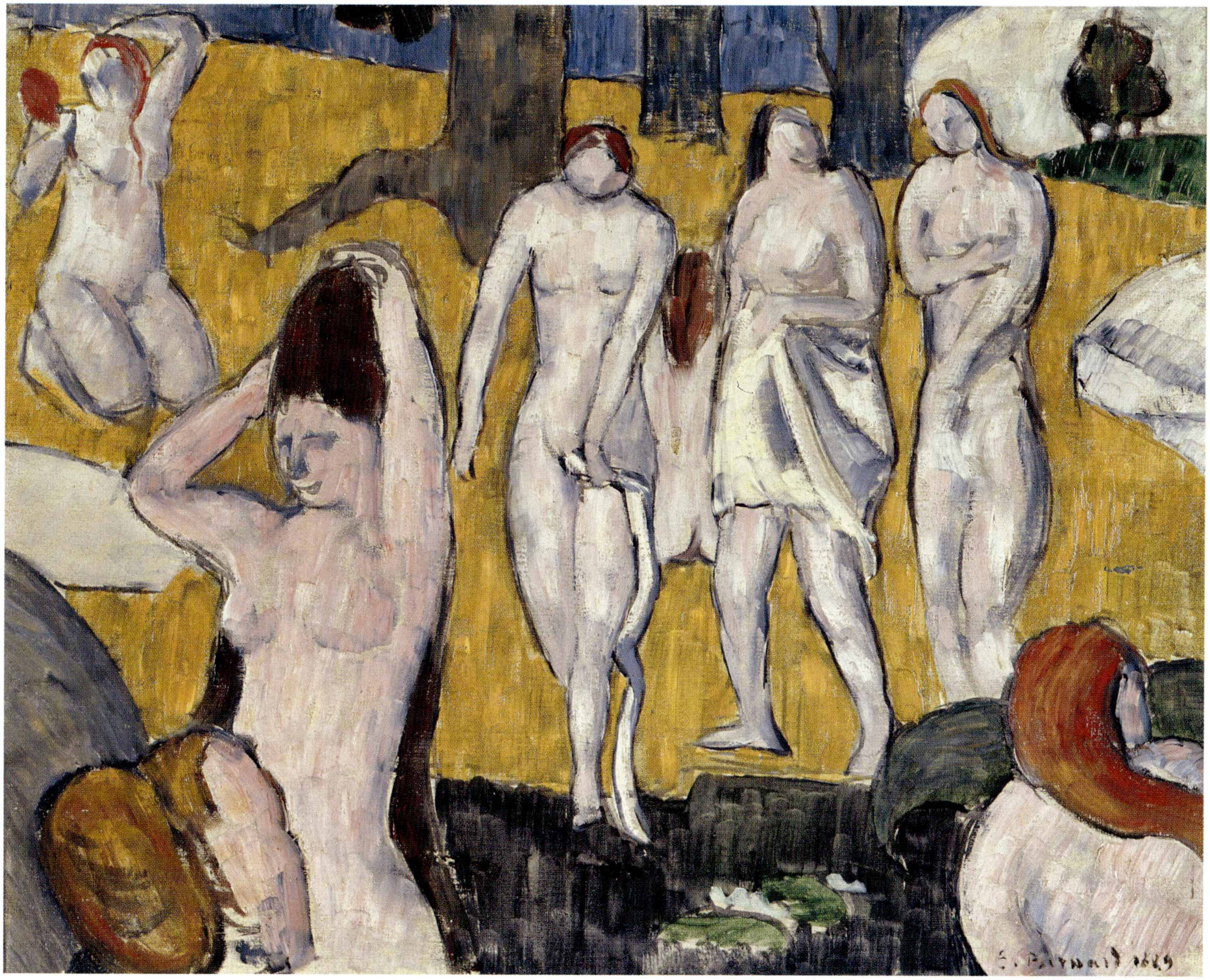

47. Émile Bernard
Women Bathing, 1889
(Baigneuses)
Oil on canvas. 47 x 57.2 cm
[Luthi n. 208]
Carmen Thyssen-Bornemisza Collection
on loan at the Museo Thyssen-Bornemisza, Madrid

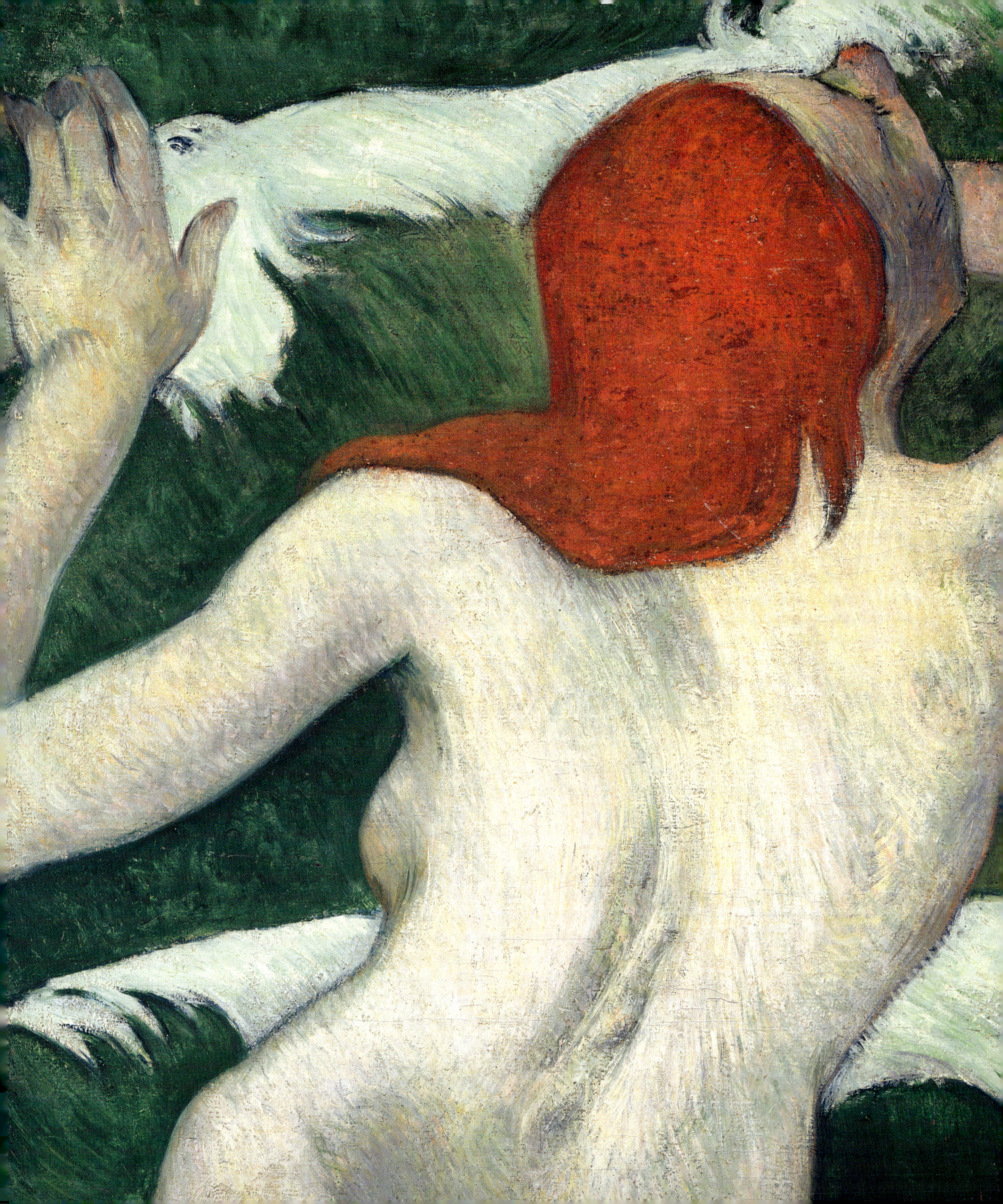

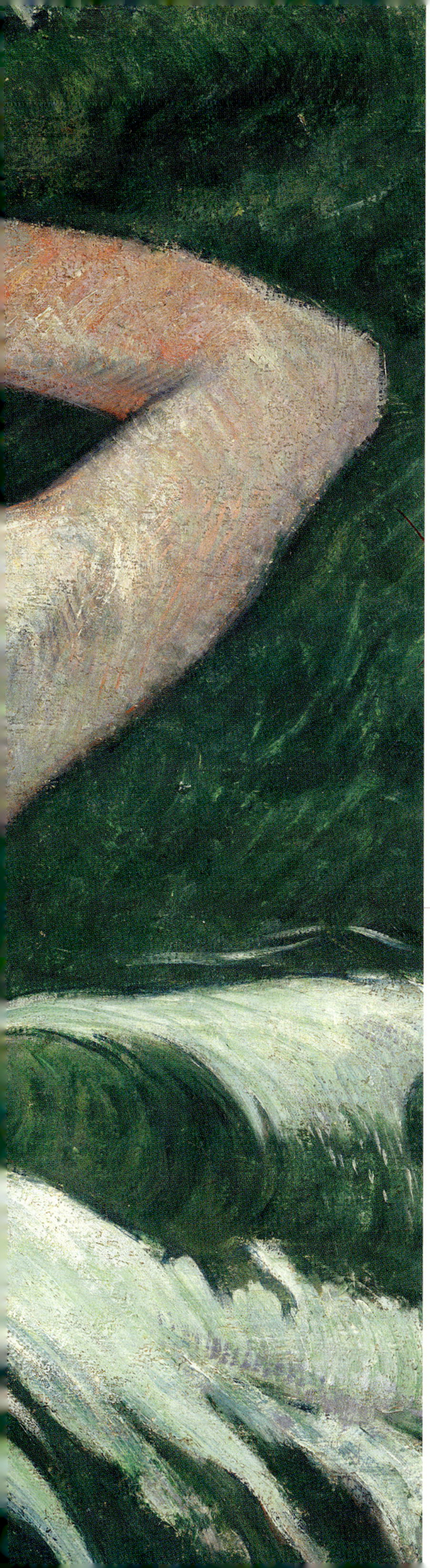

Paul Gauguin
In the waves (Ondine I), 1889
(detail)
[cat. 57]

5. Eve and the Gods

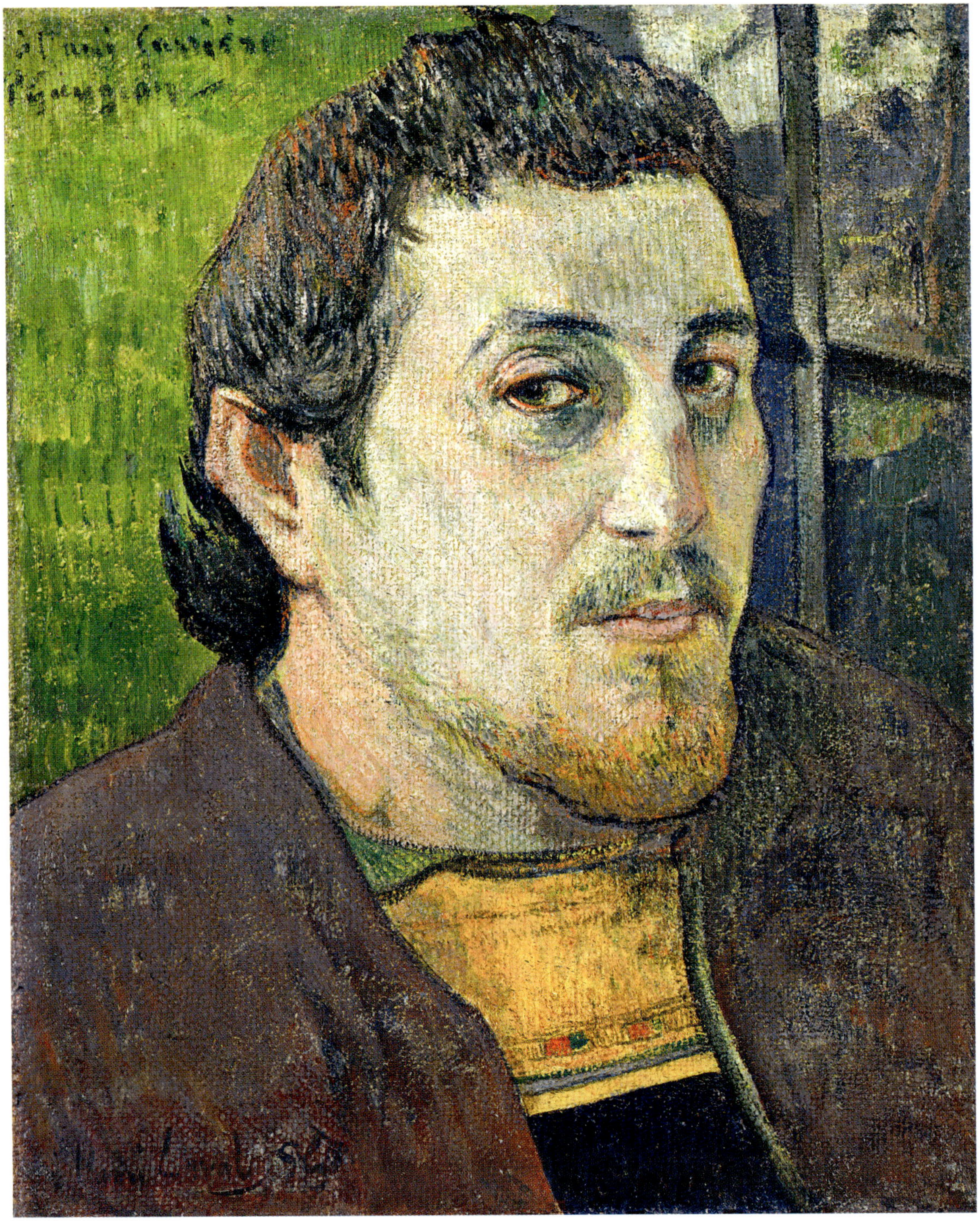

48. Paul Gauguin
Self-Portrait, 1888
(Autoportrait)
Oil on canvas. 46.5 x 38.6 cm
[Wildenstein 2001 n. 291]
National Gallery of Art, Washington
(Collection of Mr and Mrs Paul Mellon. 1985.64.20)

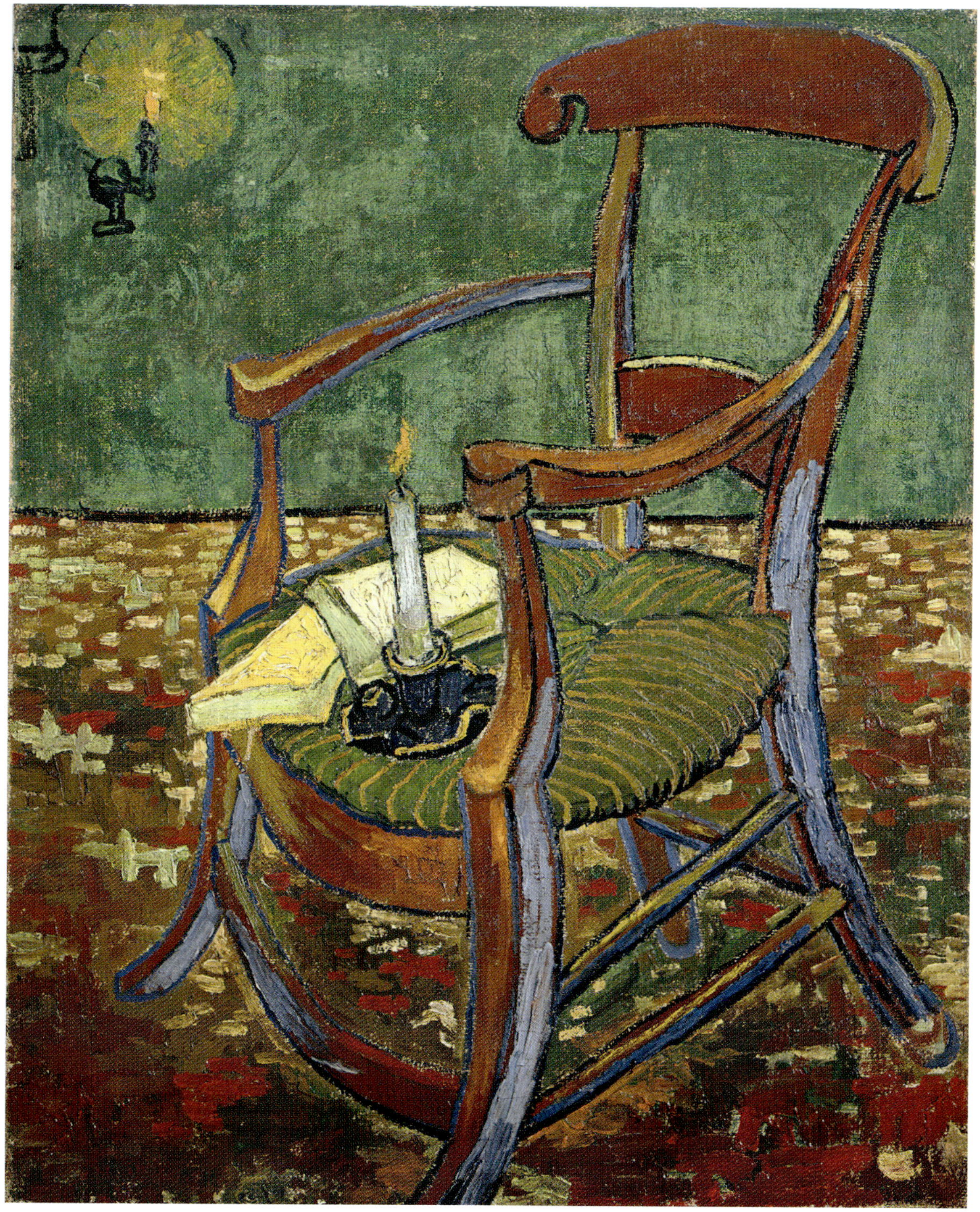

49. Vincent van Gogh
Gauguin's Chair, 1888
(Le fauteuil de Gauguin)
Oil on jute. 90.5 x 72 cm
[Faille n. 499]
Van Gogh Museum, Amsterdam
(Vincent van Gogh Foundation)

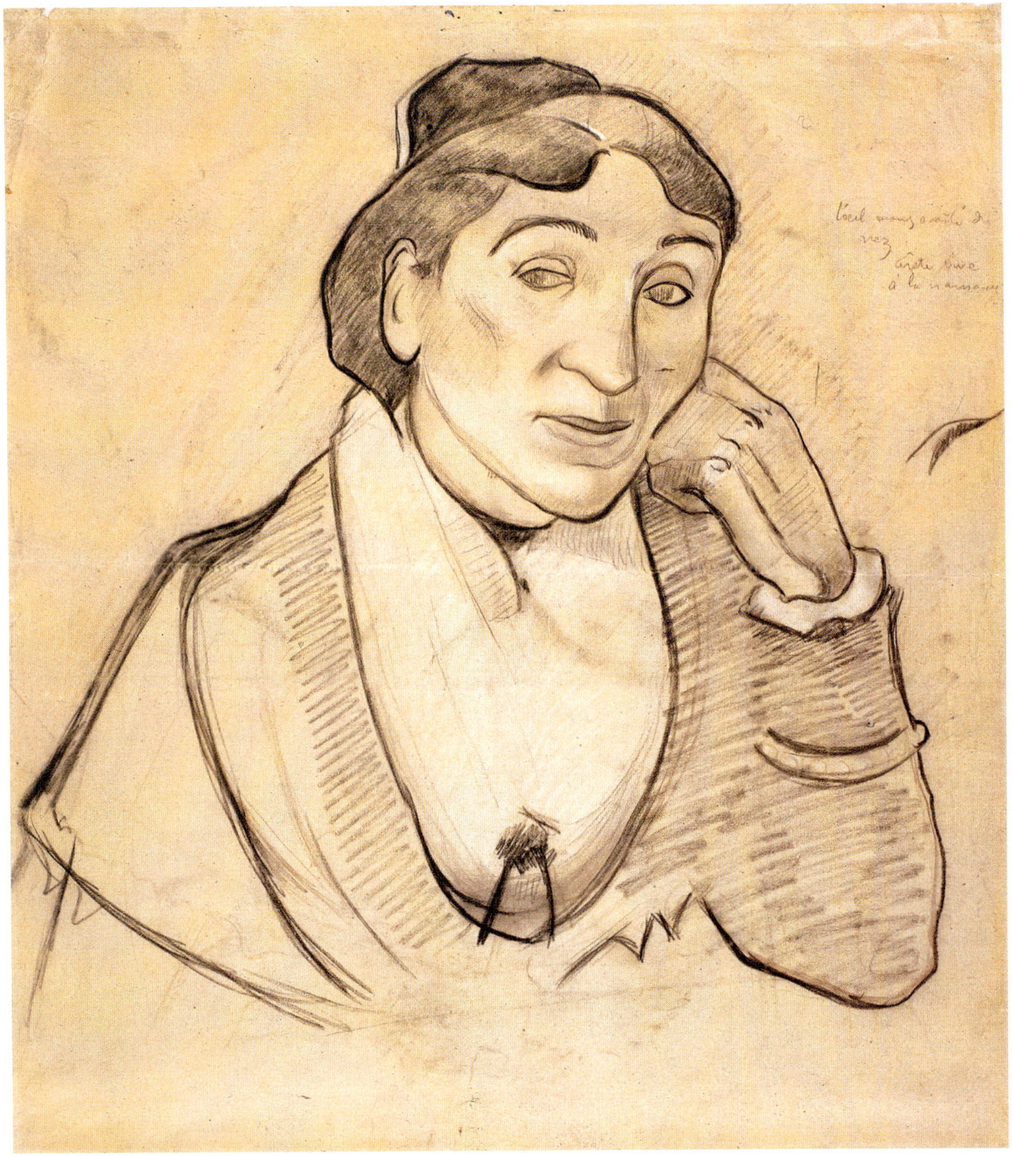

50. Paul Gauguin
L'Arlèsienne. Madame Ginoux, 1888
Coloured chalks and charcoal on paper.
56.1 x 49.2 cm
Fine Arts Museums of San Francisco,
(Memorial gift from Dr T. Edward and Tullah Hanley, Bradford, Pennsylvania 69.30.78)

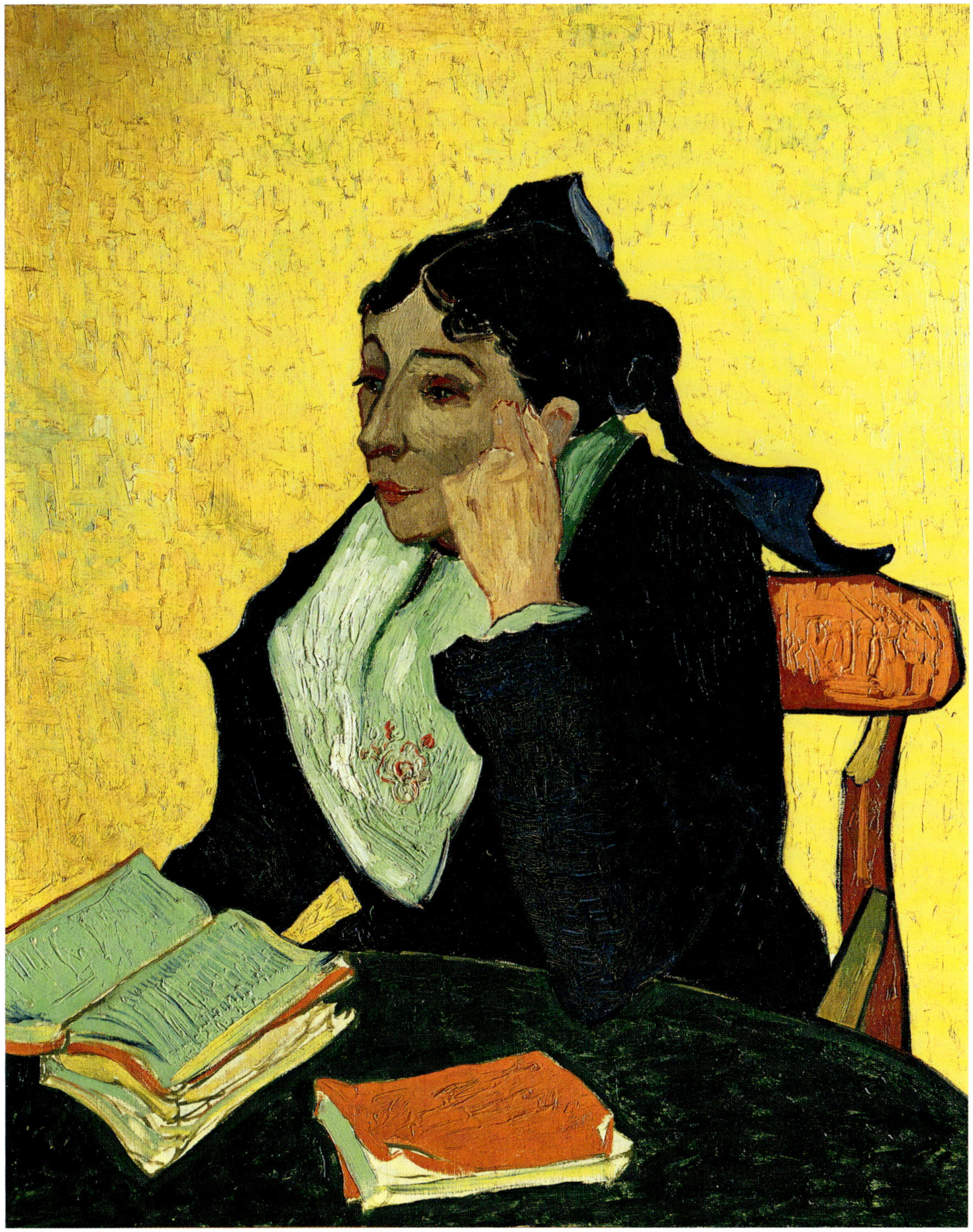

51. Vincent van Gogh
L'Arlésienne. Madame Ginoux, 1888
Oil on canvas. 91.4 x 73.7 cm
[Faille n. 488]
Metropolitan Museum of Art, New York
(Bequest of Sam A. Lewisohn, 1951 [51.112.3])

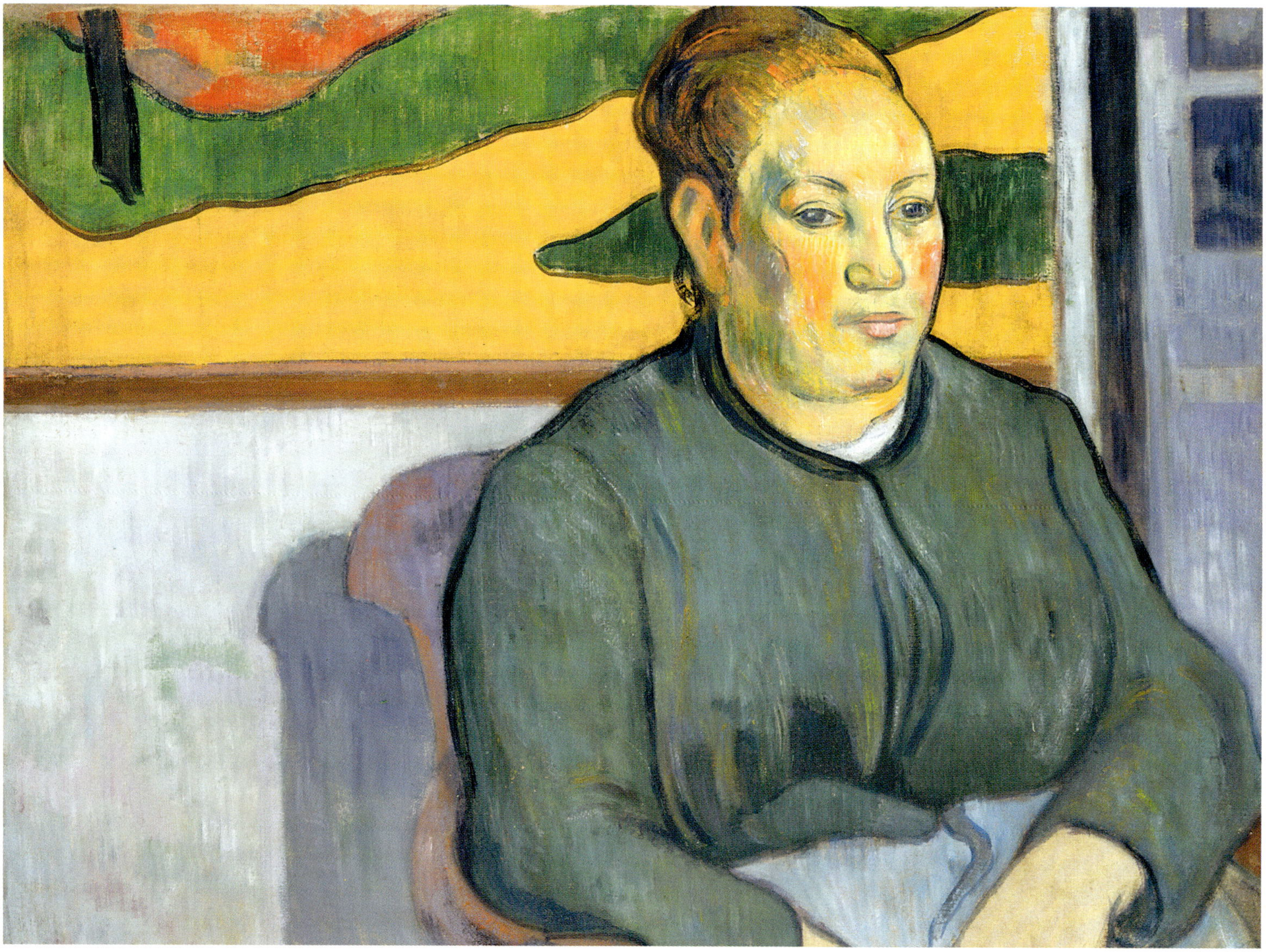

52. Paul Gauguin
Portrait of Madame Roulin, 1888
(Portrait de Madame Roulin)
Oil on canvas. 50.5 x 63.5 cm
[Wildenstein 2001 n. 327]
The Saint Louis Art Museum
(Funds given by Mrs Mark C. Steinberg)

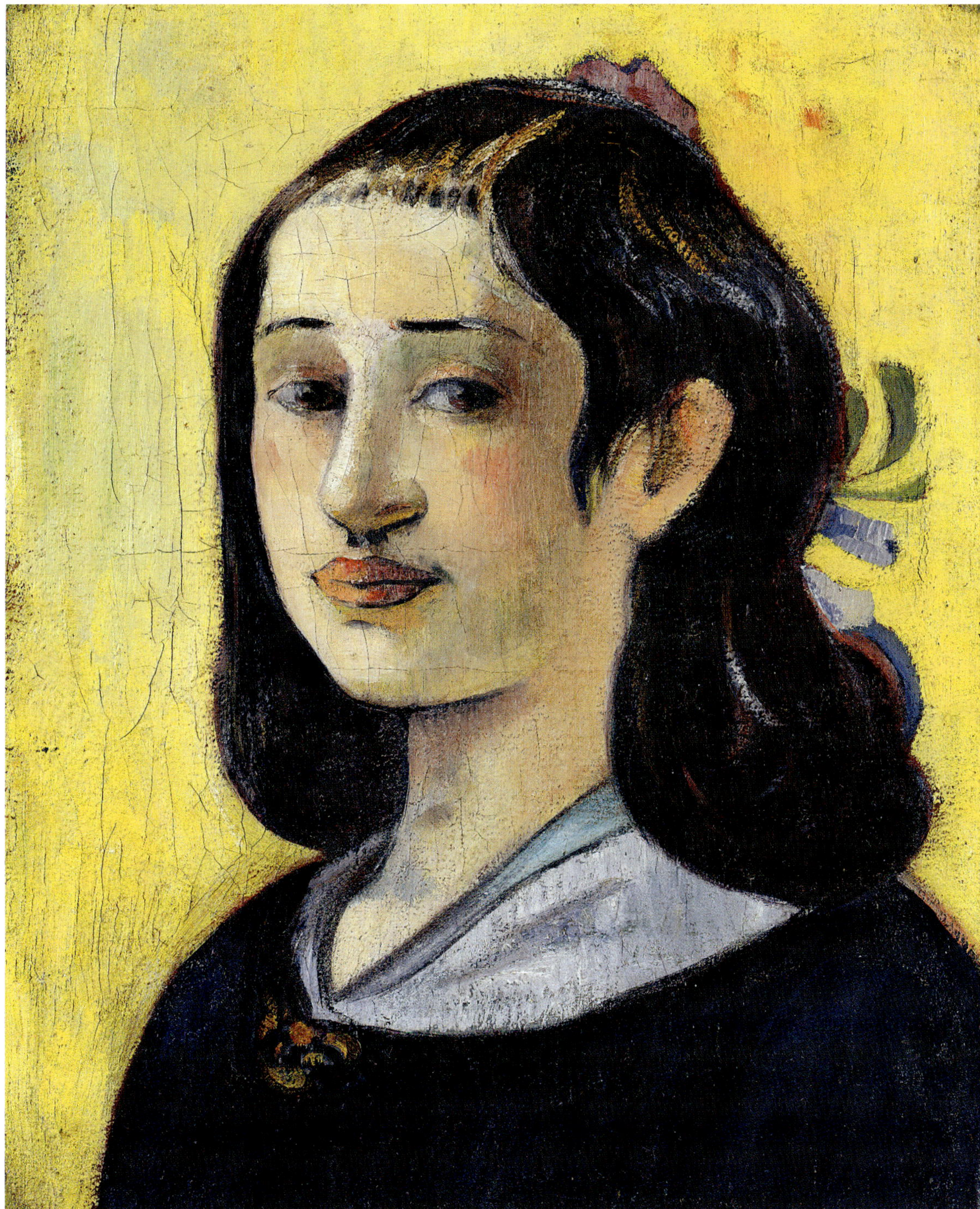

53. Paul Gauguin
The Artist's Mother, 1888
(La mère de l'artiste)
Oil on canvas. 41 x 33 cm
[Wildenstein 1964 n. 385]
Staatsgalerie Stuttgart

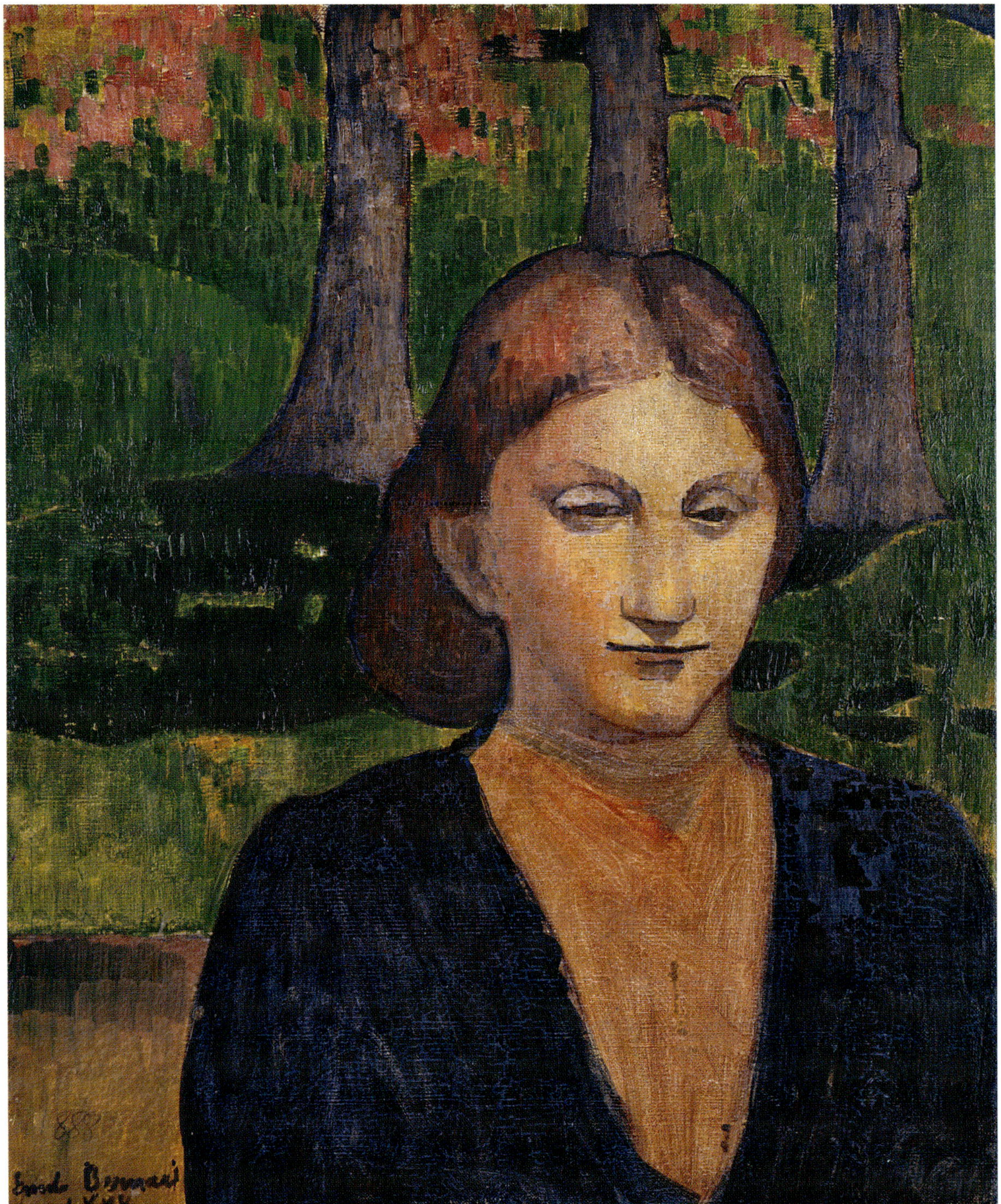

54. Émile Bernard
Portrait of Madeleine, 1888
(Portrait de Madeleine)
Oil on canvas. 61 x 50 cm
[Luthi n. 141]
Fonds national d'art contemporain, Ministère de la culture et de la communication, Paris.
In deposit at the Musée Toulouse-Lautrec, Albi
(Inv.: 16399)

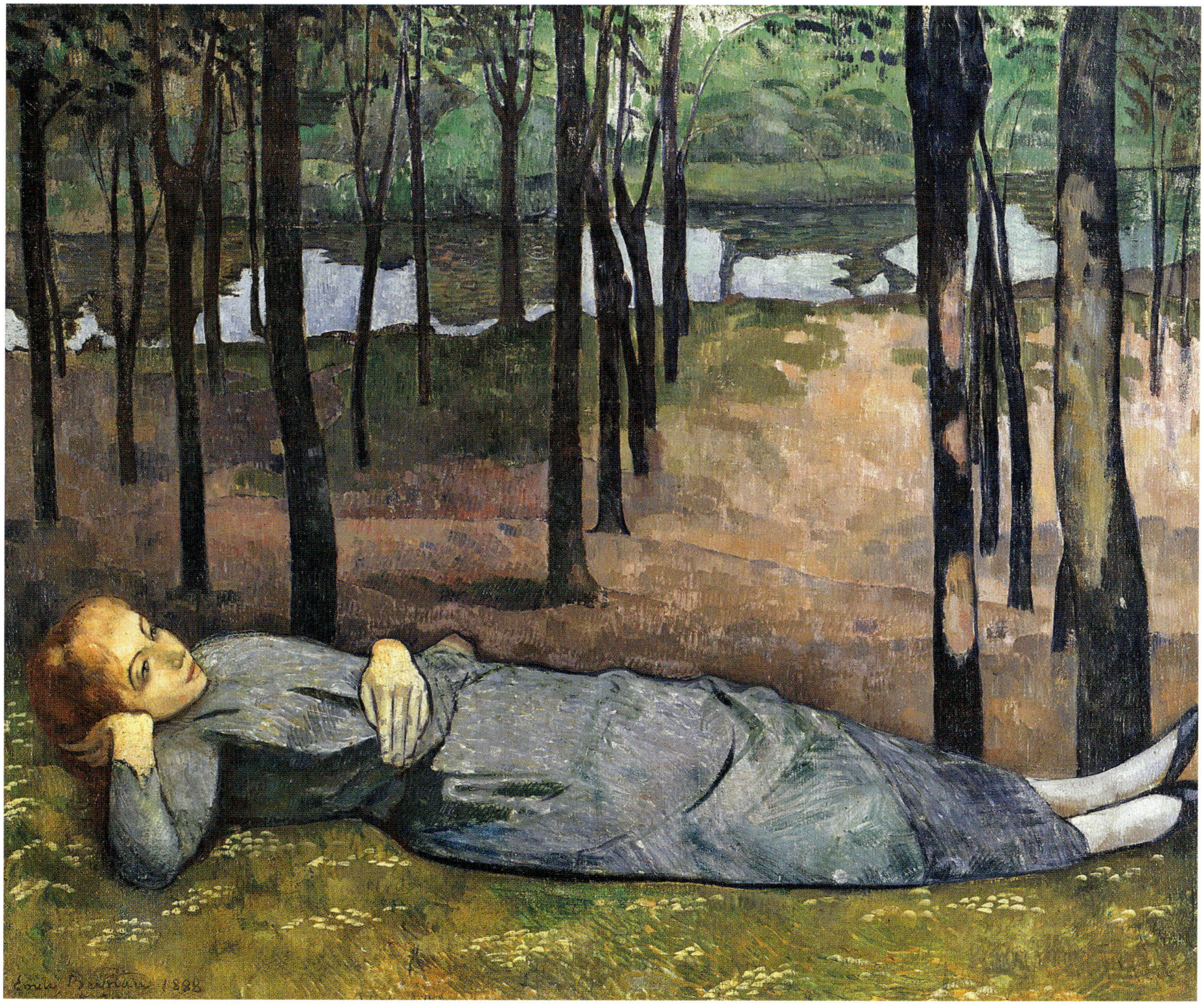

55. Émile Bernard
Madeleine in the Bois d'Amour, 1888
(Madeleine au Bois d'Amour)
Oil on canvas. 138 x 163 cm
[Luthi n. 140]
Musée d'Orsay, Paris

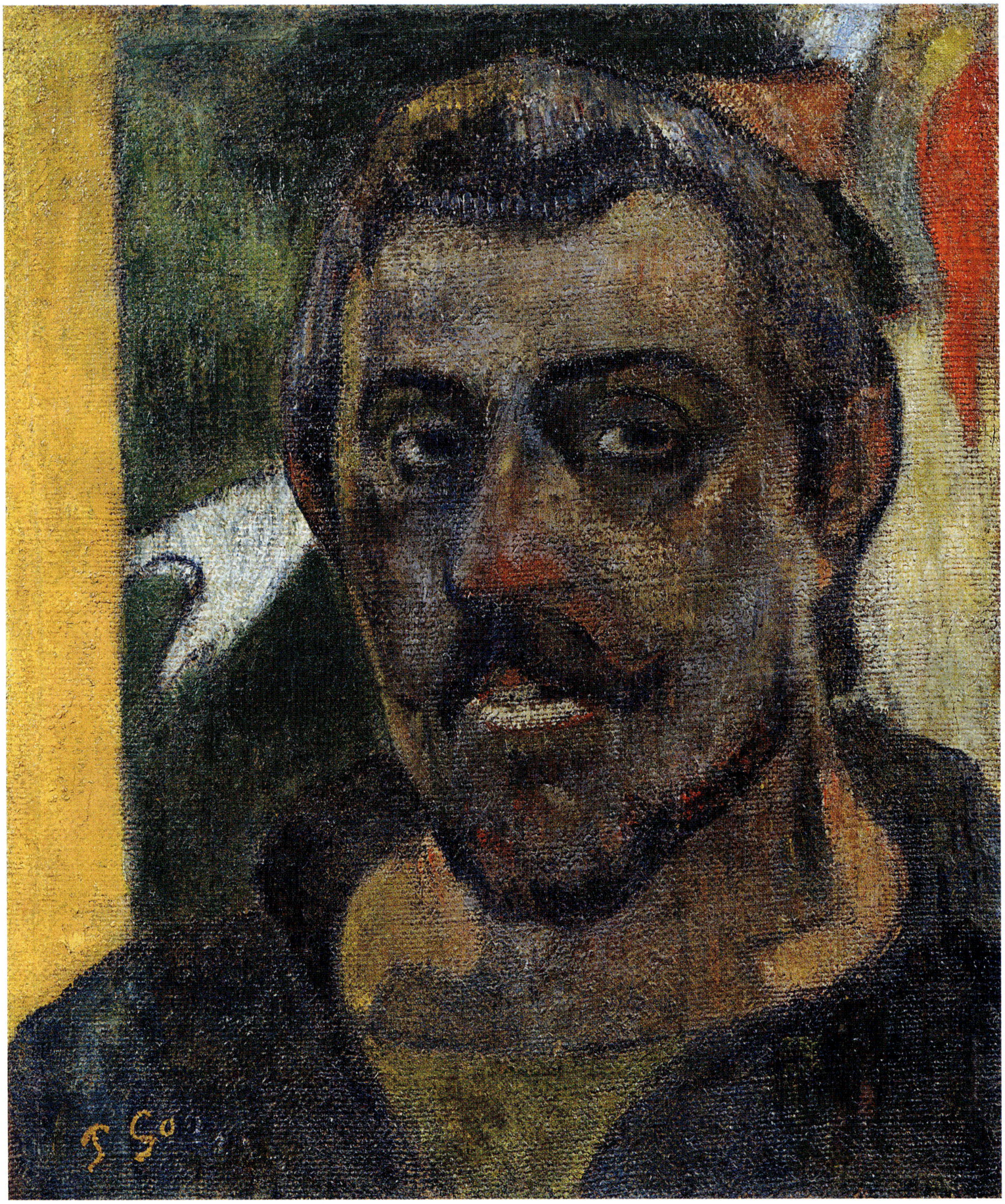

56. Paul Gauguin
Self-Portrait, 1889
(Autoportrait)
Oil on canvas. 46 x 38 cm
[Wildenstein 1964 n. 297]
State Pushkin Museum of Fine Arts, Moscow

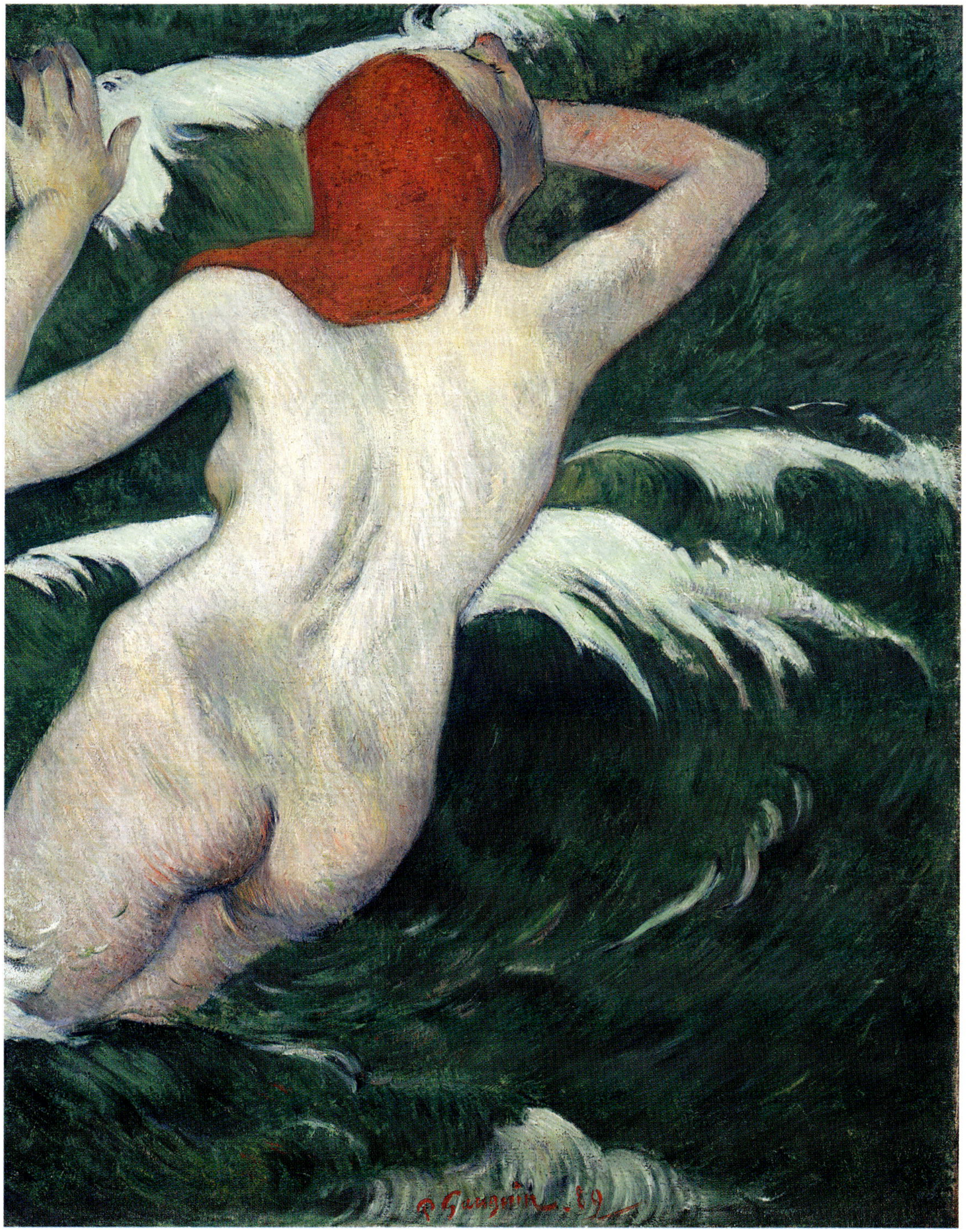

57. Paul Gauguin
In the Waves (Ondine I), 1889
(Dans les vagues [Ondine I])
Oil on canvas. 92.5 x 72.4 cm
[Wildenstein 1964 n. 336]
The Cleveland Museum of Art
(Gift of Mr and Mrs William Powell Jones, 1978.63)

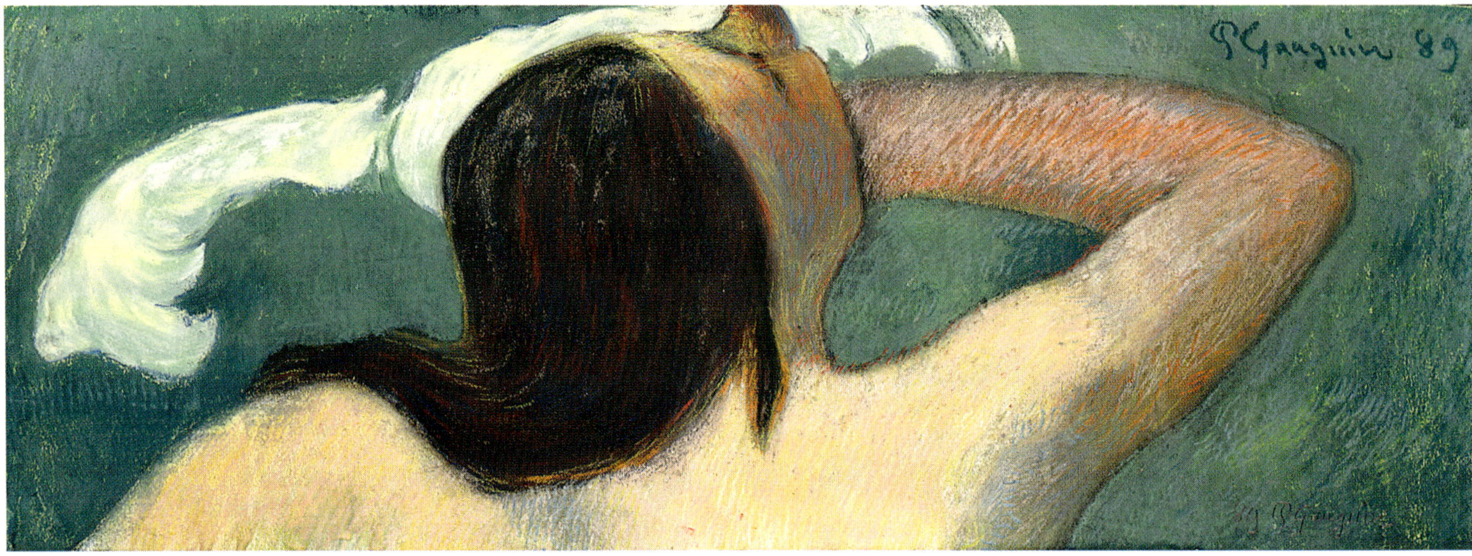

58. Paul Gauguin
Woman in the Waves (Ondine II), 1889
(Femme à la vague [Ondine II])
Pastel and gouache on paper mounted on wood panel.
18 x 48.2 cm
[Wildenstein 1964 n. 337]
Private Collection

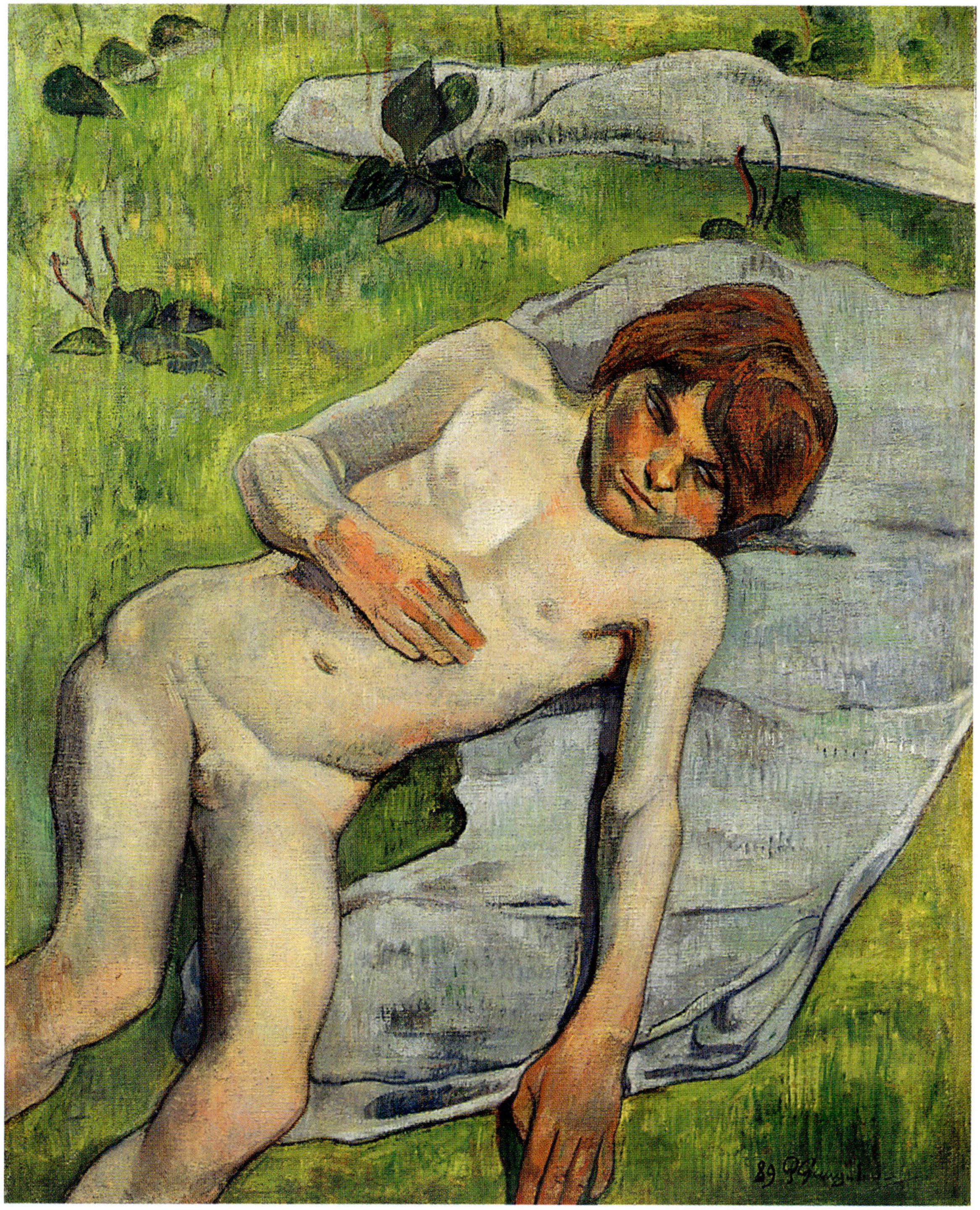

59. Paul Gauguin
Nude Breton Boy, 1889
(Petit Breton nu)
Oil on canvas. 93 x 73.5 cm
[Wildestein 1964 n. 339]
Wallraf-Richartz Museum-Fondation Corboud, Cologne

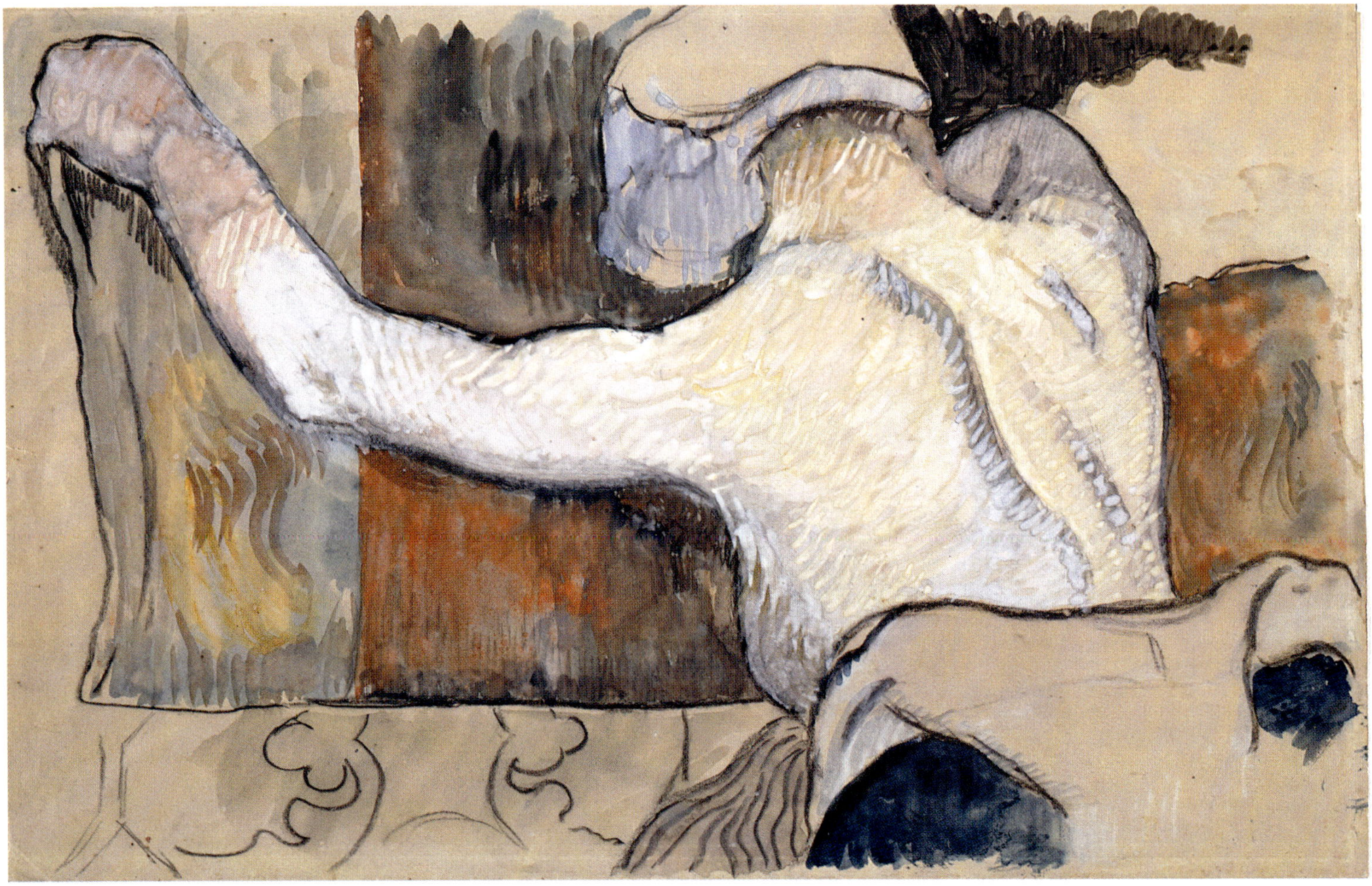

60. Paul Gauguin
Woman Seen from the Back, Study, 1888
(La Femme vue de dos, Étude)
Watercolour on paper. 26.3 x 40.4 cm
[Wildenstein 2001 p. 529]
Van Gogh Museum, Amsterdam
(Vincent van Gogh Foundation)

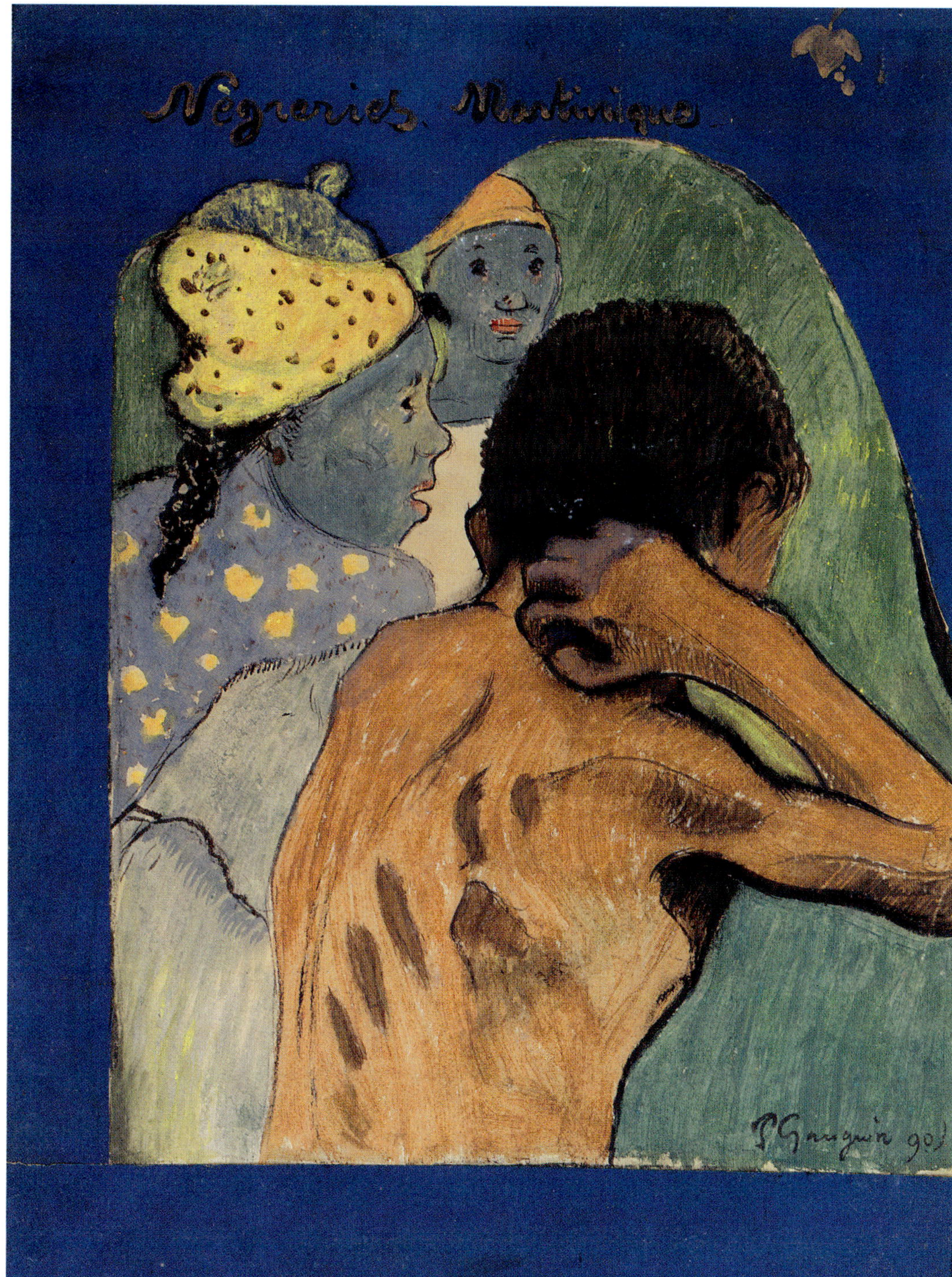

61. Paul Gauguin
Nègreries Martinique, 1890
Gouache, watercolour, ink, gold paint and collage on paper. 33.2 x 24.8 cm
[Wildenstein 1964 n. 391]
Jan and Marie-Anne Krugier-Poniatowski Collection

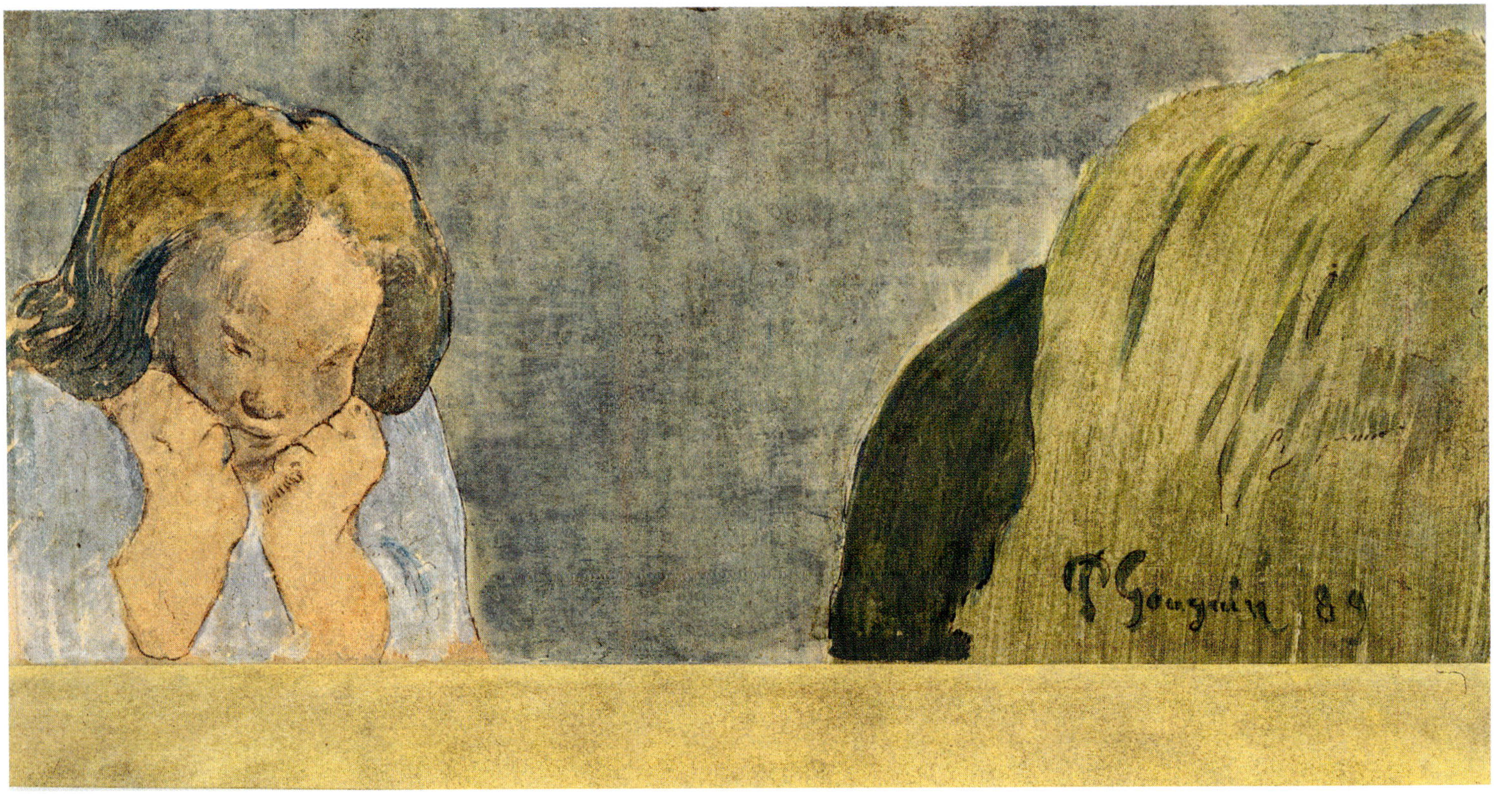

62. Paul Gauguin
Human Misery, 1889
(Misères humaines)
Watercolour and ink on paper. 20.5 x 38.5 cm
Musée Maillol, Paris

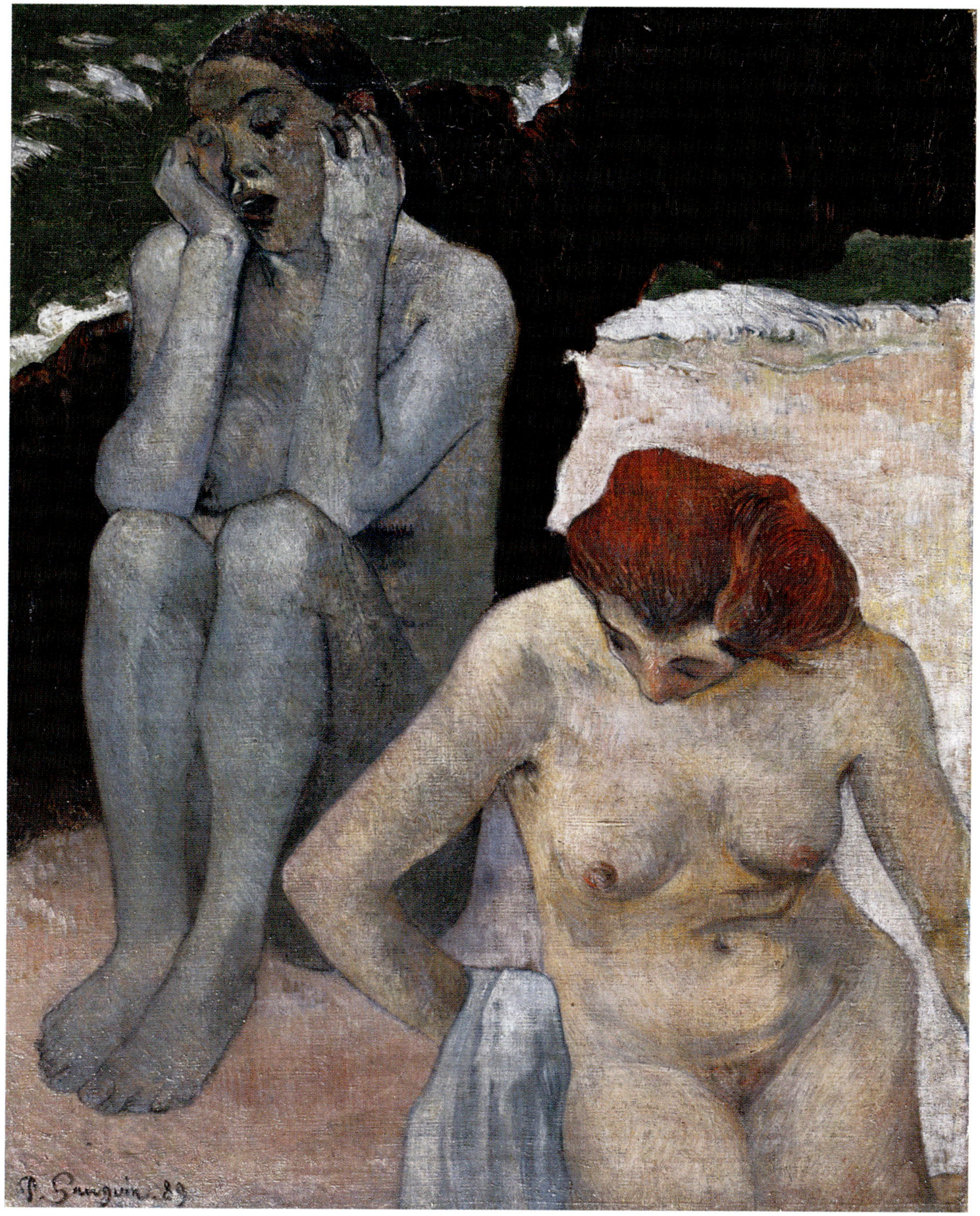

63. Paul Gauguin
Life and Death, 1889
(La vie et la mort)
Oil on canvas. 92 x 73 cm
[Wildenstein 1964 n. 335]
Mahmoud Khalil Museum, Cairo

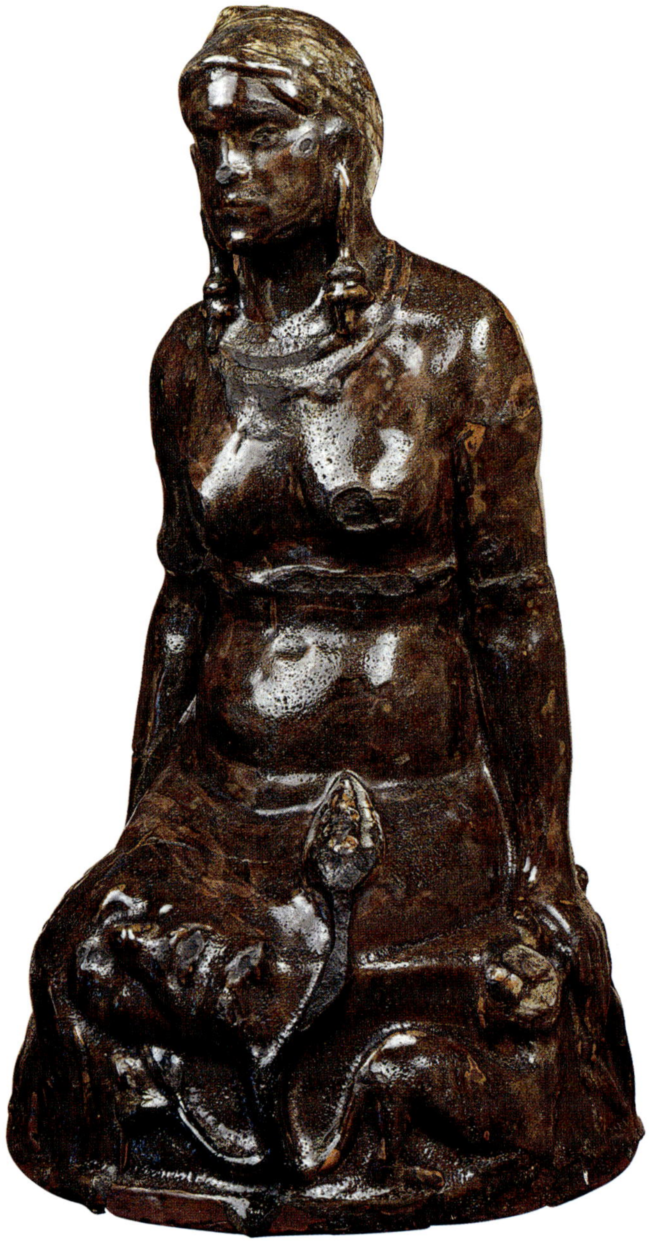

64. Paul Gauguin
Black Venus, 1889
(Vénus noire)
Glazed clay. 50 cm
Nassau County Division of Museum Services at the
Sands Point Preserve, New York

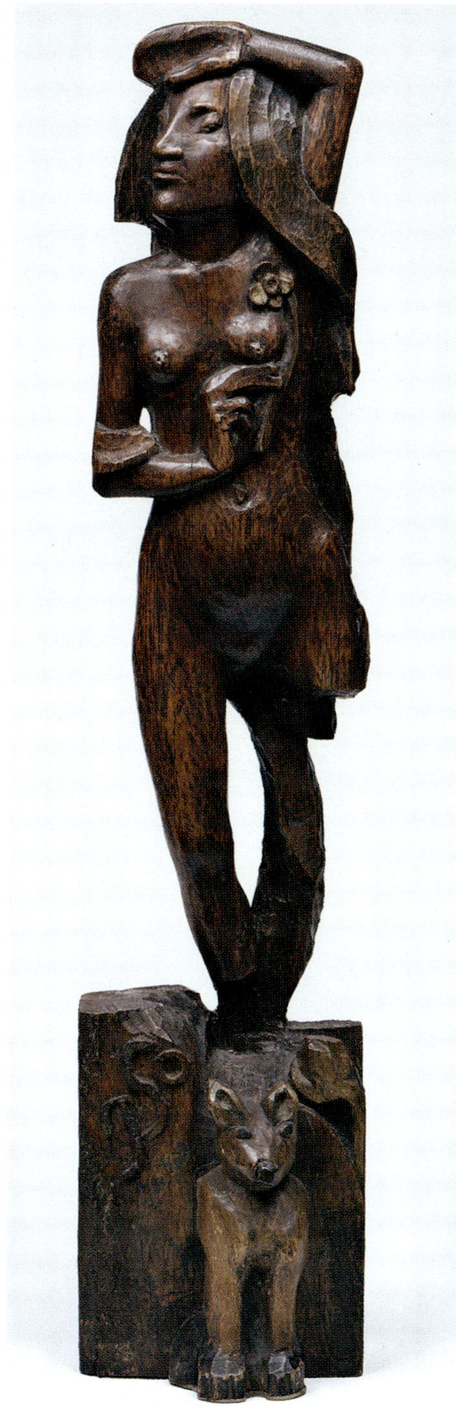

65. Paul Gauguin
Lust, 1890
(La Luxure)
Carving in polychrome and gilded pine and oak wood.
70 x 15 x 7 cm
J. F. Willumsens Museum, Frederikssund, Denmark

66. Paul Gauguin
Ictus, c. 1889–1890
Watercolour on paper. 41.6 x 56 cm
Private Collection. Courtesy Daniel Malingue, Paris

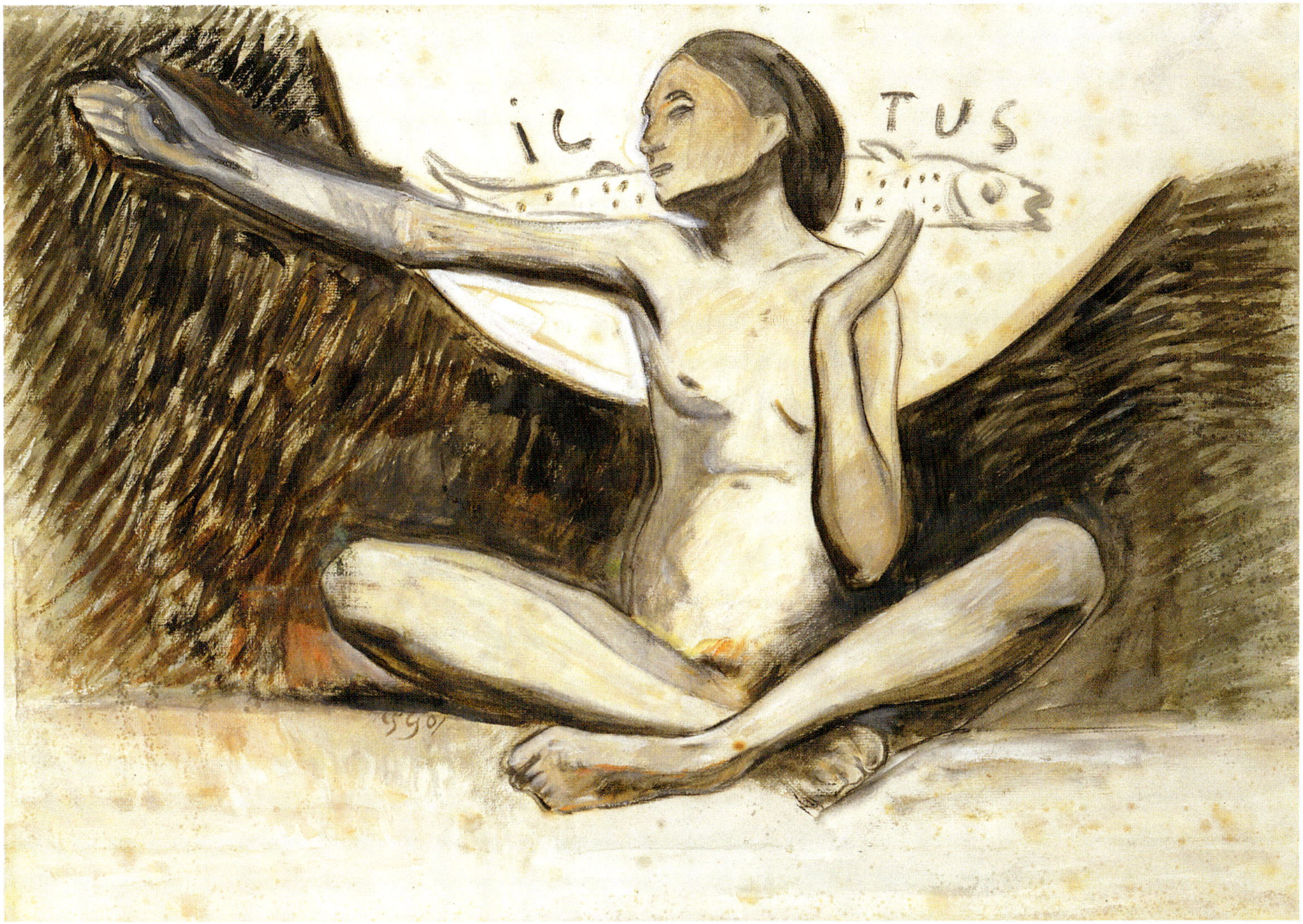
IC
TUS

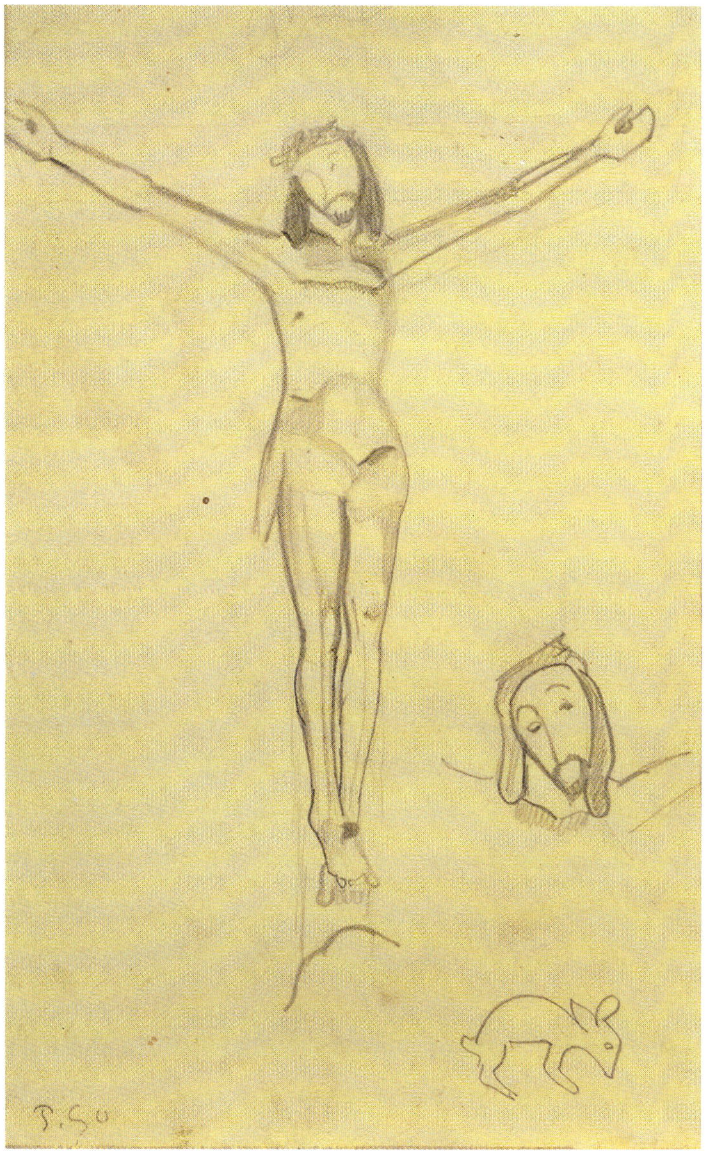

67. Paul Gauguin
Sketch for 'The Yellow Christ', 1889
(Étude pour 'Le Christ jaune')
Pencil on paper. 26.7 x 17.8 cm
Carmen Thyssen-Bornemisza Collection
on loan at the Museo Thyssen-Bornemisza, Madrid

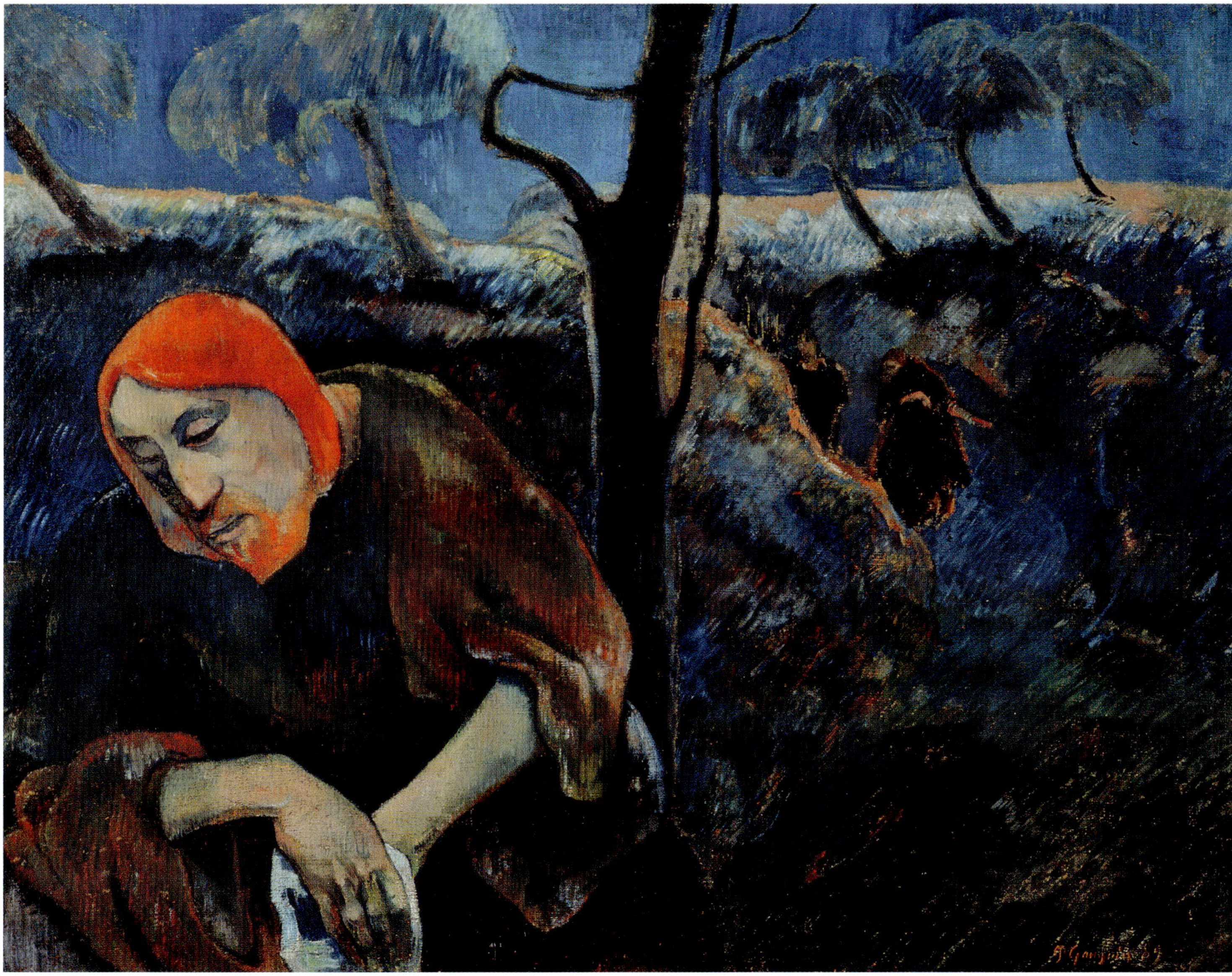

68. Paul Gauguin
Christ in the Garden of Olives, 1889
(Christ au jardin des Oliviers)
Oil on canvas. 72.4 x 91.4 cm
[Wildenstein 1964 n. 326]
Norton Gallery of Art, West Palm Beach, Florida
(Gift of Elizabeth C. Norton, 46.5)

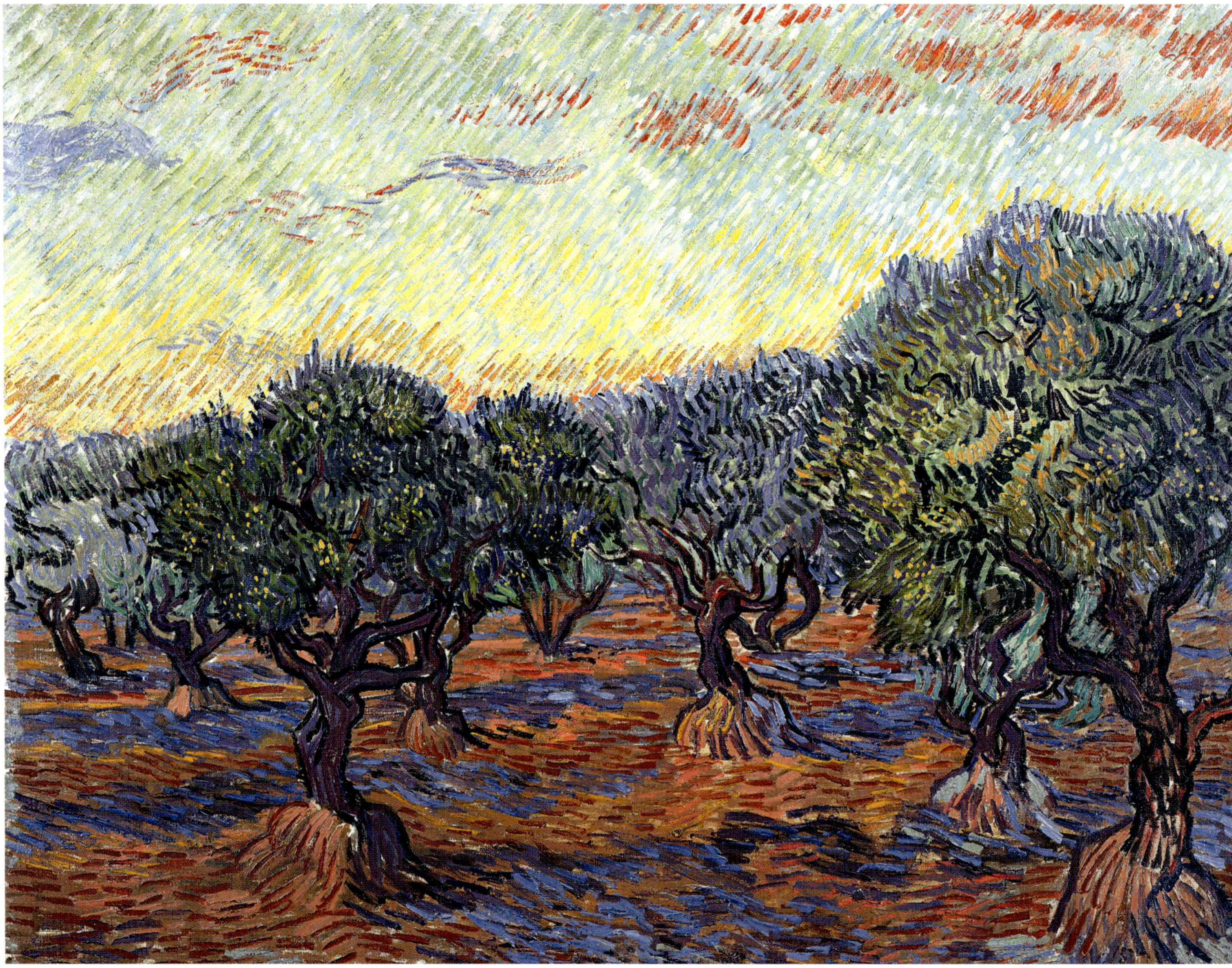

69. Vincent van Gogh
Olive Grove, 1889
(Forêt d'oliviers)
Oil on canvas. 74 x 93 cm
[Faille n. 586]
Göteborgs Konstmuseum, Sweden

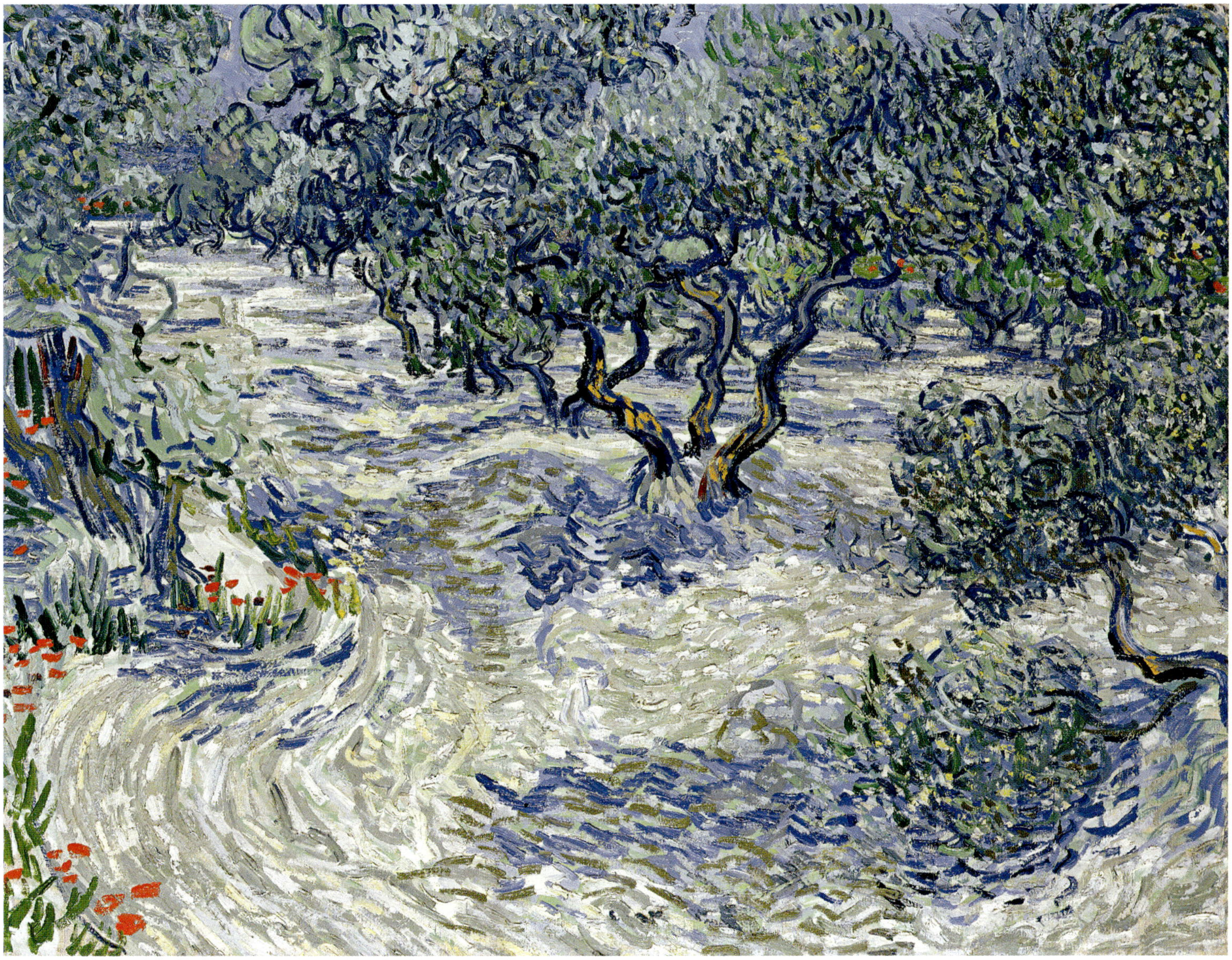

70. Vincent van Gogh
Olive Grove, 1889
(Les oliviers)
Oil on canvas. 73 x 93 cm
[Faille n. 715]
The Nelson-Atkins Museum of Art, Kansas City, Missouri
(Purchase: Nelson Trust 32-2)

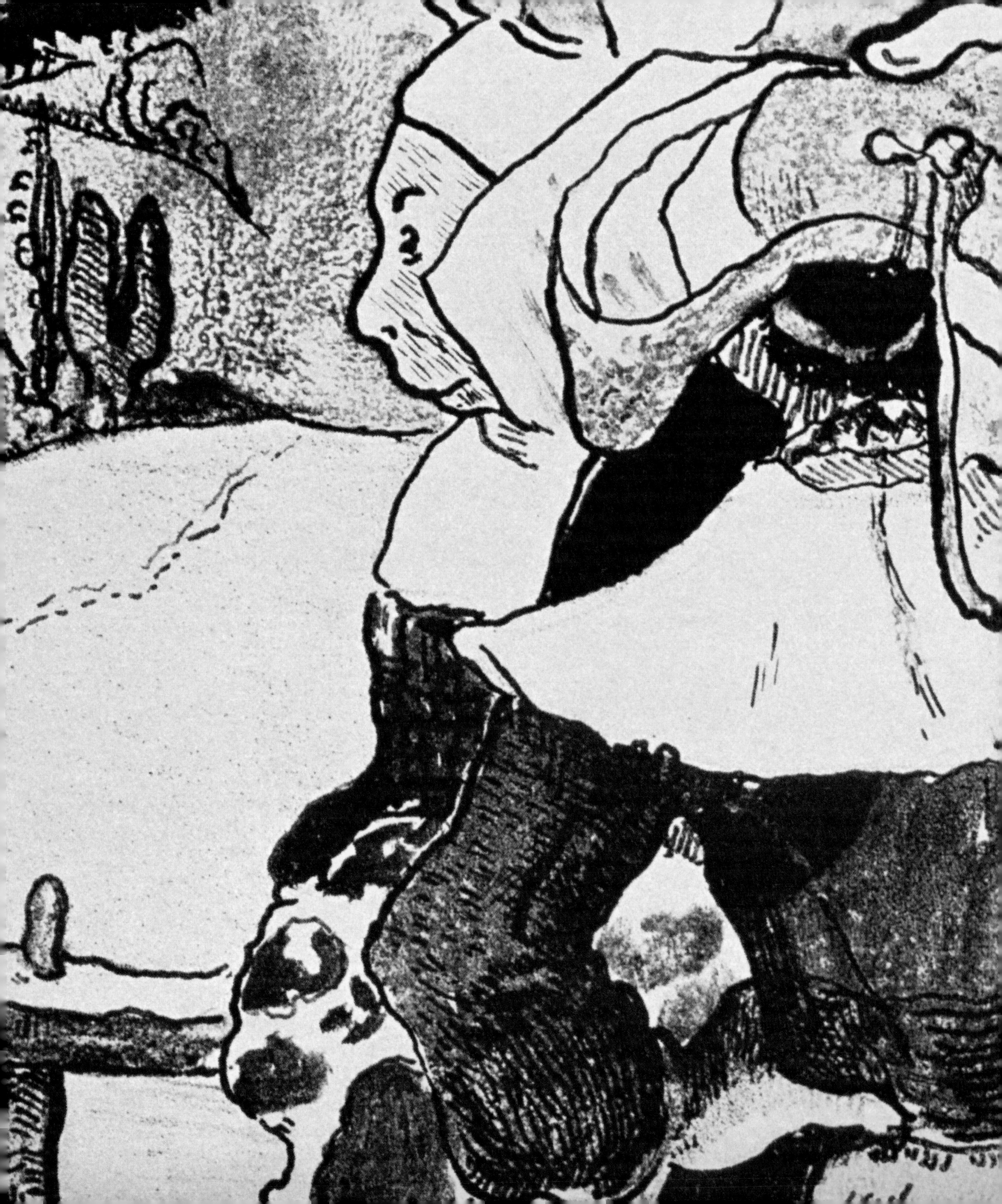

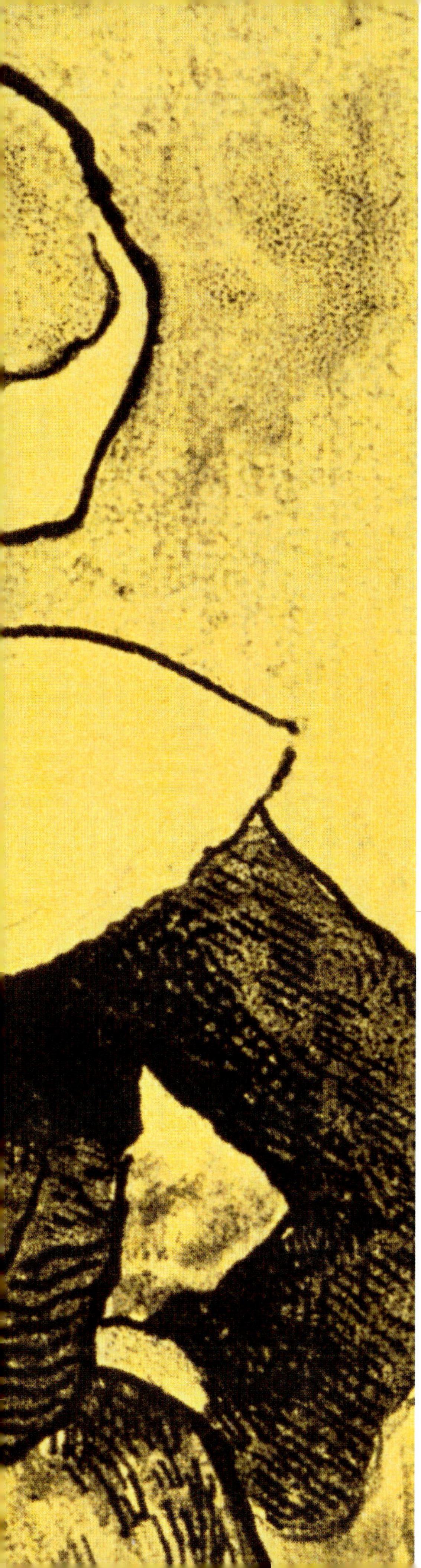

Paul Gauguin
Breton Women by a Gate, 1889
(detail)
[cat. 74]

6. Suite Volpini

71. Paul Gauguin
Leda and the Swan, 1889
(Léda et le cygne)
Zincograph. 221 x 204 mm
[Guérin n. 1]
Institut national d'histoire de l'art, Bibliothèque, collections Jacques Doucet, Paris

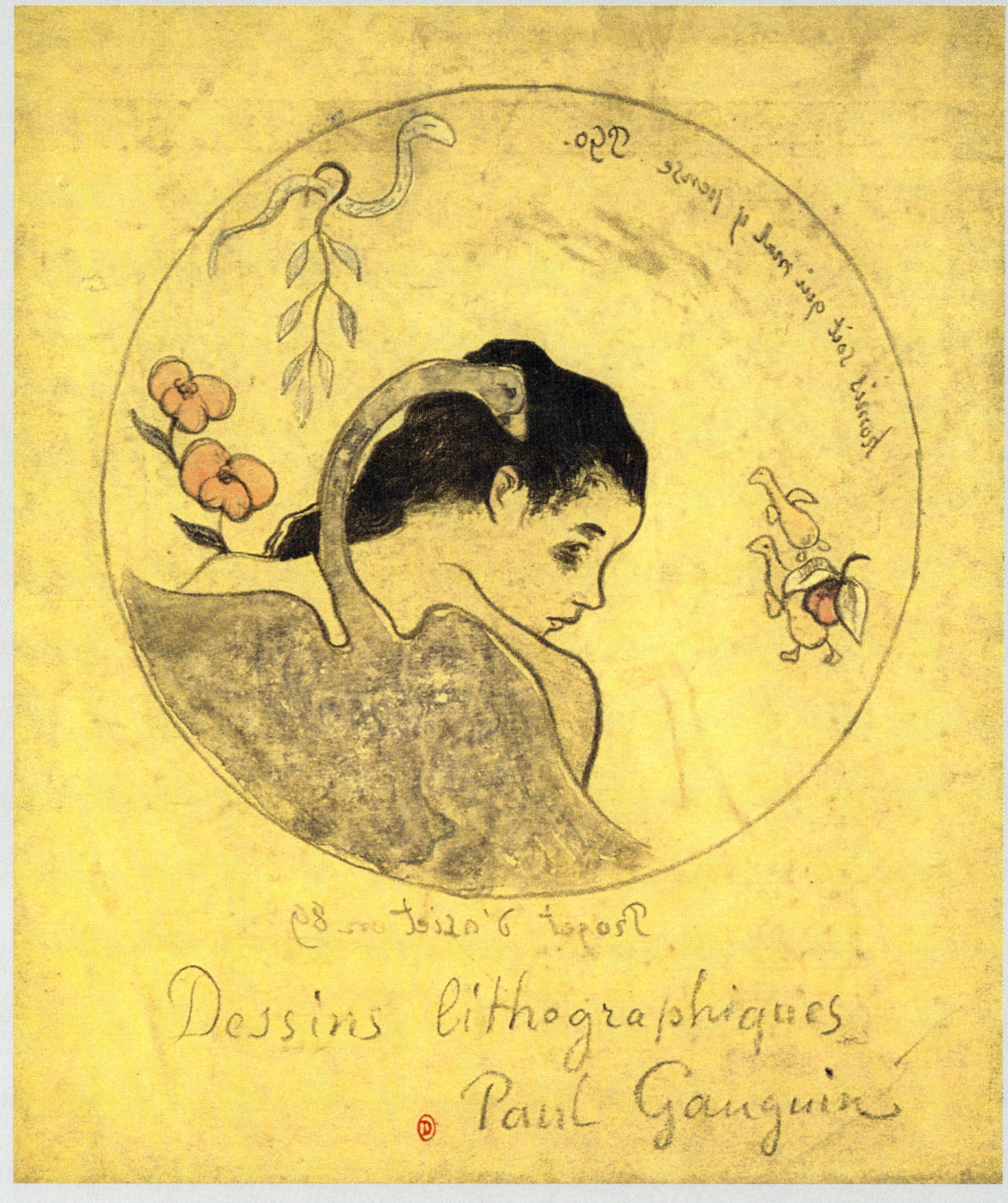
Dessins lithographiques
Paul Gauguin

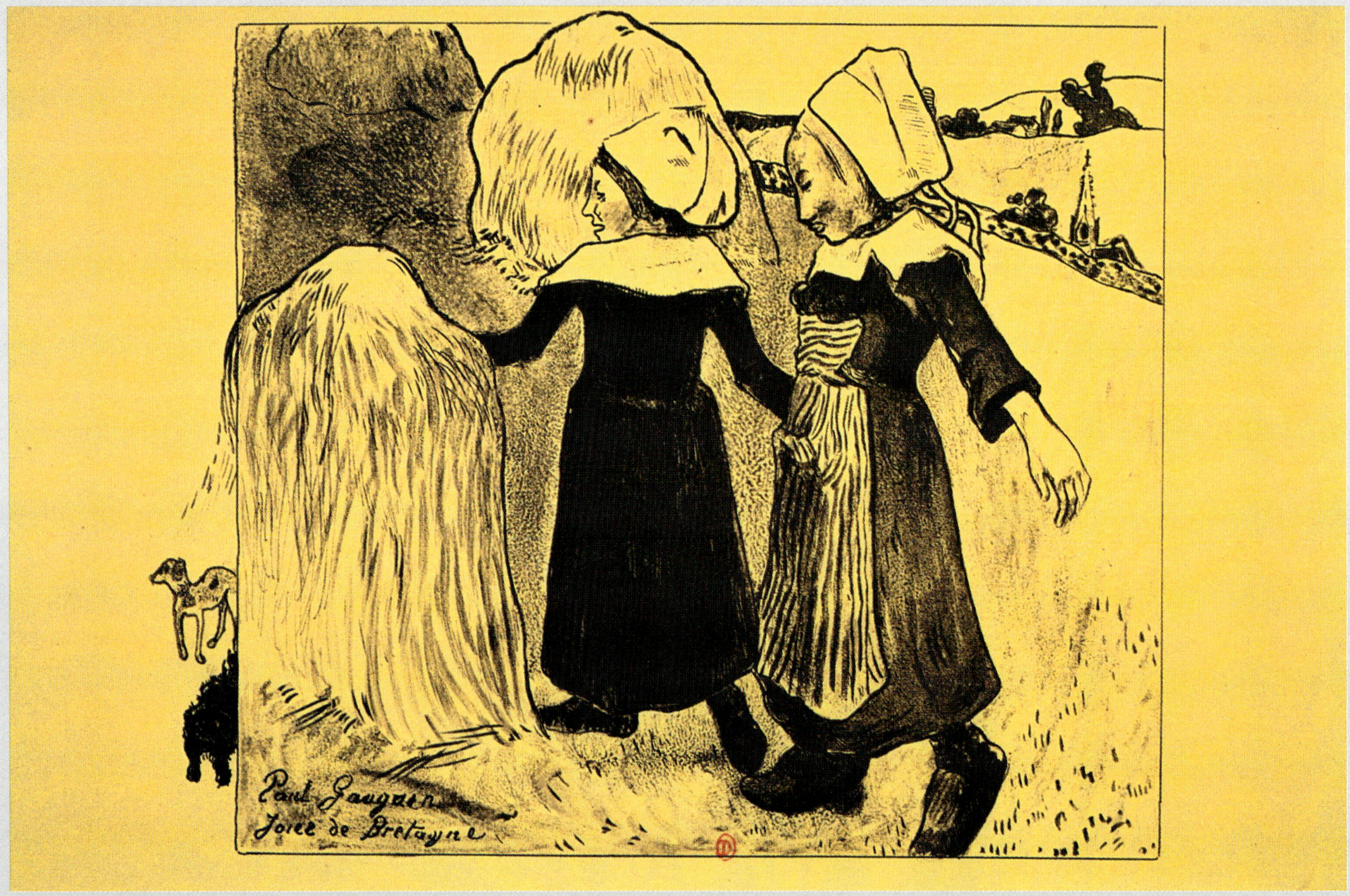

72. Paul Gauguin
The Joys of Brittany, 1889
(Joies de Bretagne)
Zincograph. 201 x 241 mm
[Guérin n. 2]
Institut national d'histoire de l'art, Bibliothèque, collections Jacques Doucet, Paris

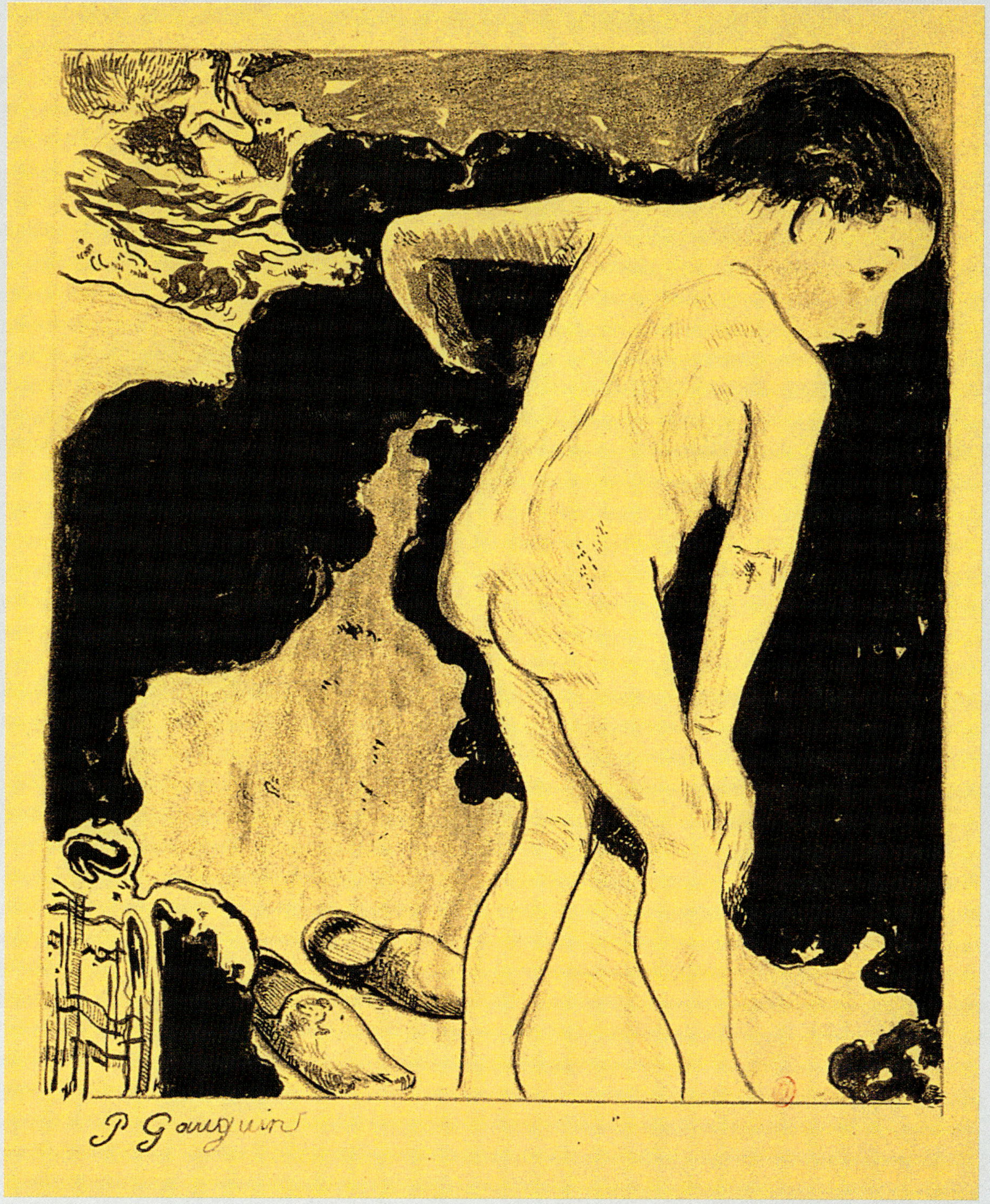

73. Paul Gauguin
Breton Bathers, 1889
(Baigneuses bretonnes)
Zincograph. 245 x 200 mm
[Guérin n. 3]
Institut national d'histoire de l'art, Bibliothèque, collections Jacques Doucet, Paris

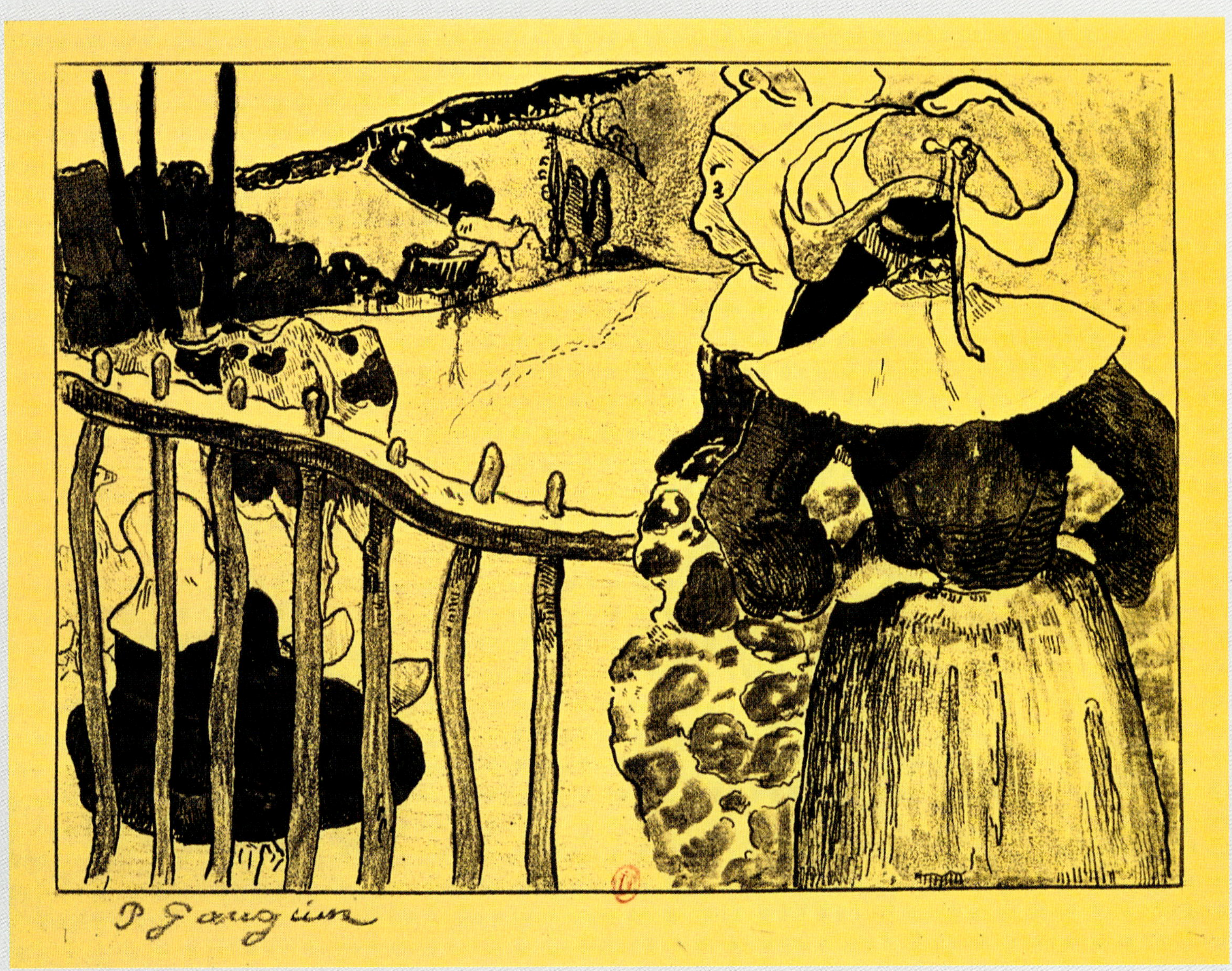

74. Paul Gauguin
Breton Women by a Gate, 1889
(Bretonnes à la barrière)
Zincograph. 170 x 215 mm
[Guérin n. 4]
Institut national d'histoire de l'art, Bibliothèque, collections Jacques Doucet, Paris

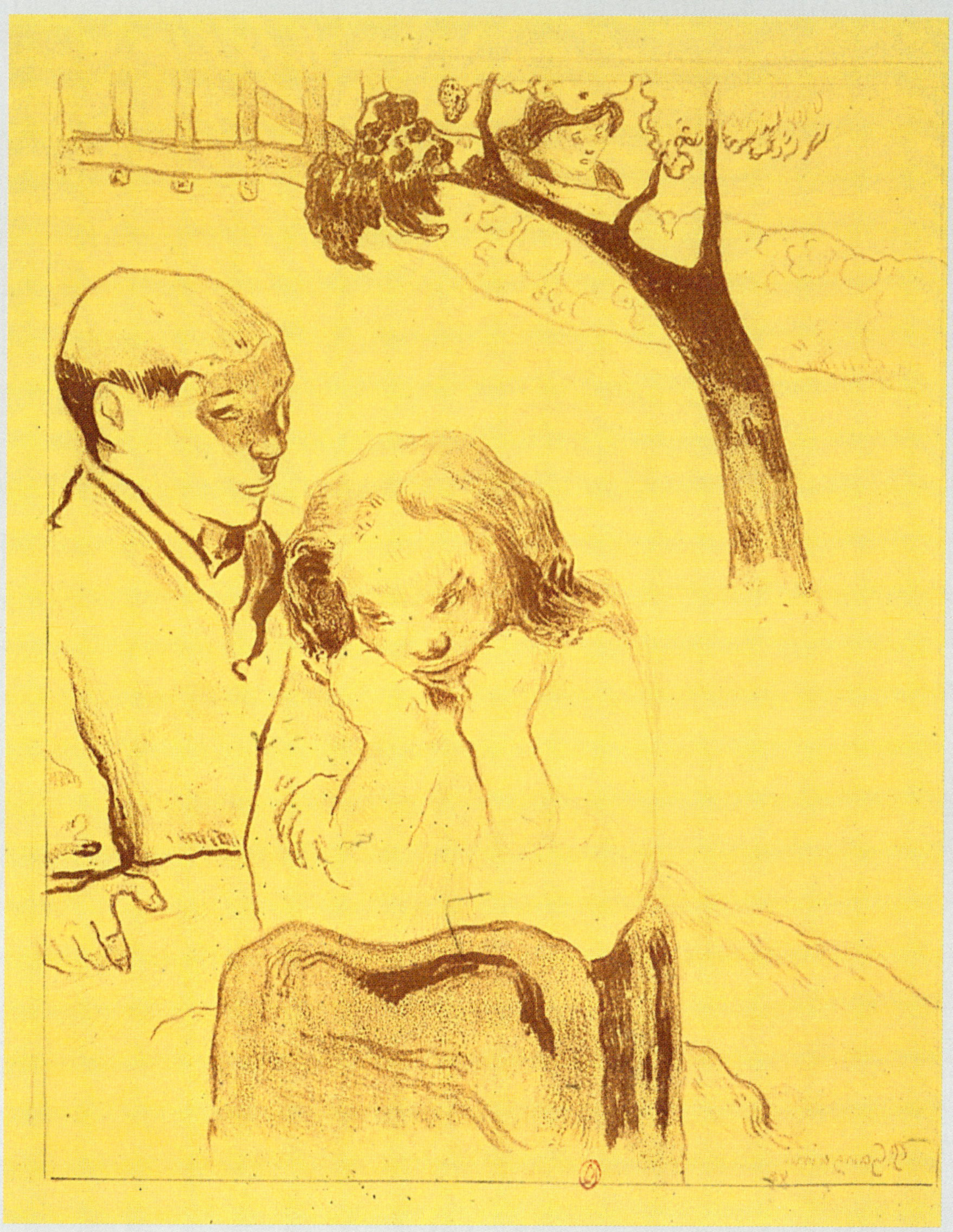

75. Paul Gauguin
Human Misery, 1889
(Misères humaines)
Zincograph. 294 x 237 mm
[Guérin n. 5]
Institut national d'histoire de l'art, Bibliothèque, collections Jacques Doucet, Paris

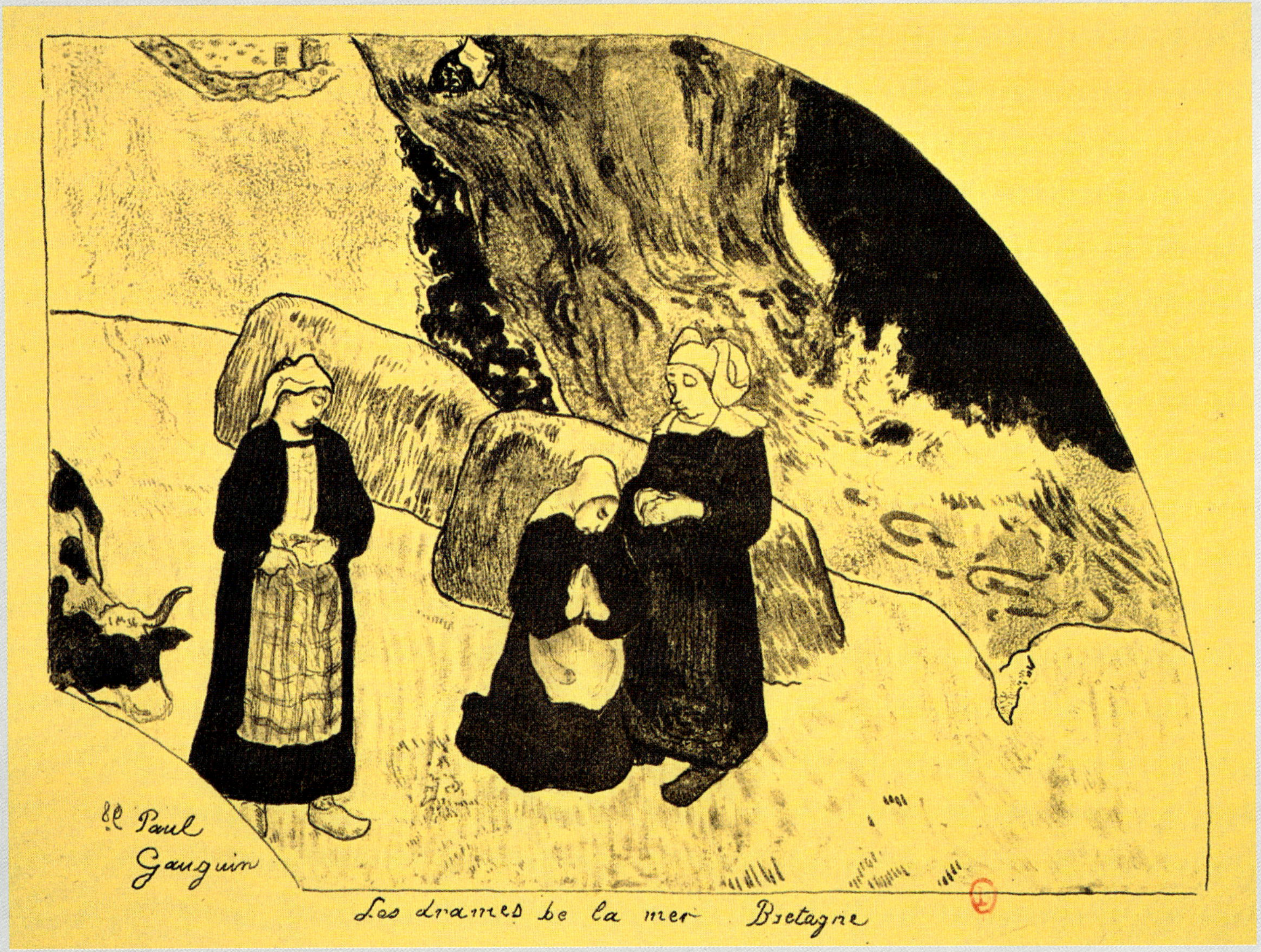

77. Paul Gauguin
Dramas of the Sea, Brittany, 1889
(Les drames de la mer, Bretagne)
Zincograph. 176 x 222 mm
[Guérin n. 7]
Institut national d'histoire de l'art, Bibliothèque, collections Jacques Doucet, Paris

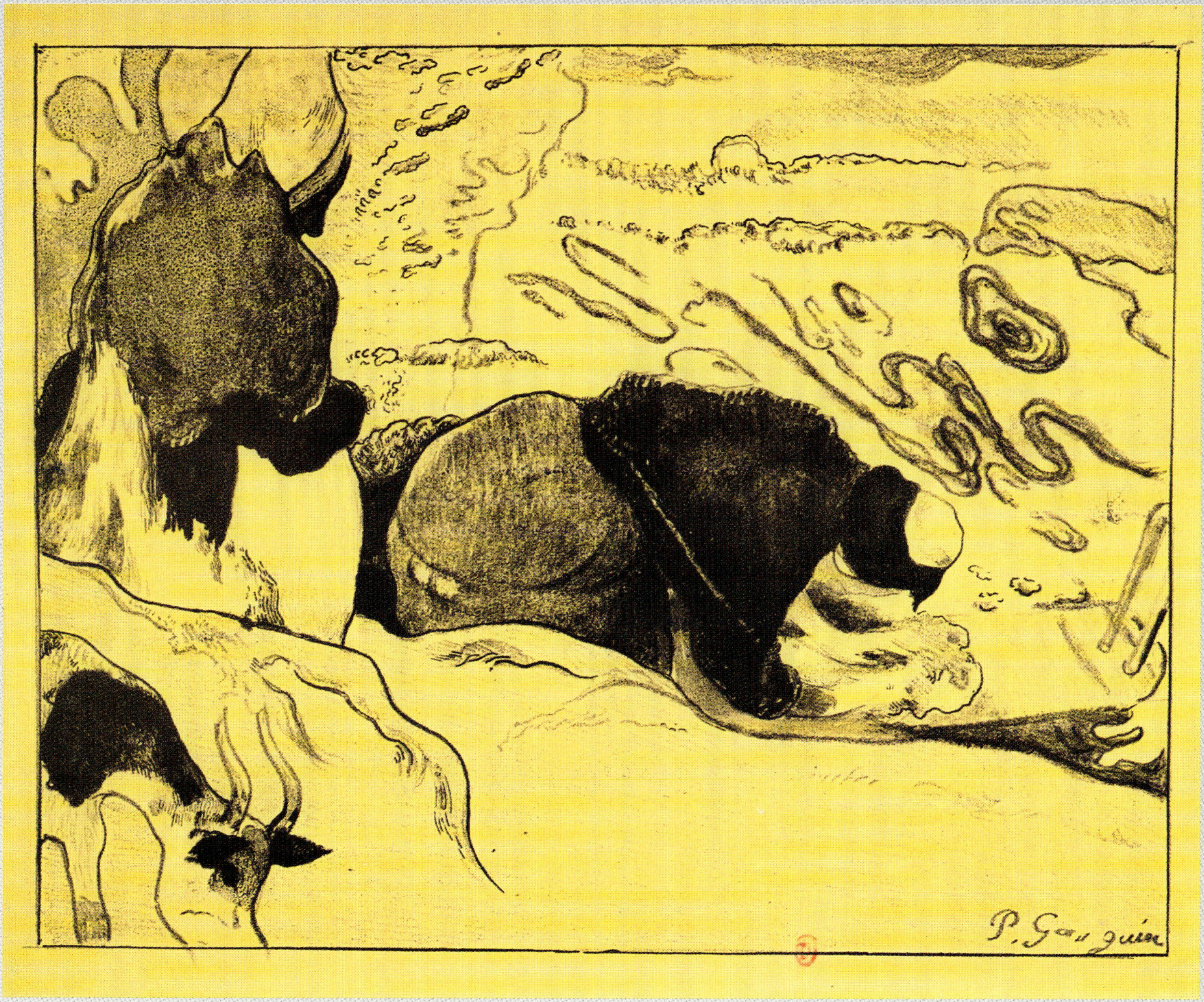

76. Paul Gauguin
Washerwomen, 1889
(Les laveuses)
Zincograph. 212 x 265 mm
[Guérin n. 6]
Institut national d'histoire de l'art, Bibliothèque, collections Jacques Doucet, Paris

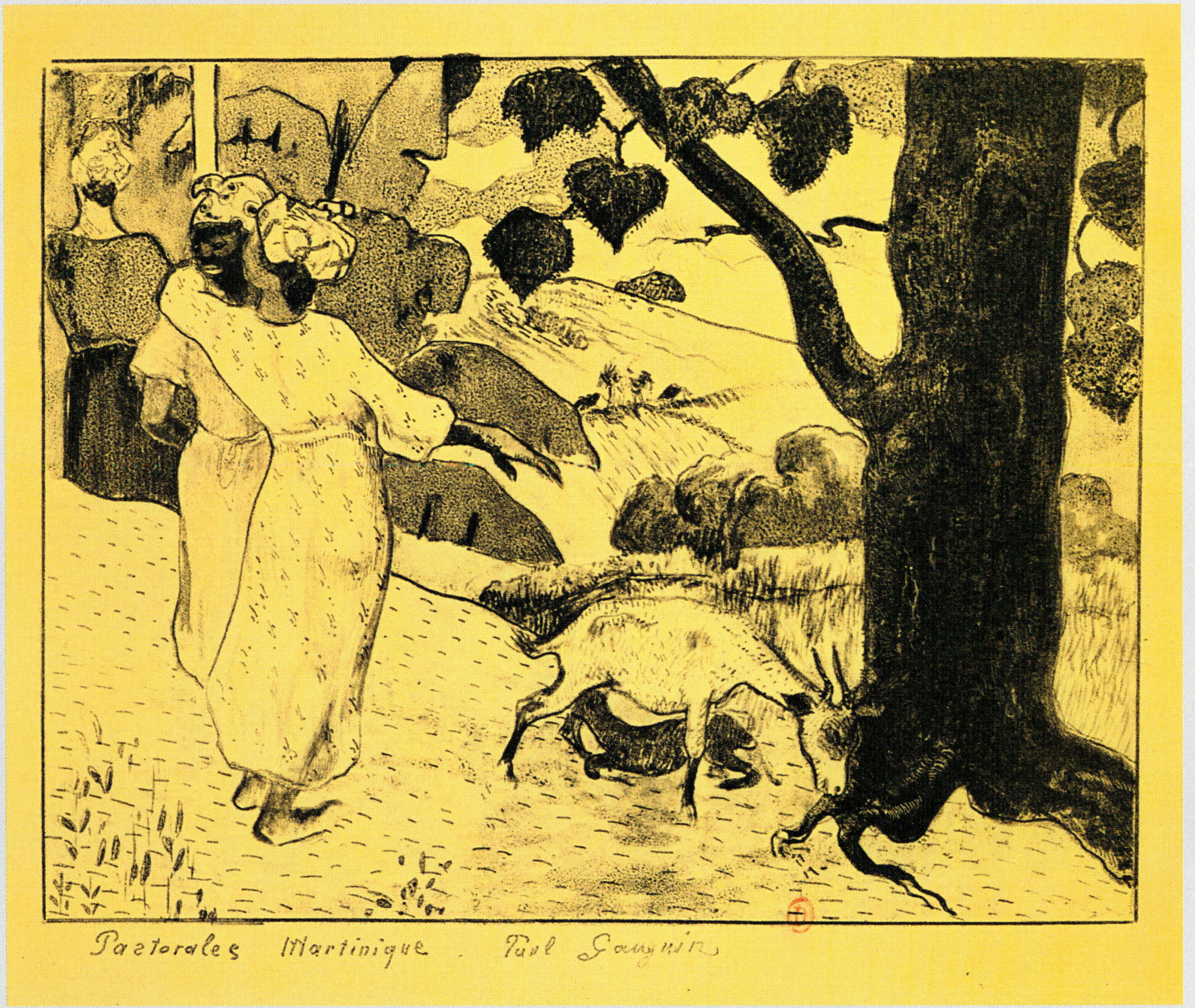

79. Paul Gauguin
Martinique Pastoral, 1889
(Pastorales Martinique)
Zincograph. 185 x 222 mm
[Guérin n. 9]
Institut national d'histoire de l'art, Bibliothèque, collections Jacques Doucet, Paris

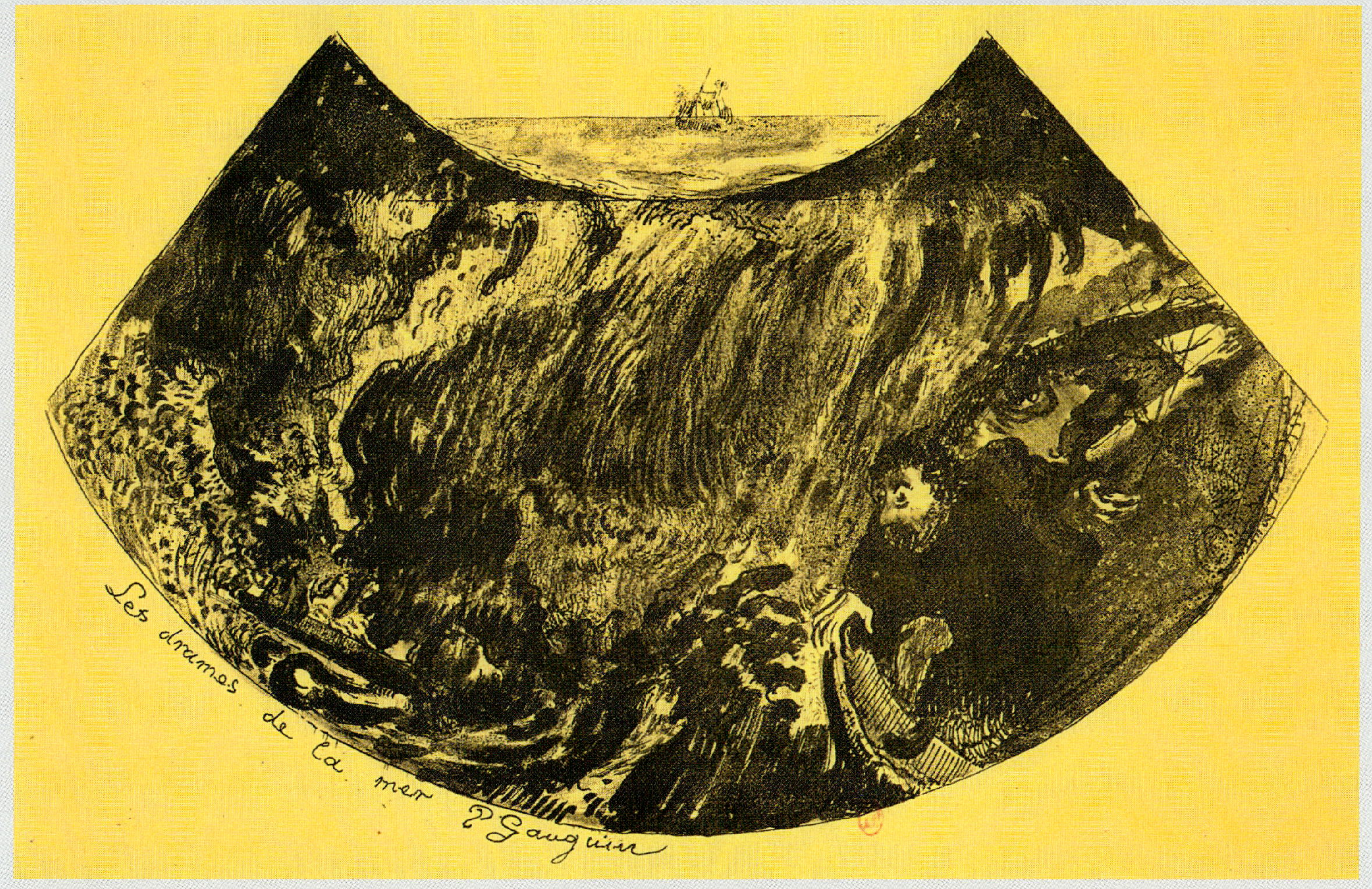

78. Paul Gauguin
Dramas of the Sea, a Descent into the Maëlstrom, 1889
(Les drames de la mer, une descente dans le Maëlstrom)
Zincograph. 180 x 272 mm
[Guérin n. 8]
Institut national d'histoire de l'art, Bibliothèque, collections Jacques Doucet, Paris

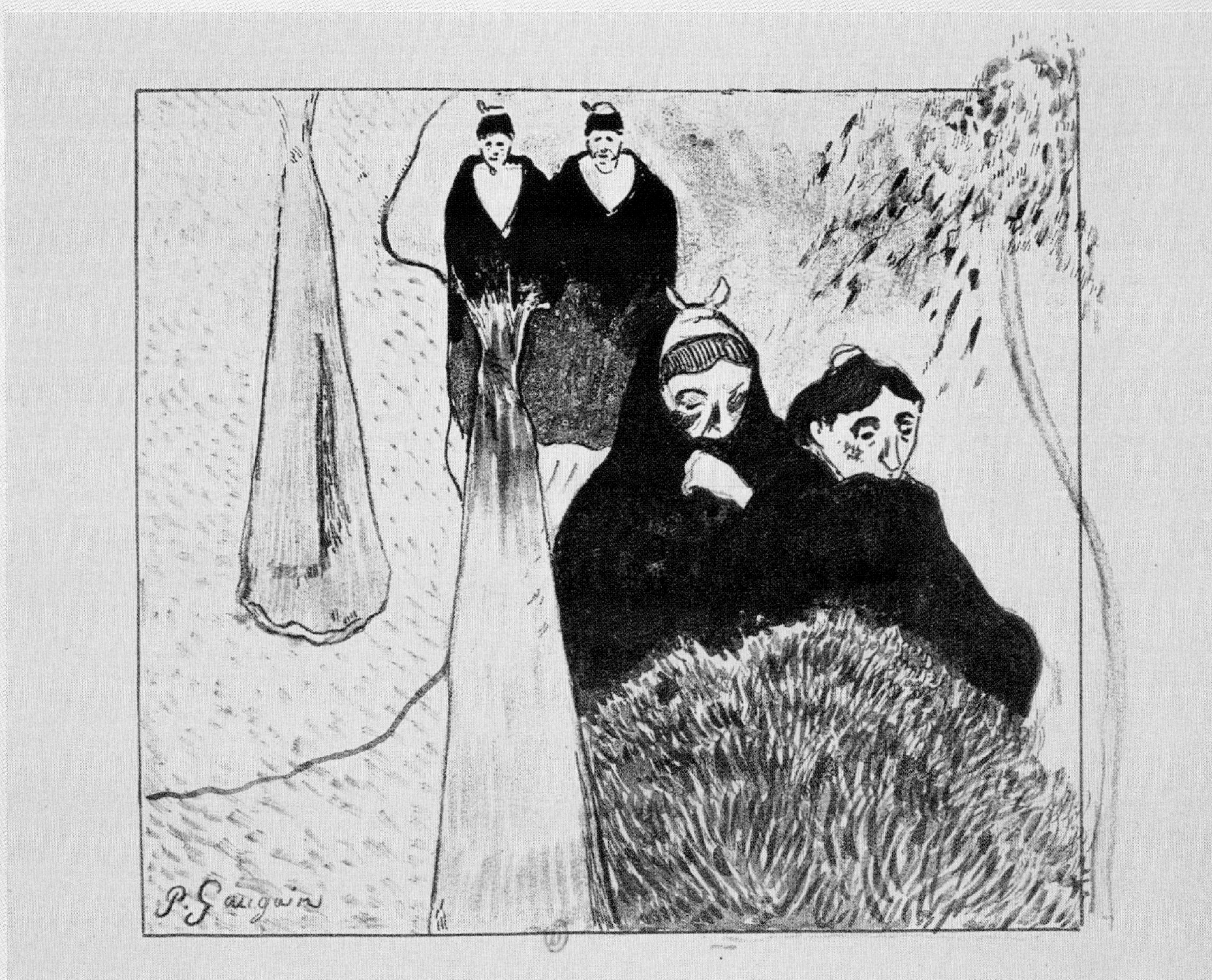

81. Paul Gauguin
Old Women in Arles, 1889
(Les vieilles filles à Arles)
Zincograph. 192 x 208 mm
[Guérin n. 11]
Institut national d'histoire de l'art, Bibliothèque, collections Jacques Doucet, Paris

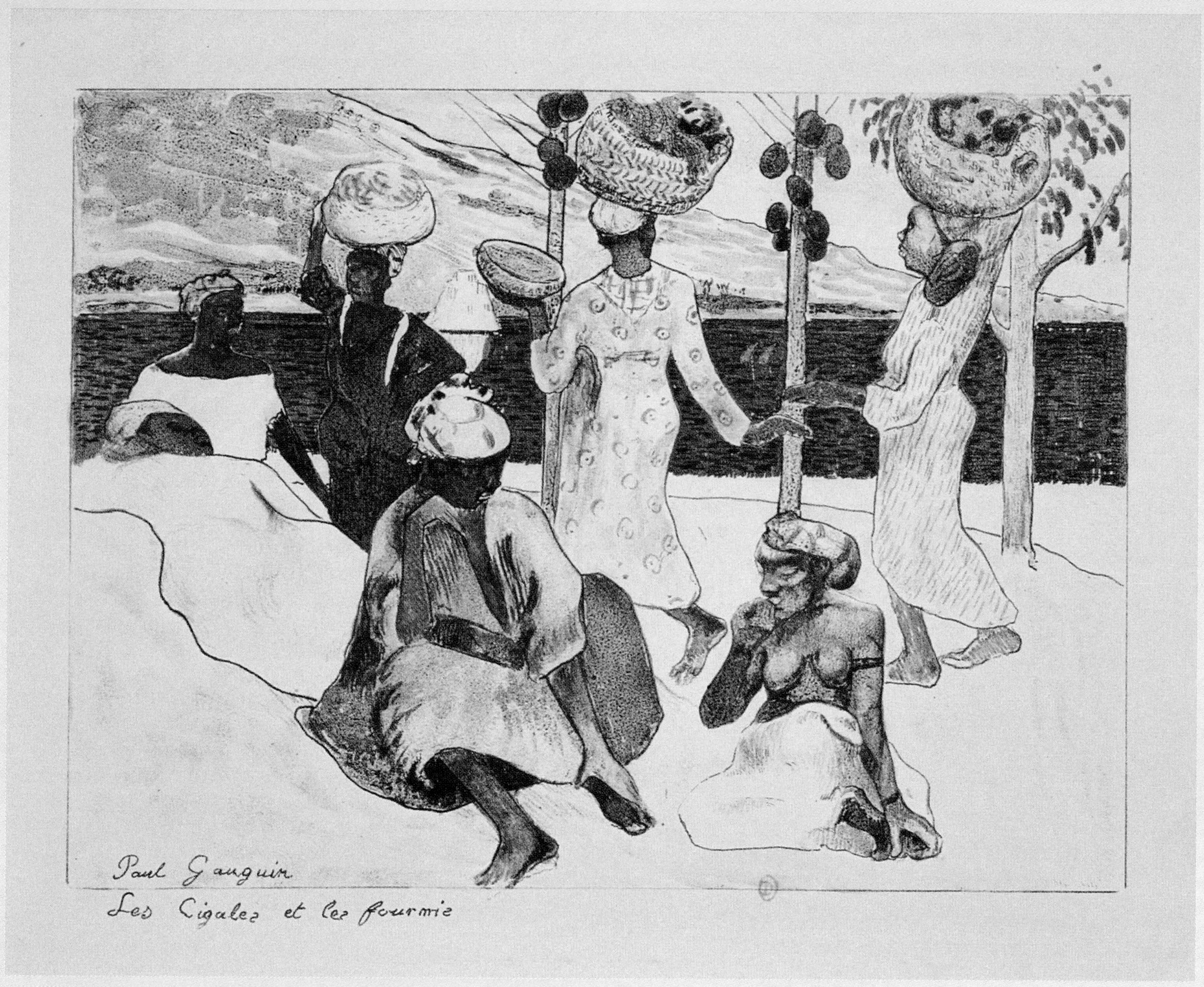

80. Paul Gauguin
The Grasshoppers and the Ants – Memories of Martinique, 1889
(Les cigales et les fourmis – Souvenir de la Martinique)
Zincograph. 216 x 261 mm
[Guérin n.10]
Institut national d'histoire de l'art, Bibliothèque, collections Jacques Doucet, Paris

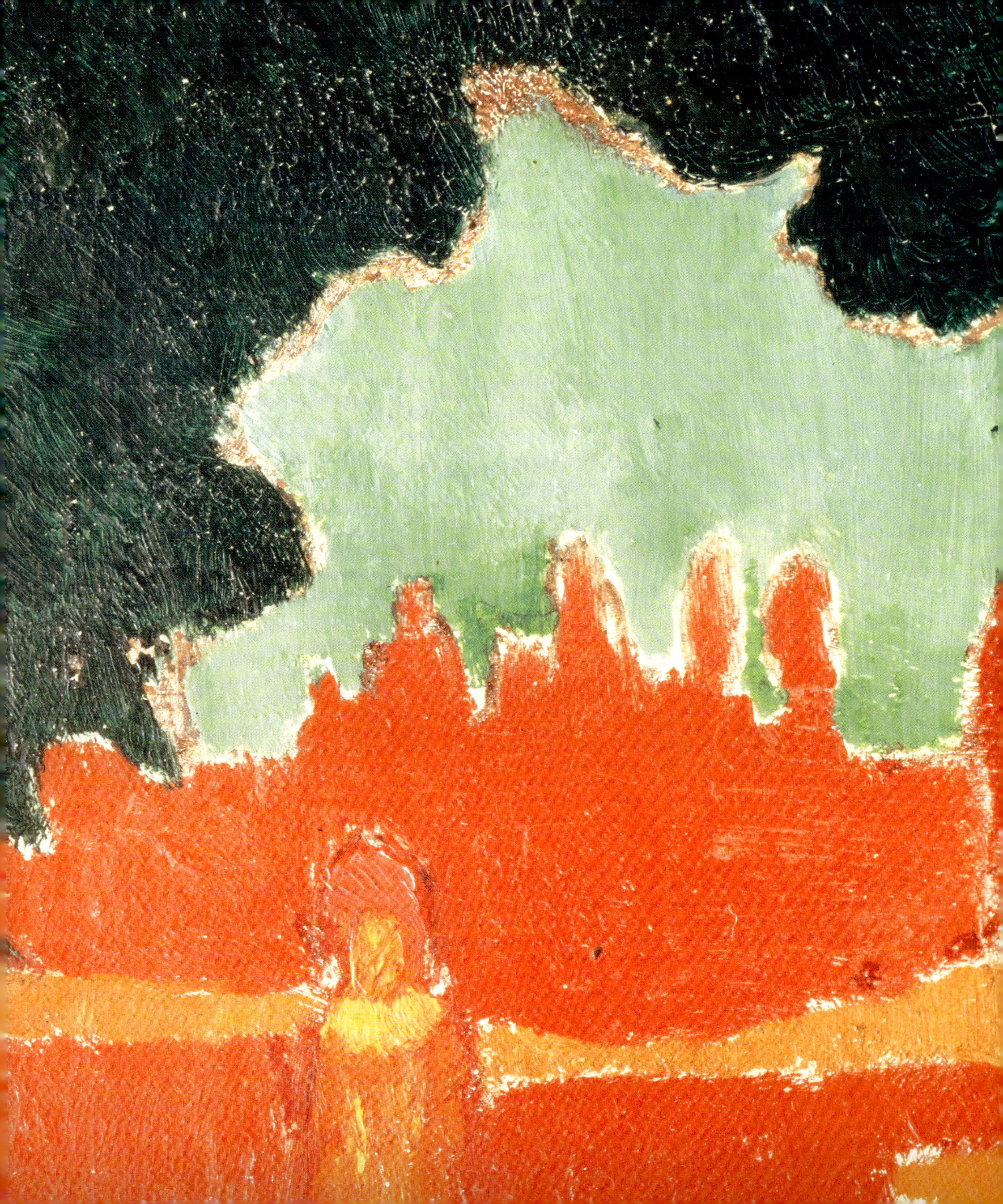

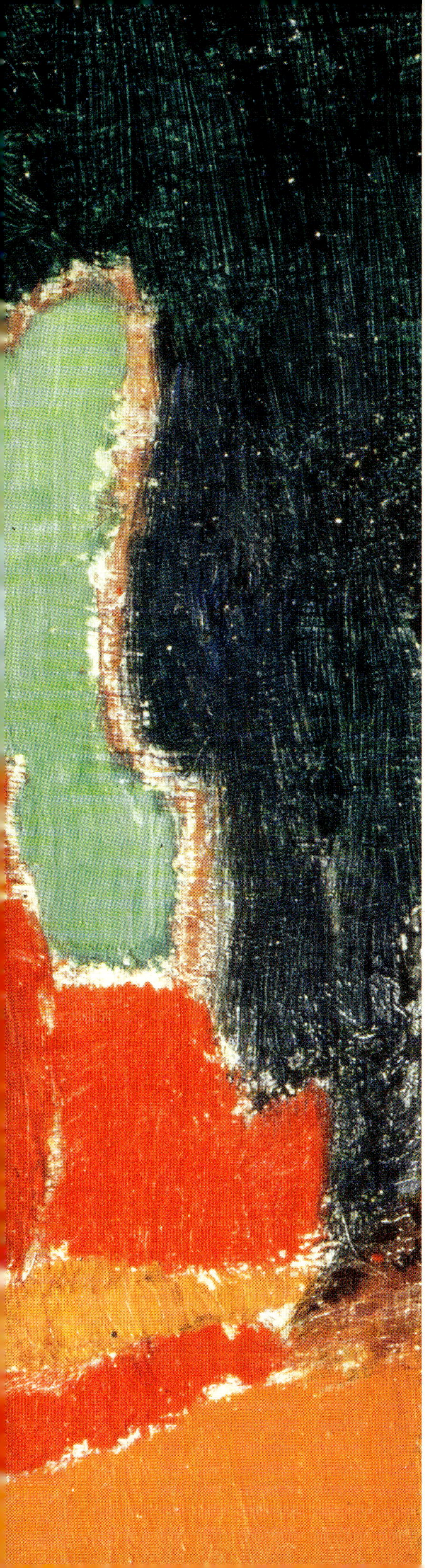

Maurice Denis
Patches of Sun on the Terrace, 1890
(detail)
[cat. 85]

7. Gauguin's Influence: From Pont-Aven to the Nabis

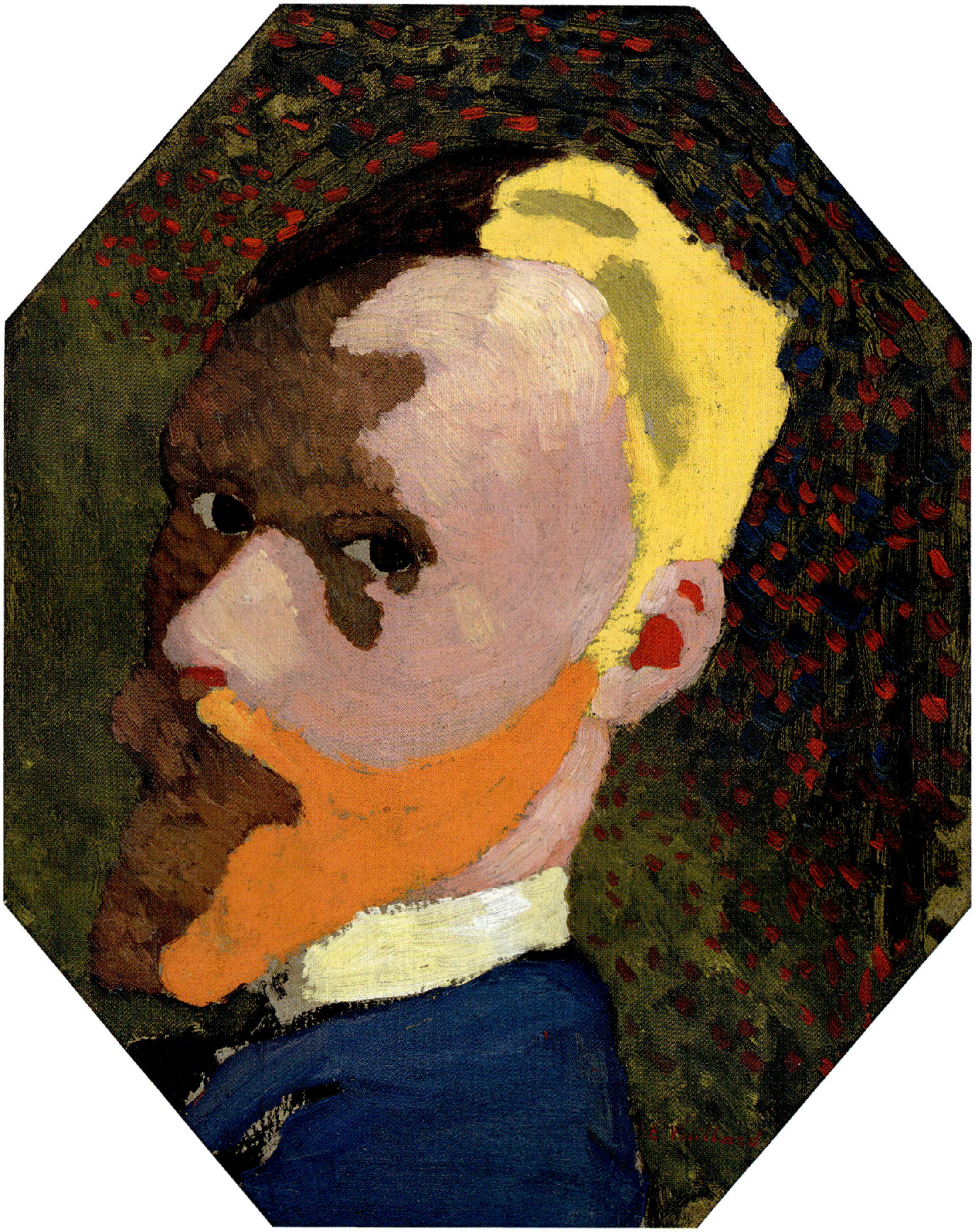

82. Édouard Vuillard
Octagonal Self-Portrait, c. 1890
(Autoportrait octogonal)
Oil on cardboard. 36 x 28 cm
[Salomon/Cogeval II n. 25]
Private Collection

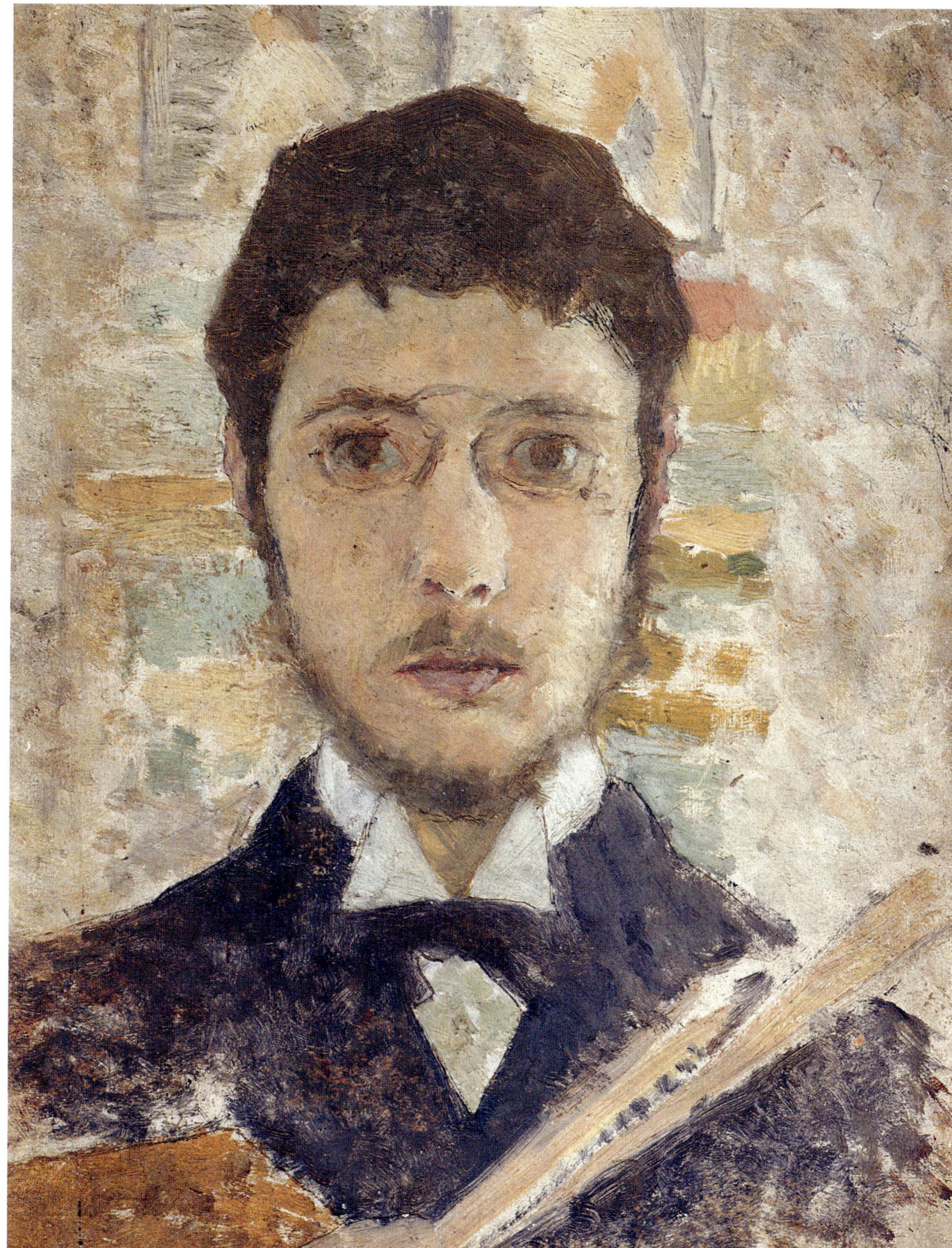

83. Pierre Bonnard
Self-Portrait. First Portrait of the Painter by Himself, 1889
(Autoportrait. Premier portrait du peintre par lui-même)
Oil on cardboard. 21.5 x 15.8 cm
[Dauberville n. 9B]
Private Collection

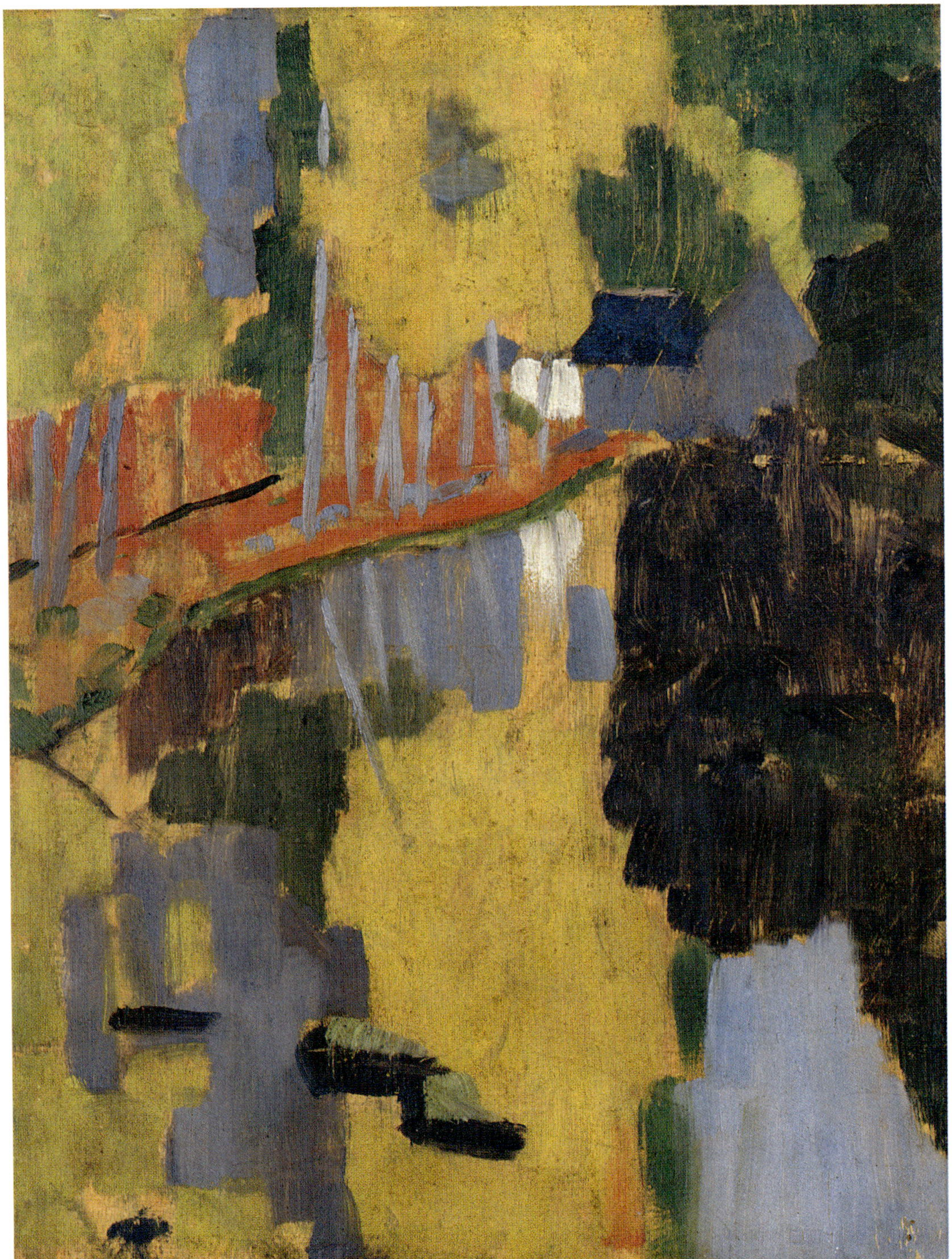

84. Paul Sérusier
The Talisman, 1888
(Le talisman)
Oil on wood panel. 27 x 21.5 cm
Musée d'Orsay, Paris

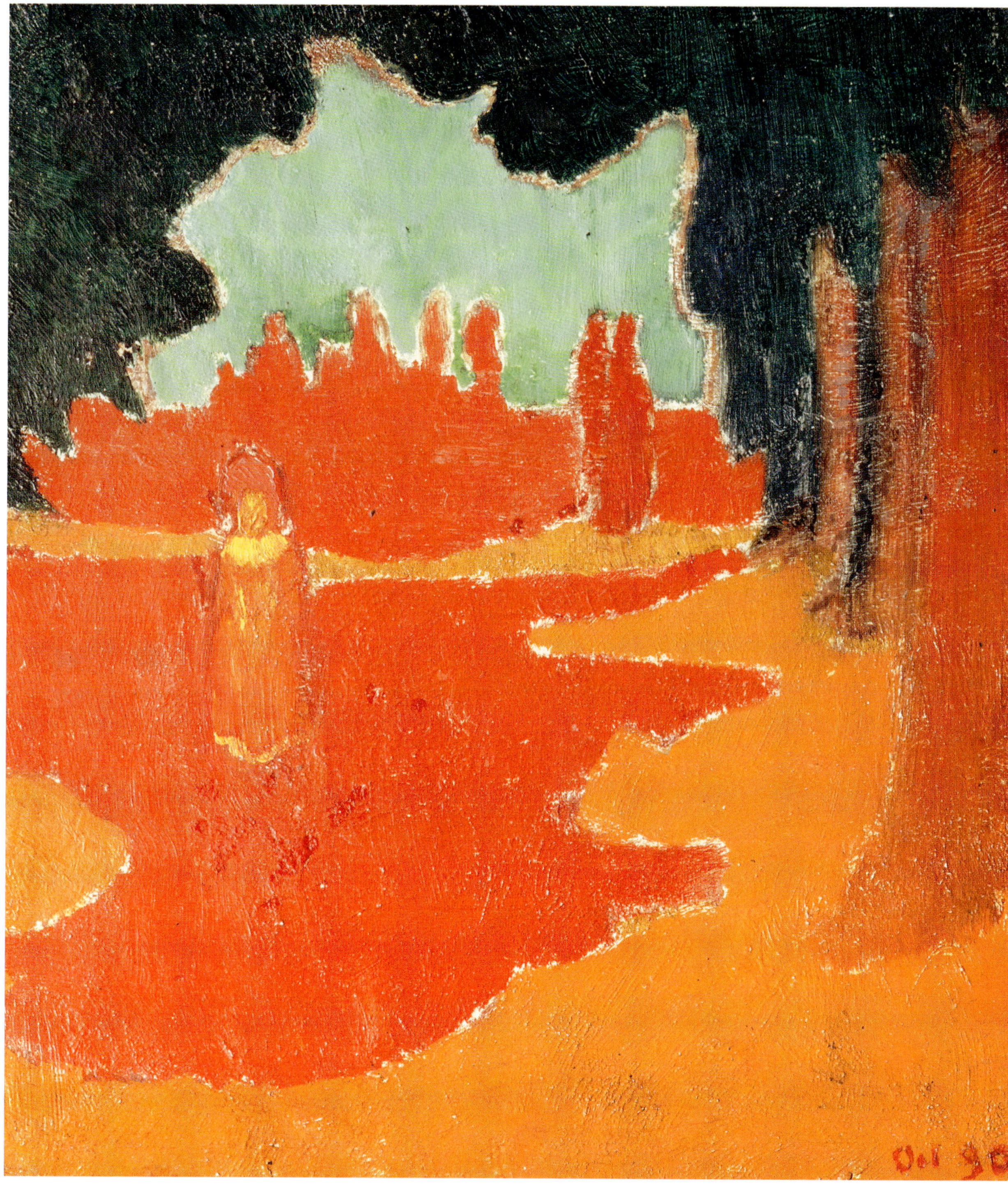

85. Maurice Denis
Patches of Sun on the Terrace, 1890
(Taches de soleil sur la terrasse)
Oil on cardboard. 24 x 20.5 cm
Musée d'Orsay, Paris

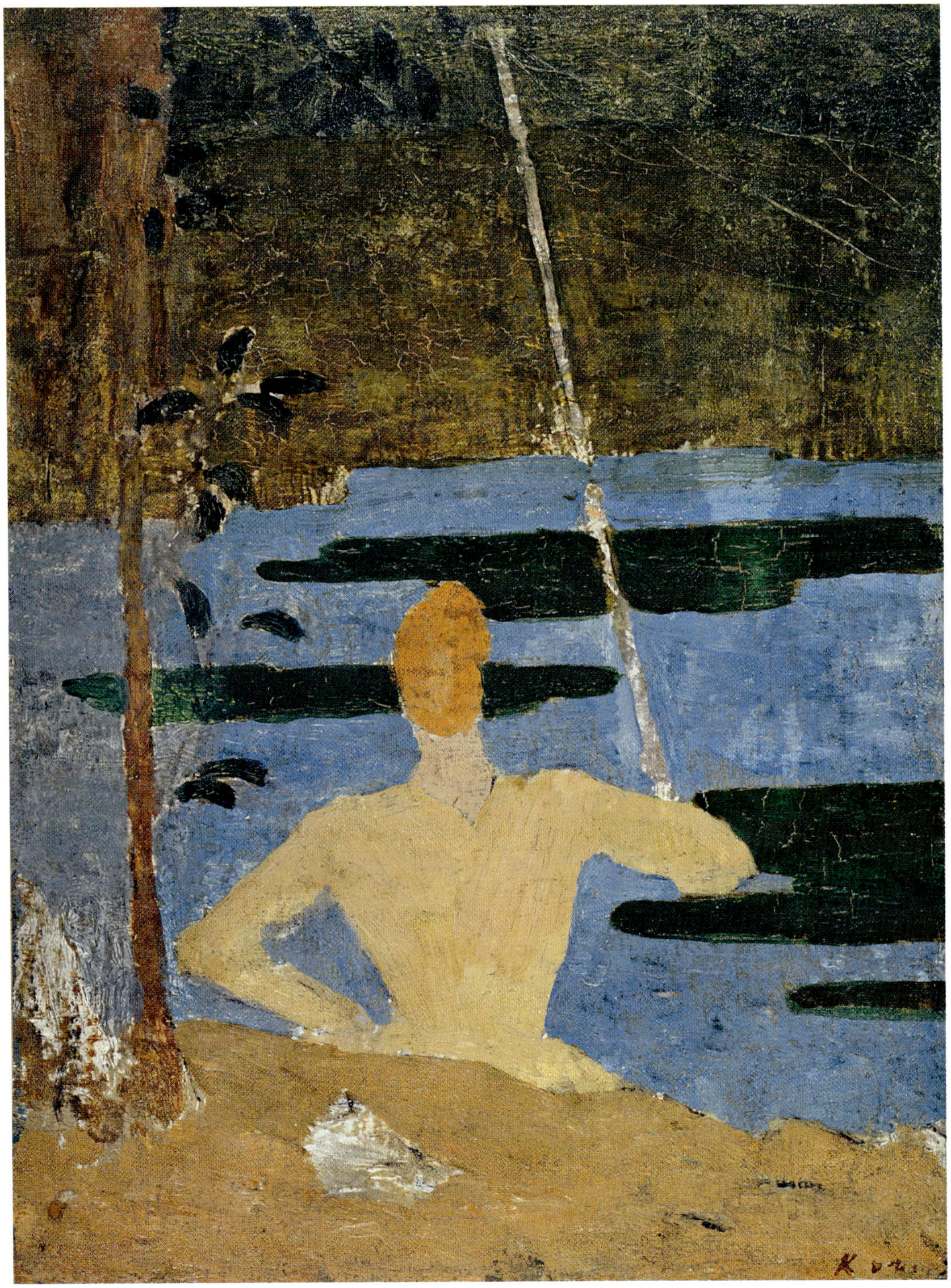

86. Ker-Xavier Roussel
The Fisherman, c. 1890–1891
(Le pêcheur)
Oil on canvas. 22 x 15 cm
Private Collection

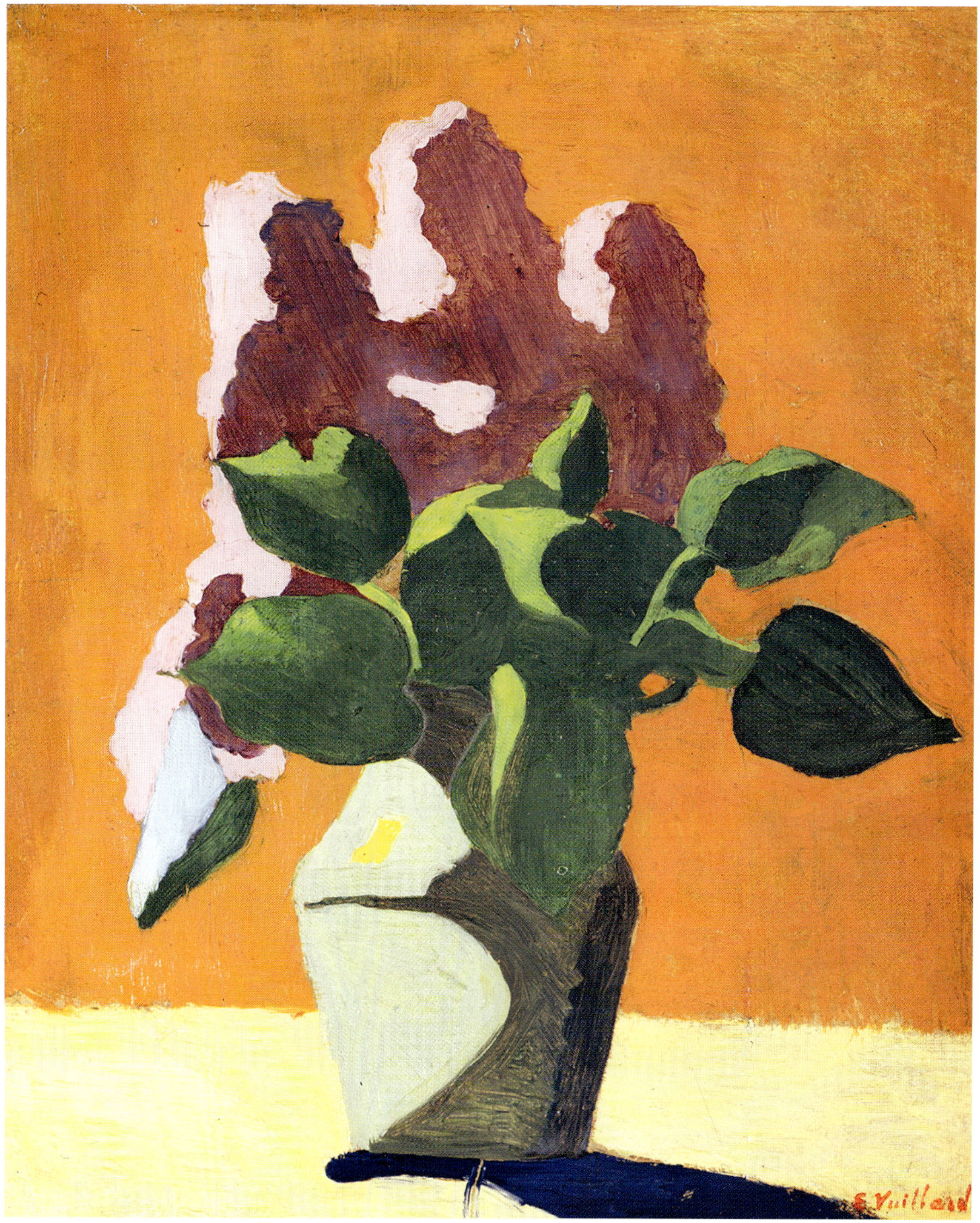

87. Édouard Vuillard
Lilacs, c. 1890
(Les lilas)
Oil on cardboard mounted on cradled panel. 35.6 x 27.9 cm
[Salomon/Cogeval II n. 28]
William Kelly Simpson Collection, New York

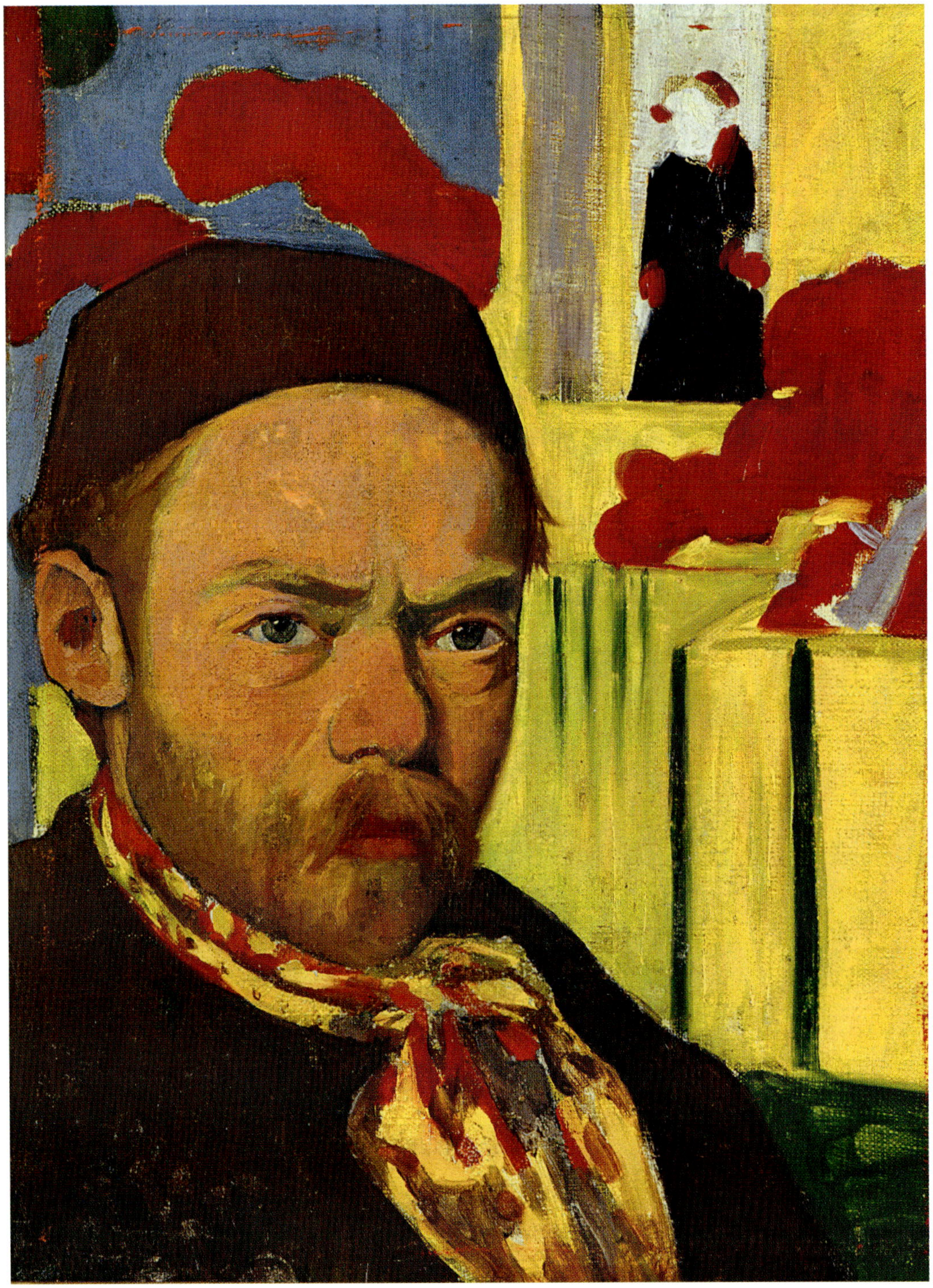

88. Jacob Meyer de Haan
Self-Portrait on Japanese Background, c. 1889–1891
(Autoportrait sur fond japonisant)
Oil on canvas . 32.4 x 24.5 cm
Triton Foundation, The Netherlands

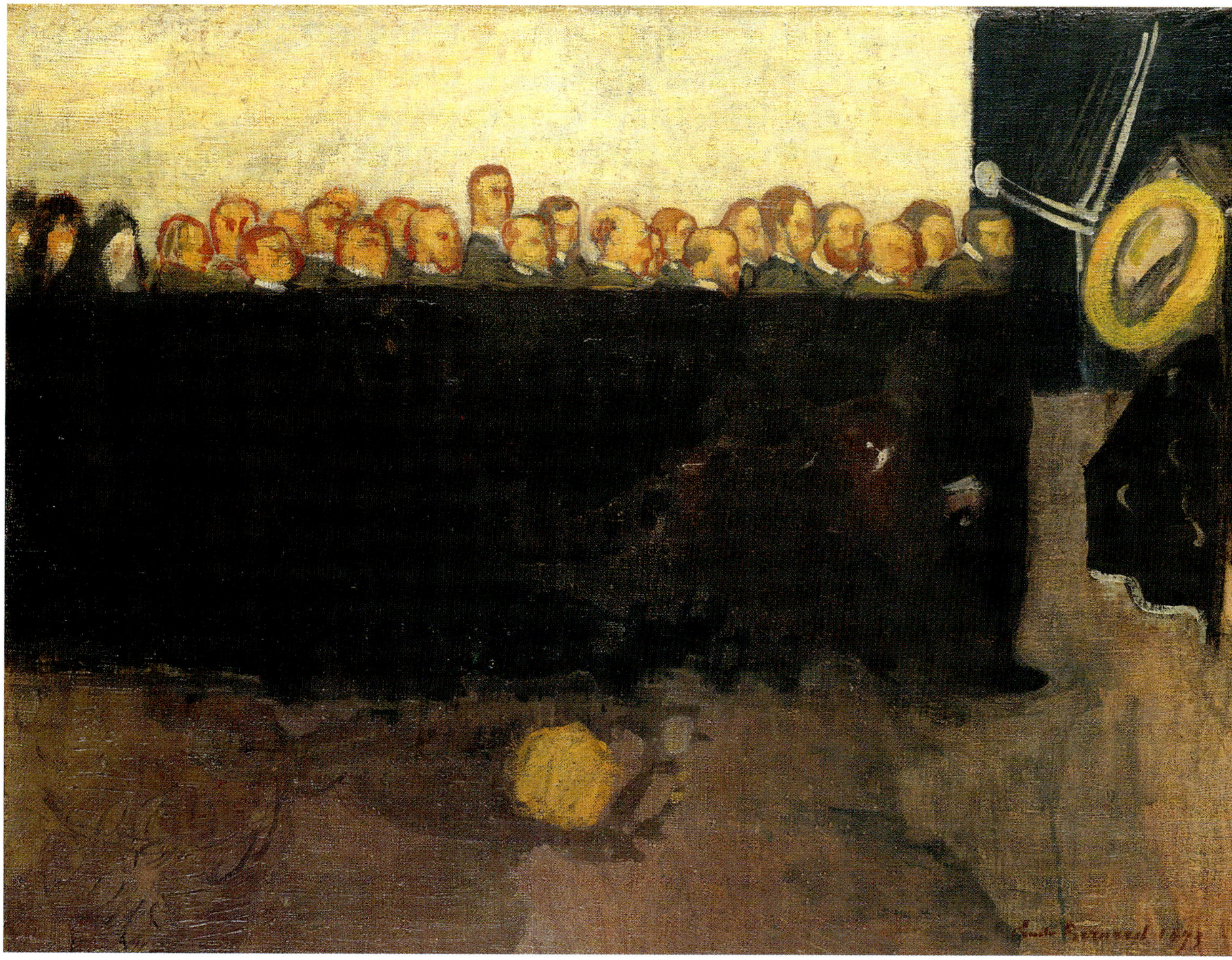

89. Émile Bernard
The Burial of Vincent van Gogh, 1893
(L'Enterrement de Vincent van Gogh)
Oil on canvas. 73 x 93 cm
[Luthi n. 397]
Private Collection

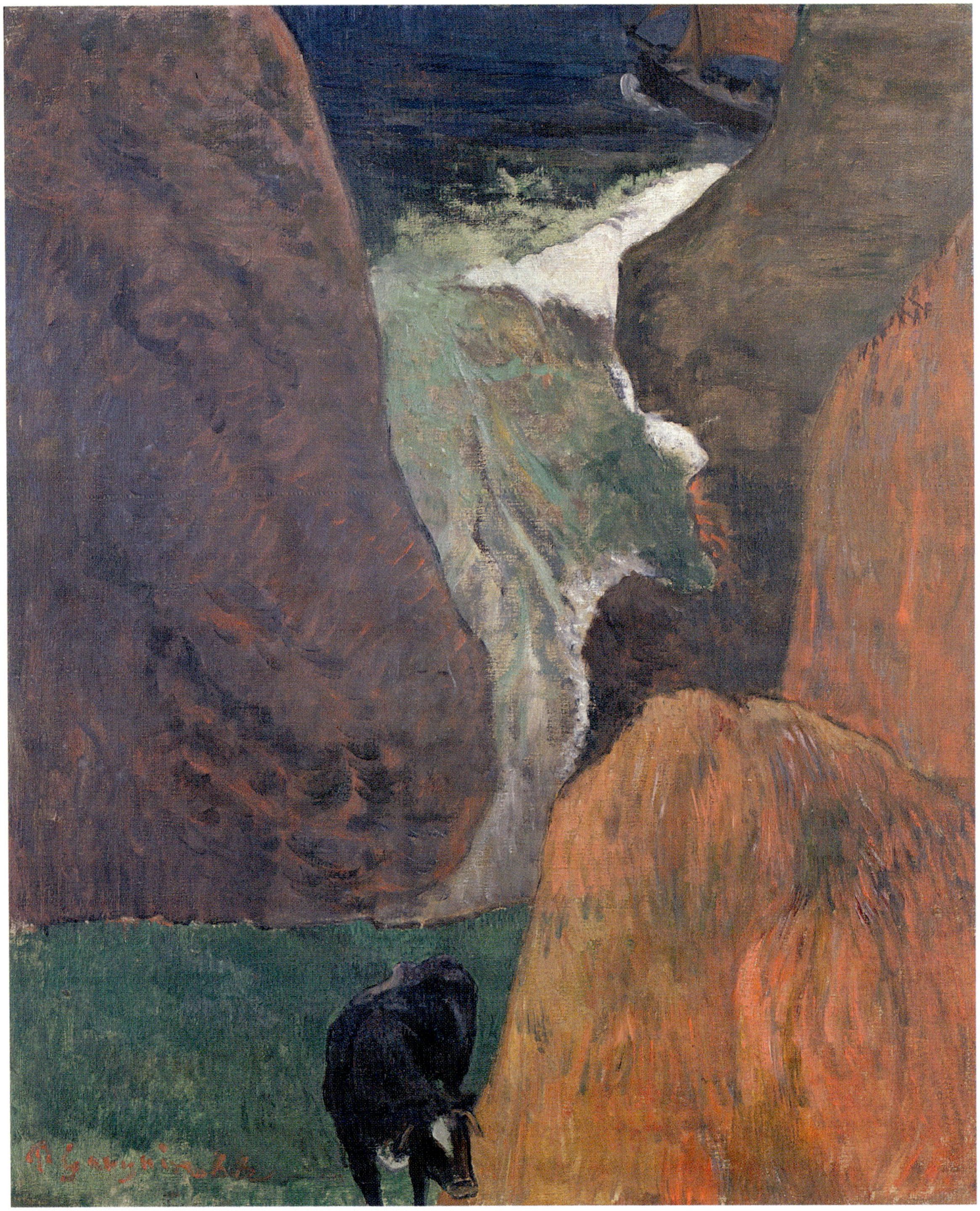

90. Paul Gauguin
Cow on the Cliffs of Porsac'h, or *Over the Abyss*, 1888
(Vache sur la falaise à Porsac'h ou Au-dessus du gouffre)
Oil on canvas. 73 x 60 cm
[Wildenstein 2001 n. 310]
Musée des Arts décoratifs, Paris

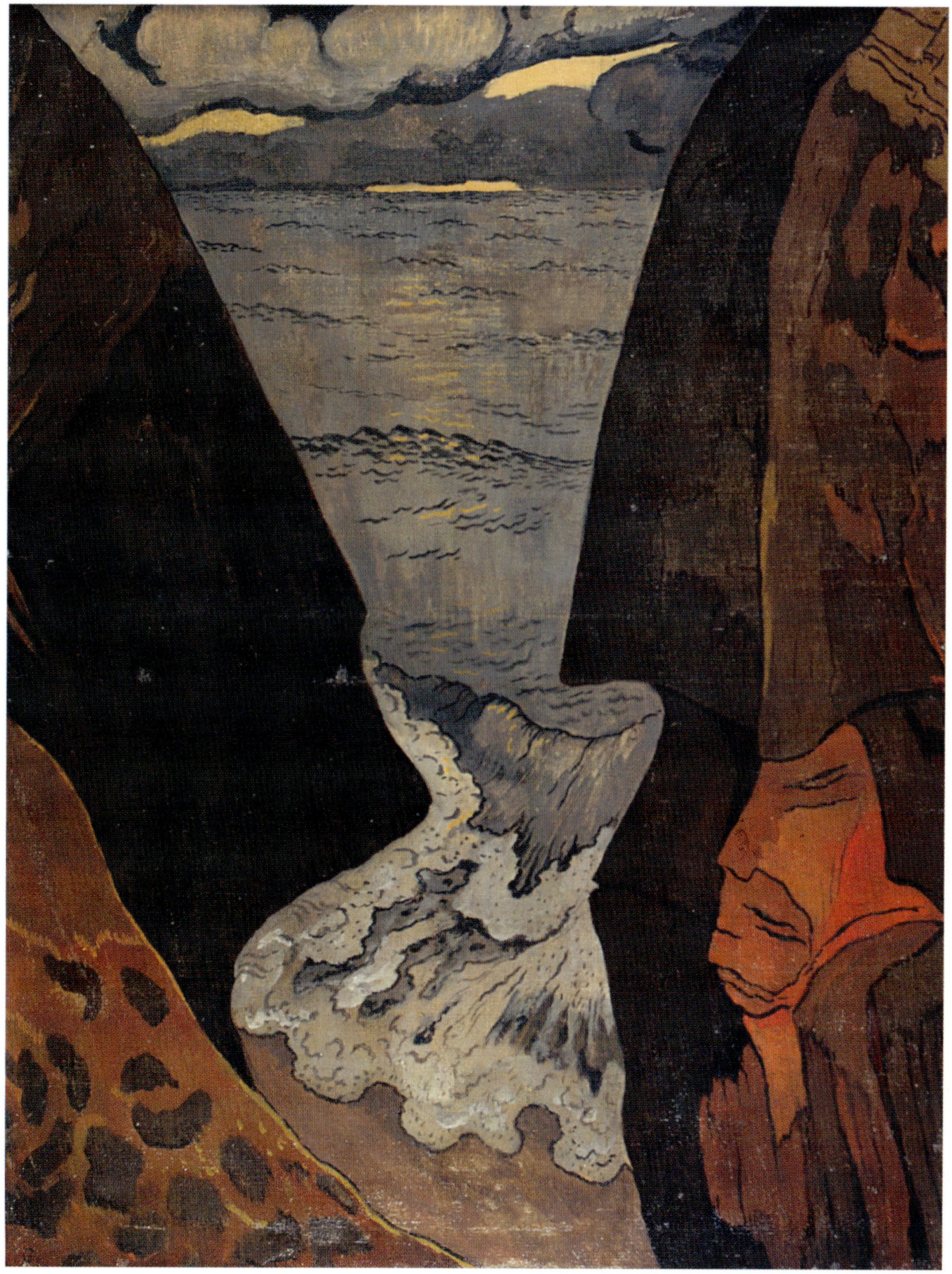

91. Georges Lacombe
Vorhor, Grey Wave, c. 1892
(Vorhor, Vague grise)
Egg tempera on canvas. 81.2 x 60.5 cm
Musée des beaux-arts de Brest

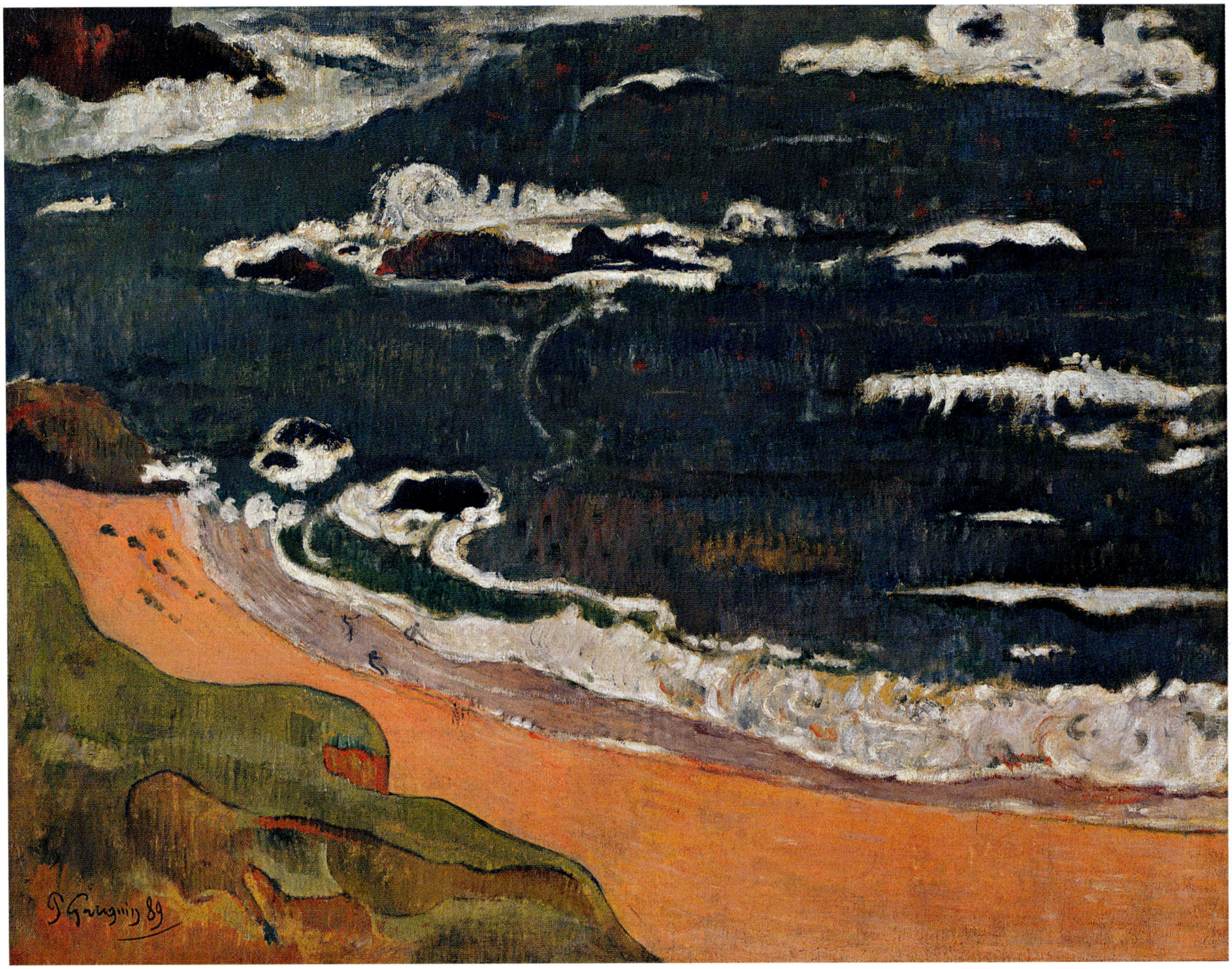

92. Paul Gauguin
The Beach at Pouldu, 1889
(La plage du Pouldu)
Oil on canvas. 73 x 92 cm
[Wildenstein 1964 n. 362]
María Amalia Lacroze de Fortabat

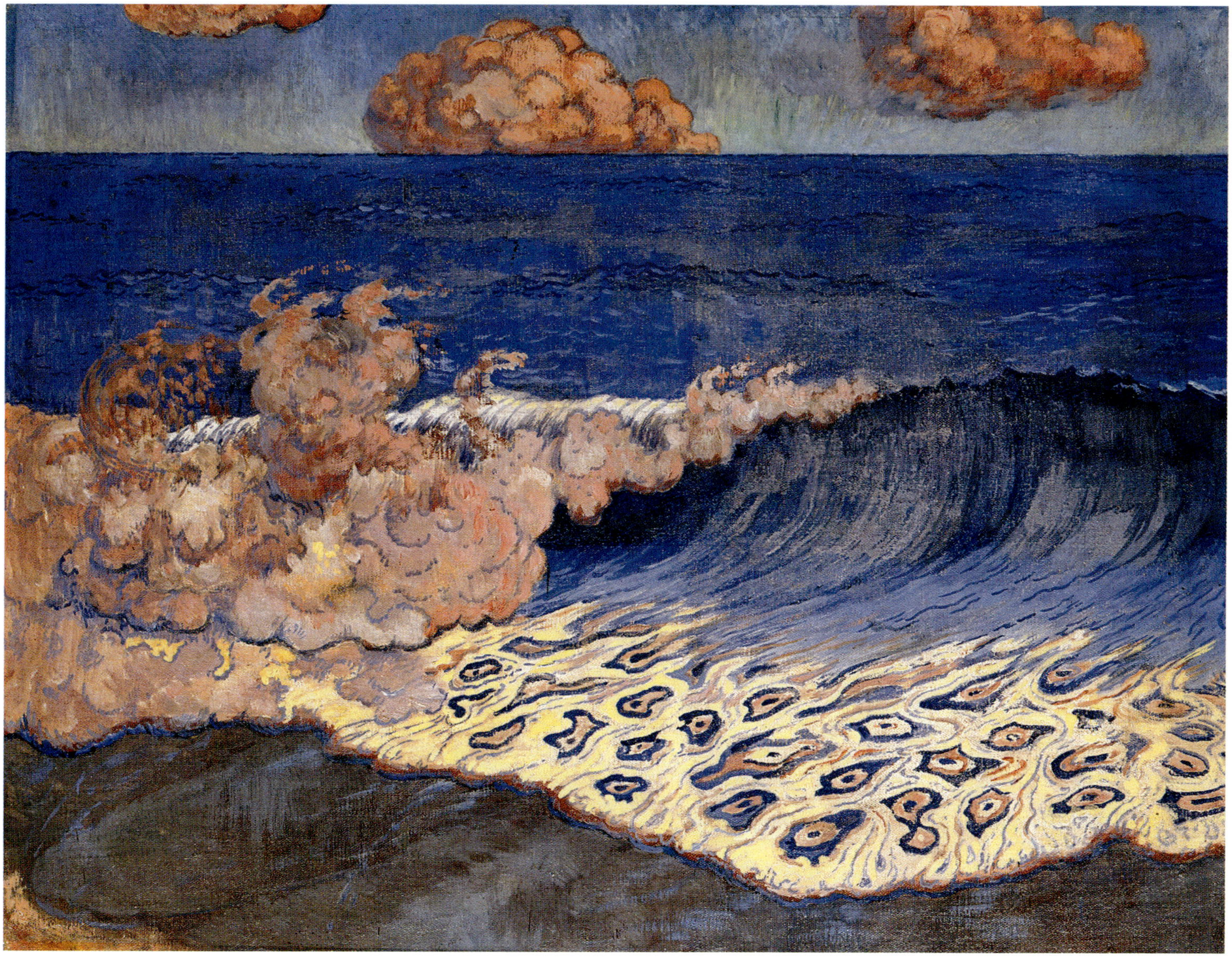

93. Georges Lacombe
Blue Seascape. Wave Effect, 1892–1894
(Marine bleue. Effet de vagues)
Tempera on canvas. 70.8 x 86.5 cm
Musée des beaux-arts de Rennes

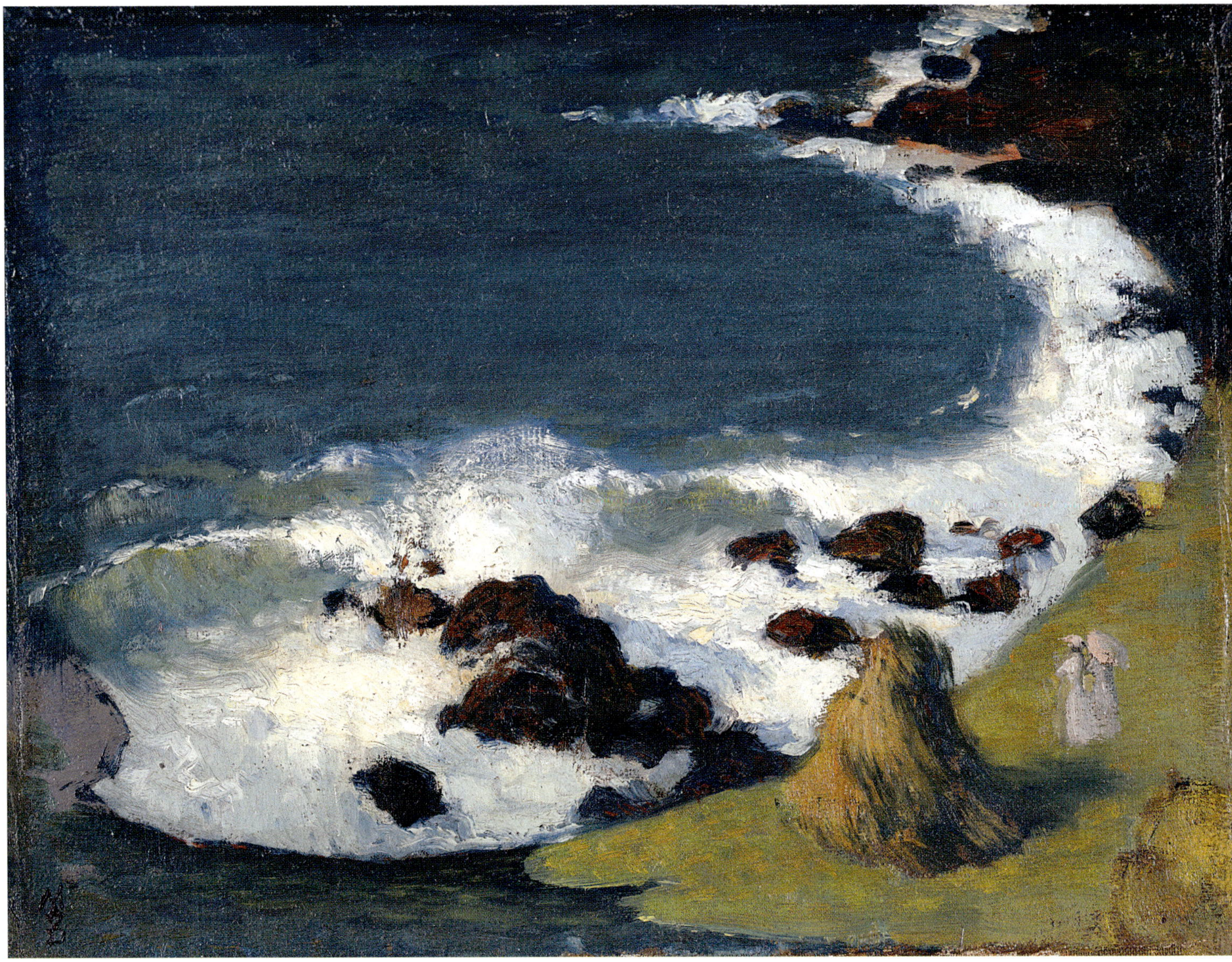

94. Maurice Denis
Sea Shore, 1891
(Bord de mer)
Oil on canvas. 20.7 x 26 cm
Private Collection. Courtesy Bellier, Paris

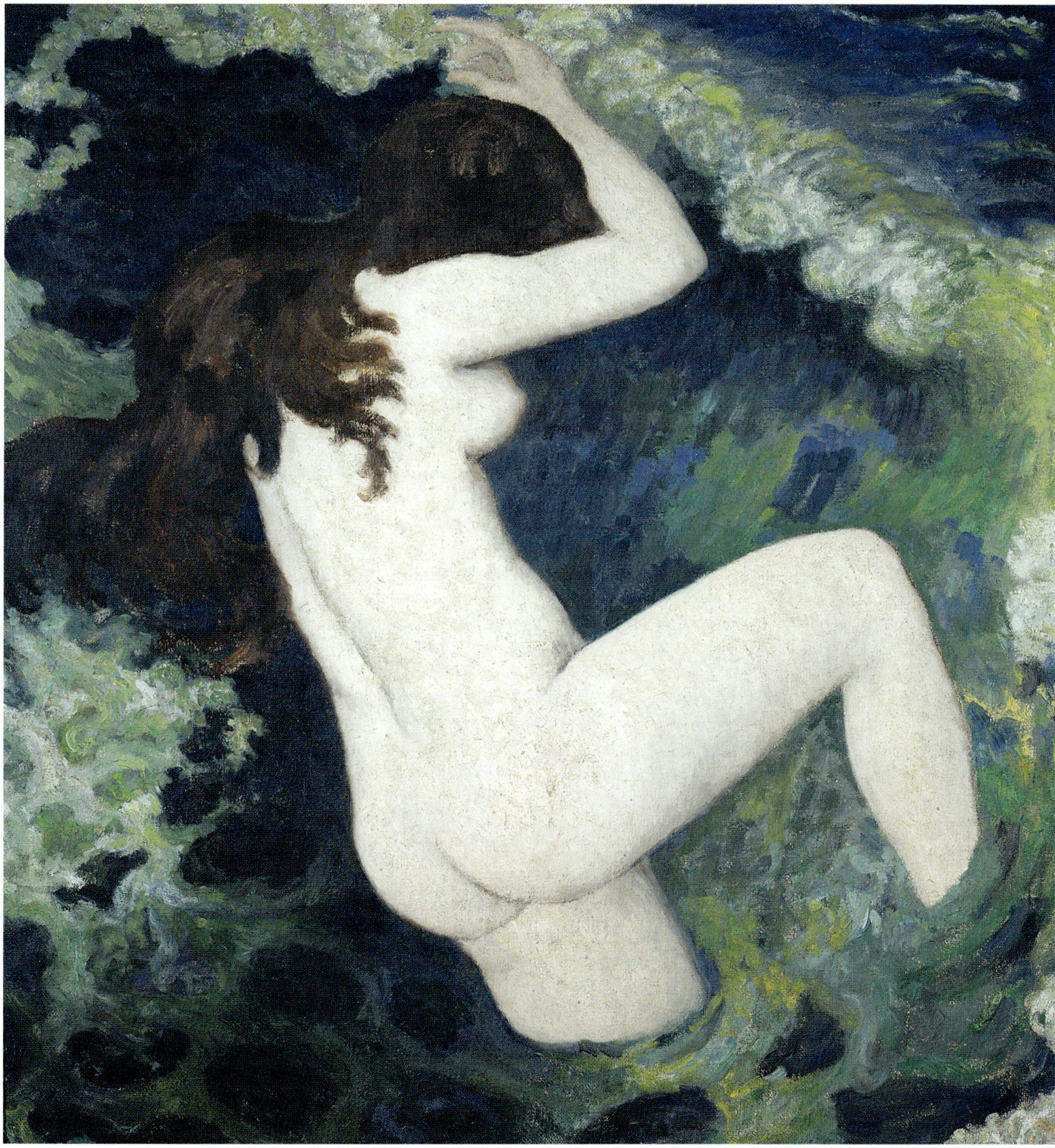

95. Aristide Maillol
The Wave, 1898
(La vague)
Oil on canvas. 99.5 x 89 cm
Petit Palais, Musée des Beaux-Arts de la Ville de Paris

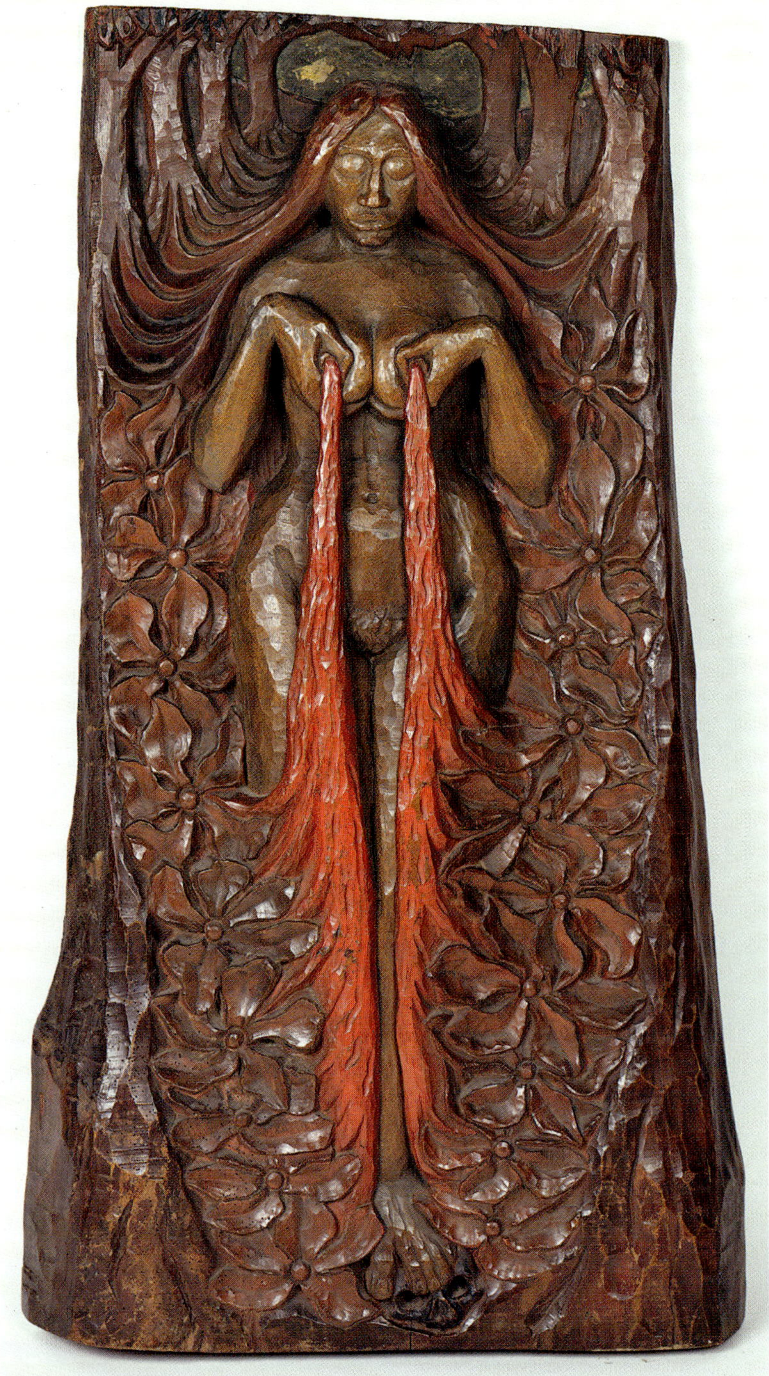

97. Georges Lacombe
Isis, 1895
Low relief in partly polychrome ebony.
111.5 x 62 x 10.7 cm
Musée d'Orsay, Paris

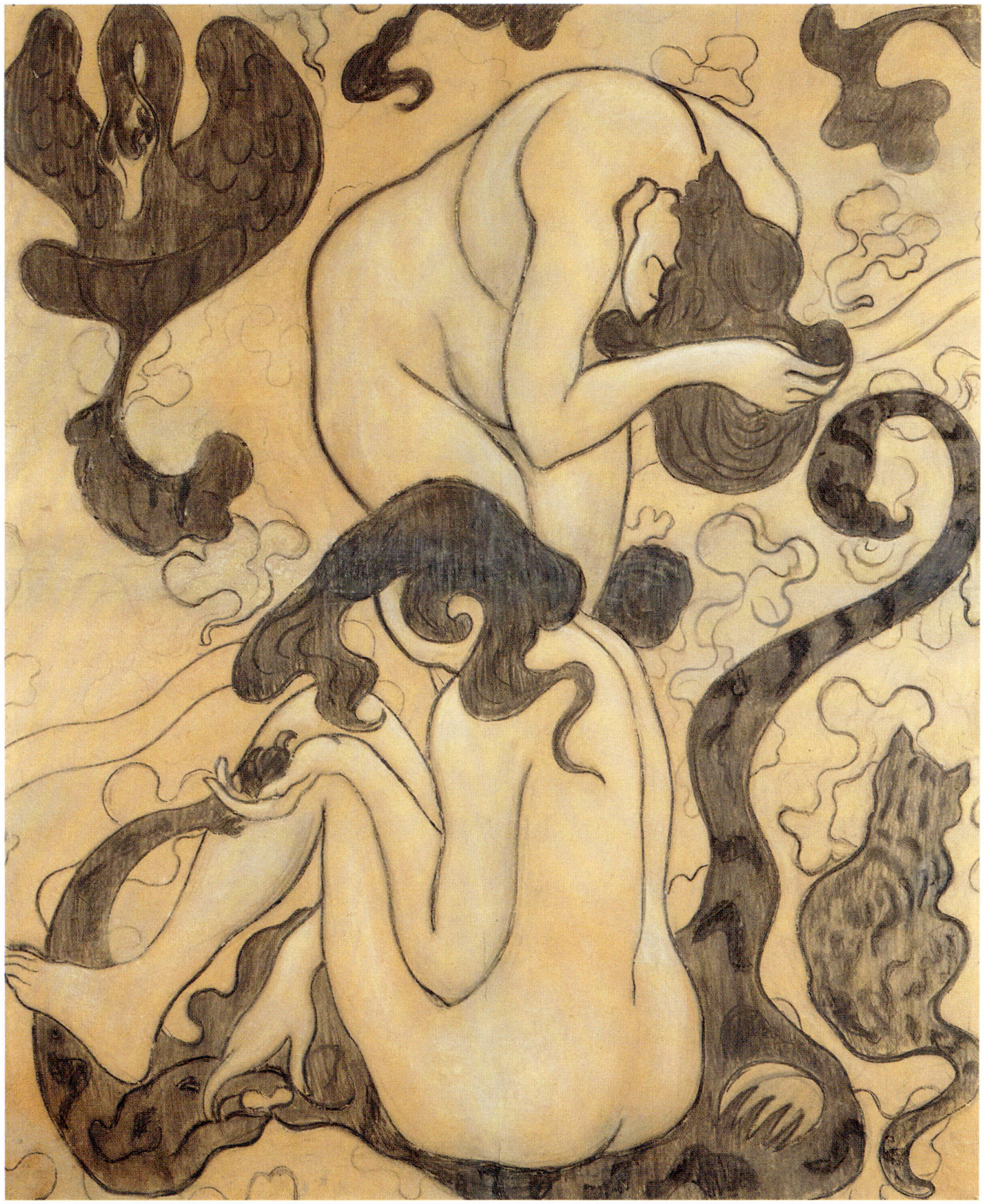

96. Paul Elie Ranson
Two Nude Women, 1890
(Deux femmes nues)
Watercolour on paper. 120 x 98 cm
Association des Amis du Petit Palais, Geneva

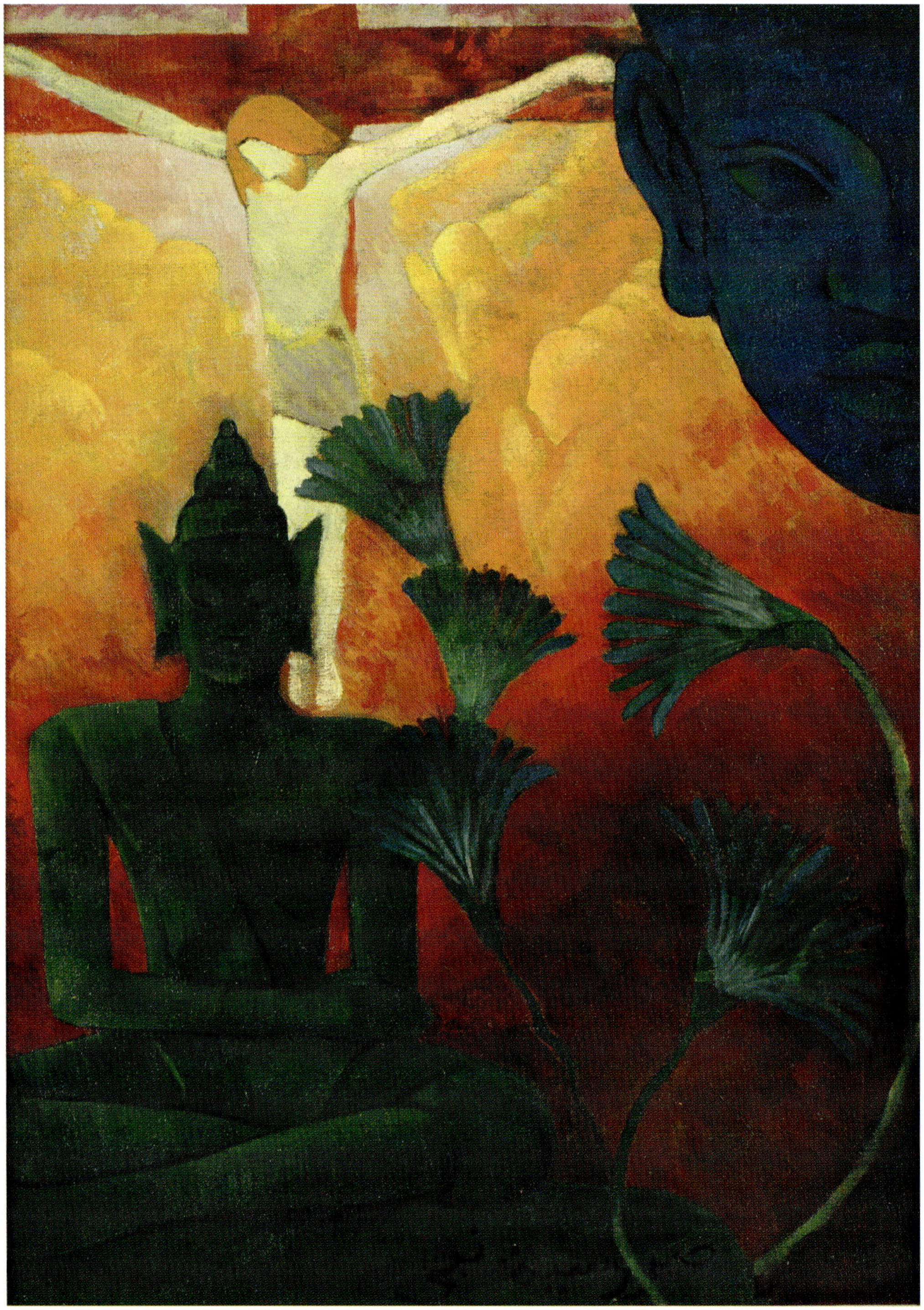

98. Paul Elie Ranson
Christ and Buddha, c. 1890
(Christ et Bouddha)
Oil on canvas. 66.7 x 51.4 cm
Triton Foundation, The Netherlands

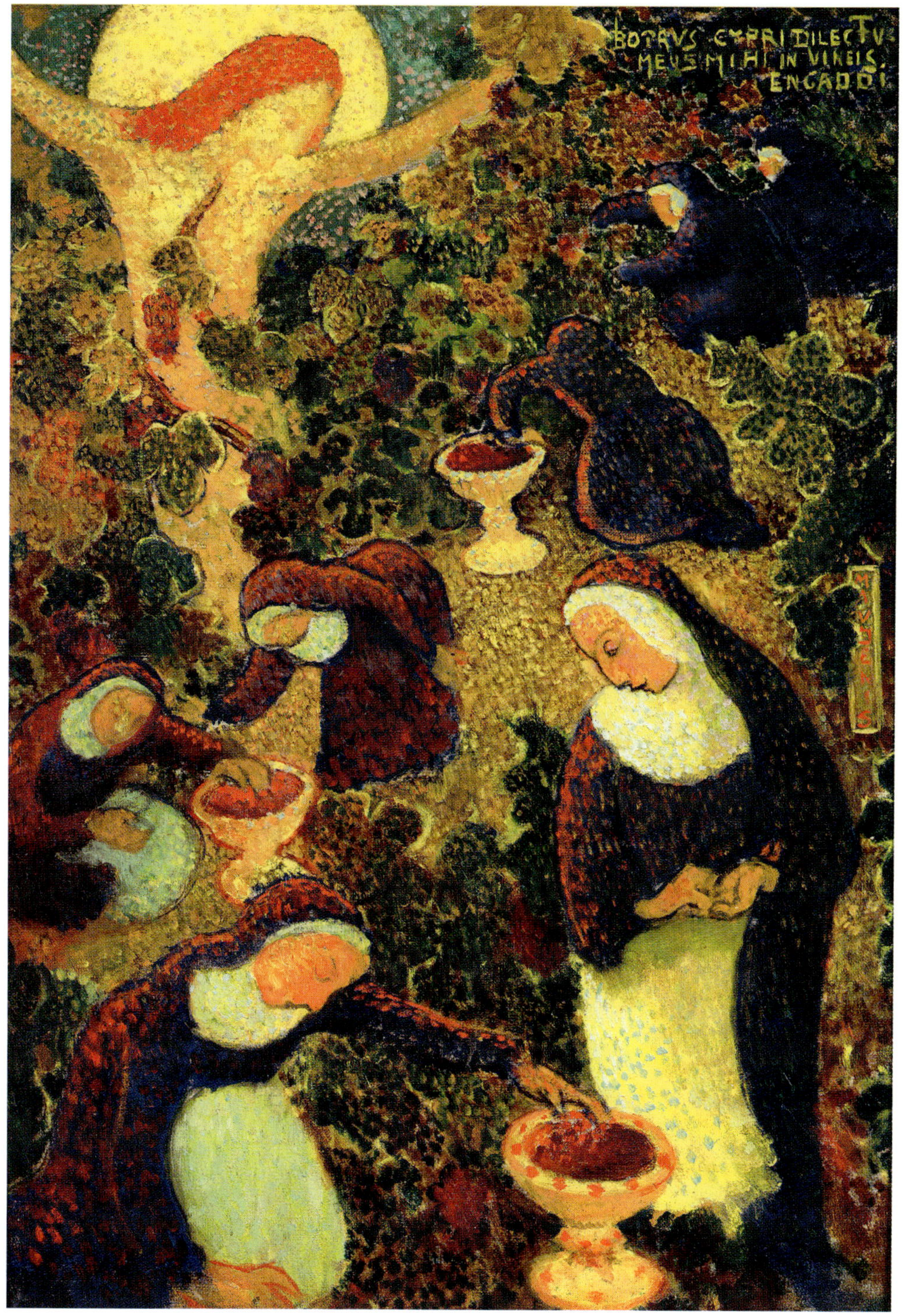

99. Maurice Denis
The Mystical Grape Harvest, c. 1890
(La vendange mystique)
Oil on canvas mounted on cardboard. 74 x 51 cm
Triton Foundation, The Netherlands

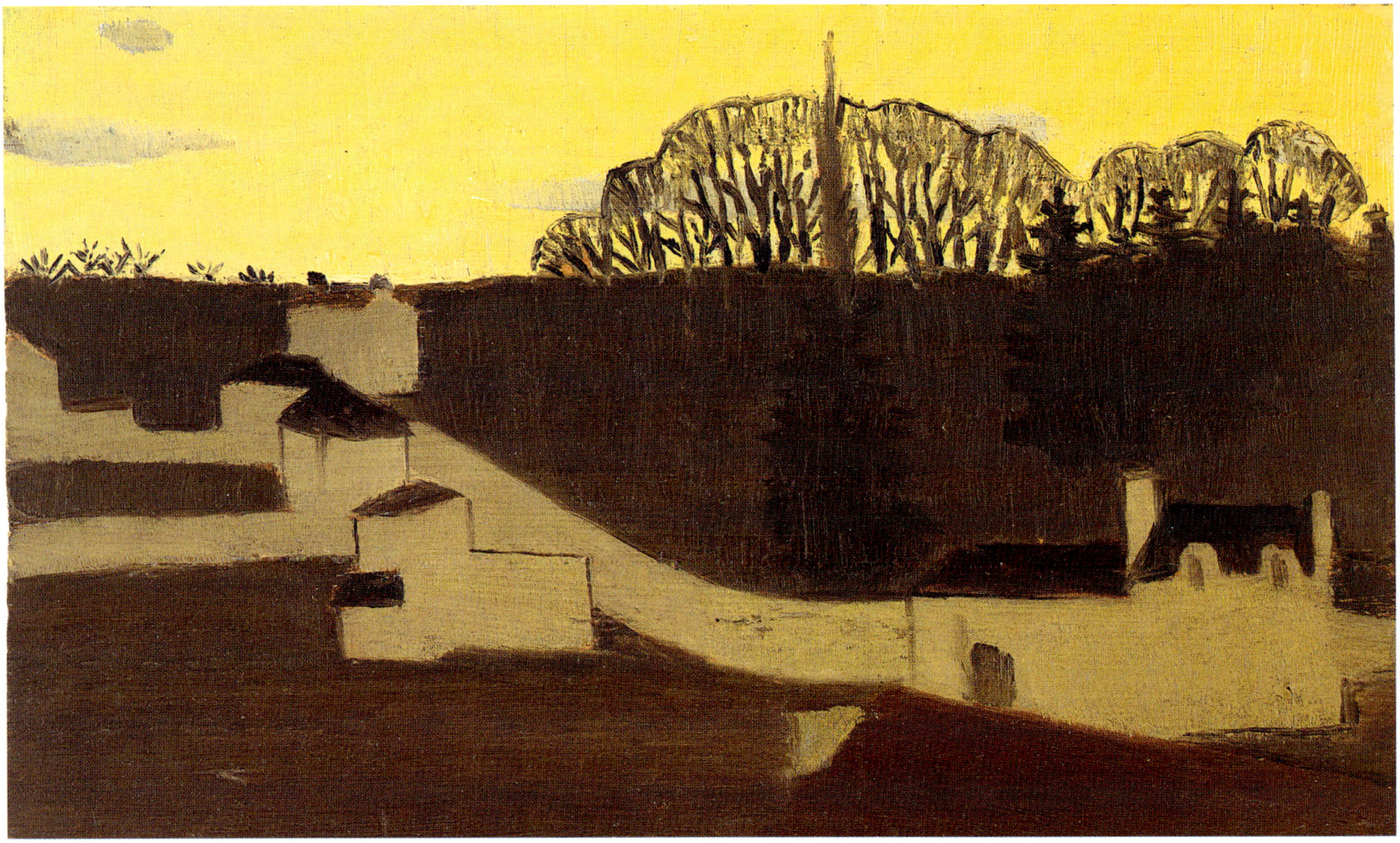

100. Maurice Denis
Yellow Evening at Fourqueux, c. 1890
(Soir jaune sur Fourqueux)
Oil on wood panel. 16 x 26.8 cm
The Montreal Museum of Fine Arts, Montreal

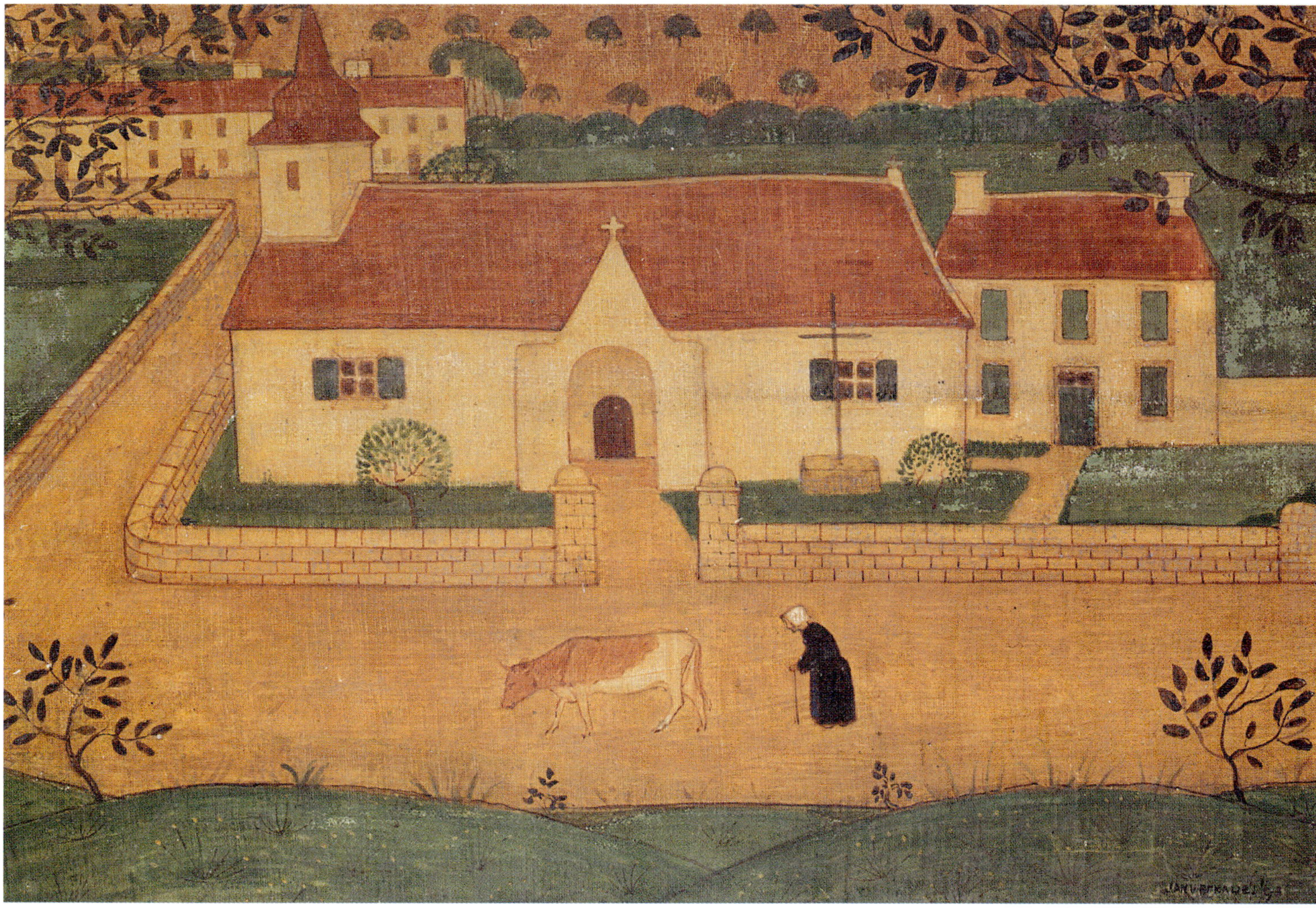

101. Jan Verkade
The Church of Saint Nolf, 1893
(L'Eglise de Saint Nolf)
Oil on canvas. 32.5 x 46 cm
Musée Départemental Maurice Denis 'Le Prieuré', Saint-Germain-en-Laye

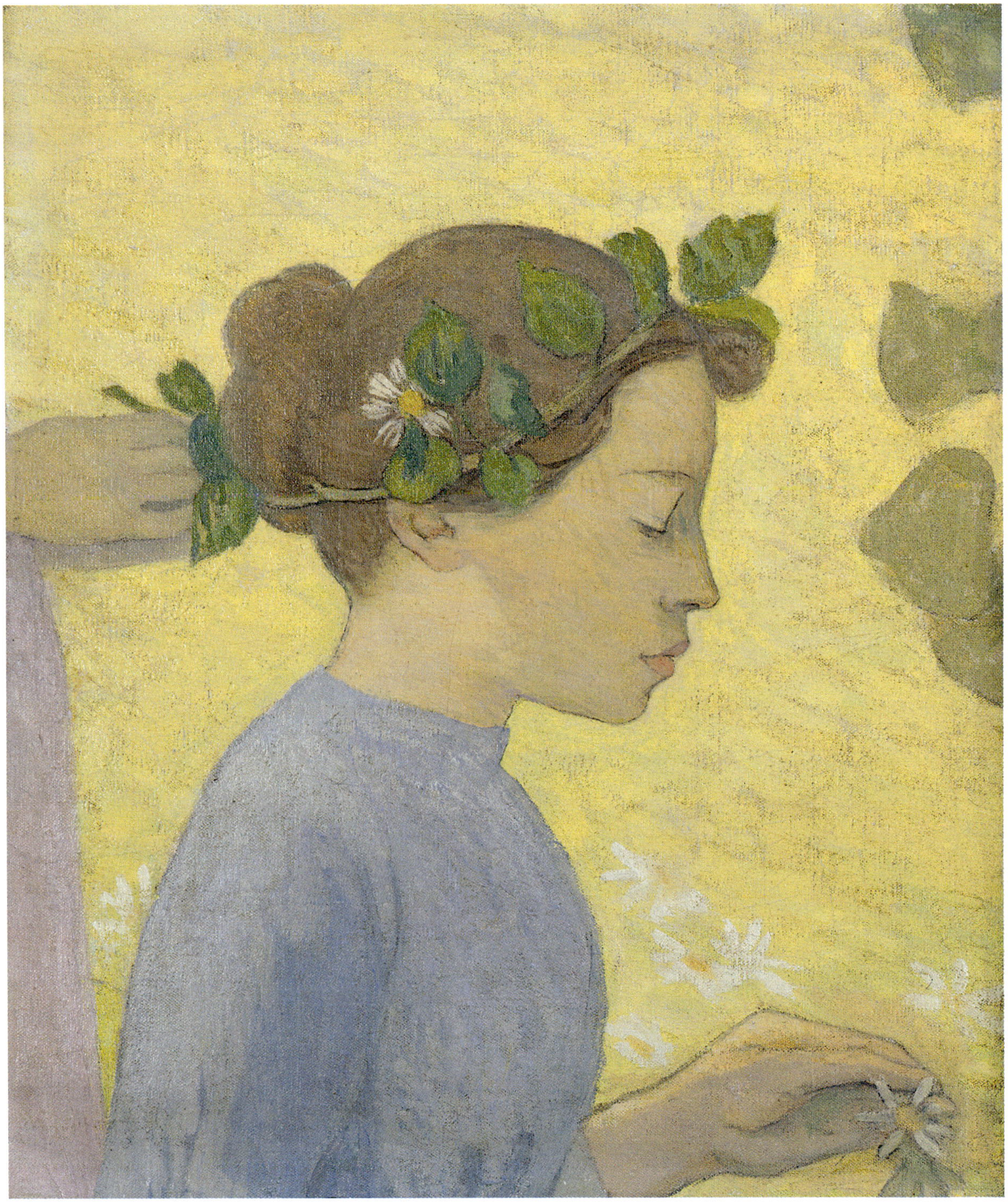

102. Aristide Maillol
Crowned Child, 1890
(L'enfant couronné)
Oil on canvas. 47 x 40 cm
Musée Maillol, Paris

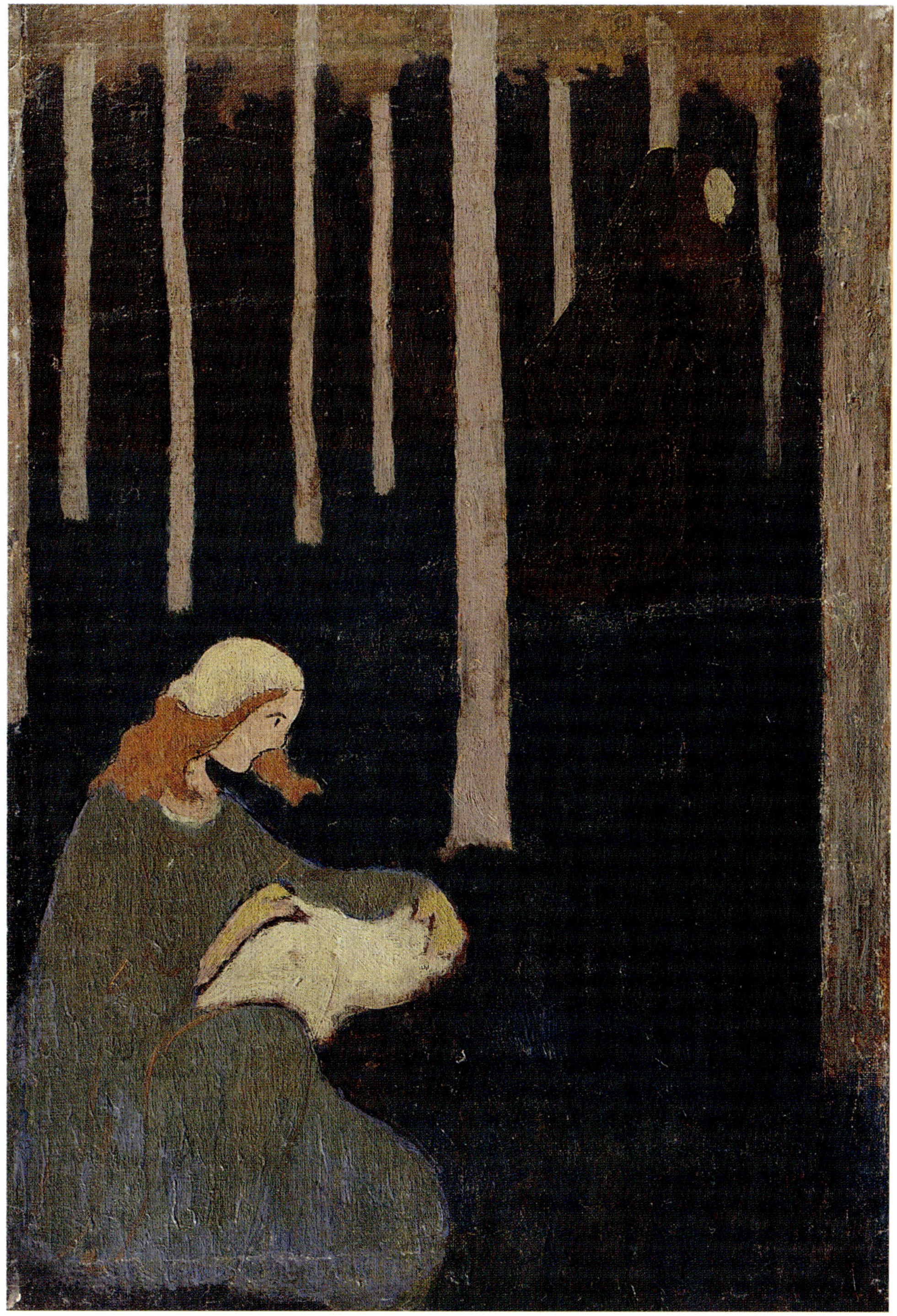

103. Ker-Xavier Roussel
Composition in the Forest, 1890–1892
(Composition dans la forêt)
Oil on canvas. 44 x 31 cm
Musée Départemental Maurice Denis 'Le Prieuré', Saint-Germain-en-Laye

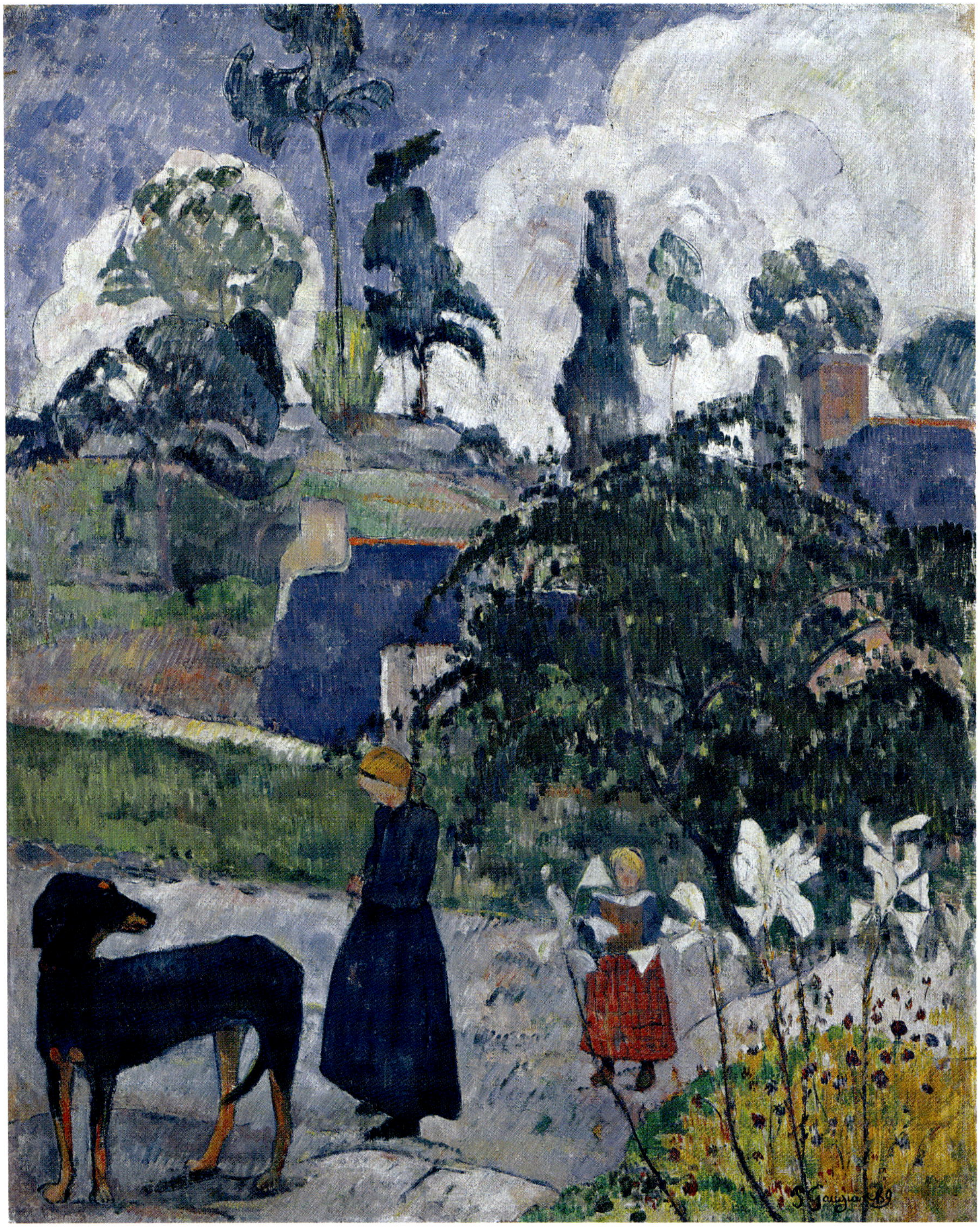

104. Paul Gauguin
Among Irises, 1889
(Entre les lys)
Oil on canvas. 92 x 73 cm
[Wildenstein 1964 n. 366]
Hilti Art Foundation, Schaan, Liechtenstein

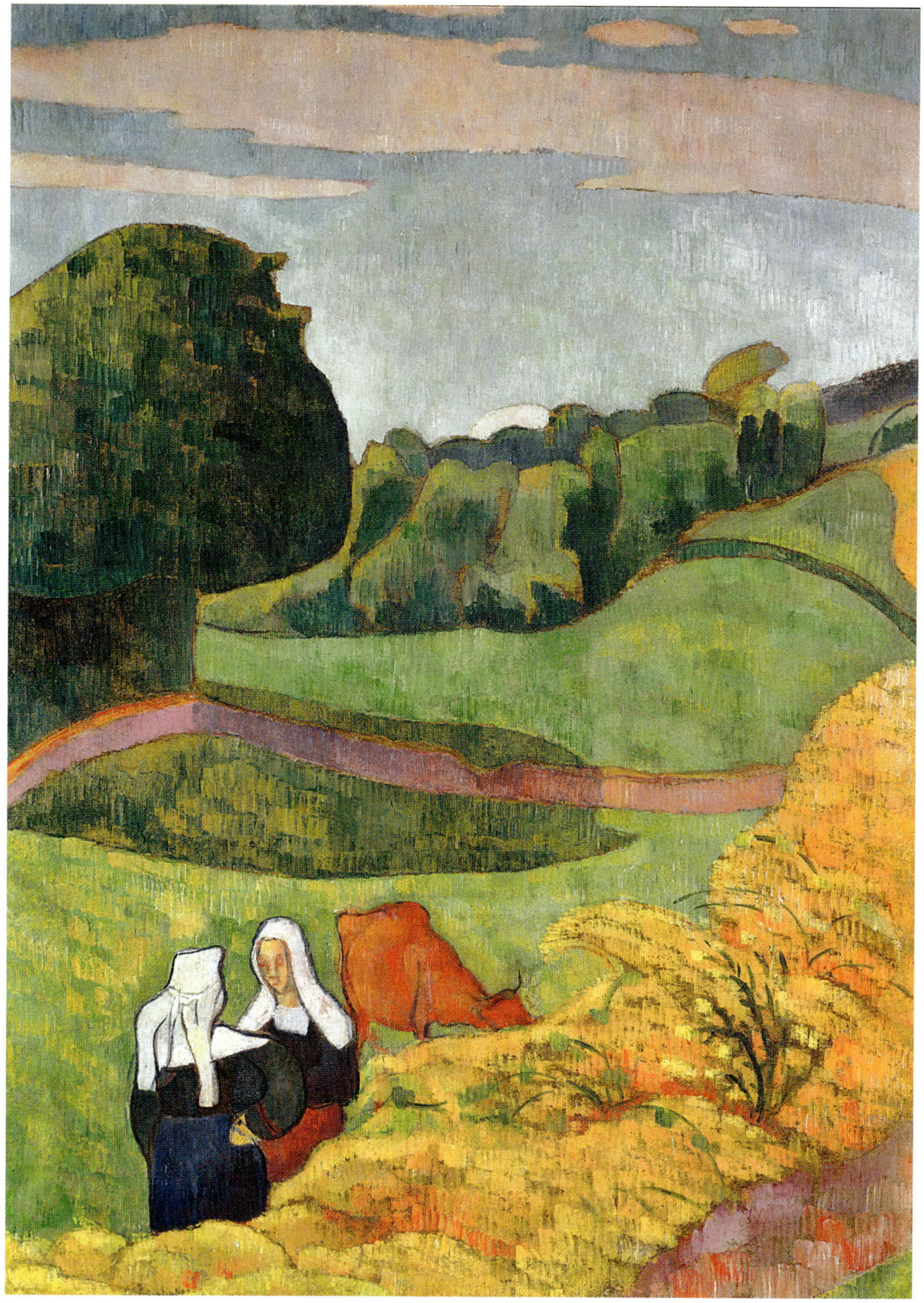

105. Émile Bernard
Landscape with Two Breton Girls, 1892
(Paysaje avec deux petites Bretonnes)
Oil on cardboard mounted on wood panel. 114.3 x 81.3 cm
[Luthi n. 329]
Triton Foundation, The Netherlands

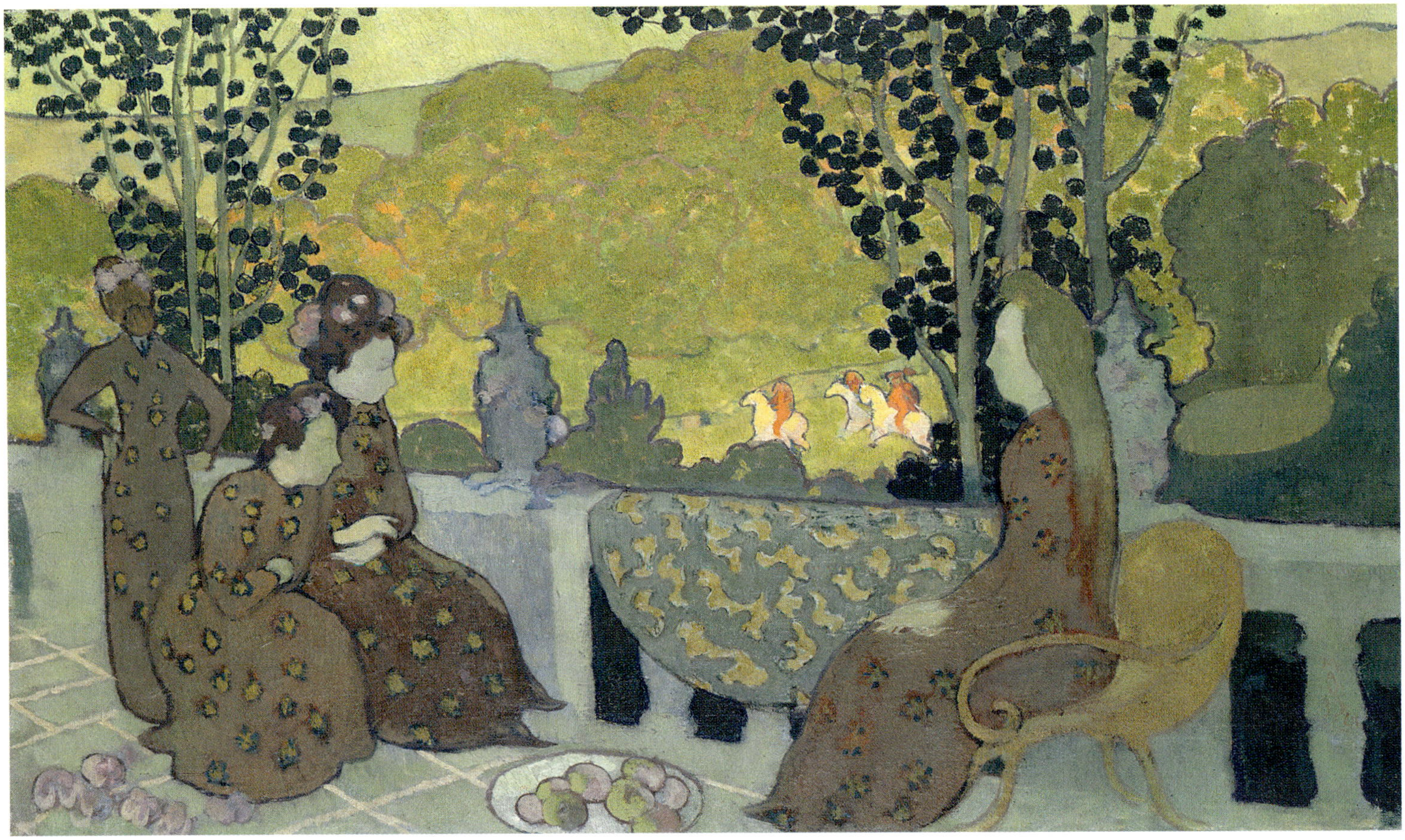

107. Maurice Denis
September: Women Seated on the Terrace, 1891
(Septembre: femmes assises à la terrasse)
Oil on canvas. 38 x 61 cm
Musée des Arts décoratifs, Paris

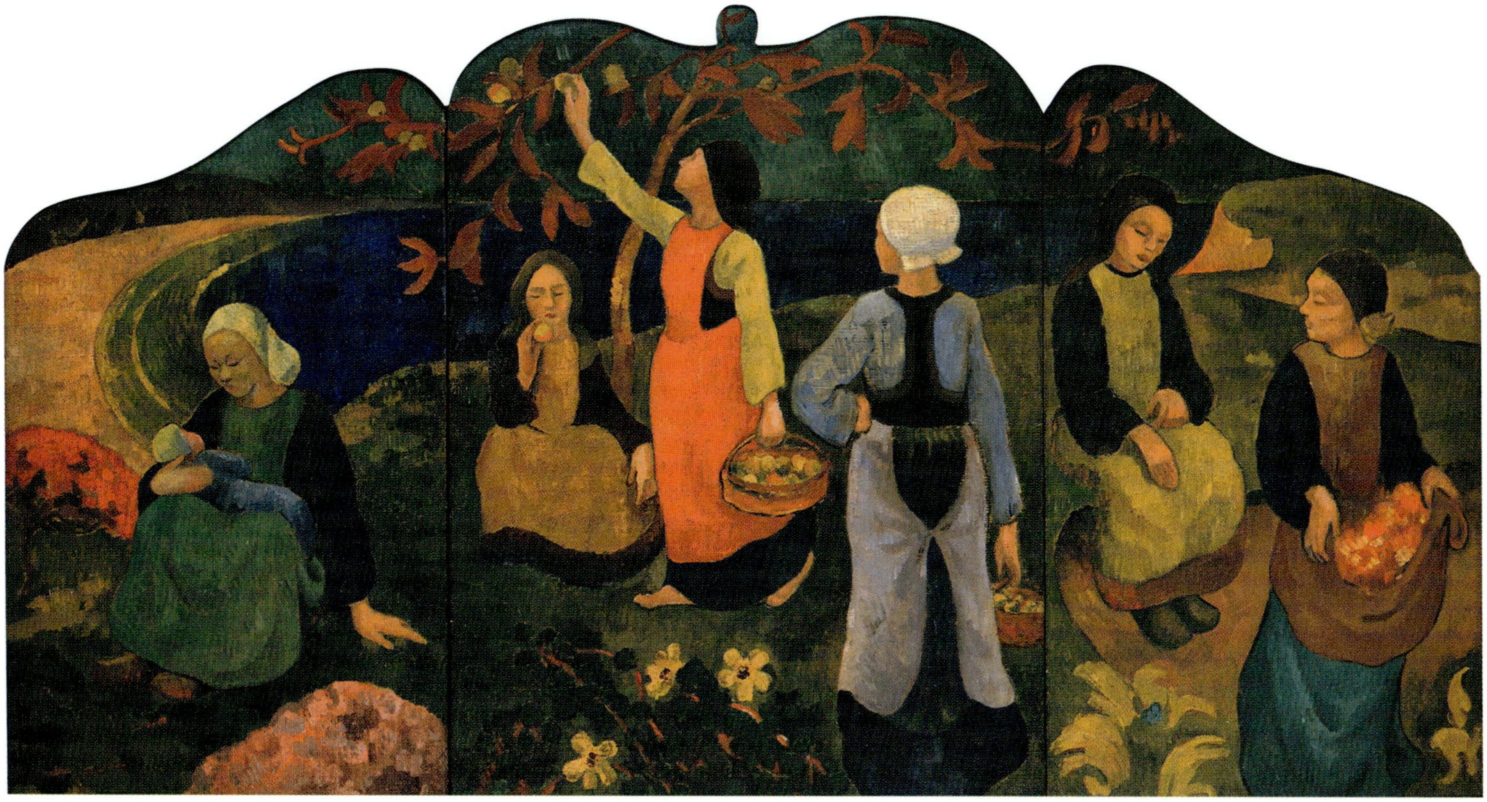

106. Paul Sérusier
Apple Harvest, c.1891
(La cueillette de pommes)
Oil on canvas. 73 x 133 cm
Triton Foundation, The Netherlands

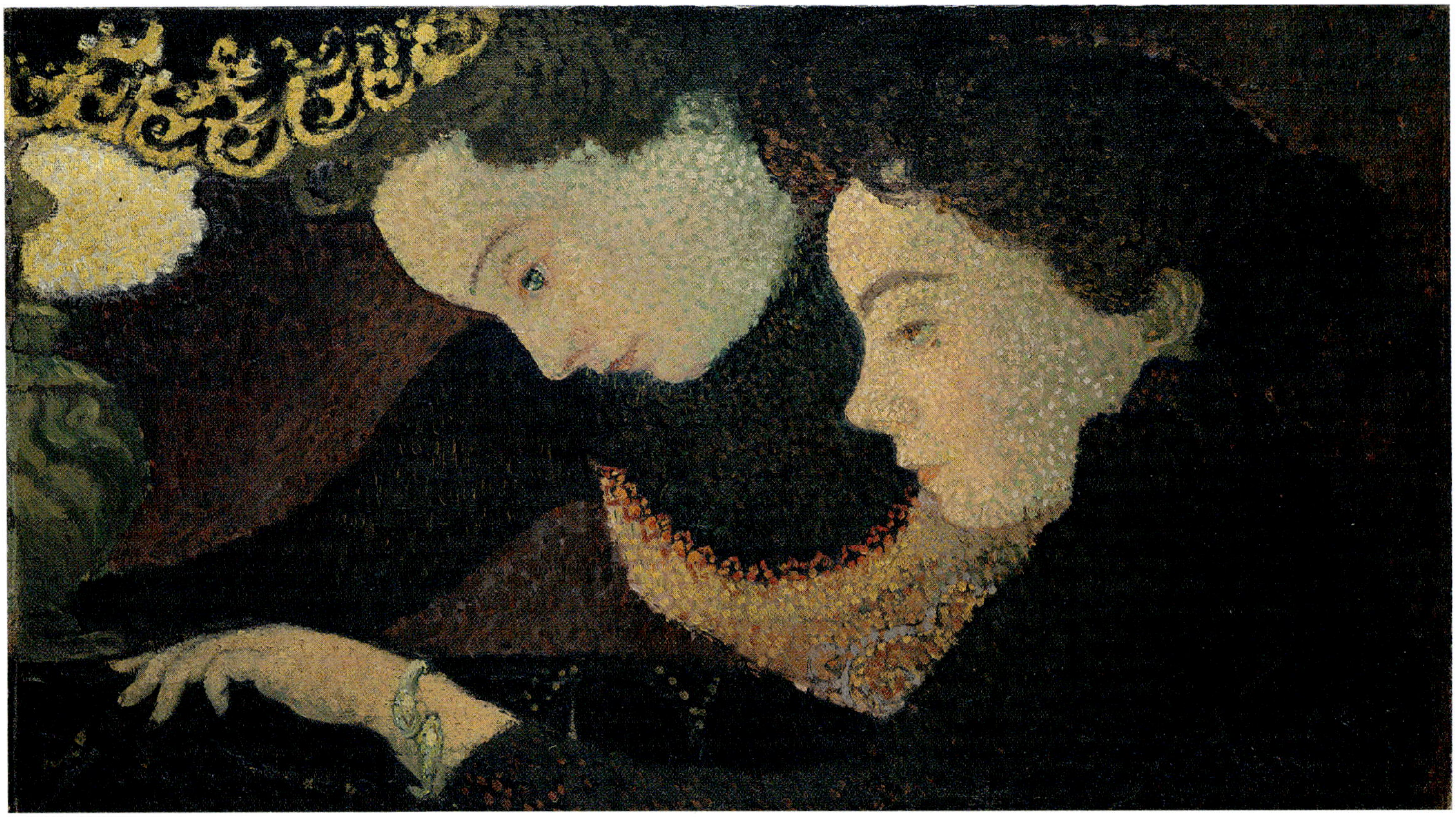

108. Maurice Denis
Young Women under a Lamp, 1891
(Les jeunes filles sous la lampe)
Oil on canvas. 36 x 25 cm
Musée des Beaux-Arts, Lyon

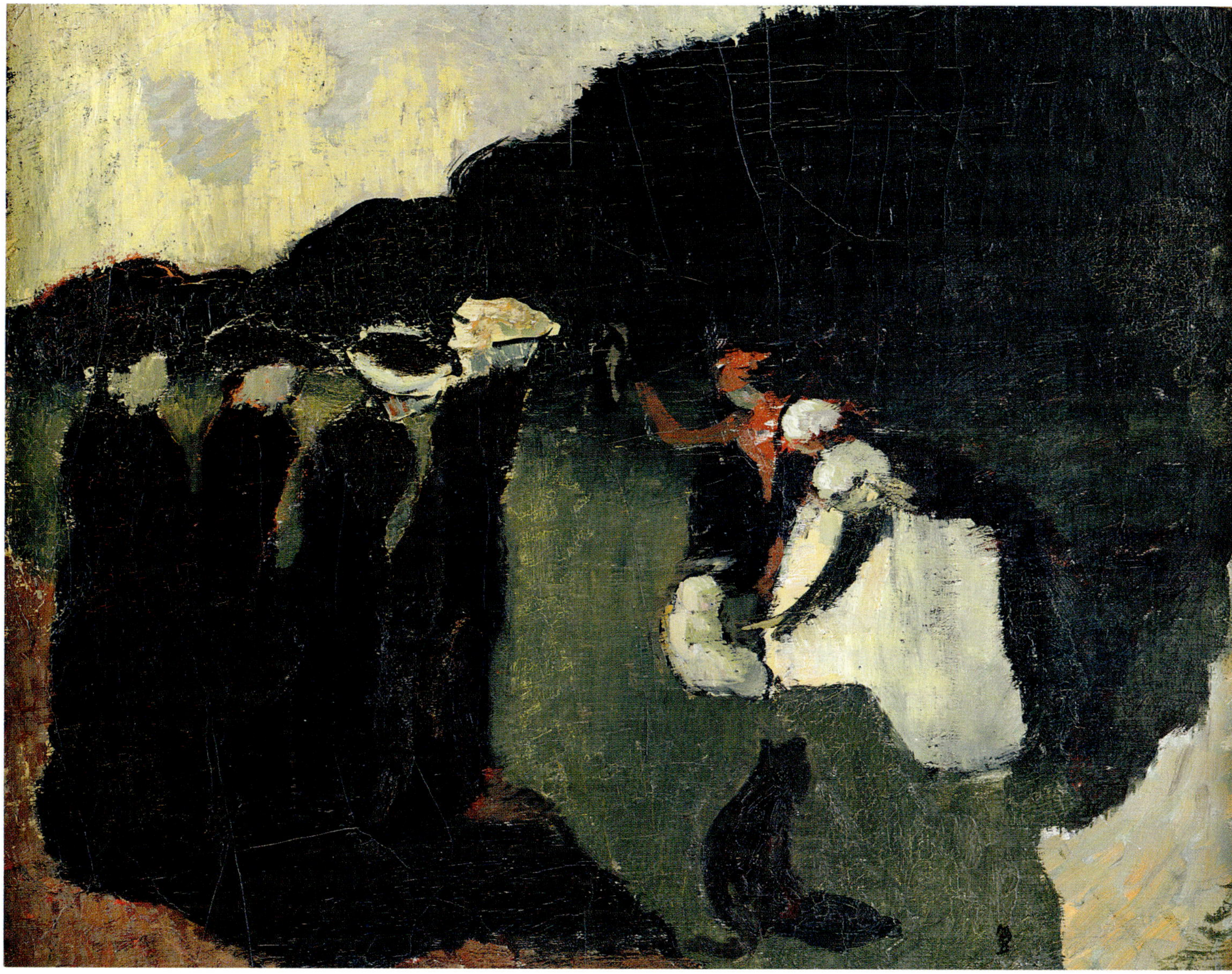

109. Maurice Denis
The Fairies, c.1891
(Les Fées)
Oil on paper mounted on canvas. 28 x 34.5 cm
Galerie Berès, Paris, France

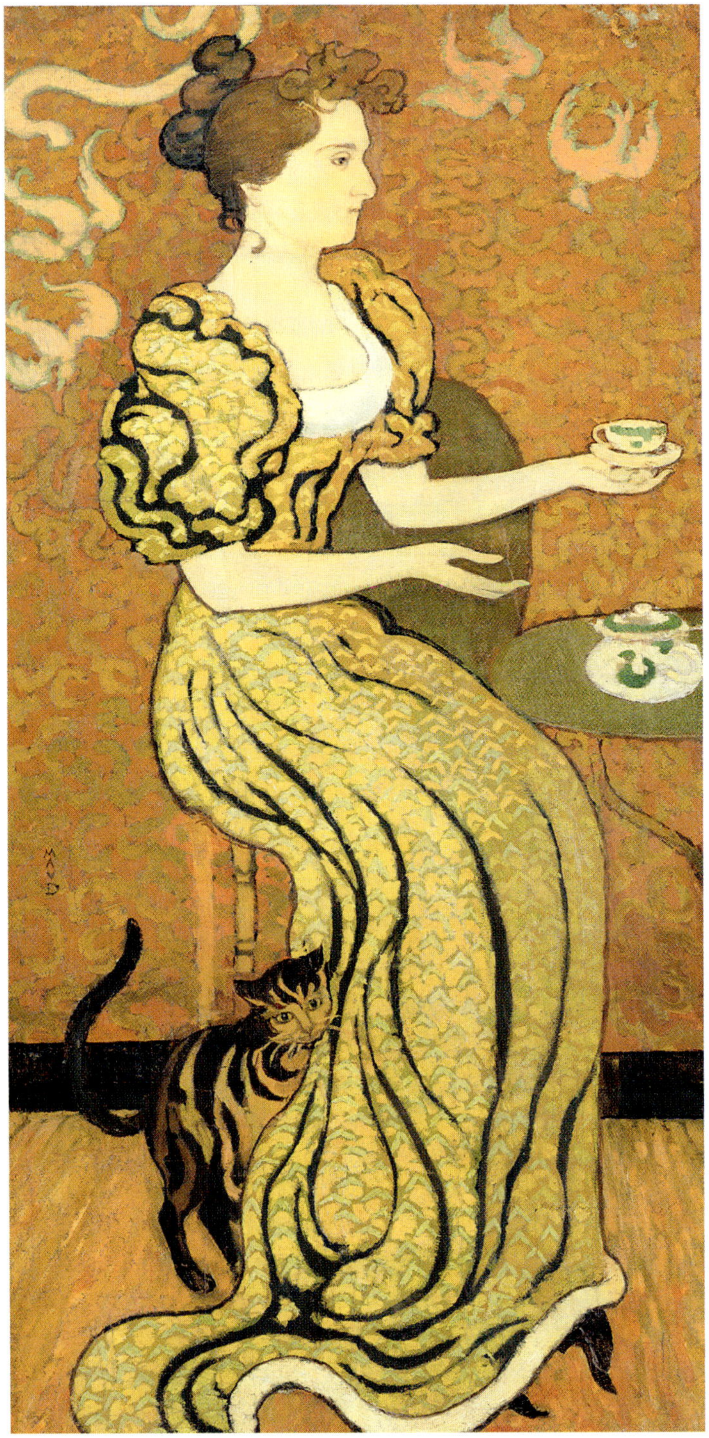

110. Maurice Denis
Madame Ranson with Cat, 1892
(Madame Ranson au chat)
Oil on canvas. 88.5 x 44 cm
Musée Départemental Maurice Denis 'e Prieuré', Saint-Germain-en-Laye

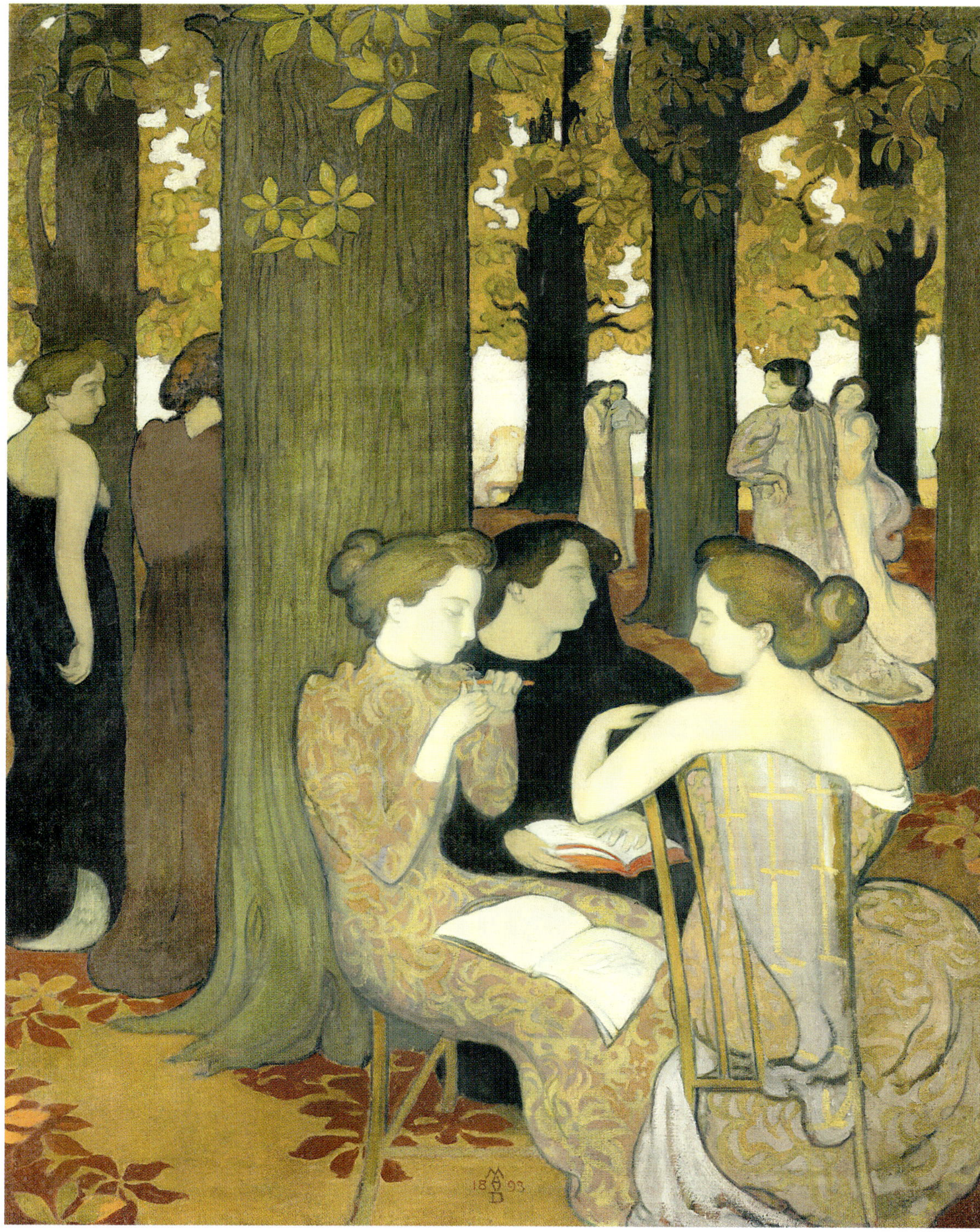

111. Maurice Denis
The Muses, 1893
(Les muses)
Oil on canvas. 171.5 x 137.5 cm
Musée d'Orsay, Paris

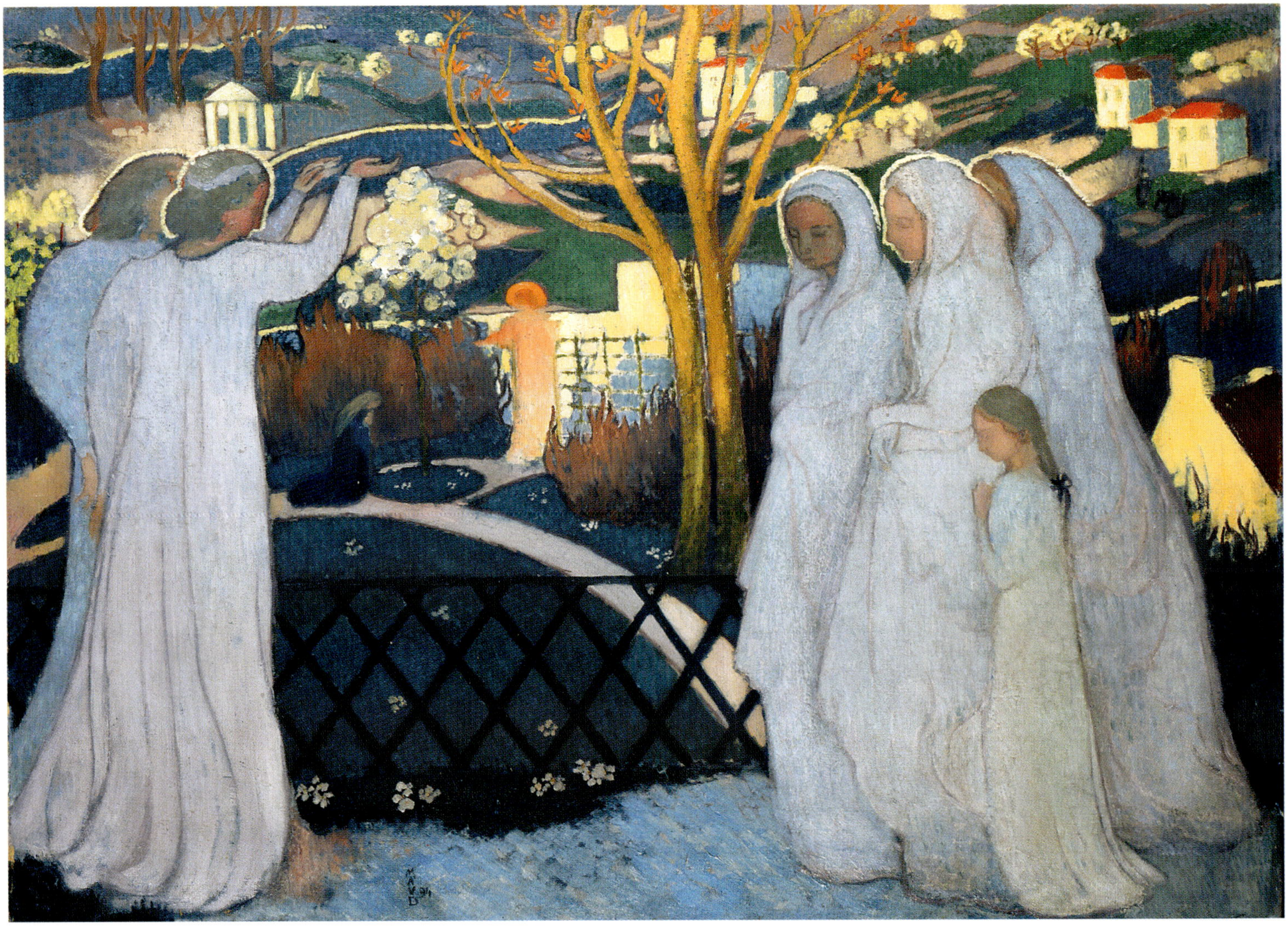

112. Maurice Denis
The Holy Women at the Tomb, 1894
(Saintes femmes au tombeau)
Oil on canvas. 74 x 100 cm
Musée Départemental Maurice Denis 'Le Prieuré', Saint-Germain-en-Laye

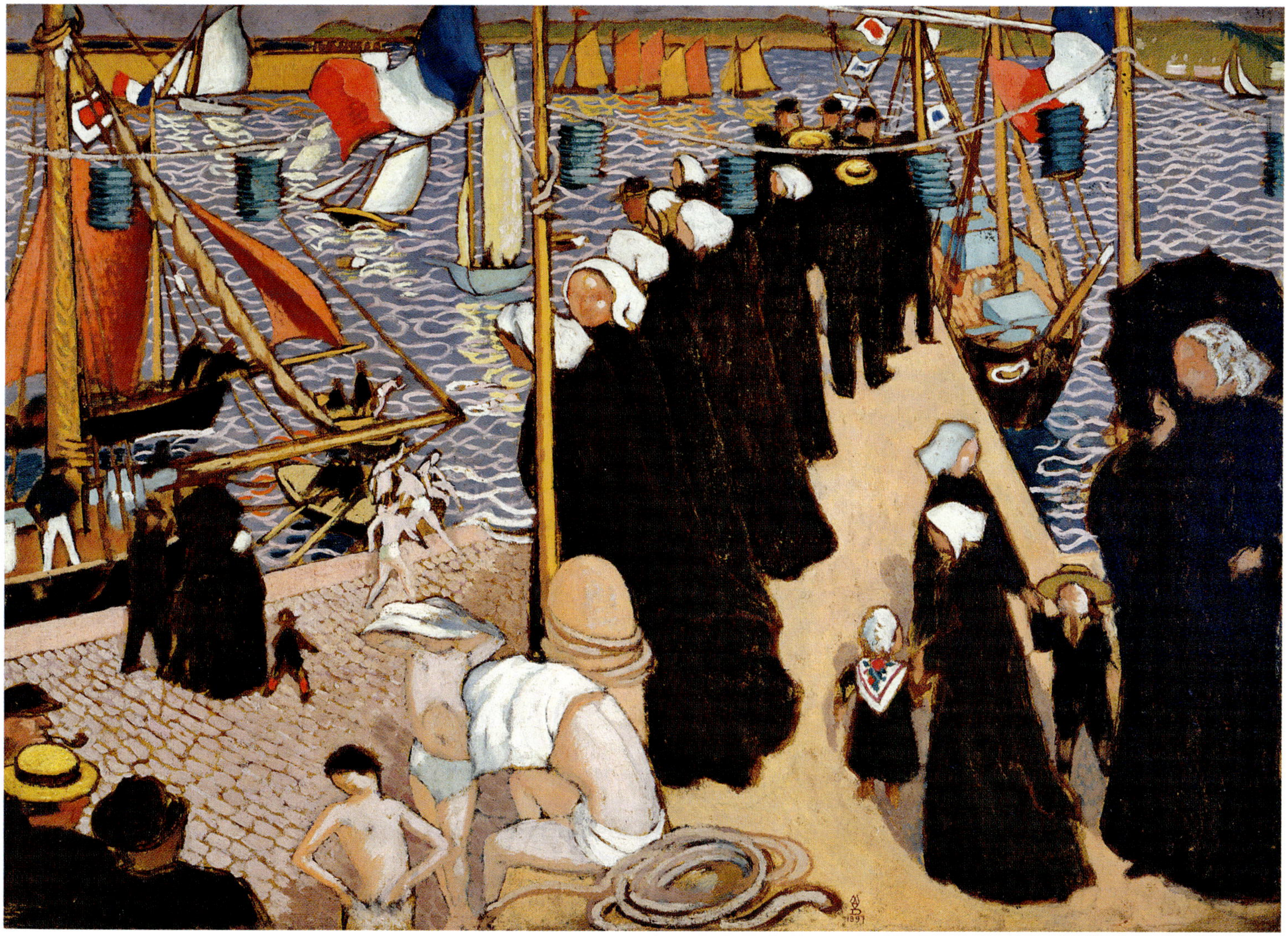

113. Maurice Denis
Regattas at Perros-Guirec Seen from the Western Wharf, 1897
(Régates à Perros-Guirec vues de la jetée ouest)
Oil on cardboard over wood panel. 73 x 100 cm
Musée Départemental Maurice Denis 'Le Prieuré', Saint-Germain-en-Laye

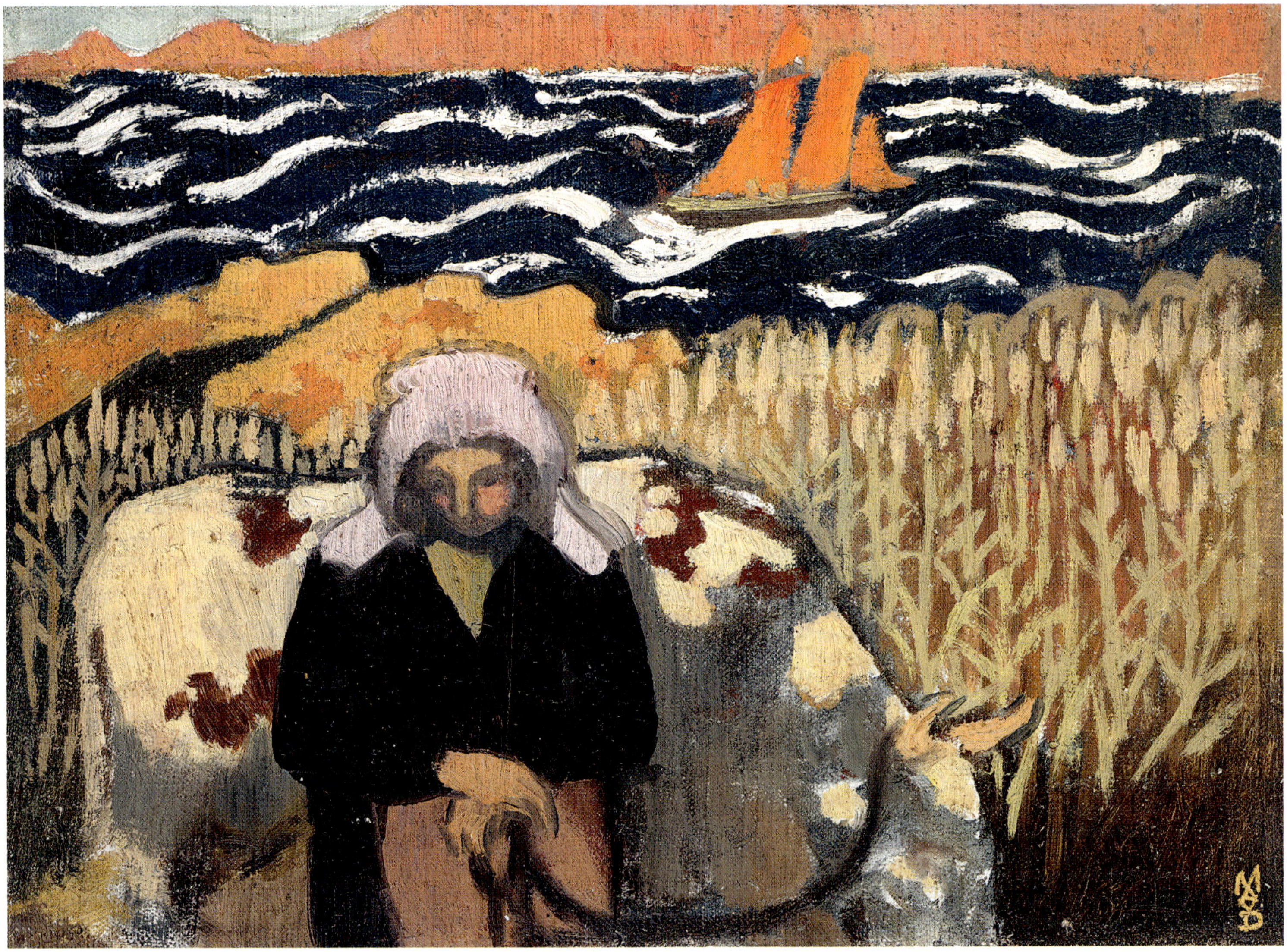

114. Maurice Denis
Peasant Woman with Cow, 1893
(La gardeuse de vache)
Oil on canvas. 20 x 27.9 cm
Indianapolis Museum of Art, Samuel Josefowitz Collection of the School of Pont-Aven, Indianapolis
(through the generosity of Lilly Endowment Inc.,
the Josefowitz Family, Mr and Mrs James M. Cornelius,
Mr and Mrs Leonard J. Betley, Lori and Dan Efroymson, and other Friends of the Museum)

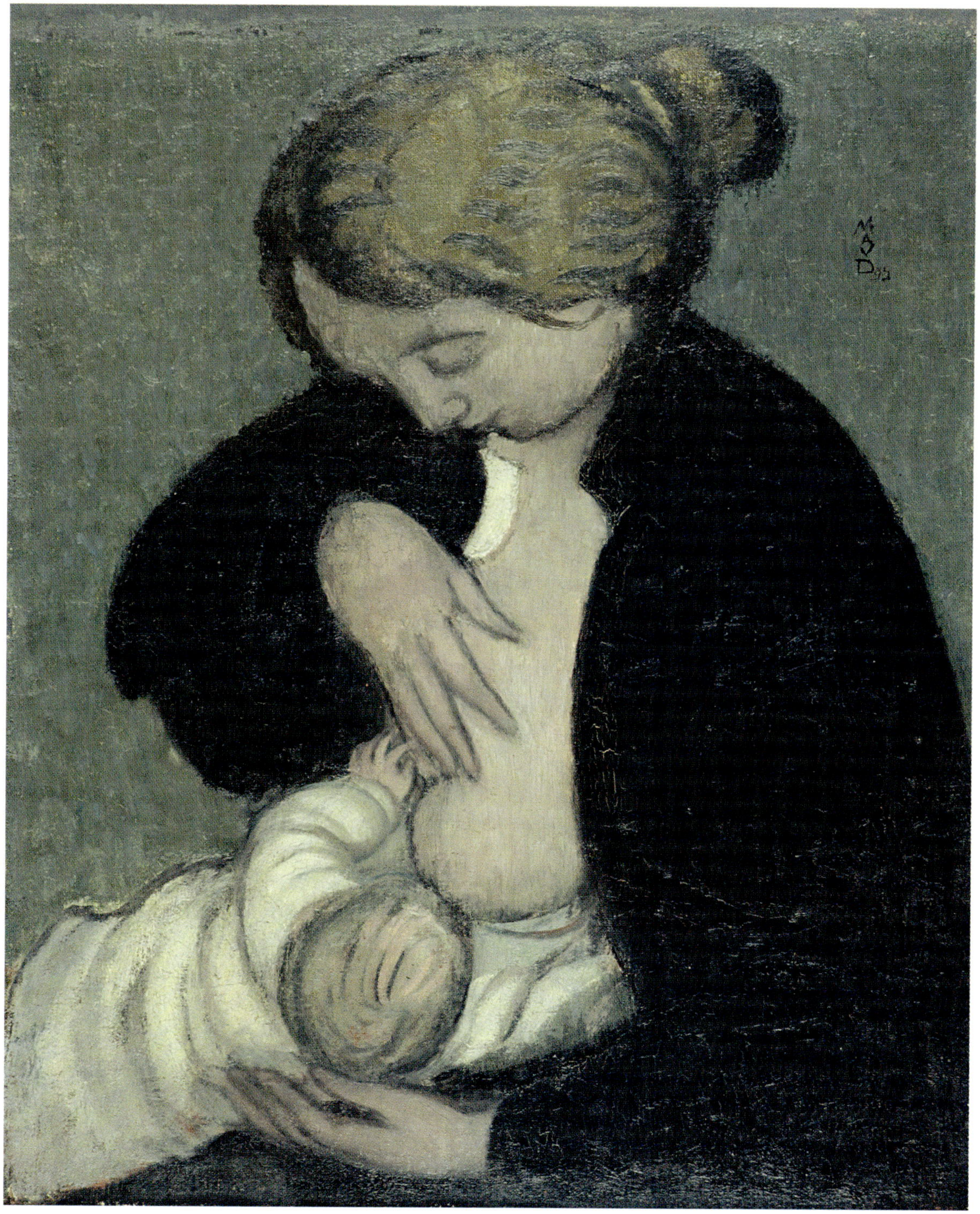

115. Maurice Denis
Mother in Black Blouse, 1895
(Mère au corsage noir)
Oil on canvas. 47 x 38 cm
Private Collection

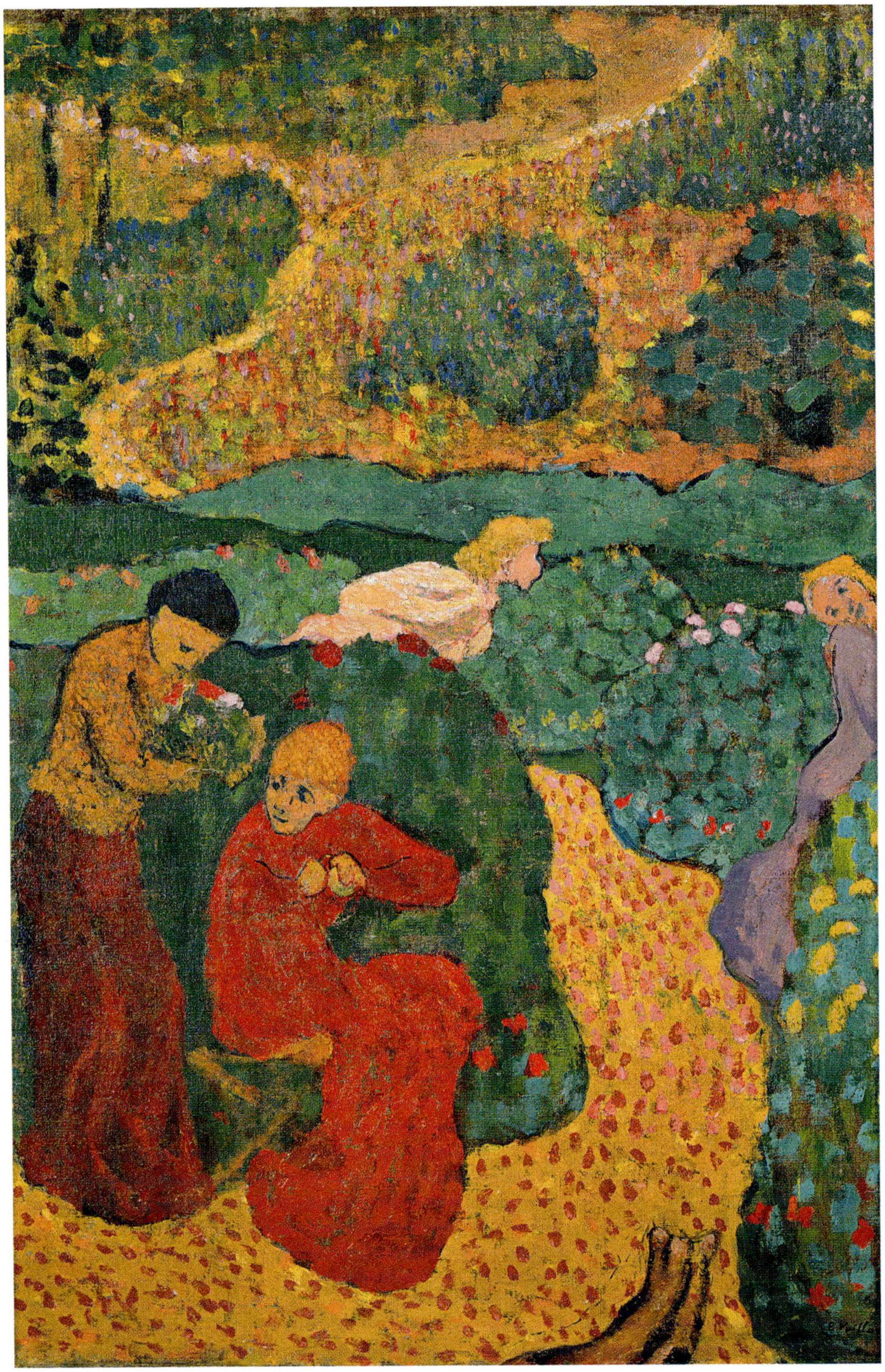

117. Édouard Vuillard
Women in the Garden or Song of Songs, 1891–1892
(Femmes au jardin ou Le Cantique des Cantiques)
Oil on canvas. 74 x 51 cm
[Salomon/Cogeval III n. 31]
Triton Foundation, The Netherlands

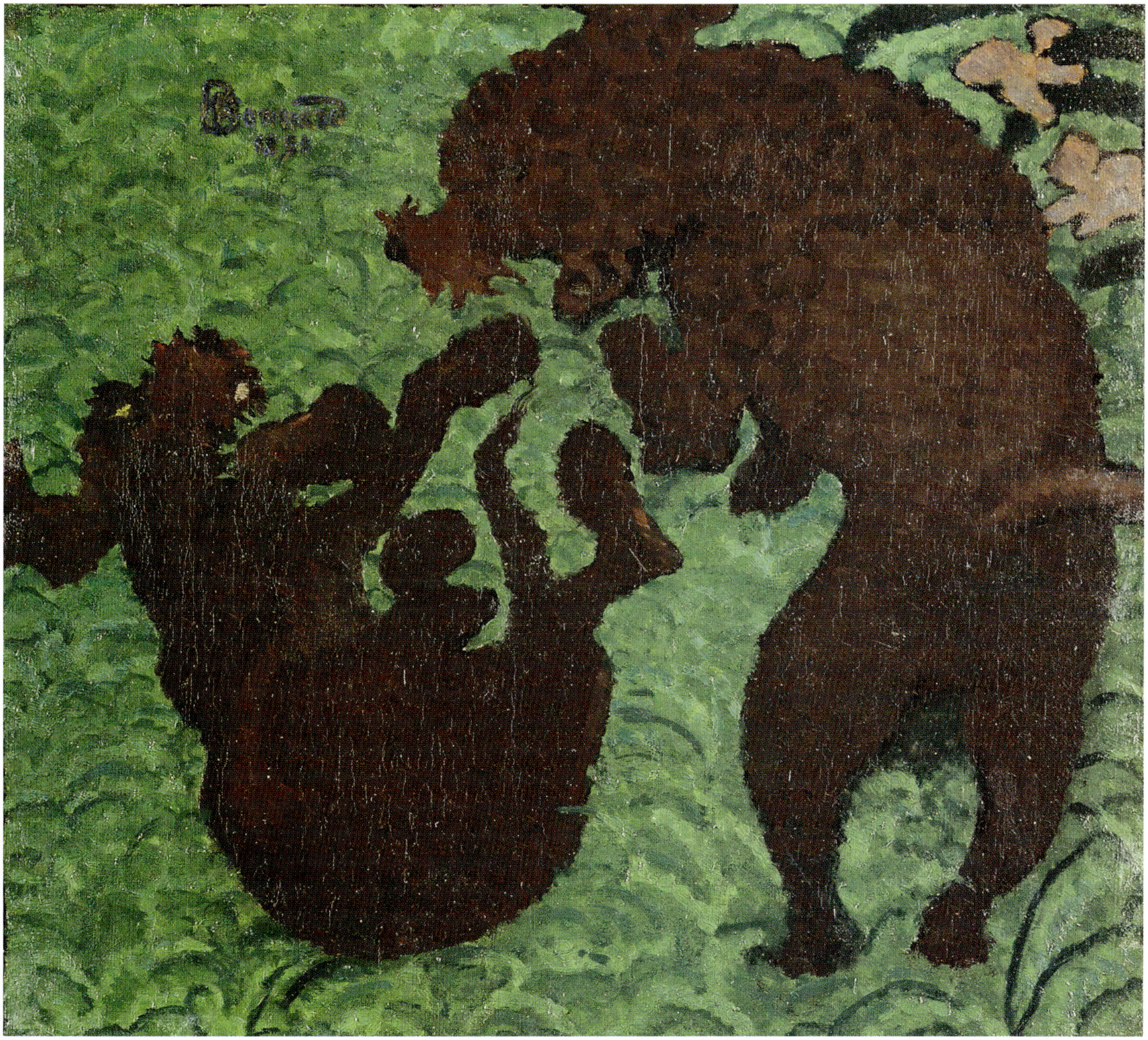

116. Pierre Bonnard
Two Dogs Playing, 1891
(Deux chiens jouant)
Oil on canvas. 37 x 39.7 cm
[Dauberville n. 27]
Southampton City Art Gallery, Southampton

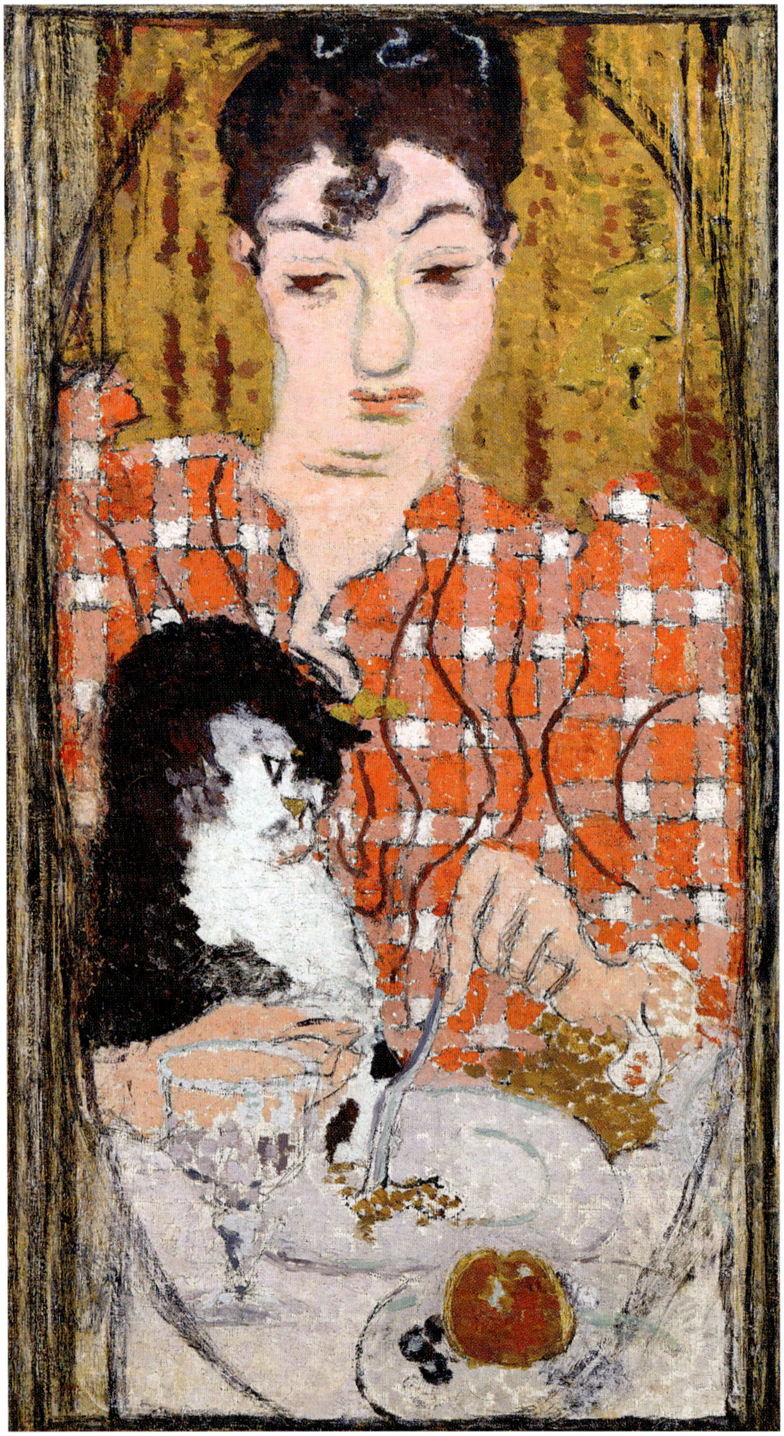

118. Pierre Bonnard
Woman in Checkered Blouse (Portrait of Mme. Claude Terrasse) c.1892
(Le corsage à carreaux [Portrait de Mme. Claude Terrasse])
Oil on canvas. 61 x 33 cm
[Dauberville n. 33B]
Reytenbagh Collection

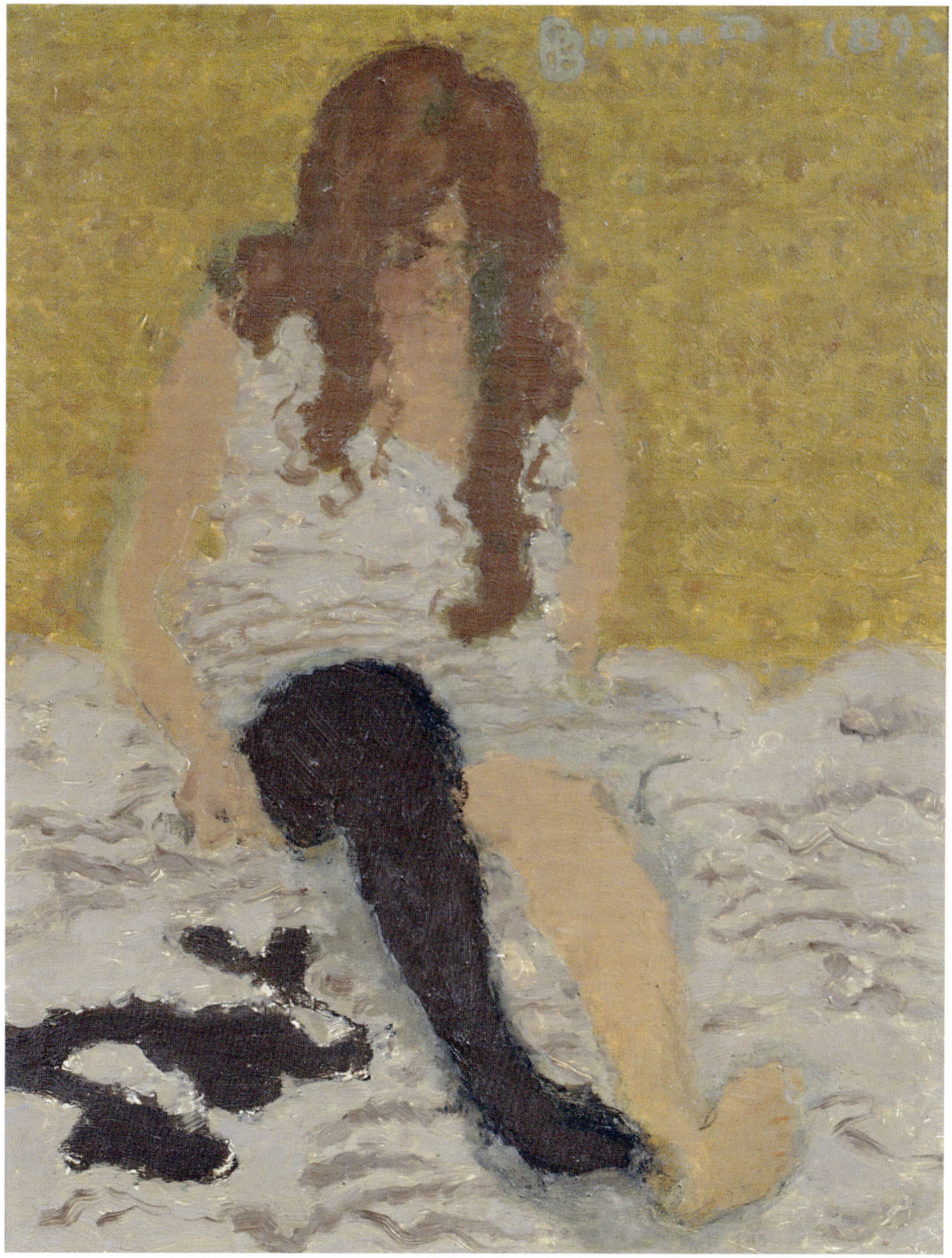

119. Pierre Bonnard
Woman Putting on her Stockings, 1893
(Femme enfilant ses bas)
Oil on wood panel. 35.2 x 27 cm
[Dauberville n. 44]
Private Collection

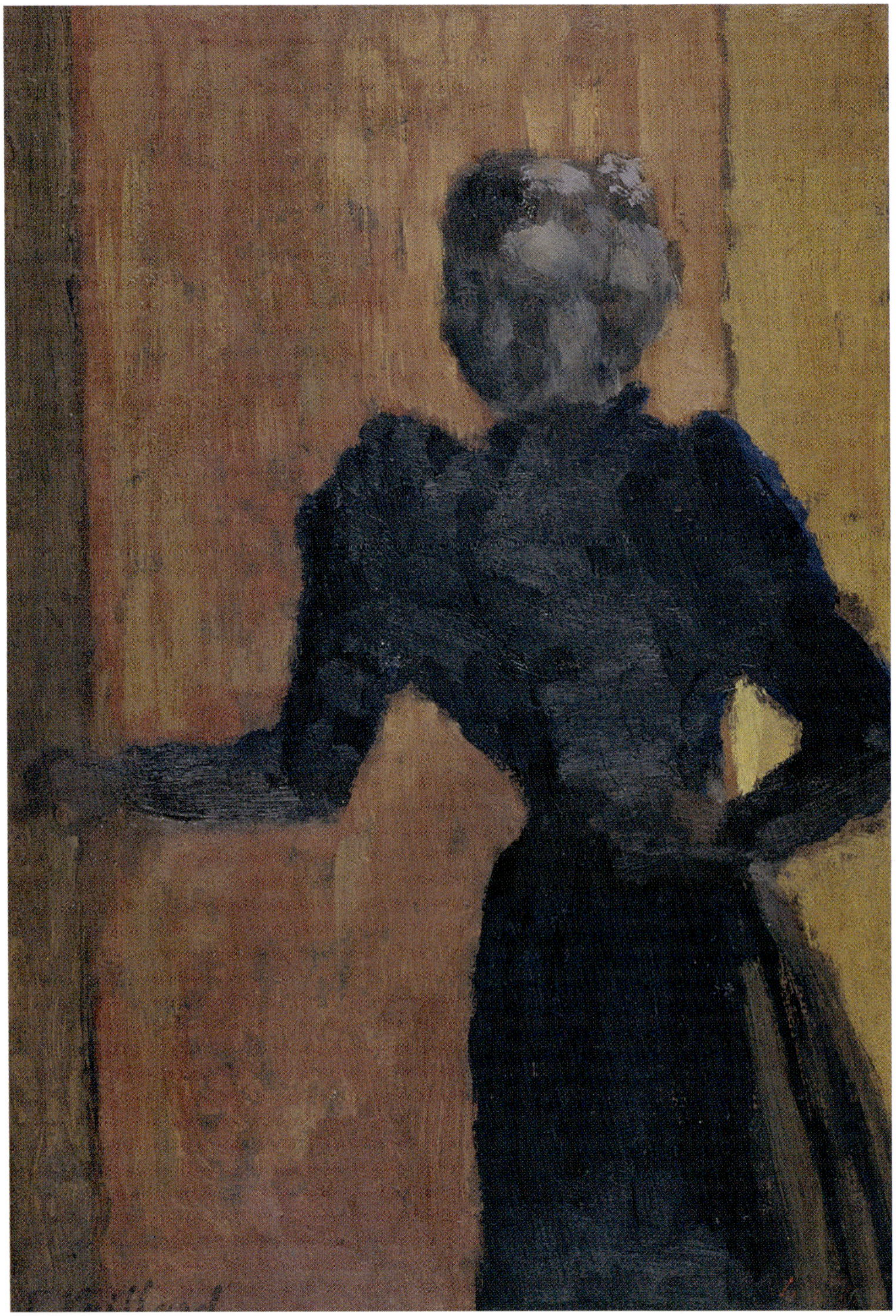

120. Édouard Vuillard
Woman in an Interior, 1893
(Femme dans un intérieur)
Oil on cardboard mounted on wood panel. 22.7 x 15 cm
[Salomon/Cogeval IV n. 99]
Collection Fondation Pierre Gianadda, Martigny, Switzerland

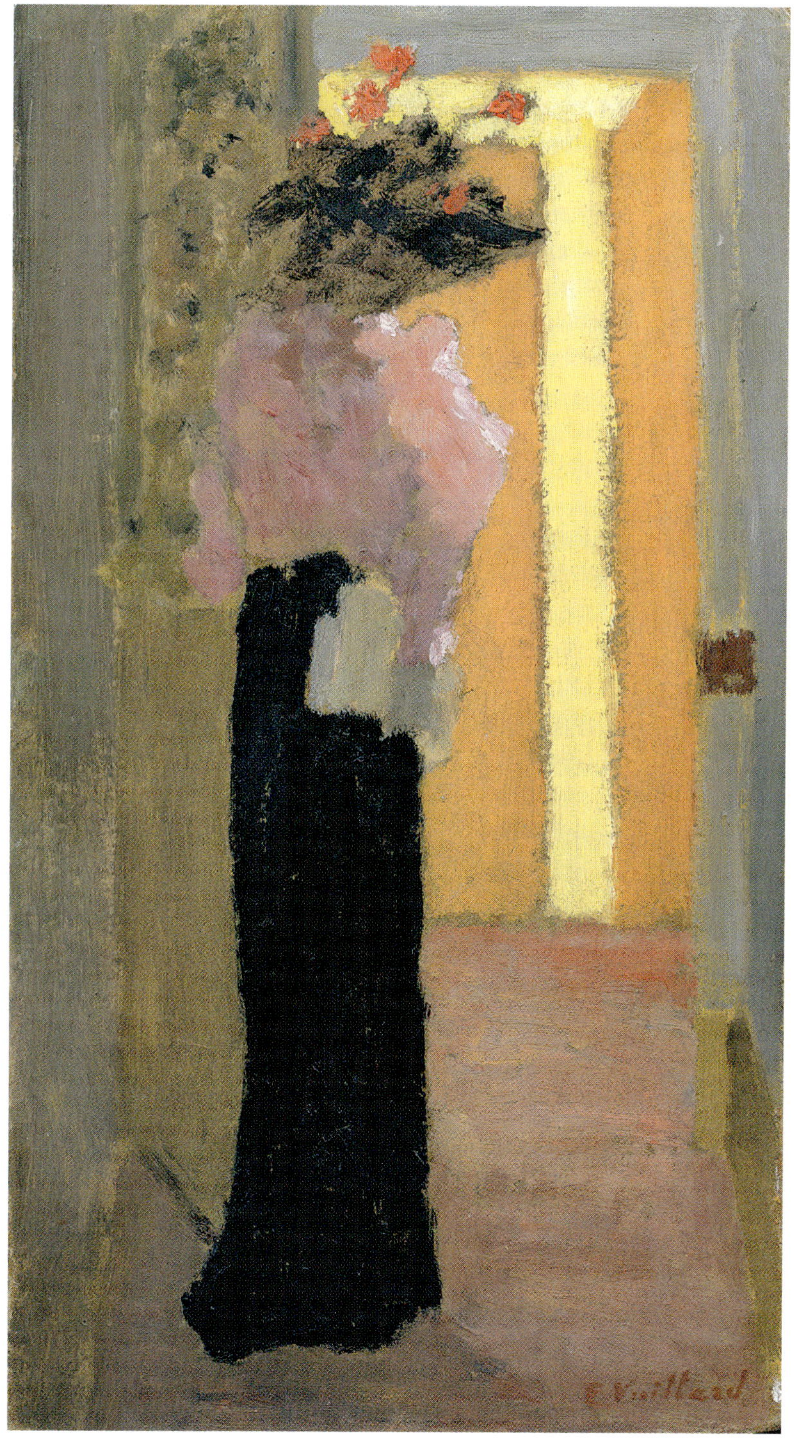

121. Édouard Vuillard
The Lady of Fashion, c. 1891–1892
(L'Élégante)
Oil over cardboard. 28.4 x 15.3 cm
[Salomon/Cogeval II n. 135]
Private Collection

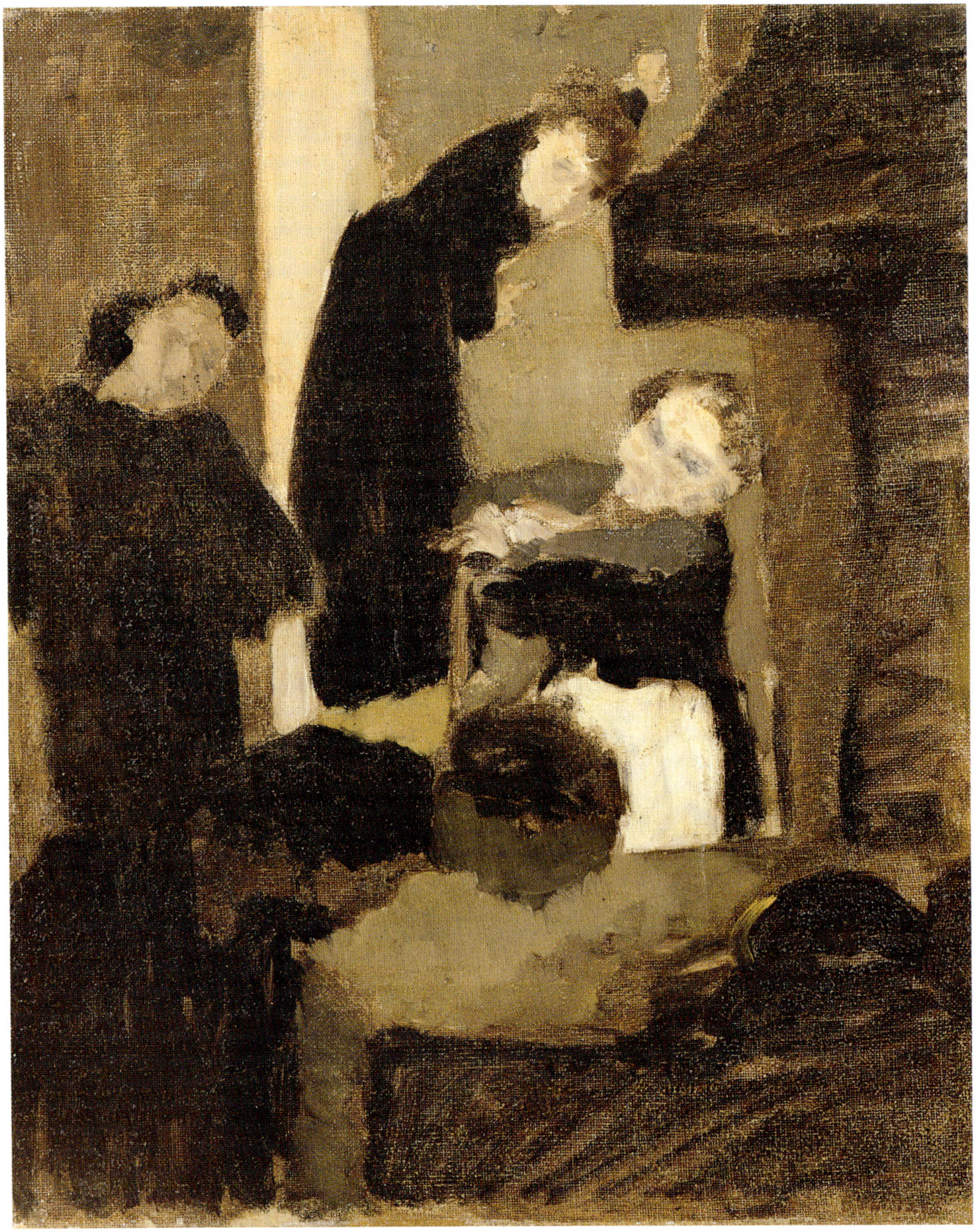

122. Édouard Vuillard
Madame Vuillard and her Employees, c.1892–1893
(Mme Vuillard et ses ouvrières)
Oil on canvas. 40.5 x 32.2 cm
[Salomon/Cogeval IV n. 56]
Galerie Berès, Paris, France

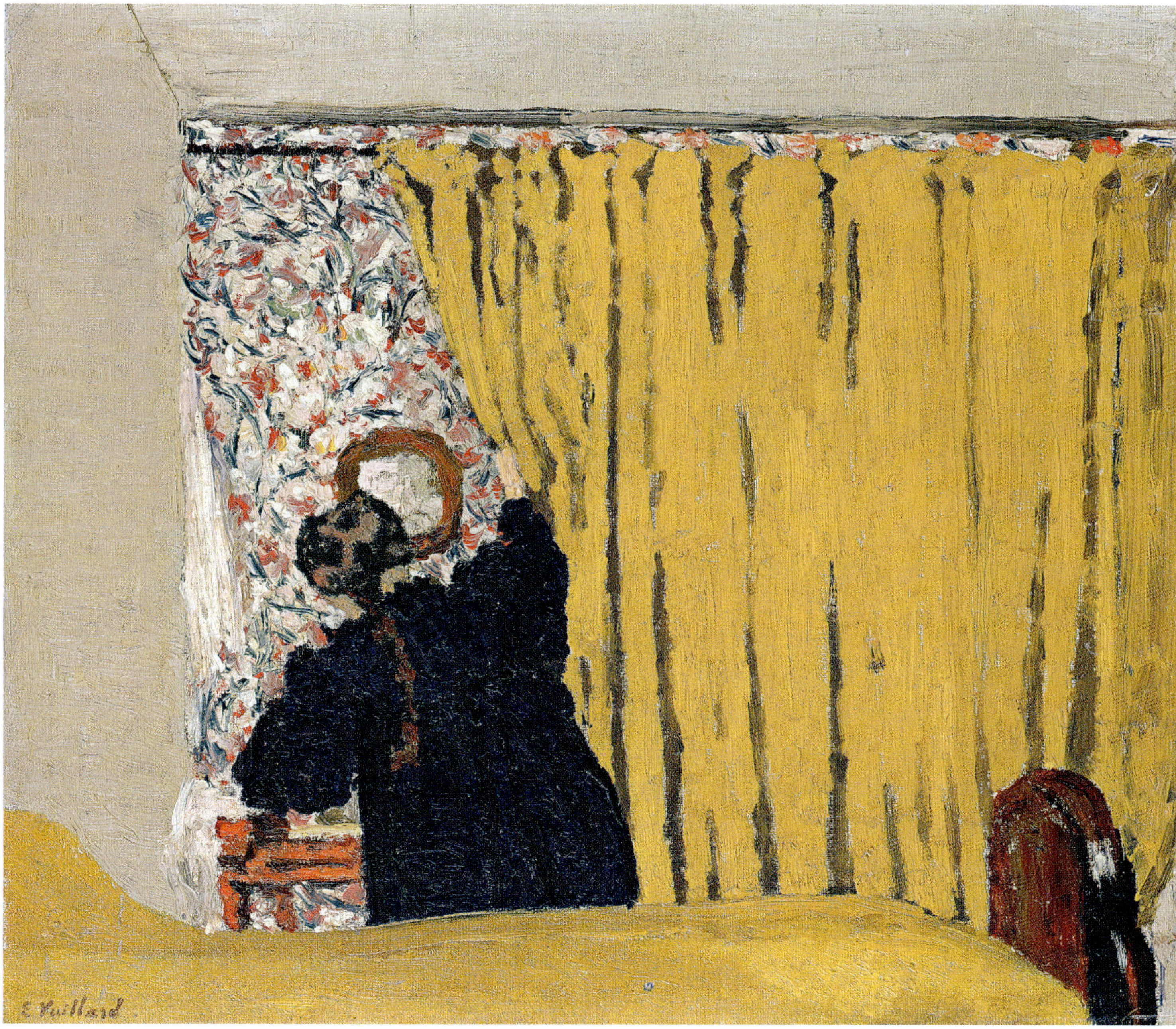

123. Édouard Vuillard
The Yellow Curtain, c. 1893
(Le Rideau jaune)
Oil on canvas. 35 x 39 cm
[Salomon/Cogeval IV n. 160]
Washington, National Gallery of Art,
Ailsa Mellon Bruce Collection 1970.17.95

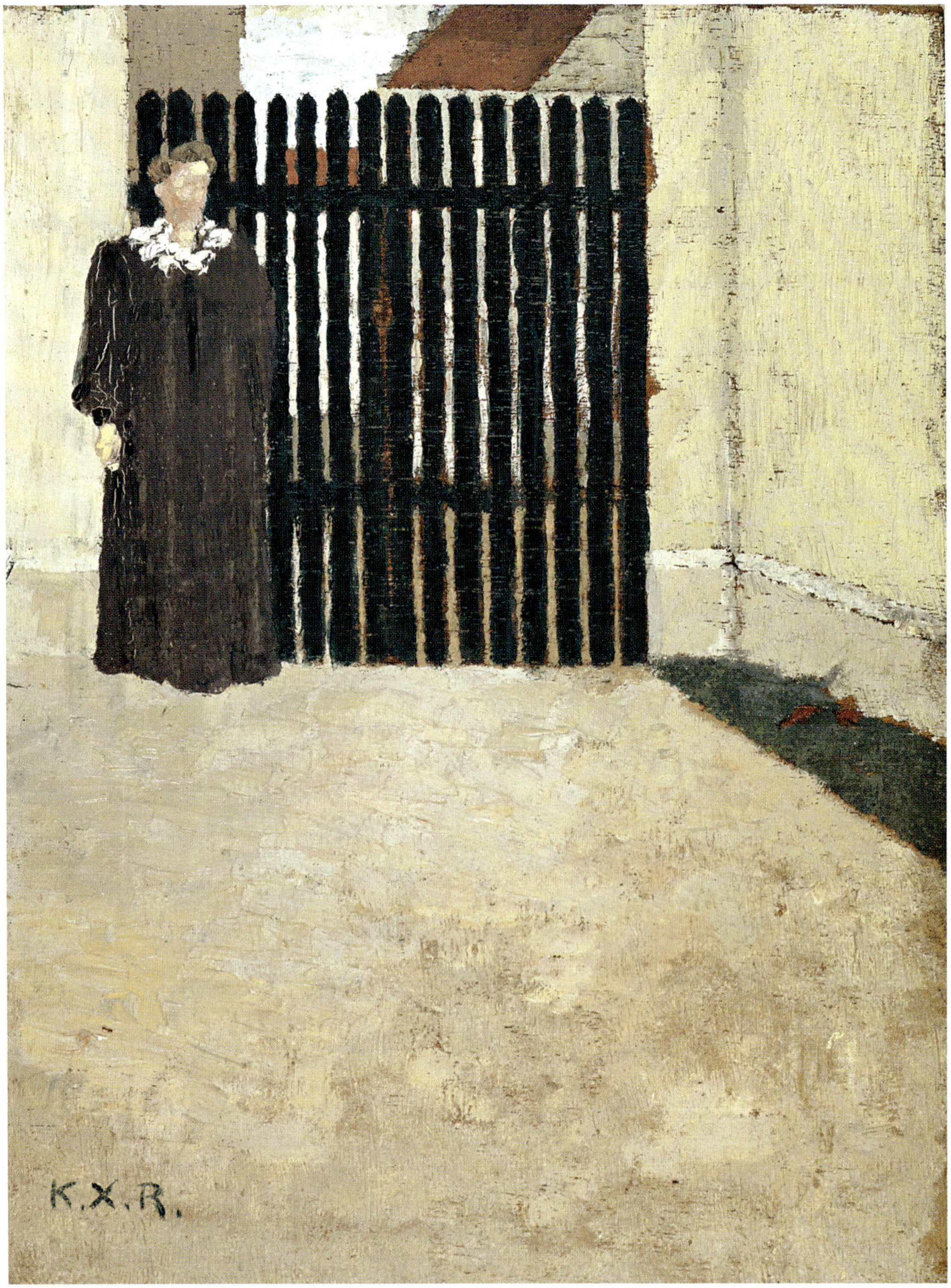

124. Ker-Xavier Roussel
Woman in front of a Green Gate, c. 1891–1893
(Femme devant un portail vert)
Oil on wood panel. 22.3 x 16.5 cm
Private Collection

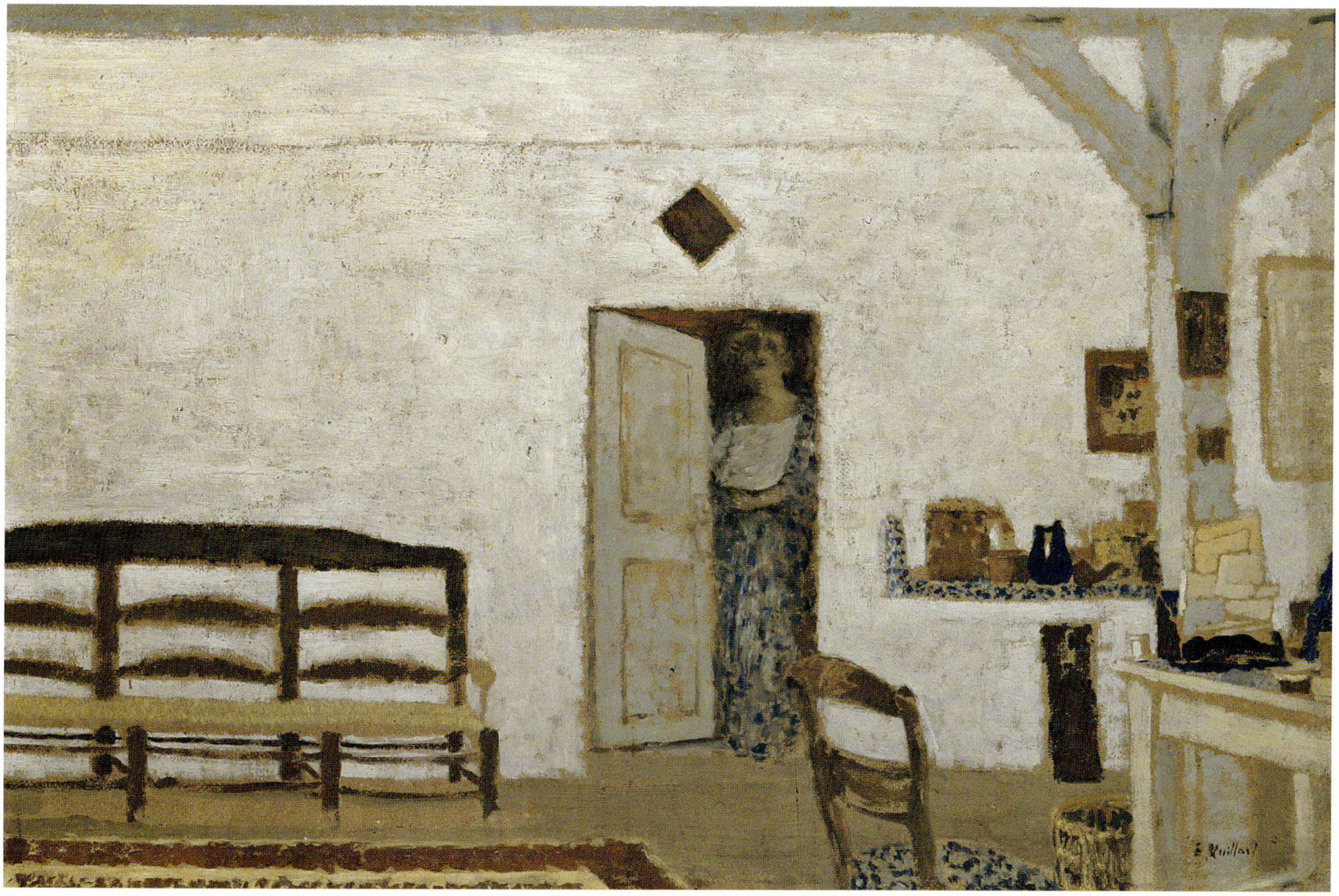

125. Édouard Vuillard
Misia at Villeneuve-sur-Yonne, 1897–1898
(Misia à Villeneuve-sur-Yonne)
Oil on canvas. 42.5 x 62.5 cm
[Salomon/Cogeval VI n. 54]
Musée des Beaux-Arts, Lyon

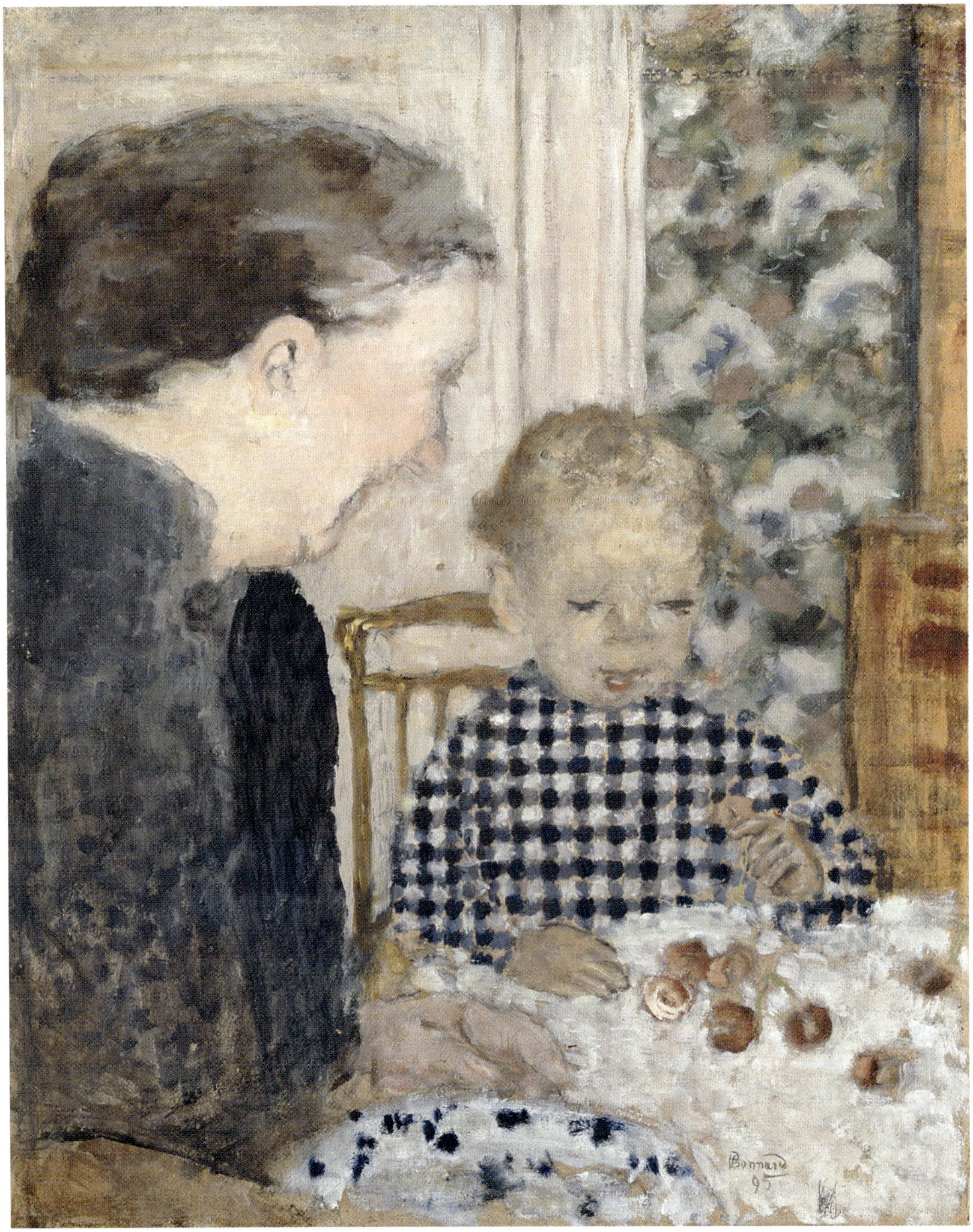

126. Pierre Bonnard
A Child Eating Cherries, 1895
(Enfant mangeant des cerises)
Oil on wood panel. 52 x 41 cm
National Gallery of Ireland, Dublin

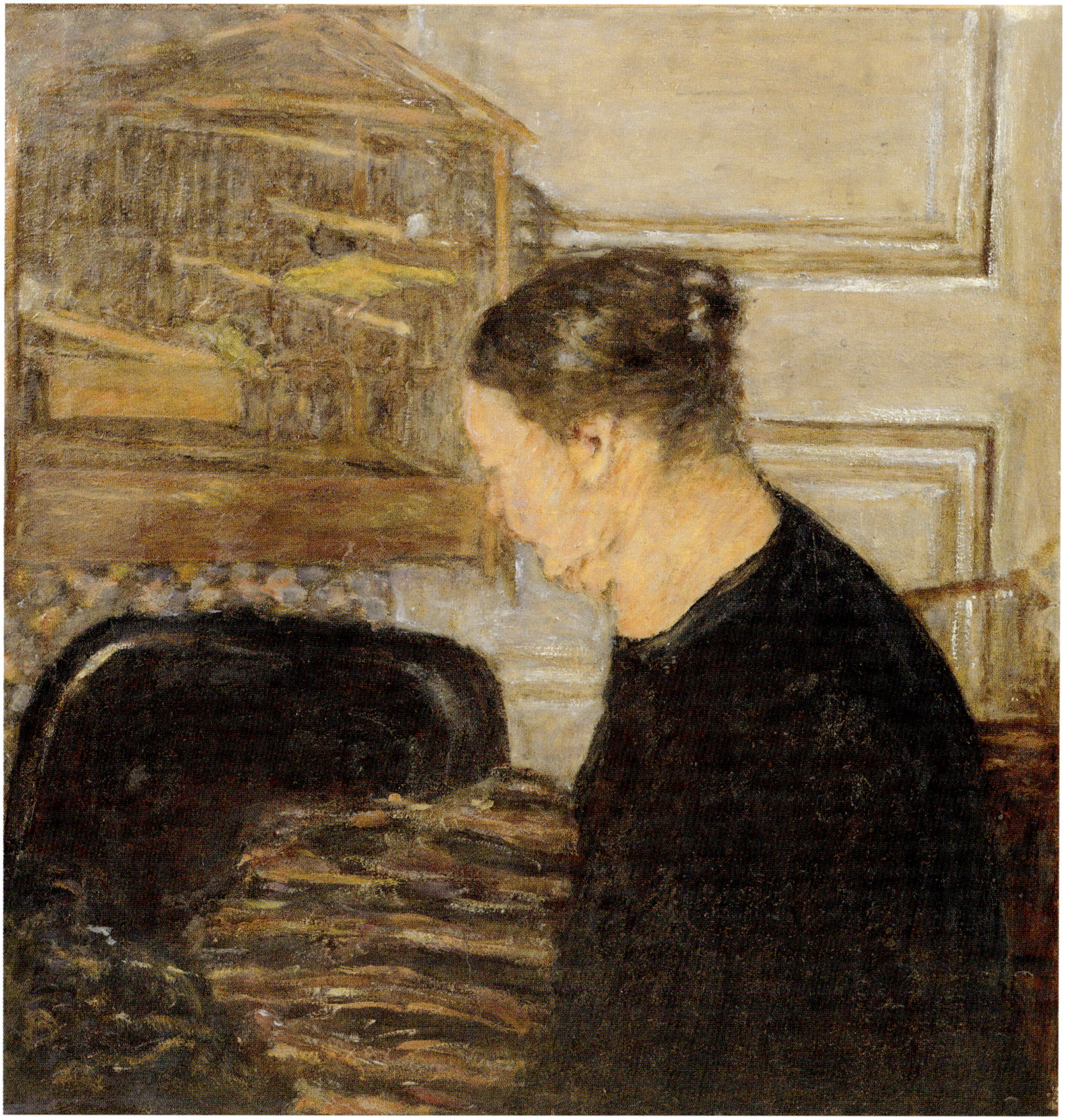

127. Pierre Bonnard
Portrait of Madame Frédéric Mertzdorff, Grandmother of the artist, 1895
(Portrait de Madame Frédéric Mertzdorff, grand-mère de l'artiste)
Oil on cardboard. 59 x 60 cm
Galerie Berès, Paris, France

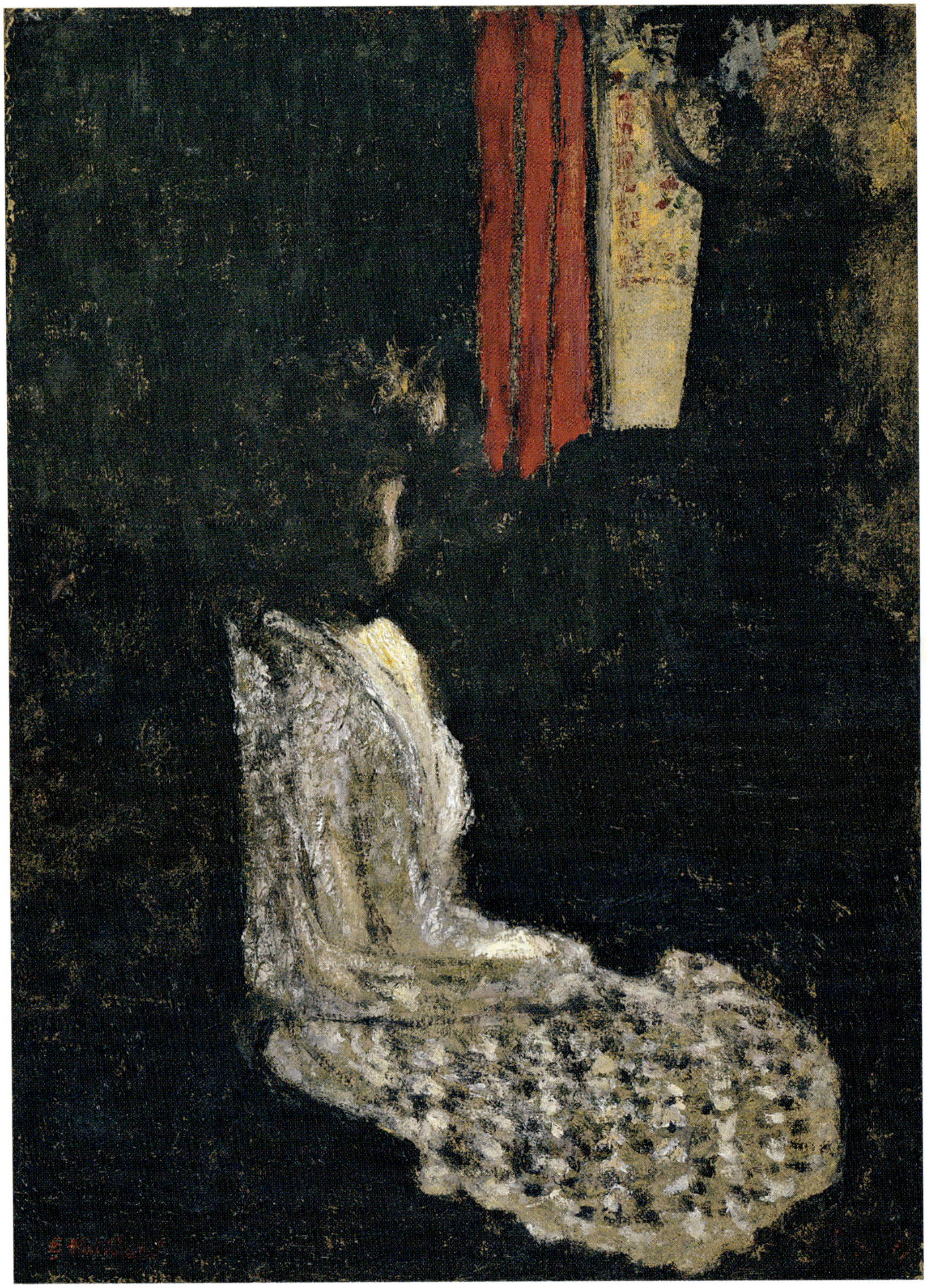

129. Édouard Vuillard
Seated Woman in a Dark Room, c. 1895
(Femme assise dans une pièce sombre)
Oil on cardboard over wood panel. 36.7 x 26.3 cm
[Salomon/Cogeval IV n. 205]
The Montreal Museum of Fine Arts, Montreal
Purchase, The Museum Campaign 1988–1993 Fund

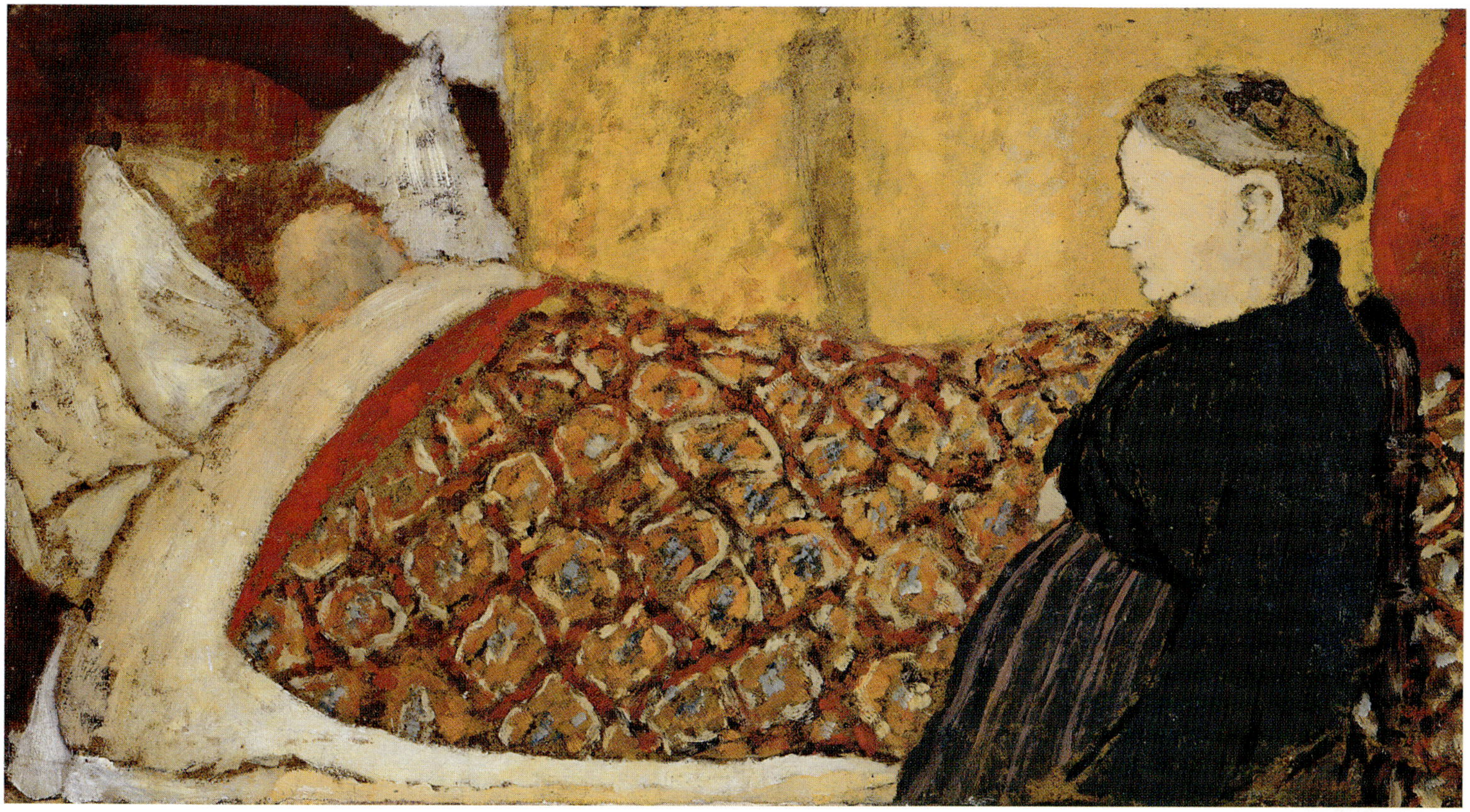

128. Édouard Vuillard
La berceuse, 1894
Oil on cardboard over wood panel. 28 x 49 cm
[Salomon/Cogeval IV n. 161]
Musée Picasso, Paris

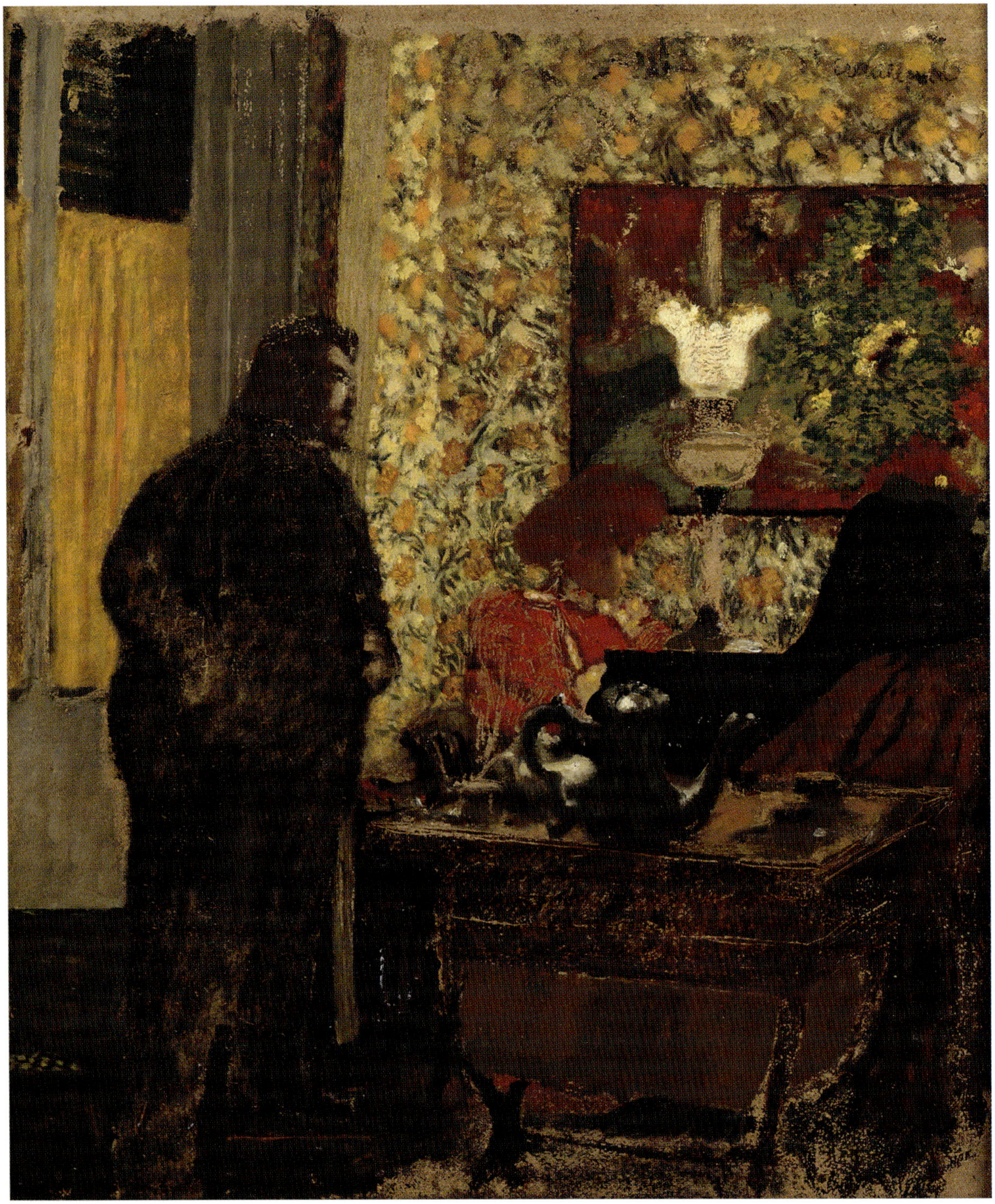

130. Édouard Vuillard
Cipa Listening to Misia Playing the Piano, 1897–1898
(Misia au piano et Cipa l'écoutant)
Oil on cardboard. 63.5 x 56 cm
[Salomon/Cogeval VI n. 38]
Staatliche Kunsthalle Karlsruhe

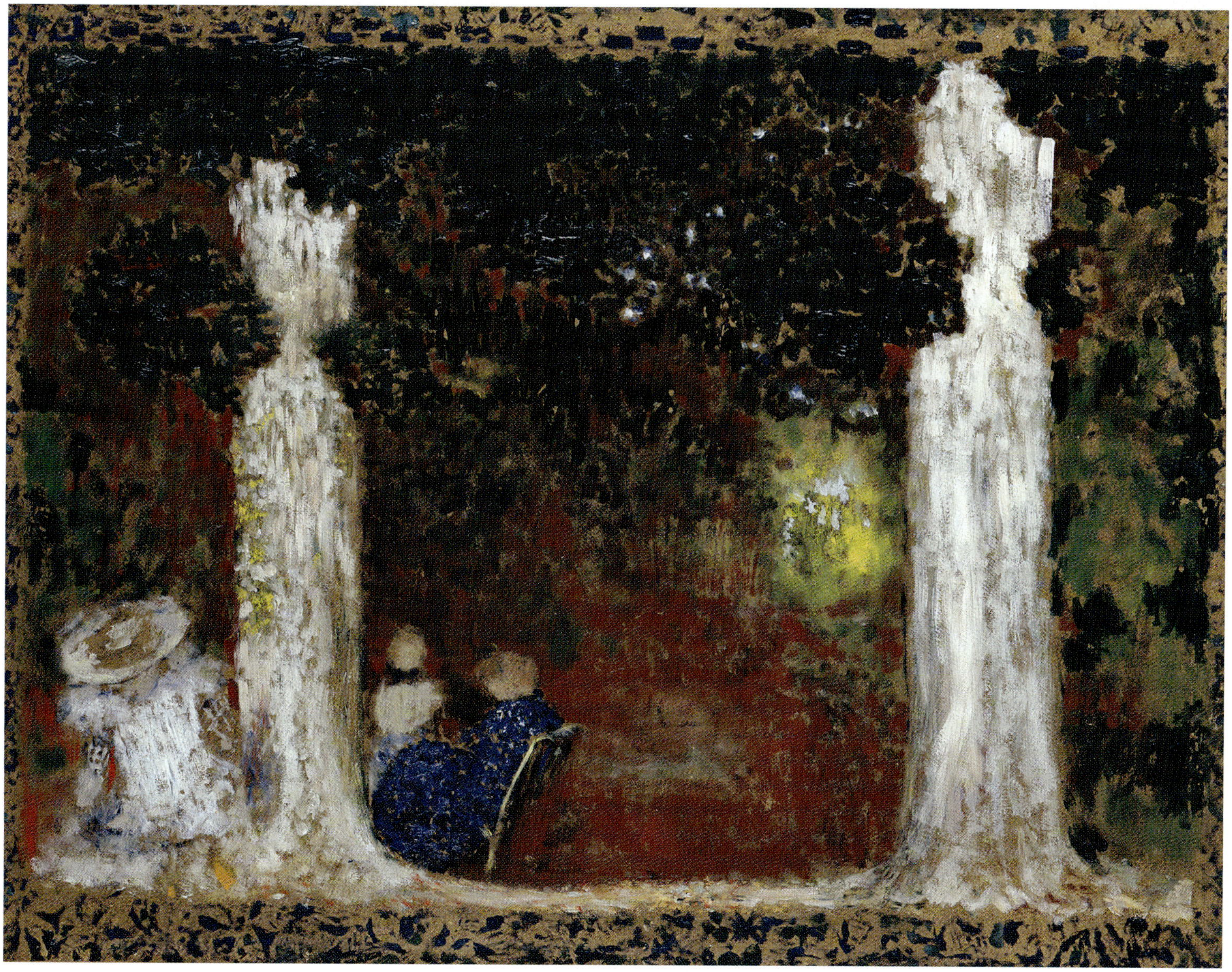

131. Édouard Vuillard
Beneath the Trees, c. 1897–1899
(Sous les arbres)
Oil on cardboard on canvas. 53 x 67 cm
[Salomon/Cogeval VI n. 94]
Carmen Thyssen-Bornemisza Collection
on loan at the Museo Thyssen-Bornemisza, Madrid

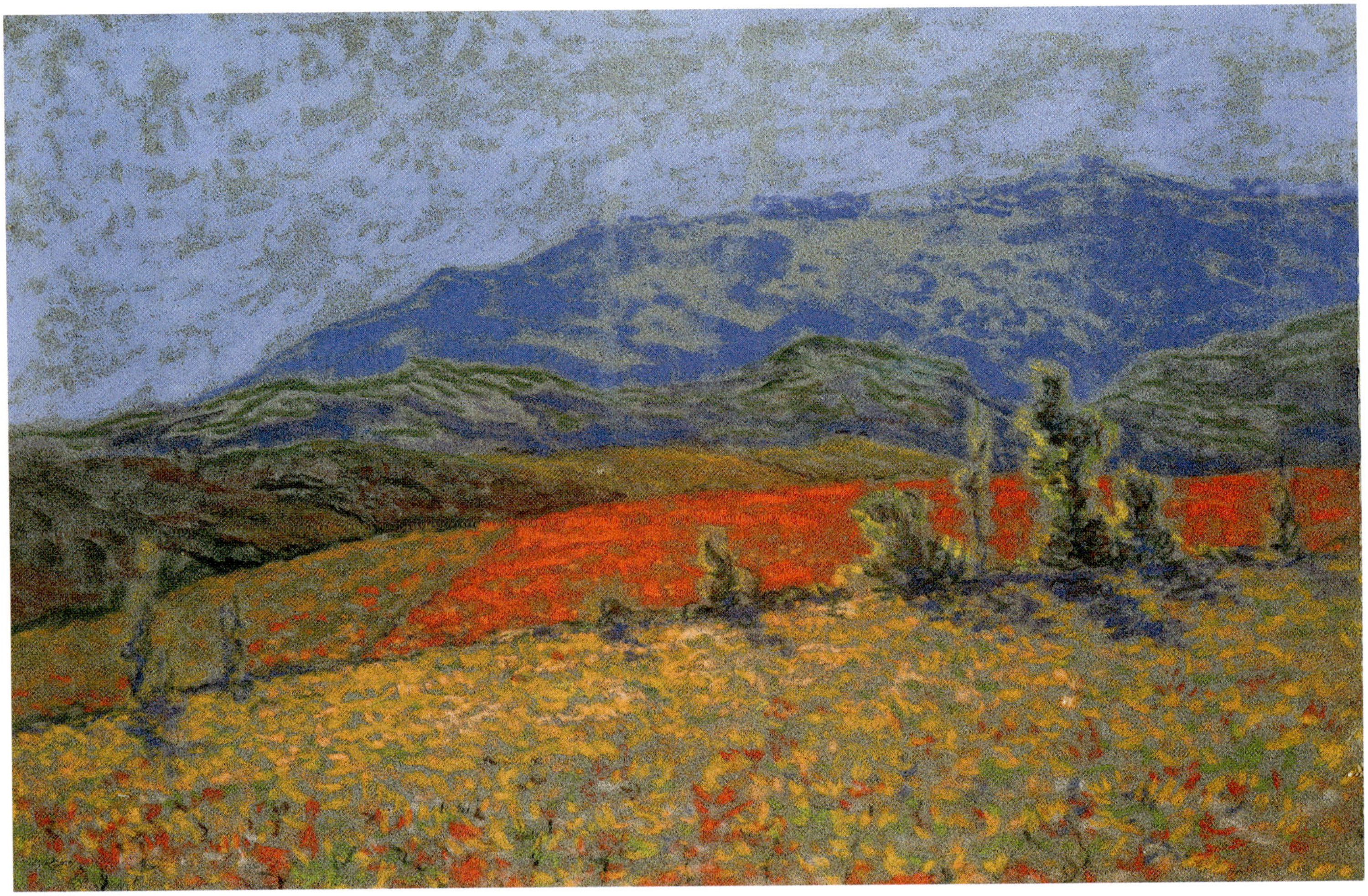

132. Ker-Xavier Roussel
Summer Landscape, 1894
(Paysage d'Été)
Pastel on cardboard. 33 x 50 cm
Association des Amis du Petit Palais, Geneva

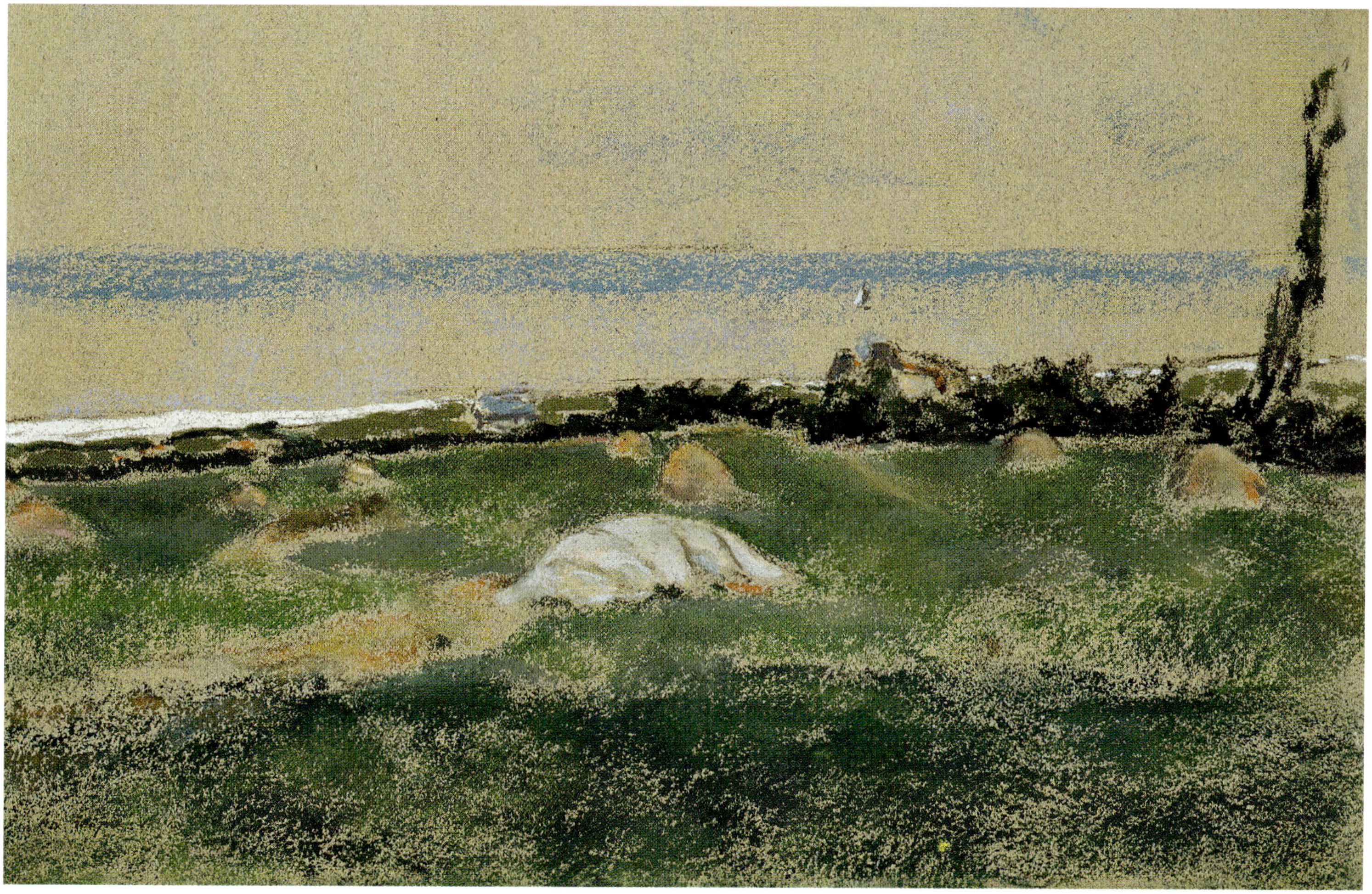

133. Ker-Xavier Roussel
Haystacks on the Sea Shore, 1894
(Les meules au bord de la mer)
Pastel on cardboard. 34 x 50 cm
Association des Amis du Petit Palais, Geneva

134. Paul Sérusier
Fabric Vendor, 1898
(La marchande d'étoffes)
Egg tempera on canvas. 73 x 92 cm
Association des Amis du Petit Palais, Geneva

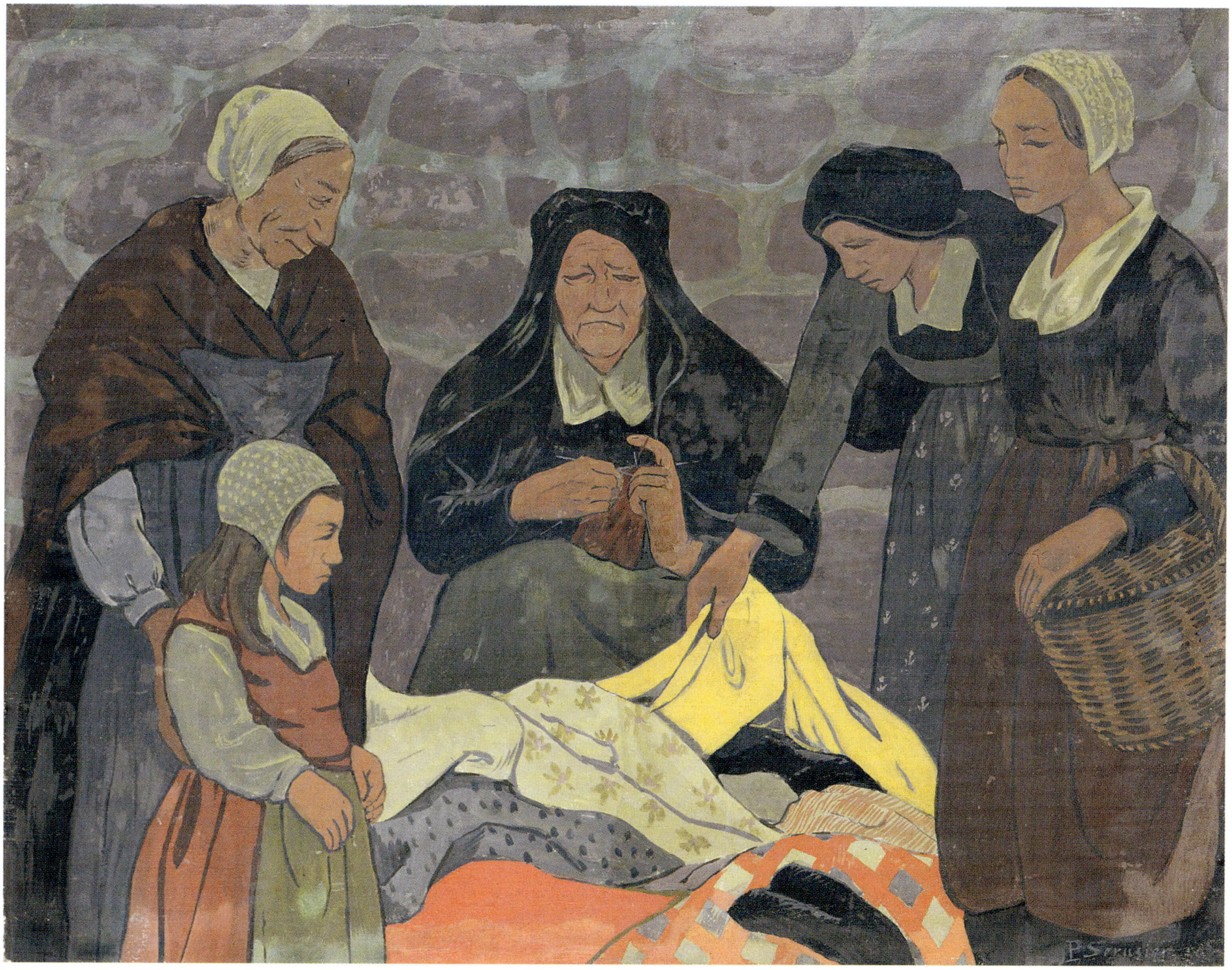

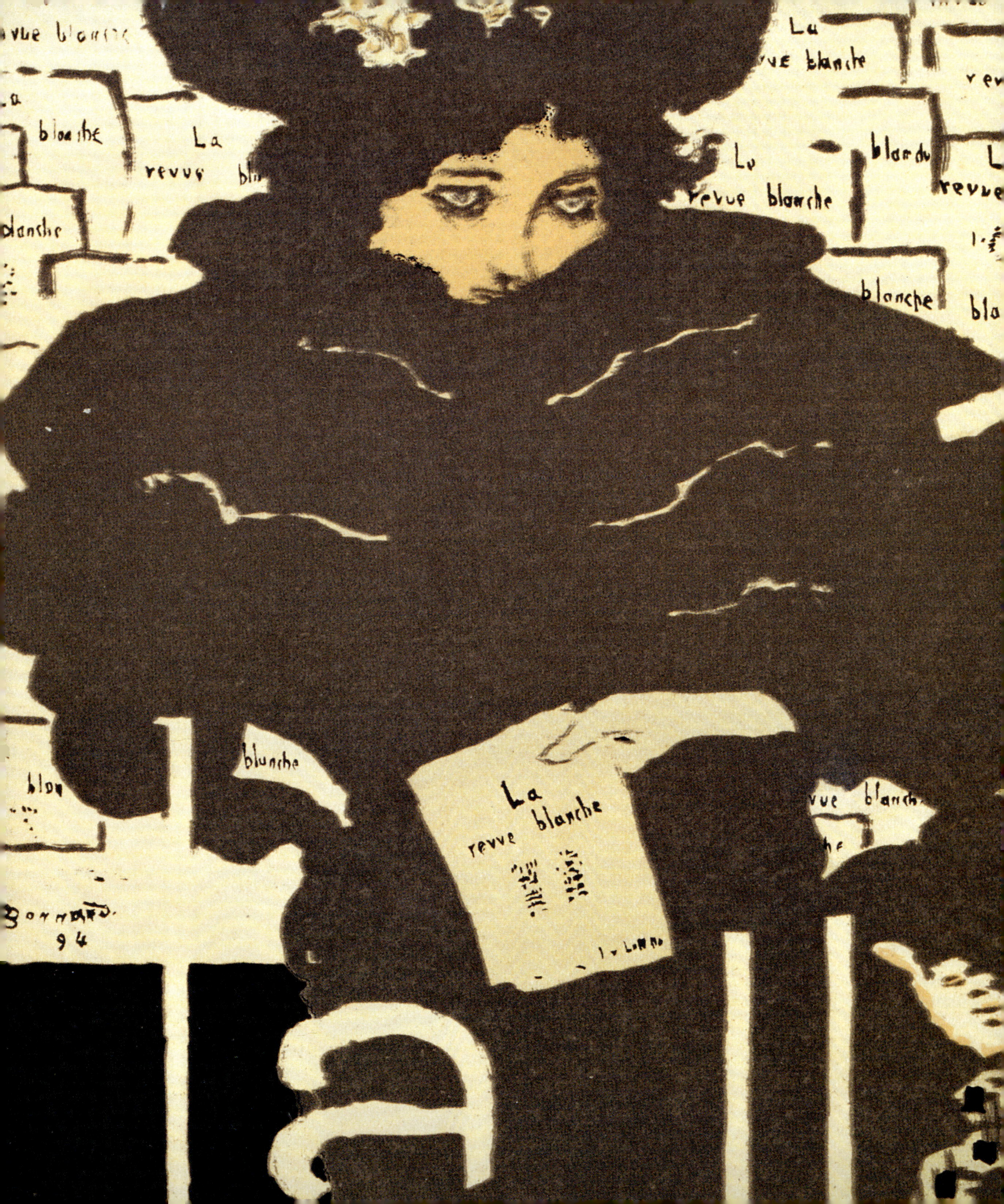
La
revue blanche
Bonnard
94

Pierre Bonnard
La Revue Blanche, 1894
(detail)
[cat. 155]

8. Prints by the Nabis Artists

135. Édouard Vuillard
At the Revue Blanche, Portrait of Félix Fénéon, 1901
(À la Revue blanche [Portrait de Félix Fénéon])
Oil on cardboard. 46.36 x 57.47 cm
[Salomon/Cogeval VI n. 106]
Solomon R. Guggenheim Museum, New York
(Gift, Solomon R. Guggenheim 41.725)

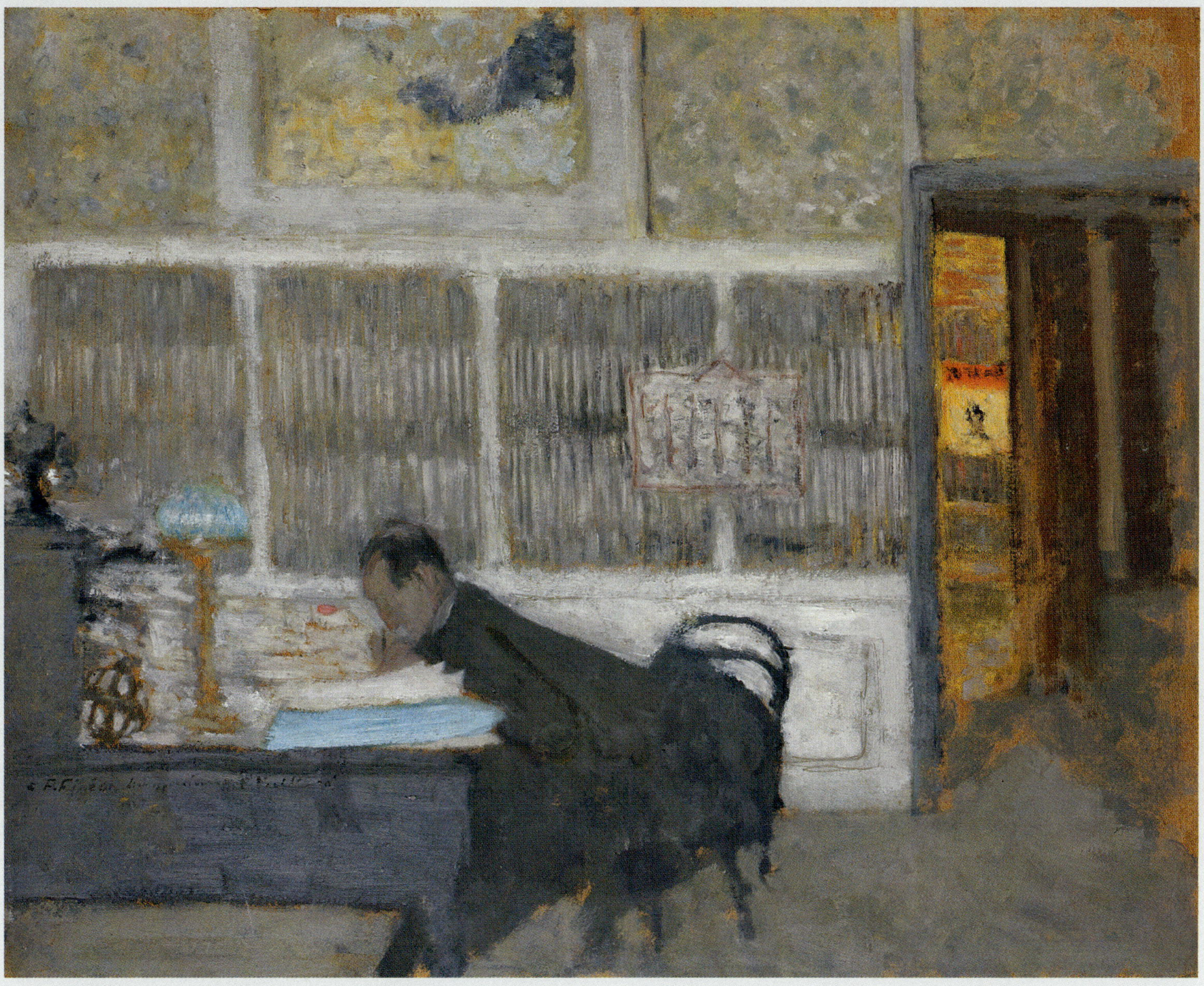

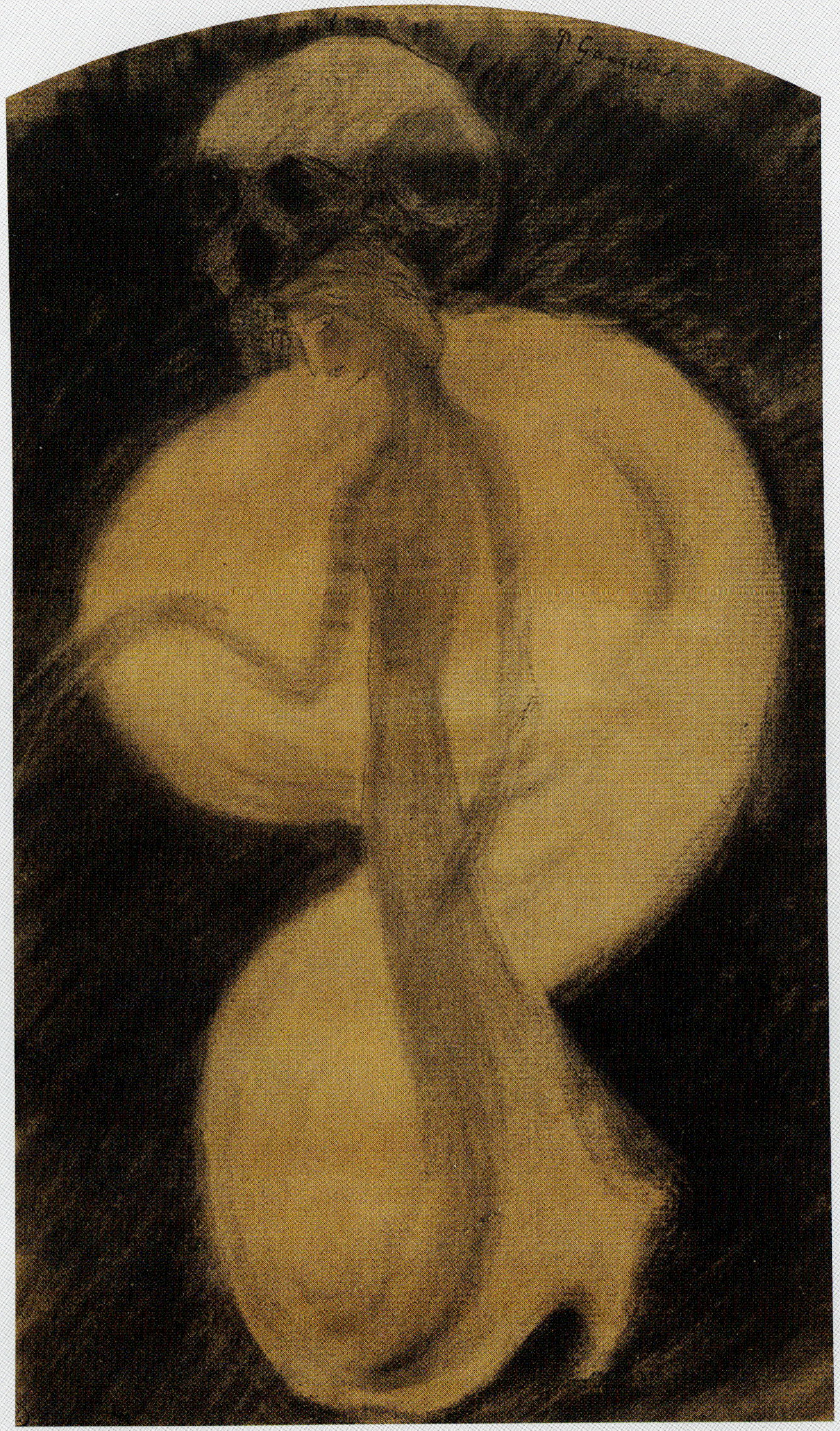

137. Paul Gauguin
Lady Death, 1891
(Madame la Mort)
Charcoal and grey wash on paper. 22.5 x 23 cm
Musée d'Orsay, in deposit at the département des Arts Graphiques del Musée du Louvre, Paris
(Gift of Yomiuri Shimbun and the Nippon Television Network Corporation, 1991)

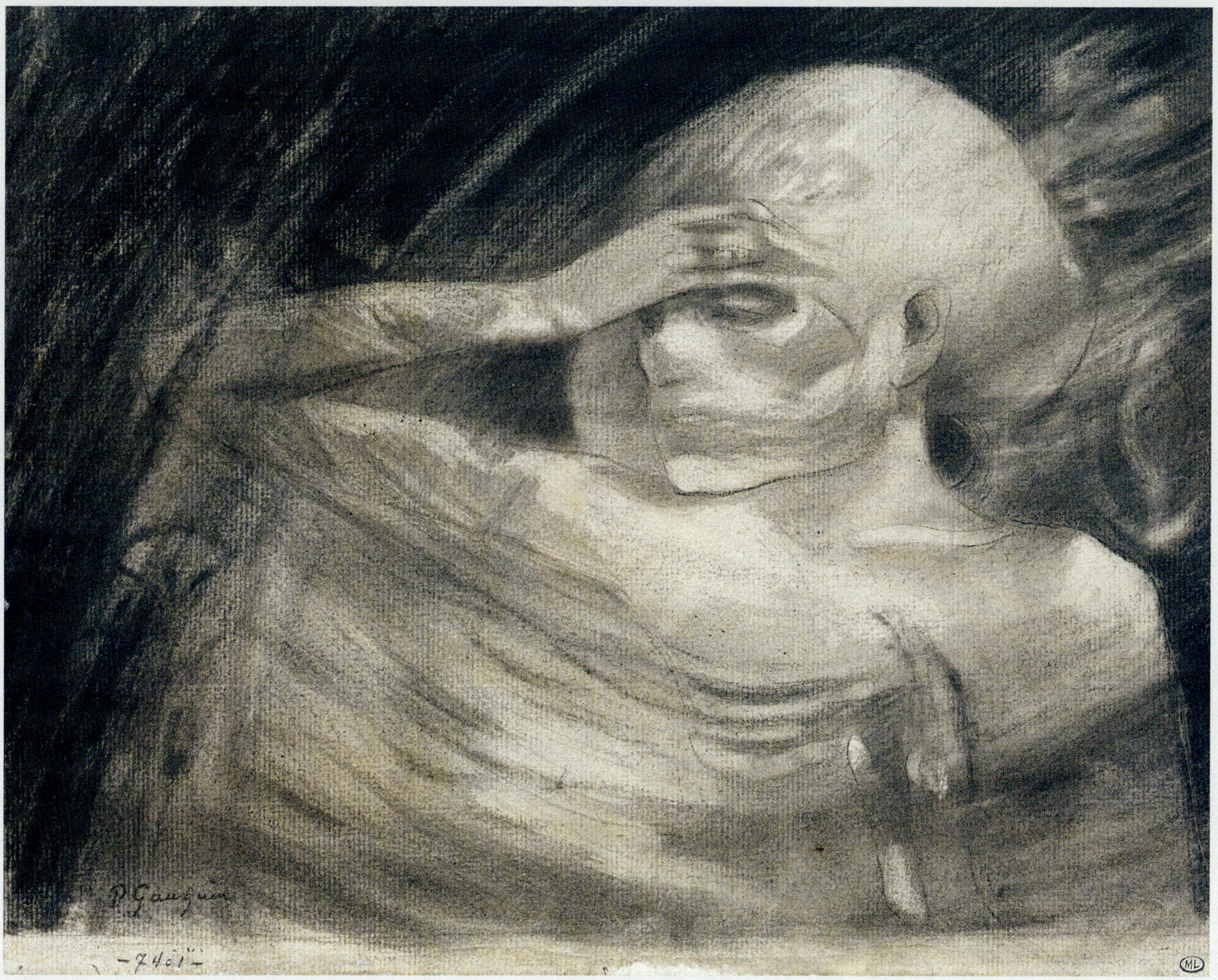

136. Paul Gauguin
Lady Death, 1891
(Madame la Mort)
Charcoal and brush on paper. 23.9 x 29.3 cm
Musée d'Orsay, in deposit at the département des Arts Graphiques del Musée du Louvre, Paris

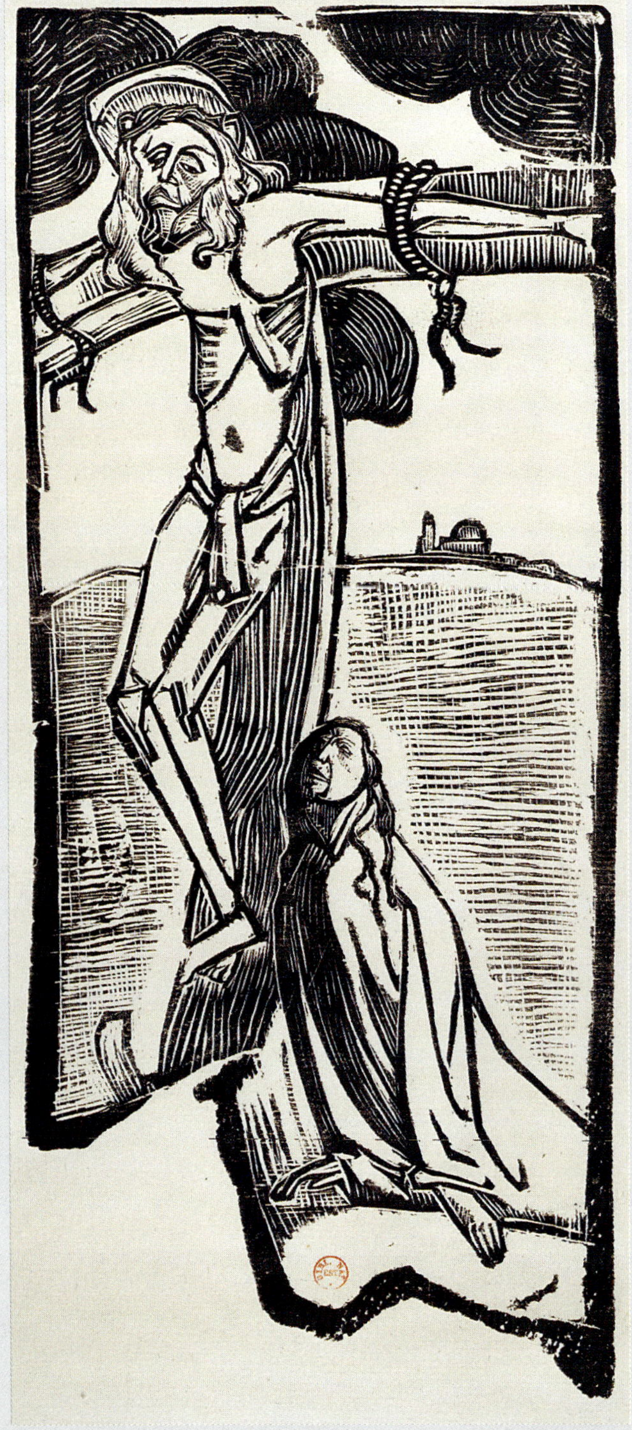

139. Émile Bernard
Crucifixion, 1890–1891
(Crucifixión)
Wood engraving. 290/350 x 150 mm
Bibliothèque nationale de France, Paris

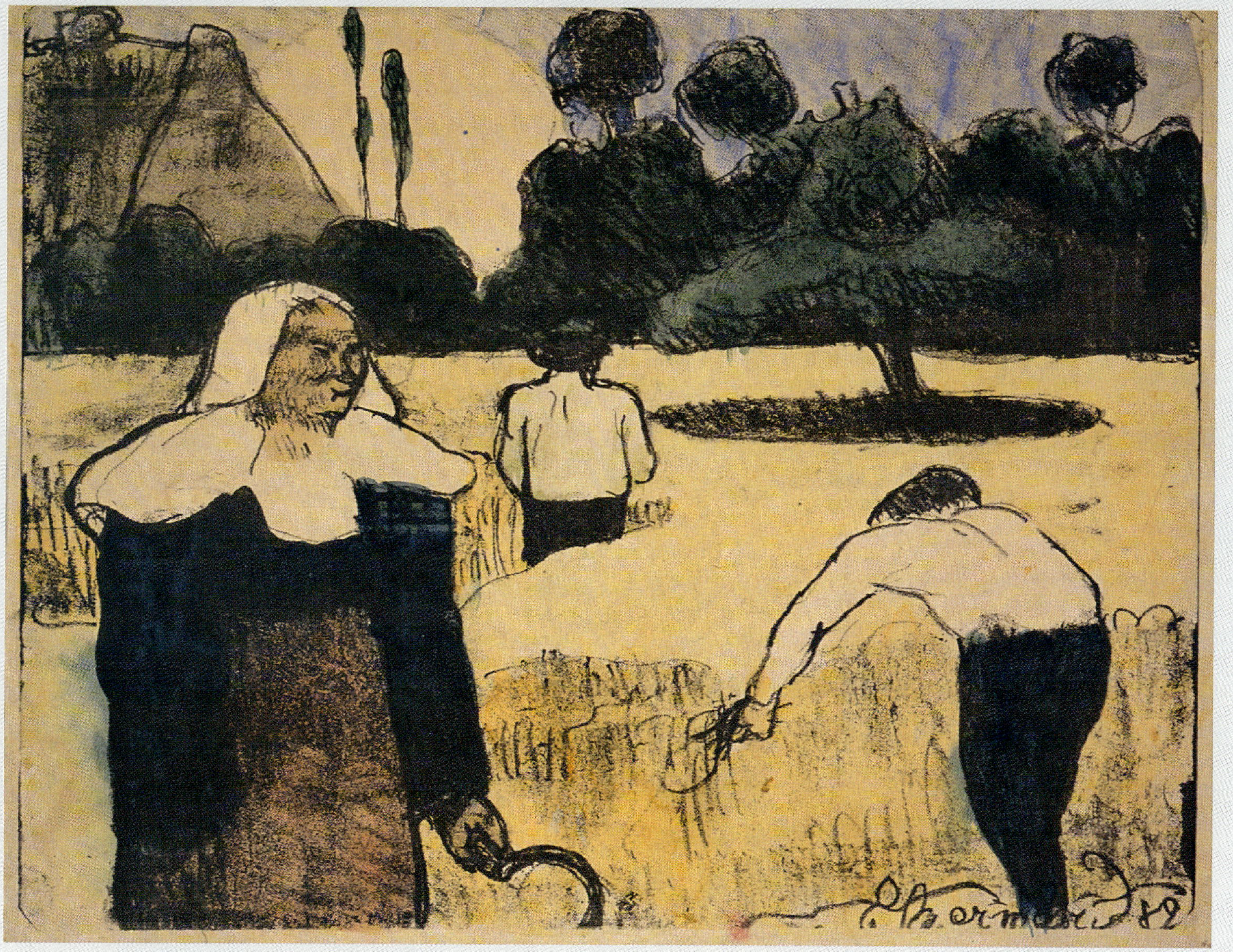

138. Émile Bernard
The Harvester, 1889
(Le moissonneur)
Zincograph. 235 x 297 mm
Institut national d'histoire de l'art, Bibliothèque,
Collections Jacques Doucet, Paris

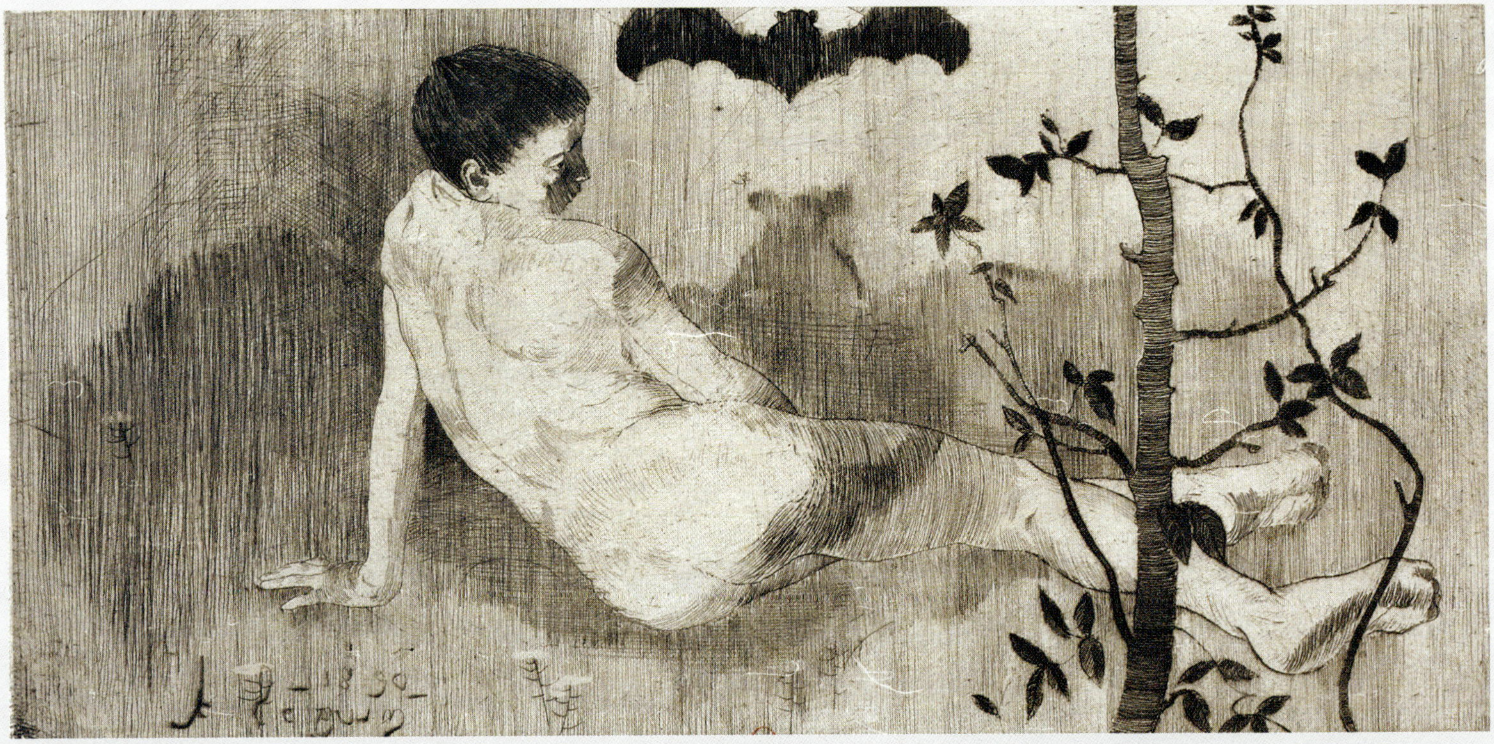

140. Armand Seguin
Nude with a Bat, 1890
(Nu à la chauve-souris)
Etching and dry point. 109 x 212 mm
[Field/Strauss/Wagstaff n. 1]
Bibliothèque nationale de France, Paris

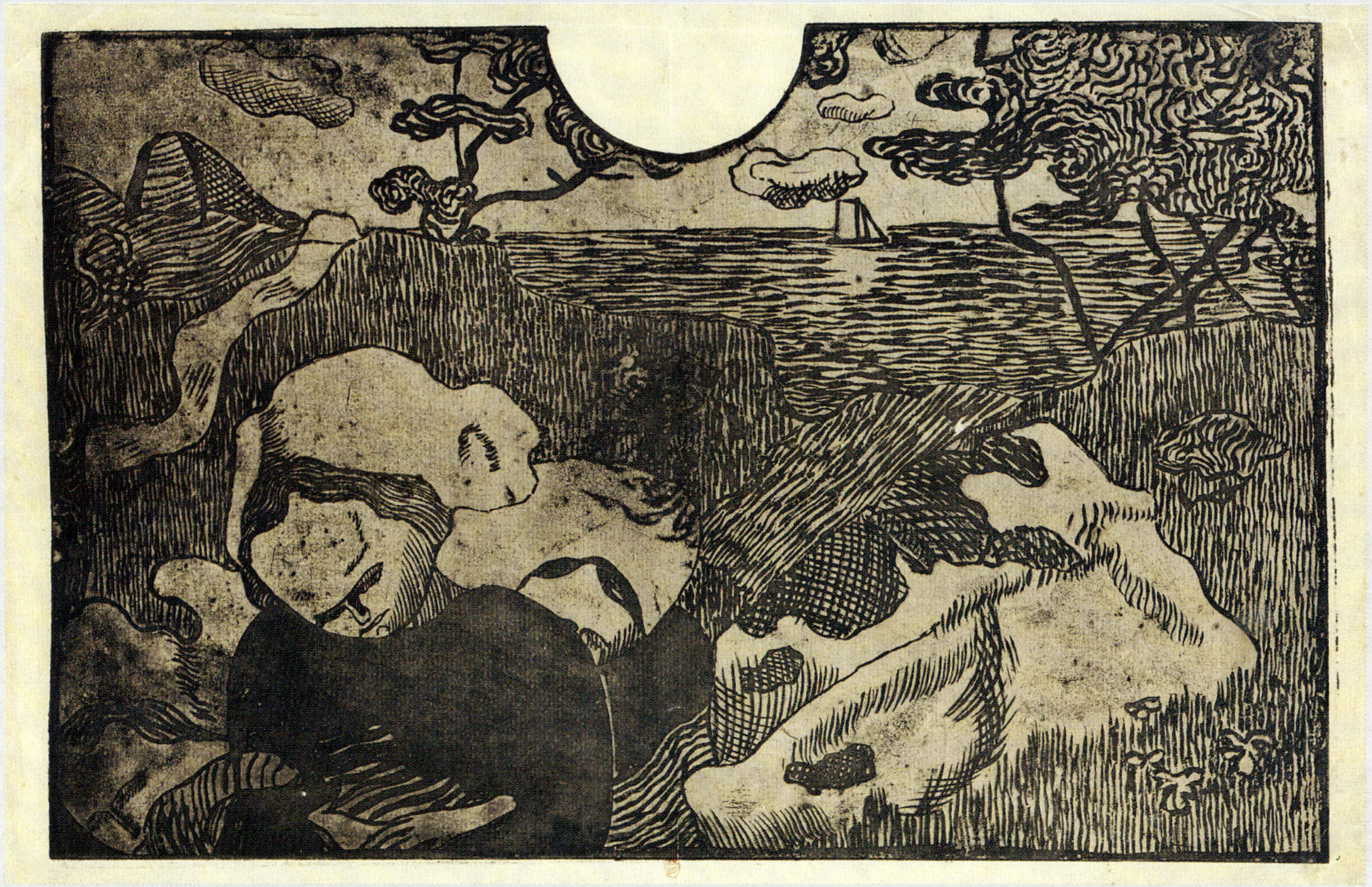

141. Armand Seguin
Decoration of Brittany. A Summer Day, c. 1894
(Décoration de Bretagne. Un jour d'été)
Etching and sugar aquatint. 245 x 372 mm
[Field/Strauss/Wagstaff n. 72]
Bibliothèque nationale de France, Paris

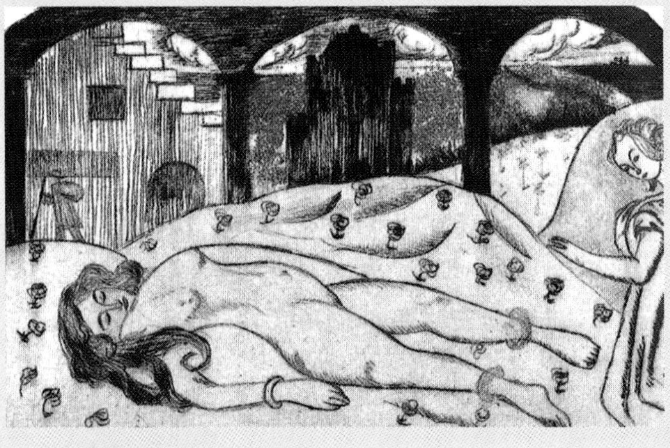

142. Armand Seguin
The Silent Pilgrim, for *Phénissa* by R. De Gourmont
(Le Pèlerin du silence)
Dry point and aquatint. 99 x 179 mm
[Field/Strauss/Wagstaff n. 91]
Bibliothèque nationale de France, Paris

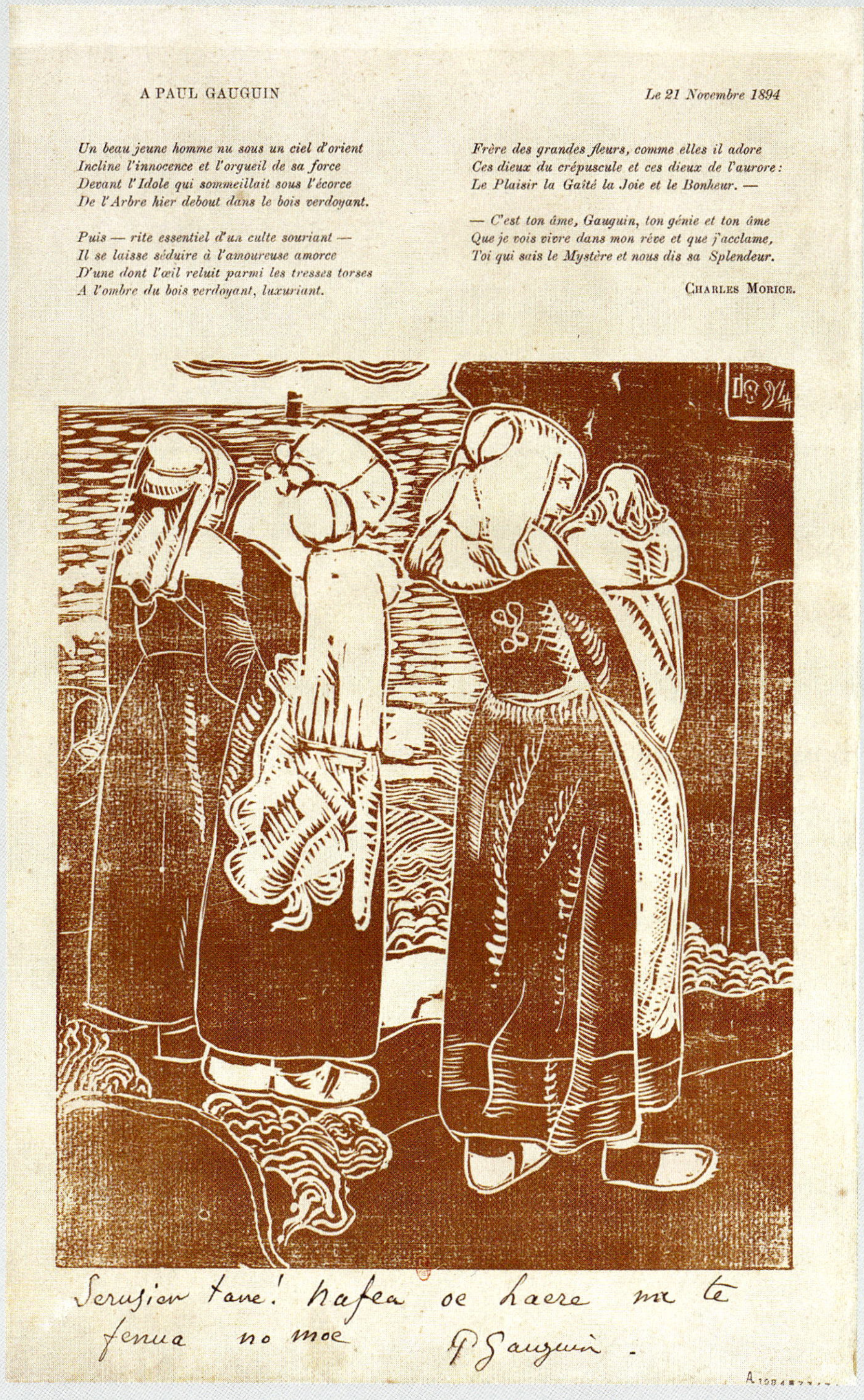

143. Armand Seguin
Breton Women, 1894
(Les bretonnes)
Wood Engraving. 229 x 186 mm
[Field/Strauss/Wagstaff n. 70]
Bibliothèque nationale de France, Paris

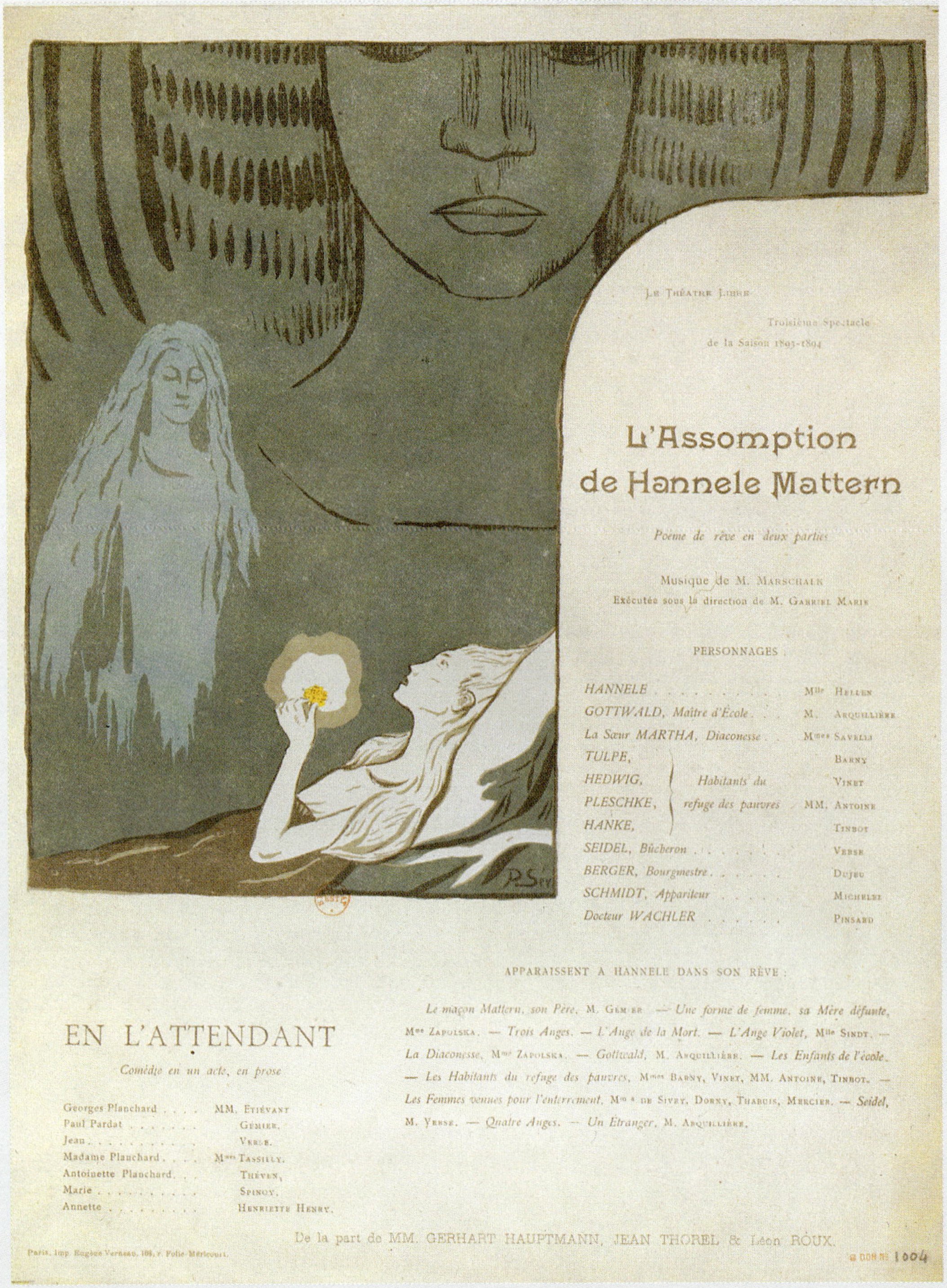

144. Paul Sérusier
Programme for *L'Assomption de Hannele Mattern*, Le Théâtre-Libre, 1893–1894
Colour lithograph. 365 x 228 mm
Bibliothèque nationale de France, Paris

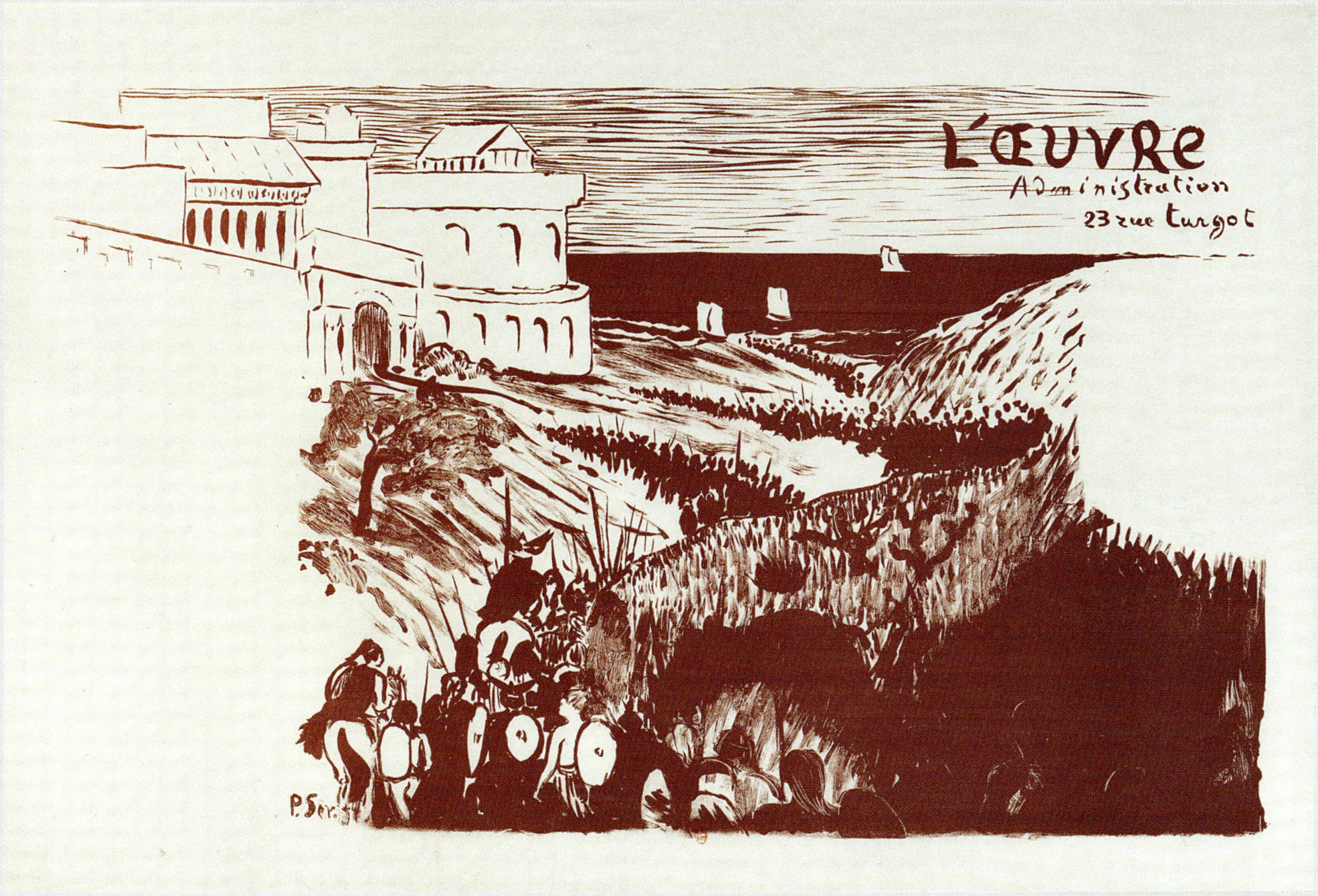

145. Paul Sérusier
Heraklea by Auguste Villeroy, Théâtre de l'Œuvre, 1896
Zincograph
Bibliothèque nationale de France, Paris

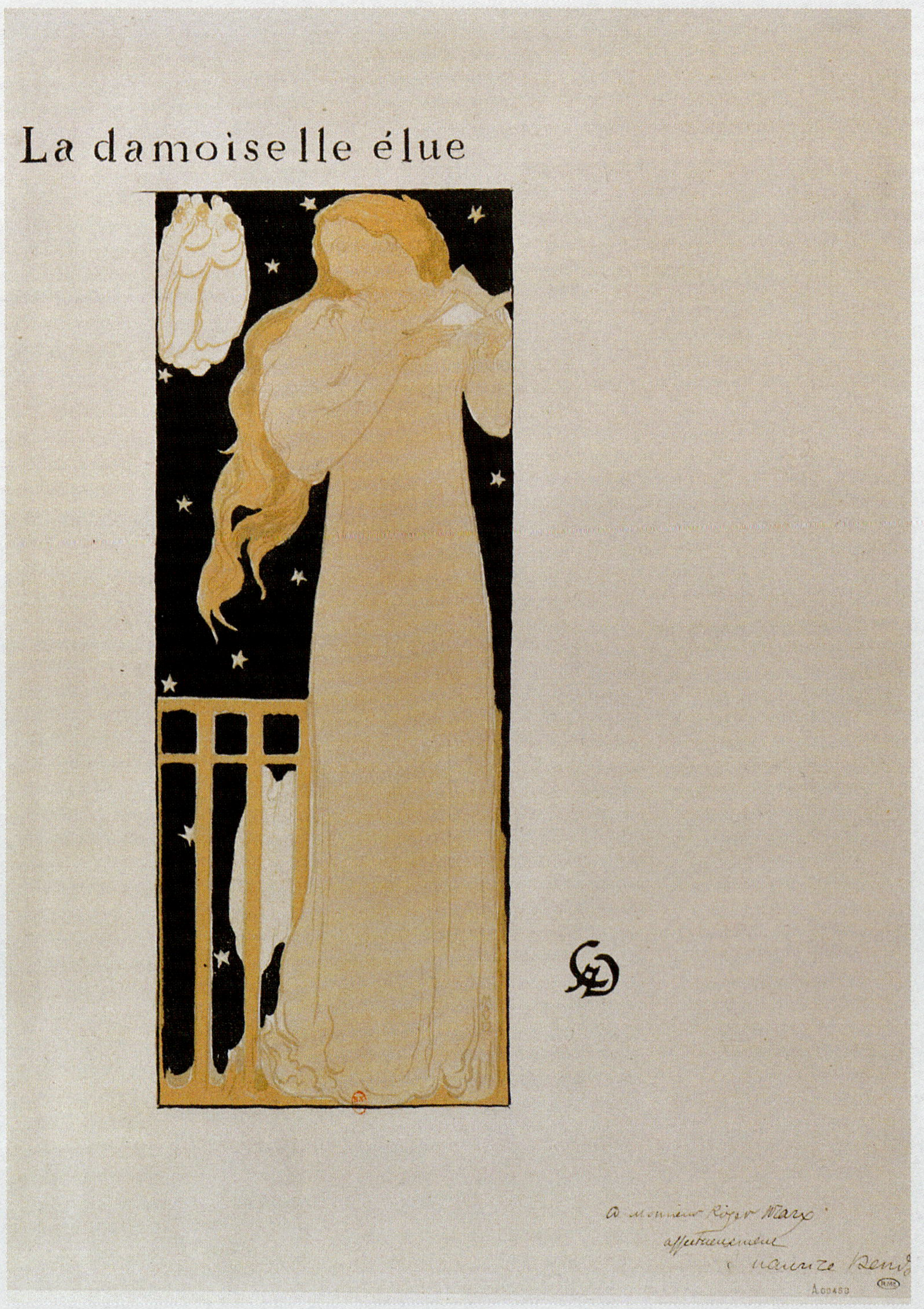

146. Maurice Denis
The Chosen Maiden, 1892
(La demoiselle élue)
Lithograph. 370 x 240 mm
Bibliothèque nationale de France, Paris

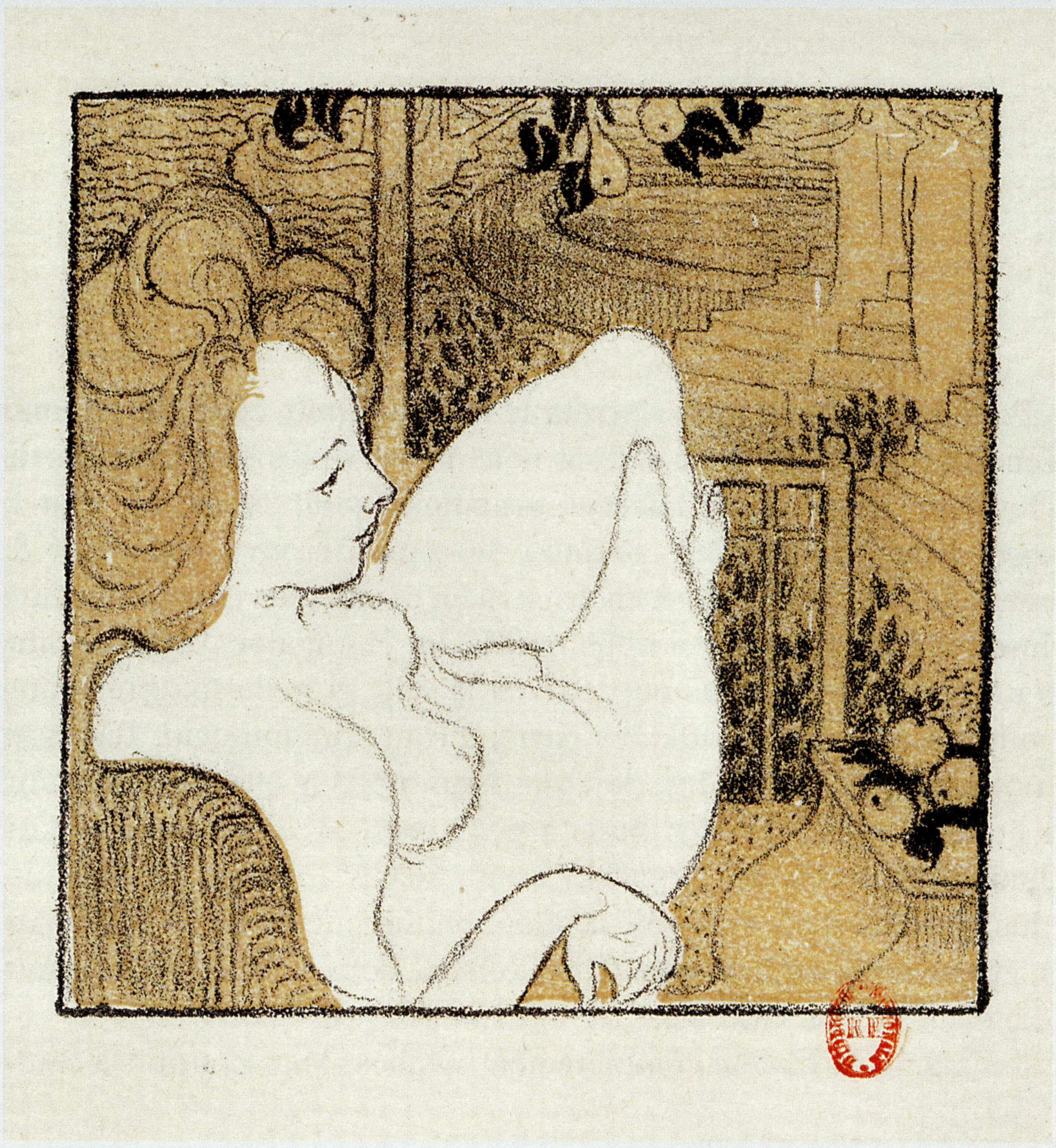

147. Maurice Denis
Le Voyage d'Urien by André Gide, 1893
1 engraving and 29 colour lithographs. 20.5 x 20.5 cm
Bibliothèque nationale de France, Paris

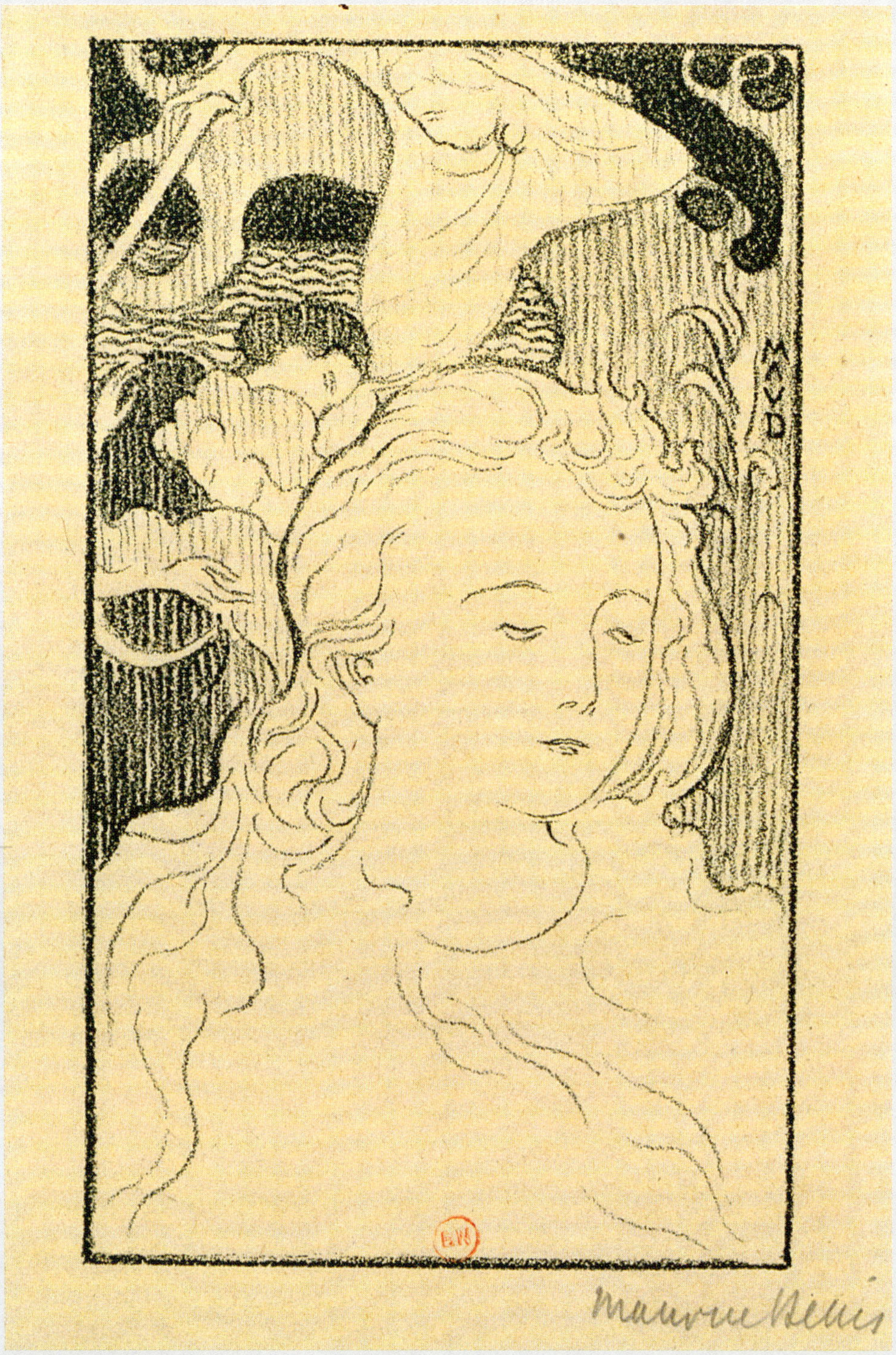

148. Maurice Denis
Programme for *Pelléas et Mélisande*, 1893
(Programme pour Pelléas et Mélisande)
Lithograph.
Bibliothèque nationale de France, Paris

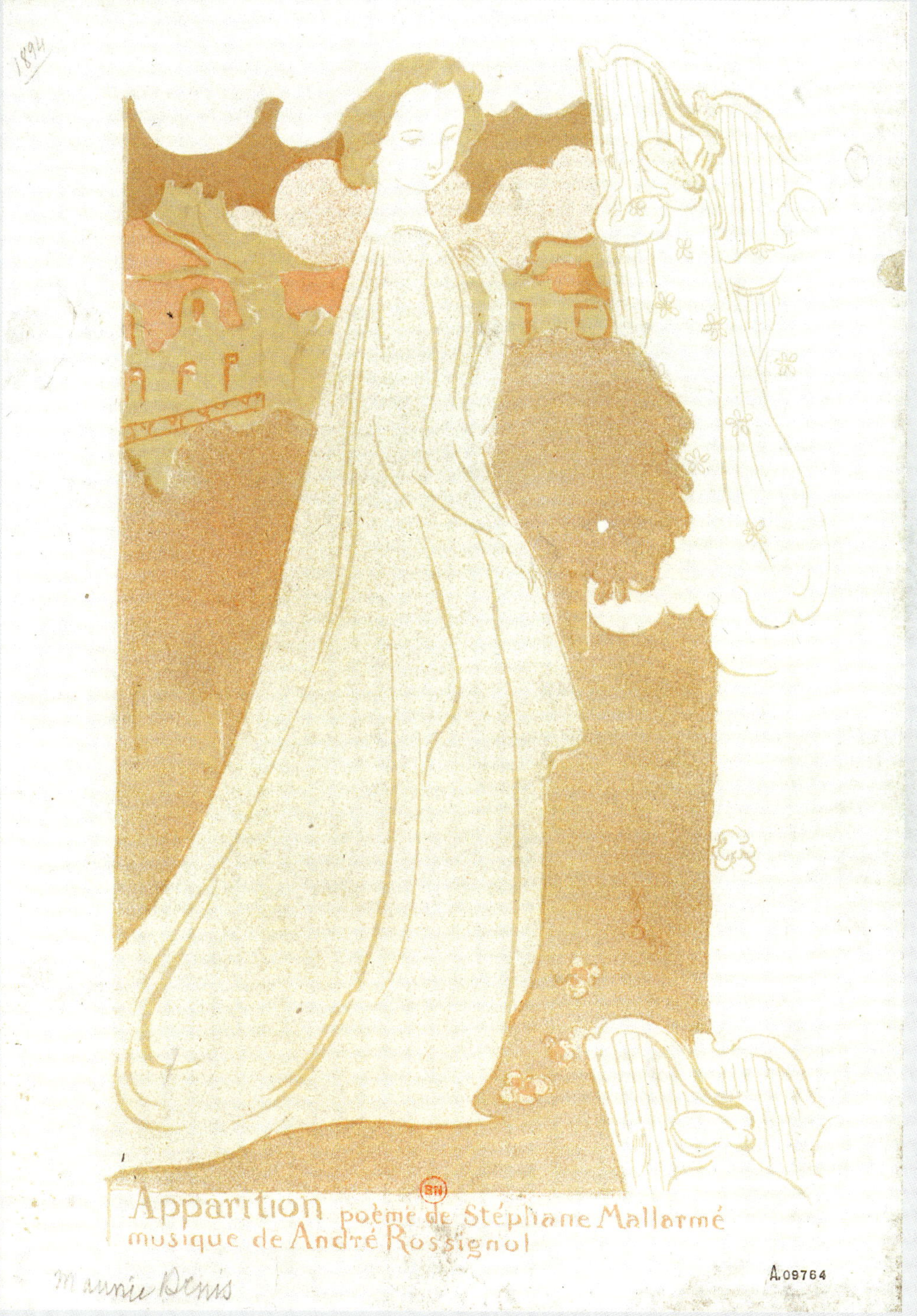

149. Maurice Denis
Front cover for the poem *Apparition* by Stéphane Mallarmé, music by André Rossignol, 1894
Bibliothèque nationale de France, Paris

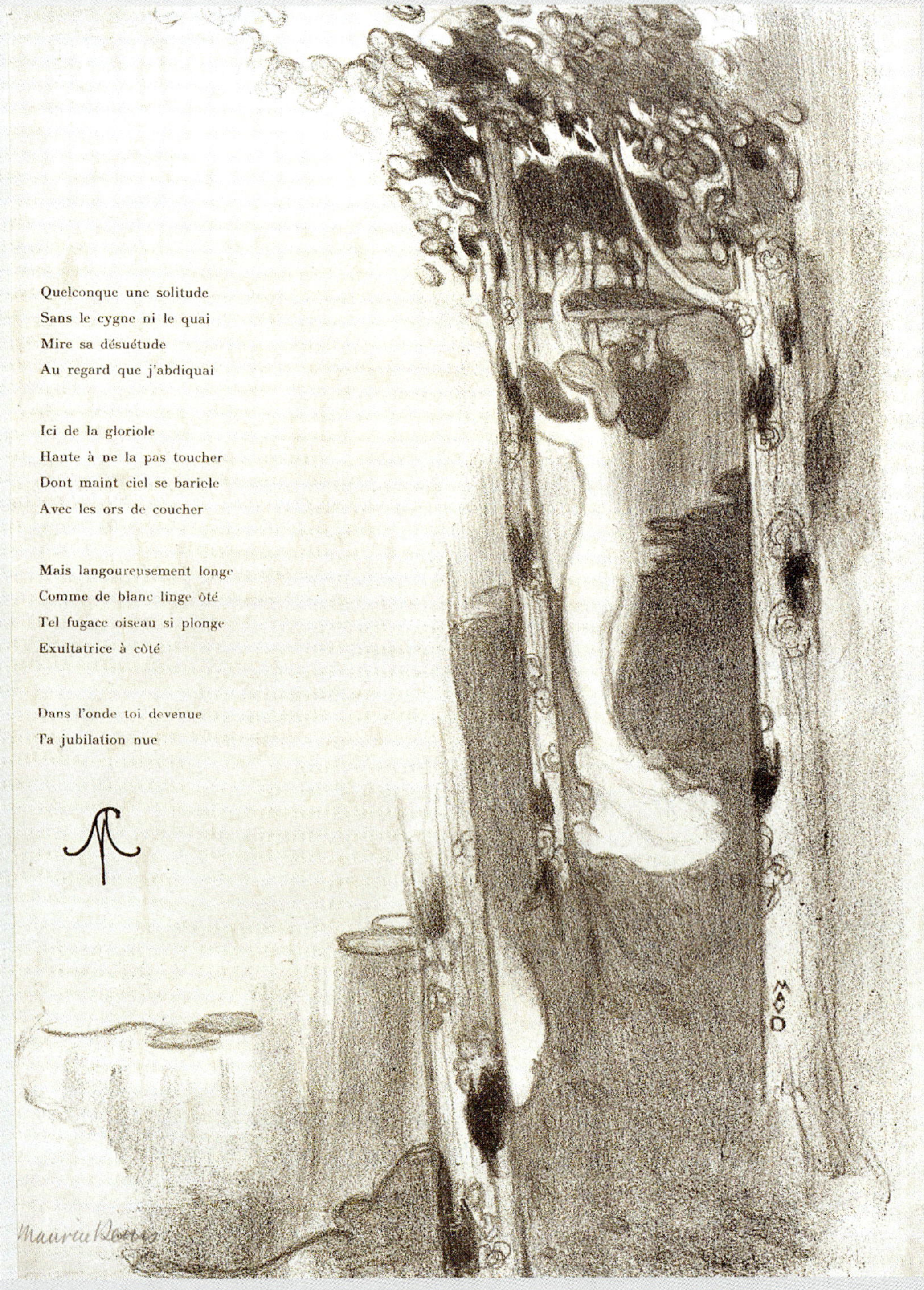

150. Maurice Denis
Poem *Sonnet ou petit air* by Mallarmé, c. 1896
Lithograph.
Bibliothèque nationale de France, Paris

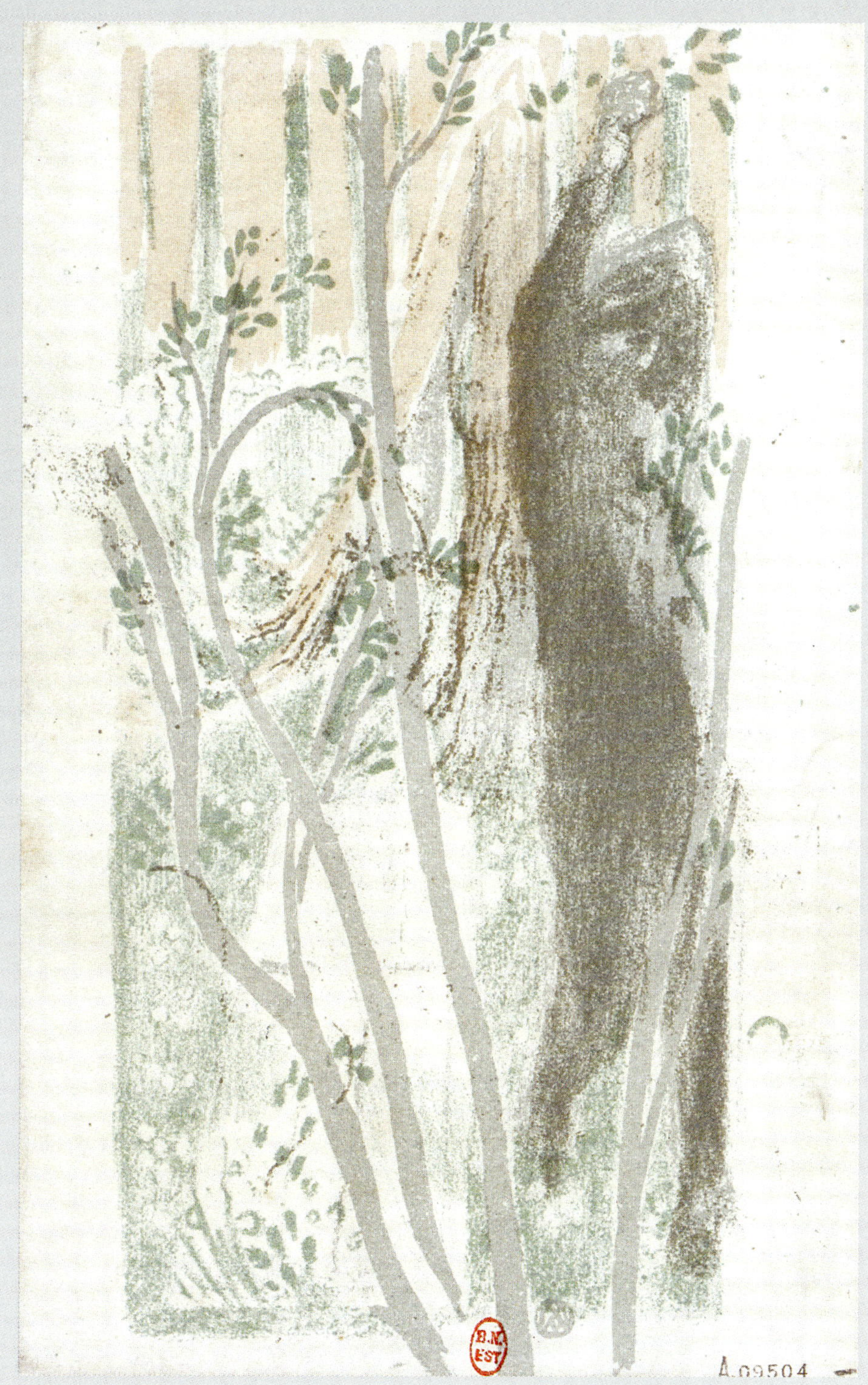

151. Maurice Denis
The Mysterious Woods, c. 1896
(La Forêt mystérieuse)
Colour lithograph
Bibliothèque nationale de France, Paris

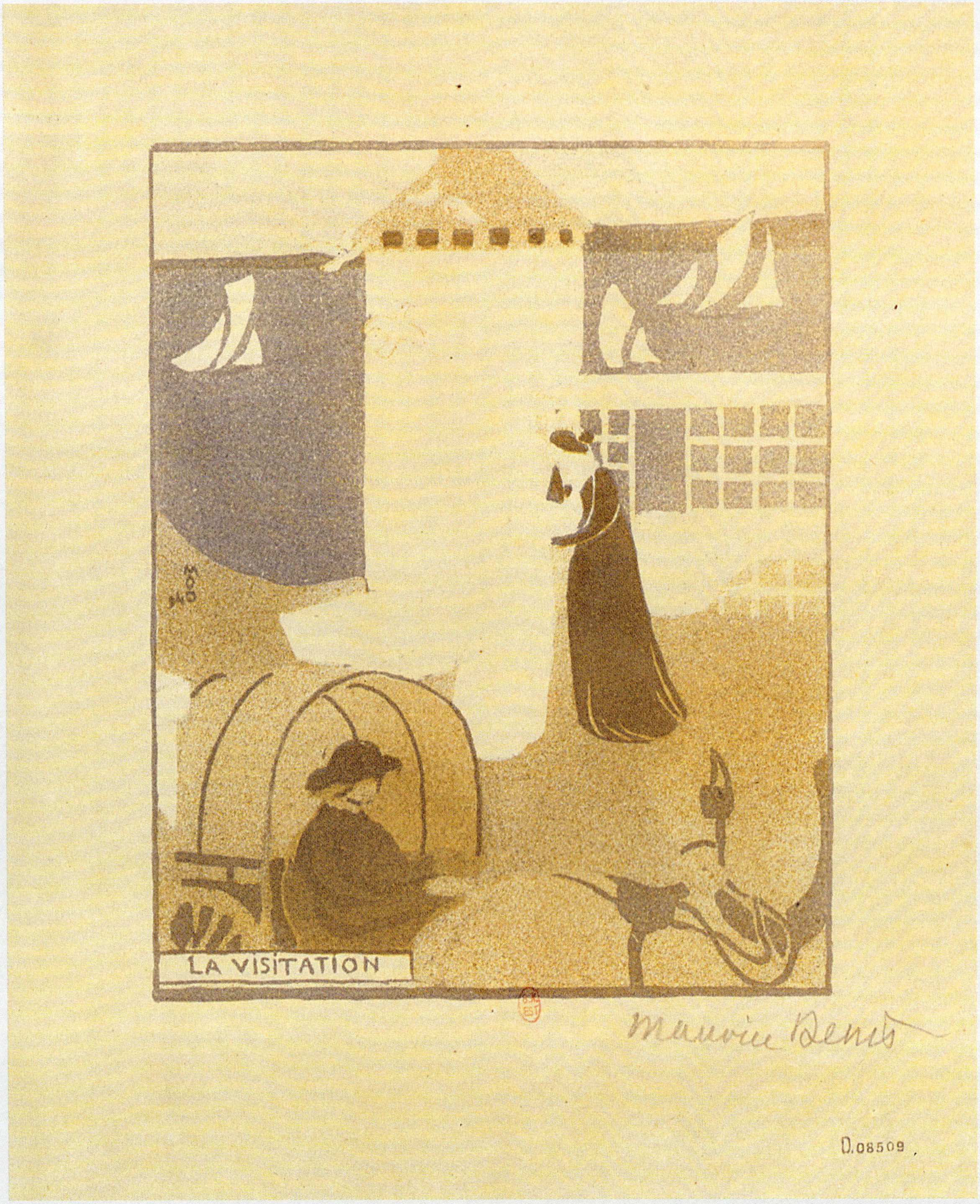

152. Maurice Denis
The Visit, 1896
(Visitation)
Colour lithograph
Bibliothèque nationale de France, Paris

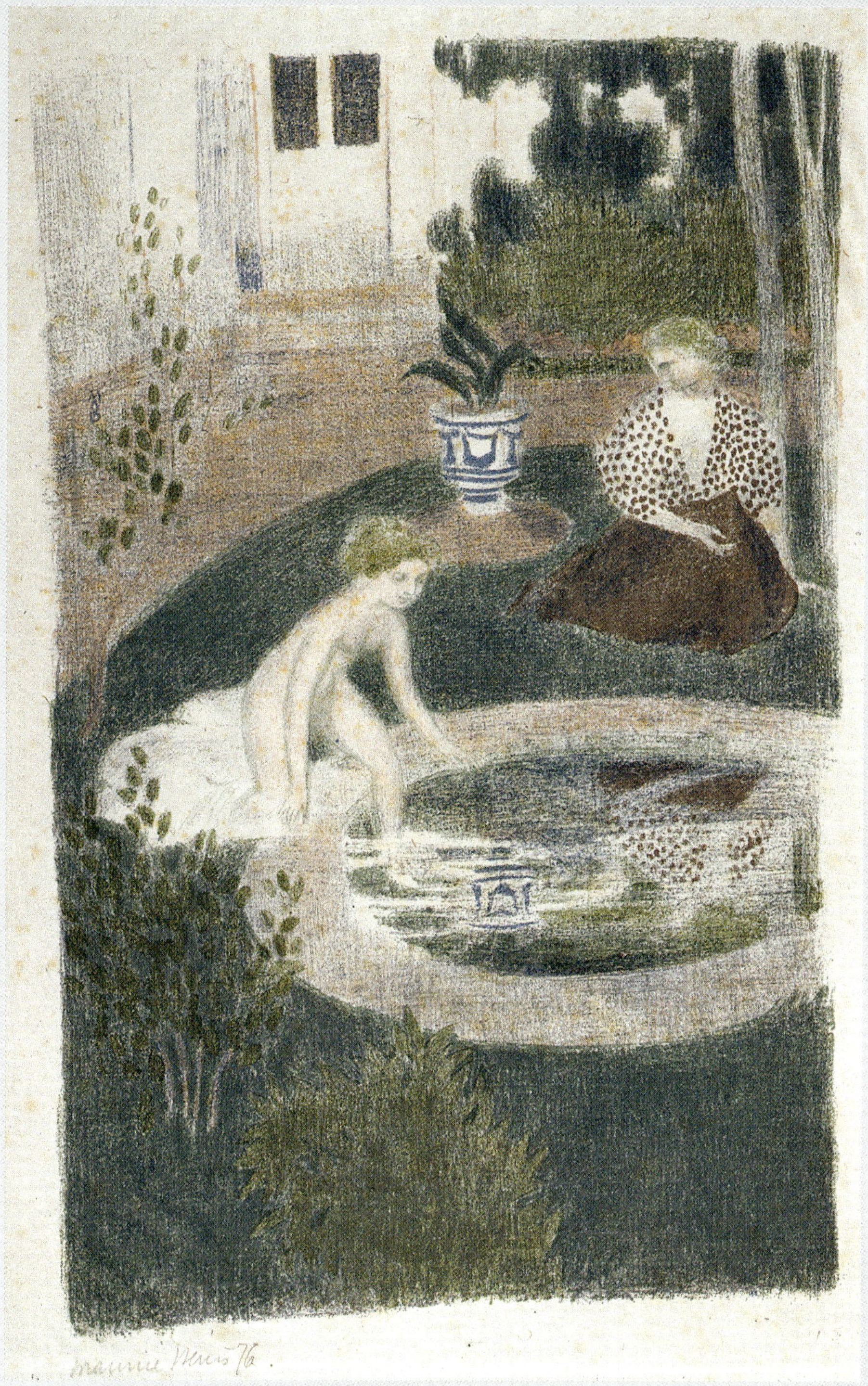

153. Maurice Denis
The Reflection in the Fountain, 1897
(Le Reflet dans la fontaine)
Lithograph in four colours. 570 x 431 mm
Galerie Berès, Paris, France

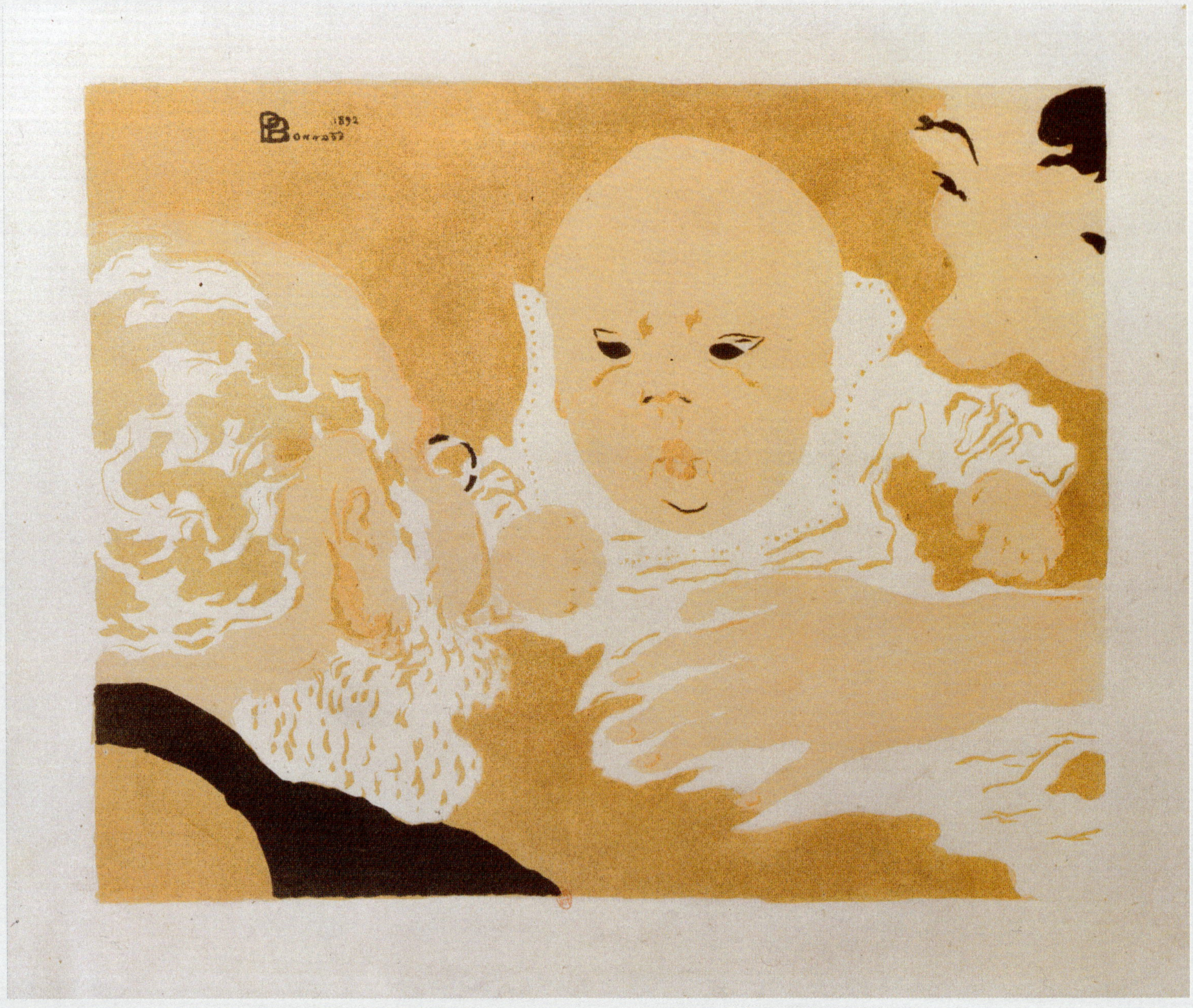

154. Pierre Bonnard
Family Scene, 1892
(Scène de famille)
Lithograph in three colours. 210 x 260 mm
[Bouvet n. 2]
Bibliothèque nationale de France, Paris

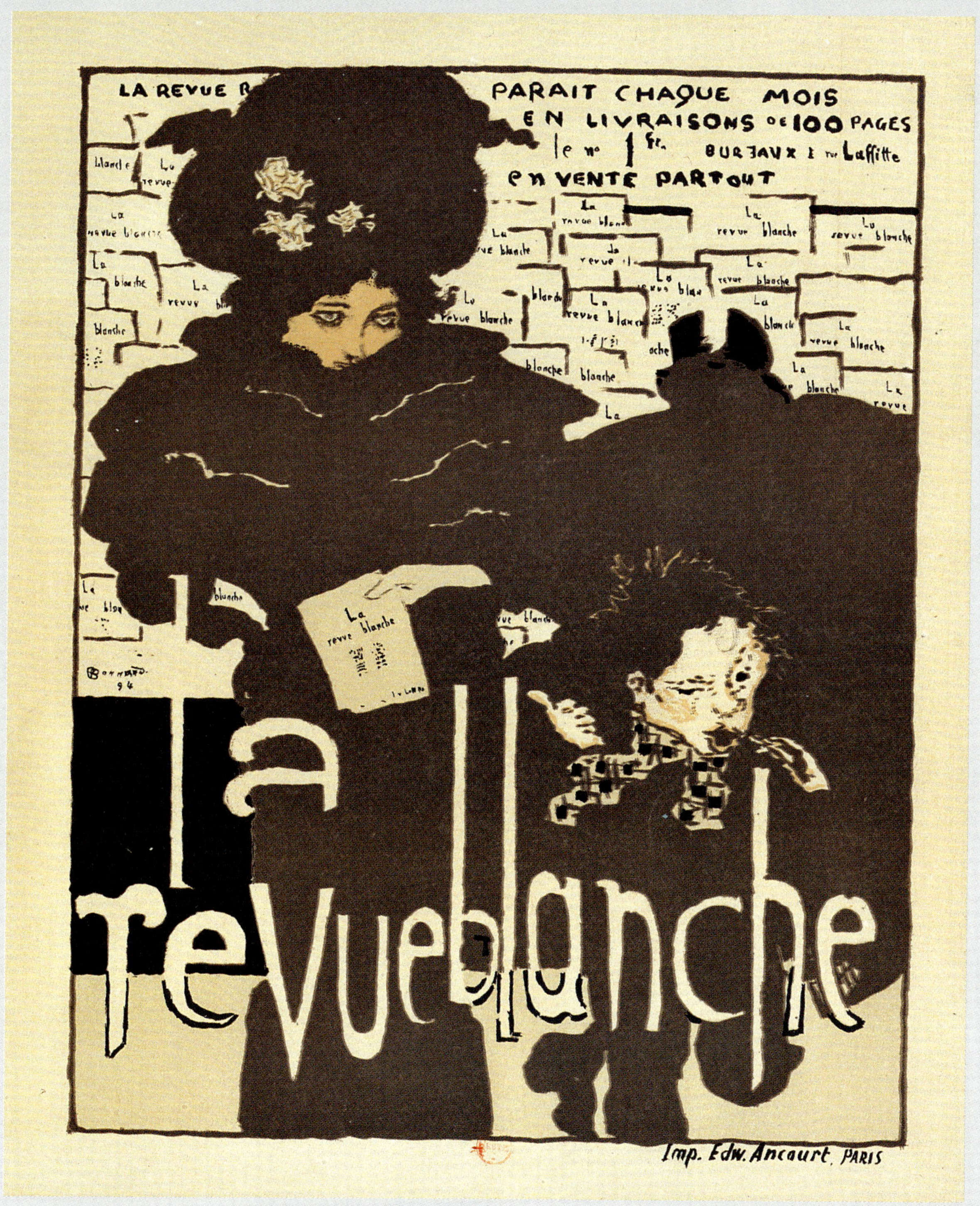

155. Pierre Bonnard
La Revue Blanche, 1894
Published in *La Revue Blanche* n. 15 and in the *Album of the Revue Blanche*
Lithograph in four colours. 800 x 620 mm
[Bouvet n. 30]
Bibliothèque nationale de France, Paris

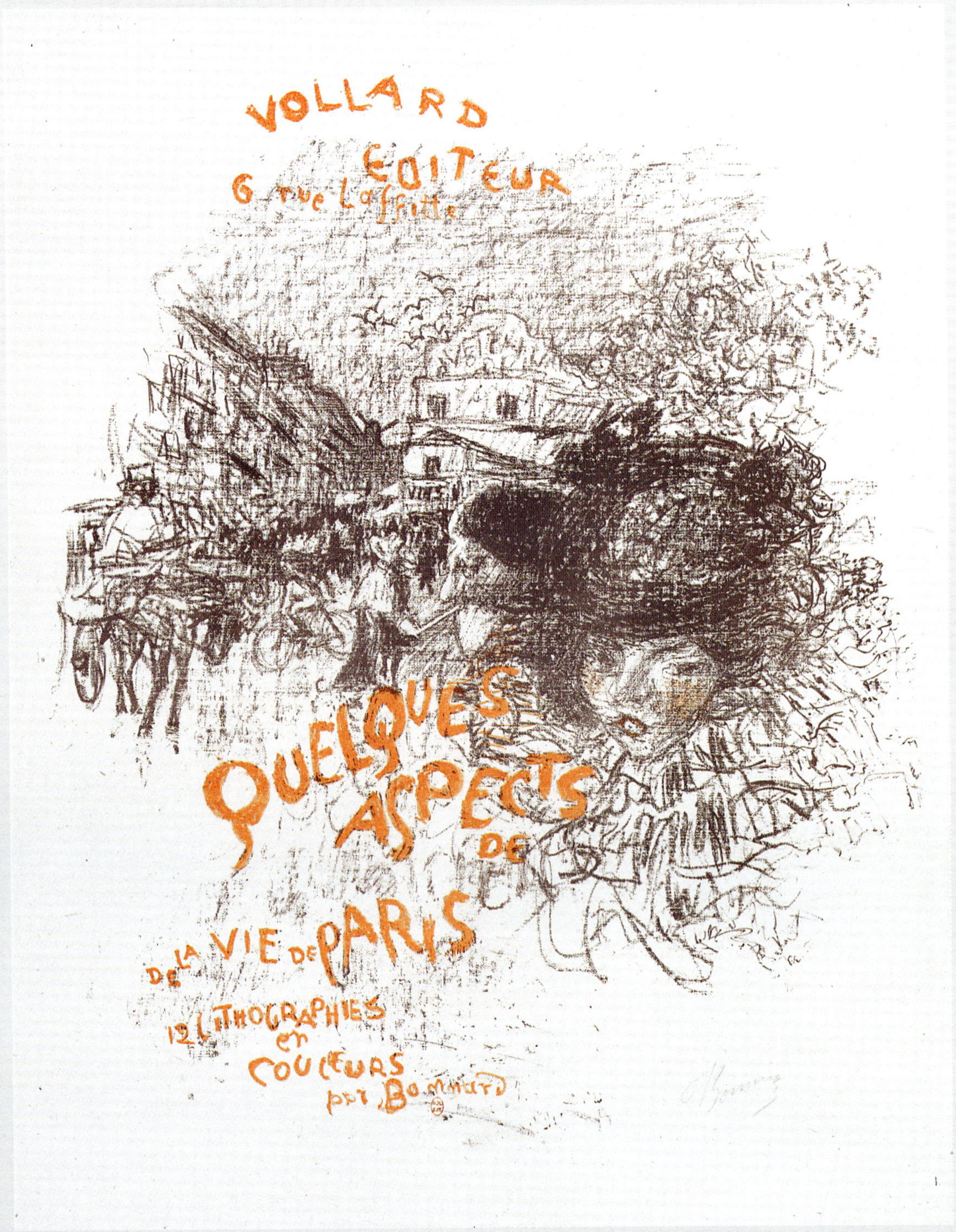

158. Pierre Bonnard
At the Theatre (Some Aspects of Parisian Life), 1899
(Au théâtre [quelques aspects de la vie de Paris])
Lithograph in four colours. 200 x 400 mm
[Bouvet n. 67]
Bibliothèque nationale de France, Paris

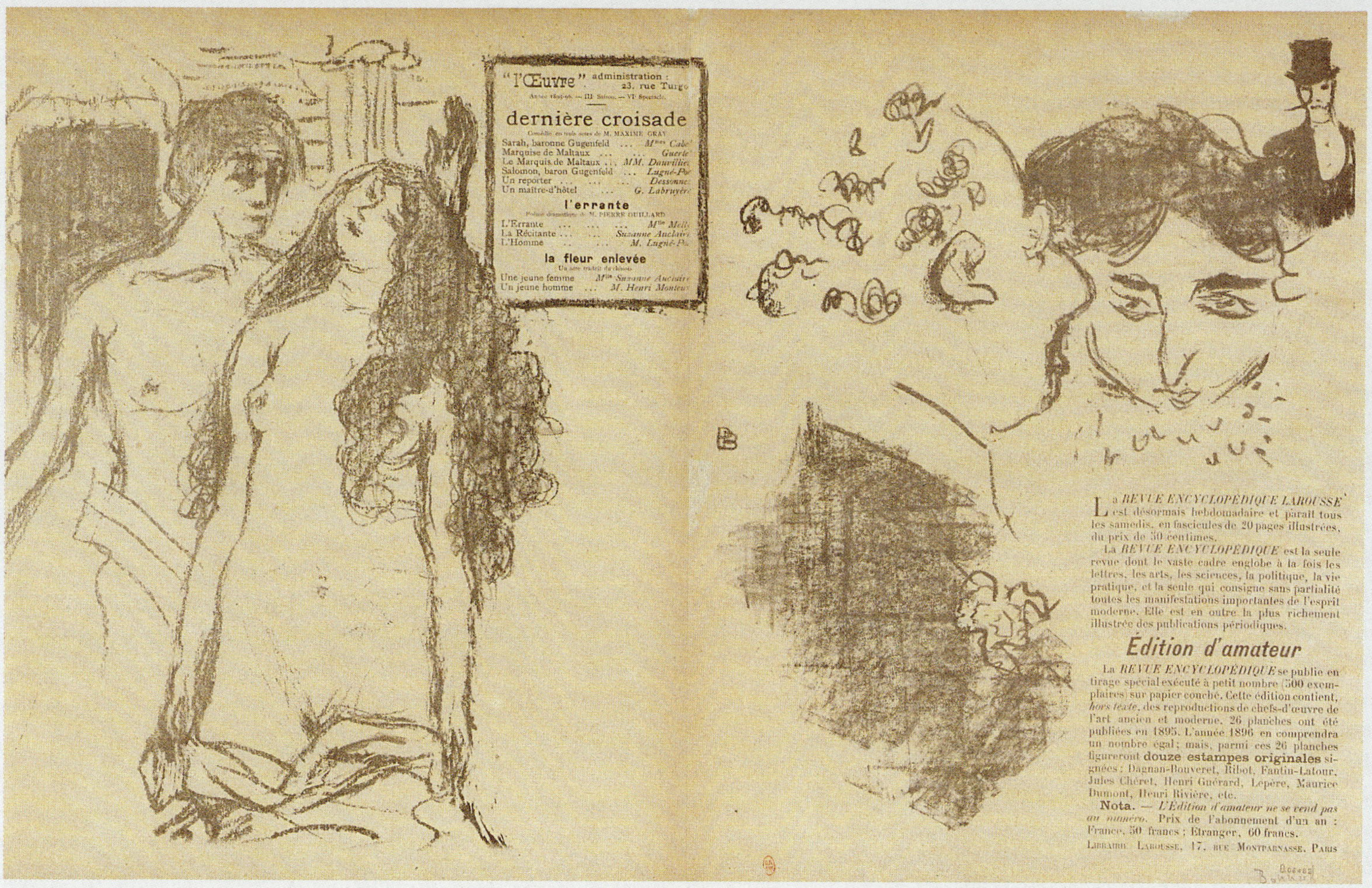

157. Pierre Bonnard
Programme for *La Dernière Croisade* by Maxime Gray, with an advertisement for the *Revue encyclopédique Larousse*, 1896
Grey lithograph. 300 x 490 mm
[Bouvet n. 37]
Bibliothèque nationale de France, Paris

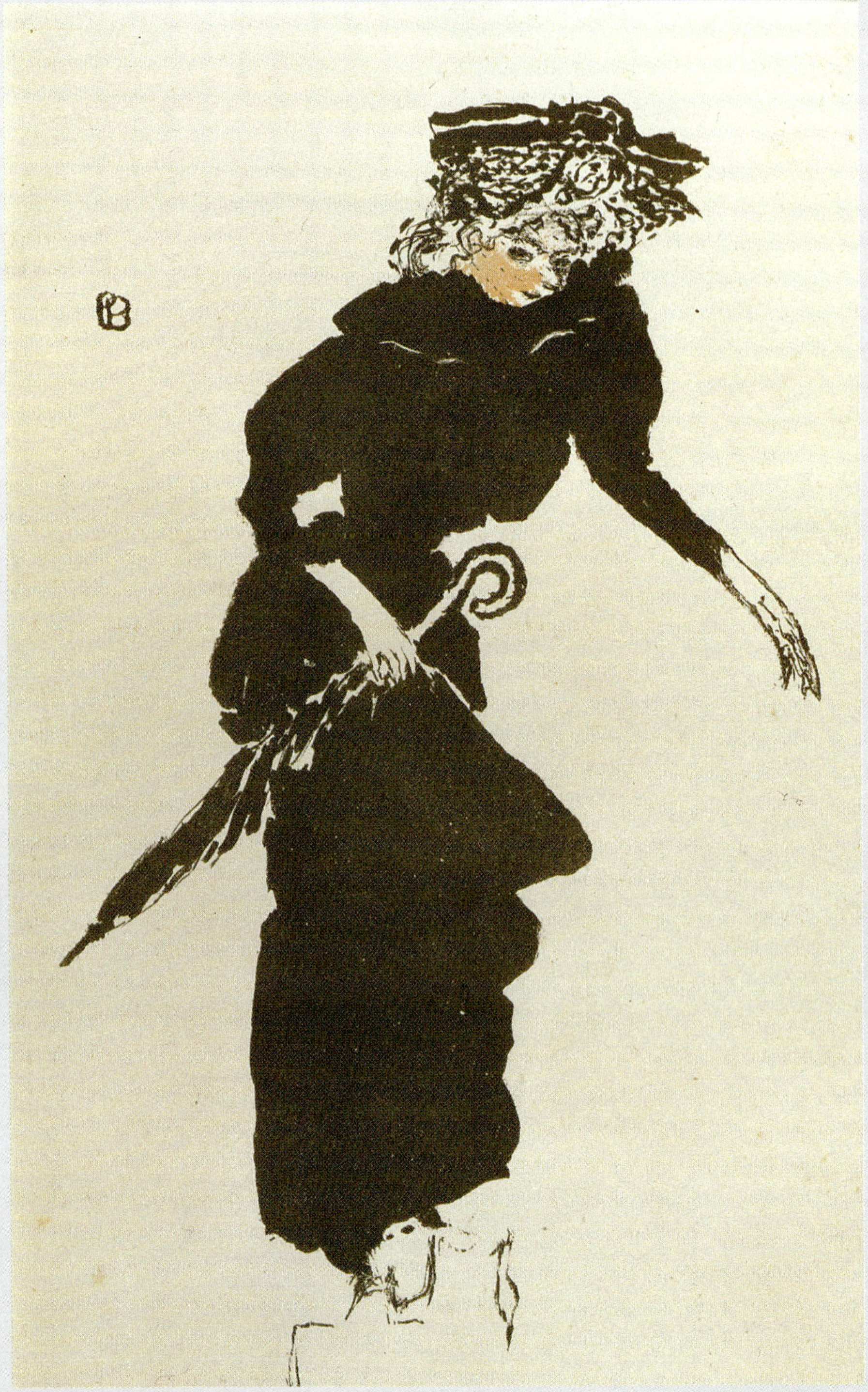

156. Pierre Bonnard
Woman with an Umbrella, 1895
(Femme au parapluie)
Lithograph in two colours. 250 x 155 mm
[Bouvet n. 33]
Bibliothèque nationale de France, Paris

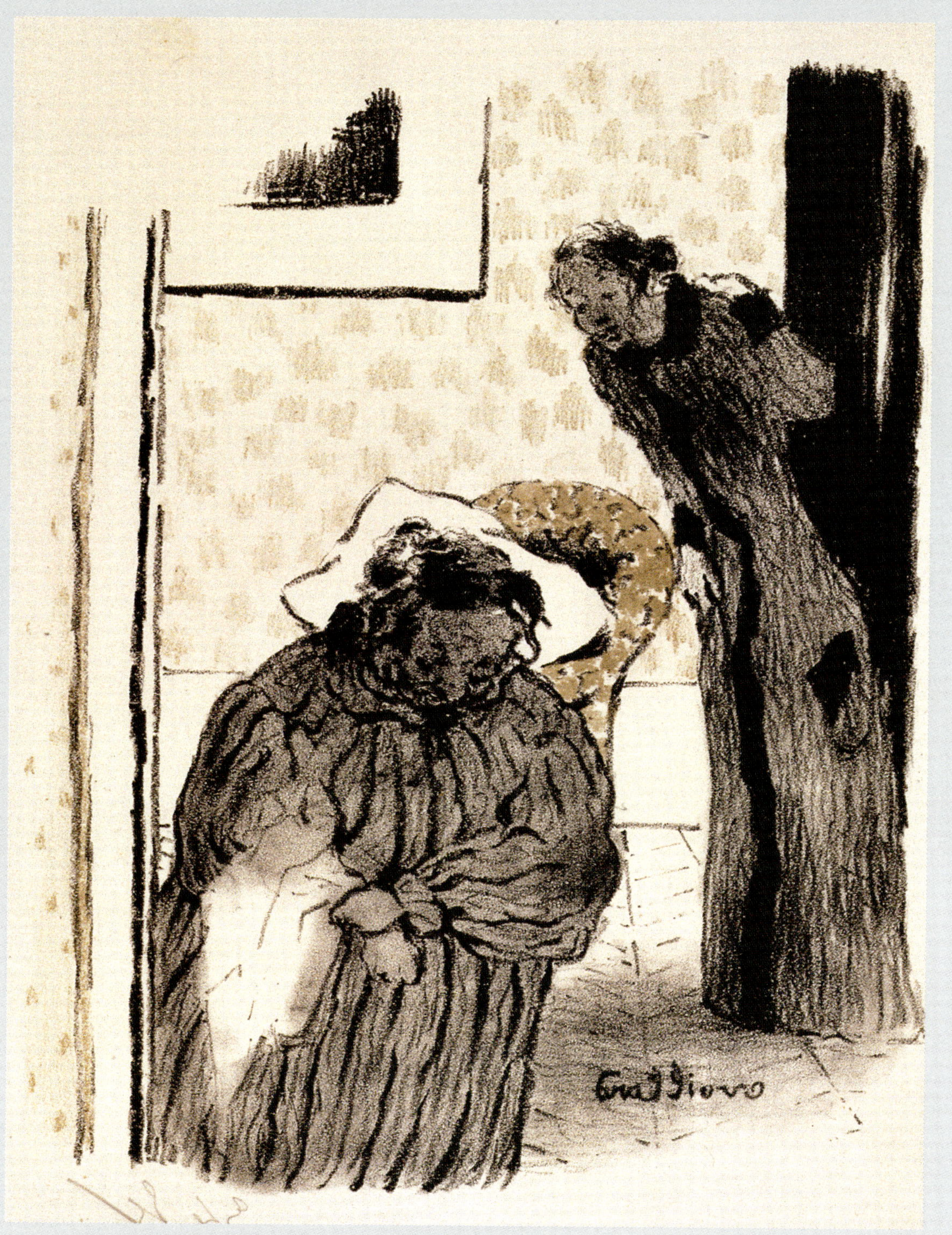

159. Édouard Vuillard
The Nap or *The Convalescent*, 1892–1893
(La sieste ou la convalescente)
Lithograph in two colours. 291 x 250 mm
Galerie Berès, Paris, France

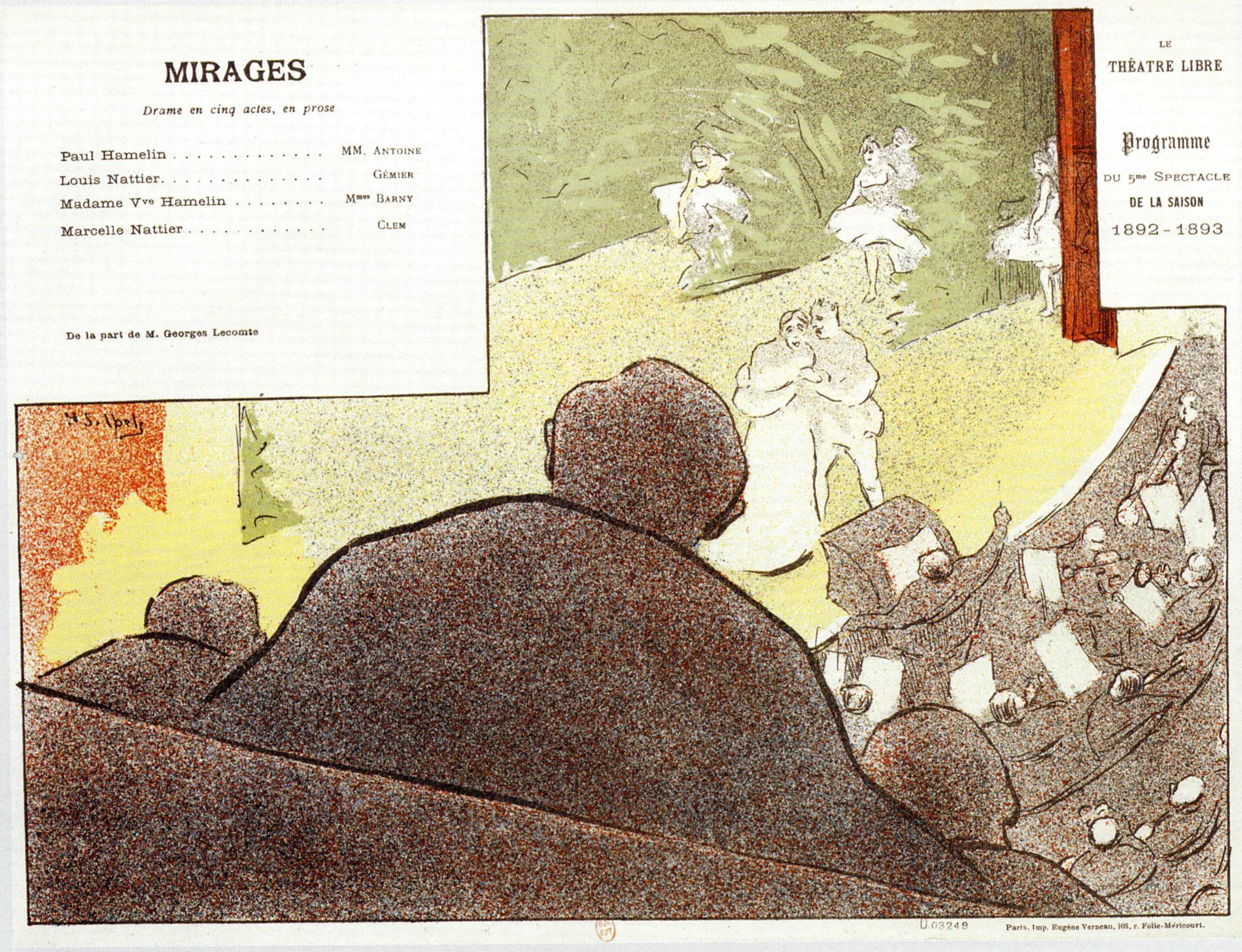

160. Henri-Gabriel Ibels
Programme for *Mirages*, Le Théâtre Libre, 1892
Colour lithograph
Bibliothèque nationale de France, Paris

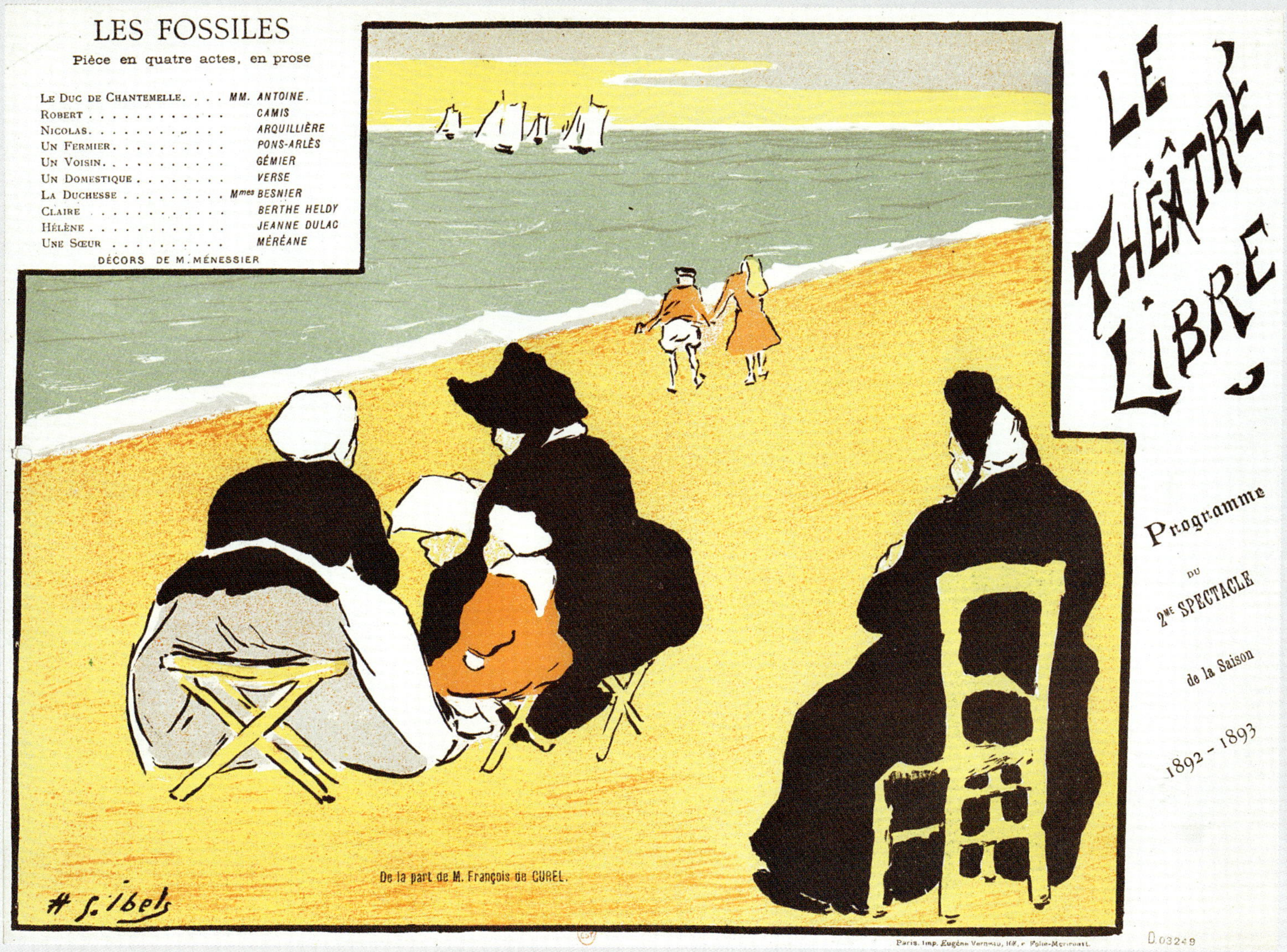

161. Henri-Gabriel Ibels
Programme for *Les fossiles*, Le Théâtre Libre, 1892
Colour lithograph
Bibliothèque nationale de France, Paris

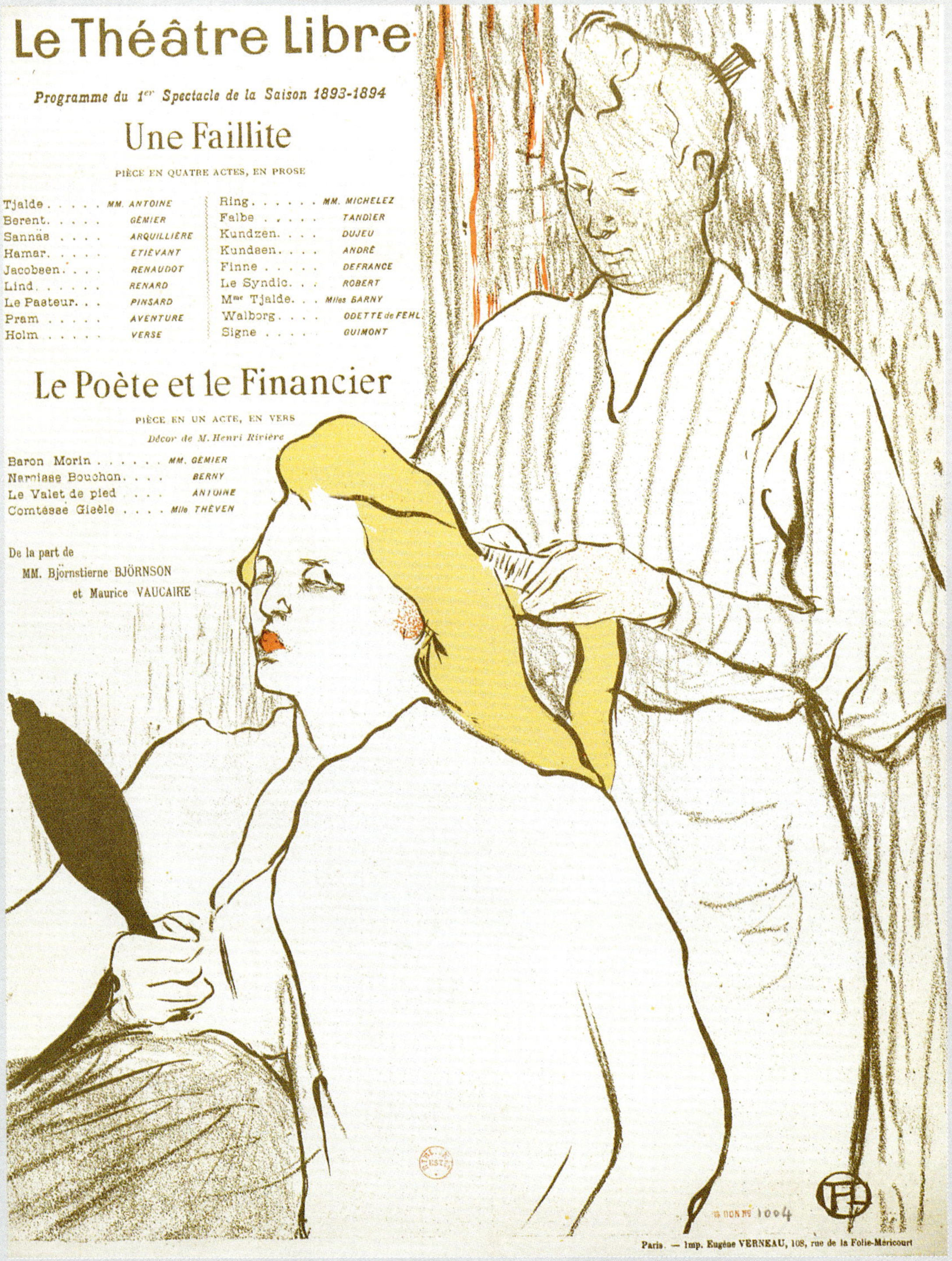

162. Henri Toulouse-Lautrec
Programme for *Le Coiffeur*, Le Théâtre Libre, 1893
Lithograph in three colours, pencil and brush. 315 x 239 mm
[W. 15 / Dc 361]
Bibliothèque nationale de France, Paris

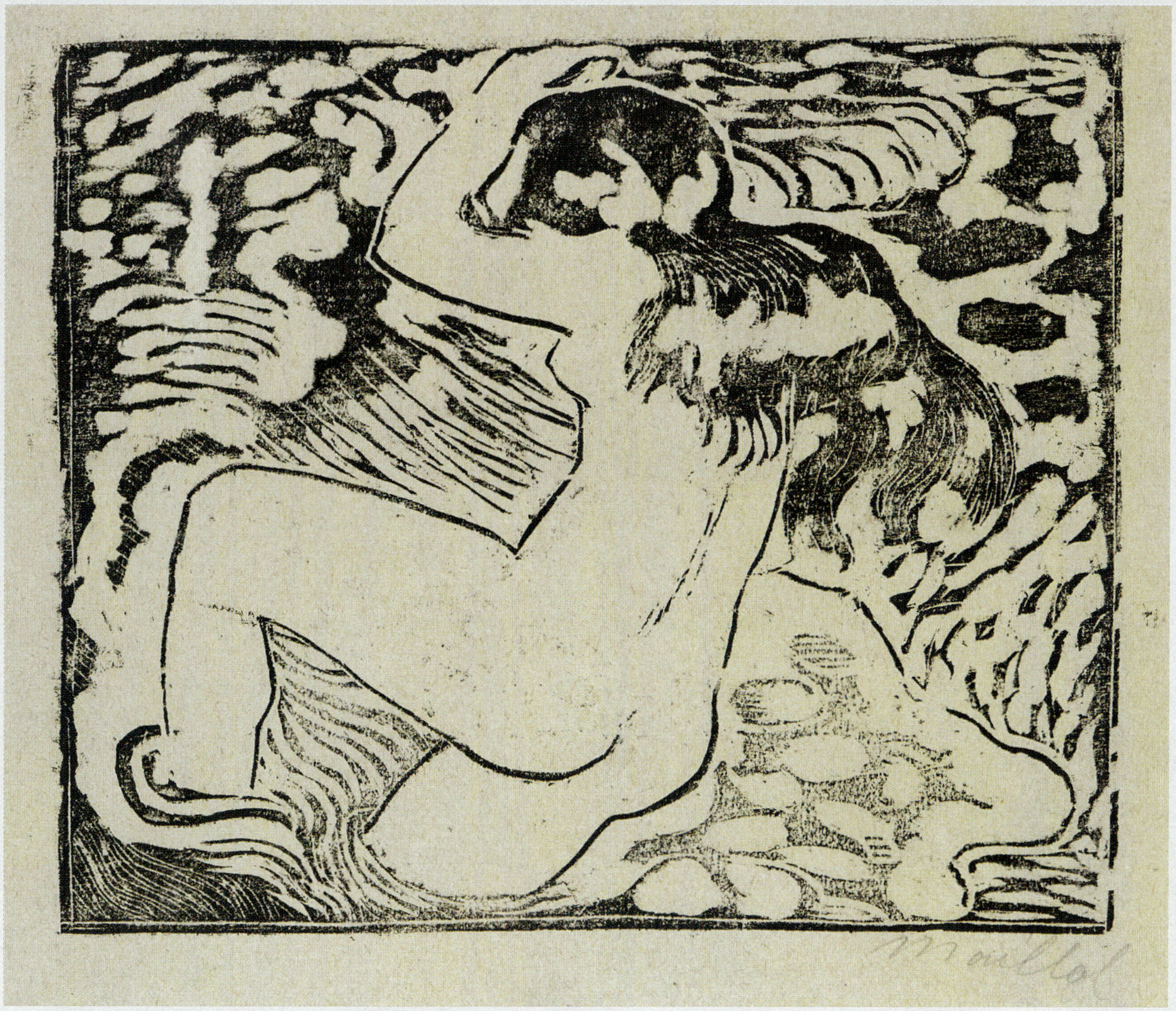

163. Aristide Maillol
Bather in the Sea, 1895
(Baigneuse en mer)
Engraving on wood. 177 x 212 mm
Musée Maillol, Paris

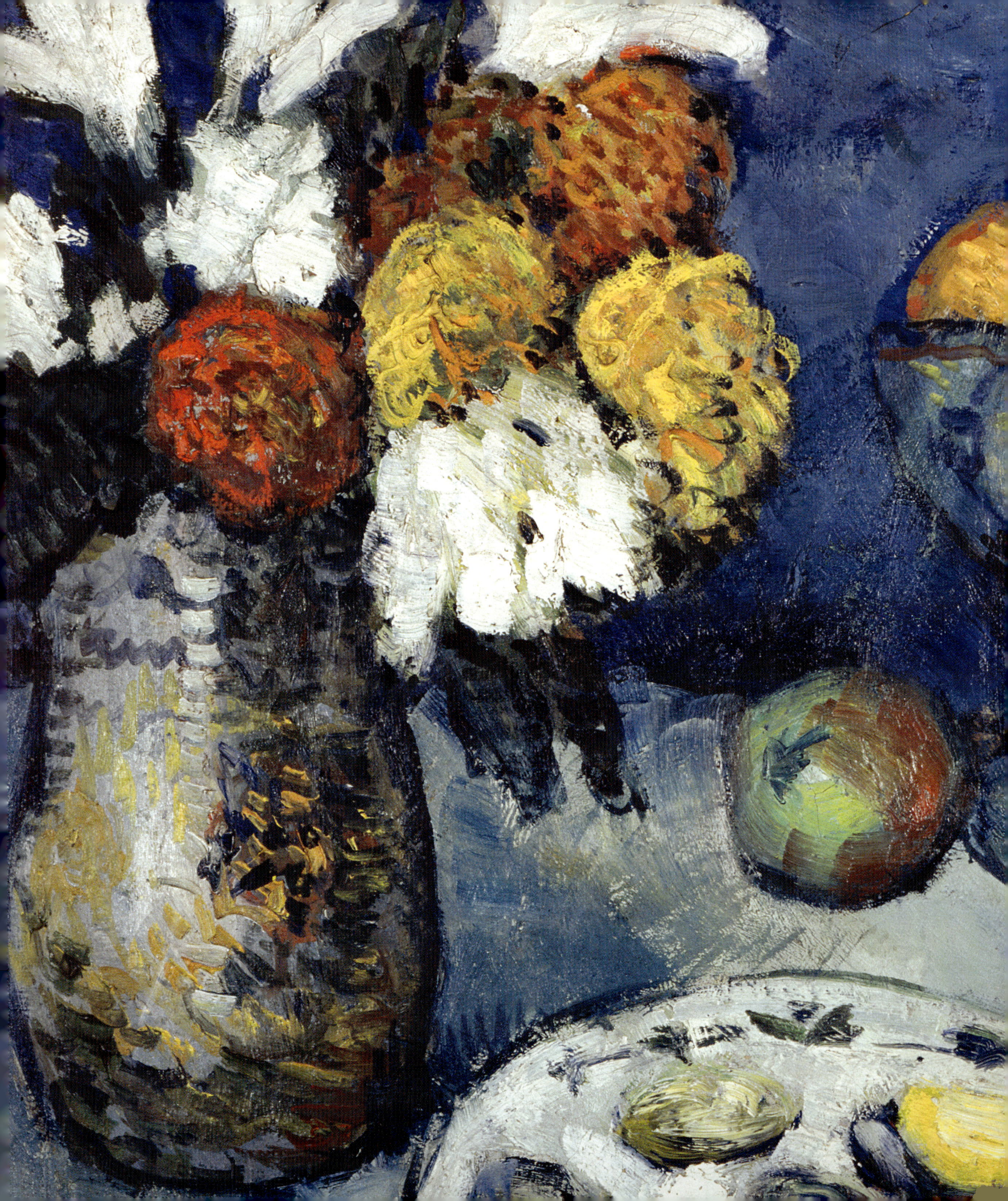

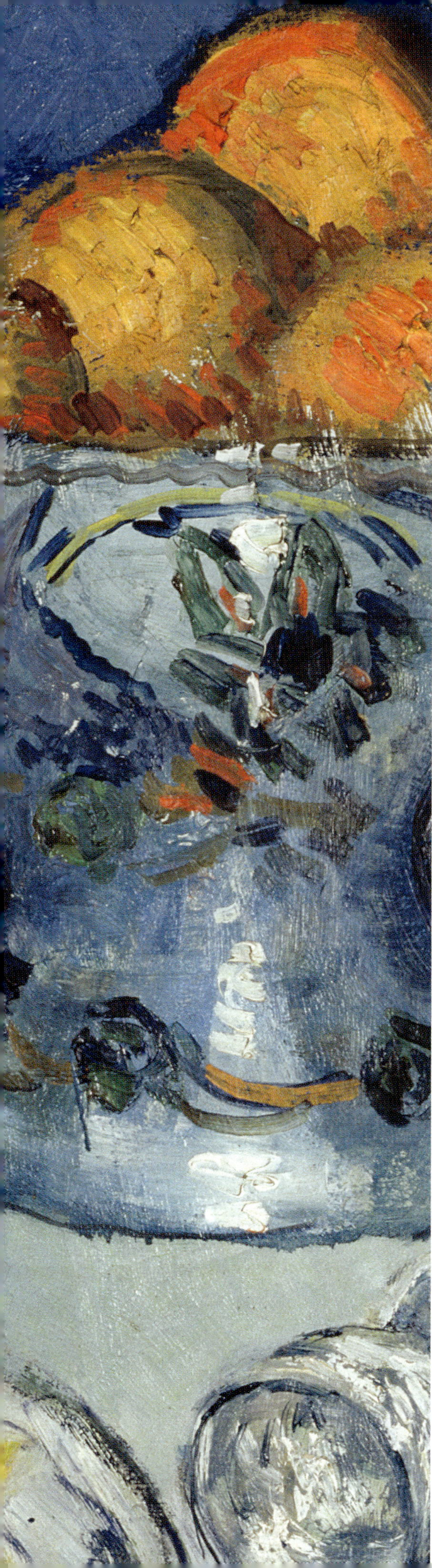

Pablo Picasso
Still Life (the Dessert), 1901
(detail)
[cat.165]

9. Gauguin and Paco Durrio, Picasso and Synthetism in Spain

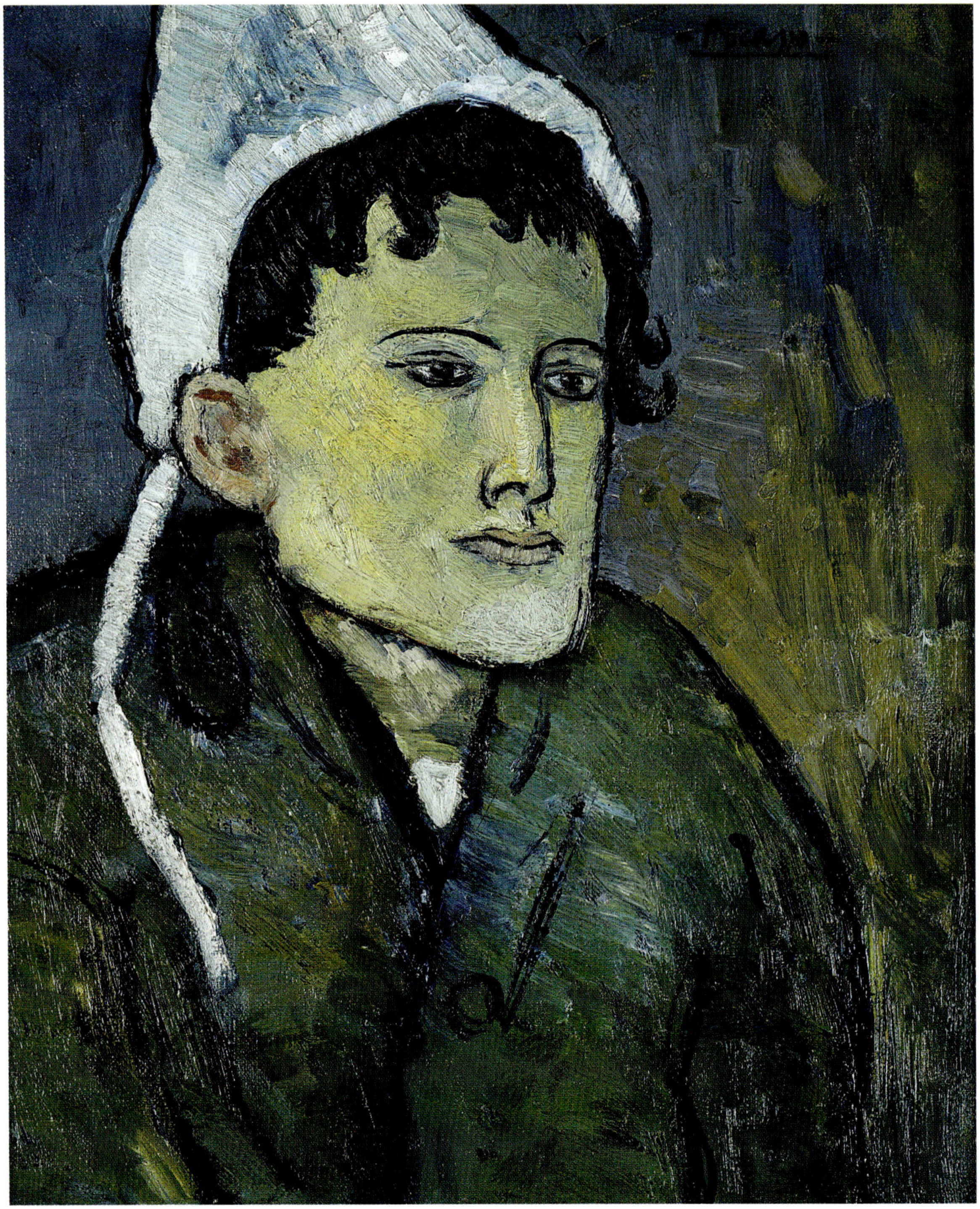

164. Pablo Picasso
Woman with Cap, 1901
(Femme au Bonnet)
Oil on canvas. 41.3 x 33 cm
[Zervos I n. 101]
Museu Picasso, Barcelona

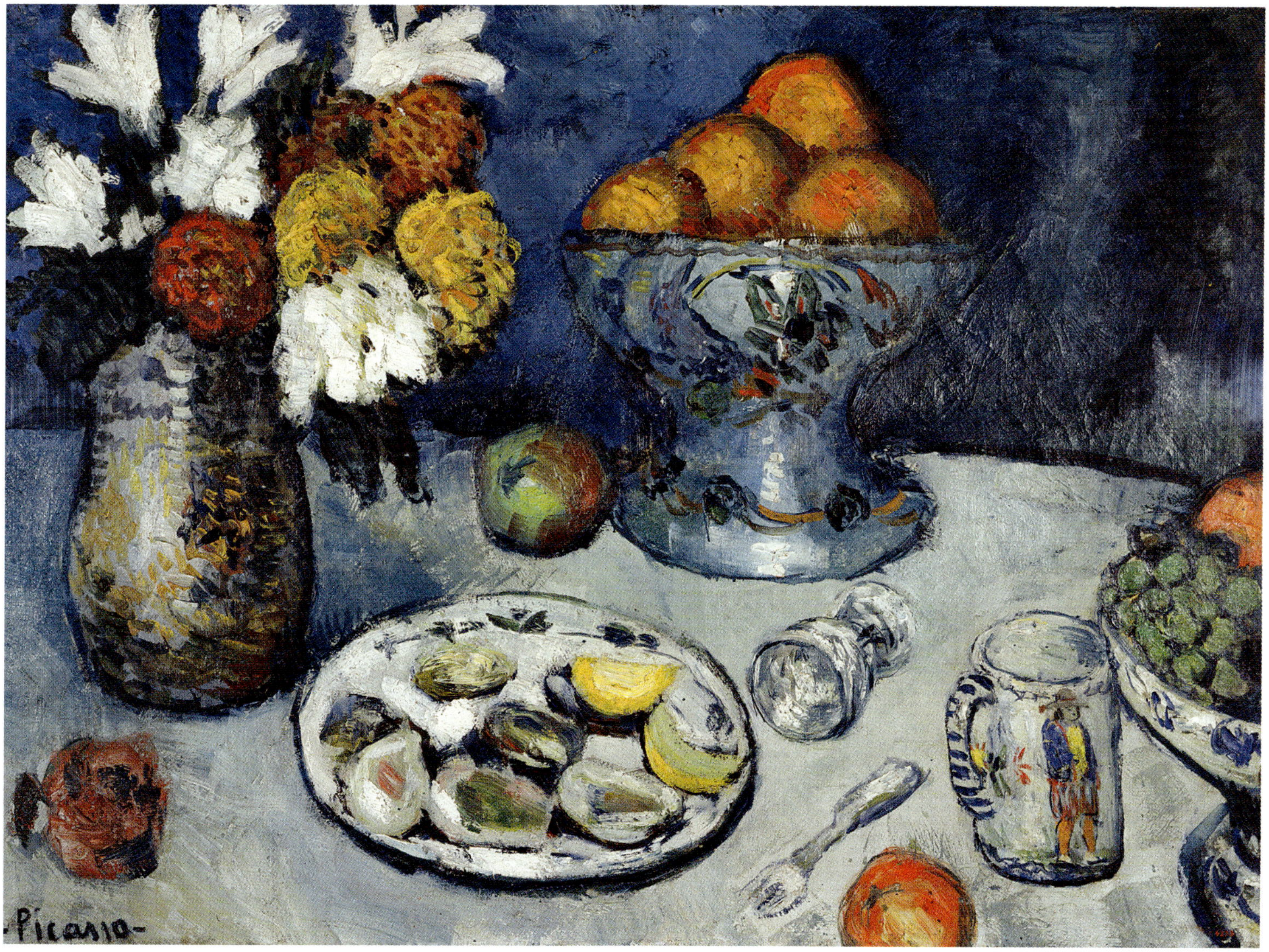

165. Pablo Picasso
Still Life (the Dessert), 1901
(Nature morte [Le dessert])
Oil on canvas. 60 x 80.5 cm
[Zervos I n. 70]
Museu Picasso, Barcelona

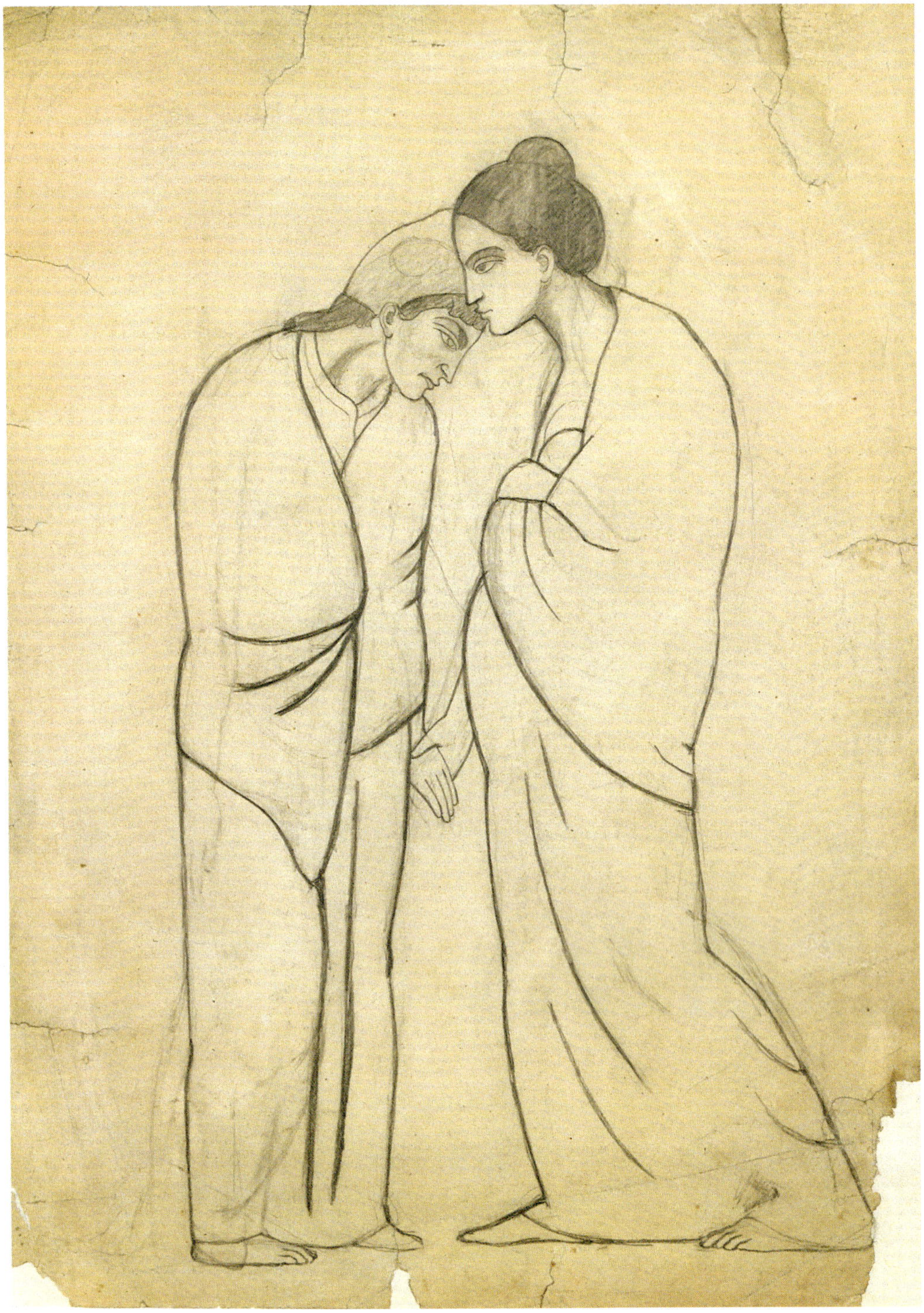

168. Pablo Picasso
Study for 'The Conversation', 1901–1902
(Étude pour 'L'entrevue')
Lead pencil on paper. 45 x 32 cm
[Zervos XXI n. 369]
Musée Picasso, Paris

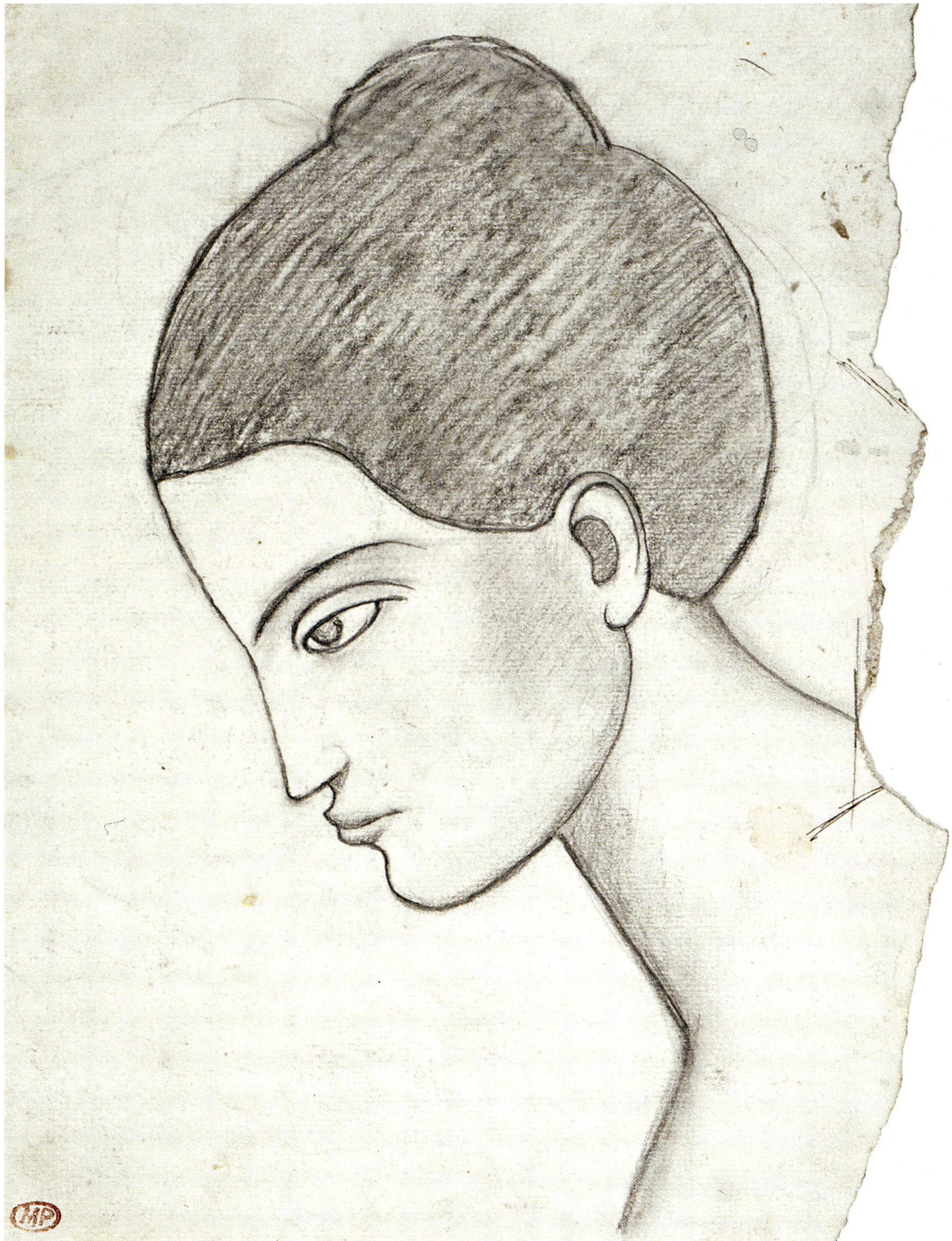

166. Pablo Picasso
Study for 'The Conversation': Woman with bun in profile, 1901–1902
(Étude pour 'L'entrevue' : profil de femme au chignon)
Lead pencil with *frottages* on paper. 21.5 x 15.8 cm
[Zervos XXII n. 37]
Musée Picasso, Paris

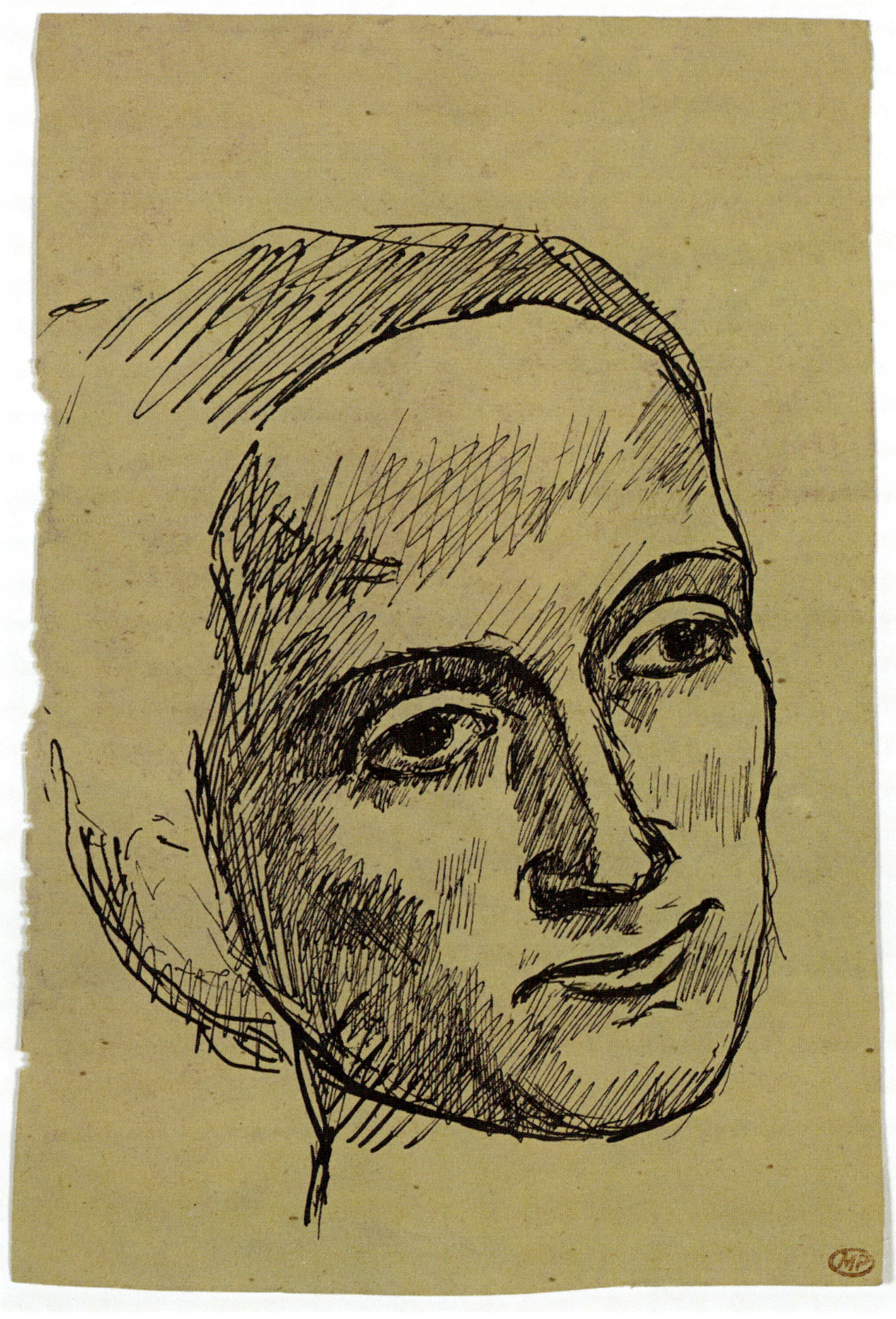

167. Pablo Picasso
Woman's Head, 1902–1903
(Tête de femme)
Pen and Indian ink on paper. 23.8 x 16.3 cm
[Zervos VI n. 466]
Musée Picasso, Paris

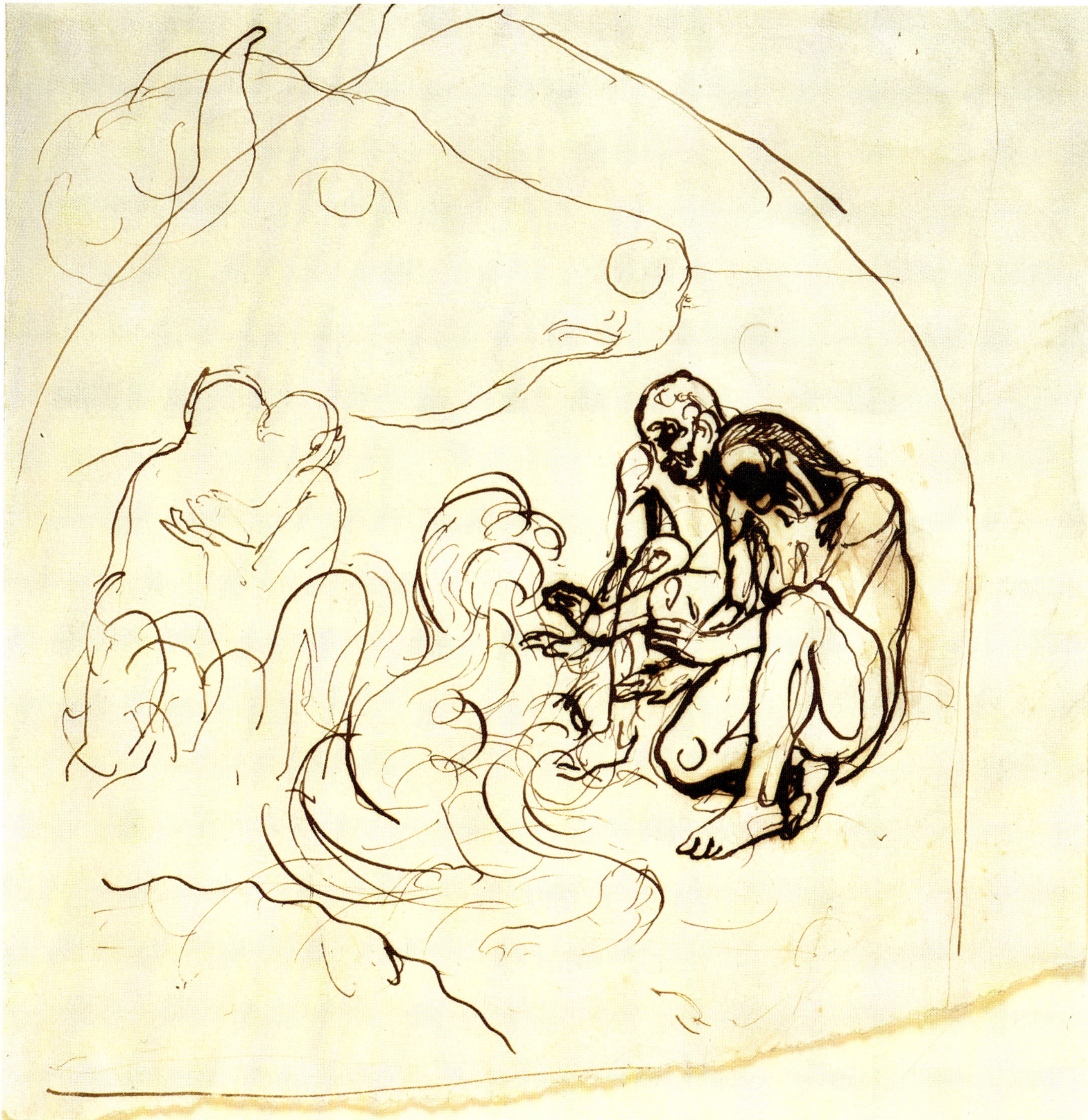

169. Pablo Picasso
Sketch for the Decoration of a Fireplace, 1903
Pen on paper. 24.5 x 23.1 cm
Museu Picasso, Barcelona

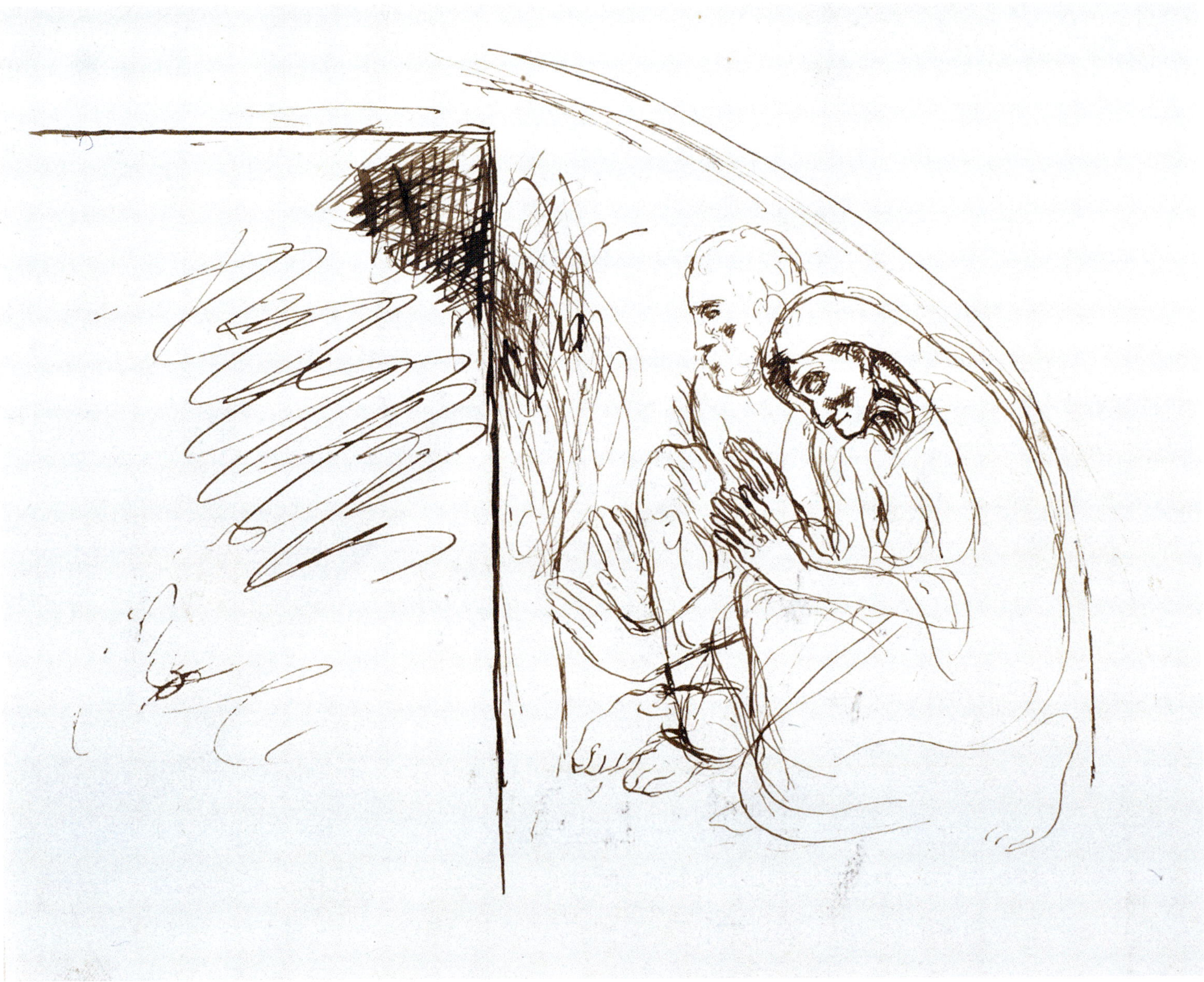

170. Pablo Picasso
Old Couple, 1903
Pen on paper. 17 x 23 cm
Museu Picasso, Barcelona

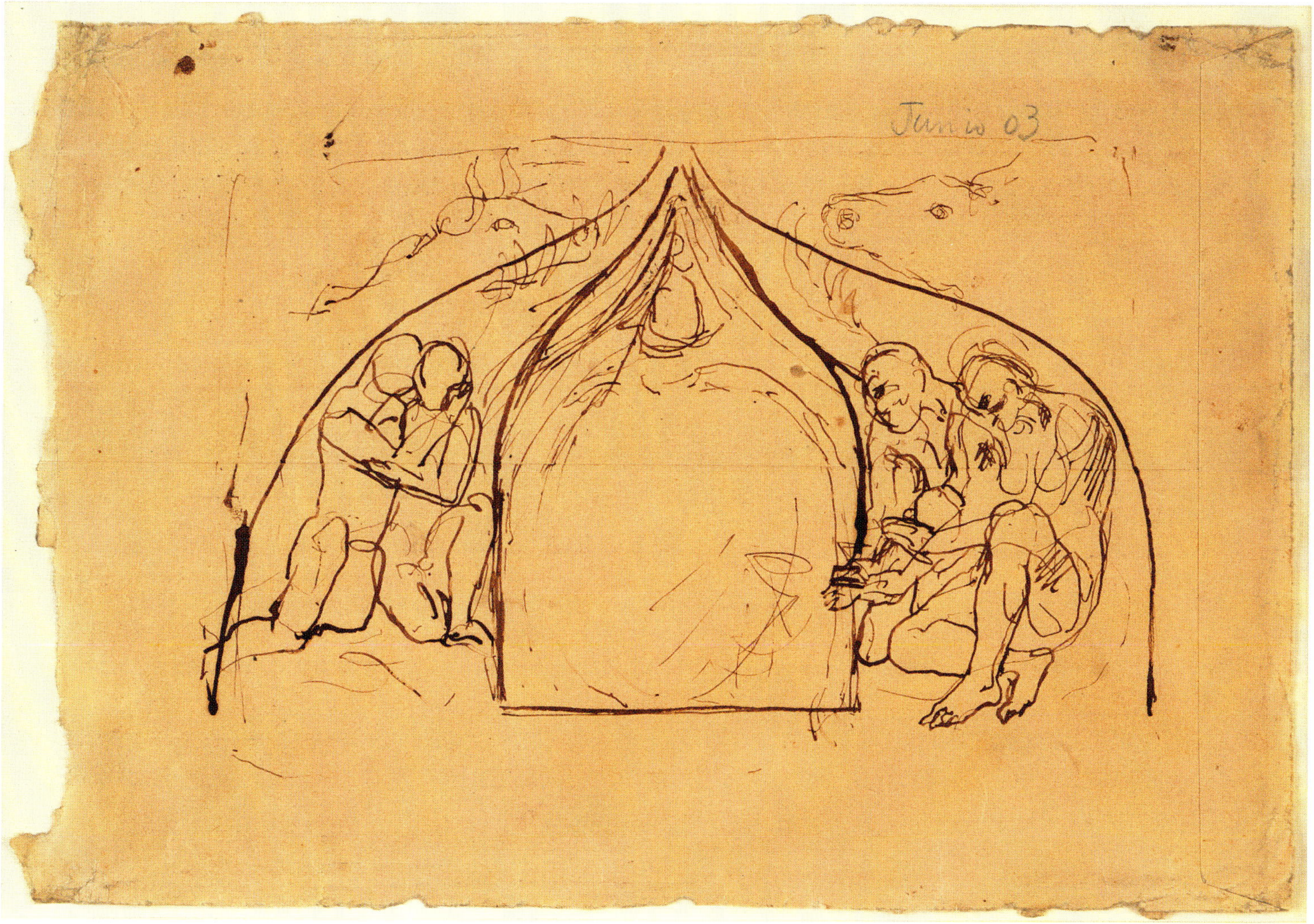

171. Pablo Picasso
Sketch for the Decoration of a Fireplace, 1903
Pen on paper. 21.3 x 30.5 cm
Museu Picasso, Barcelona

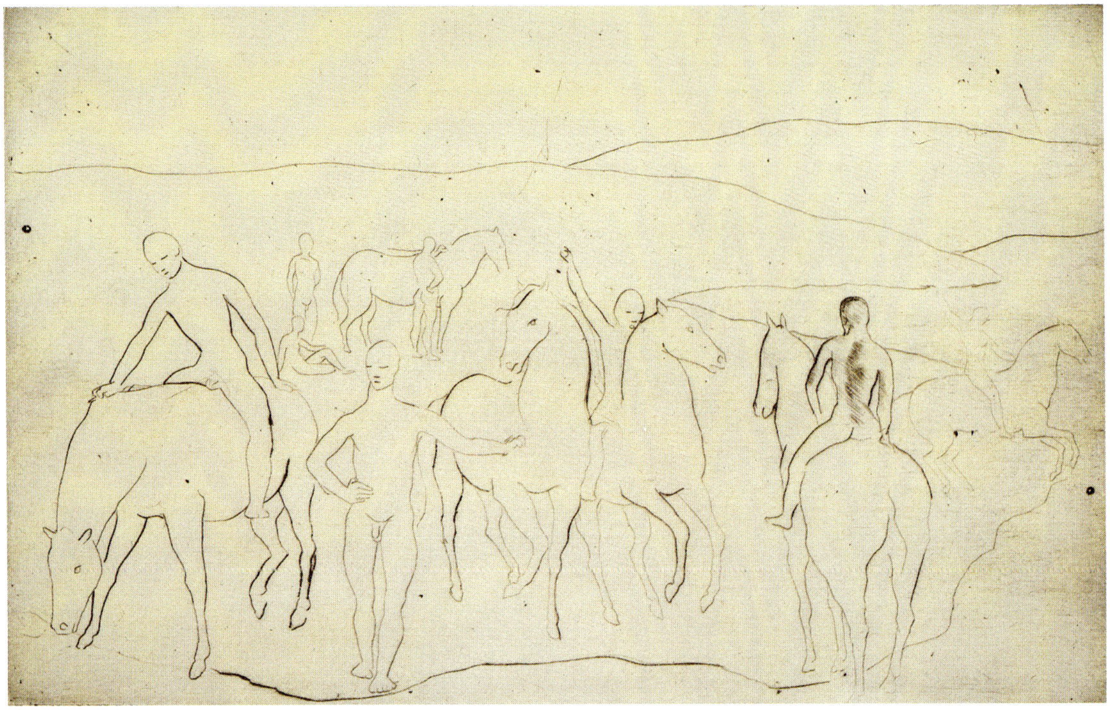

172. Pablo Picasso
The Watering-place, 1905
(L'abreuvoir)
Dry point. 12.2 x 18.8 cm
Musée Picasso, Paris

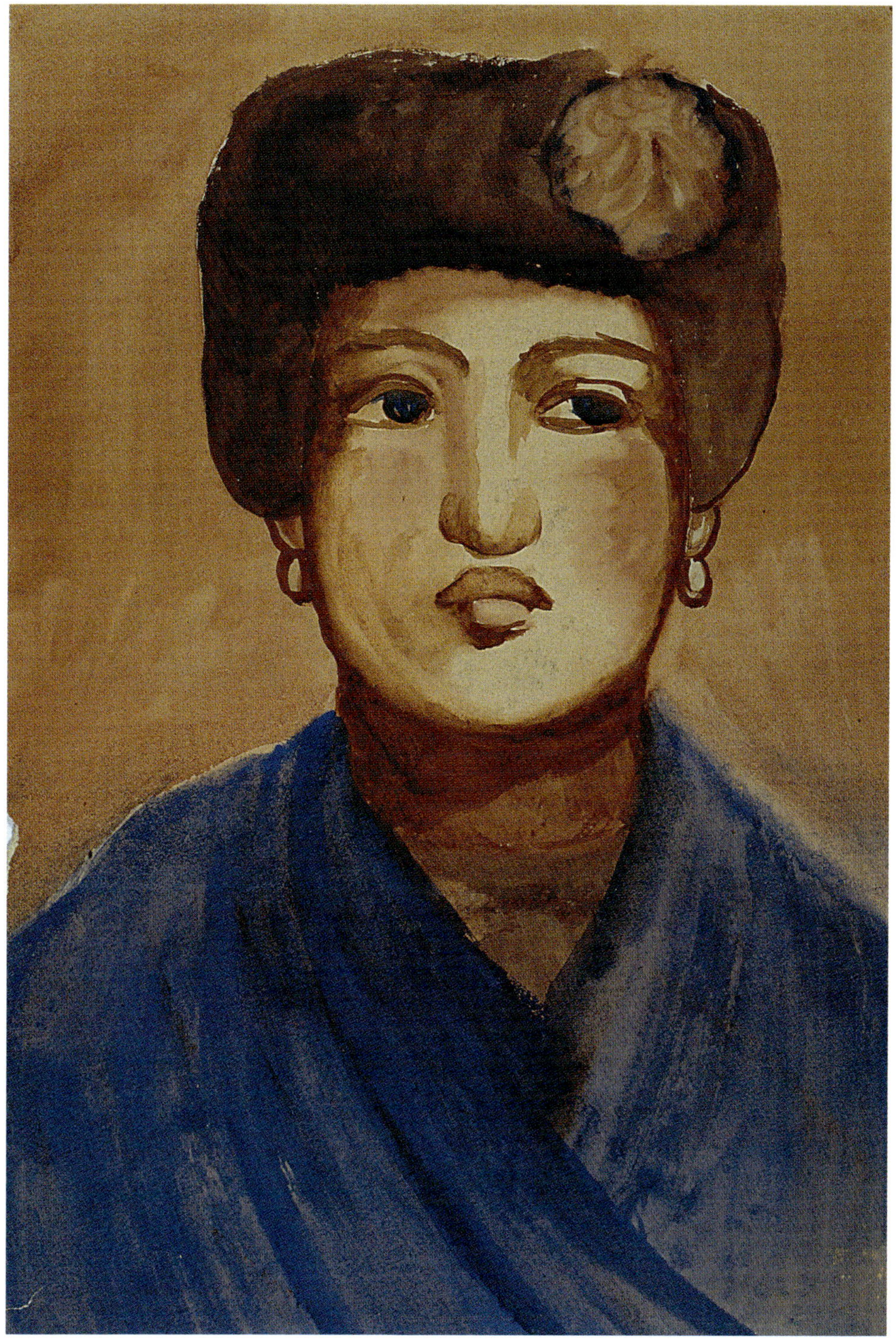

173. Joan González
Young Woman with Flower, c. 1902–1903
(Joven con flor)
Watercolour on paper. 51 x 34.6 cm
Museu Nacional d'Art de Catalunya, Barcelona

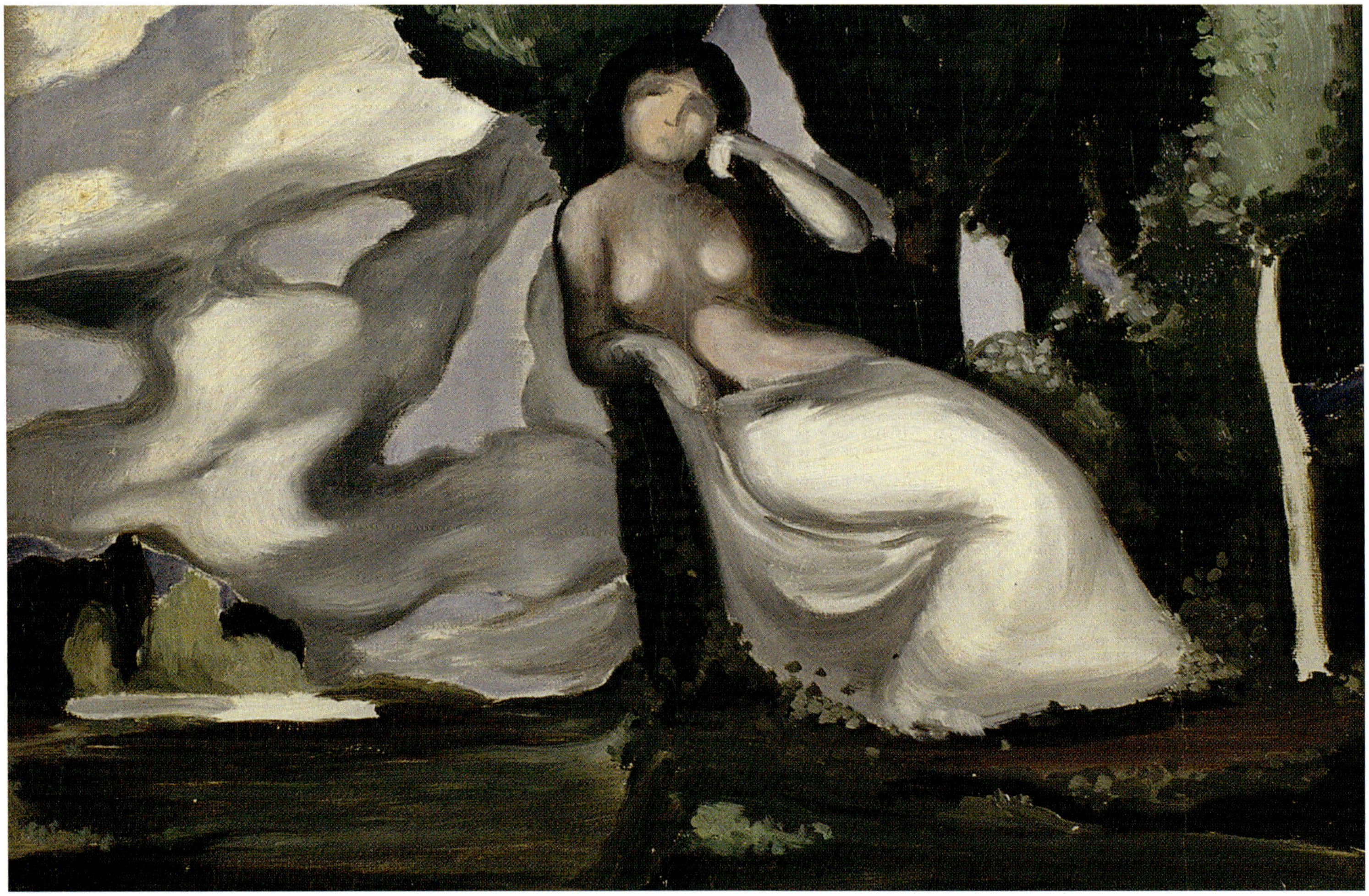

175. Joan González
Woman and Clouds, c. 1904–1906
(*Mujer y nubes*)
Oil on canvas. 26.8 x 40.8 cm
Museu Nacional d'Art de Catalunya, Barcelona

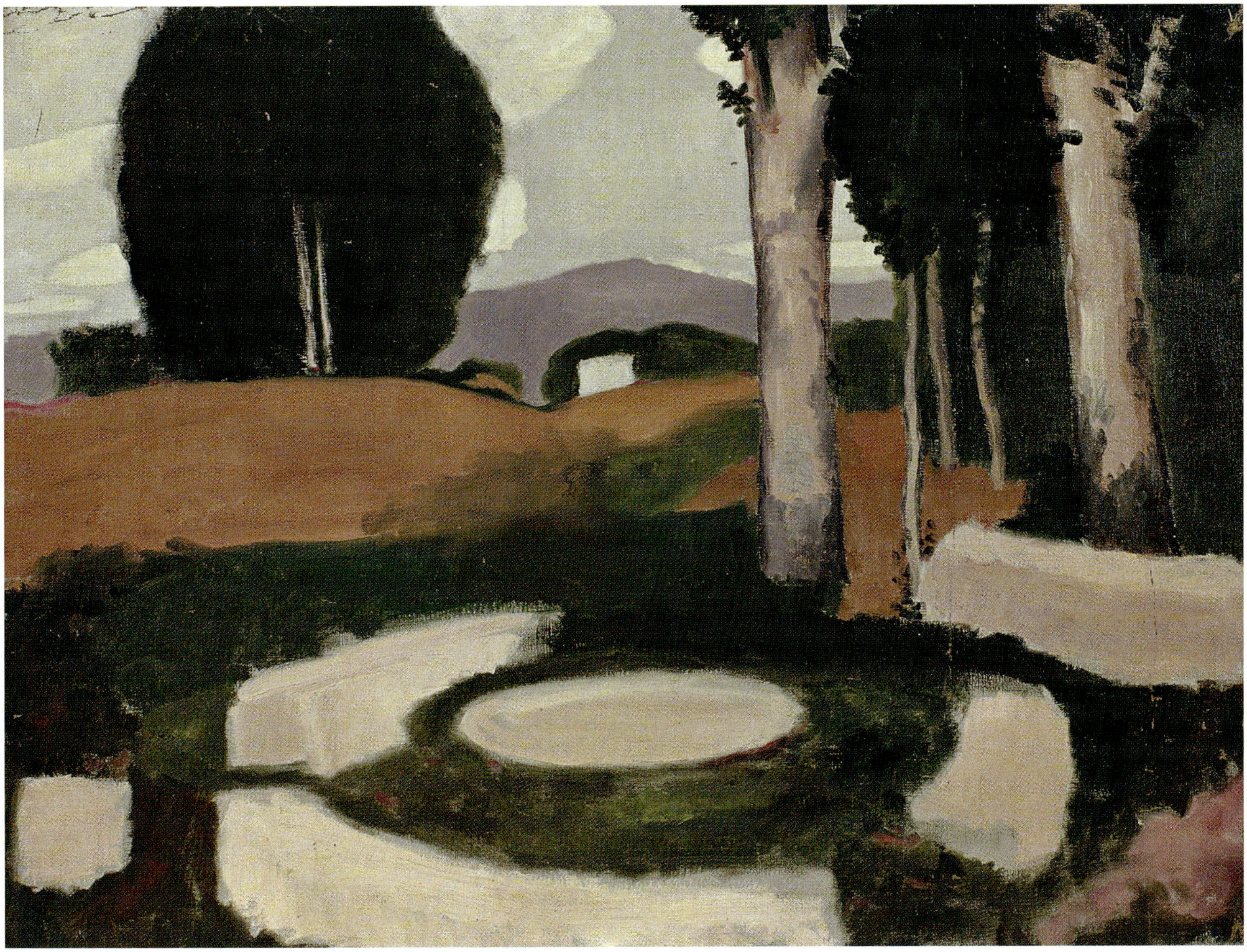

174. Joan González
Landscape, c. 1904–1905
(Paisaje)
Oil on canvas. 50 x 65 cm
Museu Nacional d'Art de Catalunya, Barcelona

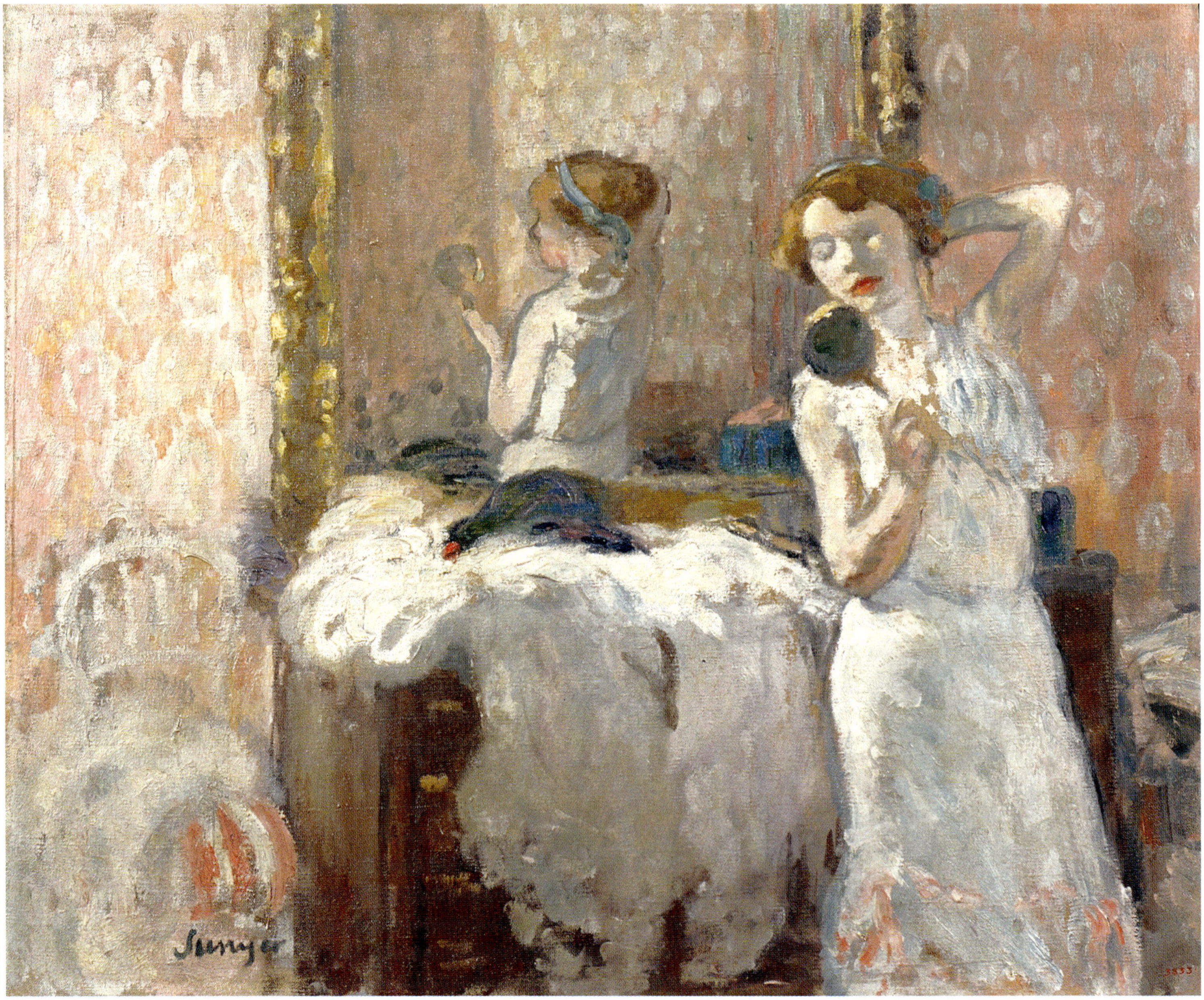

177. Joaquim Sunyer
The Mirrors, c. 1905–1907
(*Los espejos*)
Oil on canvas. 55 x 65 cm
Museu Nacional d'Art de Catalunya, Barcelona

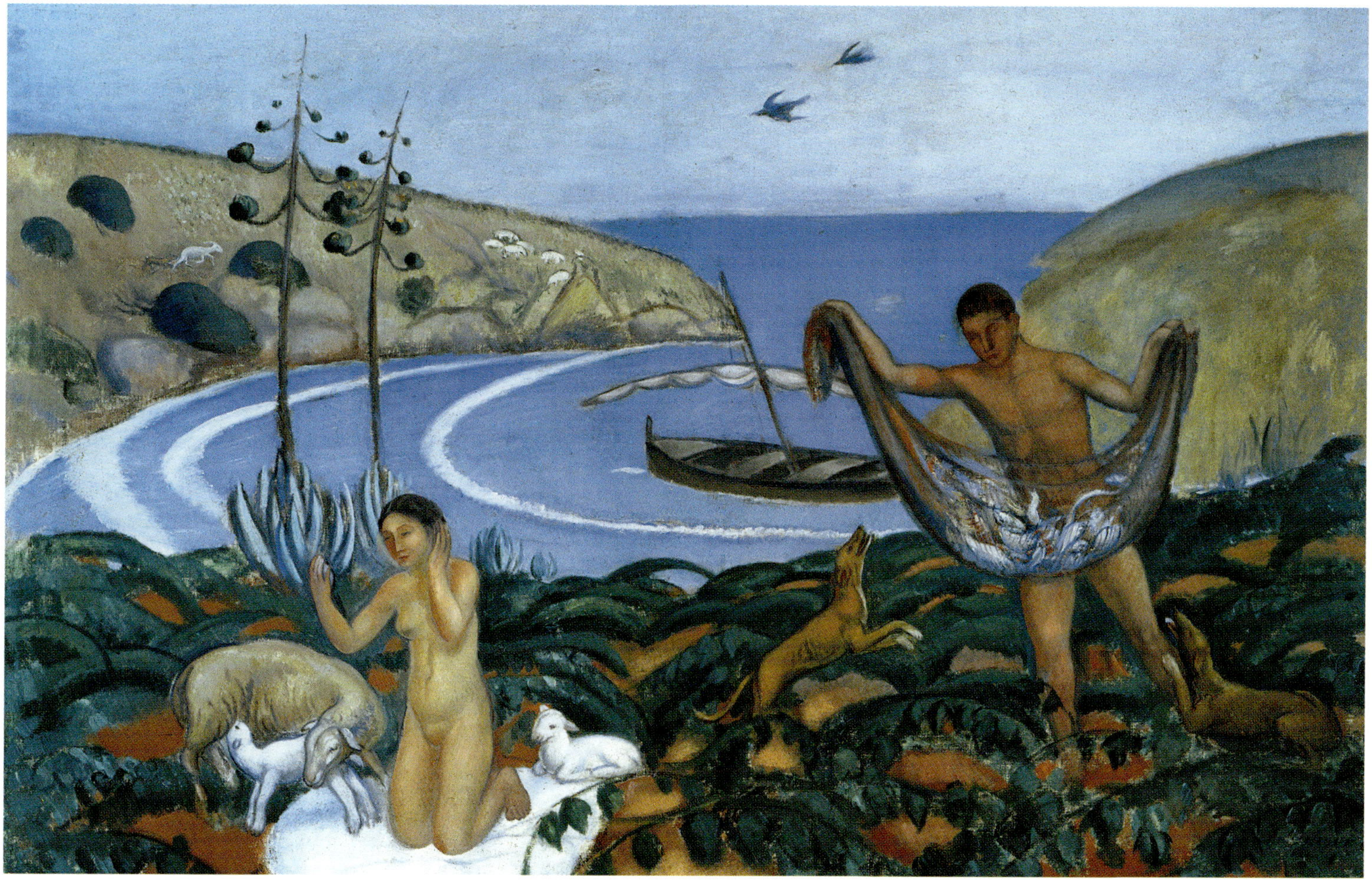

176. Joaquim Sunyer
Mediterranean, 1910–1911
(Mediterráneo)
Oil on canvas. 84 x 132 cm
Carmen Thyssen-Bornemisza Collection
on loan at the Museo Thyssen-Bornemisza, Madrid

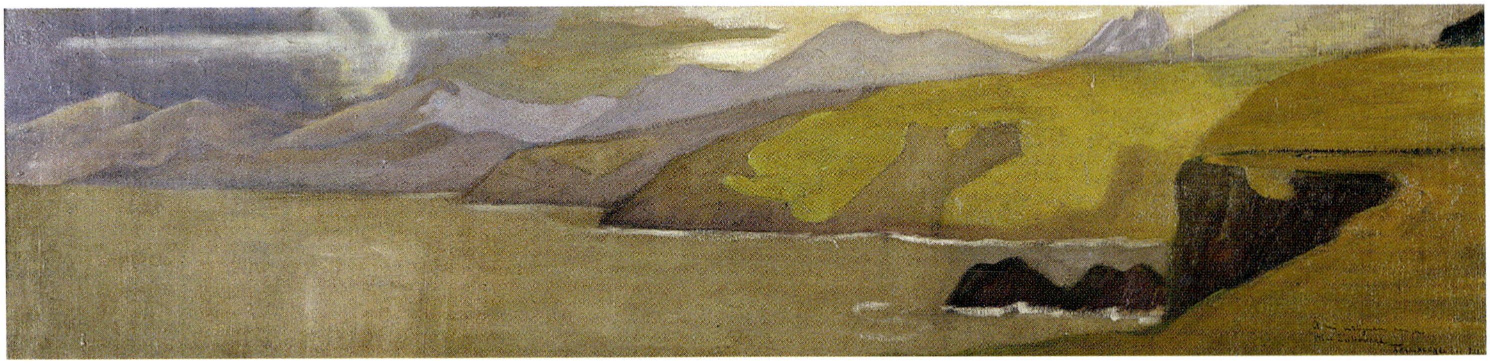

179. Julián de Tellaeche
Seascape, 1912
(Marina)
Oil on canvas. 24.5 x 100 cm
Museo Nacional Centro de Arte Reina Sofía, Madrid

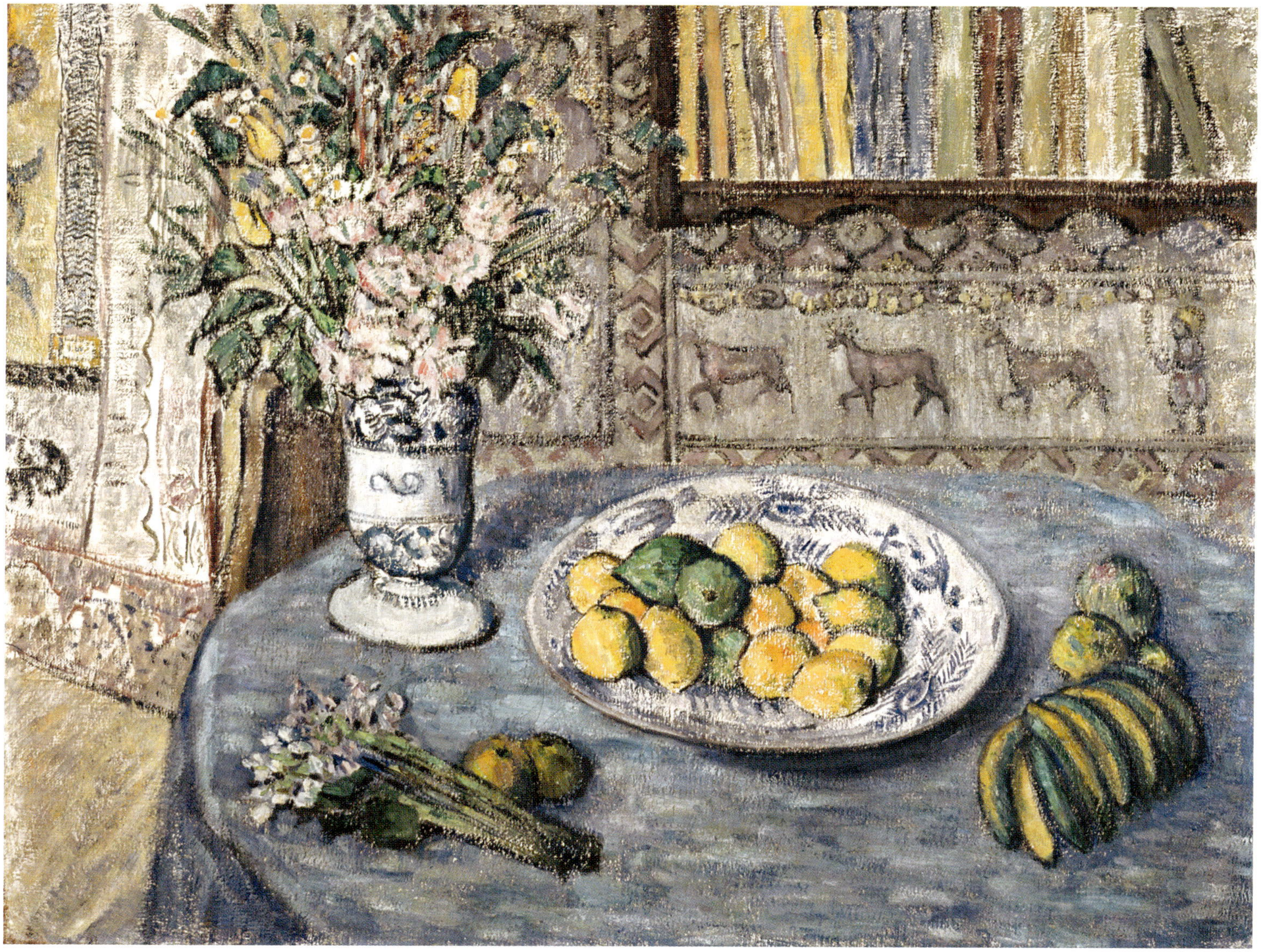

178. Juan Echevarría
Still Life, c. 1915
(*Naturaleza muerta*)
Oil on canvas. 90 x 116 cm
Museo Nacional Centro de Arte Reina Sofía, Madrid

180. Ramón de Zubiaurre
Screen, c. 1910–1911
(Biombo)
Oil on canvas. 180 x 243 cm
Private Collection

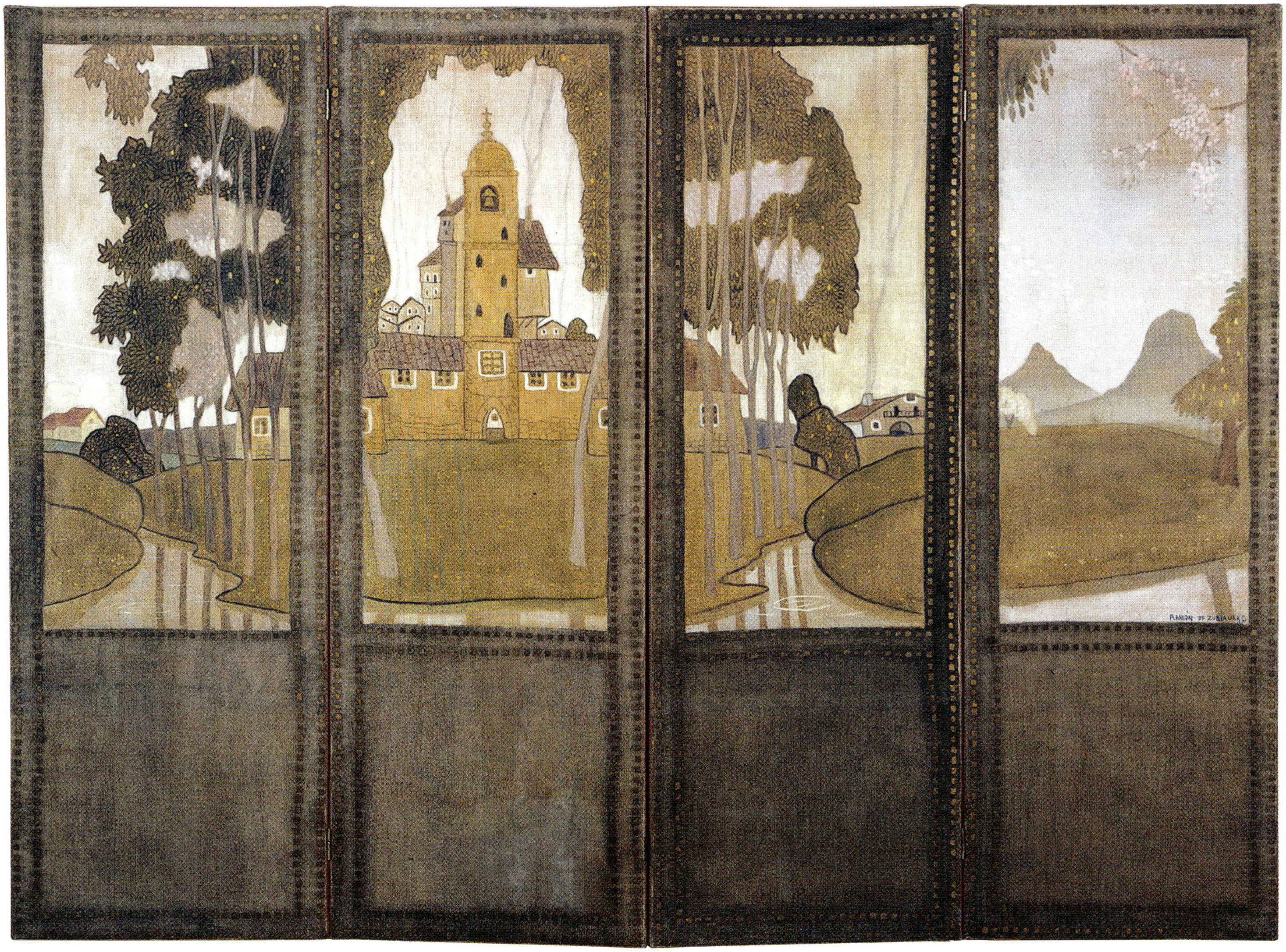

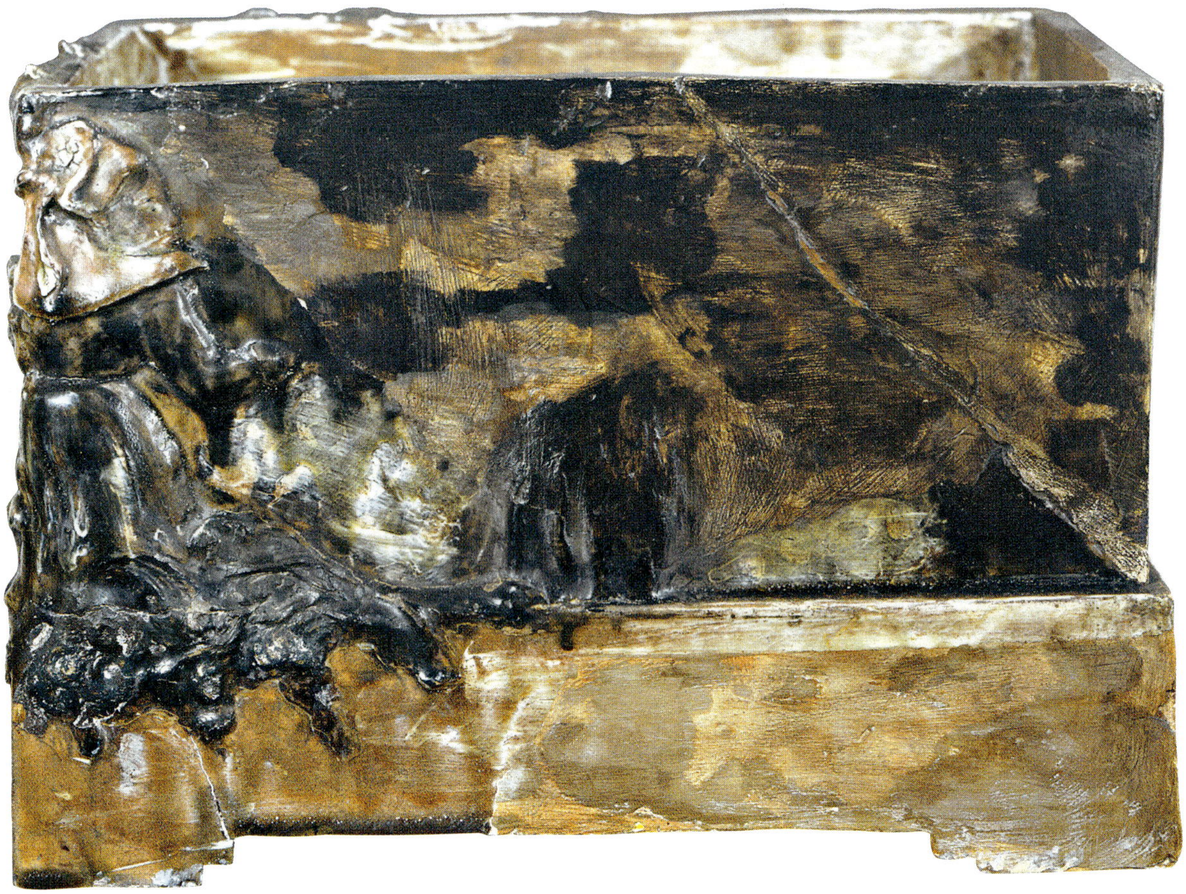

182. Paul Gauguin
Window box with Breton Scenes, 1886
(Jardinière avec scènes bretonnes)
Clay. 29 x 42 x 24 cm
Association des Amis du Petit Palais, Geneva

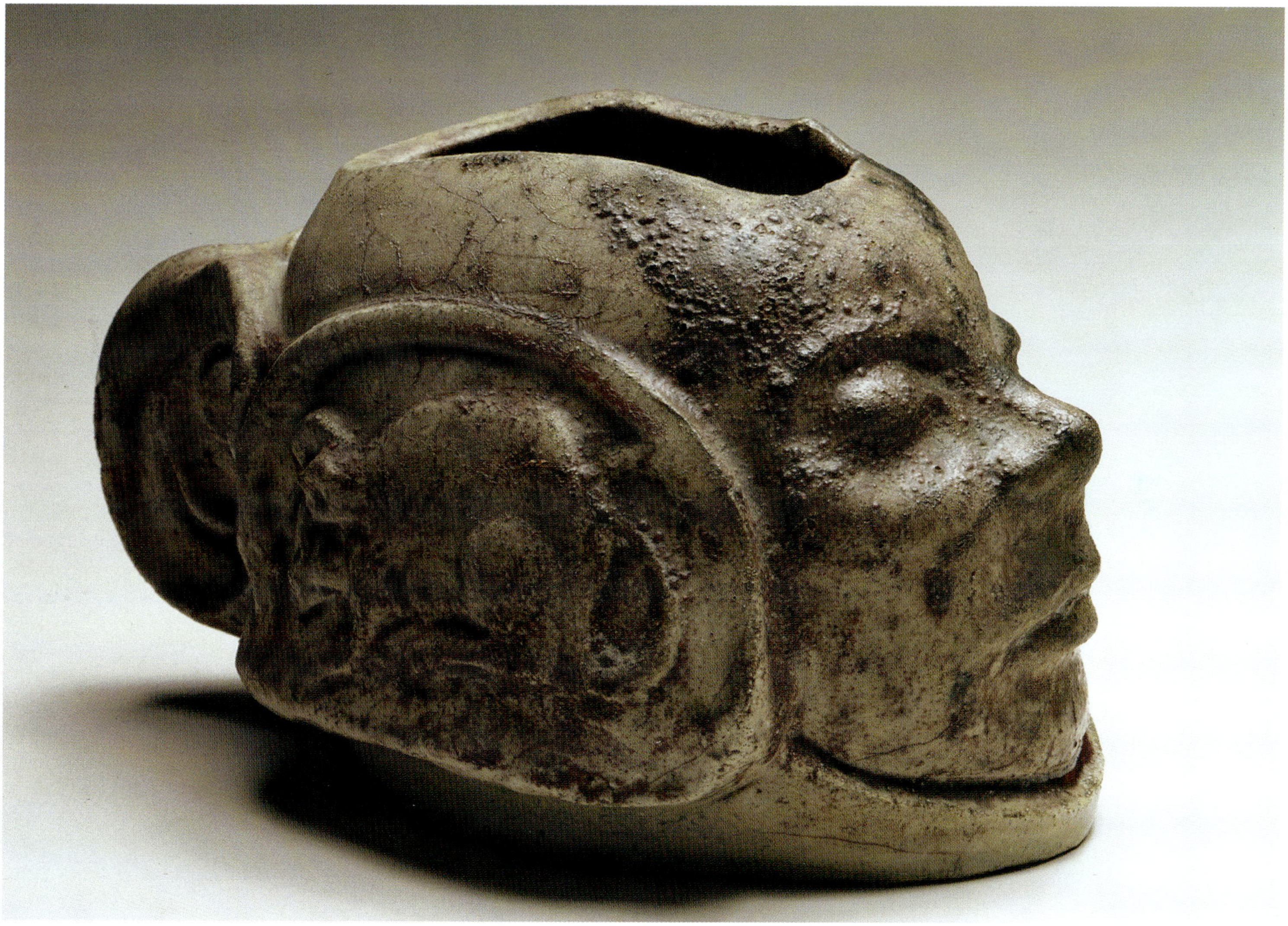

181. Paul Gauguin
Head of a Young Girl, 1893–1894
(Tête de jeune fille)
Clay, varnished and heightened in places with
dark red pigment. 15.2 x 26.18 cm
[Gray A-10]
Carmen Thyssen-Bornemisza Collection
on loan at the Museo Thyssen-Bornemisza, Madrid

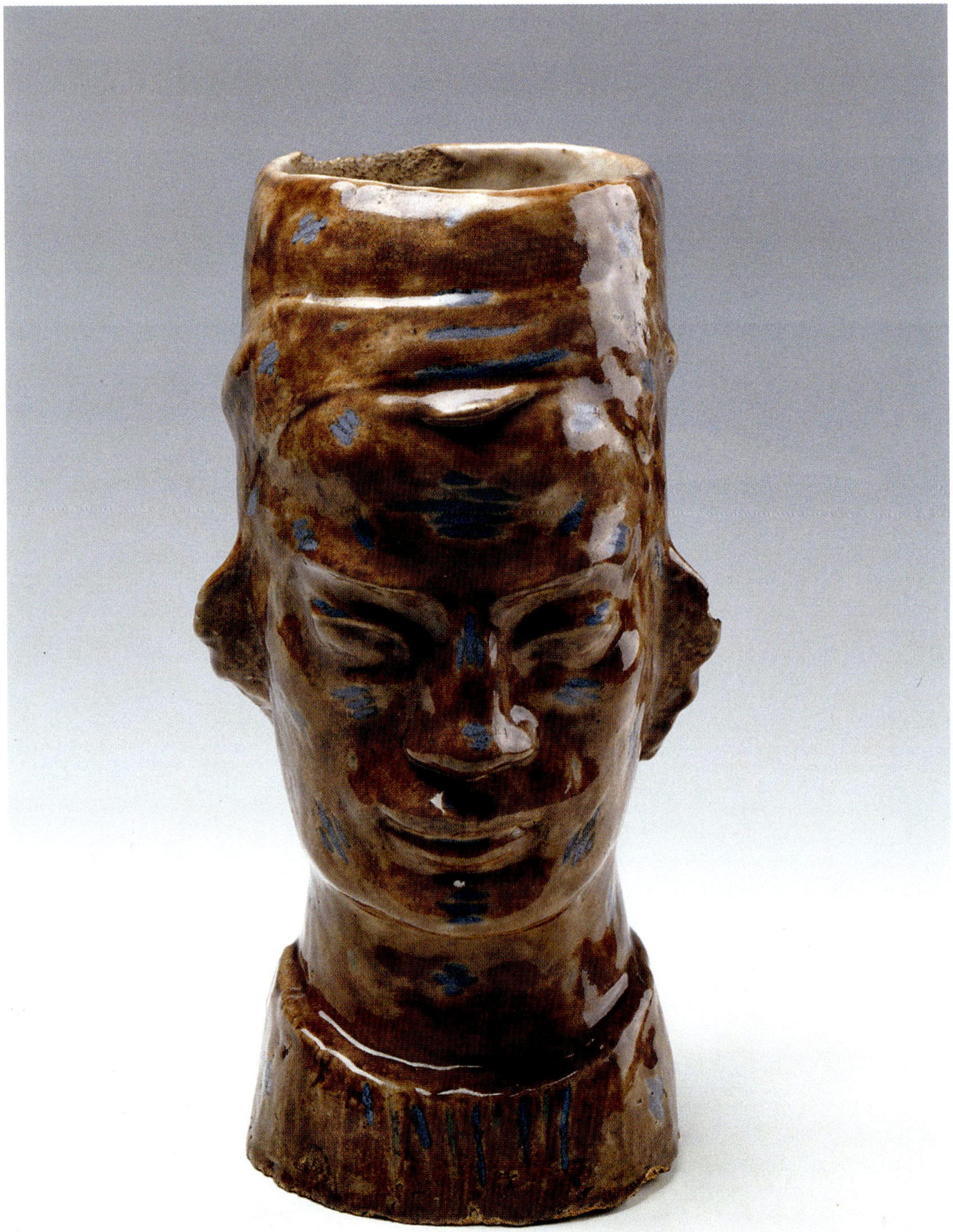

183. Paco Durrio
Head of Young Man or *Inca Head*
(Cabeza de joven o *cabeza de inca)*
Glazed clay. 30.6 x 16.5 x 18.7 cm
Museo de Bellas Artes de Bilbao

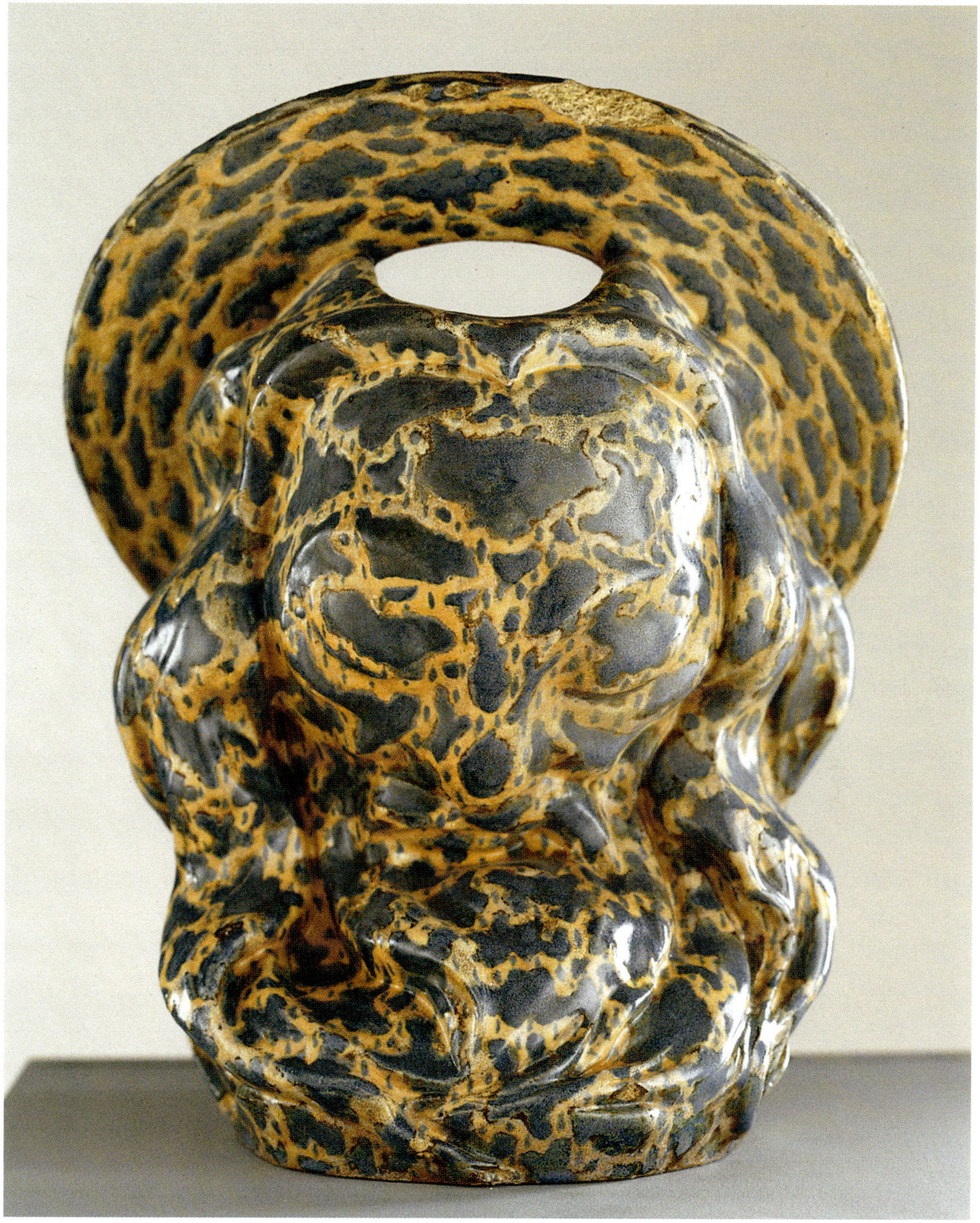

184. Paco Durrio
Head of Christ
(Cabeza de Cristo)
Glazed clay. 39.2 x 31.7 x 24.8 cm
Museo de Bellas Artes de Bilbao

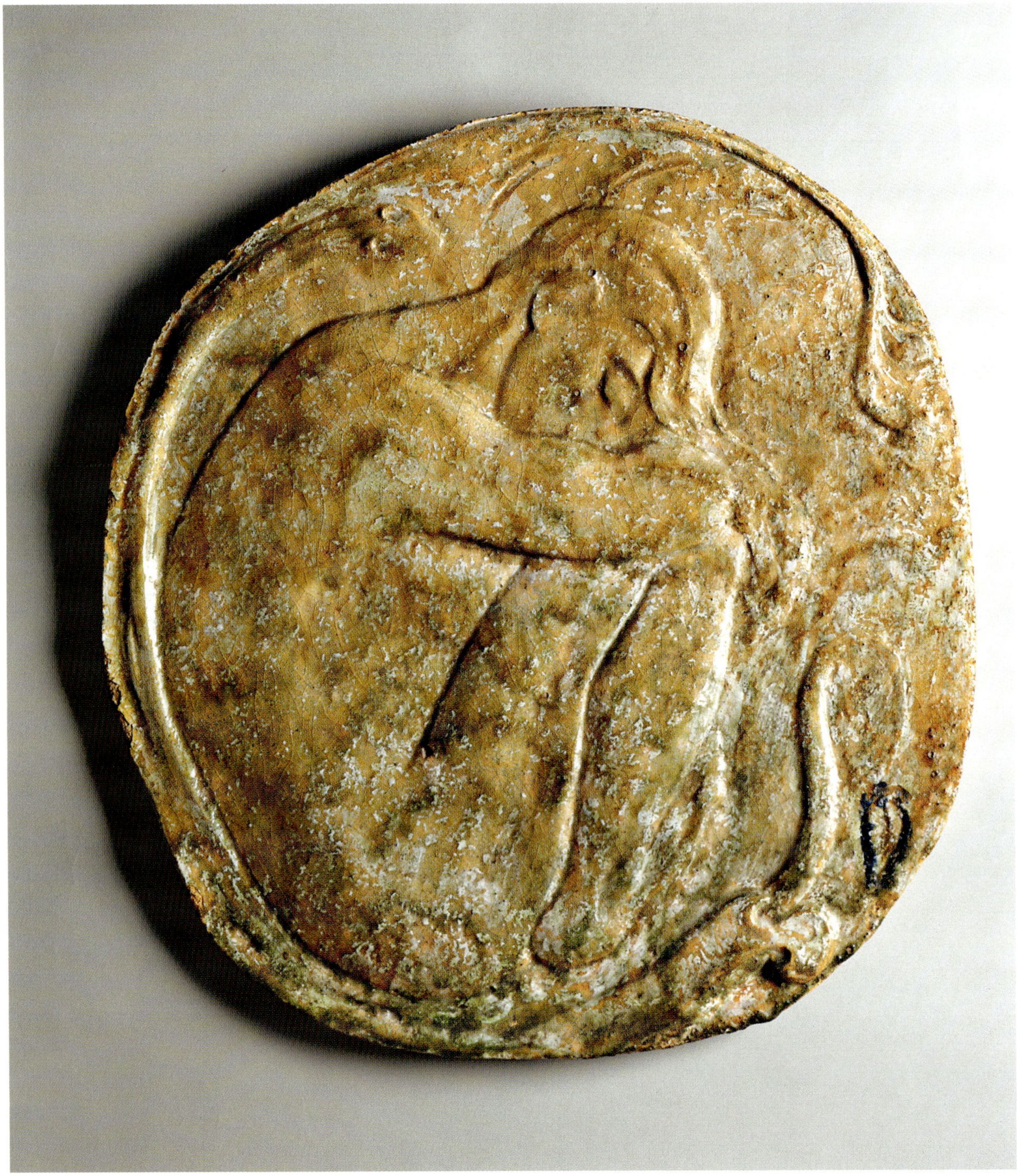

185. Paco Durrio
Large Medallion with Figure or *Eve's Dream*. c. 1908
(*Gran medallón con figura* o *El sueño de Eva*)
Glazed clay. 71.3 x 66.5 x 5.3 cm
Museo de Bellas Artes de Bilbao

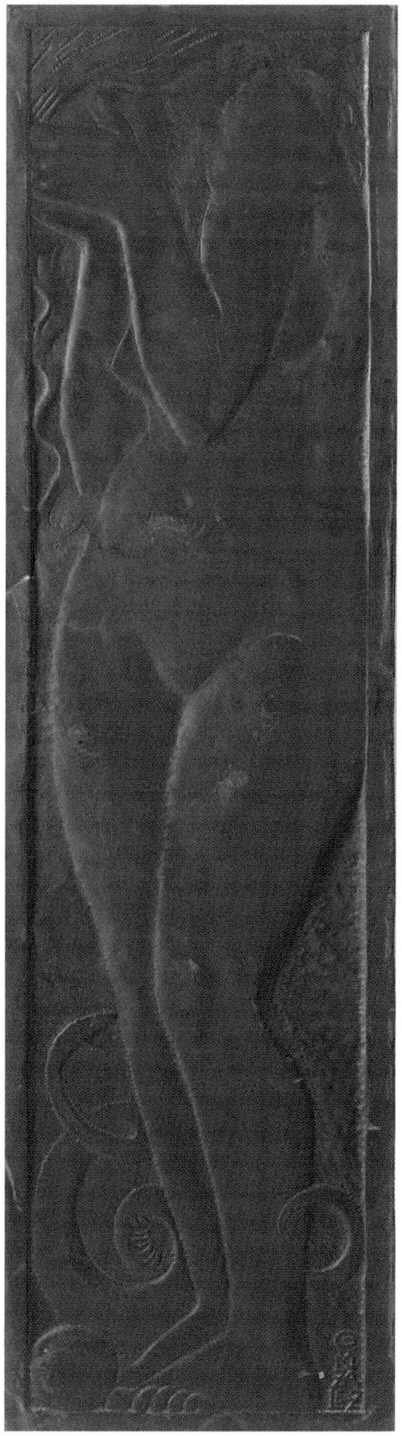

186. Julio González
Eve, c. 1900–1910
(*Eva*)
Embossed and painted copper. 131 x 37 cm
IVAM, Instituto Valenciano de Arte Moderno, Generalitat Valenciana. Donated by C. Martínez and V. Grimminger, Paris

Index of Works

cat. 155
La Revue Blanche, 1894
Published in *La Revue Blanche* n. 15 and in the *Album of la Revue Blanche*
Lithograph in four colours. 800 x 620 mm
Bibliothèque nationale de France, Paris
p. 283

cat. 156
Woman with an Umbrella, 1895
(Femme au parapluie)
Lithograph in two colours. 250 x 155 mm
Bibliothèque nationale de France, Paris
p. 286

cat. 157
Programme for *La Dernière Croisade* de Maxime Gray, with an advertisement for the *Revue encyclopédique Larousse*, 1896
Grey lithograph. 300 x 490 mm
Bibliothèque nationale de France, Paris
p. 285

cat. 158
At the Theatre (Some Aspects of Parisian Life), 1899
(Au téâtre [quelques aspects de la vie de Paris])
Lithograph in four colours. 200 x 400 mm
Bibliothèque nationale de France, Paris
p. 284

Paul Cézanne
cat. 12
Cup, Glass and Fruit II, c. 1877
(Tasse, verre et fruits, II)
Oil on canvas. 34 x 46 cm
Jan and Marie-Anne Krugier-Poniatowski Collection
p. 118

cat. 13
Fruit Bowl, Plate and Apples, 1879–1880
(Compotier, assiette et pommes)
Oil on canvas. 43.5 x 54 cm
Ny Carlsberg Glyptotek, Copenhagen
p. 120

cat. 20
Trees and Roofs, 1882–1883
(Arbres et Toits)
Pencil on paper. 32.6 x 34.5 cm
Museum Boijmans Van Beuningen, Rotterdam
p. 130

cat. 21
View of L'Estaque, 1883–1885
(Vue de L'Estaque)
Oil on canvas. 71 x 57.7 cm
Private Collection, on loan to the Fitzwilliam Museum, Cambridge
p. 131

cat. 46
Three Bathers, 1876–1877
(Trois baigneuses)
Oil on canvas. 52 x 55 cm
Petit Palais, Musée des Beaux-Arts de la Ville de Paris
p. 162

Edgar Degas
cat. 29
Peasant Girls Bathing in the Sea at Sunset, 1875–1876
(Petites paysannes se baignant à la mer vers le soir)
Oil on canvas. 61 x 81 cm
Private Collection
p. 141

cat. 30
Dancer, c. 1878
(Danseuse)
Black chalk and white highlights. 23.5 x 32.5 cm
Eugene V. Thaw, New York
p. 142

cat. 32
Dancers on Stage, 1906–1908
(Danseuses en scène)
Charcoal and pastel with tracing paper added above and below. 65 x 70 cm
Von der Heydt Museum, Wuppertal
p. 144

cat. 33
Three Nude Dancers, Resting, c. 1891–1892
(Trois danseuses nues, au repos)
Black pencil and pastel on lithograph. 19.7 x 27 cm
E. W. K. Collection
p. 145

cat. 34
Woman Washing herself with a Sponge, c. 1887
(Le bain, femme s'épongeant)
Pastel and charcoal on paper. 58 x 35.5 cm
Private Collection. Courtesy Pieter Coray
p. 146

Maurice Denis
cat. 85
Patches of Sun on the Terrace, 1890
(Taches de soleil sur la terrasse)
Oil on cardboard. 24 x 20.5 cm
Musée d'Orsay, Paris
p. 209

cat. 94
Sea Shore, 1891
(Bord de mer)
Oil on canvas. 20.7 x 26 cm
Private Collection. Courtesy Bellier, Paris
p. 218

cat. 99
The Mystical Grape Harvest, c. 1890
(La vendange mystique)
Oil on canvas mounted on cardboard. 74 x 51 cm
Triton Foundation, The Netherlands
p. 223

cat. 100
Yellow Evening at Fourqueux, c. 1890
(Soir jaune sur Fourqueux)
Oil on wood panel. 16 x 26.8 cm
The Montreal Museum of Fine Arts, Montreal
p. 224

cat. 107
September: Women Seated on the Terrace, 1891
(Septembre: femmes assises à la terrasse)
Oil on canvas. 38 x 61 cm
Musée des Arts décoratifs, Paris
p. 230

cat. 108
Young Women under a Lamp, 1891
(Les jeunes filles sous la lampe)
Oil on canvas. 36 x 25 cm
Musée des Beaux-Arts, Lyon
p. 232

cat. 109
The Fairies, c. 1891
(Les Fées)
Oil on paper mounted on canvas. 28 x 34.5 cm
Galerie Berès, Paris, France
p. 233

cat. 10
Clovis, c.1886
Oil in canvas. 56.5 x 41 cm
Collection of the Newark Museum,
Gift of Mrs Lloyd Westcott, 1960
p. 116

cat. 11
The White Bowl, 1886
(Le bol blanc)
Oil on canvas. 59.5 x 72 cm
Kunsthaus Zürich
p. 119

cat. 14
The Little One is Dreaming, 1881
(La petite rêve)
Oil on canvas. 59.5 x 74.5 cm
Ordrupgaard, Copenhagen
p. 121

cat. 15
Lilacs, 1885
(Bouquet de lilas)
Oil on canvas. 34.9 x 27 cm
Carmen Thyssen-Bornemisza Collection on loan at the Museo Thyssen-Bornemisza, Madrid
pp. 122–23

cat. 17
The Willows, 1885
(Les saules)
Oil on canvas. 89.5 x 48 cm
Private Collection. In deposit at the Musée Départemental Maurice Denis 'Le Prieuré', Saint-Germain-en-Laye
p. 127

cat. 18
An Orchard Under the Church of Bihorel, 1884
(Un verger au-dessous de l´église de Bihorel)
Oil on canvas. 65.5 x 46 cm
Carmen Thyssen-Bornemisza Collection on loan at the Museo Thyssen-Bornemisza, Madrid
p. 128

cat. 19
The Fire at the River Bank, 1886
(Le feu au bord de l'eau)
Oil on canvas. 60 x 38 cm
Carmen Thyssen-Bornemisza Collection on loan at the Museo Thyssen-Bornemisza, Madrid
p. 129

cat. 22
Cows at the Watering-place, 1885
(Vaches à l'abreuvoir)
Oil on canvas. 81 x 65 cm
Civica Galleria d'Arte Moderna, Raccolta Grassi, Milan
p. 132

cat. 23
The Inlet of Saint-Pierre seen from the Anse Turin, 1887
(La rade de Saint-Pierre vue de l'Anse Turin)
Oil on canvas. 54 x 90 cm
Ny Carlsberg Glyptotek, Copenhagen
p. 133

cat. 24
River under the Trees, Martinique, 1887
(Cours d'eau sous les arbres, Martinique)
Oil on canvas. 90 x 116 cm
Bayerische Staatgemäldesammlungen, Neue Pinakotek, Munich
p. 134

cat. 25
Coming and Going, Martinique, 1887
(Allées et Venues. Martinique)
Oil on canvas. 72.5 x 92 cm
Carmen Thyssen-Bornemisza Collection on loan at the Museo Thyssen-Bornemisza, Madrid
p. 135

cat. 26
Shepherds in a Meadow, 1888
(Berger et bergère dans le pré)
Oil on canvas. 92 x 73 cm
Musées royaux des Beaux-Arts de Belgique, Brussels
Inv. 5092
p. 136

cat. 27
Dogs Running in a Meadow, 1888
(Course de chiens dans la prairie)
Oil on canvas. 92 x 72.5 cm
Carmen Thyssen-Bornemisza Collection on loan at the Museo Thyssen-Bornemisza, Madrid
p. 137

cat. 28
La Toilette, 1882
Low relief in pear wood. 34 x 55 x 7 cm
Musée d'Art Moderne et Contemporain de Strasbourg
p. 140

cat. 31
Breton Girls Dancing, 1888
(La Ronde des petites Bretonnes)
Oil on canvas. 71.5 x 93 cm
National Gallery of Art, Washington
(Collection of Mr and Mrs Paul Mellon, 1983.1.19)
p. 143

cat. 35
Two Bathers, 1887
(Deux baigneuses)
Oil on canvas. 87.5 x 70 cm
Museo Nacional de Bellas Artes, Buenos Aires
p. 147

cat. 36
Young Breton Bathers, 1888
(Jeunes baigneurs bretons)
Oil on canvas. 92 x 73 cm
Hamburger Kunsthalle, Hamburg
pp. 148-49

cat. 40
Breton Women by a Bend in the Road, 1888
(Bretonnes au tournant d'une route)
Oil on canvas. 91 x 72 cm
Ny Carlsberg Glyptotek, Copenhagen
p. 156

cat. 41
The Vision after the Sermon, 1888
(La vision du sermon)
Oil on canvas. 73 x 92 cm
National Gallery of Scotland, Edinburgh
p. 157

cat. 42
Washerwomen in Arles, 1888
(Les lavandières à Arles)
Oil on jute. 73 x 92 cm
Museo de Bellas Artes de Bilbao
p. 158

cat. 43
The Blue Trees, 1888
(Les Arbres bleus)
Oil on jute. 92 x 73 cm
Ordrupgaard, Copenhagen
p. 159

cat. 45
The Yellow Haystacks, 1889
(Les meules jaunes)
Oil on canvas. 73 x 92 cm
Musée d'Orsay, Paris
Donated with right of usufruct by Mme Huc de Monfreid, 1951, entry in 1968
p. 161

cat. 48
Self-Portrait, 1888
(Autoportrait)
Oil on canvas. 46.5 x 38.6 cm
National Gallery of Art, Washington
(Collection of Mr and Mrs Paul Mellon. 1985.64.20)
p. 166

cat. 50
L'Arlèsienne. Madame Ginoux, 1888
Coloured chalks and charcoal on paper.
56.1 x 49.2 cm
Fine Arts Museums of San Francisco
(Memorial gift from Dr T. Edward y Tullah Hanley, Bradford, Pennsylvania 69.30.78)
p. 168

cat. 52
Portrait of Madame Roulin, 1888
(Portrait de Madame Roulin)
Oil on canvas. 50.5 x 63.5 cm
The Saint Louis Art Museum
(Funds given by Mrs Mark C. Steinberg)
p. 170

cat. 53
The Artist's Mother, 1888
(La mère de l'artiste)
Oil on canvas. 41 x 33 cm
Staatsgalerie Stuttgart, Stuttgart
p. 171

cat. 56
Self-Portrait, 1889
(Autoportrait)
Oil on canvas. 46 x 38 cm
State Pushkin Museum of Fine Arts, Moscow
p. 174

cat. 57
In the Waves (Ondine I), 1889
(Dans les vagues (Ondine I))
Oil on canvas. 92.5 x 72.4 cm
The Cleveland Museum of Art
(Gift of Mr and Mrs Wiliam Powell Jones, 1978.63)
p. 175

cat. 58
Woman in the Waves (Ondine II), 1889
(Femme à la vague [Ondine II])
Pastel and gouache on paper mounted on wood panel.
18 x 48.2 cm
Private Collection
p. 176

cat. 59
Nude Breton Boy, 1889
(*Petit Breton nu*)
Oil on canvas. 93 x 73.5 cm
Wallraf-Richartz Museum-Fondation Corboud, Cologne
p. 177

cat. 60
Woman Seen from the Back, Study, 1888
(La femme vue de dos, Étude)
Watercolour on paper. 26.3 x 40.4 cm
Van Gogh Museum, Amsterdam
(Vincent van Gogh Foundation)
p. 178

cat. 61
Nègreries Martinique, 1890
Gouache, watercolour, ink, gold paint and collage on paper. 33.2 x 24.8 cm
Jan and Marie-Anne Krugier-Poniatowski Collection
p. 179

cat. 62
Human Misery, 1889
(Misères humaines)
Watercolour and ink on paper. 20.5 x 38.5 cm
Musée Maillol, Paris
p. 180

cat. 63
Life and Death, 1889
(*La vie et la mort*)
Oil on canvas. 92 x 73 cm
Mahmoud Khalil Museum, Cairo
p. 181

cat. 64
Black Venus, 1889
(Vénus noire)
Glazed clay. 50 cm
Nassau County Division of Museum Services at the Sands Point Preserve, New York
p. 182

cat. 65
Lust, 1890
(La Luxure)
Carving in polychrome and gilded pine and oak wood. 70 x 15 x 7 cm
J. F. Willumsens Museum, Frederikssund, Denmark
p. 183

cat. 66
Ictus, c. 1889–1890
Watercolour on paper. 41.6 x 56 cm
Private Collecton. Courtesy Daniel Malingue, Paris
pp. 184–85

cat. 67
Sketch for 'The Yellow Christ', 1889
(Étude pour 'Le Christ jaune')
Pencil on paper. 26.7 x 17.8 cm
Carmen Thyssen-Bornemisza Collection on loan at the Museo Thyssen-Bornemisza, Madrid
p. 186

cat. 68
Christ in the Garden of Olives, 1889
(Christ au jardin des Oliviers)
Oil on canvas. 72.4 x 91.4 cm
Norton Gallery of Art, West Palm Beach, Florida
(Gift of Elizabeth C. Norton, 46.5)
p. 187

cat. 71
Leda and the Swan, 1889
(Léda et le cygne)
Zincograph. 221 x 204 mm
Institut national d'histoire de l'art, Bibliothèque, collections Jacques Doucet, Paris
pp. 192–93

cat. 72
The Joys of Brittany, 1889
(Joies de Bretagne)
Zincograph. 201 x 241 mm
Institut national d'histoire de l'art, Bibliothèque, collections Jacques Doucet, Paris
p. 194

cat. 73
Breton Bathers, 1889
(Baigneuses bretonnes)
Zincograph. 245 x 200 mm
Institut national d'histoire de l'art, Bibliothèque, collections Jacques Doucet, Paris
p. 195

cat. 74
Breton Women by a Gate, 1889
(Bretonnes à la barrière)
Zincograph. 170 x 215 mm
Institut national d'histoire de l'art, Bibliothèque, collections Jacques Doucet, Paris
p. 196

cat. 75
Human Misery, 1889
(Misères humaines)
Zincograph. 294 x 237 mm
Institut national d'histoire de l'art, Bibliothèque, collections Jacques Doucet, Paris
p. 197

cat. 76
Washerwomen, 1889
(Les laveuses)
Zincograph. 212 x 265 mm
Institut national d'histoire de l'art, Bibliothèque, collections Jacques Doucet, Paris
p. 199

cat. 77
Dramas of the Sea, Brittany, 1889
(Les drames de la mer, Bretagne)
Zincograph. 176 x 222 mm
Institut national d'histoire de l'art, Bibliothèque, collections Jacques Doucet, Paris
p. 198

cat. 78
Paul Gauguin
Dramas of the Sea, a Descent into the Maëlstrom, 1889
(Les drames de la mer, une descente dans le Maëlstrom)
Zincograph. 180 x 272 mm
Institut national d'histoire de l'art, Bibliothèque, collections Jacques Doucet, Paris
p. 201

cat. 79
Martinique Pastoral, 1889
(Pastorales Martinique)
Zincograph. 185 x 222 mm
Institut national d'histoire de l'art, Bibliothèque, collections Jacques Doucet, Paris
p. 200

cat. 80
The Grasshoppers and the Ants – Memories of Martinique, 1889
(Les cigales et les fourmis – Souvenir de la Martinique)
Zincograph. 216 x 261 mm
Institut national d'histoire de l'art, Bibliothèque, collections Jacques Doucet, Paris
p. 203

cat. 81
Old Woman in Arles, 1889
(Les vieilles filles à Arles)
Zincograph. 192 x 208 mm
Institut national d'histoire de l'art, Bibliothèque, collections Jacques Doucet, Paris
p. 202

cat. 90
Cow on the Cliffs of Porsac'h or *Over the Abyss*, 1888
(Vache sur la falaise à Porsac'h ou *Au-dessus du gouffre)*
Oil on canvas. 73 x 60 cm
Musée des Arts décoratifs, Paris
p. 214

cat. 92
The Beach at Pouldu, 1889
(La plage du Pouldu)
Oil on canvas. 73 x 92 cm
María Amalia Lacroze de Fortabat
p. 216

cat. 104
Among Irises, 1889
(Entre les lys)
Oil on canvas. 92 x 73 cm
Hilti Art Foundation, Schaan, Liechtenstein
p. 228

cat. 136
Lady Death, 1891
(Madame la Mort)
Charcoal and brush on paper. 23.9 x 29.3 cm
Musée d'Orsay, on deposti at the département des Arts Graphiques del Musée du Louvre, Paris
p. 265

cat. 137
Lady Death, 1891
(Madame la Mort)
Charcoal and grey wash on paper. 22.5 x 23 cm
Musée d'Orsay, on deposit at the département des Arts Graphiques del Musée du Louvre, Paris
(Gift of Yomiuri Shimbun and the Nippon Television Network Corporation, 1991)
p. 264

cat. 181
Head of a Young Girl, 1893–1894
(Tête de jeune fille)
Clay, varnished and heightened in places with dark red pigment. 15.2 x 26.18 cm
Carmen Thyssen-Bornemisza Collection on loan at the Museo Thyssen-Bornemisza, Madrid
p. 313

cat. 182
Window Box with Breton Scenes, 1886
(Jardinière avec scènes bretonnes)
Clay. 29 x 42 x 24 cm
Association des Amis du Petit Palais, Geneva
p. 312

Joan González
cat. 173
Young Woman with Flower, c. 1902–1903
(Joven con flor)
Watercolour on paper. 51 x 34.6 cm
Museu Nacional d'Art de Catalunya, Barcelona
p. 303

cat. 174
Landscape, c. 1904–1905
(Paisaje)
Oil on canvas. 50 x 65 cm
Museu Nacional d'Art de Catalunya, Barcelona
p. 305

cat. 175
Woman and Clouds, c. 1904–1906
(Mujer y nubes)
Oil on canvas. 26.8 x 40.8 cm
Museu Nacional d'Art de Catalunya, Barcelona
p. 304

Julio González
cat. 186
Eve, c. 1900–1910
(Eva)
Embossed and painted copper. 131 x 37 cm
IVAM, Instituto Valenciano de Arte Moderno, Generalitat Valenciana. Donated by C. Martínez y V. Grimminger, Paris
p. 317

cat. 5
The Cabbage Field, Pontoise, 1873
(Le champ de choux, Pontoise)
Oil on canvas. 60 x 80 cm
Carmen Thyssen-Bornemisza Collection on loan at the Museo Thyssen-Bornemisza, Madrid
p. 112

cat. 16
Woodland Scene (Spring) 1878
(Paysage avec de grands arbres [Printemps])
Oil on canvas. 73 x 54 cm
Ny Carlsberg Glyptotek, Copenhagen
p. 126

Paul Elie Ranson
cat. 96
Two Nude Women, 1890
(Deux femmes nues)
Watercolour on paper. 120 x 98 cm
Association des Amis du Petit Palais, Geneva
p. 221

cat. 98
Christ and Buddha, c. 1890
(Christ et Bouddha)
Oil on canvas. 66.7 x 51.4 cm
Triton Foundation, The Netherlands
p. 222

Ker-Xavier Roussel
cat. 86
The Fisherman, c. 1890–1891
(Le pêcheur)
Oil on canvas. 22 x 15 cm
Private Collection
p. 210

cat. 103
Composition in the Forest, 1890–1892
(Composition dans la forêt)
Oil on canvas. 44 x 31 cm
Musée Départemental Maurice Denis 'Le Prieuré', Saint-Germain-en-Laye
p. 227

cat. 124
Woman in front of a Green Gate, c. 1891–1893
(Femme devant un portail vert)
Oil on a wood panel. 22.3 x 16.5 cm
Private Collection
p. 248

cat. 132
Summer Landscape, 1894
(Paysage d'Été)
Pastel on cardboard. 33 x 50 cm
Association des Amis du Petit Palais, Geneva
p. 256

cat. 133
Haystacks on the Sea Shore, 1894
(Les meules au bord de la mer)
Pastel on cardboard. 34 x 50 cm
Association des Amis du Petit Palais, Geneva
p. 257

Armand Seguin
cat. 140
Nude with a Bat, 1890
(Nu à la chauve-souris)
Etching and dry point. 109 x 212 mm
Bibliothèque nationale de France, Paris
p. 268

cat. 141
Decoration of Brittany. A Summer Day, c. 1894
(Décoration de Bretagne. Un Jour d'été)
Etching and sugar aquatint. 245 x 372 mm
Bibliothèque nationale de France, Paris
p. 269

cat. 142
The Silent Pilgrim, for *Phénissa by* R. De Gourmont
(Le Pélerin du silence)
Dry point and aquatint. 99 x 179 mm
Bibliothèque nationale de France, Paris
p. 270

cat. 143
Breton Women, 1894
(Les Bretonnes)
Wood engraving. 229 x 186 mm
Bibliothèque nationale de France, Paris
p. 271

Paul Sérusier
cat. 84
The Talisman, 1888
(Le talisman)
Oil on wood panel. 27 x 21.5 cm
Musée d'Orsay, Paris
p. 208

cat. 106
Apple Harvest, c. 1891
(La cueillette de pommes)
Oil on canvas. 73 x 133 cm
Triton Foundation, The Netherlands
p. 231

cat. 134
Fabric Vendor, 1898
(La marchande d'étoffes)
Egg tempera on canvas. 73 x 92 cm
Association des Amis du Petit Palais, Geneva
pp. 258–59

cat. 144
Programme for *L'Assomption de Hannele Mattern*, Le Théâtre-Libre, 1893–1894
Colour lithograph. 365 x 228 mm
Bibliothèque nationale de France, Paris
p. 272

cat. 145
Heraklea by Auguste Villeroy, Théâtre d'L'Œuvre, 1896
Zincograph
Bibliothèque nationale de France, Paris
p. 273

Joaquim Sunyer
cat. 176
Mediterranean, 1910–1911
(Mediterráneo)
Oil on canvas. 84 x 132 cm
Carmen Thyssen-Bornemisza collection on loan at the Museo Thyssen-Bornemisza, Madrid
p. 307

cat. 177
The Mirrors, c. 1905–1907
(Los espejos)
Oil on canvas. 55 x 65 cm
Museu Nacional d'Art de Catalunya, Barcelona
p. 306

Julián de Tellaeche
cat. 179
Seascape, 1912
(Marina)
Oil on canvas. 24.5 x 100 cm
Museo Nacional Centro de Arte Reina Sofía, Madrid
p. 308

Photographic Credits

ARGENTINA
BUENOS AIRES Museo Nacional de Bellas Artes: cat. no. 35

CANADA
MONTREAL The Montreal Museum of Fine Arts. Photography: Brian Merrelt: cat. no. 100
The Montreal Museum of Fine Arts. Photography: Christine Guest: cat. no. 129
The Montreal Museum of Fine Arts: cat. nos. 86, 124
OTTAWA Photo © National Gallery of Canada, Ottawa: cat. no. 3

DENMARK
COPENHAGEN Ny Carlsberg Glyptothek: cat. no. 13; p. 31
Ny Carlsberg Glyptothek: Photographies: NCG / Ole Haupt: cat. nos. 16, 23
Ordrupgaard © Klemp & Woldbye: cat. no. 14
Ordrupgaard: cat. no. 43
FREDERIKSSUND J. F. Willumsens Museum Frederikssund. Photography: SMK: cat. no. 65

EGYPT
CAIRO Museo Mahmoud Khalil : cat. no. 63

FRANCE
ALBI Musée Toulouse-Lautrec, Albi, France: cat. no. 54
BREST Musée des beaux-arts de Brest: cat. no. 91
STRASBOURG Musée d'Art Moderne et Contemporain de Strasbourg. Photography: N. Bertola: cat. no. 28
GRENOBLE Photographie © Musée de Grenoble: p. 47
LYON Musée des Beaux-Arts de Lyon © Studio Basset: cat. no. 125
ORLEANS Cliché musée des Beaux-Arts d'Orléans: p. 68
PARIS Archives Vuillard, Paris: cat. nos. 82, 121
Cliché Bibliothèque nationale de France, Paris: cat. nos. 139, 140, 141, 142, 143, 144, 145, 146, 147, 148, 149, 150, 151, 152, 154, 155, 156, 157, 158, 160, 161, 162
Cortesía Bellier, Paris: cat. no. 94
Cortesía Daniel Malingue, Paris: cat. no. 66
Galerie Bères, Paris, France: cat. nos. 109, 122, 127, 153, 159
© cliché Institut national d'histoire de l'art, bibliothèque (collections Jacques Doucet): cat. nos. 71, 72, 73, 74, 75, 76, 77, 78, 79, 80, 81, 138
Musée des Arts décoratifs, Paris. Tous droits réservés. Photography: Laurent-Sully Jaulmes: cat. nos. 90, 107
Photo © RMN – Hervé Lewandowski: cat. nos. 45, 84, 85, 111; pp. 26, 61
Photo © RMN – Bulloz: cat. nos. 46, 95
Photo © RMN – Arnaudet: cat. no. 55
Photo © RMN – C. Jean: cat. nos. 97, 136
Photo © RMN – R. G. Ojeda: cat. no. 128
Photo © RMN – Gérard Blot: cat. no. 137
Photo © RMN – B. Hatala: cat. nos. 166, 172
Photo © RMN – Thierry Le Mage: cat. no. 167
Photo © RMN: cat. no. 168
Musée Maillol: cat. nos. 62, 102, 163
QUIMPER © Musée des Beaux-Arts de Quimper (France): cat. no. 44
RENNES Musée des beaux-arts de Rennes. Photography: Adélaïde Beaudoin: cat. no. 93
SAINT-GERMAIN-EN-LAYE
© Le Musée départemental Maurice Denis Le Prieuré, Saint-Germain-en-Laye (France): cat. nos. 9, 101, 103, 110, 112, 113

GERMANY
BREMEN Kunsthalle Bremen: p. 67
COLOGNE © Rheinisches Bildarchiv Köln: cat. no. 59
HAMBURG © Hamburger Kunsthalle / bpk. Photography: Elke Walford: cat. no. 36
KARLSRUHE Staatliche Kunsthalle Karlsruhe: cat. no. 130
MUNICH Bayerische Staatsgemäldesammlungen, Neue Pinakothek Munich and Kunstdia – Archiv ARTOTHEK, D-Weilhem: cat. no. 24
STUTTGART Staatsgalerie Stuttgart: cat. no. 53
WUPPERTAL Von der Heydt-Museum Wuppertal: cat. no. 32

GREAT BRITAIN
CAMBRIDGE Photograph © Copyright Fitzwilliam Museum, University of Cambridge: cat. no. 21
EDINBURGH © The National Gallery of Scotland: cat. no. 41
LONDON The Bridgeman Art Library: pp. 16, 25, 30, 32 34, 50, 53, 54, 72
Victoria & Albert Museum: p. 35
SOUTHAMPTON Southampton City Art Gallery. Cortesy Bridgeman Art Library, Londres: cat. no. 116

ITALY
MILAN © Comune di Milano – tutti I diritti di legge riservati. Foto Saporetti: cat. nos. 22, 39

IRELAND
DUBLIN Courtesy of the National Gallery of Ireland
© Courtesy of the Artist's Estate: cat. no. 126

JAPAN
TOKYO the National Museum of Western Art : p. 33

LIECHTENSTEIN
SCHAAN Oeffentliche Kunstsammlung Basel. Photography: Martin Bühler: cat. no. 104

RUSSIA
MOSCOW © The State Pushkin Museum of Fine Arts, Moscow: cat. no. 56; pp. 48, 68

SPAIN
BARCELONA © MNAC – Museu Nacional d'Art de Catalunya. Barcelona. 2004. Photographers: Calveras/Mérida/Sagristà: cat. nos. 173, 174, 175, 177
Museu Picasso: cat. nos. 164, 165, 169, 170, 171
BILBAO Argazkiak, Bilbao: cat. no. 180
© de la fotografía Museo de Bellas Artes de Bilbao / Archivo fotográfico del Museo de Bellas Artes de Bilbao: cat. no. 42
MADRID AGE Fotostock: pp. 4, 93, 95
Archivo Fotográfico Museo Nacional Centro de Arte Reina Sofía, Madrid: cats. 178, 179; p. 99
Archivo Fotográfico Museo Thyssen-Bornemisza: pp. 16, 19, 22, 31, 36, 49, 55, 66, 67, 82, 83, 84, 85, 91, 103
Colección Carmen Thyssen-Bornemisza. Photographies: José Loren: cats. 2, 4, 5, 7, 15, 18, 19, 25, 27, 47, 67, 131, 176, 181; p. 103
Museo Thyssen-Bornemisza, Madrid. Photography: José Loren: cat. 6; p. 22
Oronoz: pp. 96, 101
VALENCIA © IVAM. Institut Valencià d'Art Modern. Generalitat Valenciana. España: cat. no. 186

SWEEDEN
GOTEBORG Göteborgs Konstmuseum. Photography: Lars Noord: cat. no. 69

SWITZERLAND
BERN Cortesy E. W. K. Collection: cat. no. 33
GENEVA Studio Monique Bernaz, Genève: cat. nos. 8, 96, 132, 133, 134
Gallerie Jan Krugier, Ditesheim & Cie: cat. nos. 12, 61
MARTIGNY Fondation Pierre Gianadda, Martigny, Suisse: cat. no. 120
MONTAGNOLA Cortesy Galleria Pieter Coray: cat. no. 34
ZURICH © 2004 Kunsthaus Zürich. All rights reserved: cat. no. 11, p. 67

THE NETHERLANDS
AMSTERDAM B. V. 't Lanthuys - Vincent van Gogh Foundation: cat. nos. 49, 60; pp. 57, 59, 74
BRUSSELS Musées royaux des Beaux-Arts de Belgique, Bruxelles. Photography: Speltdoorn cat. no. 26; pp. 38, 76
GOOREIND Triton Foundation, The Netherlands: cat. nos. 88, 98, 99, 105, 106, 117
OTTERLO © kröller-müller museum: p. 61
ROTTERDAM Museum Boijmans Van Beuningen: cat. no. 20
Cortesy Reytenbagh Collection: cat. no. 118

UNITED STATES
BOSTON © 2004 Museum of Fine Arts. All Rights Reserved: p. 94
BROOKLYN The Brooklyn Museum of Art: pp. 30, 41
CHICAGO Photograph © 2000. The Art Institute of Chicago. All Rights Reserved: p. 88
CLEVELAND © The Cleveland Museum of Art: cat. no. 57
FORT WORTH Copyright© 2004 Kimbell Art Museum. Photography: Michael Bodycomb '97: cat. no. 1
HARTFORD Wadsworth Atheneum Museum of Art, Hartford, CT.: cat. no. 37
INDIANAPOLIS Indianapolis Museum of Art: cat. no. 114
KANSAS CITY © 1997 The Nelson Gallery Foundation. Photography: Robert Newcome: cat. no. 70
NEWARK The Newark Museum: cat. no. 10
NEW HAVEN Yale University Art Gallery: p. 37
NEW YORK Cortesy Eugene V. Thaw: cat. no. 30
Cortesy William Kelly Simpson Collection: cat. no. 87
Photograph © 1979 The Metropolitan Museum of Art: cat. no. 51
Photograph by David Heald © The Solomon R. Guggenheim Foundation, New York: cat. no. 135
PORT WASHINGTON
Nassau County (N.Y.) Division of Museum Services, Sand Point Preserve. Photography: Eric Pollitzer: cat. no. 64
SAN FRANCISCO © Fine Arts Museums of San Francisco: cat. no. 50
SAINT LOUIS The Saint Louis Art Museum: cat. no. 52
WASHINGTON Image © Board of Trustees, National Gallery of Art, Washington: cat. nos. 31, 48, 123
WEST PALM BEACH Norton Museum of Art, West Palm Beach, Florida: cat. no. 68